PERSPECTIVES ON SENTENCE PROCESSING

PERSPECTIVES ON SENTENCE PROCESSING

Edited by
Charles Clifton, Jr.
Lyn Frazier
Keith Rayner
University of Massachusetts at Amherst

Psychology Press
Taylor & Francis Group

New York   London

First Published by
Lawrence Erlbaum Associates, Inc., Publishers
365 Broadway
Hillsdale, New Jersey 07642

Transferred to Digital Printing 2009 by Psychology Press
270 Madison Ave, New York NY 10016
27 Church Road, Hove, East Sussex, BN3 2FA

Library of Congress Cataloging-in-Publication Data

Perspectives on sentence processing / edited by Charles Clifton, Jr.,
Lyn Frazier, and Keith Rayner.
p.   cm.
Selected papers from a conference held at the University of
Massachusetts at Amherst in March, 1993.
Includes bibliographical references and indexes.
ISBN 0-8058-1581-3 (cloth) — ISBN 0-8058-1582-1 (paper)
1. Psycholinguistics—Congresses.   I. Clifton, Charles, 1938–
II. Frazier, Lyn. 1952–   .   III. Rayner, Keith.
P37.P475   1994
401'.9—dc20   94-6096
                                                        CIP

Publisher's Note
The publisher has gone to great lengths to ensure the quality of this reprint
but points out that some imperfections in the original may be apparent.

Contents

List of Contributors

Markus Bader   Institut fuer Germanistische Sprachwissenschaft, Universitaet Jena, Leutragraben 1, UHH, 8, Stock, D-07743, Jena, Germany

Stephen Barton   Department of Psychology, University of Glasgow, 56 Hillhead Street, Glasgow G12 9YR, Scotland.

Colin Brown   Max Planck Institute for Psycholinguistics, P.O. Box 310, NL 6500 AH Nijmegen, The Netherlands.

Charles Clifton, Jr.   Department of Psychology, University of Massachusetts, Amherst, MA 01003.

Cynthia M. Connine   Psychology Department, State University at New York at Binghamton, Binghamton, NY 13760.

Laura Conway   Department of Linguistics, University of Connecticut, Storrs, CT 06268.

Stephen Crain   Department of Linguistics, University of Connecticut, Storrs, CT 06268.

Matthey W. Crocker   Department of Artificial Intelligence, 80 South Bridge, Edinburgh EH1 1HN, Scotland.

Lyn Frazier   Department of Linguistics, University of Massachusetts, Amherst, MA 01003.

Simon Garrod   Human Communication Research Center, Department of Psychology, University of Glasgow, Glasgow G12 9YR, Scotland.

Edward Gibson   Department of Brain and Cognitive Sciences, Massachusetts Institute of Technology, Cambridge, MA 02139.

Peter Hagoort   Max Planck Institute for Psycholinguistics, P.O. Box 310, NL 6500 AH Nijmegen, The Netherlands.

Aravind K. Joshi   Department of Computer and Information Science, University of Pennsylvania, Philadelphia, PA 19103.

Ingeborg Lasser   Max Planck Institute for Psycholinguistics, P.O. Box 310, NL 6500 AH Nijmegen, The Netherlands.

Simon P. Liversedge   Department of Psychology, University of Dundee, Dundee DD1 4HN, Scotland.

Maryellen C. MacDonald   Neuroscience Program, University of Southern California, Los Angeles, CA 90089–2520.

Wayne S. Murray   Department of Psychology, University of Dundee, Dundee DD1 4HN, Scotland.

Weijia Ni   Department of Linguistics, University of Connecticut, Storrs, CT 06268.

Lee Osterhout   Department of Psychology NI-25, University of Washington, Seattle, WA 98195.

Neal J. Pearlmutter   Beckman Institute, University of Illinois, 405 N. Matthews, Urbana, IL 61801.

Martin Pickering   Department of Psychology, University of Glasgow, 56 Hillhead Street, Glasgow G12 9YR, Scotland.

Owen Rambow   Department of Computer and Information Science, University of Pennsylvania, Philadelphia, PA 19103.

Keith Rayner   Department of Psychology, University of Massachusetts, Amherst, MA 01003.

Julie Sedivy   Department of Linguistics, University of Rochester, Rochester, NY 14627.

Edward P. Stabler   Department of Linguistics, UCLA, 405 Hilgard Ave., Los Angeles, CA 90024.

Michael K. Tanenhaus   Department of Psychology, University of Rochester, Rochester, NY 14627.

John C. Trueswell   Department of Psychology, University of Pennsylvania, 3815 Walnut Street, Philadelphia, PA 19104

Pienie Zwitserlood   Westf. Wilhelms-Universität Münster, Psychologisches Institut II, Fliednerstrasse 21, D48149 Münster, Germany

Preface

One of the liveliest forums for sharing psychological, linguistic, philosophical, and computer science perspectives on psycholinguistics has been the annual meeting of the City University of New York (CUNY) Sentence Processing Conference. The initial meeting of this conference was held at the CUNY Graduate Center in New York City in March 1988 and featured papers that represented nearly all the disciplines that contribute to psycholinguistics. Discussion of these papers repeatedly juxtaposed the insights of multiple disciplines, sometimes clashing, but more often complementing, one another. The next meeting of the conference added a poster session, at which participants learned how to distinguish the linguists' posters from the computer scientists' from the psychologists' by the style of their graphics and by the presence or absence of a pile of handouts. They also learned to dive into a poster from any discipline and expect to learn something interesting from it.

This interdisciplinary flavor has persisted through all the CUNY conferences that followed the initial one. The meeting of the sixth CUNY conference was held at the University of Massachusetts at Amherst in March 1993, giving the organizers at the CUNY Graduate Center a year's break. It held true to form. The papers and posters that were presented at this meeting represented the disciplines of linguistics, psychology, and computer science, many blending two or three disciplines in a single presentation. The organizers of this conference, who are the editors of this book, selected a subset of the presented papers and invited their authors to contribute them to a book. We intended to represent the main themes that ran through the 1993 conference, as well as honoring the breadth of presentations at the conference. We also hoped to highlight some of the most exciting current developments in the field of sentence processing, and even to glimpse what might be exciting in the next few years. The inability of some invited authors to provide a final manuscript by the tight deadline with which this book was prepared resulted in some narrowing of perspective and some underrepresentation of an important theme or two. Nonetheless, we hope readers agree that the chapters in this volume present the state of the art in several important approaches to sentence processing. We also hope the book rekindles in participants at the conference some of the excitement they felt when the conference was taking place.

The 1993 conference could not have taken place without the generous support of several institutions, including the University of Massachusetts/Amherst Training Program in Psycholinguistics and the University of Massachusetts/Amherst Graduate School, the Computational Linguistics Program of the Carnegie-Mellon University, the Institute for Research in Cognitive Science of the University of Pennsylvania, the Cognitive Science Program of the University of Arizona, and the Cognitive Science Program of the University of Rochester. Preparation of this volume was supported, in part, by grants to the University of Massachusetts (HD-07327 and HD-18708 from NIH, and DB-9121375 from NSF). The editors (both as editors and organizers of the conference) owe a great debt of thanks to Tom Maxfield, who helped organize and run the conference and pull this book together. We also thank Judi Amsel of Lawrence Erlbaum Associates for her help and encouragement in bringing this book to completion.

Charles Clifton, Jr.
Lyn Frazier
Keith Rayner

1 Introduction

Charles Clifton, Jr.
Lyn Frazier
Keith Rayner
University of Massachusetts at Amherst

The topics of how people produce and comprehend sentences and how they learn to do so have played a central role in the development of cognitive psychology and cognitive science. Demonstrations of the utter inadequacy of behavioral theory to deal with language comprehension, production, and acquisition (e.g., Chomsky, 1959; Miller, Galanter, & Pribram, 1960) led to its demise and fueled the cognitive revolution (Gardner, 1985; Johnson-Laird, 1988). A decade later, psycholinguistics was one of the core topics addressed by the new interdisciplinary field of cognitive science (Stillings et al., 1987). One reason that the psycholinguistics of sentence processing has played such a central role is the importance of language to the human state: How is it that we are so outstandingly successful at using language, given all our other inadequacies? Another reason is that the topic of sentence processing has proved to be a field that specialists in cognitive psychology, linguistics, computer science, and philosophy (and undoubtedly other disciplines) can study from their own perspective. In addition, it has proved to be a field in which researchers in one discipline can profit from the insights provided by researchers in the other disciplines.

This volume contains chapters that were presented at the sixth meeting of one of the liveliest forums for exploring interdisciplinary approaches to psycholinguistics—the City University of New York (CUNY) Sentence Processing Conference. We have organized the volume into six sections: (a) Sentence Processing and the Brain; (b) Phonological Processing; (c) Syntactic Processing: Information Flow and Decision Making; (d) Syntactic Processing and Computational Models; (e) Referential Processing; and (f) Sentence Processing and Language Acquisition. We provide a brief preview of the chapters in each of these sections, commenting just a bit here and there on how they fit into what is happening in the field as a whole. We conclude with some brief comments on current trends in sentence-processing research.

ORGANIZATION OF THIS BOOK

Sentence Processing and the Brain

Chapters on event-related potentials (ERPs) by Osterhout (chapter 2) and Hagoort and Brown (chapter 3) emphasize that ERPs provide an on-line technique not dependent on button pushing or any other secondary task. They also emphasize the multidimensional nature of the ERP waveforms and its continuous real-time nature. Both chapters show how syntactic violations result in components (P600 and sometimes left anterior negativity) that are distinct from the component known to attend semantic anomalies—the N400.

Osterhout notes that the P600 is apparent not only with phrase-structure and subcategorization violations, but also empty-category principle (ECP) and subjacency violations. The P600 begins earlier for these latter violation types, however, arguing against any temporal delay in the application of bounding constraints relative to phrase-structure constraints, and making the findings of Pickering, Barton, and Shillcock (chapter 9, this volume) concerning initial violation of island constraints quite surprising. Number- and gender-agreement violations also exhibit P600s, suggesting that they pattern with other syntactic violations. Both P600 and N400 are observed in examples where a syntactic violation results in an irrevocably ungrammatical and uninterpretable sentence. However, in garden-path sentences like "The boat floated down the river sank during the storm," the disambiguating word gives rise to either a P600 (for most subjects) or an N400 (for a few subjects), but never to both within a single individual.

The underlying source of the P600 versus N400 remains unclear, however, as Osterhout emphasizes. The P600 might directly reflect the processes underlying syntactic analysis, or the process of responding to syntactic violations, or processes of reanalysis. Hagoort and Brown echo this caution, and argue that certain violations (e.g., subcategorization) can be syntactic in origin but nevertheless have semantic consequences (e.g., on the interpretation of a lexical item's argument structure). They also present ERP data on lexical- and syntactic- ambiguity resolution, and they discuss how the ERP data compare with data obtained using other techniques.

Phonological Processing

Most work on sentence comprehension has used visual rather than auditory presentation. This can be justified by the intrinsic interest that the process of reading holds. Nonetheless, the real reason for the emphasis on reading is methodological and technical. It is technically easier to prepare well-controlled visual than auditory stimuli, it is hard to know how to describe an auditory signal properly without a good theory of prosody, and the methods used to probe the reading process are far more advanced than those available for studying auditory-sentence comprehension.

The roadblocks to studying listening are disappearing. Advances in microcomputer technology have brought most laboratories the capability of preparing and presenting auditory sentences, interesting and promising theories of prosody are appearing, and theories of auditory-word recognition have advanced far enough to permit serious development of theories of how people comprehend sentences they hear. This is fortunate because the field of auditory-sentence comprehension has the potential of providing important new insights into sentence processing. To take just two possible avenues of exploration, questions of how sentence context affects auditory-word recognition and how prosody affects sentence processing seem to be of unquestionable interest.

The two contributors to this volume who deal with auditory-language processing, Zwitserlood (chapter 4) and Connine (chapter 5), do not tackle questions of auditory-sentence comprehension head on, although both of these authors are known for contributions they have made to such topics. Rather, they both emphasize basic questions of how individual words are dealt with. Zwitserlood extends the work she has done on the topic of priming in auditory-word recognition to build a bridge to questions of spoken-word production (naming). She notes that, just as auditory-sentence processing has lagged as a field behind visual-sentence processing, the entire field of language production has lagged behind the field of language comprehension (and for rather similar reasons). She reviews the auditory phonological priming literature, looking at both facilitation and inhibition in word recognition, and argues that little evidence exists for true perceptual facilitation, whereas a rich variety of inhibitory effects have been demonstrated. She also reviews the phonological priming literature concerning language production, finding substantial evidence for facilitatory effects. Finally, she sketches a series of new experiments, looking at priming effects in both comprehension and production. She argues that the dissociation of effects in comprehension versus production suggests that the tasks use the same representations of linguistic form, but recruit different processing mechanisms. Partial overlap between the form of a prime and the form of a target item can facilitate phonological encoding in production via activation of lexical representations of words similar to but distinct from a target, but this same lexical activation, together with the deactivation of forms that minimally mismatch a prime, will have negative consequences for comprehension.

Connine addresses the question of why people are so good at recognizing auditory words when the problem seems to be so hard in the abstract. Why don't small distortions in the speech signal eliminate the intended word from the cohort of words compatible with the signal (cf. Marslen-Wilson & Tyler, 1980)? Utilizing both cross-modal priming and generalized phoneme-detection techniques, Connine shows that the degree of phonological similarity between an input and a target, the confusability of a target with other lexical entries, and the degree of redundancy in a target item all affect how much a given input activates a target lexical entry. Connine also introduces the concepts of *vertical* and *horizontal* *similarity*. Vertical similarity is (roughly) the degree of match between an acoustic–phonetic event and the corresponding lexical representation, and horizontal similarity is (again, roughly) the summed similarity between a lexical representation and all of its immediate phonological neighbors. There appear to be clear interactions between these two variables. For example, a high degree of vertical similarity between a nonword prime and a lexical target seems to result in more activation of a target item when horizontal similarity of the target to its neighbors is low than when it is high. Connine concludes that the process of auditory-word recognition can be a relatively gradual one, in which a preferred candidate emerges at a rate modulated by both vertical and horizontal similarity.

Syntactic Processing: Information Flow and Decision Making

Some of the most stimulating work in sentence processing is coming out of the laboratories at the University of Southern California (USC) and the University of Rochester. This work is guided by a theoretical perspective that emphasizes how various factors activate competing linguistic representations and how a constraint-satisfaction process chooses among them. It is notable for the variety of demonstrations it has provided of how sentence processing is sensitive to a wide range of extrasyntactic factors. The chapters by MacDonald, Pearlmutter, and Seidenberg (chapter 6) and Trueswell and Tanenhaus (chapter 7), together with other chapters elsewhere in this volume, provide an extended summary of the current state of this work.

MacDonald et al. argue a point that seems to be shared by most people working in the Rochester/USC tradition: Lexical-ambiguity resolution and syntactic-ambiguity resolution basically work the same way. They deny the widely held view (see, e.g., Rayner & Morris, 1991) that different processes hold in these two domains because lexical representations are retrieved, whereas syntactic representations are constructed. MacDonald et al. argue that a variety of variables, including frequency and semantic context, affect both types of ambiguity resolution in a similar fashion. They provide a striking analysis of published studies of the resolution of "horse-raced" sentences (the reduced-relative vs. past-tense ambiguity), suggesting that whether context overrides the preference for the simpler and generally more frequent past-tense reading depends on whether the verbs that were used occur more frequently in print in the past-participle or the past-tense form. Verbs that are frequently used as past participles are interpreted as such when the context supports it; verbs that are used less than 60% of the time as past participles are initially interpreted as past-tense verbs.

Trueswell and Tanenhaus provide their own arguments for an interactive (they use the term *constraint-based*) model of sentence comprehension. Like Mac-Donald et al., they emphasize the richness of the information provided by pre-stored lexical items, and focus on how the activation of a prestored item is determined by its likelihood given the input. This orientation encourages them to examine the frequency and plausibility of various structures and how such variables relate to comprehension difficulty. Also, like MacDonald et al., they emphasize how parsing difficulty should be a graded effect, not the more discrete effect that serial parsing models such as the garden-path model (Frazier, 1987) seem to suggest. Their research has led them to look at previously studied constructions, such as *that*-complements, in much greater detail than has been done previously, and to uncover some subtle and intriguing effects of argument-structure frequency, lexical preferences for specific linguistic forms (e.g., presence vs. absence of an overt *that* complementizer), and thematic-structure preferences.

The empirical effects discovered by researchers such as MacDonald et al. and Trueswell and Tanenhaus must clearly be accounted for by any adequate model of sentence processing. As these authors make clear, their own theorizing is still in a very preliminary and formative stage. The types of theories they are developing clearly can be sensitive to effects of frequency and preexisting biases they are demonstrating. Whether they can simultaneously be sensitive to the refined distinctions captured by the grammars of human languages may turn out to be a question of whether grammar can be reduced to prestored lexical structures that are activated by input.

Gibson and Pearlmutter (chapter 8) present one kind of research that must be done in developing theories of the sort envisioned by MacDonald et al. and Trueswell and Tanenhaus. They examine the relationship between the frequency of different resolutions of an ambiguity involving noun phrase (NP) modification and the ease of comprehending these different constructions. They suggest that frequency in a corpus should reflect the same complexity that can be measured in a comprehension-time experiment, and they provide evidence for this claim. In doing so, they are forced to filter their corpus sample in a variety of ways, graphically illustrating the nontrivial difficulty of doing proper frequency counts. They provide a useful discussion of the difficulty of interpreting the direction of causality in the relationship between frequency and comprehensibility. They note that, although one could claim that more frequent constructions are comprehended more easily because they are more frequent, one could equally well (given our current knowledge) posit that common underlying processes could underlie both comprehension and production, resulting in a common source of processing difficulty that appears as lower frequency of production and increased difficulty of comprehension.

Pickering, Barton, and Shillcock (chapter 9) examine a different kind of syntactic decision making and propose a different kind of theory. They examine the processing of sentences with "moved" constituents ("filler-gap" constructions), although here, as in previous work, they assume a direct relation between displaced constituents and their subcategorizers. Thus, they interpret the evidence without reference to the notion of *gap* or *trace*. They present evidence that effects of a potential gap are found inside syntactic islands, such as a relative clause, as well as outside them. They argue that this supports a parsing mechanism that first overgenerates possible structures and then filters structures that violate island constraints, although without traces, it remains unclear what is overgenerated and filtered. Specifically, Pickering et al. show that reading times in both self-paced and eye-movement studies are longer for the verb *painted* in (1a) and (1c) than in (1b) or (1d) (where the position where the true gap would appear is represented by a ___).

(1) a. I realized what the artist painted the larger mural with ___ today.
    b. I realized that the artist painted the larger mural with ___ skill.
    c. I realized what the artist who painted the larger mural ate ___ today.
    d. I realized that the artist who painted the larger mural ate ___ cakes.

This longer reading time may reflect the process of assigning a "filler" as an argument of a potential (but erroneous) argument assigner, or it may reflect very quick-acting processes of rejecting such an assignment. Pickering et al. discuss some differences between their findings and previous findings, including the position at which a "false gap" effect occurs (cf. Stowe, 1986). They also make some interesting proposals for further research, focusing on how the possibility of interpreting a string of words as a full clause or a potential end of sentence might affect filler-gap processing (Goodluck, Finney, & Sedivy, 1991).

Bader and Lasser (chapter 10) address the nature of the grammar that the human sentence-processing mechanism (HSPM) exploits. They propose that it is a principle-based grammar, but deny that the parser must be a head-driven licensing parser of the kind sometimes associated with principle-based parsing. They report a study of German parsing that shows that structure is postulated before the head of a phrase is received. They show that an NP is taken as subject of a verb-final complement clause before the other elements of the clause, including its head, have been encountered. Further, the NP is not taken as the direct object of an immediately following verb, but instead is initially taken as the subject of a subsequent verb. This result argues against the view that a constituent is structured with reference to the first available licensor because the NP in Bader and Lasser's sentences could have been licensed as object of the following verb. Concretely, German readers read sentences ending in (2a), in which the NP is taken as object of the first (more deeply embedded verb, V1), more slowly than sentences ending in (2B), in which the NP is taken as the subject of V2.

(2) ... daß NP PP V1 V2

    a. $[_{CP2}$daß $[_{CP1}$ NP PP V1] V2]   NP is object of V1

    b. $[_{CP2}$daß NP $[_{CP1}$ PP V1] V2]   NP is subject of V2

Bader and Lasser's findings argue against a view of parsing as licensing. They also show that a certain amount of top–down postulation of phrase structure is required in the human sentence-processing mechanism. Specifically, the verb phrase (VP) of the complement clause CP2 must be postulated before its head V (or I) is encountered, so that the NP can be taken as its subject.

Syntactic Processing and Computational Models

The chapters in this section contain additional new proposals about the structure of the HSPM that are motivated, in part, by a desire to design and implement computational models of sentence parsing. These chapters continue the discussion of the nature of the grammar that the HSPM exploits, begun in the previous section by Bader and Lasser—specifically whether it is a principle-based grammar (Crocker, chapter 11) or a tree-adjoining grammar (TAG; Rambow & Joshi, chapter 12). They also continue to address questions of whether phrase structure is projected: (a) strictly bottom–up using only information from the head of the phrase, (b) using any licensing information from the first available licensor, or (c) in a top–down fashion using requirements imposed by functional items but not lexical items. Also, they introduce new proposals concerning the processing of displaced constituents, further examining a topic introduced by Pickering et al.

Crocker's proposal (that the requirements of functional items such as the complementizer *that* give rise to top–down postulation) offers one means by which Bader and Lasser's results could be handled in a parser exploiting a government-and-binding (GB) or principle-based grammar. A complementizer like *daß* is required to take a clausal complement, which could lead to postulation of the complement clause before the head of the complement clause is encountered. Crocker's suggestion that the requirements of only functional items, not lexical content items, give rise to top–down node postulation is interesting, but we suspect that it may not be consistent with facts (see Adams, Clifton, & Mitchell, 1993, in particular).

Concerning the parsing of displaced constituents, Crocker proposes that the parsing system postulates traces according to the active trace strategy (ATS), which allows traces to be postulated before all lexical items preceding the trace in the terminal string have been encountered. This account fits naturally with certain intuitions about processing, but should be checked experimentally. Further, Crocker's ATS proposal raises interesting additional questions about the parsing of traces versus other empty categories such as *pro* (see DeVincenzi, 1991, for a system that treats traces like other kinds of empty categories).

Rambow and Joshi also deal with the processing of displaced constituents, drawing a sharp distinction between German topicalization, which they argue is constrained by the grammar, and long-distance scrambling, which they argue is constrained by the parsing mechanism. Thus, although there are constraints on topicalization, there is no bound on either the number of elements that may scramble or the number of clauses over which an element may scramble. Using a tree-adjoining grammar (TAG), their system parses in a bottom–up fashion, and thus contrasts with Bader and Lasser's conclusions. The passing of subcategorization restrictions between one verb and a governing verb permits the governing verb to take an additional argument—the scrambled argument. This allows each argument to be "unwrapped" and stored with the appropriate predicate. Because constituents must be held in memory until they may be unwrapped (i.e., combined with their argument assigner), multiple scramblings will rapidly lead to greater processing complexity and diminished acceptability judgments. The complexity metric that Rambow and Joshi propose correctly predicts that Dutch cross-serial dependencies will be easier to process than their center-embedded German counterparts (Bach, Brown, & Marslen-Wilson, 1986). Within German, it predicts the ease of extraposition, as well as the difficulty of long-distance topicalization. The results of their study provide a powerful argument for TAGs, which are crucial to the explanations that Rambow and Joshi proffer.

In his chapter, Stabler (chapter 13) proposes the bounded connectivity hypothesis, which claims that the processing complexity of a structure increases quickly when more than one relation of any given type connects a (partial) constituent α (or any element of α) to any constituent external to α. Assuming that A' extraction of an NP with a particular case forms a relevant relation, extraction of two NPs with the same case is predicted to be unacceptable—even in a language like Hindi, where extraction of two NPs with distinct cases is acceptable. Examples like (3), attributed to Mahajan, support the prediction.

(3) ??? kis-ko[1]   rām-ne   kis-ko[2] t_1 t_2 kahā- ki sar dard h∈
     who-ACC   Ram-erg   who-ACC   tell that head pain is
     Who did Ram tell that who has a headache?

Similar support for the bounded connectivity hypothesis is found in 'morphological' causatives, assuming that they are derived from V-raising in the syntax. Each causative verb is raised to amalgamate with the higher verb. Stabler notes that a bound on the number of morphological causatives in a single construction is found widely in V-initial languages (Amharic, Arabic), as well as V-final ones like Quechua. Sentence (4), to be compared with (5), comes from Quechua:

(4) *Riku-chi-chi-chi-ni   (chi = causative)

(5) Riku-chi-chi-ni
     see-make-make-1Sg
     I have shown it.

Presenting new data, Stabler argues against a linguistic account of the bound on morphological causatives. Semantic explanations also fail to account for the bound on repeated application of the causative, given the acceptability of periphastic causatives where no V-raising occurs (e.g., "The president made the general make the sergeant make the private kill the reporter").

In addition to offering a psycholinguistic explanation for data that have not been discussed previously in the psycholinguistic literature, Stabler also explains Dutch and German V raising by appeal to the bounded connectivity hypothesis. Unlike Rambow and Joshi's concern, which is to distinguish the relative increase in difficulty of the German versus Dutch pattern with successively more embeddings, Stabler explains why the jump from two verbs to three verbs creates noticeable difficulty in both languages. Stabler emphasizes that the bounded connectivity constraint is a sufficient, not a necessary, cause of psychological complexity, thus leaving room for other operations to also influence complexity. His approach is a novel one that opens up an entirely new set of questions about the subtrees implicated in parsing and the relations that can connect them, as well as expanding the empirical coverage of psycholinguistic complexity metrics. It also implies a view of 'constructed' memory that is both novel and intriguing.

Referential Processing

One issue that has received a great deal of attention in the last few years is the extent to which contextual and pragmatic information influences on-line parsing decisions. Four chapters on referential processing deal with this issue.

Garrod (chapter 14) is concerned with the general issue of anaphor resolution. He points out that much of the psycholinguistic literature has treated anaphor interpretation as an isolated process that is only rather loosely related to the processes involved in interpreting sentences and discourse. On the other hand, he notes that, in the linguistic literature, different anaphoric devices have been associated with a range of discourse functions that signal different ways in which a sentence should be resolved. Garrod's goal is to reconsider some of the processing assumptions about anaphor resolution in light of various linguistic analyses.

Garrod describes a referential hierarchy for identifying three dimensions by which anaphors vary. The first is contextual presupposition: the degree to which the interpretation of an expression is solely determined by the linguistic context. The second is referential function: the degree to which an expression is used to maintain reference to focused antecedents. The third is antecedent identifiability: the degree to which an expression uniquely specifies its antecedent reference. In his chapter, Garrod describes a number of interesting experiments relative to these distinctions.

The other three chapters in this section are all concerned with how contextual information influences the resolution of temporary syntactic ambiguities. Articles by Rayner, Carlson, and Frazier (1983), Crain and Steedman (1985), and

Altmann and Steedman (1988) set the stage for the debate that is currently raging. Rayner et al. presented evidence suggesting that pragmatic information does not influence the initial parsing of a syntactically ambiguous sentence. Rather, they argued that parsing decisions are made on structural grounds and that contextual and pragmatic information influences reanalysis processes. On the other hand, Crain and Steedman, as well as Altmann, argued that contextual information can override structural decisions.

All participants in the debate concerning the extent to which contextual and discourse factors influence parsing decisions acknowledge that contextual information has an effect. At issue is whether or not such information guides the selection of the first structural hypothesis.

Murray and Liversedge (chapter 15), Sedivy and Spivey-Knowlton (chapter 16), and Spivey-Knowlton and Tanenhaus (chapter 17) continue this debate. Murray and Liversedge report the results of a series of experiments that lead them to come down on the side that referential context does not affect on-line, immediate parsing decisions. On the other hand, Sedivy and Spivey-Knowlton and Spivey-Knowlton and Tanenhaus report evidence leading them to the other conclusion: Contextual and referential information interact with lexical information to determine initial parsing decisions.

It is encouraging that there is now so much interest in the general issue of the influence of discourse information on parsing decisions. Given the wide range of results that have been reported, it seems most appropriate at the moment to determine the situations in which context does and does not have an influence on parsing, rather than continue the debate of *when* context has its impact.

Sentence Processing and Language Acquisition

Crain, Ni, and Conway (chapter 18) provide an extremely stimulating discussion of the relation between adult processing and the language-acquisition device (LAD). They argue that language would be unlearnable if kids assigned "minimal-commitment" interpretations to sentences. No positive evidence could force a revision of a minimal-commitment interpretation. Rather, children must assign maximally disconfirmable interpretations (e.g., letting *only* associate with the largest possible contrast set). However, they argue that adult processing strategies lead to analyses that amount to minimal-commitment interpretations, suggesting a dissociation between language acquisition and adult sentence-processing principles. This proposal is fascinating. It raises issues about the distinctness of LAD and the sentence-parsing module, as well as many issues concerning the semantic preferences exhibited by the adult sentence-processing system. One might have thought that the assignment of focus would determine the interpretation of *only*, and that pragmatic relevance, not minimal disconfirmability, might influence the interpretation of the contrast set for *only*. Regardless of the outcome of future studies of these questions, the Crain et al. proposal moves the field ahead by being so bold and stimulating.

APPROACHES TO RESEARCH IN SENTENCE PROCESSING

Most readers of this volume are aware that there is now a wide variety of methodologies used to study sentence processing. This is very encouraging, and we hope that converging evidence emerges. In the past, the resolution of some critical theoretical issues has seemed to revolve around different methodologies being used. To take an obvious example, early research demonstrating that contextual and pragmatic factors do not influence initial parsing decisions utilized eye-movement data (see Ferreira & Clifton 1986; Rayner et al., 1983) and some self-paced reading data (Ferreira & Clifton, 1986), whereas evidence in favor of contextual information influencing such decisions was based exclusively on self-paced reading data (see Altmann & Steedman, 1988; Taraban & McClelland, 1988). Self-paced reading does not give the experimenter as much opportunity to discriminate first-pass effects from reanalysis effects. That is, the form of self-paced reading that is most diagnostic (see Rayner, Sereno, Morris, Schmauder, & Clifton, 1989) involves the presentation of one word at a time. Hence, readers cannot look back in text and must process each word more completely when first reading it. Therefore, arguments concerning the effects of contextual information on parsing had an inherent confound: Data against the efficacy of such information were based largely on one methodology, whereas data on the other side of the debate were based on a different methodology.

As the chapters in this volume make clear, there are now a number of laboratories that have eye-movement recording devices to study sentence processing. In addition, it is encouraging that ERP studies are now dealing with sentence processing (see the chapters by Osterhout and Hagoort and Brown). As we pointed out earlier, the roadblocks to studying sentence processing as people listen to sentences are disappearing. We think all of these developments are positive because they allow for the possibility of obtaining converging evidence to examine how people comprehend sentences. Thus, perhaps a clearer picture of various issues will emerge by examining results from eye-movement studies, self-paced reading studies, ERP studies, and listening experiments.

At a more general level, sentence-processing research has always involved interdisciplinary work: Psychologists, linguists, computer scientists, and philosophers (and others) have deep and abiding interests in language processing. Researchers from these different disciplines often bring differing theoretical orientations to the field, moving the study of language processing forward by focusing on different aspects of the problem.

Besides reflecting differences in theoretical orientation, the chapters in the present volume exemplify how researchers can have very different theoretical goals. An interesting dichotomy is developing between various researchers interested in language processing. Some think that theories should be molded by data, so that their theories are often at a formative stage. Others think that theories should be explicitly formulated and then tested against data. The chapters in this volume reflect both sides of this dichotomy. In the end, the differences in the way psycholinguists choose to investigate issues related to sentence processing may be primarily a matter of taste, but it is clear that the goal of the work described in this volume is to arrive at a comprehensive theory of language processing.

REFERENCES

Adams, B. C., Clifton, C., Jr., & Mitchell, D. C. (1993). *Lexical guidance in sentence processing: Further evidence for a filtering account.* Manuscript submitted for publication.

Altmann, G., & Steedman, M. (1988). Interaction with context during human sentence processing. *Cognition, 30,* 191–238.

Bach, E., Brown, C., & Marslen-Wilson, W. (1986). Crossed and nested dependencies in German and Dutch. *Language and Cognitive Processes, 1,* 249–262.

Chomsky, N. (1959). Review of *verbal behavior. Language, 35,* 26–58.

Crain, S. & Steedman, M. (1985). On not being led up the garden path: The use of context by the psychological parser. In D. Dowty, L. Kartunnen, & A. Zwicky (Eds.), *Natural language parsing* (pp. 320–358). Cambridge: Cambridge University Press.

DeVincenzi, M. (1991). *Syntactic parsing strategies in Italian.* Dordrecht: Kluwer Academic Publishers.

Ferreira, F., & Clifton, C., Jr. (1986). The independence of syntactic processing. *Journal of Memory and Language, 25,* 348–368.

Frazier, L. (1987). Sentence processing: A tutorial review. In M. Coltheart (Ed.), *Attention and performance* (pp. 559–586). Hillsdale, NJ: Lawrence Erlbaum Associates.

Gardner, H. (1985). *The mind's new science: A history of the cognitive revolution.* New York: Basic Books.

Goodluck, H., Finney, M., & Sedivy, J. (1991). Sentence completeness and filler-gap dependency parsing. In P. Coopmans, B. Schouten, & W. Zonneveld (Eds.), *OTS Yearbook 1991* (pp. 19–31). Utrech, The Netherlands: University of Utrecht Press.

Johnson-Laird, P. N. (1988). *The computer and the mind.* Cambridge, MA: Harvard University Press.

Marslen-Wilson, W. D., & Tyler, L. (1980). The temporal structure of spoken language comprehension. *Cognition, 8,* 1–72.

Miller, G. A., Galanter, E., & Pribram, K. (1960). *Plans and the structure of behavior.* New York: Holt.

Rayner, K., Carlson, M., & Frazier, L. (1983). The interaction of syntax and semantics during sentence processing: Eye movements in the analysis of semantically biased sentences. *Journal of Verbal Learning and Verbal Behavior, 22,* 358–374.

Rayner, K., & Morris, R. (1991). Comprehension processes in reading ambiguous sentences: Reflections from eye movements. In G. B. Simpson (Ed.), *Understanding word and sentence* (pp. 175–198). Amsterdam, The Netherlands: Elsevier Science Publishers.

Rayner, K., Sereno, S., Morris, R., Schmauder, R., & Clifton, C., Jr. (1989). Eye movements and on-line language comprehension processes. *Language and Cognitive Processes, 4,* 21–50.

Stillings, N. A., Feinstein, M. H., Garfield, J. L., Rissland, E. L., Rosenbaum, D. A., Weisler, S. E., & Baker-Ward, L. (1987). *Cognitive science: An introduction.* Cambridge, MA: MIT Press.

Stowe, L. (1986). Parsing wh-constructions: Evidence for on-line gap location. *Language and Cognitive Processes, 1,* 227–246.

Taraban, R., & McClelland, J. R. (1988). Constituent attachment and thematic role assignment in sentence processing: Influences of content-based expectations. *Journal of Memory and Language, 27,* 597–632.

I
SENTENCE PROCESSING AND THE BRAIN

2 Event-Related Brain Potentials as Tools for Comprehending Language Comprehension

Lee Osterhout
University of Washington

Even a cursory consideration of language comprehension is likely to lead to several conclusions about the psychological processes underlying comprehension. Perhaps most notably, comprehension is remarkably rapid, occurring essentially in "real time." Furthermore, despite its rapidity (and despite our intuitions to the contrary), comprehension is not instantaneous, but is instead a continuous process distributed over time. And if one assumes that formal descriptions of language provide even a rough approximation of the informational types and representations that are functionally involved in comprehension, then language comprehension must involve multiple levels of analysis (e.g., phonological, lexical, syntactic, semantic, pragmatic). The results of these multileveled analyses are then somehow integrated into a single coherent interpretation with incredible rapidity. Finally, these processes occur largely outside of our conscious awareness, and indeed remain (for the most part) inaccessible to consciousness.

A substantive model of language comprehension explains how all of this happens. But it is precisely because comprehension is a rapid, multileveled, unconscious process that gaining a substantive understanding of it has proved so difficult (cf. Swinney, 1981, 1982). As eloquently noted by Swinney (1981), to understand comprehension, we must examine the process as it occurs in real time, rather than describing the end-state results of comprehension (i.e., memory representations) or the underlying structure of the language (as provided by linguistic theory). One might surmise that the ideal tool for examining language comprehension mirrors the properties of comprehension itself. Such a tool would combine on-line, continuous, and nonintrusive measurement with a differential sensitivity to events occurring at distinct levels of analysis. Such a tool would also not rely on overt, conscious judgments made by the comprehender.

These ideal properties pose a formidable methodological challenge. Unfortunately, most of the commonly used methods lack many or all of these crucial properties. (One notable exception is the use of eye tracking to monitor reading; cf. Rayner, Sereno, Morris, Schmauder, & Clifton, 1989.) Many of the available methods involve measurements made *after* the process (e.g., word, phrase, or sentence reading time; grammatical judgments) or at a discrete moment *during* the process (e.g., the cross-modal priming technique; cf. Swinney, Onifer, Prather, & Hirshkowitz, 1979). These measurements typically require the use of a secondary task (e.g., button pressing) in addition to the primary task of language comprehension, and the secondary task often requires a conscious decision on the part of the subject (e.g., Is this stimulus a word?). Finally, none of the commonly used measures has been demonstrated to be differentially sensitive to events occurring at distinct levels of analysis. These measures typically respond similarly to events at any level. For example, sentence-reading times increase in the presence of either syntactic or semantic anomaly.

One method that at least in principle approximates the ideal tool as outlined is the recording of event-related potentials (ERPs) elicited during comprehension. ERPs are negative and positive voltage changes in the ongoing electroencephalogram that are time-locked to the onset of a sensory, motor, or cognitive event. Certain negative- and positive-going deflections in the ERP waveform (called *components*) have been shown to be sensitive to specific cognitive processes (for review, see Hillyard & Picton, 1987). The advantages of ERPs as measures of real-time cognition are clear: ERPs provide a continuous, on-line record of the brain's electrical activity that occurs during the process under study. Measurement of ERPs requires neither a potentially contaminating secondary task nor a conscious judgment on the part of the subject. And since ERPs provide at least a rough estimate of localization and lateralization of brain activity, they offer the added prospect of tying behavior and cognitive models more closely to brain function.

Of course, these salutary properties of ERPs are irrelevant unless it can be shown that ERPs are sensitive to the process of interest. The goal of this chapter is to selectively review evidence that ERPs are, in fact, quite sensitive to certain language-related events. Most intriguingly, some of this evidence allows one to speculate that ERPs (perhaps uniquely among current methods) are indeed differentially sensitive to events occurring at distinct levels of linguistic analysis during comprehension. This review focuses on recent findings, particularly those relating to syntactic aspects of comprehension. ERP studies of phonological processes (e.g., Kramer & Donchin, 1987; Polich, McCarthy, Wang, & Donchin, 1983; Rugg, 1985), repetition priming (Rugg, 1984a, 1985b), and semantic priming (e.g., Bentin, 1987; Bentin, McCarthy, & Wood, 1985) are not reviewed. For a general overview of the N400 component of the ERP, see one of several excellent recent reviews (Kutas & Van Petten, 1988; Fischler, 1990; Fischler & Raney, 1991).

METHODOLOGICAL CONSIDERATIONS

A few words concerning ERP methodology are in order. One methodological issue concerns the strategies available for studying cognition with ERPs. ERP researchers typically adopt one of two strategies (see also Coles, Gratton, & Fabiani, 1990; Kutas & Van Petten, 1988; Osterhout & Holcomb, 1993). The first strategy is to identify as precisely as possible the cognitive processes underlying some known ERP component. This can be accomplished (in principle) by determining the necessary and sufficient conditions for altering the component's waveform characteristics (amplitude and latency). The benefits of this strategy are substantial: With an electrophysiological marker of some cognitive process in hand, one can infer changes in the underlying cognitive process directly from changes in the ERP component. For example, prior work led Van Petten and Kutas (1987) to conclude that the amplitude of one ERP component, the N400, reflects a word's "activation level" in memory. More specifically, they concluded that highly activated words elicit small N400s, whereas less activated words elicit large N400s. These reasonable conclusions allowed them to investigate the effects of context on the processing of polysemous words, by measuring the N400s elicited by target words related to the contextually appropriate or inappropriate meanings of a polysemous word (e.g., "The gambler pulled an ace from the bottom of the DECK," followed by the target words *cards* or *ship*). The contextually inappropriate target words elicited a larger amplitude N400 than did the contextually appropriate target words, and (within the window normally associated with the N400) ERPs to inappropriate targets were indistinguishable from ERPs to control words that were not related to any meaning of the ambiguous word. Given the assumptions of Van Petten and Kutas concerning the processes underlying N400, these results seem to indicate that the contextually appropriate meanings of the polysemous word were selectively activated in memory. Although this approach to ERP research has considerable appeal, the mapping between changes in an ERP component and putative cognitive processes is often far from transparent. Importantly, experimental designs that assume knowledge of underlying cognitive processes carry with them the significant risk associated with a misidentification of these processes. If N400 amplitude reflects some aspect of cognition other than word activation, the set of interpretations one would consider in explaining the Van Petten and Kutas findings would probably change dramatically.

The second strategy for using ERPs to study cognition is to use a known ERP component to study some cognitive process even if the cognitive and neural events underlying that component are unknown. All that is needed for this approach to work is that some component must be shown to systematically covary with manipulations of stimuli, task, or instructions that are known or posited to influence the process under study. Having uncovered such a covariation, one can make certain inferences about relevant psychological processes based on between-condition differences in the ERP waveform. For example, several researchers have observed a slow positive-going wave (labeled the *P600* by Osterhout & Holcomb, 1992) in the ERP response to syntactically anomalous words. The specific cognitive events underlying the P600 are not known, and there is scant evidence that the P600 is in any sense a direct manifestation of syntactic processes. Regardless, all that is needed for the P600 to act as a useful tool for investigating syntactic analysis is evidence that the P600 reliably co-occurs with a syntactic anomaly. One can then use the P600 as an electro-physiological indicator of syntactic processing difficulty. The work reviewed next has, by and large, adopted this second approach to ERP research.

Another important methodological issue concerns the temporal information inherent in ERPs. Given the continuous, on-line quality of ERPs, they promise to reveal a great deal about the timing and ordering of language-related events. The critical temporal marker is often the moment in time at which the ERPs from two conditions begin to diverge significantly, rather than the peak latency of a particular component (see also Fischler, 1900; Osterhout & Holcomb, 1993). For example, the peak of one language-sensitive component, the N400, reliably occurs at about 400 ms after presentation of a word. Furthermore, the peak amplitude of the N400 is reliably larger for contextually inappropriate words than for contextually appropriate words (Kutas & Hillyard, 1980). However, divergences in the waveforms elicited by appropriate and inappropriate words typically emerge around 200–250 ms following word onset. The importance of this distinction becomes clear when considering whether N400 amplitude reflects processes associated with lexical access. If the peak amplitude of the N400 is taken as the relevant temporal marker, most researchers would argue that the component occurs too late to reflect lexical access (see, e.g., Sabol & De Rosa, 1976). However, if the onset of divergences in waveforms is taken to be the relevant temporal marker, the N400 is much closer to the temporal window thought to be associated with lexical access.

What sorts of inferences, then, can one make about the timing of cognitive processes based on ERP data? In practice, such inferences are fraught with danger, particularly if the ERP effects are relatively late occurring. For example, consider again the P600 effect associated with a syntactic anomaly. This effect often has an onset around 500 ms after presentation of the anomaly (Osterhout & Holcomb, 1992; Osterhout, Holcomb, & Swinney, in press; Osterhout & Mobley, 1993). This finding by no means licenses the inference that the assignment of syntactic roles to words occurs only 500 ms after word presentation. The P600 might reflect syntactic processes only indirectly; hence, the onset of the effect could be temporally distant from the syntactic processes themselves. Fortunately, very early onsets of ERP effects can sometimes license reasonably strong inferences about the timing of cognitive processes. A good example of this is provided by Holcomb and Neville (1991), who reported that the ERPs to contextually inappropriate words in spoken sentences begin to diverge from those to contextually appropriate words long before the entirety of the word has been encountered by the listener. This indicates quite clearly that the interaction between word recognition and context occurs long before the word can be recognized based on the acoustic input alone.

A separate issue concerns the use of items analyses as a procedure for generalizing the results beyond the particular set of items used in the experiment (cf. Clark, 1973). Although such analyses have become a standard procedure within psycholinguistics, they are rarely performed in ERP research. One reason for this is related to the signal-to-noise issue inherent in the signal-averaging procedure used to obtain the ERP (cf. Hillyard & Picton, 1987). In the subjects analyses, ERP researchers studying language-related components typically average over a minimum of 30 trials for each subject to extract the "signal" (the ERP) from the "noise" (randomly occurring EEG). This provides a sufficient signal-to-noise ratio when the ERP effect of interest is reasonably large (e.g., greater than 2 μV). To obtain an equivalent signal-to-noise ratio in the items analyses, experimenters would be required to run at least 30 subjects per experiment—a number far greater than that necessary to derive stable, reliable ERP averages over subjects. (In practice, the required number of subjects is likely to be greater than the number of items, for several reasons; e.g., the fact that between-subject variance is almost always greater than within-subject variance.) Running the required number of subjects for items analyses is often deemed prohibitively expensive in terms of the use of resources. Nor is the signal-to-noise issue the only problem associated with items analyses. For example, such analyses typically require tremendous quantities of computer memory and disk space— quantities that are simply too large for the typical ERP laboratory. Faced with these and other equally severe problems, most ERP researchers rely on replications across different sets of items to determine the generalizability of the effects of interest.

Finally, an important methodological concern in any examination of sentence processing is the mode of stimulus presentation. Because measurement of ERPs does not require an intrusive secondary task, in principle this method allows presentation to more closely approximate a "normal" comprehension environment. Indeed, several researchers have recently recorded ERPs during the comprehension of sentences presented as natural, continuous speech (Holcomb & Neville, 1990, 1991; Osterhout & Holcomb, 1993). Others have linked ERP measurements with eye saccades during "normal" reading (Marton & Szirtes, 1988). However, the standard method in most of the existing literature (and in most of the work reviewed here) has involved the visual presentation of sentences in a sequential, word-by-word manner, with typical word-onset asynchronies ranging from 300 to 650 ms. This stimulus presentation mode has been chosen because it allows an examination of an extended period of ERP activity to individual words that is uncontaminated by the ERPs to subsequent words. Although this precaution was reasonable as a first step, more recent work (e.g., Osterhout & Holcomb, 1993) indicates that it is not always necessary.

ERPS AND LANGUAGE

Correspondence Between Formal Theories and Comprehension Processes

One fundamental issue confronting psycholinguistic attempts to model language comprehension concerns the correspondence between formal theories of language and the cognitive-neural processes underlying comprehension. Linguistic theories of grammatical structure often distinguish among several levels of analysis (e.g., phonetic, syntactic, semantic, etc.). Perhaps the most basic distinction is that between syntax (sentence form) and semantics (sentence content). From a linguist's point of view, sentences that violate syntactic constraints (e.g., "John slept the bed") are quite distinct from sentences that violate semantic or pragmatic constraints (e.g., "John buttered his bread with socks"). Whether or not these levels of description apply to the psychological processes underlying language comprehension remains a point of dispute. A common assumption in much recent psycholinguistic work is that separable processes derive distinct syntactic and semantic representations of a sentence (cf. Berwick & Weinberg, 1983; Fodor, Bever, & Garrett, 1974). However, a popular alternative view (one that has gained considerable ground with the advent of "neural net" models) is that semantic interpretations can be derived directly, without an intervening syntactic level (Ades & Steedman, 1982; Bates, McNew, MacWhinney, Devescovi, & Smith, 1982; Johnson-Laird, 1977; McClelland & Kawamoto, 1986; Riesbeck & Schank, 1978).

This fundamental question has been difficult to address with standard measures, largely because, as noted, these measures tend to respond similarly to anomalies at different levels (Fischler & Bloom, 1980; Rayner et al., 1989; Stanovitch & West, 1983; Wright & Garrett, 1984). The multidimensional nature of ERPs might make them a more efficacious tool for addressing this issue, given two key assumptions. One assumption is that the processes associated with a given level of analysis are distinct from those associated with other levels. A second assumption is that cognitively distinct processes are mediated by neurally distinct brain systems. Given these assumptions, evidence that syntactic and semantic anomalies elicit dissimilar patterns of brain activity could be construed to support the claim that separable syntactic and semantic processes exist (Neville, Nicol, Barss, Forster, & Garrett, 1991; Osterhout & Holcomb, 1992).

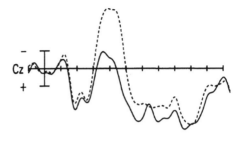

FIG. 2.1. Grand-average ERPs (averaged over subjects and items) recorded over site Cz to semantically anomalous words (dashed line) and nonanomalous control words (solid line) embedded within sentences. Onset of the critical words is indicated by the vertical calibration bar. Each hashmark on the horizontal axis represents 100 ms. Negative voltage is plotted up. Adapted from Osterhout (1990).

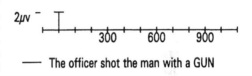

The pioneering work of Kutas and her associates over the past 15 years has demonstrated that the brain's electrophysiological response is measurably sensitive to at least one form of semantic-pragmatic anomaly. Kutas and Hillyard (1980a, 1980b, 1980c, 1983, 1984) found that contextually inappropriate words elicit a large-amplitude negative-going wave with a peak amplitude around 400 ms poststimulus (the N400 component; see Kutas & Van Petten, 1988, for review). A typical N400 response, elicited by words like *moon* in the sentence "The officer shot the man with a *moon* last night," is shown in Fig. 2.1. Although the precise cognitive (and neural) events underlying the N400 remain unclear, N400 amplitude appears to be a function of the semantic fit between the target word and preceding context.

Subsequent work has left little doubt that N400 amplitude is (at least in many situations) associated with semantic aspects of comprehension. The question, then, is whether the N400 also functions as a metric of syntactic processes, or if such processes are associated with a different (or any) ERP component. This question was addressed by Osterhout and Holcomb (1992). We presented sentences containing apparent violations of verb subcategorization or violations of phrase-structure constraints, as in (1) and (2):

(1) The broker hoped *to* sell the stock.

(2) *The broker persuaded *to* sell the stock.

The clausal complement "to sell the stock" can be easily attached to the fragment "The broker hoped" in Sentence (1). However, when used in its active form, the

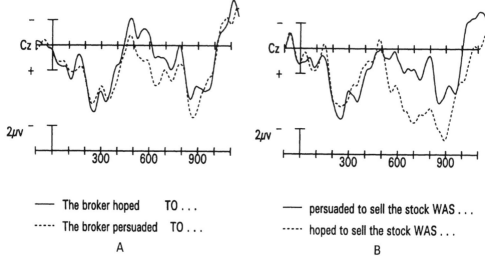

FIG. 2.2. (A) ERPs to apparent violations of verb subcategorization (dashed line) and grammatical control words (solid line). (B) ERPs to phrase-structure violations (dashed line) and grammatical controls words (solid line). Adapted from Osterhout and Holcomb (1992).

transitive verb *persuade* does not allow an argument beginning with the word *to* (i.e., a prepositional phrase [PP] or an infinitival clause) to occur immediately adjacent to the verb. Hence, the infinitival marker *to* in (2) is likely to be perceived as a violation of verb subcategorization, assuming readers do not initially attempt a reduced-relative clause analysis of the sentence. Fig. 2.2A plots the ERPs elicited by the infinitival markers in (1) and (2). The waveforms elicited by the grammatical and ungrammatical sentences clearly diverge between roughly 500 and 800 ms following presentation of the infinitival markers. However, the response to the syntactically anomalous case is not the negative-going N400, but is instead a positive-going wave. Because the positivity had a midpoint around 600 ms, we labeled this wave *P600*.

This finding suggests that a syntactic anomaly does elicit a brain response, but that this response is quite distinct from the N400 elicited by a semantic anomaly. In a second study, we presented lengthened versions of the sentences used in our first experiment, as illustrated in (3) and (4):

(3) *The broker hoped to sell the stock *was* sent to jail.

(4) The broker persuaded to sell the stock *was* sent to jail.

In (3) the added phrase cannot be attached to the initial part of the sentence without violating the phrase structure rules of English. Thus, (3) is ungrammatical and becomes so at the auxiliary verb *was*. Conversely, the added phrase can be attached to the initial part of Sentence (4); the verb *persuade* can be passivized, and this allows a reduced-relative clause interpretation of the sentence (corresponding to "The broker [who was] persuaded to sell the stock was sent to jail"). Under such an analysis, the auxiliary verb can be attached as part of the main clause ("The broker was sent to jail") and a syntactic anomaly is avoided. Therefore, if the P600 is associated with a syntactic anomaly, then the word *was* in (3) should elicit a P600 relative to the ERPs to the same word in sentences like (4). ERPs to the auxiliary verbs in both sentences types are shown in Fig. 2.2B. As predicted, the auxiliary verbs in the ungrammatical sentences elicited a large P600. These words also elicited a left-hemisphere, anterior negativity between 300 and 500 ms (not observable in Fig. 2.2B). Similar results have been reported by Hagoort, Brown, and Groothusen (1993), who used Dutch sentences as stimuli.

The basic distinction between syntax and semantics is not the only relevant distinction made by formal theories of grammar. For example, government-and-binding (GB) theory (Chomsky, 1981, 1986) posits the existence of multiple modules of grammatical knowledge within the syntactic domain. GB includes one module for specifying constraints on the phrase structure of sentences (X-bar theory) and other modules (theta theory, case theory, subjacency, empty category principle, etc.) that constrain "movement" of sentence elements for question and relative-clause formation. It is conceivable that a direct mapping exists between the grammar and the comprehension system, such that these modules of grammatical knowledge (or some subset of these modules) are encoded in cognitively and neurally distinct processing systems. (For claims in this direction, see Ferreira & Clifton, 1986; Frazier, 1990; Freedman & Forster, 1985). If these modules of knowledge are, in fact, instantiated in distinct processing modules within the brain, then one prediction is that each type of violation will elicit a distinct brain response. Two recent studies have examined this possibility. McKinnon and Osterhout (1993) examined the response to violations subsumed under the subjacency principle and the empty-category principle (ECP). Examples of violations of these constraints are presented in Sentences (5) and (6):

(5) *I wonder which of his staff members$_i$ the candidate was annoyed *when* his son was questioned by _____ $_i$.
(subjacency violation)

(6) *John$_i$ seems *that* it is likely _____ $_i$ to win.
(ECP violation)

The underlined word in each sentence marks the first point at which subjects might note the ungrammaticality of these sentences. The blank spaces represent "gaps" formed by movement of a sentence constituent (the "filler") from its canonical position. The subscripts index the gap to the filler. It is sufficient for present purposes to note that, within the GB framework, (5) is ungrammatical

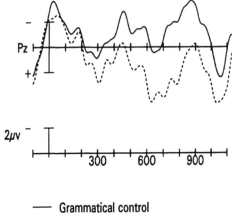

FIG. 2.3. ERPs to subjacency
violations. (dashed line) and
grammatical controls (solid
line).

—— Grammatical control

····· Subjacency violation

because the filler is too distant from its gap. More accurately, the structure
intervening between the filler and the gap prevents a coindexation of the two (cf.
Chomsky, 1981, 1986). Sentence (6) is ungrammatical because the gap does not
maintain the proper structural relation to its filler or other proper governor
(Lasnik & Saito, 1992).

The response to both types of anomalies was highly similar. (The response to
subjacency violations is shown in Fig. 2.3.) Both anomalies elicited a positive-
going wave similar in its component characteristics to the P600 effect reported by
Osterhout and Holcomb (1992). The major difference was that the response to the
subjacency and ECP violations had an onset around 200 ms. In contrast, the
onset of the response to phrase-structure and subcategorization violations reported by Osterhout and Holcomb was not evident until about 500 ms.

Similar data have been reported by Neville et al. (1991). These investigators
measured the response to violations of three distinct constraints: (a) phrase-
structure rules, (b) subjacency, and (c) a third constraint known as the specificity
constraint, which stipulates that a *wh*-phrase cannot be moved out of a noun
phrase (NP) with specific reference (consider the unacceptability of "What$_i$ did
the man admire Don's sketch *of* ____ $_i$?"). As in the Osterhout and Holcomb
study, phrase-structure violations elicited both an enhanced negativity between
300 and 500 ms over left-hemisphere sites and a large positive-going wave
beginning at about 500 ms. Subjacency violations elicited a positivity with an
onset around 200 ms. Specificity violations elicited a slow negative-going potential that was most evident in the left hemisphere and that had an onset as early as
125 ms at some sites.

Whether or not these results indicate the operation of distinct processing modules has been a matter for debate. To date, all syntactic anomalies tested so far (excepting specificity violations) have elicited a broad-based positive-going wave (the P600), beginning between 200 and 500 ms after presentation of the anomaly. Assuming that similar brain responses reflect similar cognitive states, these data seem to indicate that many syntactic anomalies engender a similar processing response. This response is quite distinct from that elicited by a semantic anomaly (cf. McKinnon & Osterhout, 1993). At the same time, differences do exist among the responses to these different violations, particularly in the portion of the waveforms preceding P600 onset. For example, phrase-structure violations were associated with a left-hemisphere negativity not seen in the response to other anomalies, and P600 onset was much more rapid for subjacency violations than for phrase-structure violations. These differences can be construed as evidence that separable processing systems exist for each type of constraint (cf. Neville et al., 1991). Of course, there is nothing inconsistent in maintaining both claims simultaneously. It is certainly possible that, although the syntactic anomalies produce a common end state (reflected in the P600), this end state is reached via nonidentical sets of processes (reflected in the ERP differences preceding the P600).

The previous data exemplify situations in which formal theories of language structure have informed processing theories. One might ask whether opportunities exist for the converse situation to apply, that is, data from processing studies informing formal theory construction. In particular, one might conceivably use ERPs to provide an empirical, evidential basis for identifying the level of analysis at which certain phenomena occur within the processing system. As noted by Radford (1988), this is not always obvious. In examining the status of the anomalous sentences such as "The boy next door never loses her temper with anyone," Radford notes that the proper characterization of such oddities is open to argument. One could claim that the sentence is *syntactically* anomalous, that is, that agreement between a pronoun and its antecedent in gender is stipulated as part of the formal, rule-governed grammar. Alternatively, one could claim that the sentence is *semantically* anomalous, i.e., that part of the meaning of the noun *boy* denotes a male human, whereas part of the meaning of the pronoun *she* denotes a female human, leading to a contradiction in meaning if these two entities are taken to be co-referential. This ambiguity is mirrored in linguists' theoretical treatments of agreement (cf. Barlow & Ferguson, 1988). Traditional grammars (and many modern grammars) treat agreement as part of the syntactic (form-driven) system (Chomsky, 1986; Quirk & Greenbaum, 1973). But other recent accounts propose a semantic or discourse-function (content-driven) account of agreement (Givon, 1976; Reid, 1991).

Clearly, if our previous interpretations are correct, ERPs might prove helpful in deciding this issue from an empirical basis. The question is simple: Do violations of agreement elicit a brain response that is more similar to that elicited by a syntactic or semantic anomaly? That is, will such anomalies elicit the P600 (syntactic anomaly) or the N400 (semantic anomaly)? We (Osterhout & Mobley, 1993) recently addressed this issue by presenting sentences similar to (7)–(9):

(7) *Many doctors *claims* that insurance rates are too high.
(8) *The hungry guests helped *himself* to the delicious meal.
(9) *The successful woman congratulated *himself* on the promotion.

All three sentences contain an agreement violation. In Sentence (7), the verb disagrees with its subject in number. In (8) and (9), the reflexive disagrees with its antecedent in number and gender, respectively. Of interest are the ERPs elicited by the italicized words in each sentence. All three anomaly types elicited a large positive-going wave similar to the P600 component discussed previously. One could interpret these data as indicating that agreement is encoded as part of the syntactic, rule-governed constraints on well formedness. Similar results have been obtained with agreement violations that were presented to Dutch speakers (Hagoort et al., in press).

ERPs and On-Line Syntactic Analysis

One of the more notable trends within psycholinguistics over the past decade has been the resurgence of interest in the on-line syntactic analysis of sentences. This resurgence has been fueled largely by the seminal work of Frazier and Rayner (1982; Rayner, Carlson, & Frazier, 1983) and their associates (e.g., Ferreira & Clifton, 1986; Ferreira & Henderson, 1990). These researchers have compellingly demonstrated that, given an appropriate tool (eye tracking in this case), one can observe even those comprehension processes that occur with great speed. Because ERPs appear to be sensitive to syntactic aspects of comprehension, it becomes feasible to attempt to use ERPs as another on-line tool for investigating the psychological and neural processes underlying syntactic analysis during sentence comprehension.

One particularly productive line of research has entailed examining the processing response to syntactic ambiguity (i.e., situations in which more than one well-formed syntactic analysis is available for a string of words). For example, consider Sentence (10):

(10) The lawyer charged (that) the defendant *was* lying.

Without the complementizer *that,* the proper grammatical role of the NP "the defendant" is temporarily ambiguous between an "object of the verb" role and a "subject of an upcoming clause" role. The fact that the NP is actually the subject of a clausal complement becomes certain only when the syntactically disambiguating auxiliary verb *was* is encountered. In contrast, the presence of the overt complementizer immediately indicates (prior to encountering the NP) that the subject role is the appropriate role for the upcoming NP. Considerable evidence (mostly involving measurements of eye movements during reading) has indicated that readers experience processing difficulty upon encountering the auxiliary verb in sentences like (10) when no complementizer is present (Rayner & Frazier, 1987). These results have been taken to indicate that readers initially (and erroneously) assign the object role to the ambiguous NP (i.e., readers seem to pursue a single syntactic analysis even when confronted with syntactic ambiguity). Under a direct-object analysis, the phrase "was lying" cannot be attached to the preceding sentence fragment, and therefore a syntactic garden path results; the reader must attempt a reanalysis of the sentence.

Data from the few ERP studies that have examined this issue are, by and large, consistent with this serial parsing model. The results reported by Osterhout and Holcomb (1992), discussed earlier, are consistent with the claim that readers initially computed a simple-active analysis when confronted with a simple-active/reduced-relative clause ambiguity. Further work by Osterhout et al. (in press) provided additional evidence. Osterhout et al. presented sentences similar to Sentence (10). The auxiliary verb in sentences without an overt complementizer elicited a P600-like positivity, relative to ERPs to the same words in sentences with a complementizer. One could interpret this result as indicating that readers initially pursued the direct-object analysis of the reduced sentences, leading to a syntactic anomaly (a garden-path effect) upon encountering the disambiguating auxiliary verb.

If readers initially pursue a single analysis for syntactically ambiguous sentences, what factors determine which analysis is attempted first? Two distinct (and mutually exclusive) generalizations have been proposed regarding this question. Frazier and her colleagues have persuasively argued for a "minimal-attachment" strategy, in which the simplest analysis (as determined by the number of nodes in the phrase structure) is always attempted first, with backtracking and reanalysis when the minimal-attachment analysis turns out to be incorrect (Frazier, 1987; Frazier & Rayner, 1982). Other theorists have argued for a "lexical-preference" parser, in which the parser initially pursues the analysis that is consistent with the "preferred" subcategorization frame of the matrix verb in the sentence (Fodor, 1978; Ford, Bresnan, & Kaplan, 1982; Tanenhaus & Carlson, 1989). Implications of these two approaches are illustrated by Sentences (11)–(14):

(11) The doctor hoped the patient *was* lying.
(12) *The doctor forced the patient *was* lying.
(13) The doctor believed the patient *was* lying.
(14) The doctor charged the patient *was* lying.

These sentences are distinguished by the subcategorization properties associated with the main verb in each sentence. The intransitive verb *hope* in Sentence (11) does not allow a direct-object NP, unambiguously indicating that the NP is the subject of an upcoming clause. The transitive verb *force* in Sentence (12) requires a direct object, forcing the postverbal NP to play the object role. This results in ungrammaticality when the auxiliary verb *was* is encountered. The verbs in Sentences (13) and (14) can be used with or without a direct object. This introduces temporary syntactic ambiguity—the postverbal NP might be acting either as object of the verb or as subject of an upcoming clause. Because the object interpretation is syntactically simpler (Frazier & Rayner, 1982), a minimal-attachment parser would initially (and erroneously) assign the object role to the NP. This would lead to the apparent ungrammaticality due to a garden-path effect at the auxiliary in both sentences. In contrast, a lexical-preference parser would initially choose the analysis consistent with the verb's biases. The verb in Sentence (13) is biased toward intransitive use, whereas the verb in Sentence (14) is biased toward transitive use. Hence, a lexical-preference parser would initially pursue the correct verb–subject analysis of Sentence (13), but would erroneously pursue the verb–NP analysis of (14), leading to a garden-path effect at the auxiliary verb.

Sentences similar to Sentences (11)–(14) were visually presented (in a word-by-word manner) by Osterhout et al. (in press). ERPs to the final three words in each sentence type (postverbal noun, auxiliary verb, and the sentence-ending verb) are shown in Fig. 2.4. Arrows indicate the onset of each word. As expected, the auxiliary verbs in sentences containing "pure" transitive verbs elicited a large P600 effect, relative to the same words in sentences containing "pure" intransitive verbs. Less expectedly, these auxiliary verbs also elicited an enhanced N400 component. This observation is a challenge to our claim that the P600 and N400 effects are elicited as a function of syntactic and semantic anomalies, respectively. One reasonable explanation that allows us to maintain this claim hinges on the observation that the auxiliary verbs in these sentences rendered the sentence irrevocably ungrammatical (hence, uninterpretable). In contrast, the auxiliary verb in sentences like Sentences (10) and (14) simply force the parser to consider a less preferred analysis. Hence, ERPs to the auxiliary verb in Sentence (12) might contain the response to both a syntactic anomaly and the response to the semantic anomaly engendered by the ungrammaticality (and resulting uninterpretability) of the sentence.[1]

---

[1]Given such an interpretation, the relative onsets of the N400 (around 200 ms) and P600 (around 500 ms) become somewhat paradoxical. According to most accounts, syntactic analysis precedes semantic analysis (and indeed the semantic anomaly here is the result of the syntactic anomaly). Yet the brain response to semantic anomaly is actually preceding the response to syntactic anomaly. Since we cannot at present precisely identify the cognitive events underlying these effects, the resolution to the paradox is not clear. However, we would note that these effects may not directly reflect the processes involved in constructing syntactic and semantic representations; rather, it is likely that these

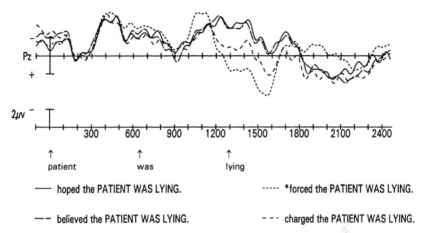

↑ patient   ↑ was   ↑ lying

—— hoped the PATIENT WAS LYING.   ····· *forced the PATIENT WAS LYING.

— — believed the PATIENT WAS LYING.   - - - charged the PATIENT WAS LYING.

FIG. 2.4.   ERPs to the final three words in each of the four sentence types: intransitive, transitive, intransitively biased, and transitively biased. Onset of the critical word (the auxiliary verb, penultimate in the sentence) is indicated by the second arrow under the horizontal axis. Adapted from Osterhout, Holcomb, and Swinney (in press).

Fig. 2.4 also indicates that auxiliary verbs in sentences containing transitively biased verbs also elicited a P600, although reduced in amplitude and more restricted in distribution than the P600 elicited by pure transitive-verb sentences. In striking contrast, ERPs to auxiliary verbs in sentences containing *intransitively* biased verbs were indistinguishable from those elicited by the same words in "pure" intransitive sentences (i.e., the auxiliary verbs in these sentences did not elicit a P600 effect). Clearly, P600 amplitude was a function of the verb-subcategorization information associated with the matrix verbs in these sentences. These findings suggest that the putative verb biases exist and have processing relevance at least under some comprehension environments.[2] Perhaps more importantly, these results provide compelling evidence that P600 amplitude is a function of syntactic aspects of comprehension.

Another type of syntactic ambiguity concerns the processing of "filler-gap" relations within sentences. As noted, these sentences contain a constituent (the filler) that has been "moved" from its canonical position within the sentence (the

---

components are indeterminately removed from the syntactic and semantic processes themselves. Also, this explanation is seemingly inconsistent with the results observed by Osterhout and Holcomb (1992). In that study, the phrase structure violations rendered the sentence irrevocably ungrammatical; yet, the response to the anomaly was a monophasic positivity.

[2]For a discussion concerning whether this evidence indicates that verb information is used to determine the *initial* syntactic analysis pursued by the parser or, alternatively, to aid in the re-analysis of an initial parse (as, e.g., predicted by models of parsing operating under a minimal attachment principle; cf. Frazier, 1987), see Osterhout et al. (in press).

gap). Considerable evidence indicates that the comprehension system attempts to match up fillers with the appropriate gaps during comprehension (cf. Bever & McElree, 1988; MacDonald, 1989; Nicol & Swinney, 1989; Osterhout & Swinney, 1993). However, this process of gap filling is far from trivial, as there is often uncertainty concerning the proper location of the gap. For example, the sentence fragment "The mother found out which book the child read. . . ." can be continued in several ways, each with a different gap location. Two models have been proposed to account for how the processing system deals with such uncertainty (cf. Fodor, 1978; Garnsey, Tanenhaus, & Chapman, 1989). A *first-resort parser* assigns a filler to the first possible gap, whereas a *last-resort parser* waits until there is unambiguous information about gap location. Garnsey et al. conducted a clever experiment to contrast these parsing models. They presented sentences similar to Sentences (15) and (16):

(15) The businessman knew which customer$_i$ the secretary called _____ $_i$ at home.
(16) The businessman knew which article$_i$ the secretary called _____ $_i$ at home.

The first possible gap location in these sentences is immediately after the verb (in direct-object position). However, the sentences could continue in such a way that the gap actually occurs at a different location (e.g., "The businessman knew which article the secretary called about _____"). A first-resort parser would posit a gap immediately after the verb, whereas a last-resort parser would wait until the proper gap location could be identified with certainty. The logic of the experiment was as follows: The noun *customer* is a plausible object of the verb *call*, whereas the noun *article* is not. If the parser immediately posits a gap after the verb and associates the gap with the filler, and if that filler is an implausible object, the verb might be expected to elicit an N400 component. This is precisely what Garnsey et al. observed, providing support for the first-resort parsing model.

Also relating to filler-gap sentences is the posited distinction between processes that derive phrase-structure representations (constituent-analysis processes) and those that determine relations among phrasal types (such as the "binding" between a gap and its antecedent). There are theoretical and empirical reasons for believing that these two tasks are distinct and separable (Frazier, 1990; Freedman & Forster, 1985; Forster, 1987). One theoretical reason for anticipating such a distinction within the processing system is that this distinction is explicit within GB theory. Furthermore, within GB there is an implied sequentiality in the operation of these processes; the phrase-structure representation must be constructed before relationships among phrasal constituents can be checked. This has led to the hypothesis that listeners and readers might "overgenerate" constituent structures that are locally well formed but that violate constraints on relationships among constituents. And indeed there have been claims of evidence purporting to show that readers "overgenerate" sentence structures in just this way (Freedman & Forster, 1985; Forster, 1987; Forster & Stevenson, 1987; but see Crain & Fodor, 1987). There is also evidence that certain aphasics can generate complete constituent structures, but cannot perform binding operations and other semantic processes over these structures (Linebarger, 1989).

If constituent analysis and binding operations are indeed separable and sequential, one might anticipate evidence that binding constraints are applied only after some measurable delay (cf. Weinberg, 1987). Some evidence bearing on this prediction is provided by the studies by McKinnon and Osterhout (1993) and Neville et al. (1991). In both experiments, sentences were presented that contained violations of constraints on movement (i.e., subjacency and ECP). As noted earlier, both types of anomaly elicited a P600-like positivity. Critically, the onset of this positivity was actually much more rapid for subjacency and ECP violations than for phrase-structure and verb subcategorization violations (compare Fig. 2.2B and 2.3).[3] These results are difficult to reconcile with the claim that binding constraints are applied after phrase-structure constraints.

Are These Language-Related ERP Effects Language Specific?

One of the standard doctrines within modern neuropsychology is the existence of language-specific brain systems (cf. Geschwind, 1979). Therefore, it is reasonable to ask whether the ERP components that are sensitive to language processes (e.g., N400 and P600) are in any sense language specific. Such claims have been made recently with respect to the N400 component (Holcomb, 1988; Holcomb & Neville, 1990). With respect to the P600, the most salient alternative to the language-specificity hypothesis is the possibility that the P600 is a member of the family of late positive components (P300 and related components) often observed following unexpected stimuli (Donchin, 1979, 1981; Duncan-Johnson & Donchin, 1977; Hillyard & Picton, 1987; Ritter & Vaughan, 1969). The amplitude of the P300 is a function of both the subjective probability and the task relevance of the eliciting stimulus. Because the P300 is elicited by a wide variety of stimuli, it is clearly not language specific. One could easily justify the claim that the syntactic anomalies in the experiments reviewed previously acted as "unexpected events," either by virtue of the general rarity of ungrammaticality or because readers generate expectations concerning upcoming sentence constituents.

---

[3]This comparison is somewhat complicated by the fact that in the Osterhout and Holcomb (1992) study, words were presented at a rate of 650 ms per word, while in the McKinnon and Osterhout study words were presented at a rate of 400 ms per word.

There are at least three ways to evaluate the possibility that the P600 is "just another" P300.[4] First, one can directly compare the scalp distributions of the P300 and P600 components. It is generally agreed that ERP components with distinct scalp distributions must be generated by neurally distinct brain systems (cf. Johnson, 1993). Second, one can attempt to determine if P600 amplitude is affected by the same manipulations known to affect P300 amplitude. If not, one has grounds for arguing that the effects are functionally distinct. Third, and most critically, one can determine whether the P600 and P300 components are *additive* in their effects. This can be accomplished by presenting stimuli that are expected to simultaneously elicit both components, and comparing this response to the ERP response to each anomaly type in isolation. Additivity in such situations strongly implies functional and neural independence (see, e.g., Kutas & Hillyard, 1980a).

An investigation of the relationship between P600 and P300 is currently underway in our laboratory. In an initial experiment, we manipulated both anomaly type and the task relevance of the anomalies. The stimuli include three sentence types: well-formed sentences with no anomalies; sentences containing a verb that disagreed with the subject noun in number (which should elicit the P600); and well-formed sentences containing a word in uppercase letters (the type of "physical" anomaly known to elicit the P300-like effects). This allowed direct comparisons of the scalp distributions of the ERP response to each anomaly type. Additionally, the subjects' task was manipulated in a between-subjects manner. One group of subjects was asked to make "sentence acceptability" judgments following each sentence. Subjects were explicitly told that an anomaly of any type was sufficient to render the sentence "unacceptable"; hence, both types of anomalies were directly task relevant. A second group of subjects was asked to passively read each sentence. Presumably, the anomalies in this condition were less task relevant than in the first condition.

ERPs to the critical words in each sentence type are shown in Fig. 2.5A (acceptability-judgment condition) and 2.5B (passive-reading condition). In both conditions, as expected, the uppercase words elicited a large positive wave with an onset around 200 ms and with a peak amplitude around 400 ms (similar to previous reports of the P300 component; cf. Donchin, 1981). The agreement violations elicited a positivity with an onset around 500 ms and a peak amplitude around 700 ms (the P600 component). Although the amplitudes, onsets, and peak latencies of these effects differed, the scalp distributions of these effects were very similar. Furthermore, the manipulation of task relevance had a similar

---

[4]Recent work has indicated that there might be many "P300-like" components, each with an independent neural source (cf. Johnson, Jr., 1993). Therefore, a better way to phrase this question might be to ask whether the brain response to anomalies that involve formal, rule-governed aspects of language is distinct from the response to anomalies that do not. In the present discourse, one can think of the terms "P600" and "P300" as shorthand for these two categories of anomaly.

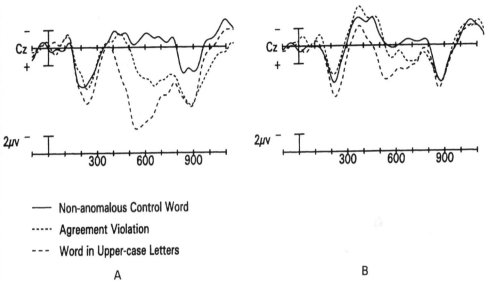

— Non-anomalous Control Word

····· Agreement Violation

- - - Word in Upper-case Letters

A   B

FIG. 2.5. ERPs to uppercase words (long dashes), agreement violations (short dashes), and nonanomalous control words (solid line). (A)
ERPs elicited during the acceptability-judgment task; (B) ERPs elicited
during the passive-reading task.

influence on the response to both anomaly types. The amplitude of both responses was greatly reduced in the passive-reading condition, relative to the
acceptability-judgment condition.

These findings seem to indicate that the P600 might indeed be another manifestation of the P300 family of positivities. However, preliminary results from a
second experiment lead us to suspect that the contrary claim is correct. In this
experiment, we presented the sentences described earlier, plus a fourth sentence
type that contained a "doubly anomalous" word (i.e., a verb that disagrees with
its subject in number and that is also in uppercase letters). The goal was to
determine whether the P300 and P600 are additive. We evaluated this by comparing the observed waveform elicited by the doubly anomalous words to a composite waveform created by adding the ERP response to agreement violations and
uppercase words (when these anomalies were presented independently) to the
waveform elicited by the nonanomalous control sentences. The composite waveform was remarkably similar to (and did not differ significantly from) the observed waveform (Fig. 2.6). We believe that this striking preliminary result
represents compelling evidence that the P300 and P600 components have additive effects. The clear implication of this result is that the P300 and P600 are
indeed independent. Of course, this claim in turn does not *necessarily* imply that
the P600 is language specific.

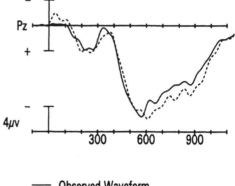

FIG. 2.6. ERPs to words that were in uppercase letters and that indicated an agreement violation (solid line) and composite waveform (dashed line).

—— Observed Waveform

····· Composite Waveform

Caveats and Complications

Perhaps the most important caveat attached to the previous work is the artificiality introduced by the relatively slow word-by-word visual presentation of sentences. Simply put, people do not usually comprehend language in this manner. Therefore, one must ask whether these results will generalize to more natural comprehension situations. Although a complete answer to this question is not yet available, early indications are encouraging in this regard. In particular, Osterhout and Holcomb (1993) replicated their earlier study (Osterhout & Holcomb, 1992), replacing word-by-word visual presentation with sentences presented as continuous, natural speech. Violations of verb subcategorization and phrase-structure constraints elicited a positive-going wave similar to that elicited during comprehension of the visual sentences, indicating that mode of presentation is not a critical factor.

A second issue concerns a possible alternative interpretation of these ERP effects. In the work reviewed earlier, large N400s have been elicited by content words (nouns and verbs), whereas the P600 has been elicited by function words (e.g., infinitival markers and auxiliary verbs).[5] Hence, the possibility exists that the N400 and P600 are elicited as a function of word class, rather than anomaly type; i.e., anomaly type has been confounded with word class). Closed class words serve primarily as vehicles of phrasal construction, whereas open class words are primarily agents of reference. A considerable amount of evidence from diverse lines of investigation suggests that these two classes are treated differently during comprehension, and might indeed involve the operation of neurally

---

[5]Note that in the Osterhout and Mobley (1993) study discussed above, in some sentences the critical words were (open class) verbs. However, the critical comparisons involved erroneous plurality markers, which are often considered to be closed class morphemes.

distinct systems (e.g., Bradley, Garrett, & Zurif, 1980; Friederici, 1983; Neville, 1992). Perhaps a syntactic anomaly engenders a processing response that is similar to that engendered by a semantic anomaly, but the similarity in responses is obscured by differences in the responses to tokens of the two word classes. To investigate this possibility, we recently presented garden-path sentences similar to Sentence (17):

(17) The boat sailed down the river *sank* during the storm.

Considerable prior work suggests that subjects will initially attempt a simple-active interpretation of the sentence, rather than the appropriate reduced-relative clause analysis (e.g., Bever, 1970; Frazier & Rayner, 1982). Under a simple-active analysis, the sentence becomes ungrammatical at the verb *sank,* which is a content word. If the N400 and P600 are elicited as a function of anomaly type, this word should elicit the P600. Conversely, if these effects are elicited as a function of word class, this word should elicit a large N400 effect.

Grand-average ERPs to the critical words (and to matched control words in sentences such as "The boat sailed down the river and *sank* during the storm") are shown in Fig. 2.7A. Inspection of this figure seems to indicate that the anomaly elicited a *biphasic response,* i.e., *both* an N400 and P600 effect within the same epoch. However, inspection of individual waveforms revealed that *no individual subject showed a biphasic response* to these anomalies. Rather, the majority of subjects showed a *monophasic* response to the anomalous word. In the majority of these subjects (nine subjects), the anomaly elicited a very clear P600 effect (Fig. 2.7B); in four subjects, the anomaly elicited an enhanced N400 (Fig. 2.7C); and in two subjects, the response to the anomaly did not differ from that of controls.[6] When averaged together, these monophasic responses took on the appearance of a biphasic response.

These findings are quite disturbing from a methodological point of view because averaging over subjects is a standard procedure for ERP researchers. At the minimum, these findings suggest that researchers should examine individual subject averages, rather than relying exclusively on averages over subject. A corollary of this is that researchers should present sufficient numbers of items in each condition so that the signal-to-noise ratio for each subject is sufficient to allow inspection of individual subject data.

From a theoretical perspective, the apparent existence of individual differences in subjects' responses to this type of anomaly raises some fascinating questions. For example, do these differences among subjects reflect differences in linguistic processes and capacities (e.g., differences in the grammatical com-

---

[6]It is not the case that the subgroup of subjects who elicited an N400 response to these anomalies would not produce a P600 response to any anomaly. Embedded within the list were agreement anomalies, which elicited a P600-like response in most subjects.

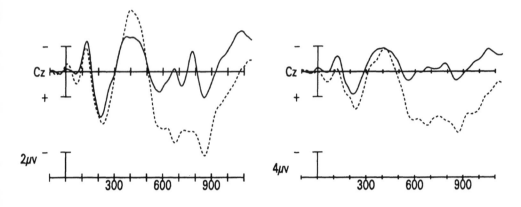

A   B

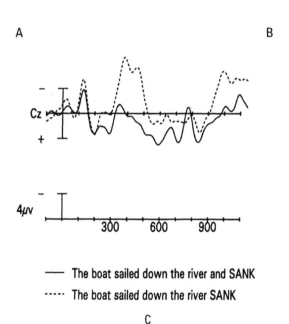

——— The boat sailed down the river and SANK

----- The boat sailed down the river SANK

C

FIG. 2.7. (A) ERPs (over 15 subjects) to syntactic anomalies (dashed line) and control words (solid line). (B) ERPs averaged over nine subjects who showed a P600 response to syntactic anomalies. (C) ERPs averaged over four subjects who showed an N400 response to syntactic anomalies.

petence or in linguistic processing strategies)? If so, what is the etiology underlying these differences? Obviously, at present we lack even speculative answers to these questions, and they deserve some further investigation.

These findings also suggest that our claim that the N400 and P600 are elicited as a function of anomaly type is too broadly stated, if one defines anomaly type with reference to a static theory of linguistic structure and linguistic processing. One might speculate that the specific processing strategies and linguistic competences that subjects bring with them to the lab may, in part, determine both the category some particular event falls into and the brain response elicited by that event. But this would extend rather than limit the utility of ERPs because such a situation would allow a careful examination of individual differences associated with linguistic processes to a static theory of linguistic structure and linguistic processing. One might speculate that the specific processing strategies and linguistic competences that subjects bring with them to the lab may, in part, determine both the category some particular event falls into and the brain response elicited by that event. But this would extend rather than limit the utility of ERPs, since such a situation would allow a careful examination of individual differences associated with linguistic processes.

Another challenge to the generalization that syntactic and semantic anomalies elicit the P600 and N400 effects, respectively, comes from several very recent studies reporting a negative-going wave in the ERP response to syntactic anomalies, rather than a P600. For example, Munte, Heinze, and Mangun (1993) recorded ERPs to the second word of word pairs. In the semantic condition, these pairs were either semantically related (e.g., "gangster-robber") or unrelated ("parliament-cube"). In the syntactic condition, the pairs were either "grammatical" (e.g., "you-spend") or "ungrammatical" ("your-write"). Target words in the semantically unrelated condition elicited a negative-going wave with a centroparietal distribution (an enhanced N400), whereas targets in the ungrammatical condition elicited a negative-going wave largest over frontal and left-hemisphere sites, relative to controls. In a separate study, Rosler, Friederici, Putz, and Hahne (1993) presented sentences that ended either in a semantically or a syntactically anomalous word. Subjects made lexical decisions to the sentence-final words. Both anomalies elicited a negative-going wave. As in the Munte et al. paper, the response to semantic anomalies were posteriorly distributed whereas the response to ungrammaticality was frontal and largest over the left hemisphere.

The proper interpretations of these findings, and the caveats they might necessitate with respect to the claim that syntactic anomalies elicit the P600, are not yet clear. For example, word pairs might not fully engage the sentence-processing system, and we do not know how the decision processes associated with the lexical decision task interact with the response to syntactic and semantic anomalies. But most importantly, in both of these experiments the critical word was the *last stimulus presented* prior to the subject's overt response, and in the

Rosler et al. study the critical word was in sentence-final position. There are a number of reasons for suspecting that sentence position (sentence-final *vs.* sentence-embedded) might influence the ERP waveform elicited in response to an anomalous word. For example, a large corpus of psycholinguistic work has indicated that the processes engaged in responding to a sentence-final word are, to some extent, distinct from those engaged in responding to an embedded word (e.g., Just & Carpenter, 1987). This is indicated by differences in a variety of responses to these two classes of words (e.g., eye fixations and lexical decisions are longer to sentence-final words than to other words). Further, ERPs to sentence-final words are known to differ from those to embedded words (Friedman, Simson, Ritter, & Rapin, 1975). Finally, recent work (Hagoort et al., 1993; McKinnon & Osterhout, 1994; Osterhout, 1990; Osterhout & Holcomb, 1992, 1993; Osterhout & Mobley, 1993) has shown that final words in sentences typically judged to be unacceptable elicit an N400-like effect, *even when the final word itself is not anomalous.* Thus, a sentence containing a syntactic anomaly embedded within the sentence typically elicits two large responses—a P600 to the syntactically anomalous word and an N400-like response to the final word in the sentence (McKinnon & Osterhout, 1994; Osterhout & Holcomb, 1992, in press; Osterhout & Mobley, 1993). Although the cognitive events underlying this sentence-ending negativity are unknown, Osterhout and Holcomb (1992; see also Osterhout & Holcomb, 1990) have speculated that it reflects the difficulty associated with semantically interpreting an ungrammatical sentence.

Evidence that sentence position does indeed have an influence on the ERP waveform elicited by syntactic anomalies is reported in one recent study (Osterhout, 1994). I directly compared the response to syntactic anomalies that were either embedded within sentences or in sentence-final position. Such words elicited a large P600 response when embedded within the sentence and an N400-like response when in sentence-final position. The correct interpretation of this sentence-position effect remains uncertain. One possibility is that the cognitive processes responding to an anomaly in sentence-final position differ from those that respond to the same anomaly when it is embedded within the sentence. For example, perhaps the P600 reflects the parser's attempts to derive a grammatical analysis of the sentence after encountering an apparent syntactic violation (cf. Osterhout et al., in press). Attempts at reanalysis might be common when the anomaly is embedded within the sentence, but less common when the anomaly occurs at the end of the sentence. The N400-like effect elicited by the anomalous sentence-final words might reflect the difficulty in deriving a coherent message-level interpretation from an ill-formed structure (Osterhout & Holcomb, 1992). Another quite (quite distinct) possibility is that the cognitive and neural response to syntactic anomalies is similar across sentence positions, but that the brain response to anomalies in sentence-final position is confounded with sentence wrap-up, decision, and response processes. It is possible that such words elicit two responses: a P600 to the syntactic anomaly, and an enhanced N400 by virtue of being the final word in an unacceptable sentence. Since these effects have opposite polarities and are temporally close, the resulting response to the word might look like neither the N400 nor the P600 effect when each of these effects is elicited in isolation from the other. (See Osterhout, 1994, for more discussion of this issue.)

Regardless of the proper interpretation of this sentence-position effect, it is clear that the claim that syntactic anomalies elicit a positive-going wave does not obviously apply to anomalous words in sentence-final position. At the same time, one cannot at present dismiss the possibility that by presenting the anomalous word in sentence-final position, one runs the risk of confounding the response to the anomaly with sentence wrap-up, decision, and response processes.

CONCLUSIONS

In this brief review, I have described two measurable ERP components that seem to be sensitive to certain cognitive and neural events underlying language comprehension. One component (N400) seems to be sensitive to the semantic-pragmatic content of the message. A second component (P600) seems to be sensitive to the syntactic form of the input. The anomalies eliciting these two components tend to bifurcate in precisely the manner that many linguists would predict, with semantic anomalies (e.g., contextually inappropriate words) eliciting a large N400 and syntactic anomalies (e.g., verb-subcategorization, phrase-structure, subjacency, and agreement violations) eliciting the P600. One could interpret these findings as (empirical) mutual support both for the linguists' categories and for the claim that ERPs are differentially sensitive to these categories.

An observant reader will have noted what has *not* been said concerning a set of hypothetical cognitive processes manifested by these components. The absence of such a discussion is not a matter of design, but rather an acknowledgment that we lack even the rudiments of an understanding concerning the cognitive-neural underpinnings of these ERP effects. For example, we do not know whether the P600 directly reflects the processes underlying syntactic analysis, or the processes that respond to syntactic anomaly, or the processes that attempt a reanalysis subsequent to an anomaly, and so on. We *do* know that the cognitive processes that follow a syntactic anomaly are distinct from those that follow a semantic anomaly, given the reasonable assumption that distinct patterns of brain response necessarily index different cognitive processes. And the preliminary evidence seems to indicate that the P600 is indexing a different set of processes than those reflected in the P300, since the two components seem to be independent. However, we have very little positive evidence concerning the precise identity of the cognitive events that do underlie the P600 component. Because the utility of these effects will likely increase as our knowledge of the underlying cognitive events increases, one challenge for the next few years will be to identify these cognitive processes.

However, the work reviewed herein indicates that, even without a substantive understanding of the specific cognitive correlates of these ERP effects, they can be used productively to study the process of comprehension. In particular, the accumulating evidence is largely consistent with the claim that, in addition to the acknowledged advantages of on-line, continuous, nonintrusive measurement, ERPs are differentially sensitive to events occurring at the syntactic and semantic levels of analysis. Whether a similar sensitivity exists with respect to other linguistic levels (e.g., phonological) remains to be seen.

ACKNOWLEDGMENTS

The author wishes to thank Phil Holcomb for his collaboration and support in much of the work reviewed herein. Also, thanks to the Cognitive Psychophysiology Research Group at the University of Washington (Dawn Aiken, Mike Bersick, Marty Blount, Vicka Corey, Rick McKinnon, Linda Mobley, and Sherri Sipe) for help in designing and conducting portions of this research, and for comments on earlier versions of this manuscript. Preparation of this chapter was supported in part by NIH grant DC01947 and by a GSRF grant from the University of Washington.

REFERENCES

Ades, A., & Steedman, S. (1982). On the order of words. *Linguistics and Philosophy, 6,* 517–558.

Barlow, M., & Ferguson, C. A. (1988). *Agreement in natural language.* Menlo Park, CA: CSLI.

Bates, E. S., McNew, B., MacWhinney, A., Devescovi, A., & Smith, S. (1982). Functional constraints on sentence processing. *Cognition, 11,* 245–299.

Bentin, S. (1987). Event-related potentials, semantic processes, and expectancy factors in word recognition. *Brain & Language, 31,* 308–327.

Bentin, S., McCarthy, G., & Wood, C. C. (1985). Event-related potentials associated with semantic priming. *Electroencephalography and Clinical Neurophysiology, 60,* 343–355.

Berwick, R. C. & Weinberg, A. (1983). The role of grammars as components of models of language use. *Cognition, 13,* 1–61.

Bever, T. G. (1970). The cognitive basis for linguistic structure. In J. R. Hayes (Ed.), *Cognition and the development of language* (pp. 279–362). New York: Wiley.

Bever, T. G., & McElree, B. (1988). Empty categories access their antecedents during comprehension. *Linguistic Inquiry, 19,* 35–45.

Bradley, D. C., Garrett, M. F., & Zurif, E. B. (1980). Syntactic deficits in Broca's aphasia. In D. Caplan (Ed.), *Biological studies of mental processes* (pp. 269–286). Cambridge, MA: MIT Press.

Chomsky, N. (1981). *Lectures on government and binding.* Dordrecht, The Netherlands: Foris.

Chomsky, N. (1986). *Knowledge of language.* New York: Praeger.

Clark, H. H. (1973). The language-as-fixed-effect fallacy: A critique of language statistics in psychological research. *Journal of Verbal Learning and Verbal Behavior, 12,* 335–359.

Coles, M. G. H., Gratton, G., & Fabiani, M. (1990). Event-related brain potentials. In J. T. Cacioppo & L. G. Tassinary (Eds.), *Principles of psychophysiology* (pp. 413–455). Cambridge, England: Cambridge University Press.

Crain, S., & Fodor, J. D. (1987). Sentence matching and overgeneration. *Cognition, 26,* 123–169.

Donchin, E. (1979). Event-related brain potentials: A tool in the study of human information processing. In: H. Begleiter (Ed.), *Evoked Brain Potentials and Behavior* (pp. 13–75). New York: Plenum Press.

Donchin, E. (1981). Surprise? . . . Surprise! *Psychophysiology, 18,* 493–513.

Duncan-Johnson, C. C., & Donchin, E. (1977). On quantifying surprise: The variation in event-related potentials with subjective probability. *Psychophysiology, 14,* 456–467.

Ferreira, F., & Clifton, C., Jr. (1986). The independence of syntactic processing. *Journal of Memory and Language, 25,* 348–368.

Ferreira, F., & Henderson, J. M. (1990). Use of verb information during syntactic parsing: Evidence from eye movements and word-by-word self-paced reading. *Journal of Experimental Psychology: Learning, Memory, & Cognition, 16,* 555–568.

Fischler, I. S. (1990). Comprehending language with event-related potentials. In J. W. Rohrbaugh, R. Parasuraman, & R. Johnson, Jr. (Eds.), *Event-related brain potentials* (pp. 165–177). New York: Oxford University Press.

Fischler, I. S., & Bloom, P. (1980). Rapid processing of the meaning of sentences. *Memory and Cognition, 8,* 216–225.

Fischler, I. S., & Raney, G. E. (1991). Language by eye: Behavioral, autonomic and cortical approaches to reading. In J. R. Jennings & M. G. H. Coles (Eds.), *Handbook of cognitive psychology: Central and autonomic nervous system* (pp. 511–574). New York: Wiley.

Fodor, J. A., Bever, T. G., & Garrett, M. F. (1974). *The psychology of language.* New York: McGraw-Hill.

Fodor, J. D. (1978). Parsing strategies and constraints on transformations. *Linguistic Inquiry, 9,* 427–473.

Ford, M., Bresnan, J., & Kaplan, R. (1982). A competence based theory of syntactic closure. In J. Bresnan (Ed.), *The mental representation of grammatical relations* (pp. 797–828). Cambridge, MA: MIT Press.

Forster, K. I. (1987). Binding, plausibility, and modularity. In J. L. Garfield (Ed.), *Modularity in knowledge representation and natural language understanding* (pp. 63–82). Cambridge, MA: MIT Press.

Forster, K. I., & Stevenson, B. J. (1987). Sentence-matching and well-formedness. *Cognition, 26,* 171–186.

Frazier, L. (1987). Sentence processing: A tutorial review. In M. Coltheart (Ed.), *Attention and Performance XII.* (pp. 559–585). Hillsdale, NJ: Lawrence Erlbaum Associates.

Frazier, L. (1990). Exploring the architecture of the language-processing system. In G. T. M. Altmann (Ed.), *Cognitive models of speech processing* (pp. 409–433). Cambridge, MA: MIT Press.

Frazier, L., & Rayner, K. (1982). Making and correcting errors during sentence comprehension: Eye movements in the analysis of structurally ambiguous sentences. *Cognitive Psychology, 14,* 178–210.

Freedman, S. A., & Forster, K. I. (1985). The psychological status of overgenerated sentences. *Cognition, 19,* 101-131.

Friederici, A. D. (1983). Levels of processing and vocabulary types: Evidence from online comprehension in normals and agrammatics. *Cognition, 19,* 133–166.

Friedman, D., Simson, R., Ritter, W., & Rapin, I. (1975). The late positive component (P300) and information processing in sentences. *Electroencephalography and Clinical Neurophysiology, 38,* 255–262.

Garnsey, S. M., Tanenhaus, M. K., & Chapman, R. M. (1989). Evoked potentials and the study of sentence comprehension. *Journal of Psycholinguistic Research, 18,* 51–60.

Geschwind, N. (1979). Specializations of the human brain. In *The Brain* (pp. 108–119). New York: W. H. Freeman.

Givon, T. (1976). Topic, pronoun, and grammatical agreement. In C. N. Li (Ed.), *Subject and topic.* New York: Academic Press.

Hagoort, P., Brown, C., & Groothusen, J. (1993). The syntactic positive shift as an ERP measure of syntactic processing. *Language and Cognitive Processes, 8,* 337–364.

Hillyard, S. A., & Picton, T. W. (1987). Electrophysiology of cognition. In F. Plum (Ed.), *Handbook of physiology. Section 1: Neurophysiology.* New York: American Physiological Society.

Holcomb, P. J. (1988). Automatic and attentional processing: An event-related brain potential analysis of semantic priming. *Brain and Language, 35,* 66–85.

Holcomb, P. J., & Neville, H. J. (1990). Semantic priming in visual and auditory lexical decision: A between modality comparison. *Language and Cognitive Processes, 5,* 281–312.

Holcomb, P. J., & Neville, H. J. (1991). The electrophysiology of spoken sentence processing. *Psychobiology, 19,* 286–300.

Johnson, R., Jr. (1993). On the neural generators of the P300 component of the event-related brain potential. *Psychophysiology, 30,* 90–97.

Johnson-Laird, P. (1977). Psycholinguistics without linguistics. In N. S. Sutherland (Ed.), *Tutorial essays in psychology. Vol. 1.* Hillsdale, NJ: Lawrence Erlbaum Associates.

Just, M. A., & Carpenter, P. A. (1987). *The psychology of reading and language comprehension.* Boston: Allyn and Bacon.

Kramer, A., & Donchin, E. (1987). Brain potentials as indices of orthographic and phonological interaction during word matching. *Journal of Experimental Psychology: Learning Memory and Cognition, 13,* 76–86.

Kutas, M., & Hillyard, S. A. (1980a). Event-related brain potentials to semantically inappropriate and surprisingly large words. *Biological Psychology, 11,* 99–116.

Kutas, M., & Hillyard, S. A. (1980b). Reading between the lines: Event-related brain potentials during natural sentence processing. *Brain and Language, 11,* 354–373.

Kutas, M., & Hillyard, S. A. (1980c). Reading senseless sentences: Brain potentials reflect semantic incongruity. *Science, 207,* 203–205.

Kutas, M., & Hillyard, S. A. (1983). Event-related brain potentials to grammatical errors and semantic anomalies. *Memory and Cognition, 11,* 539–550.

Kutas, M., & Hillyard, S. A. (1984). Brain potentials during reading reflect word expectancy and semantic association. *Nature, 307,* 161–163.

Kutas, M., & Van Petten, C. (1988). Event-related brain potential studies of language. In P. K. Ackles, J. R. Jennings & M. G. H. Coles (Eds.), *Advances in psychophysiology* (pp. 138–187). Greenwich, Cn: JAI Press.

Lasnik, H., & Saito, M. (1992). *Move alpha: Conditions on its application and output.* Cambridge, MA: MIT Press.

Linebarger, M. C. (1989). Neuropsycholinguisitic evidence for linguistic modularity. In G. N. Carlson & M. K. Tanenhaus (Eds.), *Linguistic structure in language processing* (pp. 197–238). Dordrecht, the Netherlands: Kluwer.

MacDonald, M. C. (1989). Priming effects from gaps to antecedents. *Language and Cognitive Processes, 4,* 35–46.

Marton, M., & Szirtes, J. (1988). Context effects on saccade-related brain potentials to words during reading. *Neuropsychologia, 26,* 453–463.

McClelland, J. L., & Kawamoto, A. H. (1986). Mechanisms of sentence processing: Assigning roles to constituents. In J. L. McClelland and D. E. Rumelhart (Eds.), *Parallel distributed processing: Exploration in the microstructure of cognition. Vol 2* (pp. 272–325). Cambridge, MA: MIT Press.

McKinnon, R., & Osterhout, L. (1994). Modularity in syntax reconsidered: Evidence for the rapid use of constraints in sentence processing. Manuscript submitted for publication.

Munte, T. F., Heinze, H., & Mangun, G. (1993). Dissociation of brain activity related to syntactic and semantic aspects of language. *Journal of Cognitive Neuroscience, 5,* 335–344.

Neville, H. J. (1992). Fractionating language: Different neural systems with different sensitive periods. *Cerebral Cortex, 2,* 244–258.

Neville, H. J., Nicol., J., Barss, A., Forster, K. I., & Garrett, M. F. (1991). Syntactically based processing classes: Evidence from event-related brain potentials. *Journal of Cognitive Neuroscience, 3,* 151–165.

Nicol, J., & Swinney, D. A. (1989). The role of structure on coreference assignment during sentence comprehension. *Journal of Psycholinguistic Research, 18,* 5–20.

Osterhout, L. (1990). *Event-related potentials elicited during sentence comprehension.* Unpublished doctoral dissertation, Tufts University, Medford, MA.

Osterhout, L. (1994). *Effects of sentence position and word class on the brain response to syntactic anomalies.* Manuscript submitted for publication.

Osterhout, L., & Holcomb, P. J. (1990). Event-related potentials elicited by grammatical anomalies. In C. H. M. Brunia, A. W. K. Gaillard, & A. Kok (Eds.), *Psychophysiological brain research* (pp. 299–302). Tilburg, the Netherlands: Tilburg University Press.

Osterhout, L., & Holcomb, P. J. (1992). Event-related brain potentials elicited by syntactic anomaly. *Journal of Memory and Language, 31,* 785–806.

Osterhout, L., & Holcomb, P. J. (1993). Event-related potentials and syntactic anomaly: Evidence of anomaly detection during the perception of continuous speech. *Language and Cognitive Processes, 8,* 413–438.

Osterhout, L., & Holcomb, P. J. (in press). Event-related brain potentials and language comprehension. In M. D. Rugg & M. G. H. Coles (Ed.), *Electrophysiological studies of human brain function.* Oxford: Oxford University Press.

Osterhout, L., Holcomb, P. J., & Swinney, D. A. (in press). Brain potentials elicited by garden-path sentences: Evidence of the application of verb information during parsing. *Journal of Experimental Psychology: Learning, Memory, and Cognition.*

Osterhout, L., & Mobley, L. A. (1993). *Event-related brain potentials elicited by failure to agree.* Manuscript submitted for publication.

Osterhout, L., & Swinney, D. A. (1989). On the role of the simplicity heuristic during language processing: Evidence from structural and inferential processing. *Journal of Psycholinguistic Research, 18,* 533–562.

Osterhout, L., & Swinney, D. A. (1993). On the temporal course of gap-filling during comprehension of verbal passives. *Journal of Psycholinguistic Research, 22,* 273–286.

Polich, J., McCarthy, G. Wang, W. S., & Donchin, E. (1983). When words collide: Orthographic and phonological interference during word processing. *Biological Psychology, 16,* 155–180.

Radford, A. (1988). *Transformation syntax.* Cambridge, England: Cambridge University Press.

Quirk, R., & Greenbaum, S. (1973). *A concise grammar of contemporary English.* London: Longman.

Rayner, K., Carlson, M., & Frazier, L. (1983). The interaction of syntax and semantics during sentence processing: Eye movements in the analysis of semantically biased sentences. *Journal of Verbal Learning and Verbal Behavior, 22,* 358–374.

Rayner, K., & Frazier, L. (1987). Parsing temporarily ambiguous complements. *Quarterly Journal of Experimental Psychology, 39A,* 657–673.

Rayner, K., Sereno, S. C., Morris, R. K., Schmauder, A. R., & Clifton, C. (1989). Eye movements and on-line language comprehension processes. *Language and Cognitive Processes, 4,* SI21–SI50.

Reid, W. (1991). *Verb and noun number in English: A functional explanation.* London: Longman.

Riesbeck, C. K., & Schank, R. C. (1978). Comprehension by computer: Expectation-based analysis of sentences in context. In W. J. M. Levelt & G. B. Flores d'Arcais (Eds.), *Studies in the perception of language* (pp. 247–293). New York: John Wiley & Sons.

Ritter, W., & Vaughan, Jr., H. G. (1969). Average evoked responses in vigilance and discrimination. *Science, 164,* 326–328.

Rosler, F., Friederici, A., Putz, P., & Hahne, A. (1993). Event-related brain potentials while encountering semantic and syntactic constraint violations. *Journal of Cognitive Neuroscience, 5,* 345–362.

Rugg, M. D. (1984a). Event-related potentials in phonological matching tasks. *Brain & Language, 23,* 225–240.

Rugg, M. D. (1984b). Event-related potentials and the phonological processing of words and nonwords. *Neuropsychologia, 22,* 435–443.

Rugg, M. D. (1985). The effects of semantic priming and word repetition on event-related potentials. *Psychophysiology, 22,* 642–647.

Sabol, M. A., & De Rosa, D. V. (1976). Semantic encoding of isolated words. *Journal of Experimental Psychology: Human Learning and Memory, 2,* 58–68.

Stanovitch, K., & West, R. F. (1983). On priming by a sentence context. *Journal of Experimental Psychology: General, 112,* 1–36.

Swinney, D. A. (1981). The process of language comprehension: An approach to studying issues in cognition and language. *Cognition, 10,* 307–312.

Swinney, D. A. (1982). The structure and time course of information interaction during speech comprehension: Lexical segmentation, access, and interpretation. In J. Mehler, E. C. T. Walker, & M. Garrett (Eds.), *Perspectives on mental representation.* Hillsdale, NJ: Lawrence Erlbaum Associates.

Swinney, D. A., Onifer, W., Prather, P., & Hirshkowitz, M. (1979). Semantic facilitation across sensory modalities in the processing of individual words and sentences. *Memory and Cognition, 7,* 159–165.

Tanenhaus, M. K., & Carlson, G. N. (1989). Lexical structure and language comprehension. In W. D. Marslen-Wilson (Ed.), *Lexical representation and process* (pp. 529–561). Cambridge, MA: MIT Press.

Van Petten, C., & Kutas, M. (1987). Ambiguous words in context: An event-related potential analysis of the time course of meaning activation. *Journal of Memory and Language, 26,* 188–208.

Wright, B., & Garrett, M. F. (1984). Lexical decision in sentences: Effects of syntactic structure. *Memory and Cognition, 12,* 31–45.

3 Brain Responses to Lexical Ambiguity Resolution and Parsing

Peter Hagoort
Colin Brown
*Max Planck Institute for Psycholinguistics, Nijmegen,
The Netherlands*

We present two sets of event-related potential (ERP) data on separate aspects of sentence processing. The first set focuses on the disambiguation of *biased* ambiguous words by right-context information (biased ambiguous words are words that have a clearly dominant and subordinate meaning). The ERP data provide both converging and contrasting evidence with results obtained in eye-movement studies. The ERP data converge with these studies by showing that when the right-context is consistent with the subordinate meaning, processing effects are observed at the point of disambiguation, whereas no effect is seen when the dominant meaning is confirmed (cf. Dopkins, Morris, & Rayner, 1992; Frazier & Rayner, 1990). The ERP data contrast with eye-movement data (cf. Rayner & Duffy, 1986) by showing that processing effects do obtain at the level of biased ambiguous words preceded by neutral sentential contexts.

The second set of ERP data focuses on neurophysiological manifestations of syntactic processing. These data show an ERP effect to syntactic violations that is qualitatively different from the well-known N400 effect to violations of semantic constraints. Next to the ERP effect elicited by the word that renders the sentence ungrammatical, N400 effects are observed further downstream in sentences that can be interpreted semantically (i.e., normal prose), but not in sentences that are very hard to interpret (i.e., syntactic prose). This shows that syntactic and semantic ERP effects can be dissociated. In addition, these data suggest that a syntactic problem has immediate consequences for the semantic integration of words following the occurrence of a parsing problem. Finally, probably due to the semantic consequences of the lexically specified argument structure of verbs, the pattern of results for subcategorization violations is different from that of the other two syntactic violations in this experiment (i.e., agreement violations and phrase-structure violations).

Before discussing our experimental work, we briefly describe the ERP method, and specify its relevant features for sentence-processing research.

Scalp-recorded ERPs reflect the summation of the synchronous post-synaptic activity of many neurons. ERPs differ from background EEG in that they reflect brain electrical activity time-locked to particular stimulus events. Establishing a reliable ERP trace normally requires averaging over a series of ERP recordings to tokens of the same stimulus type. The resulting average waveform typically includes a number of positive and negative peaks, sometimes referred to as *components*. Usually the peaks in the ERP waveform are labeled according to their polarity (*N* for negative, *P* for positive) and their average latency in milliseconds relative to the onset of stimulus presentation (e.g., *N400, P600*). In some cases, the ERP peaks get a functionally defined label (*SPS* for syntactic positive shift; *ERN* for error-related negativity). ERPs are recorded from a number of leads distributed over the scalp, and often have a characteristic distribution, showing larger amplitudes at some leads than at others. These distributional characteristics can be helpful in identifying a certain component.

For the purposes of psycholinguistically oriented ERP research, the most informative ERP peaks belong to the class of the so-called "endogenous" components. Endogenous components are relatively insensitive to variations in physical stimulus parameters (e.g., size, intensity), but highly responsive to the cognitive processing consequences of the stimulus events. The modulations in amplitude or latency of an endogenous ERP peak as a consequence of some experimental manipulation, usually form the basis for making inferences about the nature of the underlying cognitive processing events. In terms of experimentation, the ways in which to elicit the relevant experimental effects are not essentially different from other research paradigms in psycholinguistics.

The moment at which the ERP method showed a first glimpse of its potential relevance for sentence-processing research is clearly demarcated in time by the 1980 publication of a paper in *Science* by Kutas and Hillyard. These researchers presented subjects with a variety of sentences either ending in a word that was semantically congruous with the sentence context (e.g., "He shaved off his mustache and beard") or ending in a semantic anomaly (e.g., "I take coffee with cream and dog"). The semantically anomalous words elicited a negative component with a centro-parietal maximum on the scalp, and a latency that peaked around 400 ms. This component has since become known as the *N400,* and the difference between the N400 amplitude in the experimental and the control conditions has become known as the *N400 effect.* It is now clear that N400 effects can be obtained with a variety of paradigms and using a variety of language stimuli, by no means restricted to violations.

Today, the following general characteristics are known to hold for the N400: (a) Each open-class word elicits an N400. (b) The amplitude of the N400 is inversely related to the cloze probability of a word in sentence context. The better the semantic fit between a word and its context, the more reduced the amplitude of the N400 (Kutas, Lindamood, & Hillyard, 1984). (c) The amplitude of the N400 varies with word position, such that the first content word in a sentence produces a larger negativity than content words in later positions (Kutas, Van Petten, & Besson, 1988). This amplitude reduction is most likely due to the increasing semantic constraints throughout the sentence. (d) N400 effects are obtained in sign language (Kutas, Neville, & Holcomb, 1987; Neville, Mills, & Lawson, 1992), but not with violations of contextual constraints in music (Besson & Macar, 1987; Paller, McCarthy, & Wood, 1992). (e) N400 effects are observed both for written- and spoken-language input, although with slightly different time courses (e.g., Connolly, Stewart, & Phillips, 1990; Holcomb & Neville, 1991). For language comprehension, the processing nature of the N400 has recently been claimed to be related to lexical-semantic integration processes (Brown & Hagoort, 1993). That is, once a word has been accessed in the mental lexicon, its meaning has to be integrated into an overall representation of the current word or sentence context. The easier this integration process is, the smaller the amplitude of the N400 becomes.

Although the past 15 years have seen an increase in ERP research on language processing, most of the research has been dedicated to determining the parameters that modulate language-relevant ERP components such as the N400. These were necessary steps in preparing the ground for ERP research aimed at explicitly testing specific theoretical proposals on different aspects of language processing. Only in recent years have ERP studies directly addressed central issues in sentence-processing research (e.g., Garnsey, Tanenhaus, & Chapman, 1989; Kluender & Kutas, 1993; Osterhout, chapter 2, this volume; Van Petten & Kutas, 1987).

The reason for being optimistic about possible contributions of ERP research to studies of sentence processing arises from some of the characteristics of brain waves as a dependent measure. We discuss two of the most relevant ones for purposes of studying higher order sentence-processing operations.

The first is the *multidimensional* nature of the ERP waveform. ERPs can vary along a number of dimensions: specifically, the latency at which an ERP component occurs relative to stimulus onset, its polarity, its amplitude, and its amplitude distribution over the recording sites. On the basis of these characteristics it is reasonable to assume that different types of ERP peaks are generated by different neural systems. Insofar as the involvement of different neural systems implies qualitatively different processing events, in principle these processing events can show up as qualitatively different in the ERP waveform. This characteristic makes ERPs a useful addition to the recording of unidimensional measures, such as reading times. For instance, if the electrophysiological signatures of semantic integration processes and parsing operations turn out to be qualitatively different, ERPs might provide us with a crucial tool for testing how and at what moments in time the process of assigning a structure to the incoming string of words and interpreting this string semantically, influence each other. Recent evidence suggests that aspects of syntactic processing do indeed elicit ERP responses qualitatively different from those of semantic integration processes (e.g., Hagoort, Brown, & Groothusen, 1993; Kluender & Kutas, 1993; Münte, Heinze, & Mangun, 1993; Neville, Nicol, Barss, Forster, & Garrett, 1991; Osterhout & Holcomb, 1992; Rösler, Pütz, Friederici, & Hahne, 1993).

The second important characteristic of ERPs is that they provide a *continuous, real-time* measure. Like speeded reaction-time (RT) measures in the more classical psycholinguistic tasks, such as naming, lexical decision, and word monitoring, ERPs are tightly linked to the temporal organization of ongoing language-processing events. But in contrast to RT measures, ERPs provide a continuous record throughout the total processing epoch and beyond (as is the case with eye-movement registration). Therefore, it is possible to monitor not only the immediate consequences of a particular experimental manipulation (e.g., a syntactic or semantic violation), but also its processing consequences further downstream. As we will show, this feature enabled us to show that the impossibility of assigning the preferred structure to an incoming string of words has consequences for lexical-semantic integration processes further downstream in the sentence (Hagoort et al., 1993).

In the remainder of this chapter, we illustrate the usefulness of these characteristics of ERPs by presenting the two datasets mentioned previously. We consider neither of the experiments decisive for central debates in their respective domains of sentence-processing research. At the same time, both are not entirely without consequences for some of the current positions in these domains.

THE RESOLUTION OF LEXICAL AMBIGUITY BY RIGHT-CONTEXT INFORMATION

In the absence of a well-defined theory of the semantics of natural languages, it is notoriously difficult to develop processing models of the integration of words in message-level representations. Both at the word-meaning level and the message level, it is unclear exactly what these representations are and, hence, what the nature of the eventual end product of the comprehension process is. One way that psycholinguistic researchers have sidestepped some of the problems involved here is to investigate the meaning selection of lexically ambiguous words in sentential contexts. Here at least we have two (or more) clearly distinct meanings for a given lexical form, whatever theory of semantics eventually turns out to hold. With these different meanings in hand, it is possible to investigate the time course of their activation, both as a function of their relative meaning frequency and of the preceding and/or following contextual information. This kind of experimental program is important because it focuses on the integration of words into higher order meaning representations, and thereby, on the interface between the mental lexicon and sentence-processing systems, an interface that lies at the heart of language understanding.

Over the past two decades, a quite stable picture has emerged of the processing of lexically ambiguous words in neutral sentential contexts. This picture has primarily been built up on the basis of RT research with the cross-modal priming paradigm. The data indicate that, initially, all meanings of an ambiguous word are activated, followed by the selection of a single meaning (e.g., Seidenberg, Tanenhaus, Leiman, & Bienkowski, 1982; Simpson, 1981; Simpson & Krueger, 1991). The time course of meaning selection is influenced by the relative meaning frequency of the distinct meanings of an ambiguous word, and the overall thrust of the results reported in the literature is that dominant meanings are accessed prior to, and remain activated longer than, subordinate meanings (e.g., Simpson & Burgess, 1985; Simpson & Krueger, 1991).

The impact of preceding biasing sentential-context information on ambiguity resolution is still a matter of some debate. There is evidence for multiple meaning activation irrespective of contextual bias, followed by context-sensitive selection (e.g., Duffy, Morris, & Rayner, 1988; Kintsch & Mross, 1985; Onifer & Swinney, 1981; Swinney, 1979). However, contrary findings have been reported. These mainly concern results from studies using biasing contexts for dominant meanings, showing that in these circumstances subordinate meanings are not necessarily activated (e.g., Dopkins et al., 1992; Simpson, 1981, 1984; Simpson & Krueger, 1991; Tabossi, 1988a, 1988b; Tabossi, Colombo, & Job, 1987; Tabossi & Zardon, 1993; Van Petten & Kutas, 1987).

In the present experiment, we focus on the effects of so-called right-context information on meaning selection for ambiguous words with clearly dominant and subordinate meanings (cf. Duffy et al., 1988; Frazier & Rayner, 1990; Rayner & Frazier, 1989). Subjects read sentences that contained words with two distinct meanings. The ambiguities were preceded by neutral sentential information, and were followed (several words downstream) by a word that disambiguated either for the dominant or the subordinate meaning of the preceding ambiguous word. This approach yields two datasets that can contribute to a more detailed characterization of the meaning-selection process as it occurs in real-time. On the one hand, it provides data on the possible processing consequences that derive from multiple meaning representations associated with one lexical form (cf. Rayner & Duffy, 1986). On the other hand, it provides data on possible processing effects at the level of the disambiguating word. Such effects can reveal the extent to which the relative meaning frequency determines the time course of meaning selection and decay; that is, whether the interpretative process is best characterized as one of immediate or delayed meaning selection (cf. Frazier & Rayner, 1990; Rayner & Frazier, 1989). The manipulation of right-context information exploits one of the appealing characteristics of the ERP method that we mentioned earlier; namely, the fact (which it shares with eye-movement registration) that ERPs can be obtained over the entire processing span of a sentence (or sequence of sentences) without having to interrupt the comprehender's ongoing linguistic analysis.

Method

Thirty-six university students read 360 Dutch sentences. Of this set, 120 are test sentences containing an ambiguous word, 120 are control sentences for the ambiguous test sentences, 60 are sentences containing a high-cloze probability word, and 60 are sentences containing a low-cloze probability word. The following sentences exemplify the materials for the ambiguity manipulation (the ambiguous word is in bold roman, the control word is in bold italics, and the disambiguating word is in plain italics):

Concordant with Dominant Meaning

Ambiguous: Mijn oom heeft de **as** van zijn *sigaar* snel opgeruimd.
                (My uncle has the **ash** of his *cigar* quickly
                [cleared away].)
Unambiguous: Mijn oom heeft de ***peuk*** van zijn *sigaar* snel opgeruimd.
                (My uncle has the ***stub*** of his *cigar* quickly
                [cleared away].)

Concordant with Subordinate Meaning

Ambiguous: Mijn oom heeft de **as** van zijn *auto* opnieuw gelast.
                (My uncle has the **axle** of his *car* again welded.)
Unambiguous: Mijn oom heeft de ***knalpijp*** van zijn *auto* opnieuw gelast.
                (My uncle has the ***muffler*** of his *car* again welded.)

The meaning dominance of the ambiguous words was assessed via an association test on 70 university students. The dominant meaning frequency is 81.3%, and the subordinate meaning frequency is 11.7%.

The 60 high-cloze and 60 low-cloze probability sentences were constructed to elicit a standard N400 effect. Given that the present study is the first study to our knowledge to look at brain-potential manifestations of the consequences of right-context information for the processing of lexically ambiguous words, we thought it prudent to establish a standard N400 effect within the same subject population, so as to have a basis for comparing possible morphological differences in the ERP waveforms elicited in the ambiguity conditions.

The high- and low-cloze sentences were identical, with the exception of the high- and low-cloze target words that occurred in sentence-medial position. The cloze probability is 0.58 for the high-cloze words and 0.07 for the low-cloze words. The following two sentences exemplify the two cloze conditions (the target word is in bold):

High cloze: Jenny stopte het snoepje in haar **mond** na afloop van de les.
(Jenny put the sweet in her **mouth** after the lesson.)
Low cloze: Jenny stopte het snoepje in haar **zak** na afloop van de les.
(Jenny put the sweet in her **pocket** after the lesson.)

Two lists of 180 sentences each were made. Each list contains 30 right-context dominant-concordant sentences, 30 right-context subordinate-concordant sentences, 60 control sentences, 30 high-cloze sentences, and 30 low-cloze sentences. Within each list, only one version of an ambiguous context occurred (i.e., either dominant or subordinate), with its corresponding control sentence occurring in the same sequential position in the other list. Each list was presented to 18 subjects.

All sentences were displayed word by word on a high-resolution computer screen. Each word replaced the preceding one, and was presented for 300 ms, with an Inter-Stimulus-Interval (ISI) of 300 ms.[1] Subjects were instructed to attentively read the sentences for comprehension. No additional task demands were imposed.

Results

For each subject, average waveforms are computed for each condition and electrode site separately, over all trials that are free of artifacts. Mean amplitudes are calculated per subject, per condition, and per electrode for latency windows specified later. These amplitude values are entered into repeated measures analyses of variance (ANOVA). Before turning to the ambiguity data, we briefly present the waveforms for the cloze manipulation. These data establish a standard N400 effect.

ERPs to High- and Low-Cloze Words in Sentence-Medial Position.   In Fig. 3.1 and 3.2, 2400-ms epochs are shown for the high- and low-cloze words. This epoch contains three word positions: one word preceding the high- or low-cloze

---

[1] EEG activity was recorded using an Electrocap with seven scalp tin electrodes, each referred to the left mastoid. Three electrodes were placed according to the International 10–20 system (Jasper, 1958), at frontal (Fz), central (Cz), and parietal (Pz) sites. Symmetrical anterior-temporal electrodes were placed halfway between F7 and T3 (anterior left: AL), and F8 and T4 sites (anterior right: AR), respectively. Symmetrical posterior-temporal electrodes were placed lateral (by 30% of the interaural distance) and 12.5% posterior to the vertex (posterior left: PL; posterior right: PR). Vertical eye movements and blinks (EOG) were monitored via a supra- to sub-orbital bipolar montage. A right to left canthal bipolar montage was used to monitor horizontal eye movements. The EEG and EOG recordings were amplified with Nihon Kohden AB-601G bioelectric amplifiers, using a Hi-Cut of 30 Hz and a time constant of 8 sec. The EEG and EOG were digitized on-line with a sampling frequency of 200 Hz. Sampling started 150 ms before the presentation of the first word of each sentence, with a total sampling epoch of 9000 ms.

HIGH CLOZE vs. LOW CLOZE PROBABILITY WORDS

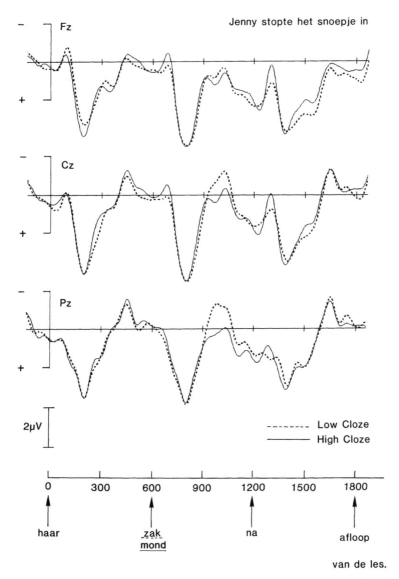

FIG. 3.1. Cloze-probability data. Grand-average waveform for each of the three midline electrode sites, for the high- and the low-cloze words. The cloze target is preceded and followed by one word. The translation of the example sentence is "Jenny put the sweet in her pocket/mouth after the lesson." Negativity is up in this and all subsequent figures.

HIGH CLOZE vs. LOW CLOZE PROBABILITY WORDS

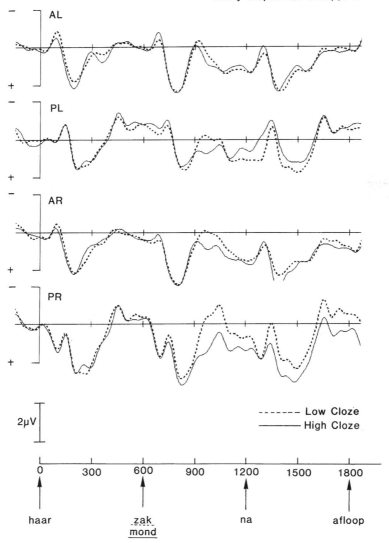

FIG. 3.2. Cloze-probability data. Grand-average waveform for each of the four lateral electrode sites, for the high- and the low-cloze words. The cloze target is preceded and followed by one word. The translation of the example sentence is "Jenny put the sweet in her pocket/mouth after the lesson."

word, the high- or low-cloze word itself, and one following word. Figure 3.1 shows the midline electrode sites, and Fig. 3.2 shows the lateral sites. The waveforms for the high- and low-cloze words show the by-now standard and well-established N400 effect, reflecting the degree to which the words can be readily integrated within the higher order representation of their preceding sentential-semantic context (cf. Brown & Hagoort, 1993). Statistical analyses were done on the standard time window for analysis of N400 effects. The ERP for the low-cloze words shows a significant negative enhancement in the 300–500-ms latency range following word onset, compared with the high-cloze words $[F(1, 33) = 5.60, MSe = 10.39, p = .024]$. The distribution of the effect follows the standard topography of the N400 to visual stimulation: largest over centro-parietal electrode sites, larger over posterior than anterior sites, with a slight increase over the right as compared with the left hemisphere. This fits well with previous reports in the literature (e.g., see overviews in Kutas & Van Petten, 1988; Van Petten & Kutas, 1991). No significant differences are predicted to emerge at the preceding word position because at this position the two cloze conditions are identical. None emerge, which demonstrates that the ERP registrations are reliable. Similarly, the waveforms for the position following the target word do not differ from each other.

ERPs to the Ambiguous Word.   For this analysis, the data for the dominant- and subordinate-material sets are collapsed because the factor Dominance is only relevant with respect to the disambiguating word. Figures 3.3 and 3.4 contain 1800-ms epoch waveforms for the ambiguous words and for their controls. Figure 3.3 shows the midline electrode sites, and Fig. 3.4 shows the lateral sites. All words in both conditions elicit an N400, with the standard topography for visual stimulation.

The ERPs elicited in the Ambiguous and Unambiguous conditions at the word position preceding the ambiguity lie on top of each other. This is as it should be because the sentences in the two conditions are identical at this point. Significant differences are observed for the ambiguous word in comparison with its unambiguous control. The overall ANOVA shows a main effect of Ambiguous–Unambiguous $[F(1, 33) = 9.16, MSe = 4.87, p = .005]$. However, it should be noted that the distribution of the effect over the scalp does not fit with the standard topography observed for N400 effects. In particular, the ambiguity effect has a frontal, largely lateralized distribution. There is some separation between the Ambiguous and Unambiguous conditions at Fz, but the largest effects emerge at the anterior left (AL) and anterior right (AR) sites. The posterior left (PL) site shows some effect, whereas at the posterior right (PR) site there is no difference between the two conditions. The most sustained separation holds over the left hemisphere: The effects at AL and PL sites are still present at the onset of the following word. This is not the case for the right lateral sites. Leaving aside imponderables concerning the meaning of this particular topo-

PROCESSING LEXICALLY AMBIGUOUS WORDS

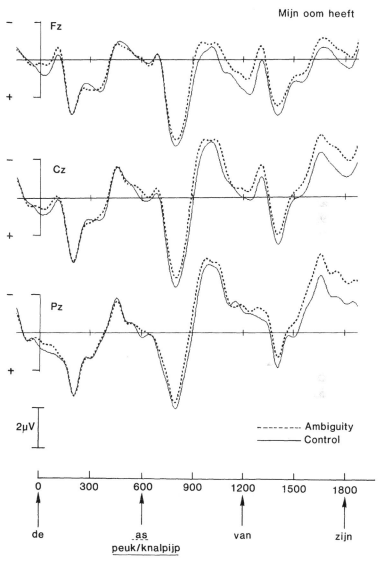

FIG. 3.3. ERPs for the ambiguous words. Grand-average waveform for each of the three midline electrode sites, for the ambiguous words and their controls. These words are preceded and followed by one word. The translation of the example sentence is "My uncle has the (ash/axle)/(stub/muffler) of his (cigar quickly cleared away/car again welded)."

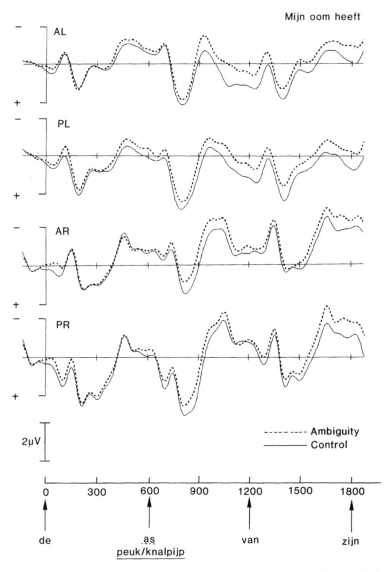

FIG. 3.4. ERPs for the ambiguous words. Grand-average waveform for each of the four lateral electrode sites, for the ambiguous words and their controls. These words are preceded and followed by one word. The translation of the example sentence is "My uncle has the (ash/axle)/(stub/muffler) of his (cigar quickly cleared away/car again welded)."

graphical deviation from the standard distribution of the N400 effect, the overall significant difference between the Ambiguous and Unambiguous conditions indicates that there are processing consequences associated with the reading of biased ambiguous words preceded by neutral sentential contexts.

The processing effects of the ambiguous word carry over into the processing of the word following the ambiguity. Here again, a statistically significant difference exists between the Ambiguous and Unambiguous conditions [$F(1, 33)$ = 5.45, MSe = 8.77, p = .026]. Unlike the effect for the ambiguous word, this effect shows a topography that is more in line with the standard topography for N400 effects.

ERPs to the Word Disambiguating for the Dominant Meaning.   Figure 3.5 contains 1200-ms epoch waveforms for the three midline electrode sites for the disambiguating words in the Ambiguous and Unambiguous conditions (i.e., either with an ambiguous or an unambiguous word in the preceding context).[2] As for the previously reported epochs, clear N400s were elicited by each word, and their topography is in line with the standard distribution of the N400 over the scalp.

Although there is a slight separation between the Ambiguous and Unambiguous conditions at the level of the disambiguating word, this does not reach significance. Likewise, for the following word, no significant differences emerge. So, it is clear that when the right-context information as conveyed by the disambiguating word is in accordance with the dominant meaning of a previously encountered ambiguous word, no differential processing consequences are observed. As we shall now see, this does not hold for right-contexts that are in accordance with the subordinate meaning.

ERPs to the Word Disambiguating for the Subordinate Meaning.   Figure 3.6 contains 1200-ms epoch waveforms for the three midline electrode sites for the disambiguating words in the Ambiguous and Unambiguous conditions. Again, clear N400s are observed on each word, with the standard topography. At the level of the N400 to the disambiguating word, a statistically reliable negative enhancement emerges for the Ambiguous compared with the Unambiguous condition [$F(1, 33)$ = 10.65, MSe = 7.93, p = .003]. This effect is restricted to the disambiguating word: No significant Ambiguous–Unambiguous differences are present for the following word. The effect at Fz is somewhat larger than usually observed with N400 effects, but overall the topography matches the standard distribution. Here, then, in contrast to the contexts for the dominant meaning of an ambiguous word, an N400 effect is observed when the disambiguating information accords with the subordinate meaning of a previously processed ambiguous word.

---

[2]In this and the following figure, we do not present the lateral sites because no hemispheric differences emerged in the size of the effects.

LEXICAL AMBIGUITY: Right context biases dominant meaning

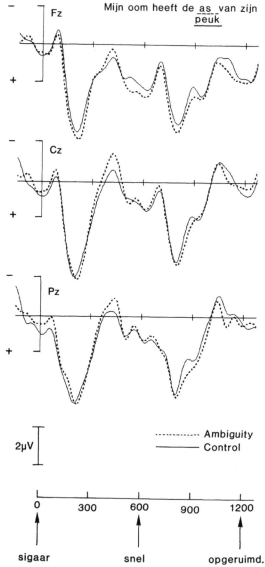

FIG. 3.5. ERPs to the word that disambiguates for the dominant meaning of the ambiguous word. Grand-average waveform for each of the three midline electrode sites. The disambiguating word is followed by one word. The translation of the example sentence is "My uncle has the ash/stub of his cigar quickly (cleared away)."

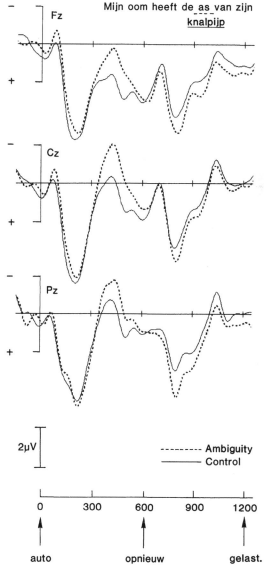

FIG. 3.6. ERPs to the word that disambiguates for the subordinate meaning of the ambiguous word. Grand-average waveform for each of the three midline electrode sites. The disambiguating word is followed by one word. The translation of the example sentence is "My uncle has the axle/muffler of his car again welded."

Discussion

We begin with a discussion of the effects at the level of the ambiguous word, and then turn to the effects of the disambiguation. The significant negative enhancement for the ambiguous words compared with their unambiguous controls indicates that some differential processing is associated with the ambiguous words. This finding is in line with eye-movement data reported by Frazier and Rayner (1990), showing that fixation times are longer on words with multiple meanings compared with words with multiple senses. However, the ERP results are at odds with eye-movement data on balanced versus biased homographs (i.e., homographs with two equally likely meanings, vs. one highly likely and one unlikely meaning). The eye-movement data show that when the preceding context is neutral, readers fixate longer on balanced homographs compared with control words. This fixation difference is not observed for biased homographs (e.g., Duffy et al., 1988; Pacht & Rayner, 1993; Rayner & Duffy, 1986). Contrary to these findings, our ERP results do show a processing effect for biased homographs preceded by neutral sentential contexts. This effect might be due to unknown lexical differences between the ambiguous words and their controls (as could be the case for the pattern of effects obtained in the eye-movement studies). Alternatively, the effect might be reflecting some differential sensitivity between eye-movement and brain-potential data. We did not include balanced homographs in the present experiment, therefore full clarification of this issue awaits further research.

One possible reason for the present ERP effect is that accessing ambiguous words entails accessing multiple meanings, and thereby multiple lexical representations, which is not the case for the control words. Multiple access could be associated with greater processing costs, and this emerges in the ERP waveform. Alternatively, the ERP effect could be reflecting the processing costs associated with computing separate higher order message representations to accommodate the separate meanings of the ambiguity (i.e., multiple integration). Either way, if we accept that the control conditions are appropriate, the implication of the effect is that both meanings of the ambiguous word are activated, and that both are available within a time span of some 300 ms.

Two caveats need to be made here. First, although the ambiguous and the control words are matched on lexical characteristics, it is unclear how to control for, in particular, the lexical frequency of the two classes of words, given the different dominant and subordinate meanings of the ambiguous word (cf. Rayner & Frazier, 1989). However, it is unlikely that differences in lexical frequency underlie the observed effect, since work by Van Petten and Kutas (1990) has shown that the impact of word frequency on the ERP waveform is eliminated after the first two or so words in a sentence. Second, the exact nature of the neurophysiological effect we observed on the ambiguous word is as yet unclear. As we pointed out, the topography of the effect is quite different from the standard distribution of the N400, and this indicates that we are perhaps not dealing with an N400 effect here. Clearly, further research is required before any substantial statements can be made about possible neurophysiological effects related to the processing of ambiguous words preceded by neutral sentential contexts. With these caveats in mind, though, the results do indicate that representational aspects of the mental lexicon—in the present case the lexical complexity of ambiguous words—are manifest in the ERP waveform in the absence of any kind of explicit and interfering task demands (such as those associated with RT tasks).

The pattern of effects at the level of the disambiguating word is much clearer. No processing effects are observed when the dominant meaning of the ambiguous word is in accordance with the disambiguating information, but effects are observed for the subordinate meaning. These results fit well with integration-based accounts of the processing of ambiguous words with clearly dominant and subordinate meanings (cf. Rayner & Frazier, 1989). That is, upon encountering an ambiguous word preceded by a neutral sentential context, the processor integrates the dominant meaning with the prior context. This default assignment occurs either because the dominant meaning is accessed first, or because it receives more activation during a multiple-access process. If subsequent information indicates that the subordinate meaning is in fact the appropriate one, reanalysis processes have to be invoked. Claims about the nature of these reanalysis processes depend on the kinds of assumptions that are made about the time course of the access and integration process. In the integration model proposed by Rayner and Frazier, it is assumed that integration of the dominant meaning with prior context precedes, and if enough of a time lag exists before the subordinate meaning arrives, thereby terminates access to the subordinate meaning. Hence, the reanalysis process will often involve some kind of reaccessing process of the subordinate meaning. The nature of this process is unclear and has not been specified in any of the available models. The results are also compatible with reordered access models (cf. Dopkins et al., 1992). But because we used neutral left-sentential contexts in our experiment, we cannot contrast integration-based accounts with reordered access models. Alternatively, both the dominant and subordinate meanings of an ambiguous word might be accessed in parallel. In this scenario, multiple message-level representations are computed and held in working memory until such a moment in time when disambiguating information comes in. The effect of meaning frequency is then explained by positing differential activation levels for the higher order representations, possibly linked with differential activation-decay functions.

All of the accounts we have described are compatible with the brain-potential data presented in this chapter. In fact, these accounts are, to date, compatible with all of the available data on the effects of right-context information on the processing of ambiguous words that are preceded by neutral sentential contexts. Although the activation and decay functions of the dominant and subordinate meanings in neutral contexts are reasonably well established (e.g., Simpson & Burgess, 1985; Simpson & Krueger, 1991), it is still a matter of debate how these activation and decay functions are modulated by either left- or right-biasing contexts. To determine the nature of the interaction between context and the lexical activation and decay characteristics of the alternative meanings, we need tightly time-locked measures with which we can track on a momentary basis the activational status of the dominant and subordinate meanings over the sentence. Only by using these measures will we be able to determine the time course of the interaction between the activation level(s) of the lexical meaning(s) and the incoming left- or right-context information. Partly due to the relatively slow presentation rate, the present ERP results do not provide sufficient information about this time course, and thereby about the nature of the interaction between context and lexical information. However, what these results clearly demonstrate is that it is possible to pick up on neurophysiological effects that reflect computations at the interface between the mental lexicon and higher order processing systems. Given this demonstration, the challenge now ahead for language researchers using the ERP method is to work out ways of further capitalizing on the on-line, continuous character of the ERP signal, and to attempt to build up a real-time processing profile of ambiguity resolution.

THE BRAIN'S RESPONSE TO PARSING

Most ERP studies on the processing of syntactic information have investigated the ERP effects of various types of syntactic violations in visually presented sentence materials. Although ERP studies of syntactic processing are still relatively limited in number, on the whole, the results suggest that the ERP responses to violations of syntactic preferences are qualitatively different from the classical N400 (Hagoort et al., 1993; Kluender & Kutas, 1993; Kutas & Hillyard, 1983; Münte et al., 1993; Neville et al., 1991; Osterhout & Holcomb, 1992; Rösler et al., 1993).

Existing electrophysiological studies of sentence processing and parsing suggest at least two candidate ERP effects that appear to be related to syntactic analysis: (a) a negative shift that is maximal over left-anterior recording sites (LAN); and (b) a large, broad, symmetric, positive-going shift that has been variously labeled the *P600* (Osterhout & Holcomb, 1992) or the syntactic positive shift (SPS; Hagoort et al., 1993).

Frontal negativities (as well as a small P600) were observed for the first time by Kutas and Hillyard (1983) to words indicating mismatches in number agreement between an adjective and a noun (e.g., "six apple" instead of "six apples") or to illegal tense marking (e.g., "Ice begins to grew" instead of "Ice begins to grow"). Neville et al. (1991) observed LAN effects for violations of phrase-structure constraints, which were realized by changing the obligatory word order of the head noun and a preposition in a noun phrase (e.g., "Ted's about films America"). More complex patterns of results were observed to two additional violation types in the Neville et al. study. Finally, LAN effects were also observed by Kluender and Kutas (1993) in a number of different sentence types, including filler-gap constructions.

Because the extent to which these various LANs are related is unclear, a unifying account of what leads to their elicitation must await further research. It will be especially important to determine what underlies the reported variations in the onset and distributional characteristics of the LAN effects. What is clear, however, is that LAN effects are qualitatively different from the typical N400 effects seen following violations of semantic constraints.

A clearer picture emerges for the SPS/P600 that has been observed to diverse syntactic violations in English and Dutch (Hagoort et al., 1993; Osterhout & Holcomb, 1992). In one of their conditions, Hagoort et al. compared ERPs to Dutch sentences that violated the agreement between the subject NP and the finite verb, as in the following example sentences (literal translation in English between brackets; the word that renders the sentence ungrammatical (the Critical Word [CW]) and its counterpart are italicized):

Het verwende kind *gooit* het speelgoed op de grond.
(The spoiled child *throws* the toys on the floor.)
*Het verwende kind *gooien* het speelgoed op de grond.
(The spoiled child *throw* the toys on the floor.)

The basic pattern of results that we observed is shown in Fig. 3.7 for the posterior midline site (Pz). The CW is preceded by two words and followed by three words.

As can be seen, the ERP waveform to the incorrect CW shows a positive shift in comparison with its correct counterpart. This positive shift is widely distributed over the recording sites and has a centro-parietal maximum. The onset of the positive shift, which we labeled *SPS* (i.e., Syntactic Positive Shift), is at about 500 ms after presentation of the incorrect CW. As can be seen, the SPS is replaced by a negative shift on word positions following the CW. These are N400 effects.

A similar pattern of results is obtained for a completely different syntactic violation. In the phrase-structure violation, the obligatory word order in Dutch of adjective–adverb–noun sequences was violated by changing the order of the adjective and the adverb, as in the following example sentences (the CW is italicized):

De echtgenoot schrikt van de nogal emotionele *reactie* van zijn vrouw.
(The husband [is startled] by the rather emotional *response* of his wife.)

AGREEMENT CONDITION, Electrode Pz

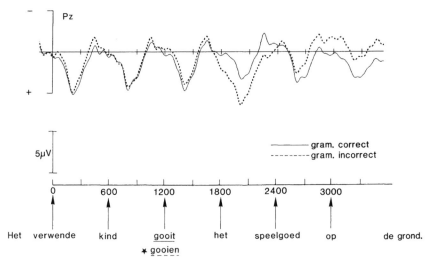

FIG. 3.7.   Agreement condition, normal prose. Grand-average wave-form for electrode site Pz, for the grammatically correct and incorrect CWs. The CW is preceded by two and followed by three words. The translation of the example sentence is "The spoilt child throws/throw the toy on the ground."

*De echtgenoot schrikt van de emotionele nogal *reactie* van zijn vrouw.)
(The husband [is startled] by the emotional rather *reaction* of his wife.)

For these sentences, again, an SPS was observed, followed by a negative shift to words after the noun that rendered the sentence ungrammatical in the incorrect version. However, there was one major difference with the agreement violation. For the phrase-structure violation, the SPS was already observed to the adverb preceding the noun. At this position, the sentence still could have been continued in a syntactically legal way by adding another adjective (e.g., "the emotional rather aggressive reaction").

This suggests that the positive shift is not an ERP response to violations only. Therefore, we have proposed that the SPS is elicited to the word in the sentence that renders the assignment of the preferred structure (e.g., the less complex, more frequent one) impossible.

To test the independence of SPS and N400 effects, we ran a follow-up study in which sentential-semantic constraints are reduced as much as possible. This was done by constructing syntactic-prose versions of the sentences that were used in the previous study. These sentences are structurally identical to the ones from which they were derived, but are constructed in such a way as to be semantically uninterpretable. In the syntactic-prose version of the experiment, the same syntactic-violation types are used as in the normal-prose version. If SPS and N400 are related to qualitatively different processing events, this experiment should dissociate them because, in the syntactic-prose sentences, we do not expect the syntactic violations to have detectable consequences for (attempts to construct) a semantic interpretation of the sentences. Therefore, in this experiment we expected to see an SPS to the syntactic violations, but no N400 effects for words following the violations.

In addition, this experiment should give us more information about possible reasons for the absence of an SPS to the third kind of syntactic violation we tested in the previous experiment. In this subcategorization violation, we violated the constraint that obligatory intransitive verbs cannot take a noun as direct object. The following sentences are examples of this violation (the CW is italicized):

De zoon van de rijke industrieel leent de *auto* van zijn vader.
(The son of the rich industrialist borrows the *car* of his father.)
*De zoon van de rijke industrieel pocht de *auto* van zijn vader.
(The son of the rich industrialist boasts the *car* of his father.)

For this violation, no effect was observed to the incorrect CW in comparison with the CW in the correct companion sentences. Thus, this violation behaved differently than the other two. However, some consequences of this violation showed up in the N400 effects to words following the CW, reminiscent of the N400 effects for the other two syntactic-violation types.

We speculated that the absence of an SPS might result from the occurrence of an SPS and an N400 effect in the same latency range. Because these are two opposing effects in terms of their electrical polarity, they cancel each other out, with the absence of a significant difference on the CW as the net result. The reason that these opposing effects occur in the same latency range might be due to the intricate relationship between the verb's semantic specifications and its subcategorization frame. Recent empirical evidence suggests that part of the verb's semantic specifications are encoded in its subcategorization frame (Fisher, Gleitman, & Gleitman, 1991). This fits with several linguistic accounts claiming that subcategorization frames are relatively straightforward projections from certain semantic features (Bresnan, 1979; Chomsky, 1981; Jackendoff, 1978).

Exactly how intricate the relationship between subcategorization frame and semantic specifications is could become clear in the syntactic-prose version of this experiment, by removing the semantic consequences of the syntactic violation with respect to the overall interpretation of the sentence. This was another reason for running a syntactic-prose version of the experiment reported in Hagoort et al. (1993).

Method

Three hundred and sixty Dutch sentences were constructed. All sentences were derived from the set of sentences in the normal-prose version of the experiment (Hagoort et al., 1993). For each sentence in the normal-prose version, the lexical items were replaced by other lexical items of the same word class. The replacements were chosen so as to make the sentences semantically uninterpretable. That is, the usual semantic context constraints no longer applied in these syntactic-prose sentences. However, all of the sentences had the same constituent structure as their source sentences in the normal-prose version of this experiment.

As in the normal-prose experiment, half of the sentences are grammatically correct, and half contain a grammatical violation. Each sentence in the violated set is derived from a sentence in the correct set, such that the only difference with the companion correct sentence is the word violating the syntactic constraints. Three kinds of grammatical violations are used: (a) violation of verb–noun number agreement, (b) violation of verb subcategorization, and (c) violation of phrase structure.

The *agreement violations* consist of number violations between verbs and nouns within subject–verb–object (SVO) or verb–subject–object (VSO) sentences. The following example gives both the grammatically correct and incorrect version of an SVO agreement violation (literal translation in English between brackets; the CW and its correct counterpart are in italics):

> De gekookte gieter *rookt* de telefoon in de poes.
> (The boiled watering-can *smokes* the telephone in the cat.)
> *De gekookte gieter *roken* de telefoon in de poes.
> (The boiled watering-can *smoke* the telephone in the cat.)

The *subcategorization violations* involve obligatory intransitive verbs followed by a noun that has to be assigned the grammatical role of direct object. The correct companion sentence contains a transitive verb at the CW position. For example:

> De haargrens in de gewassen boterham leent de *wortel* van zijn krant.
> (The hair-line in the washed bread borrows the *root* of his newspaper.)
> *De haargrens in de gewassen boterham pocht de *wortel* van zijn krant.
> (The hair-line in the washed bread boasts the *root* of his newspaper.)

The *phrase-structure violations* consist of nouns preceded by transpositions of adverbs and adjectives. In Dutch, like English, it is a violation of phrase-structure constraints to have a noun preceded by an adjective–adverb sequence. For example (the CW is italicized):

De hiel valt over de nogal bewoonde *poes* op zijn broekzak.
(The heel tripped over the rather inhabited *cat* on his pocket.)
*De hiel valt over de bewoonde nogal *poes* op zijn broekzak.
(The heel tripped over the inhabited rather *cat* on his pocket.)

Note that the actual violation occurs on the noun following the adverb (i.e., on *poes*) because the adjective–adverb sequence can be part of a larger and grammatically legal adjective–adverb–adjective–noun sequence (e.g., "the inhabited rather talkative cat"). However, in the normal-prose experiment, an SPS was already obtained to the adverb preceding the noun. This is probably because the adverb forces the parser to entertain the possibility of the more complex (less frequent) and, therefore, less preferred adjective–adverb–adjective–noun structure. If this account is correct, also in this experiment the SPS should already be observed to the adverb (i.e., *nogal*) that precedes the noun (i.e., *poes*) in the CW position.

The additional criteria that had to be met in constructing the materials, and the way in which the materials were divided over two lists and three blocks, were exactly the same as in the normal-prose experiment (for details, see Hagoort et al., 1993).

Grammaticality Judgment Pretest

Before running the ERP experiment, the test sentences were pretested in a grammaticality judgment experiment, using a Go/NoGo task, in which subjects were instructed to respond whenever they detected a grammatical violation. The purpose of this pretest was to establish whether subjects were as sensitive to the three types of violations in syntactic-prose sentences as they had been for the normal-prose sentences.

The sentences were displayed word by word in the center of a high-resolution computer screen. Each word was presented for 200 ms, and replaced by the next word in the sentence after a 500-ms blank-screen period. The subjects were told that the sentences they had to read were difficult to understand, but that nevertheless they should try to read each sentence for comprehension. In addition, subjects were instructed to press a button whenever they encountered a grammatical error.

Table 3.1 summarizes the results of the grammaticality pretest for the syntactic-prose sentence and those on a parallel grammaticality pretest for the normal-prose version of these sentences. The percentages indicate the number of times that subjects detected a violation of a certain type on either the CW or the word following it.

In general, compared with the normal-prose sentences, subjects were a little less but still highly accurate in the on-line detection of agreement violations and phrase-structure violations that were embedded in syntactic-prose sentences. In

TABLE 3.1
Performance on the Grammaticality Judgment Task

Condition	Normal Prose (%)	Syntactic Prose (%)
Agreement Violation	90	73
Subcategorization Violation	74	21
Phrase-Structure Violation	86	73

Note. Percentage of violation detections at the CW position and the following word position for the normal and syntactic prose experiment.

contrast, the performance on the subcategorization-violation sentences decreased dramatically for the syntactic-prose version. This suggests that, unlike with agreement violations and phrase-structure violations, subjects do not recognize the subcategorization violations as purely syntactic in nature. This fits well with the empirically supported claim that part of the verb's semantic specifications are encoded in its subcategorization frame (Fisher et al., 1991). Because the subcategorization violations we created are not only syntactic violations but also semantic violations, they probably are not recognized as different from the other words in the sentences that also violated the standard semantic constraints (such as selectional restrictions).

For the agreement and phrase-structure violations, however, the results of the grammaticality judgment pretest indicate the relatively immediate salience of the ungrammaticalities even in sentences that are difficult to interpret semantically.

The ERP Experiment

Display of the stimuli, including presentation durations of the words, was identical to that of the ambiguity experiment and the normal-prose version of the current experiment. Subjects were informed that they would see sentences that were difficult to understand, but that they nevertheless should read for comprehension. No additional task demands were imposed. Subjects were told that some sentences would be grammatically incorrect, but they were given no information concerning the kinds of grammatical errors that would occur.

Results

For all subjects ($N = 40$), average waveforms are computed over all artifact-free trials, for the correct and incorrect sentences of the three violation types separately. Mean amplitudes are calculated per subject, per condition, and per electrode for the critical time ranges given later.

To check whether the differences obtained in the critical time ranges might be due to some spurious effects, we also analyzed two word-epochs preceding the critical areas for each of the three violations. Significant differences were not obtained in any of these cases. This further substantiates the claim that the ERP differences between the CWs in the correct and incorrect sentences are real.

Agreement. Figure 3.8 shows the grand-average waveforms for the three midline sites[3] (Fz, Cz, and Pz) in the correct and incorrect agreement conditions. As can be seen in the waveforms, an SPS emerges to the CWs in the incorrect version compared with the CWs in the correct version. The SPS starts at around 500 ms following the onset of the CW, and continues throughout the following word.

To test the SPS to the incorrect CWs, an ANOVA was performed on the mean amplitudes in the 500–1200-ms range following the onset of the CW. This includes the positivity to the incorrect CW itself and its carry-over effect into the processing range of the next word.[4] The analysis yielded a main effect of Grammaticality [$F(1, 39) = 6.82$, MSe $= 26.04$, $p = .013$].

Although the SPS in the normal-prose sentences was followed by a negative shift toward the end of the sentences, this negative shift was absent in the incorrect agreement sentences in this experiment. Analyses on penultimate and sentence-final words did not result in significant N400 effects. We return to this difference between the normal-prose and the syntactic-prose experiments in the discussion.

Subcategorization.   Figure 3.9 shows the grand-average waveforms for the three midline sites (Fz, Cz, and Pz) in the correct and incorrect subcategorization condition. Inspection of the waveforms suggests the absence of any difference between the correct and incorrect conditions, both to the CW and to the words preceding and following it. A statistical analysis on the mean amplitudes in the 500–1200-ms range following the onset of the CW did not result in a significant effect of Grammaticality. Just as in the normal-prose experiment, no SPS was manifest on the noun following the obligatorily intransitive verbs.

Although in the normal-prose experiment increased N400 amplitudes were

---

[3]For all three violation types, the recording sites over the left and right hemisphere showed the same pattern of results as the midline sites. In addition, no hemispheric differences were obtained in the size of the effects.

[4]In the normal-prose version of this experiment, a smaller latency window was used for statistical analysis (see Hagoort et al., 1993). This window went from 500 ms after onset of the CW (or the word preceding the CW in the phrase-structure condition), until 700 ms, which is approximately until the N1 to the following word. Certainly in the current experiment, with the absence of negative shifts following the SPS, the positivity was much more extended than this small 200-ms period. However, we also analyzed the results for the mean amplitude in this reduced latency window. For this reduced window, the effects of Grammaticality failed to reach significance in the Agreement condition. In the phrase-structure condition, the effect of Grammaticality was significant [$F(1, 39) = 11.28$, MSe $= 16.29$, $p = .002$].

AGREEMENT CONDITION, Midline Electrodes

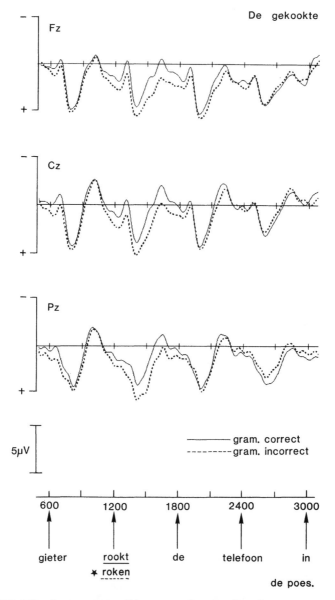

FIG. 3.8. Agreement condition, syntactic prose. Grand-average wave-form for each of the three midline electrode sites, for the grammatically correct and incorrect CWs. The CW is preceded by one and followed by two words. The translation of the example sentence is "The boiled watering-can smokes/smoke the telephone in the cat."

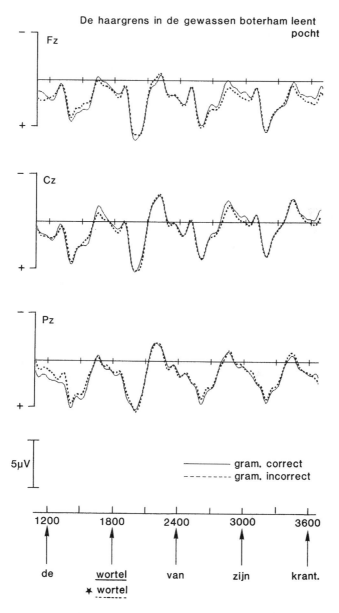

FIG. 3.9. Subcategorization condition, syntactic prose. Grand-average waveform for each of the three midline electrode sites, for the grammatically correct and incorrect CWs. The CW is preceded by one and followed by two words. The translation of the example sentence is "The hair-line in the washed bread borrows/boasts the carrot of his newspaper."

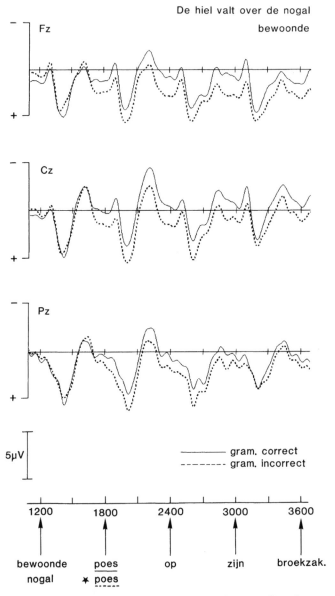

FIG. 3.10. Phrase-structure condition, syntactic prose. Grand-average waveform for each of the three midline electrode sites, for the grammatically correct and incorrect CWs. The CW is preceded by one and followed by two words. The translation of the example sentence is "The heel tripped over the rather inhabited/inhabited rather cat on his pocket."

seen to the penultimate and sentence-final words in the ungrammatical condition, this negative shift was absent in the syntactic-prose sentences. In summary, then, the subcategorization violation did not result in any visible difference between the waveforms of the grammatically correct and incorrect conditions.

Phrase Structure.   Figure 3.10 shows the grand-average waveforms for the three midline sites (Fz, Cz, and Pz) in the correct and incorrect phrase-structure conditions. The waveforms show that a positive shift is present in the incorrect phrase-structure sentences compared with their correct counterparts. As in the normal-prose experiment, this positive shift is already elicited by the adverb that precedes the CW. The positivity carries on throughout the epoch of the CW into the following word. An ANOVA was performed for a window that started 500 ms after onset of the adverb preceding the CW and included the CW epoch until the onset of the word following the CW (i.e., 1200 ms after onset of the word that preceded the CW). This analysis results in a highly significant effect for Grammaticality [$F(1, 39) = 10.74$, MSe = 15.83, $p = .002$].

No differences between the two conditions were observed for penultimate and sentence-final words. This contrasts with the negativities at the same word positions in the incorrect normal-prose version of the sentences.

Discussion

The first major result of this study is the widely distributed positivity that is elicited by two of the three types of syntactic violations. This effect is very similar to the SPS that we obtained in the normal-prose version of this experiment, and to the P600 reported by Osterhout and Holcomb (1992).

Figure 3.11 shows the difference waveforms between the grammatically incorrect and the grammatically correct conditions for the agreement and phrase-structure violations. Difference waveforms are presented for the syntactic-prose experiment and for the normal-prose experiment to allow for a comparison of the results in both experiments. The difference waveforms give a straightforward picture of the commonalities and differences in effects between the normal-prose and the syntactic-prose experiment for the two syntactic violations that show an SPS.

A comparison of the two difference waveforms shows two aspects worth mentioning. The first one is that, to the very same word positions for the very same violation types (i.e., the agreement violation and the phrase-structure violation), an SPS is observed in both normal-prose and syntactic-prose sentences. The effect is slightly smaller in the syntactic prose, but has the same onset latency (500 ms after word onset) for the two prose types.

The second aspect is that in the syntactic prose the absence of a negative shift following the SPS near the sentence is striking because a negative shift is so clearly present in the normal-prose difference waveforms. In the normal-prose

DIFFERENCE WAVEFORMS: Grammatical – Ungrammatical

AGREEMENT CONDITION

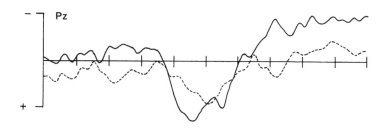

PHRASE STRUCTURE CONDITION

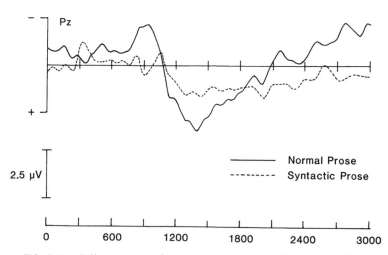

FIG. 3.11. Difference waveforms at electrode site Pz between the grammatically incorrect and correct conditions for the agreement and phrase-structure violations, in the normal-prose and syntactic-prose experiments.

experiment, it was even present for the subcategorization-violation condition, which did not reveal an SPS.

A number of conclusions follow from the results of this experiment, in combination with the results obtained for the normal-prose sentences. First, the SPS that we obtained in this experiment to two different syntactic violations occurred in the absence of N400 effects to words following the syntactic violations. This further substantiates the claim that the SPS is qualitatively different from the negative shift (the N400), which we believe to be especially sensitive to semantic integration processes (Brown & Hagoort, 1993). That is, the processing of syntactic information has a neurophysiological signature that is clearly different from that for the processing of semantic information. This result is difficult to account for in sentence-processing models that deny that qualitatively different constraints (i.e., syntactic and semantic) make qualitatively different contributions to the construction of an interpretation for the whole utterance (e.g., McClelland, St. John, & Taraban, 1989).

Second, the results of the phrase-structure condition show that the presence of a syntactic violation is not a precondition for the SPS to be elicited. In the phrase-structure condition, the SPS was observed to the word that rendered the assignment of a preferred structure (i.e., determiner–adjective–noun) impossible. The adverb following the adjective forces the parser to entertain the possibility of an alternative structure, which is the less frequent and more complex NP structure (i.e. determiner–adjective–adverb–adjective–noun). The result of the phrase-structure condition fits with the proposal that, by default, the parser assigns only one structure to the incoming string of words. This preferred structure is determined on the basis of some computational economy principle (see Frazier, 1987), or on the basis of the frequency of alternative syntactic constructions. The preferred structure gets revised if it is rendered untenable by further incoming words. In general, the SPS seems to arise to the word in the sentence that indicates that the preferred structural assignment is an incorrect syntactic analysis for the incoming string of words.

The presence of N400 effects to words more or less immediately following the syntactic violation in the normal-prose sentences, and their absence in syntactic prose, can be explained in terms of recent proposals about the processing nature of the N400 (Brown & Hagoort, 1993; Osterhout & Holcomb, 1992). According to these proposals, the N400 is especially sensitive to the integration of lexical meaning into an overall representation of the word or sentence context. With the normal sentential-semantic context constraints in place, the syntactic violations seem to have an immediate consequence for the semantic integration of following words into a coherent overall message-level representation of the whole sentence. This integration process becomes more difficult, resulting in an increase of the N400 to words following the syntactic violation. The situation is clearly different for the syntactic-prose sentences. The absence of sentential-semantic constraints probably prevents the construction of a coherent message-level representation. Therefore, the semantic integration process might be extremely difficult, if not impossible. In these circumstances, the syntactic violation probably has no additional disadvantageous consequences for semantic integration processes. Therefore, the syntactic violation does not lead to increased N400 amplitudes to words further downstream.

Finally, the absence of an SPS to subcategorization violations replicates the result for the normal-prose sentences. We explained the absence of an effect for Grammaticality in the normal-prose version of this experiment as resulting from the opposing overlapping effects of an SPS and an N400 in the same latency range. The opposite polarity of these two effects results in the disappearance of both effects in the averaged waveforms. We speculated that, unlike the agreement and phrase-structure violations, in the subcategorization-violation condition the CW renders the sentence ungrammatical via its semantic properties. By removing to a large extent the semantic constraints in the syntactic-prose sentences, we hoped to get a clearer picture of the purely syntactic consequences of subcategorization violations. However, the results of the grammaticality pretest already suggested that this would not work. Subjects are not able to detect subcategorization violations as purely syntactic anomalies. This confirms our earlier suggestion (Hagoort et al., 1993) that verb meaning and the syntactic aspects of the verb that are specified on the subcategorization frames are tightly intertwined (see Fisher et al., 1991, for empirical support). Therefore, the subcategorization violations that we used in both studies are not only syntactic violations, but by necessity also semantic violations. As a result, in syntactic prose they probably get processed in the same way as the semantically anomalous prose in which they are embedded.

In conclusion, the results of the syntactic-prose experiment further substantiate the existence of 'syntactic' ERP components within the domain of language-related ERP effects. The SPS that we observed might either reflect the computation of a separate level of syntactic representation during the process of language understanding, or the initiation of a syntactic reanalysis after a first-pass structural assignment has failed to provide a well-formed structure. Further research is needed to specify the exact processing nature of the SPS within the context of current parsing proposals. However, the clearly syntactic nature of the SPS holds promise for its use in testing more subtle differences between competing parsing theories.

CONCLUDING REMARKS

In this chapter, we have presented ERP data from two experiments that address very different issues in language comprehension research. Both issues, however, have in common that they are related to higher order integration processes. Although in recent years there has been something of an upsurge in experimental work on syntactic and semantic integration processes, on the whole, systems that lie beyond the mental lexicon have not been the focus of on-line investigation, in part because the existing RT techniques pose problems in tracking the comprehension process as it develops across the sentence or discourse. With the advent of eye trackers, a first continuous record was obtained of the normal reading process, in the absence of irrelevant task demands. We hope to have demonstrated that the registration of ERPs presents an additional and insightful tool with which to observe the language comprehension system as it operates in real-time. However, as we pointed out in the general introduction, it is important to emphasize that the present ERP data are but first steps in a psycholinguistic research program on brain manifestations of sentence processing. Before the full potential of the signal characteristics of ERPs can be realized within psycholinguistics, a number of issues need to be addressed, two of which we mention here.

A first issue concerns the relatively slow presentation rates that have been used in the ERP experiments reported here (and in general in the ERP and language literature), which lag far behind the normal reading rate. The main reason for using relatively slow presentation rates is that this minimizes the problem of overlapping components in the waveform. However, this is not a principled problem, as has been shown by Kutas (1987). She registered ERPs to semantically congruous and incongruous words in sentence-final position in sentences presented at a rate of 10 words per second (i.e., about twice as fast as the normal reading rate), and obtained essentially the same N400 effect as when the words of the same sentences were presented once every 700 ms. Furthermore, and clearly contrary to claims about nonlinguistic effects of unnatural rates on language-related ERPs, similar N400 effects have been observed in our laboratory and by others for semantically incongruous words in naturally produced connected speech (Connolly et al., 1990; Holcomb & Neville, 1991). So, the available evidence indicates that rate effects do not severely contaminate the ERP results. Nevertheless, it is clear that researchers using the ERP method will have to move toward more standard presentation rates in reading experiments, certainly when focusing on higher order integration processes. At present, we are running a Rapid Serial Visual Presentation (RSVP) version (one word every 250 ms) of the normal-prose version reported in Hagoort et al. (1993) to ensure that the SPS is also present with more normal reading rates. At the same time, we are running a connected speech version of this experiment to see whether the SPS obtains across modalities, which is to be expected on the basis of work by Osterhout and Holcomb (1993) on ERPs and syntactic processing in connected speech. We believe this kind of simultaneous approach is necessary to test the validity of language-related ERP effects.

A second issue concerns the temporal relationship between the real-time electrophysiological signal and the ongoing linguistic analysis. As we pointed out earlier, an appealing characteristic of ERPs is that they are a real-time signal with which to observe a real-time process. However, before ERPs can be used to obtain a truly on-line processing profile of language comprehension, a better understanding is required of the exact time-locking relationships between the ERP waveform and the presumed underlying comprehension process. This implies that we have to come to grips with the complex problem of the exact moment in time at which a particular component emerges in the ERP waveform. For components like the N400 and the SPS, it is relatively straightforward to determine at what moment after stimulus onset they reach their peak amplitude. However, the latencies of these peak amplitudes clearly overestimate the moment in time at which the components have their onset relative to the onset of the linguistic stimulation that elicits them, and it is exactly these onset moments that provide critical information about the time course of the ongoing comprehension process. This aspect of the time-locking issue poses a real challenge for psycholinguists working with the ERP method.

In conclusion, it is clear that several problems have to be solved before all the promises that ERPs hold for psycholinguistics will be obtained. But we believe that it is equally clear that the ERP method is already a very useful and revealing tool with which to investigate language processes.

ACKNOWLEDGMENTS

We would like to thank Aafke Deckers and Jolanda Groothusen for their assistance in all phases of the work reported here, and Lyn Frazier for her comments on an earlier version of this chapter. This research was supported by a grant from the Volkswagen Foundation (Hannover, Germany) and by the Max Planck Society (München, Germany). The authors contributed equally to this publication, and their order of mention is arbitrary.

REFERENCES

Besson, M., & Macar, F. (1987). An event-related potential analysis of incongruity in music and other non-linguistic contexts. *Psychophysiology, 24,* 14–25.

Bresnan, J. (1979). *Theories of complementation in English syntax.* New York: Garland.

Brown, C. M., & Hagoort, P. (1993). The processing nature of the N400: Evidence from masked priming. *Journal of Cognitive Neuroscience, 5,* 34–44.

Chomsky, N. (1981). *Lectures on government and binding.* Dordrecht, The Netherlands: Foris.

Connolly, J. F., Stewart, S. H., & Phillips, N. A. (1990). The effects of processing requirements on neurophysiological responses to spoken sentences. *Brain and Language, 39,* 302–318.

Dopkins, S., Morris, R. K., & Rayner, K. (1992). Lexical ambiguity and eye fixations in reading: A test of competing models of lexical ambiguity resolution. *Journal of Memory and Language, 31,* 461–476.

Duffy, S. A., Morris, R. K., & Rayner, K. (1988). Lexical ambiguity and fixation times in reading. *Journal of Memory and Language, 27,* 429–446.

Fisher, C., Gleitman, H., & Gleitman, L. R. (1991). On the semantic content of subcategorization frames. *Cognitive Psychology, 23,* 331–392.

Frazier, L. (1987). Sentence processing: A tutorial review. In M. Coltheart (Ed.), *Attention and performance XII: The psychology of reading* (pp. 559–586). Hillsdale, NJ: Lawrence Erlbaum Associates.

Frazier, L., & Rayner, K. (1990). Taking on semantic commitments: Processing multiple meanings vs. multiple senses. *Journal of Memory and Language, 29,* 181–200.

Garnsey, S. M., Tanenhaus, M. K., & Chapman, R. M. (1989). Evoked potentials and the study of sentence comprehension. *Journal of Psycholinguistic Research, 18,* 51–60.

Hagoort, P., Brown, C. M., & Groothusen, J. (1993). The Syntactic Positive Shift (SPS) as an ERP-measure of syntactic processing. *Language and Cognitive Processes. 8,* 439–483.

Holcomb, P. J., & Neville, H. J. (1991). Natural speech processing: An analysis using event-related brain potentials. *Psychobiology, 19,* 286–300.

Jackendoff, R. (1978). Grammar as evidence for conceptual structure. In M. Halle, J. Bresnan, & G. Miller (Eds.), *Linguistic theory and psychological reality* (pp. 201–228). Cambridge, MA: MIT Press.

Jasper, H. H. (1958). Report to the committee on methods of clinical examination in electroencephalography: Appendix. The ten-twenty system of the International Federation. *Electroencephalography and Clinical Neurophysiology, 10,* 371–375.

Kintsch, W., & Mross, E. F. (1985). Context effects in word identification. *Journal of Memory and Language, 24,* 336–349.

Kluender, R., & Kutas, M. (1993). The interaction of lexical and syntactic effects in the processing of unbounded dependencies. *Language and Cognitive Processes. 8,* 573–633.

Kutas, M. (1987). Event-related brain potentials (ERPs) elicited during rapid serial visual presentation of congruous and incongruous sentences. In R. Johnson, Jr., J. W. Rohrbaugh, & R. Parasuraman (Eds.), *Current trends in event-related potential research* (pp. 406–411). Amsterdam: Elsevier.

Kutas, M., & Hillyard, S. A. (1980). Reading senseless sentences: Brain potentials reflect semantic incongruity. *Science, 207,* 203–205.

Kutas, M., & Hillyard, S. A. (1983). Event-related brain potentials to grammatical errors and semantic anomalies. *Memory & Cognition, 11,* 539–550.

Kutas, M., Lindamood, T., & Hillyard, S. A. (1984). Word expectancy and event-related potentials during sentence processing. In S. Kornblum & J. Requin (Eds.), *Preparatory states and processes* (pp. 217–238). Hillsdale, NJ: Lawrence Erlbaum Associates.

Kutas, M., Neville, H. J., & Holcomb, P. J. (1987). A preliminary comparison of the N400 response to semantic anomalies during reading, listening and signing. In R. J. Ellingson, N. M. F. Murray, & A. M. Halliday (Eds.), *The London Symposium* (pp. 325–330). Amsterdam: Elsevier.

Kutas, M., & Van Petten, C. (1988). Event-related brain potential studies of language. In P. K. Ackles, J. R. Jennings, & M. G. H. Coles (Eds.), *Advances in psychophysiology* (Vol. 3, pp. 139–187). Greenwich, CT: JAI Press.

Kutas, M., Van Petten, C., & Besson, M. (1988). Event-related potential asymmetries during the reading of sentences. *Electroencephalography and Clinical Neurophysiology, 69,* 218–233.

McClelland, J. L., St. John, M., & Taraban, R. (1989). Sentence comprehension: A parallel distributed processing approach. *Language and Cognitive Processes, 4,* 287–335.

Münte, Th. F., Heinze, H.-J., & Mangun, G. R. (1993). Dissociation of brain activity related to syntactic and semantic aspects of language. *Journal of Cognitive Neuroscience, 5,* 335–344.

Neville, H., Mills, D. L., & Lawson, D. S. (1992). Fractionating language: Different neural subsystems with different sensitive periods. *Cerebral Cortex, 2,* 244–258.

Neville, H., Nicol, J. L., Barss, A., Forster, K. I., & Garrett, M. F. (1991). Syntactically based sentence processing classes: Evidence from event-related brain potentials. *Journal of Cognitive Neuroscience, 3,* 151–165.

Onifer, W., & Swinney, D. A. (1981). Accessing lexical ambiguities during sentence comprehension: Effects of frequency of meaning and contextual bias. *Memory & Cognition, 9*, 225–236.

Osterhout, L., & Holcomb, P. J. (1992). Event-related brain potentials elicited by syntactic anomaly. *Journal of Memory and Language, 31*, 785–806.

Osterhout, L., & Holcomb, P. J. (1993). Event-related potentials and syntactic anomaly: Evidence of anomaly detection during the perception of continuous speech. *Language and Cognitive Processes. 8*, 413–437.

Pacht, J. M., & Rayner, K. (1993). The processing of homophonic homographs during reading: Evidence from eye movement studies. *Journal of Psycholinguistic Research, 22*, 257–271.

Paller, K. A., McCarthy, G., & Wood, C. C. (1992). Event-related potentials elicited by deviant endings to melodies. *Psychophysiology, 29*, 202–206.

Rayner, K., & Duffy, S. A. (1986). Lexical complexity and fixation times in reading: Effects of word frequency, verb complexity, and lexical ambiguity. *Memory & Cognition, 14*, 191–201.

Rayner, K., & Frazier, L. (1989). Selection mechanisms in reading lexically ambiguous words. *Journal of Experimental Psychology: Learning, Memory, and Cognition, 15*, 779–790.

Rösler, F., Pütz, P., Friederici, A., & Hahne, A. (1993). Event-related brain potentials while encountering semantic and syntactic constraint violations. *Journal of Cognitive Neuroscience, 5*, 345–362.

Seidenberg, M. S., Tanenhaus, M. K., Leiman, J. M., & Bienkowski, M. (1982). Automatic access of the meanings of ambiguous words in context: Some limitations of knowledge-based processing. *Cognitive Psychology, 14*, 489–537.

Simpson, G. B. (1981). Meaning dominance and semantic context in the processing of lexical ambiguity. *Journal of Verbal Learning and Verbal Behavior, 20*, 120–136.

Simpson, G. B. (1984). Lexical ambiguity and its role in models of word recognition. *Psychological Bulletin, 96*, 316–340.

Simpson, G. B., & Burgess, C. (1985). Activation and selection processes in the recognition of ambiguous words. *Journal of Experimental Psychology: Human Perception and Performance, 11*, 28–39.

Simpson, G. B., & Krueger, M. A. (1991). Selective access of homograph meanings in sentence context. *Journal of Memory and Language, 30*, 627–643.

Swinney, D. A. (1979). Lexical access during sentence comprehension: (Re)Consideration of context effects. *Journal of Verbal Learning and Verbal Behavior, 18*, 645–659.

Tabossi, P. (1988a). Accessing lexical ambiguity in different types of sentential contexts. *Journal of Memory and Language, 27*, 324–340.

Tabossi, P. (1988b). Sentential context and lexical access. In S. L. Small, G. W. Cottrell, & M. K. Tanenhaus (Eds.), *Lexical ambiguity resolution* (pp. 331–342). San Mateo, CA: Morgan Kaufmann.

Tabossi, P., Colombo, L., & Job, R. (1987). Accessing lexical ambiguity: Effects of context and dominance. *Psychological Research, 49*, 161–167.

Tabossi, P., & Zardon, F. (1993). Processing ambiguous words in context. *Journal of Memory and Language, 32*, 359–372.

Van Petten, C., & Kutas, M. (1987). Ambiguous words in context: An event-related brain potential analysis of the time course of meaning activation. *Journal of Memory and Language, 26*, 188–208.

Van Petten, C., & Kutas, M. (1990). Interactions between sentence context and word frequency in event-related brain potentials. *Memory & Cognition, 18*, 380–393.

Van Petten, C., & Kutas, M. (1991). Electrophysiological evidence for the flexibility of lexical processing. In G. B. Simpson (Ed.), *Understanding word and sentence* (pp. 129–174). North-Holland: Elsevier Science Publishers.

II PHONOLOGICAL PROCESSING

4

Access to Phonological-Form Representations in Language Comprehension and Production

Pienie Zwitserlood
University of Münster
Germany

Functionally speaking, language has two modes: production and comprehension, both in their primary (speaking and speech perception) and secondary (writing and reading) modalities. Perception and production are intimately linked in the normal language user: Every speaker is a listener, and vice versa. It is surprising that, in psycholinguistic research, the two modes of language use have been studied in street separation for a long time. The reasons for this are manifold (see MacKay, Allport, Prinz, & Scheerer, 1987). It is due, in part, to a Cartesian philosophical tradition that treated action as inferior to perception, and the study of language production has always been the poor cousin. Language comprehension is a fully established research area with its own questions and methods, whereas the upsurge of experimental studies on the processes involved in production is of a more recent date. But the separation is not as strict as it seems because research into one language mode frequently relies on the subjects' smooth performance in the other. Much research on word recognition uses *pronunciation* or *naming* (i.e., the speaking out loud of a stimulus word) as a measure of comprehension processes. Conversely, word-production studies using the picture–word paradigm rely on the influence on production processes of stimuli that are presented for comprehension. Nevertheless, few attempts have been made to study aspects of language performance under the unified view of one system for language use.

In this chapter, I try to integrate what is known about access to word forms in language comprehension and production, assuming that information about the form of words is shared by production and comprehension—an assumption that I motivate later. In what follows, I first provide some background information on process and representation in comprehension and production as a context for the question of shared or separate representations of lexical form. Next, I summarize the evidence from comprehension and production studies on phonological-form priming. Then I present some of my own data on differences and commonalities between comprehension and production at the level of lexical form. Finally, I discuss the implications of comprehension and production data with respect to processing mechanisms underlying access to form representations in each language mode.

GENERAL ISSUES CONCERNING LANGUAGE COMPREHENSION AND PRODUCTION

Models of production and comprehension agree, to a large extent, on the functional components involved in producing or understanding language. Production models such as Levelt's (1989) or Garrett's (1980, 1988) distinguish semantic, syntactic, morphological, phonological, and articulatory-phonetic components, and the same is true for most models of language understanding (Forster, 1979; Marslen-Wilson, 1987). In models for both language modes, a crucial role is reserved for the mental lexicon and for the types of information it contains.

The mental lexicon contains information about semantic and syntactic properties of words. A word's morphological makeup is also considered to be lexically represented, and so is information about what words sound or look like. The latter information is stored in terms of abstract representations of lexical form. Such representations can be labeled *phonological*[1] if we are dealing with speech, or *orthographic* if we are dealing with reading and writing. For spoken words, the input to, and the output from, the form level consists of speech. The phonological representations in the form lexicon do not code all information present in the speech signal. They abstract away from differences between speakers, speech rate, and other surface variation; they might even be underspecified for information that can be inferred by rule (Lahiri & Marslen-Wilson, 1991). Similarly, orthographic representations are insensitive to surface variability due to writing style or typesetting.

It is obvious that the description of the form of words has to be different for the auditory and visual modality: for listening and speaking on the one side, and reading and writing on the other side. The focus of this chapter is not on modality-specific input or output processing, but on differences and commonalities between the two language modes—comprehension and production—

---

[1]The term *phonological* is used here as neutral with respect to the exact form of the code (see Besner & Davelaar, 1982). Phonological representations are defined as abstract, mode-independent, long-term memory codes, and their existence does not preclude the existence of other, more peripheral auditory or articulatory representations or computations. I use the terms *phonological representation* and *word form* interchangeably.

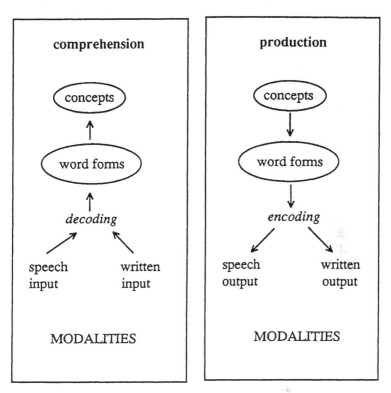

FIG. 4.1.   Language modes (production and comprehension) and modalities (speech and writing).

concerning the ways in which phonological representations are addressed in the mental lexicon, and concerning the mechanisms operating at the phonological level. Because phonological representations are at issue, I confine myself to one modality: the situation in which speech, rather than written language, is perceived or produced.

As illustrated in Fig. 4.1, the pathways between conceptual and word-form information are different for language comprehension and production. In comprehension, the direction of information flow is from speech to concepts or meaning. To understand what a word means, the listener first has to identify exactly which word was spoken: was it /haːt/ (heart) or /haːd/ (hard)? The word-recognition system uses information contained in the speech input to access phonological forms in the mental lexicon, and to decide which of these representations best matches the input. These two processes, access to form representations and selection of the best match, are incorporated in most models of word recognition, although the models differ in the ways in which the mechanisms are implemented (cf. Forster, 1976, 1979; Marslen-Wilson, 1987; McClelland & Elman, 1986).

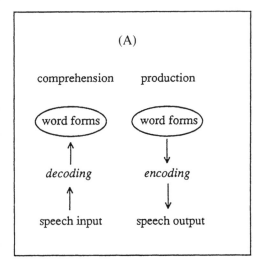
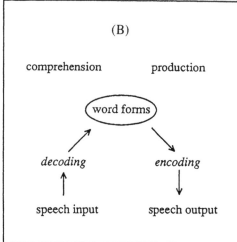

FIG. 4.2.   Separate or shared representations of lexical form.

In language production, the direction is from meaning to speech. The speaker first has to decide what he or she is going to say (i.e., to select a concept or word meaning) before the corresponding word form can be retrieved from the lexicon. Analogous to comprehension, speech production involves access and selection, but selection occurs at the conceptual-semantic level, rather than at the phonological level. As with comprehension models, models of speech production incorporate these processes, albeit in computationally different ways (cf. Dell, 1986, 1988; Levelt, 1989).

This comparison of comprehension and production focuses on processing rather than on representation. I attempt to integrate findings concerning access to lexical forms in comprehension and production under the assumption that representations are shared, but that processes might differ. It has often implicitly been assumed that memory representations are shared between the two language modes (see Fig. 4.2B), but this is by no means self-evident. The issue of shared or separate levels of phonological form for comprehension and production has been studied by examining certain types of speech errors (Fay & Cutler, 1977), experimental data from normal subjects (Clarke & Morton, 1983; Shallice, McLeod, & Lewis, 1985), but mainly data from the language impaired (see Allport, 1984; Caplan, 1992; Friedrich, 1990; Shallice, 1988, for overviews).

Some researchers argue in favor of a single phonological level (Allport, 1984; Allport & Funnell, 1981; Caramazza, Berndt, & Basili, 1983; Liberman & Mattingly, 1985; MacKay, 1987), whereas others (Monsell, 1987; Shallice et al., 1985) interpret the available evidence as speaking against it. These two positions are illustrated in Fig. 4.2. It is often very difficult to decide whether the data from normal subjects or from patients speak on the issue of shared or separate repre-

sentations, or of shared or distinct processing mechanisms. Process and representation are notoriously hard to distinguish empirically, and evidence against
shared representations is often also compatible with the view that because comprehension and production have different mechanisms operating on the same
representations. The idea of a single level of phonological representation is
compelling for reasons of parsimony and refutability, whereas a separation of the
mechanisms involved in speaking and understanding is quite plausible, given
their radically different functionality.

PHONOLOGICAL EFFECTS IN COMPREHENSION
AND PRODUCTION

There is a clear asymmetry between comprehension and production concerning
empirical studies on phonological processing and representation: The work in
comprehension is abundant, whereas the production literature is rather meager.
Summarizing the major outcomes in each field, I confine myself to research on
speech, leaving out the literature on orthographic priming. Although this research is very informative about phonological recoding and automatic activation
of phonological information during reading, it does not address the question that
mechanisms operate on phonological forms.[2]

The research summarized next is evaluated with respect to the following
questions. Under what circumstances are phonological forms accessed (or activated), and by means of which input? What is the nature of effects (facilitatory,
inhibitory) obtained with different experimental manipulations, and what do
these effects tell us about the mechanisms operating on phonological representations? Also, is it possible to distinguish between effects caused by the subjects'
strategic behavior and genuine on-line processing effects? For comprehension
and production, the experimental technique par excellence seems to be the priming paradigm, in which primes are presented that are related in form, but not in
meaning, to subsequently presented targets. But the tasks that subjects have to
perform vary between studies, and the outcome of experiments varies with the
tasks.

Phonological Priming in Language Comprehension

Form-priming studies in comprehension can be divided along a number of dimensions: task (identification in noise, lexical decision, shadowing, or pro-

---

[2]The issues of phonological recoding and activation, of connections between orthographic and
phonological representations at a lexical level, or between graphemes and phonemic segments at a
prelexical level, are not central to this chapter, although some of the experiments discussed later,
including our own, present spoken primes and visual targets, thus relying on the existence of such
connections.

nouncing the target), word status of primes and targets (words or pseudowords), timing of prime and target presentation (in terms of shorter or longer intervals [ISIs] or onset asynchronies [SOAs] between primes and targets), modality of prime or target presentation (both auditorily; prime or target visually), position of form overlap between prime and target (onset overlap, e.g., /mInt/-/mInk/, or rhyme overlap, e.g., /li:d/-/ri:d/), and, finally, the way in which activation of word forms is measured (through direct form overlap between primes and targets, or mediated via semantic relations). All of these factors play a role, as is seen later. I discuss word-onset overlap and rhyme overlap separately.

Primes and Targets Overlapping at Word Onset.   In one of the earlier studies looking at onset similarity (Jakimik, Cole, & Rudnicky, 1985), spoken target words were presented that were fully contained in spoken prime words. Primes and targets were separated by long intervals, and the task was lexical decision. Jakimik et al. found facilitation when primes and targets were both orthographically and phonologically similar (*pillow*–PILL), but not for mere phonological (*spider*–SPY) or orthographic (*legislate*–LEG) similarity.[3] Their conclusion was that spelling plays a role in spoken-word recognition. However, given the long prime–target intervals, they acknowledged the possibility that their results could reflect strategic processing in terms of a postperceptual assessment of the orthographic congruency between primes and targets. With similar materials (*tinsel*–TIN, *bulletin*–BULLET), Marslen-Wilson, Tyler, Waksler, and Older (1994) did not find any facilitation of lexical decisions to visual targets by spoken primes. Importantly, their form-related prime–target pairs formed only a small subset of the trials, and targets were presented immediately at the offset of the primes, in a different modality. Such factors make orthographic congruency checking unlikely.

Slowiaczek and Pisoni (1986) could not replicate the Jakimik et al. results in a lexical decision study with auditory primes and targets presented with shorter ISIs. Contrary to the prime–target pairs of Jakimik et al. and Marslen-Wilson et al., targets were not fully contained in the primes. The overlap between primes and targets varied from one phoneme to complete identity (e.g., target BLACK paired with *burnt, bleed, bland,* and *black*). In addition to facilitation for complete identity, inhibitory trends were found when prime and target shared a large number of segments (*bland*–BLACK). Inhibition was also found by Marslen-Wilson (1990), with auditory primes and visual targets (*feed*–FEEL) when the task was lexical decision, and by Brown (1990), with Dutch words (*stoep*–STOEL; *pavement-chair*) using pronunciation instead of lexical decision. But with an untimed task, identification of spoken words presented in noise, Slowiaczek, Nusbaum, and Pisoni (1987) did obtain phonological priming. Word

---

[3]In all examples, primes are in italics, targets in uppercase, independent of the modality in which they are presented.

primes that shared two or more phonemes with the target produced significant facilitation.

Goldinger, Luce, Pisoni, and Marcario (1992) questioned why facilitation is obtained with identification in noise, but only under certain conditions with other tasks. With identification in noise, Goldinger et al. replicated the phonological facilitation of Slowiaczek et al. (1987), but the effect was much attenuated when the percentage of related trials was small. The null effects of Slowiaczek and Pisoni with lexical decision were also replicated, but when lexical decisions had to be made on targets presented in noise, facilitation reappeared. This effect remained stable when primes and targets were separated by long intervals, and, again, its presence crucially depended on a high number of related trials. Such persistence over time and dependence on the amount of related trials are notorious indicators of strategic influences (cf. Neely, 1991), and Goldinger et al. concluded that phonological facilitation with both tasks is not a perceptual, but a bias, effect.

Radeau, Morais, and Dewier (1989) similarly argued that the untimed identification-in-noise task invites guessing strategies, and that lexical decision is notorious for postlexical bias effects. They opted for a different on-line task: *shadowing* (i.e., the repeating out loud of a spoken target word). Radeau et al. compared results from lexical decision and shadowing for the same set of materials. When words were primed by words, lexical decision showed interference, replicating the trends found by Slowiaczek and Pisoni. Inhibition was also found with shadowing, although of a smaller magnitude. When words were primed by pseudowords, a facilitatory trend was observed in lexical decision, but only when primes and targets shared a large amount of overlap. When pseudowords primed pseudoword targets, inhibition again was found. The shadowing data showed no effects for pseudoword primes and/or targets. Radeau et al. interpreted the inhibition with lexical decision when primes and targets had the same (word or pseudoword) status as evidence for congruency-checking procedures, and thus as bias effects.

Slowiaczek and Hamburger (1992) found that shadowing responses were faster when primes and targets shared the first segment (*smoke*–STILL) than in a control condition (*dream*–STILL). But when primes and targets shared the first three segments (*stiff*–STILL), shadowing latencies were slower than in the shared first-segment condition, although they were not different from the control condition. The interference, relative to the shared first-segment condition, was dependent on the lexical status of the prime because pseudowords that shared three segments with their target (*stitt*–STILL) showed no inhibition. The evidence for form priming with overlap at word onset is summarized in Table 4.1.

No facilitation is ever found when the so-called "mediated-priming technique" is used to study the activation of a word's phonological code by a word with which it shares word-initial segments. With mediated priming, activation of the form representation of a word such as *street* by an input such as *streak* is

TABLE 4.1
Summary of Initial Overlap Effects in Comprehension

Study	Prime	Target	Task	Timing	Results
Jakimik et al. (1985)	W	W aud	LD aud	SOA 2,000	*spider*–SPY: no effect *pillow*–PILL: fac
Slowiaczek & Pisoni (1986)	W/PW aud	W/PW aud	LD	ISI 50 500	1–3 segments: no effect (*bland*–BLACK)
Marslen-Wilson et al. (1993)	W aud	W vis	LD	ISI 0	*tinsel*–TIN: inh
Marslen-Wilson (1990)	W aud	W vis	LD	ISI 0	*feed*–FEEL: inh
Brown (1990)	W aud	W vis	NAM	ISI 0	*stoep*–STOEL: inh
Slowiaczek et al. (1987)	W/PW aud	W aud	ID/ noise	ISI 50	1 segment: no effect (2), 3 segments: fac
Goldinger et al. (1992)	W aud	W aud	ID/ noise	ISI 50	1 segment (*run*–RAM) 50% related: fac 10% related: no effect
	W	W/PW	LD		−noise: no effect +noise: = as ID/noise
Radeau et al. (1989)	W/PW aud	W/PW aud	SHAD	SOA 700 850	1 segment: no effect W–W: 2 segments: inh W–PW: no effect PW–W: no effect PW–PW: no effect
			LD		W–W: 1,2 segments: inh W–PW: no effect PW–W: 3 segments: fac PW–PW: 2,3 segments: inh
Slowiaczek & Hamburger (1992)	W aud	W aud	SHAD	ISI 500	1 segment: fac. 2,3 segments: no effect, but slower than 1 segment

Note. W = word; PW = pseudoword; aud = auditory; vis = visual; LD = lexical decision; NAM = naming; ID/noise = identification in noise; SHAD = shadowing; fac = facilitation; inh = inhibition.

assessed by auditorily presenting *streak* as prime, followed by a visual target that is semantically related to *street* (e.g., ROAD). The logic is that, if the lexical form of *street* is primed by the overlap it shares with *streak,* this activation should spread to the semantic level. Zwitserlood (1989), for Dutch, and Marslen-Wilson (1993), for English, found that word fragments (e.g., *stree*–ROAD) facilitated target recognition, whereas no facilitation was ever observed for full real-word primes (*streak*–ROAD). Connine, Blasko, and Titone (1993) demonstrated that pseudoword primes do produce facilitation with mediated priming (*dandeliom*–FLOWER).

Primes and Targets That Rhyme.   Far fewer studies have used the direct form priming paradigm to investigate primes and targets that share rhyme overlap rather than word-initial information. There is an extensive literature on phonological recoding or activation during reading, using rhyming pairs (*mint*–TINT) and orthographically similar nonrhyming pairs (*couch*–TOUCH), but these studies do not address the issue of processing at the level of phonological form (see Meyer, Schvaneveldt, & Ruddy, 1974; Humphreys, Evett, & Taylor, 1982). One early study with spoken primes and visual targets by Tanenhaus, Flanigan, and Seidenberg (1980) used a Stroop color-naming interference paradigm to investigate rhyme priming. It took subjects longer to name the color in which a target word was printed when it was preceded by a spoken rhyming word (*toes*–NOSE) than when it was preceded by an unrelated word. The fact that interference was found is probably inherent to the Stroop paradigm, and should not be interpreted in terms of lexical inhibition. In fact, Hillinger (1980) found facilitation of lexical decision responses to visual targets that rhymed with their spoken primes (*pitch*–DITCH).[4] When primes and targets were both presented auditorily, Emmorey (1989) and Praamstra and Stegeman (1993) found facilitation with lexical decision, as did Slowiaczek et al. (1987) with the identification in noise task.

Another line of research looks at rhyme priming by means of the mediated-priming technique, combining spoken primes (*cattle* or *yattle*) with targets (WAR) that are semantically related to words (*battle*) that rhyme with the primes. With primes that were phonologically maximally distinct (in terms of a difference in distinctive features) from the word form they were intended to prime, Marslen-Wilson and Zwitserlood (1989) found no significant mediated priming, and this was replicated by Connine et al. (1993). But priming did occur with pseudowords, provided that their first segment was phonologically close to the target representation (Connine et al., 1993; Marslen-Wilson, 1993; Marslen-Wilson, Moss, & van Halen, 1993).

Facilitation and Inhibition in Comprehension.   The evidence for word primes sharing word-initial information with their targets, summarized in Table 4.1, shows that direct-form priming facilitates lexical decisions, provided that a large number of related trials is used. Most researchers conclude that this facilitation is due to strategic, postlexical bias because effects are observed over a broad range of interstimulus intervals and do not survive when the percentage of related trials is small. Some also acknowledge that such bias effects are not necessarily restricted to lexical decision. It is argued that the identification of spoken words in noise similarly reflects bias because phonological facilitation is much reduced

---

[4]Hillinger (1980) obtained a similar result when both the prime and target were presented visually, but others have been unable to replicate this (Martin & Jensen, 1988; Peter, Lukatela, & Turvey, 1990).

when fewer related trials are used. So, there is general agreement to treat facilitory phonological priming obtained for primes and targets that are both words as strategic in nature.

Inhibition effects are interpreted in a different way. Provided that real-word primes and targets share a large amount of form overlap, interference is found with lexical decision, with pronunciation of visually presented targets, as well as with the shadowing task. Such inhibition is often interpreted as truly perceptual in origin, and as resulting from lexical competition within a framework of word recognition allowing for the activation of multiple word forms during lexical access (see Colombo, 1986; Goldinger et al., 1992; but also see O'Seaghdha, Dell, Peterson, & Juliano, 1992, for a different approach). The idea is that a prime will initially activate all words with which it shares form information. When the prime is a real word, its activation level will eventually exceed that of other word forms (i.e., it wins the competition and is ready to be recognized). This recognition leads to the suppression of other word forms that were initially activated. When the subsequently presented target word shares (a large amount of) phonological overlap with the prime, the target is most likely one of the suppressed candidates, and its (re)activation and recognition will be delayed.

This interpretation can also explain why sometimes facilitation, but no interference, is found for pseudoword primes. Although pseudowords will activate similar real-word forms, pseudowords do not have a representation at the form level at which word forms compete. Consequently, there is no winner among the set of activated forms, and the diffuse activation of a number of word forms, including the target word, might produce some facilitation, but most of the times no measurable effects are obtained.

Facilitation is observed with the shadowing task when the prime and target only share the first segment (e.g., *smoke*–STILL). Slowiaczek and Hamburger (1992) interpreted this effect as truly perceptual, reflecting the bottom–up activation of phonemic segments shared by the prime and target. This can happen when the target is not a strong competitor to the prime: They merely share one word-initial segment. An alternative explanation would be that what is in fact primed is the speech-production component. Shadowing involves producing the spoken word, and similar first-phoneme effects have been found for visually presented primes and targets when subjects have to pronounce the target word (Forster & Davis, 1991).

Similar arguments apply for rhyme overlap as for word-onset overlap: The facilitation observed with lexical decision and identification in noise could be due to a strategic comparison of primes and targets, leading to faster or more accurate responses in cases of form overlap. But such strategies are useless for mediated priming because there is no form relation between primes and targets. Nevertheless, rhyme priming is observed with this paradigm, albeit under restricted circumstances. The prime has to be close to the form representation of the intended word in terms of shared features, and a critical factor is the lexicality of the prime. As with onset overlap, no priming is observed with this task when the prime is a word, and thus a potential lexical competitor to the target.

Taken together, the evidence for truly perceptual facilitation from word primes to form-similar word targets is rather thin for both onset and rhyme overlap. Only pseudowords can prime lexical forms, provided that they overlap with the target representation in all but a few features. More interesting are the inhibitory effects that are evident in a number of tasks and paradigms. If their origin is truly perceptual, they can be interpreted as an index of the initial lexical activation of the target word by the prime. If information contained in the prime does not activate the phonologically similar target at some point during prime processing, the target does not enter into lexical competition, and thus null effects are the expected outcome. As argued previously, competition between form-related lexical representations can explain inhibition, but interference might also be caused by the fact that the prime contains information that mismatches the phonological specification of the target: The /k/ in *streak* mismatches the representation of *street*. Pseudoword primes that mismatch the targets' specification by no more than one feature are nevertheless always less effective primes as word fragments, or as the target itself (Connine et al., 1993; Marslen-Wilson, 1993). This is indicative of the reality of mismatch effects, an issue that I return to later.

Phonological Priming in Language Production

The technique preeminently used to look at form priming in word production is the picture–word paradigm. In a typical experiment, subjects see pictures, usually line drawings of objects, and their task is to say the word that denotes the pictured object. This is picture naming. At some point before, during, or after the presentation of the picture, another stimulus is presented either visually, superimposed on the picture, or auditorily. This stimulus can be form related to the picture's name. Sometimes subjects are asked to perform a secondary task on these stimuli (e.g., lexical decision), but in most experiments the subjects only have to name the pictured objects. The latter situation is similar to the direct-form priming paradigm used in comprehension research because the spoken or visual stimuli serve as primes to the name of the picture.

Visually Presented Primes.   Using pictures with superimposed printed letter strings, Rayner and Posnansky (1978; Posnansky & Rayner, 1978; Rayner & Springer, 1986) observed that picture naming was facilitated when the printed string maintained the overall shape of the picture name (e.g., *bcnrc* with the picture of a horse), when a printed word shared the first letter or phoneme with the picture (*home*–HORSE), and when a pseudoword string had the same pronunciation as the picture name (*hoars*–HORSE).[5] Lupker (1982) followed up this line of research with superimposed printed words that were either shape related to the picture's name, orthographically related (*blood*–FOOD), phonologically related (*brain*–PLANE), or orthographically and phonologically related (*cane*–PLANE). Mere shape relatedness did not facilitate picture-naming latencies, but orthographic similarity, phonological similarity, and a combination of both did (see also Underwood & Briggs, 1984, for similar results).

Facilitation of picture naming was also obtained by Lupker and Williams (1989), who presented prime words before the picture targets, instead of superimposing them. Lupker and Williams used a rhyming relationship between words and picture names, but they did not distinguish between mere phonological and combined phonological–orthographic similarity. Another difference from earlier work was that subjects also reacted to the prime words. When printed primes and picture names both had to be pronounced, a large facilitory effect of form relatedness was obtained in picture naming. This facilitation was reduced by half when a semantic categorization (i.e., Does the word specify a natural or an artificial object?) had to be made on the word primes. To put it differently, the actual speaking out loud of the prime word substantially increased the facilitation obtained for picture naming.

Auditorily Presented Primes.   Glaser and Duengelhoff (1984) and Rayner and Springer (1986) have shown that the strength of effects obtained with the picture–word paradigm crucially depends on the timing of word and picture presentation. Semantic and form effects seem to have a different time course. Semantic relations between words and pictures typically have an influence when the word precedes the picture, whereas form priming tends to be stronger when word and picture are presented simultaneously, or when the picture precedes the word. Such observations, together with evidence from speech errors (see Butterworth, 1989; Garrett, 1988), corroborate a separation of content-based and form-based processing during language production, incorporated in two-stage models (Garrett, 1980; Kempen & Huijbers, 1983; Levelt, 1989; but see Dell, 1986, for a different proposal). The first stage in such models involves access to semantic and syntactic information about words. This is *lemma access,* in Kempen and Huijbers' terminology. Selection occurs at this stage: The lemma appropriate for

---

[5]Unless stated otherwise, in this in all following experiments on picture naming, effects of form relatedness are assessed against an unrelated condition, not against the situation that a picture has to be named without any additional stimulus. The picture–word paradigm is, in essence, an interference paradigm. Relative to naming latencies for pictures presented alone, latencies for pictures with an accompanying stimulus are longer. That is why these stimuli are usually labeled *distractors.* But relative to the picture-alone baseline, a form-related prime generally produces less interference than a completely unrelated stimulus. When I speak about facilitation in conditions of form relatedness, it is in comparison to another stimulus that shares no form overlap with the picture's name. Also, I use the terms *inhibition* and *interference* interchangeably.

the expression of the intended message is selected from a set of activated lemmas (Roelofs, 1992). The second stage involves word-form (*lexeme*) retrieval and phonological encoding.

The timing of the influence of semantic and phonological factors was systematically investigated in a series of experiments with auditory primes (Levelt et al., 1991; Schriefers, Meyer, & Levelt, 1990). Schriefers et al. presented spoken words and pictures with three onset asynchronies: the word preceding the picture by 150 ms, simultaneous presentation, and the word following picture onset after 150 ms. Words and pictures could be semantically related (*cockroach*–SPIDER), phonologically related (*spiral*–SPIDER), or unrelated (*radio*–SPIDER). Picture-naming latencies were differentially affected by semantic and form-related primes. Relative to the unrelated prime, reliable semantic interference was obtained at SOA −150 only. Phonological facilitation was found at SOAs 0 and +150, but not at SOA −150. The early semantic and the later phonological effects provide clear support for two-stage models.

Levelt et al. (1991) used a variant of the picture–word paradigm with a dual-task situation. Pictures had to be named and a manual lexical decision was required for the spoken words. In fact, lexical-decision latencies, not picture-naming latencies, were analyzed to assess effects of the relationship between words and pictures. SOA was dependent on the time it took to recognize each picture when it was presented in isolation. The onset of the spoken words was either 500 or 200 ms before, or 100 ms after, the mean recognition latency for each picture. The results revealed a phonological effect at each SOA, but a semantic effect only at the earliest SOA, in part supporting a two-stage model. A further prediction of two-stage models was tested. If selection occurs at the lemma level, and if phonological information is retrieved for the selected lemma only, there should be no phonological activation of other lemmas that are supposed to be activated by the picture before selection occurs. To test this, pictures (e.g., SHEEP) were combined with words that were phonologically related to a semantic associate of the picture (*wood*, related to wood) or to a semantic alternative of the picture (*goal*, related to goat). No effect was found in either condition, demonstrating that only the selected lemma, not lemmas that are semantically related to the target lemma, is phonologically encoded.

Concentrating on phonological processing during picture naming, Meyer and Schriefers (1991) investigated onset and rhyme similarity between spoken words and picture names over a range of SOAs. For onset similarity, significant facilitation of picture-naming latencies was obtained for SOAs −150 to +150, with the strength of the effect increasing toward positive SOAs. For rhyme overlap, facilitation was found only at the −150 SOA. As the term indicates, *onset asynchronies* align the presentation of pictures relative to the *onset* of the spoken word. By definition, rhyming words have their phonological overlap with the picture name not at word onset, but somewhat later in the spoken word. When the presentation of the pictures was aligned relative to the onset of the shared segments, a different pattern emerged. Rhyming words facilitated picture naming at SOAs 0 and +150, and this is more in agreement with the pattern for onset similarity. In general, however, facilitation was larger when word and picture name shared the same onset as when they rhymed. Also, onset overlap still produced earlier effects than rhyme overlap.[6] This led Meyer and Schriefers to propose a particular locus for their priming effects: the process of *phonological encoding,* which I come back to later.

Facilitation in Production.   Picture–word studies clearly show that phonological similarity between a prime word and the name of the picture facilitates picture naming. This is a robust phenomenon, and it is obtained with visual and auditory prime-presentation. It is worth noting that semantic relatedness between words and pictures produces interference, relative unrelated conditions, whereas form similarity results in facilitation. As argued in the context of the interference found for form priming in comprehension, inhibition might be a good index of competition between representations at the level that is tapped by the prime. For semantic interference in production, this would imply that lemmas compete, and that selection is accomplished, at the semantic level, not at the form level. If this is so, it leaves us with only one activated phonological form during production— a conclusion that is supported by the absence, in Levelt et al. (1991), of form priming for words that are semantically related to the picture.

When spoken words are presented with pictures, the timing of word and picture presentation plays a crucial role in determining the time course of phonological priming. A form-related spoken word can influence picture-naming latencies during some, but not all, phases of picture naming. The largest effects are found toward the moment of pronunciation of the picture's name (i.e., at later processing stages). Which aspects of producing a picture's name could be sensitive to form-related priming? In principle, two alternatives offer themselves. The first would be the moment at which the form lexicon is accessed (i.e., the retrieval of the lexeme or word form of the picture's name). The prime word that is phonologically related to this word form enters the form lexicon through the perceptual system, and activates its own form representation as well as other word forms with which it shares phonological overlap. Among these will certainly be the picture's phonological representation. On the comprehension side, the picture's word form might compete with the prime word for recognition. But the picture-naming task does not tap into comprehension mechanisms; it measures processes involved in producing a picture name. On the production side, there is no competition at the form level because selection has already been

---

[6]As is seldom done in production studies, Meyer and Schriefers (1991) looked at the influence of the percentage of related trials on facilitation. Because facilitation effects did not diminish when the relatedness percentage was reduced from 50% to 20%, they concluded that facilitation of picture naming was not caused by guessing strategies or checking procedures.

accomplished at the lemma level. Only the picture's word form need be retrieved from the form level, and the fact that this representation has recently received activation from the spoken word might make it more readily available. This could speed up picture naming.

A second potential locus of the facilitation effects is the phase of *phonological encoding*. According to most researchers in speech production, it is not the case that word forms, once retrieved from the lexicon, are translated into articulatory gestures as a whole. Speech-error evidence (see Fromkin, 1971; Shattuck-Hufnagel, 1979) shows that speakers make sound errors that could not arise if complete word forms were translated into articulatory packages. Errors such as *fleaky squoor*, where *squeaky floor* was intended, demonstrate that units smaller than complete phonological forms are involved in speech production, and empirical support comes from priming studies (Meyer, 1990, 1991). Thus, phonological encoding is the construction process by which sublexical units (segments or sequences of segments), specified by the phonological representation of a word, are selected and combined into larger units (see Dell, 1988; Levelt, 1989; Shattuck-Hufnagel, 1979).

The earlier impact of word-onset similarity, compared with rhyme overlap, even when the onset of picture presentation was aligned with the onset of overlapping segments, led Meyer and Schriefers (1991) to believe that the locus of phonological priming in production resides in the phonological-encoding stage. In particular, they interpreted their results as evidence for a phonological-encoding process that operates in a left-to-right manner, with the onset of a word being encoded before its end. But differences between onset and rhyme overlap could also arise at the level of word forms. Onset relatedness has a stronger impact in comprehension studies, where it produces interference. It could be that asymmetries between onset and rhyme priming observed in production reflect differences in the activational state of the picture names at the level of lexical form, as a function of the position of overlap between spoken words and picture names. At present, however, the locus of phonological priming in language production seems to be undecided.

Finally, an interesting phenomenon should be mentioned in relation to the production–comprehension issue. The study by Levelt et al. (1991) involved both lexical decision to spoken words and picture naming, but lexical-decision responses were used to investigate what happens during the production of the picture's name. Now, lexical decision is by all means a comprehension task. Of course, it is perfectly viable to use such a measure as an index of what the speaker is accessing, generating, or computing during the process of picture naming, in which he or she is also involved. What is intriguing is that this is the only production study discussed here that shows interference, not facilitation, due to form overlap between primes and pictures.[7] In the Levelt et al. study,

---

[7]Bock (1987) found inhibition in an experiment in which complex pictures of actions involving

lexical-decision latencies are longer in form-related than in unrelated conditions. They are even longer than in semantic conditions, which notoriously produce interference when picture-naming latencies are measured.

I believe what this mirrors is the inhibition found in comprehension experiments. Phonological relatedness of a picture's name and a spoken word produces interference because the lexical-decision task taps into the comprehension system. But the Levelt et al. dual task, as in all studies that demonstrate form priming when input to the comprehension system is combined with output from the production system, clearly shows that there is cross talk between comprehension and production. The fact that phonological facilitation is found for picture naming, and interference for comprehension tasks, is strongly suggestive of different processes—not of different representations—involved in comprehension and production. Therefore, the cross talk most likely arises at the level of form representations. This issue was explicitly addressed in our own research that I briefly summarize now.

SOME NEW DATA ON FORM EFFECTS IN
COMPREHENSION AND PRODUCTION

In a series of experiments recently run in collaboration with Meyer and van Turennout, we looked at phonological priming in comprehension and production with the same basic set of materials. In the production experiments, the picture–word paradigm was used. Pictures were shown on a monitor, accompanied by spoken primes. Subjects ignored the spoken primes, and their task was to name the pictures. The comprehension experiments involved a cross-modal paradigm, combining the spoken primes with printed words (the pictures' names) presented on a monitor. Subjects ignored the spoken primes, and either pronounced the visually presented target or performed a lexical decision. Although at the input side printed words and pictures look very different, pronouncing a printed word and naming a picture share an output component: The word's form has to be produced, to be spoken out loud, in both cases. This is not true for lexical decision. Given that we used exactly the same stimuli in comprehension and production experiments, either in pictured or printed form, the patterning of the data can tell us whether picture and word pronunciation group together, or whether pronunciation and lexical decision show similar results.

---

two objects (e.g., *man, bee*) were preceded by a spoken or visual prime word that was phonologically similar to the name of one of the objects (e.g., *mat*). Subjects named the objects, but the dependent measure was not response time, but the frequency with which the primed word was produced before or after the unprimed one. Primes inhibited the production of phonologically similar words. Primed words were more often produced after than before unprimed words. This was independent of whether the subjects overtly produced, silently mouthed, or merely read the prime.

The overlap between the spoken prime and the picture's name, and thus between the spoken prime and the printed target word, was always at word onset, and we varied the type of spoken primes. With a picture of a tower, or with the printed target word TOWER, spoken primes were either real words (*towel*), word fragments (*towe*), or pseudowords (*towes*). All three types of prime were used in picture naming and in word pronunciation, but the pseudoword primes were not included in the lexical decision study. In control conditions, the targets were combined with phonologically unrelated primes (e.g., *scissors*–TOWER).

The timing relation between primes and targets was varied in production and comprehension experiments, but a direct comparison of the SOAs used in comprehension and production was not intended. The reason to vary the timing relation between primes and targets was to investigate the time course of the activation of phonological information, for comprehension as well as for production. The processing stages at which phonological information provided by a spoken prime might be useful are not the same in the two language modes (see Fig. 4.1). Access to word forms is early in comprehension because the input is an acoustic signal. Access to phonological information is relatively late during picture naming in production because the picture is first processed at a conceptual/semantic level. This has consequences for the timing relation between primes and targets, and this is why we used different SOAs in comprehension and production studies.

A clear pattern emerged for production: Picture naming was facilitated by all prime types. At the SOAs at which phonological effects are typically found in production (0 and +150), we obtained strong facilitation of picture naming from word primes (about 95 ms), word fragments (85 ms), and numerically somewhat weaker effects for pseudoword primes (50 ms). All priming effects decreased in size when the spoken words were presented 300 ms after the onset of picture presentation. Thus, when picture processing is well on its way, the influence of a form-related prime diminishes. This corroborates evidence cited earlier (Meyer & Schriefers, 1991; Schriefers et al., 1990) concerning the time course of phonological priming in production.

The comprehension experiments showed a qualitatively different overall pattern of results. First, priming effects were much smaller. Second, there were differential effects as a function of prime type. With both pronunciation and lexical decision, a clear difference was found between word-fragment primes and real-word (and pseudoword) primes. Word fragments always produced facilitation, independent of the task and the timing relation between primes and targets (the SOAs used were −300, −150, and 0). With the pronunciation task, real-word and pseudoword primes did not produce facilitation when primes preceded the target (SOA −300). Facilitation started to emerge at SOA −150, and when prime and target were presented simultaneously (SOA 0), the effects were as strong as for word fragments. With lexical decision, we only contrasted real-word and fragment primes, using the same three SOAs as with pronunciation.

Word primes did not facilitate lexical decisions, with one exception. A subset of our word primes, bisyllabic words, produced a facilitation effect at SOA 0.

How can we interpret this difference in comprehension between word fragments (*towe*) and real-word (*towel*) and pseudoword (*towes*) primes? What is important is that the duration of spoken words and pseudowords ranged from 350 to 650 ms, and that the mean pronunciation latencies for the visual targets was about 440 ms. When spoken primes are presented shortly before, or concurrent with, the target, not all information contained in the spoken prime will be available when subjects initiate the pronunciation response. In fact, it is quite likely that the subjects had not fully identified the primes at the time the response was given. With primes and targets overlapping at word onset, the crucial mismatching information that distinguishes word fragments from word and pseudoword primes (/l/ in *towel*, /s/ in *towes*) comes too late to influence pronunciation responses. We believe that this is why word fragments, word primes, and pseudoword primes behaved exactly the same at SOA 0. The chance that all information about the spoken word has been perceived before a response is given is much larger when the prime precedes the target (SOA −300). We did not find any facilitation for primes containing information that mismatches the phonological specification of the target word. The same arguments apply for the bisyllabic real-word primes that caused facilitation in lexical decision. Given their duration, the mismatching information was probably not perceived in time to influence the response.

When mismatch is perceived, it prevents priming in comprehension with lexical decision as well as with word pronunciation. It is interesting that we did not obtain any inhibition in our comprehension experiments. One reason could be that inhibition, resulting from lexical competition, takes time to develop (see Bock, 1987; Colombo, 1986, for similar arguments). The comprehension studies in which inhibition was obtained all presented primes well before targets, and this was not the case here. We found effects of a mismatch between the spoken input and the target's form specification independently of the lexical status of the stimulus that contained the mismatching information. It should be kept in mind that word fragments, and word and pseudowords whose mismatching information comes too late to influence the response, do produce facilitation, indicating that the target's word form is indeed activated by matching input. But when mismatching information is detected, it has negative consequences on lexical processing in comprehension, and this mismatch effect is measurable before the consequences of lexical competition. Our data do not provide positive evidence for competitive processing during comprehension, but they also do not speak against it. What we have shown is that form representations can be primed reliably in comprehension, provided that no mismatching information is detected between the spoken prime and the form representation of the target word.

In summary, we obtain clear phonological facilitation when subjects have to produce the name of a picture, and this effect is as strong for word fragments as for words, although the latter contain information that mismatches the phonological specification of the picture's name. The facilitation found in production is unaffected by the presence or absence of mismatching information. The comprehension data show a different pattern: Word fragments produce phonological facilitation and real words and pseudoword primes do not, provided that their full specification is available by the time the response is initiated. This data pattern shows a dissociation between comprehension and production. How can we explain this discrepancy between comprehension and production effects? In principle, there are two options: one that maintains the idea of shared form representations for comprehension and production, and one that locates the cross talk between the two language modes at a different level. I discuss both, and see how they fare in the light of the evidence presented previously.

DIFFERENT FORM REPRESENTATIONS OR DIFFERENT MECHANISMS?

First and foremost, when an input to the comprehension system is combined with an output from the production system, as is the case in picture–word experiments, phonological effects are a prime demonstration of contact between the two modes of language use at some level. But which level might this be? If production and comprehension operate on the same form representations, how can it be that we observe strong facilitation in one mode and no facilitation in the other? A solution might be the following.

In comprehension, word forms are activated by sensory information that matches their specification. But word recognition involves selection at the level of form representations. To decide that *towel,* and not *tower,* was heard, the word-recognition system has to rely on information in the speech signal to differentiate between activated word forms. To accomplish selection, the sensory information eventually has to agree with only one word form, not many word forms. What I propose here is that the mechanism of selection that operates at the form level in comprehension actively uses mismatching information to accomplish its task. The relative level of activation of word forms is of course affected by the degree of overlap with a spoken input, but not by the consequences of the mechanism of selection. Such an interpretation clearly locates negative effects of mismatching information, and, in principle, lexical competition inside a processing procedure, not in the activational status of lexical forms. The information, or activation, is there, but the mechanism of selection and recognition is blind to it, at least for a short period of time.

When negative effects of mismatching information are caused by processing mechanisms particular to comprehension, we can maintain shared-form representations between comprehension and production. When a picture's name has to be retrieved from this shared form lexicon, its form representation might not available for comprehension procedures temporarily, but it is fully accessible to mechanisms of word production. As argued earlier, production does not involve selection at the form level; it merely involves the retrieval of one word form from the lexicon. In picture naming with form-related primes, the information contained in such primes activates related form representations through the comprehension system. As argued earlier, this has negative consequences for their availability to the word-recognition system, but the production process does not suffer from this. It merely retrieves a word form whose activational status is enhanced by its form relation to the prime. The postulation of different mechanisms, not of different representations for comprehension and production, can explain the dissociation in priming effects between comprehension and production.

An alternative explanation is to assume separate levels of form representation for production and comprehension, each with their own dedicated processing mechanisms. But we have to explain at which level the contact between comprehension and production that produces considerable facilitation in picture naming is established. A likely locus for the facilitation in production is the phonological-encoding stage. Phonological encoding is a computation that is particular to production, and the segmental information it operates on is delivered by the one phonological-form representation retrieved from the lexicon. A prime that is presented for comprehension could facilitate phonological encoding in production, if one assume's that, during speech perception, segmental information is made available to be mapped onto the comprehension representations of lexical form.

If contact between comprehension and production is at a segmental level, rather than at the word-form level, this could explain why facilitation if found in picture naming, but not in our comprehension experiments. Phonological encoding operates on segments, not on holistic word forms. Phonological encoding inserts the segments that have been made available by the picture's word form into their appropriate positions in the frame or code that is under construction. Assuming that speech perception makes available the segments of the spoken prime, and assuming that segmental representations are shared between production and comprehension, phonological encoding of a picture name could profit from segmental similarity to a spoken prime. The presence of mismatching segments between prime and picture name would not negatively affect the process of phonological encoding because computations at this level are insensitive to mismatch; they only operate on segments that are part of the word that has to be produced.

There is one problem for this temptingly elegant locus of form facilitation in production. As argued earlier, naming a picture and pronouncing a printed word share an output component—the word has to be phonologically encoded and pronounced in both cases. Why then, if facilitation in production is located at the segmental level, do we not find any priming with word pronunciation? Of course, the printed word that has to be pronounced enters the comprehension system, where the prior presentation of a form-related prime might have made its representation temporarily less accessible. But even if word pronunciation is negatively influenced by comprehension mechanisms, at the stage of phonological encoding we would expect the same facilitory effects as for picture naming. Given that the size of these effects is considerable, the net result should be observable facilitation in word pronunciation. But this is not what we found. On the contrary, very similar results were found for pronunciation and lexical decision—a task that does not tax the speech-output component.

With respect to the two possible loci of contact between comprehension and production, this absence of facilitation in word pronunciation tips the balance in favor of shared form representations, at least for the time being. The emerging picture on phonological processing and representation in language comprehension and production is compatible with a view that form representations are shared, whereas processing mechanisms are radically different. In production, selection takes place at the level of meaning representations, and only the phonological form for the selected word is retrieved. The activation of this word form by a prior prime facilitates the retrieval process. The status of mismatching information is the same as of missing information: The word form belonging to the picture's name receives more activation the more overlap it shares with the prime (cf. Meyer, 1991).

Compared with missing information, mismatching segments do have negative consequences in comprehension. The locus of this effect seems to reside inside the mechanisms operating on phonological representations during word recognition. In comprehension, selection has to be accomplished at the level of lexical form, and mismatching information is actively used by the selection mechanism to ensure that one and only one word will be recognized.

ACKNOWLEDGMENTS

I am grateful to Liesbeth Meijer and Sibrand van Coillie for their assistance in preparing the materials and running the experiments of the project with Antje Meyer and Miranda van Turennout, and to Dirk Vorberg for his comments on an earlier version of this chapter. I also thank Antje Meyer for luring me into the realm of language production.

REFERENCES

Allport, D. A. (1984). Speech production and comprehension: One lexicon or two? In W. Prinz & A. F. Sanders (Eds.), *Cognition and motor processes.* (pp. 209–228). Berlin: Springer.
Allport, D. A., & Funnell, E. (1981). Components of the mental lexicon. In D. E. Broadbent, J.

Lyons, & C. Longuet-Higgins (Eds.), *Psychological mechanisms of language* (pp. 183–196). London: The Royal Society.

Besner, D., & Davelaar, E. (1982). Basic processes in reading: Two phonological codes. *Canadian Journal of Psychology, 36,* 701–711.

Bock, K. (1987). An effect of the accessibility of word forms on sentence structure. *Journal of Memory and Language, 26,* 119–137.

Brown, C. M. (1990). *Spoken-word processing in context.* Unpublished doctoral dissertation, University of Nijmegen, The Netherlands.

Butterworth, B. (1989). Lexical access in speech production. In W. Marslen-Wilson (Ed.), *Lexical representation and process.* (pp. 108–135). Cambridge, MA: MIT Press.

Caplan, D. (1992). *Language: Structure, processing, and disorders.* Cambridge, MA: MIT Press.

Caramazza, A., Berndt, R. S., & Basili, A. G. (1983). The selective impairment of phonological processing: A case study. *Brain and Language, 18,* 128–174.

Clarke, R., & Morton, J. (1983). Cross-modality facilitation in tachistoscopic word recognition. *Quarterly Journal of Experimental Psychology, 35A,* 79–96.

Colombo, L. (1986). Activation and inhibition with orthographically similar words. *Journal of Experimental Psychology: Human Perception and Performance, 12,* 226–234.

Connine, C. M., Blasko, D. G., & Titone, D. (1993). Do the beginnings of words have a special status in auditory word recognition? *Journal of Memory and Language, 32,* 193–210.

Dell, G. S. (1986). A spreading activation theory of retrieval in sentence production. *Psychological Review, 93,* 283–321.

Dell, G. S. (1988). The retrieval of phonological forms in production: Tests of predictions from a connectionist model. *Journal of Memory and Language, 27,* 124–142.

Emmorey, K. D. (1989). Auditory morphological priming in the lexicon. *Language and Cognitive Processes, 4,* 73–92.

Fay, D. A., & Cutler, A. (1977). Malapropisms and the structure of the mental lexicon. *Linguistic Inquiry, 8,* 505–520.

Forster, K. I. (1976). Accessing the mental lexicon. In R. J. Wales & E. C. T. Walker (Eds.), *New approaches to language mechanisms.* (pp. 257–287). Amsterdam: North-Holland.

Forster, K. I. (1979). Levels of processing and the structure of the language processor. In W. E. Cooper & E. C. T. Walker (Eds.), *Sentence processing: Psycholinguistic studies presented to Merrill Garrett.* (pp. 27–85). Hillsdale, NJ: Lawrence Erlbaum Associates.

Forster, K. I., & Davis, C. (1991). The density constraint on form-priming in the naming task: Interference effects from a masked prime. *Journal of Memory and Language, 30,* 1–25.

Friedrich, F. (1990). Multiple phonological representations and verbal short-term memory. In G. Vallar & T. Shallice (Eds.), *Neuropsychological impairments of short-term memory.* (pp. 74–93). Cambridge, England: Cambridge University Press.

Fromkin, V. A. (1971). The non-anomalous nature of anomalous utterances. *Language, 47,* 27–52.

Garrett, M. F. (1980). Levels of processing in sentence production. In B. Butterworth (Ed.), *Language production: Vol. 1. Speech and talk.* (pp. 177–220). London: Academic Press.

Garrett, M. F. (1988). Processes in language production. In F. J. Newmeyer (Ed.), *Linguistics: The Cambridge survey: Vol. III. Psychological and biological aspects of language.* (pp. 69–96). Cambridge, MA: Harvard University Press.

Glaser, W. R., & Duengelhoff, F. J. (1984). The time course of picture-word interference. *Journal of Experimental Psychology: Human Perception and Performance, 10,* 640–654.

Goldinger, S. D., Luce, P. A., Pisoni, D. B., & Marcario, J. K. (1992). Form-based priming in spoken word recognition: The roles of competition and bias. *Journal of Experimental Psychology: Learning, Memory, and Cognition, 18,* 1211–1238.

Hillinger, M. L. (1980). Priming effects with phonemically-similar words: The encoding-bias hypothesis reconsidered. *Memory & Cognition, 8,* 115–123.

Humphreys, G. W., Evett, L. J., & Taylor, D. E. (1982). Automatic phonological activation in visual word recognition. *Memory & Cognition, 10,* 115–123.

Jakimik, J., Cole, R. A., & Rudnicky, A. I. (1985). Sound and spelling in spoken word recognition. *Journal of Memory and Language, 24,* 165–178.

Kempen, G., & Huijbers, P. (1983). The lexicalization process in sentence production: Indirect election of words. *Cognition, 14,* 185–209.

Lahiri, A., & Marslen-Wilson, W. (1991). The mental representation of lexical form: A phonological approach to the recognition lexicon. *Cognition, 38,* 243–294.

Levelt, W. J. M. (1989). *Speaking. From intention to articulation.* Cambridge, MA: MIT Press.

Levelt, W. J. M., Schriefers, H., Vorberg, D., Meyer, A. S., Pechmann, T., & Havinga, J. (1991). The time course of lexical access in speech production: A study of picture naming. *Psychological Review, 98,* 122–142.

Liberman, A. M., & Mattingly, I. G. (1985). The motor theory of speech revisited. *Cognition, 21,* 1–36.

Lupker, S. J. (1982). The role of phonetic and orthographic similarity in picture-word interference. *Canadian Journal of Psychology, 36,* 349–367.

Lupker, S. J., & Williams, B. A. (1989). Rhyme priming of pictures and words: A lexical activation account. *Journal of Experimental Psychology: Learning, Memory, and Cognition, 15,* 1033–1046.

MacKay, D. (1987). Asymmetries in the relationship between speech perception and production. In H. Heuer & A. F. Sanders (Eds.), *Perspectives on perception and action.* (pp. 301–333). Hillsdale, NJ: Lawrence Erlbaum Associates.

MacKay, D., Allport, A., Prinz, W., & Scheerer, E. (1987). Relationships and modules within language perception and production: An introduction. In A. Allport, D. MacKay, W. Prinz, & E. Scheerer (Eds.), *Language perception and production: Relationships between listening, speaking, reading, and writing.* (pp. 1–15). London: Academic Press.

Marslen-Wilson, W. (1987). Functional parallelism in spoken word-recognition. *Cognition, 25,* 71–102.

Marslen-Wilson, W. (1990). Activation, competition, and frequency in lexical access. In G. T. M. Altmann (Ed.), *Cognitive models of speech processing.* (pp. 148–172). Cambridge, MA: MIT Press.

Marslen-Wilson, W. (1993). Issues of process and representation in lexical access. In G. T. M. Altmann & R. C. Shillcock (Eds.), *Cognitive models of speech processing: The Sperlonga meeting II.* (pp. 187–210). Hillsdale, NJ: Lawrence Erlbaum Associates.

Marslen-Wilson, W., Moss, H. E., & van Halen, S. (1993). *Perceptual distance and competition in lexical access.* Unpublished manuscript, Birkbeck College, London.

Marslen-Wilson, W., Tyler, L. K., Waksler, R., & Older, L. (1994). Morphology and meaning in the mental lexicon. *Psychological Review, 101,* 3–33.

Marslen-Wilson, W., & Zwitserlood, P. (1989). Accessing spoken words: The importance of word onsets. *Journal of Experimental Psychology: Human Perception and Performance, 15,* 576–585.

Martin, R. C., & Jensen, C. R. (1988). Phonological priming in the lexical decision task: A failure to replicate. *Memory & Cognition, 16,* 505–521.

McClelland, J., & Elman, J. (1986). The TRACE model of speech perception. *Cognitive Psychology, 18,* 1–86.

Meyer, A. S. (1990). The time course of phonological encoding in language production: The encoding of successive syllables of a word. *Journal of Memory and Language, 29,* 524–545.

Meyer, A. S. (1991). The time course of phonological encoding in language production: Phonological encoding inside the syllable. *Journal of Memory and Language, 30,* 69–89.

Meyer, A. S., & Schriefers, H. (1991). Phonological facilitation in picture-word interference experiments: Effects of stimulus onset asynchrony and types of interfering stimuli. *Journal of Experimental Psychology: Learning, Memory, and Cognition, 17,* 1146–1160.

Meyer, D. M., Schvaneveldt, R. W., & Ruddy, M. G. (1974). Functions of graphemic and phonemic codes in visual word recognition. *Memory & Cognition, 2,* 309–321.

Monsell, S. (1987). On the relation between lexical input and output pathways for speech. In A.

Allport, D. MacKay, W. Prinz, & E. Scheerer (Eds.), *Language perception and production: Relationships between listening, speaking, reading, and writing.* (pp. 273–311). London: Academic Press.

Neely, J. H. (1991). Semantic priming effects in visual word recognition. In D. Besner & G. Humphreys (Eds.), *Basic processes in reading: Visual word recognition.* (pp. 264–336). Hillsdale, NJ: Lawrence Erlbaum Associates.

O'Seaghdha, P., Dell, G. S., Peterson, R. R., & Juliano, C. (1992). Models of form-related priming in comprehension and production. In R. G. Reilly & N. E. Sharkey (Eds.), *Connectionist approaches to natural language processing.* (pp. 373–408). Hove, England: Lawrence Erlbaum Associates.

Peter, M., Lukatela, G., & Turvey, M. T. (1990). Phonological priming: Failure to replicate in the rapid naming task. *Bulletin of the Psychonomic Society, 28,* 389–392.

Posnansky, C. J., & Rayner, K. (1978). Visual vs. phonetic contributions to the importance of the initial letter in word identification. *Bulletin of the Psychonomic Society, 11,* 188–190.

Praamstra, P., & Stegeman, D. F. (1993). Phonological effects on the auditory N400. *Cognitive Brain Research, 1,* 73–86.

Radeau, M., Morais, J., & Dewier, A. (1989). Phonological priming in spoken word recognition: Task effects. *Memory & Cognition, 17,* 525–535.

Rayner, K., & Posnansky, C. J. (1978). Stages of processing in word identification. *Journal of Experimental Psychology: General, 107,* 64–80.

Rayner, K., & Springer, C. J. (1986). Graphemic and semantic similarity in the picture-word interference task. *British Journal of Psychology, 77,* 207–222.

Roelofs, A. (1992). A spreading-activation theory of lemma retrieval. *Cognition, 42,* 107–142.

Schriefers, H., Meyer, A. S., & Levelt, W. J. M. (1990). Exploring the time course of lexical access in language production: Picture-word interference studies. *Journal of Memory and Language, 29,* 86–102.

Shallice, T. (1988). *From neuropsychology to mental structure.* Cambridge, England: Cambridge University Press.

Shallice, T., McLeod, P., & Lewis, K. (1985). Isolating cognitive modules with the dual-task paradigm: Are speech perception and production separate processes? *Quarterly Journal of Experimental Psychology, 37A,* 507–532.

Shattuck-Hufnagel, S. (1979). Speech errors as evidence for a serial-order mechanism in sentence production. In W. E. Cooper & E. C. T. Walker (Eds.), *Sentence processing: Psycholinguistic studies presented to Merrill Garrett.* (pp. 295–342). Hillsdale, NJ: Lawrence Erlbaum Associates.

Slowiaczek, L. M., & Hamburger, M. B. (1992). Prelexical facilitation and lexical interference in auditory word recognition. *Journal of Experimental Psychology: Learning, Memory, and Cognition, 18,* 1239–1250.

Slowiaczek, L. M., Nusbaum, H. C., & Pisoni, D. B. (1987). Phonological priming in auditory word recognition. *Journal of Experimental Psychology: Learning, Memory, and Cognition, 13,* 64–75.

Slowiaczek, L. M., & Pisoni, D. B. (1986). Effects of phonological similarity on priming in auditory lexical decision. *Memory & Cognition, 14,* 230–237.

Tanenhaus, M. K., Flanigan, H. P., & Seidenberg, M. S. (1980). Orthographic and phonological activation in auditory and visual word recognition. *Memory & Cognition, 8,* 513–520.

Underwood, G., & Briggs, P. (1984). The development of word recognition processes. *British Journal of Psychology, 75,* 243–255.

Zwitserlood, P. (1989). The locus of the effects of sentential-semantic context in spoken-word processing. *Cognition, 32,* 25–64.

5 Vertical and Horizontal Similarity in Spoken-Word Recognition

Cynthia M. Connine
State University of New York at Binghamton

Auditory-word recognition is a remarkably robust aspect of language processing. The acoustic signal may be distorted and/or disrupted in a wide variety of ways, yet spoken-word recognition appears to proceed with little difficulty. Among those potentially problematic aspects of spoken language are (a) misarticulations in the form of speech errors, (b) dynamic processes among successive phonemes, and (c) masking of speech sounds due to environmental noise. Beyond the inherent variability in the acoustic signal, one specific observation that has been emphasized in early models of spoken-word recognition is that the speech signal is distributed over time. Unlike visual language, in which information may be obtained in parallel, information in the speech signal is available to the listener in a time-dependent manner. Simply stated, the beginnings of words reach a listener's ear prior to the ends of words. These observations concerning the physical characteristics of spoken language have influenced researchers concerned with the recognition of phonemes and with how listeners recognize spoken words. The implicit assumption in much of the research has been that the problems of ambiguity and distortion will have catastrophic consequences for word recognition. The focus of the current chapter is whether this assumption is warranted. I report data from a number of experiments that suggest perturbations in the speech signal are not major impediments to word recognition.

One particularly influential model, the cohort model, proposes that the information that reaches the listener first (word-initial information) serves to activate a set of lexical hypotheses that are consistent with it (Marslen-Wilson & Welsh, 1978). The set of words that are activated early in spoken-word recognition is determined by a strict mapping based on phoneme overlap of word-initial information. Lexical hypotheses are eliminated as soon as they deviate from the acoustic–phonetic input. Word recognition is claimed to occur when there is only one lexical hypothesis remaining in the cohort. In this version of the model, no cost to word recognition is incurred by the size of the cohort, in that the set of words that are activated based on the input do not compete with each other during recognition.

More recent conceptions of auditory-word recognition have relaxed assumptions concerning the integrity of word onsets and have emphasized the notion of the activation of a set of lexical candidates (Marslen-Wilson, 1987, 1990; McClelland & Elman, 1986; Norris, 1990). Many recent theoretical developments have focused on *horizontal similarity,* that is, the consequences of simultaneous activation of a number of lexical hypotheses on the activation of the intended word (that lexical hypothesis that maps most accurately onto the input; Marslen-Wilson, 1990). A major focus of these theories has been on the nature and consequences of the competitor environment for spoken-word recognition. A precursor to competitive processes implicit in most models is *vertical similarity.* Vertical similarity refers to the nature of the mapping process from the acoustic–phonetic input to a target-lexical representation. In a general form, the claim is that lexical activation is modulated by the degree to which there is a successful mapping of the acoustic–phonetic input to a prestored representation. The theoretical concepts of *activation* and *competition* are included in current versions of the cohort model, and are shared with the class of connectionist word-recognition models such as the TRACE model that assume interconnections within and between phoneme and lexical levels (Elman & McClelland, 1986; McClelland & Elman, 1986; see also Norris, 1990). These models differ in detail, but share the assumption that the acoustic–phonetic similarity of the input to a stored representation determines the degree to which a lexical representation is activated. In these models, horizontal and vertical similarity are related, but separable, dimensions. Horizontal similarity emphasizes the relative number of lexical items that overlap in acoustic–phonetic structure (lexical neighborhood) and the effects of neighborhood size on ease of recognition. Vertical similarity emphasizes the activation level of the target-lexical representation (that word intended by a speaker or that word probed in an empirical investigation) as a function of its overlap with the acoustic–phonetic input. In the following section, I discuss the relationship between vertical and horizontal similarity, and I present data that bear on the issue of how these two dimensions of acoustic–phonetic similarity interact.

HORIZONTAL AND VERTICAL SIMILARITY

Horizontal similarity refers to the activation of a variable number of lexical representations that are similar to the acoustic–phonetic input. The relative number of representations activated is referred to as *neighborhood density.* In the auditory domain, neighborhood density typically is operationally defined as the number of words formed from a base word using a method of one phoneme substitution. The consequences of horizontal similarity on spoken-word recognition has received increasing attention in the past few years. When effects of horizontal similarity emerge (see following discussion), a major finding is that recognition of an auditory stimulus with many neighbors (a dense neighborhood) suffers compared with an auditory stimulus with few neighbors (a sparse neighborhood). One possible theoretical instantiation of the effects of neighborhood density is in terms of lateral inhibition among activated-lexical representations (e.g., McClelland & Elman, 1986). Other models propose simple, activation-based competition in which recognition occurs when the activation of the candidate is sufficiently greater than its closest competitor (Marslen-Wilson, 1987; see Bard, 1990, for a discussion concerning the difficulty in discriminating among competition mechanisms).

Consider research that has investigated vertical similarity. Vertical similarity focuses on the relationship between the relative activation level of a given lexical representation and the degree to which the input successfully maps onto it. Vertical similarity has received generally less emphasis in theories of spoken-word recognition. Although the claim that the degree of match between the input and a lexical representation must in some way modulate word recognition may not be controversial, there is little evidence concerning constraints on vertical-similarity mapping. What evidence exists suggests that vertical similarity is a powerful determinant of lexical activation. One relevant set of results comes from a signal-detection analysis of the phoneme-restoration paradigm developed by Samuel (1981). Samuel found that a high degree of similarity between the type of noise used in the task and the phoneme that the noise masked (or replaced) resulted in a larger phoneme-restoration effect. For example, an aperiodic sound produced greater restoration for phonemes with similar acoustic properties (e.g., fricatives) than for phonemes with dissimilar properties (e.g., vowels).

More recently, we conducted an extensive series of experiments that permit a number of detailed conclusions concerning the nature of the similarity-mapping process in the vertical dimension (Connine, Blasko, & Titone, 1993; see also Milberg, Blumstein, & Dworetzky, 1988). These experiments used a cross-modal priming paradigm, in which an auditory stimulus was presented followed by a semantically related or unrelated visually presented target word. Subjects performed a lexical decision on the visually presented target. Typically, priming is demonstrated by related targets showing faster reaction times than unrelated targets. In our experiments, we created a set of derived nonwords from a set of base words by changing the initial phoneme by one or two linguistic features (minimal nonwords) or by five or more linguistic features (maximal nonwords). The derived nonwords and base words were presented auditorily in a cross-modal priming experiment where a semantically related word (a visual target that was semantically related to the base word) or an unrelated word was presented at the offset of auditory stimulus. One major finding was that the similarity relationship between the acoustic input and a lexical representation determined the robustness of the obtained priming effect. The base words showed the largest priming effect, whereas minimal nonwords showed an intermediate but significant priming effect, and maximal nonwords showed no significant priming effect (see also Marslen-Wilson & Zwitserlood, 1988, for a similar demonstration). These results suggest that nonwords with an initial phoneme similar in acoustic–phonetic structure to a base word (minimal nonwords) activated the base word lexical representation, although less robustly than the base word activated itself. If a portion of the acoustic-phonetic input is sufficiently dissimilar in acoustic–phonetic structure (maximal nonwords), the base word is not sufficiently activated to produce semantic priming.

Although the relevant simulations have not been conducted for TRACE (McClelland & Elman, 1986), Norris (1990) presented a connectionist model of spoken-word recognition that models some of our data. A major focus of Norris' model was to design a connectionist network where the time-varying aspects of speech (e.g., temporal location and duration) could be adequately captured. The specific model architecture Norris used was a recurrent net. Recurrent-net architectures have a kind of memory because the current state of the network is encoded by a set of state units (Jordan, 1986). The activation of state units is determined by the status of the network from previous cycles, as well as the current input. One relevant test of the model included presentation of stimulus sets such as *coronet, goronet* (comparable to a minimal nonword), and h*oronet* (comparable to a maximal nonword). Norris found that presentation of g*oronet* resulted in activation of *coronet,* whereas presentation of h*oronet* did not activate *coronet.*

Vertical and horizontal similarity appear to be determinants of spoken-word recognition. The degree to which a particular word may emerge as the clear winner in competition, with similar-sounding lexical hypotheses, will depend on characteristics of the input (as expressed in the activation level), as well as the structural relationships between the most highly activated lexical hypothesis and other lexical items (as expressed in the lexical neighborhood). Horizontal similarity is currently a major organizing characteristic in models of spoken-word recognition. However, there are indications that effects of horizontal similarity are intimately related to (and perhaps modulated by) vertical similarity. Competition from other similar-sounding words seems to be consistently found only under conditions where the integrity of the acoustic–phonetic input is in some way compromised. When the acoustic–phonetic input is sufficient for a single lexical hypothesis to dominate, lexical competition effects are negligible. Marslen-Wilson (1990) found competition effects for spoken words only when the acoustic signal was truncated prior to the point at which a word was unique. This result was found in a gating task, where guesses about the intended word were assessed prior to the uniqueness point, and in a cross-modal priming paradigm, when word fragments were presented prior to the uniqueness point. No competitor effects were found for words where a response was made after the entire word was heard (lexical-decision task and auditory-repetition task). Once the lexical identity of the input was unambiguous, competition effects were no longer evident. In general, lexical-density effects have been demonstrated for words presented in noise using a perceptual identification task, where the words appeared in isolation and in a phonological priming paradigm (Goldinger, Luce, & Pisoni, 1989; Luce, Pisoni, & Goldinger, 1990), and for nonwords in a lexical-decision task (Luce et al., 1990). A more recent investigation using a phonological/phonetic priming task to investigate the consequences of lexical competition provides an explicit comparison between words presented in the clear and in noise (Goldinger, Luce, Pisoni, & Marcario, 1992). Goldinger et al. found priming effects (residual inhibitory effects of a prime stimulus on identification of a similar-sounding target stimulus), but only when the target stimuli were presented in noise. Competition effects from the prime disappeared when the words were presented in the clear.

The available data suggest that lexical-neighborhood effects emerge in the auditory domain when the signal is degraded (presented in noise or only partially available) or a nonword is presented. More generally, this analysis indicates that when the acoustic–phonetic evidence for any specific lexical hypothesis is weak, competition effects are maximized. Conversely, when the acoustic–phonetic evidence for a word is robust, similar-sounding words have less of an impact on recognition of the target word. Stated somewhat differently, if a particular stretch of acoustic–phonetic input provides weak evidence for a particular lexical entry, any lexical neighbors also activated based on the input will provide a robust source of competition. In contrast, if the input provides strong evidence for a particular lexical entry, competition from lexical neighbors will be weak.

To investigate these hypotheses, we conducted a series of post-hoc analyses on the data obtained for minimal and maximal nonwords and the base words in the cross-modal priming paradigm (Connine et al., 1993). Recall that these results showed priming effects for associates to a base word only for minimal nonwords. In the analyses presented here, we examined the priming effects as a function of horizontal similarity. Given the relatively poor mapping from the input to a lexical representation afforded by a maximal nonword, competition from even a few lexical neighbors (a low-density neighborhood) may be sufficient to dampen lexical activation. The reduced activation for maximal nonwords, combined with the competition from many lexical neighbors, provides the straightforward prediction of no priming effects for maximal nonwords from high-density neighborhoods.

The relatively complete mapping from the input to a lexical representation for minimal nonwords may be sufficient to sustain lexical activation and dampen competition effects, particularly for stimuli from low-density neighborhoods.

Predictions for minimal nonwords from high-density neighborhoods are dependent on the temporal characteristics of competition effects. If the high degree of similarity of the input to a lexical representation is sufficient to decrease the effectiveness of competition effects, priming may be found for minimal nonwords from high-density neighborhoods. However, if competition from many similar-sounding words (high-density stimuli) is sufficient to dampen activation of a minimal nonword, no evidence for lexical activation will be found. Finally, the robust lexical activation given a real word should result in comparable priming effects for both high- and low-density neighborhoods.

To summarize the predictions, maximal nonwords should not show priming effects for stimuli from either high- or low-density neighborhoods. In contrast, minimal nonwords should show priming effects for stimuli from low-density neighborhoods and attenuated or absent priming effects for stimuli from high-density neighborhoods. Finally, the goodness of fit afforded by the presentation of real words should permit robust activation sufficient to dampen competitive effects from high- and low-density neighborhoods. This predicts comparable robust priming effects for stimuli from low- and high-density neighborhoods given presentation of the base words.

These predictors were examined by calculating priming effects separately for high-density (greater than five neighbors) and low-density (two neighbors) stimuli. In these analyses, lexical neighborhoods were calculated by determining the number of lexical items formed via one phoneme substitution based on the derived nonword (Luce et al., 1990; Marslen-Wilson, 1990; see also Coltheart, Davelaar, Johasson, & Besner, 1977). Neighborhood statistics were calculated using a 150,000-word on-line lexical database that contains phonetic transcriptions along with normative data for 26 psycholinguistic attributes for each entry (see Wilson, 1988).

Table 5.1 shows priming effects for maximal nonwords as a function of neighborhood density. There was a tendency for a priming effect to emerge for low-density stimuli (18 ms), but the effect was not significant [$t(34) = 1.2, p = .23$]. There was no evidence for priming for high-density stimuli ($t = .03$). These results indicate that measurable lexical activation was precluded for maximal nonwords, regardless of competitive influences from similar-sounding words.

TABLE 5.1
Lexical-Decision Reaction Times to Related and Control
Visual Targets Following Maximal Nonwords
as a Function of Lexical Density

Targets	High Density (ms)	Low Density (ms)
Related	656	649
Control	655	667

TABLE 5.2
Lexical-Decision Reaction Times to Related and Control
Visual Targets Following Minimal Nonwords
as a Function of Lexical Density

Target	High Density (ms)	Low Density (ms)
Related	655	637
Control	666	686

In contrast, clear effects of horizontal similarity were evident for minimal nonwords. Table 5.2 shows priming effects for minimal nonwords as a function of neighborhood density. A large priming effect (49 ms) was found for stimuli from low-density neighborhoods [$t(31) = 3.6, p < .01$]; no priming effect was evident for stimuli from high-density neighborhoods ($t(37) = .88, p = .61$).

These results indicate a qualifier to the claim that vertical similarity modulates lexical activation—a similar-sounding stimulus will activate a lexical representation when there are sufficiently few competing lexical representations. A dissimilar-sounding stimulus will fail to provide sufficient evidence for a particular lexical representation to permit activation, even given weak competition from similar-sounding words.

Finally, Table 5.3 shows priming effects for base words as a function of neighborhood density. Here, the priming effect was somewhat smaller for stimuli from high-density neighborhoods (high, 24 ms; low, 38 ms). However, effects of horizontal similarity were not sufficient to dampen activation even for words with many competitors [high, $t(37) = 1.91, p = .06$; low, $t(34) = 2.18, p < .05$].

Taken together, the results from the minimal, maximal, and base words indicate a complex relationship between the activation level of any given lexical item and the competitive influence of similar-sounding neighbors. A more complete mapping from the acoustic signal to a lexical representation for any given lexical item will result in more robust activation. Coupled with the activation afforded a specific lexical representation by the input are the consequences of structural

TABLE 5.3
Lexical-Decision Reaction Times to Related
and Control Visual Targets for Base Words
as a Function of Lexical Density

Target	High Density (ms)	Low Density (ms)
Related	620	618
Control	644	656

relationships in the lexicon. If the input produces weak activation for a particular lexical representation, the competitive influences of lexical representations with similar phoneme structure are more robust.

SIMILARITY MAPPING: LEXICAL AND TEMPORAL EXTENT

I have used results from cross-modal priming to argue that a word is activated in memory to the degree that there is a successful mapping of the input to a lexical representation. The cross-modal priming results suggest that maximal nonwords failed to contact a lexical representation. My colleagues and I explored this claim further in a recent series of experiments designed to investigate the contribution of two additional dimensions of spoken words. One dimension, *lexical extent,* refers to the fact that the information at the ends of some words is redundant with beginning information. A second dimension, *temporal extent,* refers to the fact that the information in spoken words is distributed across the time dimension. Spoken-word recognition processes may have evolved to incorporate these aspects of the physical signal.

Lexical Extent

The dimension of *lexical extent* has been incorporated into the Cohort model via the notion of uniqueness points and is intimately tied to the notion of sequential-multiple activation. Uniqueness point refers to the sequential point in a word where it diverges from all other words in the language. The cohort model claims that words with early uniqueness points may be recognized prior to the end of the word. According to this view, few processing resources are devoted to monitoring the information subsequent to the uniqueness point because the word has effectively been recognized.

The view presented here emphasizes a different aspect of lexical extent; I focus on the redundancy available in long words. In the presence of ambiguity and distortions in a word, the complementary redundancy available throughout a word may be crucial confirming evidence for successful recovery of the intended word. In the TRACE model (McClelland & Elman, 1986), redundancy expresses itself in the simulations via relative activation levels of long versus short words. All other things being equal, long words will always reach a higher level of activation simply due to the additional information provided by the greater number of phonemes in a long word (see Frauenfelder & Peeters, 1990, for a number of simulations that demonstrate this property of TRACE). Of particular interest are the consequences of a maximal change in words with a high degree of redundancy. The experiments were also designed to provide converging evidence for our claims concerning the general role of acoustic–phonetic similarity in modulating lexical activation.

The experiment used a phoneme-monitoring paradigm. Phoneme monitoring has been shown to be sensitive to a variety of linguistic and perceptual variables (Foss, 1969, 1975; Frauenfelder, 1992; Morton & Long, 1976). Researchers have also used the phoneme-monitoring task to investigate the relationship between speech perception and word recognition (Cutler, Mehler, Norris, & Segui, 1987). One important focus that has come out of this research is a task analysis of phoneme monitoring intended to elucidate issues concerning the contribution of lexical representations to phoneme recognition. One potential view of the role of lexical representations in the phoneme-monitoring task is that a phoneme detection is always made completely independent from a lexical representation (Foss & Gernsbacher, 1983). An alternative view of lexical contributions is that a response is made after a mandatory consultation of the lexicon (Foss & Swinney, 1973). An intermediate position states that phoneme detections can be made using either a lexical or a prelexical code. The major factor that determines which code is used is the speed with which a particular code is available: A lexical code is used if it is available first, whereas a prelexical code is used if it is available first. With this controversy in mind, Frauenfelder and Segui (1989) recently developed a version of phoneme monitoring, generalized phoneme monitoring (GPM), in which multiple-target phonemes and varying target positions are used. Frauenfelder and Segui demonstrated that maximizing uncertainty in this fashion maximizes reliance on a lexical representation for the detection responses.

We used GPM to investigate the consequences of differing degrees of acoustic–phonetic similarity for lexical activation for highly redundant words. One purpose of the experiment was to obtain converging evidence for the claim based on cross-modal priming that minimal nonwords result in a more active lexical representation than maximal nonwords and less activation than the base word. A second purpose was to determine the consequences of a high degree of redundancy on activation for maximal nonwords. In most instances, redundant words are long words so that the amount of information that contributes to lexical activation is relatively greater. The strong evidence for a specific word (possibly combined with the greater amount of time during which activation may accumulate) may be sufficient for lexical activation even in the presence of a maximal phoneme change. To test this hypothesis, we selected 48 three-syllable base words. Derived nonwords were created from the base words (e.g., *chocolate*) by changing one or two distinctive features of the initial phoneme (e.g., *shocolate; minimal nonwords*) or six or more distinctive features of the initial phoneme in the base word (e.g., *bocolate; maximal nonwords*). A final set of nonwords (e.g., *nujalate; control nonwords*) was constructed by changing the consonants and vowels excluding the final syllable. The control nonwords were spoken with the same lexical prosody as the base word. The control nonwords were included to provide a stimulus set that had very little overlap with the base words throughout their extent. This condition provided a baseline against which to assess whether maximal-change nonwords activated a lexical representation.

TABLE 5.4
Phoneme-Monitoring Reaction Time (ms)
for Words and Minimal, Maximal, and
Control Nonwords

Subject	Reaction Time (ms)
Word	494
Minimal nonword	521
Maximal nonword	547
Control nonword	567

In all nonwords, the final syllable was left intact so that the local context (syllable length, vowel length) for the phoneme detection was comparable in the four conditions. Subjects monitored for a final-stop consonant and responses were timed from the onset of the closure. Phoneme-monitoring detection times are shown in Table 5.4 for each of the four conditions. The results showed that as acoustic–phonetic similarity of the input decreased relative to the base word, phoneme-detection times increased, with word stimuli showing the fastest times followed by minimal nonwords, maximal nonwords, and control nonwords.

A one-way analysis of variance (ANOVA; stimulus-type word, minimal nonword, maximal nonword, control nonword) showed a main effect of stimulus type [$F(3, 47) = 15.06, p < .01$]. Paired comparisons showed significant differences between all possible comparisons ($p < .05$). The phoneme monitoring and priming results converge in support of the central claim that vertical similarity modulates lexical activation. More importantly, the faster monitoring times for the maximal condition, compared with the nonword control condition, suggest that these stimuli successfully activated a lexical representation.

Superficially, the phoneme-monitoring results for maximal nonwords contrast with the cross-modal priming results presented earlier. However, the evidence for activation of maximal nonwords in phoneme monitoring can be accounted for by a model where the evidence provided by the extensive confirming information in the stimulus is sufficient to permit lexical activation. A straightforward prediction of this account is that maximal nonwords that are derived from highly redundant base words should show evidence of semantic priming. This explanation of the phoneme-monitoring results was confirmed in an additional experiment where nonwords derived from redundant base words were presented in a cross-modal priming experiment. The derived nonwords were created from a new set of 44 base words, where a phoneme was altered by five or more linguistic features. The altered phoneme occurred in either the initial or final syllable. The results are shown in Table 5.5.

As is clear from Table 5.5, related targets were faster than control targets, and this was true for both early and late maximal-change nonwords. Paired compari-

TABLE 5.5
Lexical-Decision Reaction Times to Related and Control
Visual Targets Presented Subsequent to the Offset
of Maximal Nonwords Derived from Unique Base Words
as a Function of the Position of the Altered Phoneme

Target	Early Change (ms)	Late Change (ms)
Related	701	700
Control	714	718

sons showed that the priming effect for both stimulus types was significant [early change, $t(67) = 2.5$, $p < .01$; late change, $t(67) = 3.9$, $p < .01$]. Taken together, the semantic-priming and phoneme-monitoring results demonstrate that lexical extent contributes to word recognition in a fashion that permits lexical activation, even given a relatively poor input-to-lexical representation mapping.

Temporal Extent

The phoneme-monitoring and cross-modal priming results demonstrated activation for maximal nonwords. The relevant dimension thought to permit lexical activation was the redundancy in these words. Another potential contributor to activation for redundant maximal nonwords is that it was the temporal extent of these stimuli that permitted us to detect lexical activation. The nature of lexical redundancy is such that, in English, it is naturally confounded with length; words that are highly redundant tend to be long (contain more phonemes). As a consequence, there was proportionally more evidence in favor of a particular word at the point of a response in the three-syllable stimuli compared with stimuli we have used in other experiments. Further, both the phoneme-monitoring response and the cross-modal priming paradigm assessed activation in a sequentially late position in the stimuli (on or after the final phoneme). It may be crucial that activation is assessed in a task where there is sufficient temporal extent from the altered phoneme to detect measurable lexical activation for maximal-change nonwords. This view suggests that a maximal change for short stimuli does not result in a blocking of lexical activation, but rather the maximally different information modifies the rate of activation of a lexical representation. That is, maximal nonwords may activate a lexical entry, but the slope of the activation function may be less steep compared with minimal nonwords. Thus, activation may reach its peak relatively later for maximal nonwords compared with minimal nonwords. This predicts that priming effects may emerge for maximal stimuli, but relatively late in processing.

The purpose of the next experiment was to test the contribution of temporal extent to the impact of acoustic–phonetic similarity on lexical activation. The set

TABLE 5.6

Lexical-Decision Reaction Times to Related and Control
Visual Targets Presented 350 ms Subsequent to the Offset
of Maximal Nonwords as a Function of Lexical Density

Target	High Density (ms)	Low Density (ms)
Related	646	639
Control	655	667

of two-syllable maximal nonwords used in our previous cross-modal priming experiment was used (Connine et al., 1993). Recall that our previous results using short-maximal nonwords showed no evidence for lexical activation even when there was little competition from other lexical representations. To determine the contribution of lexical extent, the present experiment was conducted with a 350-ms delay between offset of the auditory stimulus and presentation of the visual target.

The priming results given a 350-ms delay contrasted strikingly with the priming results for maximal nonwords when the visual target was presented at stimulus offset. With a 350-ms delay in presentation of the visual target, a 22-ms priming effect was found [648 ms, related; 670 ms, control; $F(1, 57) = 22.3$, $p < .01$]. Table 5.6 shows a post-hoc analysis based on neighborhood density.

As is clear from Table 5.6, a robust priming effect (28 ms) was found for stimuli from low-density neighborhoods [$t(35) = 2.21$, $p < .05$]. A nonsignificant priming effect of 9 ms [$t(29) = .67$), $p = .53$ was found for stimuli from high-density neighborhoods. As in the previous experiments, neighborhood-density effects emerged when there was sufficient activation for a lexical representation.

The priming effect found for stimuli from low-density neighborhoods indicates that, with a delay, the target-lexical entry was active. This result supports the hypothesis that vertical similarity serves to modulate the rate of activation of a specific lexical representation and does not act simply to preclude activation. These results are of particular interest because they suggest a view of word recognition where a single hypothesis does not emerge as the best candidate in an all-or-none fashion. Rather, word recognition appears to be a much more gradual process, where a candidate emerges based on vertical and horizontal similarity in a time-dependent process.

CONCLUSIONS

The view of spoken-word recognition that emerges from the data presented here is a word-recognition system that is sensitive to signal-specific dimensions of spoken language—in particular, the distribution of information over time. The findings also reveal an intricate relationship between vertical and horizontal similarity, where the competitive influences of similar-sounding words become less pronounced as the mapping between the physical signal and a word permits more effective activation of a lexical representation. On a more general level, what is revealed is the remarkable resilience of spoken-word recognition in the presence of distortion.

The data presented here only begin to address the nature of the mapping from the speech signal to a lexical representation. What remains for further research is a determination of what principles exist that constrain the contribution of vertical similarity to spoken-word recognition. Of considerable interest are those principles that have their basis in language-specific structure derived from the phonotactic and phonological regularities in a language. Listeners are aware of these dimensions of the structure of their language, and it is quite likely that this knowledge is brought to bear during spoken-word recognition. One way in which this knowledge may be used is that language-specific knowledge of phonotactic and phonological structure may provide a means for constraining the general principle of activation based on acoustic–phonetic similarity.

ACKNOWLEDGMENTS

The research and preparation of this chapter were supported by NIDCD grant R29 NS26587, and additional support was provided by the Center for Cognitive and Psycholinguistic Science. This chapter is based on a talk given at a symposium on auditory-word recognition at the sixth annual CUNY Conference on Sentence Processing. My thanks to the conference organizers for the invitation. Thanks go to Dawn Blasko, Jane Ferriby, and Debra Titone for their many contributions to the experiments described herein, and to Cara Schmitt and Stacey Garsson for their assistance in running subjects.

REFERENCES

Bard, E. (1990). Competition, lateral inhibition and frequency: Comments on the chapters of Frauenfelder and Peeters, Marslen-Wilson, and others. In G. T. M. Altmann (Ed.), *Cognitive models of speech processing: Psycholinguistic and computational perspectives,* (pp. 185–210). Cambridge, MA: MIT Press.

Coltheart, M., Davelaar, E., Johasson, J. T., & Besner, D. (1977). Access to the mental lexicon. In S. Dornic (Ed.), *Attention and performance* (Vol. 6) London: Academic Press.

Connine, C. M., Blasko, D. M., & Titone, D. A. (1993). Do the beginnings of spoken words have a special status in auditory word recognition? *Journal of Memory and Language, 32,* 193–210.

Cutler, A., Mehler, J., Norris, D., & Segui, J. (1987). The syllable's differing role in the segmentation of French and English. *Journal of Memory and Language, 25,* 385–400.

Elman, J., & McClelland, J. (1986). Exploiting the lawful variability in the speech wave. In J. S.

Perkell & D. H. Klatt (Eds.), *Invariance and variability of speech processes* (pp. 360–380). Hillsdale, NJ: Lawrence Erlbaum Associates.

Foss, D. (1969). Decision processes during sentence comprehension: Effects of lexical item difficulty and position upon decision times. *Journal of Verbal Learning and Verbal Behavior, 8,* 457–462.

Foss, D. (1975). On the time-course of sentence comprehension. In F. Bresson & J. Mehler (Eds.), *Current approaches to problems in psycholinguistics.* Paris: CNRS.

Foss, D., & Gernsbacher, M. A. (1983). Cracking the dual code: Toward a unitary model of phoneme identification. *Journal of Verbal Learning and Verbal Behavior, 22,* 609–632.

Foss, D., & Swinney, D. (1973). On the psychological reality of the phoneme: Perception, identification and consciousness. *Journal of Verbal Learning and Verbal Behavior, 12,* 246–257.

Frauenfelder, U. (1992). The interface between acoustic-phonetic and lexical processing. In M. E. H. Schouten (Ed.), *The auditory processing of speech: From sounds to words.* New York: Mouton de Gruyter.

Frauenfelder, U., & Peeters, G. (1990). Lexical segmentation in TRACE: An exercise in simulations. In G. T. M. Altmann (Ed.), *Cognitive models of speech processing: Psycholinguistic and computational perspectives.* Cambridge, MA: MIT Press.

Frauenfelder, U., & Segui, J. (1989). Phoneme monitoring and lexical processing: Evidence for associative context effects. *Memory and Cognition, 17,* 134–140.

Goldinger, S., Luce, P., & Pisoni, D. (1989). Priming lexical neighbors of spoken words: Effects of competition and bias. *Journal of Memory and Language, 28,* 501–518.

Goldinger, S., Luce, P., Pisoni, D., & Marcario, J. (1992). Form-based priming in spoken word recognition: The roles of competition and bias. *Journal of Experimental Psychology: Learning, Memory & Cognition, 18*(6), 1211–1238.

Jordan, M. (1986). *Serial order: A parallel distributed processing approach* (Rep. No. 8604). San Diego: University of California.

Luce, P. A., Pisoni, D. B., & Goldinger, S. (1990). Similarity neighborhoods of spoken words. In G. T. M. Altmann (Ed.), *Cognitive models of speech processing: Psycholinguistic and computational perspectives.* Cambridge, MA: MIT Press.

Marslen-Wilson, W. (1987). Functional parallelism in spoken word recognition. *Cognition, 25,* 71–102.

Marslen-Wilson, W. (1990). Activation, competition and frequency in lexical access. In G. T. M. Altmann (Ed.), *Cognitive models of speech processing: Psycholinguistic and computational perspectives.* Cambridge, MA: MIT Press.

Marslen-Wilson, W., & Welsh, A. (1978). Processing interactions and lexical access during word recognition in continuous speech. *Cognitive Psychology, 10,* 29–63.

Marslen-Wilson, W., & Zwitserlood, P. (1988). Accessing spoken words: On the importance of word onsets. *Journal of Experimental Psychology: Human Perception and Performance, 15,* 576–585.

McClelland, J., & Elman, J. (1986). The TRACE model of speech perception. *Cognitive Psychology, 18,* 1–86.

Milberg, W., Blumstein, S., & Dworetzky, B. (1988). Phonological factors in lexical access: Evidence from an auditory lexical decision task. *Bulletin of the Psychonomic Society, 26*(4), 305–308.

Morton, J., & Long, (1976). Effect of word transitional probability on phoneme identification. *Journal of Verbal Learning and Verbal Behavior, 15,* 43–51.

Norris, D. (1990). A dynamic-net model of human speech recognition. In G. T. M. Altmann (Ed.), *Cognitive models of speech processing: Psycholinguistic and computational perspectives.* Cambridge, MA: MIT Press.

Samuel, A. (1981). Phonemic restoration: Insights from a new methodology. *Journal of Experimental Psychology: General, 110,* 474–494.

Wilson, M. D. (1988). MRC psycholinguistic database: Machine-usable dictionary, version 2.0. *Behavior Research Methods, Instrumentation, and Computers, 20,* 6–10.

III SYNTACTIC PROCESSING: INFORMATION FLOW AND DECISION MAKING

6 Syntactic Ambiguity Resolution as Lexical Ambiguity Resolution

Maryellen C. MacDonald
University of Southern California

Neal J. Pearlmutter
University of Illinois

Mark S. Seidenberg
University of Southern California

Although languages exhibit many types of ambiguity, most research on ambiguity resolution has focused on lexical and syntactic ambiguities. The theories that have dominated lexical and syntactic ambiguity resolution over the past 15 years suggest that lexical and syntactic ambiguities are resolved by very different mechanisms (e.g., Frazier, 1989; Frazier & Rayner, 1987). This chapter explores an alternative hypothesis—that lexical and syntactic ambiguity resolution operate via very similar mechanisms because much of what has been termed *syntactic ambiguity resolution* derives from lexical processes.

STANDARD VIEWS OF LEXICAL AND SYNTACTIC AMBIGUITY RESOLUTION

Lexical ambiguity research has addressed how the comprehender determines the contextually appropriate meaning of a semantically ambiguous word such as *bank* or *watch*. This research has primarily addressed how aspects of lexical structure (such as the relative frequencies of alternative meanings) and contextual information affect ambiguity resolution (see Simpson, 1981, for review). Theorizing about lexical ambiguity resolution has been heavily influenced by the finding first reported by Conrad (1974)—that subjects briefly activate multiple senses of ambiguous words even in clearly disambiguating contexts (Swinney, 1979; Tanenhaus, Leiman, & Seidenberg, 1979). On the basis of these data, researchers have argued for "multiple-access" models in which either the most common meanings of an ambiguous word (Seidenberg, Tanenhaus, Leiman, & Bienkowski, 1982) or all meanings of an ambiguous word (Swinney, 1979) are looked up in the lexicon in parallel, with contextual information used shortly afterward to select the appropriate meaning and suppress the incorrect alternatives.

Syntactic ambiguity resolution has been viewed quite differently. For example, consider the syntactic ambiguity commonly called the *main-verb/reduced-relative* (*MV/RR*) ambiguity in Sentences (1) and (2):

(1) The horse raced past the barn yesterday.
(2) The horse raced past the barn fell.

Sentence (1) is a simple sentence in which *raced* is the past-tense main verb of the sentence. Sentence (2) is Bever's (1970) well-known "garden-path" sentence in which *raced* is a past participle and introduces a reduced-relative clause construction, meaning "the horse that was raced past the barn," and *fell* is the main verb of the sentence. This temporary ambiguity is permitted in English because certain words introducing a relative clause (e.g., "that was") can be optionally omitted, and because most verbs in English are identical in their past-tense and past-participle forms.

In contrast to the multiple-access view that is dominant in lexical ambiguity resolution, the prevailing view of how syntactic ambiguities like the MV/RR ambiguity in Sentences (1) and (2) are processed is that only one interpretation is pursued. The most fully developed theory of this sort is the "garden-path" model of Frazier and her colleagues (Ferreira & Clifton, 1986; Frazier, 1979, 1989; Rayner, Carlson, & Frazier, 1983). A main feature of the garden-path model is the proposal that the first stage in the comprehension process is the computation of a phrase structure representation of the input. This analysis is the responsibility of a syntactic processor or *parser* thought to compute only a single analysis at a time. It receives as input only the grammatical categories of the words being processed (e.g., determiner, adjective, noun) and does not have access to the words' identities or meanings. When the sequence of categories that the parser is analyzing is compatible with multiple phrase structure analyses, the path it follows is determined by a processing strategy called *minimal attachment,* by which the syntactically simpler interpretation is preferred, where simplicity is indexed by the number of nodes in a phrase-structure tree. In the MV/RR ambiguity, the minimal-attachment strategy directs the parser to pursue only the main-verb interpretation of this ambiguity, as in Sentence (1). This strategy is responsible for the difficulty that comprehenders have with the alternative reduced-relative structure shown in Sentence (2).

These very different views about lexical and syntactic ambiguity resolution are summarized in Table 6.1. Many of these differences derive from assumptions about the types of knowledge involved in each domain (Frazier, 1989), and the

TABLE 6.1
Properties of Ambiguity-Resolution Systems

Lexical Ambiguity	Syntactic Ambiguity
Multiple alternatives initially considered	Single alternative initially considered
Parallel processing	Serial processing
Capacity free	Capacity limited
Context used to select appropriate meaning	Context used to confirm analysis, guide reanalysis
Meanings are stored and accessed	Syntactic structures constructed by rule

notion that language processing is accomplished via the operation of autonomous processing modules (Fodor, 1983). Lexical ambiguity is thought to involve meanings that are stored in the lexicon. Processing involves accessing this information, which is assumed to be accomplished automatically and in parallel. By contrast, syntactic structures are thought to be constructed on the basis of grammatical rules, rather than stored directly in memory. This computation is assumed to place demands on working memory and attentional resources that are limited in capacity (Frazier, 1979). Because of these limitations, the parser can pursue only a single analysis at a time. Thus, lexical ambiguity resolution is thought to routinely involve the temporary access of multiple alternatives in an autonomous lexicon, with other processing subsystems coming along later to select the contextually appropriate word meaning. In contrast, syntactic ambiguity resolution is thought to be strictly serial, with only one parse computed at a time by an autonomous parser. Other processing subsystems later confirm or disconfirm this analysis, initiating reanalyses as necessary.

CHALLENGES FOR THE STANDARD THEORIES

Both empirical and theoretical considerations have called into question the accounts of ambiguity resolution summarized in Table 6.1. We consider three different challenges to these accounts: (a) the role of context, (b) the role of frequency, and (c) the nature of lexical and syntactic representations.

Context Effects

The core finding on which the standard theory of lexical ambiguity resolution rests was the activation of multiple meanings in biasing contexts, but the results of several studies have violated this pattern (e.g., Seidenberg et al., 1982, Experiment 2; Simpson & Krueger, 1991; Swinney & Hakes, 1976; Tabossi, 1988; Tabossi, Colombo, & Job, 1987; see McClelland, 1987, for discussion).

The conflicting results were initially attributed to methodological differences between studies (Swinney, 1979), but the more recent studies such as Tabossi's used the same cross-modal priming technique as in the studies that yielded multiple access. Hence, the role of context is apparently not as simple as the standard view suggests.

Similar questions arise with regard to syntactic ambiguity. Whereas lexical ambiguity research focused on whether contextual information could override the multiple-access pattern, research on syntactic ambiguity has addressed whether contextual information could override the minimal-attachment pattern, such that a syntactically more complex interpretation of an ambiguity would be favored in a biasing context. For the MV/RR ambiguity, the question is whether a helpful context could override the preference for the main verb interpretation, so that, in context, resolving the ambiguity in favor of the reduced-relative interpretation would be no more difficult than parsing an unambiguous sentence with this same structure.

Two types of contextual manipulations favoring the reduced-relative interpretation have been investigated. The first of these, which is grounded in a similar lexically based theory (Trueswell & Tanenhaus, this volume; Trueswell, Tanenhaus & Garnsey, in press), is the relative plausibility of the two alternative interpretations. For example, in a string that introduces the MV/RR ambiguity, such as "the patient examined," the prior discourse context might affect whether it is more plausible for the patient to be examining something (the main-verb interpretation) or to be examined by someone (the reduced-relative interpretation). Similarly, in "the evidence examined," the fact that the noun *evidence* is inanimate makes the main-verb interpretation, in which the evidence would be examining something, highly implausible (Ferreira & Clifton, 1986; Trueswell, et al. in press). The second context manipulation rests on a theory of pragmatics and on the fact that the reduced-relative interpretation involves noun modification—in "the patient examined by the doctors was overweight," the phrase "examined by the doctors" modifies "the patient." Crain and Steedman (1985) and Altmann and Steedman (1988) argued that, in the absence of a specific context that makes noun modification felicitous (e.g., a situation in which the speaker wants to distinguish between two previously mentioned patients), a noun-modification interpretation is computationally more difficult than an interpretation that does not include modification. This difference in computational complexity rests at a pragmatic level, rather than at the syntactic level as in the garden-path model, yielding the prediction that the difficulty of the main-verb and reduced-relative interpretations will vary with the nature of the pragmatic context in which the ambiguity is being interpreted. On this view, the preference for the main-verb minimal-attachment reading seen in many studies is an artifact of the pragmatic context in which the ambiguities are presented.

According to the garden-path model, neither the plausibility nor the pragmatic context manipulations should affect the initial interpretation of syntactic ambiguities because initial parsing decisions are guided only by phrase-structure rules and strategies such as minimal attachment, not by context. As reviewed later, many studies of the MV/RR ambiguity have supported the garden-path model's predictions, but a number of other studies have found that context does appear to affect the earliest parsing decisions. Thus, for both lexical and syntactic ambiguity, the traditional view that context does not influence early ambiguity resolution mechanisms is only partially supported by the empirical evidence.

Frequency

The frequency with which words are used in a language has a large effect on lexical processing—a fact acknowledged by all models of the lexicon dating at least from Morton (1969). In lexical ambiguity resolution, several studies have found the multiple-access pattern for "equibased" words—those with alternative meanings that are roughly equal in frequency (Swinney, 1979; Tanenhaus et al., 1979). Most ambiguous words have alternative meanings that differ considerably in frequency, however. For example, in the Francis and Kučera (1982) corpus of American English, there are 1,366 words that occur as both nouns and verbs. These include both words whose noun and verb meanings are semantically unrelated (such as *tire* and *bluff*), and words with semantically related meanings (such as *cap* and *coin*). For 73% of these noun–verb ambiguities, one grammatical category is used at least twice as often as the other, and analyses of the words that are ambiguous between other grammatical categories yield a similar picture. It is likely that the processing system exploits these substantial differences in frequency.

Simpson (1981) reviewed a large number of studies suggesting that frequency affects the order in which the meanings of ambiguous words are accessed. An early model incorporating this idea was proposed by Hogaboam and Perfetti (1975), and Seidenberg et al. (1982) observed that the multiple-access pattern may be the special case in which the two most common meanings of a word happen to be similar in frequency. Important studies by Rayner and Duffy (1986) and Duffy, Morris, and Rayner (1988) provided additional evidence concerning the frequency factor. Using eye-tracking measures, Rayner and Duffy established that equibiased-ambiguous words (such as *pitcher*) produce longer fixation durations than matched unambiguous words in neutral contexts (i.e., contexts that do not favor either meaning). Thus, multiple access of meaning was associated with longer fixation durations. Fixation durations did not differ for nonequibiased words (such as *port*) compared with controls, suggesting that, for these words in which one meaning is much more frequent than others, only the dominant meaning is accessed and integrated with the context. Duffy et al. then examined how the processing of equibiased and nonequibiased words is affected by biasing contextual information. Contexts were constructed so as to favor one meaning of the equibiased ambiguous word and the less frequent (subordinate) meaning of the nonequibiased ambiguous word. Duffy et al. found that equibiased ambiguous words in biasing contexts act like nonequibiased words in neutral contexts. In both cases, a single meaning is accessed on line and integrated with the context, and no effect of ambiguity is observed. Thus, context can promote one meaning of the equibiased word, yielding fixation times equal to those for an unambiguous control word. Moreover, nonequibiased words in biasing contexts favoring the subordinate meaning acted like equibiased words in neutral contexts. In both of these cases, latencies were longer in the ambiguous condition than in the unambiguous control condition, indicating that multiple meanings had been accessed. Thus, contexts can promote the less frequent meaning of a biased word, but the effect is limited: Whereas the context increases the activation of the lower frequency meaning, the higher frequency meaning is still activated. Context can increase the salience of a lower frequency meaning, but it does not appear to inhibit the higher frequency meaning.

These studies provide clear evidence that the relative frequency of meaning has an impact on processing; they also indicate that contextual information can result in only one meaning of an ambiguous word being activated to a detectable level. Moreover, the two factors interact: Biasing contexts produce selective access when the alternative meanings are similar in frequency and when they are consistent with the higher frequency meanings of nonequibiased words, but not when they favor lower frequency meanings. None of these results is expected from the perspective of a modular lexicon that exhaustively accesses all meanings of an ambiguous word, independent of frequency or context.

In syntactic ambiguity resolution, the role of frequency is less clear. The garden-path model assumes that the relative frequency of alternative syntactic structures is irrelevant to the initial syntactic processing of sentences because minimal attachment is a strategy based on the relative simplicity of syntactic structures, not their relative frequencies. However, one might ask, by analogy to lexical ambiguity, whether the words that trigger a syntactic ambiguity have frequency asymmetries that affect the resolution of the ambiguities they create. Taking the MV/RR ambiguity in "the patient examined" as an example, the questions are whether the verb *examined* is used more often in simple transitive sentences (as a main verb) or in reduced relatives, whether there are verbs in which the relative frequencies are reversed, and whether the comprehension process exploits such frequency information.

Representation: Access Versus Construction

Finally, we turn to the different assumptions about lexical and syntactic representations that are embodied in the standard views of ambiguity resolution. Models of lexical ambiguity resolution have typically assumed that meanings are fixed entries that are accessed in the course of processing, but this notion has been strongly questioned on both theoretical and empirical grounds. More recent theories suggest that the meanings of words are computed as part of the recognition process (Barsalou, 1987), and the meaning that is computed may differ depending on the context in which it occurs (Merrill, Sperber, & McCauley, 1981). This view is captured by the distributed representations employed in connectionist networks. The meaning of a word can be represented as a pattern of activation over a set of units encoding semantic primitives (Hinton, 1986); each unit participates in the meaning of many words. In a system employing this type of knowledge structure, the meanings of words are not stored as separate entries, and therefore cannot be accessed. Rather, they are computed with different patterns activated in different contexts.

Kawamoto (1988, 1993) provided an application of this framework to lexical ambiguity resolution. In Kawamoto's model, each code for a word (spelling, meaning, phonology, grammatical category) is represented by a pattern of activation over a set of units encoding that type of information. The model computes patterns of activation corresponding to these codes. The model was developed using a greatly simplified domain consisting of a small number of words and contexts. The vocabulary items included homographs such as *wind* and *bass,* which have semantically unrelated meanings that are associated with different pronunciations. The architecture of the system allowed the computation of word meaning to be influenced by contextual information. However, the model computed multiple meanings of homographs even when contextual information favored one meaning. The basic reason for this outcome is very simple. Multiple meanings are computed for words such as *wind* because the association between each meaning and its sensory form (orthography or phonology) is much stronger than the association between a component meaning and the information provided by the biasing context. Thus, the model exhibits the property that Marslen-Wilson (1987) termed *bottom–up priority.*

Kawamoto's model is an important challenge to the traditional view of ambiguity resolution, insofar as it shows that the multiple-access pattern that had been taken as diagnostic of a modular lexicon could appear in a nonmodular architecture. It was simply because the contextual constraints were too weak that multiple access occurred in Kawamoto's model, not because the lexical processor was an autonomous module. The model does not show that the modular account is incorrect. Rather, it shows that the data taken as evidence for the modular view are compatible with very different theoretical conclusions.

With regard to syntactic ambiguity resolution, the analogous question is whether the data showing the minimal-attachment pattern necessarily implicate a modular parser. As in the case of lexical ambiguity, the signature finding—the garden-path effect in sentences such as "The horse raced past the barn fell"—is taken as evidence for an autonomous module in the comprehension system. Kawamoto's model alerts us to the possibility that the absence of context effects in some circumstances need not implicate a modular architecture. Indeed, the claim that some types of biasing information are merely too weak to overcome minimal attachment (e.g., McClelland, 1987; Trueswell et al., in press; Tyler, 1989) is certainly reminiscent of the demonstration in Kawamoto's model that multiple access of meaning will obtain in contexts that are too weakly constraining.

In addition to these questions about the relationship between context effects and modularity, there are additional reasons to question the view of syntactic representations that is embodied in the standard account of syntactic ambiguity resolution. The standard account was based on early work in generative grammar (up to and including the standard theory of Chomsky, 1965), which had relied on the mechanism of phrase structure rules to generate basic syntactic structures. Nothing about these rules necessarily associated them with particular lexical items, and thus the syntactic component of the linguistic system could easily be viewed as an independent module with its own idiosyncratic representations and processes. More recently, however, collections of phrase structure rules have been abandoned in favor of formulations in which lexical items are directly associated with the information used to construct a complete syntactic representation, including the X-bar structures in Government-and-binding (GB) theory (Chomsky, 1981) and predicate-argument structures in lexical-functional grammar (Bresnan, 1982). On this view, the lexicon and syntax are very tightly linked. To the extent that information required by the syntactic component is stored with individual lexical items, it will be difficult to find a neat boundary between the two systems. Thus, whereas Kawamoto's model provides an alternative to the concept of accessing a lexical entry, syntactic theory augments the role of the lexicon in syntactic representations. According to this alternative view, syntactic information is part of a word's representation in memory. These developments suggest the possibility that the computation of both "lexical" and "syntactic" information in sentence comprehension is governed by common lexical processing mechanisms. This possibility is explored next.

TOWARD AN INTEGRATED THEORY OF LEXICAL AND SYNTACTIC AMBIGUITY RESOLUTION

In this section, we develop our principal theoretical claim—that both lexical and syntactic ambiguity are governed by the same types of knowledge representations and processing mechanisms. We have just seen that very similar empirical, theoretical, and methodological issues have arisen in both the lexical and syntactic domains, including the role of frequency information, the relative degree to which contextual information constrains the interpretation of ambiguities, and whether the processing system is modular or interactive. We suggest that these parallels between the domains are not coincidental; they derive from the fact that the syntactic ambiguities in question are based on ambiguities at the lexical level. The same ambiguity-resolution mechanisms apply in both domains because both involve ambiguities over various types of lexical representations.

Theoretical Background.   In developing this framework, we have built on considerable earlier research in sentence comprehension. Bever's (1970) suggestion that syntactic ambiguities are resolved via the application of strategies that were sensitive to the individual lexical items in the sentence is clearly revived here. The idea that syntactic ambiguity resolution is guided by lexical information has been extensively discussed by Tanenhaus and his colleagues at the University of Rochester (Boland & Tanenhaus, 1991; Carlson & Tanenhaus, 1988; Tanenhaus & Carlson, 1989; Trueswell & Tanenhaus, this volume; Trueswell, et al., in press). The studies from the Rochester group have addressed many of the issues considered in this article and greatly influenced our approach. Other observations concerning the important role of lexical information in syntactic processing can be found in Fodor (1978), Ford, Bresnan & Kaplan (1982), and Tyler (1989). The view that sentence processing involves constraint satisfaction mechanisms has been proposed by a number of people, most prominently McClelland (McClelland, 1987; St. John & McClelland, 1990). Our approach is in much the same spirit as the "Competition Model" of MacWhinney and Bates (1989). Our goal has been to develop an integrative theoretical framework that rationalizes much of the existing literature and provides an orientation for future research.

We assume that comprehension is the process of concurrently deriving a number of linked representations of different types for a given input sentence or sequence of sentences. A single, appropriate representation must be computed at each level in the course of processing (although a complete record of all of this information will not necessarily have to be maintained throughout the processing of a sentence). Sentences are represented at three major levels: (a) lexical, (b) syntactic, and (c) discourse. We focus on the lexical component here, although a complete theory of language comprehension would address all levels. Following a brief sketch of some lexical representations and processing mechanisms, we then apply this model of ambiguity resolution to the structure for which there is the most behavioral evidence—the MV/RR ambiguity—showing that it accounts for a broad range of findings, including ones that were previously seen as conflicting.

The Lexicon

The standard view of the lexicon in psycholinguistics is that it is a mental dictionary containing an entry for each word in a person's vocabulary, specifying its semantics, phonology, and orthography. The lexical representations that we propose include these three types of information as well as several other types of information that are relevant to syntactic processing, including a representation of the word's grammatical features (including grammatical category), morphology (at least inflectional), argument structure, and syntactic structure (cf. Boland & Tanenhaus, 1991; Tanenhaus & Carlson, 1989; Tyler, 1989). For words that are associated with more than one representation of a particular type, all the alternatives are included as part of the word's representation in memory. Thus, we are taking the notion of representation of multiple alternatives in the lexicon that has already been proposed for semantic ambiguities (e.g., the alternative interpretations of *bank*) and extending it to include other types of lexical representation. Rather than proposing a complete model of these types of lexical representation here (see MacDonald, Pearlmutter, & Seidenberg, 1993, for a more extensive treatment of this issue), we focus on one type of information that is especially relevant to syntactic ambiguity resolution: what current syntactic theories such as GB theory (Chomsky, 1981) call *argument structures* (e.g., Grimshaw, 1990; Levin & Rappaport, 1986; Stowell, 1981).

Argument Structure.   The argument structures associated with a word serve two critical functions. First, they encode the relationships between the word and the phrases that typically occur with it (the word's *arguments*). Second, argument structures capture important facts about correlations between syntactic and semantic information. We assume that the lexical entry of (at least) each verb, preposition, noun, and adjective includes a representation of argument structure information. For example, the argument structure for the verb *put* captures English speakers' knowledge that not just any combination of a subject noun phrase (NP), an object NP, and a prepositional phrase (PP) is acceptable for this verb—the subject NP must take the role of agent (the thing doing the putting), the object NP must be the theme (the thing being put), and the PP must specify a location (where the theme is put). This course-grained semantic information about a phrase, such as the requirement that the PP mark a location of some sort, is called the *thematic role* assigned to the phrase (Chomsky, 1981; Fillmore, 1968; Gruber, 1976; Jackendoff, 1972). The conjunction of syntactic and semantic information in one representation captures interdependencies between the syntactic and semantic information that are important for language processing and ambiguity resolution (e.g., Boland & Tanenhaus, 1991; Carlson & Tanenhaus, 1988; Stowe, 1989; Tanenhaus & Carlson, 1989).

Because many words can appear with more than one configuration of arguments, they are associated with several different argument structures. The fact that such words are associated with more than one argument structure creates an ambiguity that must be resolved during the comprehension process. For example, the verb *raced* has at least two different argument structures: In the *transitive* argument structure, the verb has two arguments—both an agent (the racer) and a theme (the entity raced), whereas the *intransitive* argument structure has only one argument—the agent. When the comprehender encounters a string such as "the horse raced," one of these two argument structures for *raced* must be selected; in addition, a thematic role must be assigned to *the horse:* Either the horse is the agent (possible under either transitive or intransitive argument structures) or it is the theme (possible only with the transitive structure). Thus, much of the parsing process here involves activating the correct lexical representation of *raced*.

This example illustrates a crucial difference between our proposal and other characterizations of parsing. Some previous theories (e.g., Frazier, 1979) have emphasized syntactic phrase structure ambiguity and relegated thematic role assignment to a later stage of parsing. Syntactic structures were assumed to be built on the basis of phrase structure rules, and proposals about the architecture of the parser described strategies for dealing with ambiguities defined at this level. On this view, the syntactic ambiguity in the *raced* example concerns the sort of verb phrase to construct for *raced*. By contrast, we are claiming that the ambiguity has a fundamentally different character: It is lexical insofar as it derives from the fact that the lexical representation of a verb such as *raced* contains multiple argument structures. The ambiguity is resolved not by strategies governing the application of structure-generating rules, but rather by the processes that govern the resolution of other types of lexical ambiguities. These processes, which we argue apply equally to lexical representations of both semantic and syntactic ambiguity, are outlined in the next section.

Processing Assumptions

In keeping with the idea that syntactic ambiguities are lexically based, our processing assumptions are taken directly from recent models of word recognition, particularly the interactive-activation models of McClelland and Rumelhart (1981) and Elman and McClelland (1984) and the lexical-ambiguity resolution model of Kawamoto (1993). Our goal here is to identify basic characteristics of the system, rather than to describe how these characteristics can be implemented in specific computational models. All of the mechanisms we propose have been explored in previous modeling research, which provides a basis for assuming that they are not unrealistic with regard to their computational demands. No novel ideas about processing are being introduced here. Rather, there is the application of some familiar computational concepts in a new domain—syntactic ambiguity resolution. For an example of how such a model might be implemented, see Pearlmutter, Daugherty, MacDonald, and Seidenberg (1993), which described a constraint-satisfaction model of some aspects of thematic role assignment.

Activation. We assume a basic activation metaphor, in which units (or sets of units) corresponding to each type of information are activated in the course of processing. Although it appears innocuous and well grounded in previous modeling research, this assumption carries with it some potentially controversial implications concerning the treatment of syntactic information. In our approach, lexical-syntactic information about alternative argument structures is associated with lexical items and can be activated to differing degrees. The only requirement is that the system settle on one of the alternatives eventually for comprehension to occur. The notion of partially activating syntactically relevant information is quite foreign to the earlier approaches, although it follows naturally from the assumption that some syntactic information, such as argument structure information, is stored as parts of lexical entries. Thus, this claim blurs the distinction between accessed lexical (semantic) representations and constructed syntactic representations. In our view, all lexical representations are processed the same way, in that alternative interpretations are subject to partial activation.

Frequency.   Each component of a lexical entry carries information about its frequency of occurrence in the language. For example, the representation of the verb *raced* includes the information that it has two alternative argument structures—transitive and intransitive. The frequency with which *raced* occurs with each form would be encoded as part of this representation. If frequencies are encoded for the syntactic aspects of lexical representation in the same way that the frequencies of alternate meanings are encoded, lexical frequency information should affect syntactic ambiguity resolution in the same way that meaning frequencies affect lexical ambiguity resolution. That humans encode information about the frequencies of occurrence for a broad range of entities is well established. Here, we merely assume that they encode frequencies for all the types of information stored in the lexicon. As in many models of word recognition, we assume that frequency information is encoded by activation level, although there are other ways that this aspect of the system might be implemented (e.g., by encoding individual instances).

Constraint Satisfaction.   In resolving ambiguities, the processing system exploits three main characteristics of language: First, the different types of information associated with a word are not independent of one another. Thus, process in resolving an ambiguity at one level provides information relevant to resolving ambiguities elsewhere in the system. Second, a word will not necessarily be equally ambiguous at all levels of representation. For example, a word can be ambiguous as to tense, but unambiguous with regard to grammatical category. Third, even when the grammar admits multiple alternatives at a given level of representation, they often differ substantially in frequency, and thus a priori probability of occurrence. Therefore, ambiguity resolution is a classic example of a constraint-satisfaction problem (McClelland, Rumelhart, & Hinton, 1986): Multiple interdependent, partially redundant, probabilistic sources of information interact to allow the system to settle on an interpretation at each level. The fact that the processing system exploits these characteristics allows ambiguities to be resolved efficiently.

The computational properties of constraint-satisfaction mechanisms have been studied in considerable detail. Rumelhart (1977) provided an early, informal discussion of this type of processing in language comprehension. St. John and McClelland (1990) developed a model that applied to some of the same phenomena we consider here (see also McClelland, 1987). MacWhinney and Bates (1989) have also explored constraint-satisfaction mechanisms in language comprehension in their competition model. Constraint-satisfaction concepts are also beginning to have a significant impact on linguistic theory, particularly in morphology and phonology (Prince & Smolensky, in press, and references cited there); Stabler (1993) described an implementation of GB theory as a constraint-satisfaction system. Connectionist models provide one way of implementing constraint satisfaction, but there are nonconnectionist schemes as well. In fact, the development of constraint-satisfaction systems predates the emergence of contemporary connectionist theory (see Mackworth, 1977). Our focus is on how the constraint-satisfaction process applies to the issue of syntactic ambiguity resolution. The claims that are made are largely neutral with respect to whether this process is realized by a connectionist network, a set of symbolic rules or simultaneous equations, a production system, or some other means.

For descriptive purposes, and because we have hypothesized that syntactic ambiguity resolution can be subsumed under principles identified with lexical processing, we assume the general framework of an interactive-activation model (Elman & McClelland, 1984; McClelland & Rumelhart, 1981). A fragment of a lexical representation is provided in Fig. 6.1 for an ambiguous verb that can trigger the MV/RR ambiguity (e.g., *raced, pushed*). Only three levels of lexical representation are shown, and each has a set of units representing the alternatives

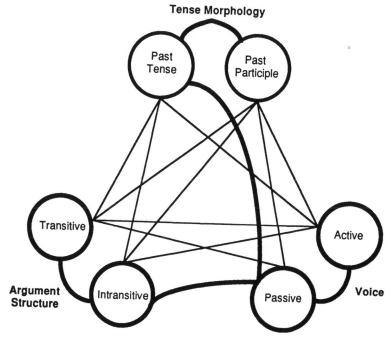

FIG. 6.1. A representation of three levels of lexical ambiguity for a verb such as *raced.*

that are available for a given word. Thus, the tense morphology level has the alternatives past tense and past participle, the voice level has the alternatives active and passive, and the argument-structure level is shown with the transitive (assigning both an agent and a theme thematic role) and intransitive (assigning only an agent role) argument structures, although many verbs will have more than two argument structure options. It should be apparent that these units are placeholders for more complex representations whose details are important but not immediately relevant to the level at which we are describing the behavior of the system. As in the TRACE model (Elman & McClelland, 1984), there are inhibitory connections between the alternatives within a given type. The connections between different types of information reflect dependencies dictated by the grammar of the language. Where the grammar permits a relationship between two types of information, the connections are assumed to be excitatory, shown by thin straight lines. Where the grammar rules out a relationship between two alternatives, the connection between the relevant units is inhibitory, shown by thick curved lines. Thus, every unit is connected to every other unit either by an excitatory connection, when the grammar allows both units to be part of a representation (e.g., passive and past participle, active and transitive), or by an inhibitory connection, when the grammar disallows the combination of units either within a level or between levels.

Figure 6.1 captures some important interdependencies between these three levels of representation, particularly that the passive voice, as in the reduced-relative construction or in simple passives such as "The horse was raced," is permissible with only one alternative at each of the other two levels of representation—the transitive argument structure and past-participle tense morphology. The conjunction of passive voice and past tense is ungrammatical, as in "The horse was rode by the man," as are passive uses with intransitive verbs, as in "The horse was slept." However, active sentences may appear with either transitive- ("The horse pulled the wagon") or intransitive-argument structures ("The horse slept"). They may occur with past-tense verbs, as in these last two examples, or with a past participle when a form of *have* is present, as in "The horse had pulled the wagon" or "The horse has slept."[1]

Figure 6.1 also illustrates several of our claims about the basic aspects of

---

[1]The excitatory and inhibitory connections in Fig. 6.1 can be interpreted in several different ways. First, they may be seen as the reflection in the lexicon of grammatical constraints that are represented elsewhere. From this view, the lexicon would come to represent the non-co-occurrence of some features with inhibitory connections, but we would also find (nonprobabilistic) constraints in the grammar prohibiting these co-occurrences. An alternative view is that the connections in Fig. 6.1 are the grammatical constraints, and there is no additional representation of the grammar. Many positions between these two views are also possible. For the purposes of this chapter, we have remained neutral with respect to these alternatives. Our primary points are that the lexicon encodes frequency information for both lexical-syntactic and lexical-semantic representations, and that this frequency information drives the lexical and syntactic ambiguity resolution processes.

processing. First, processing involves the spread of activation between units in the system (initiated by input from orthographic or phonological representations not shown in the figure). The degree of activation is an index of the amount of evidence in favor of a particular hypothesis (MacDonald, Just & Carpenter, 1992; Trueswell et al., in press), and the behavior of each unit in the system depends on the behaviors of the other units to which it is directly or indirectly connected. The net activation of a unit is dynamically updated to reflect these effects. Second, disambiguation involves activating one alternative at a given level and inhibiting all others. We envision this as a winner-take-all process of the sort implemented in previous interactive-activation models (e.g., Elman & McClelland, 1984). Third, processing is *analytically exhaustive,* meaning that disambiguation must be achieved at all levels of lexical representation. The idea here is that the comprehension system does not have the option of ignoring individual types of lexical information. Thus, sentences are processed and ambiguities are resolved at all possible levels of linguistic representation. This strong assumption will probably have to be relaxed to accommodate cases in which the communicative goals of the reader or listener can be achieved with only a partial analysis of a sentence. However, we view these as deviations from the normative situation.

Lexical Dominance and Contextual Constraint.   Given this conception of interactive processes within the lexicon, we can now consider the nature of contextual influences on these processes. Our view is that contexts operate by providing information that is relevant to resolving ambiguities at the different levels of representation within the lexicon. For example, a context might provide information about the grammatical category of a word that is ambiguous between noun and verb senses (e.g., *watch*), or it might provide information about its likely thematic role. Contexts can also provide lexical-semantic information relevant to discriminating between word meanings. Tabossi (1988) argued that this is how the contexts constrained meaning activation in her materials, and the "semantic priming" contexts of Seidenberg et al. (1982) may have affected processing in the same way. Contexts differ with respect to the amount of information they provide and the extent to which this information constrains the ambiguity resolution process.

Therefore, the scope of context effects is determined by: (a) the characteristics of interactive processing within the lexicon, (b) the extent and degree to which natural language contexts provide information relevant to resolving different types of ambiguities, and (c) the ways in which the different sources of constraint combine. The constraints that come from within the lexicon and from the broader context vary continuously in strength. For example, contexts vary from being very unconstraining (following "The next word in the sentence is," any word could occur) to very constraining ("I drink my coffee with cream and . . ."). Thus, we would expect to observe a broad range of outcomes from the interaction between lexical and contextual sources of constraint with regard to the course of the ambiguity-resolution process. In the well-studied area of meaning ambiguity, this broad range of outcomes has been obtained. Some studies have shown activation of multiple meanings of ambiguous words in biasing contexts (e.g., Swinney, 1979; Tanenhaus et al., 1979), whereas other studies using similar methodologies have yielded evidence for selective activation of the contextually appropriate meaning (Simpson &Krueger, 1991; Tabossi et al., 1987).

With this broad range of outcomes, the functional characteristics of lexical-contextual interactions will depend on both the structure of the lexicon and the nature of the context. Some general tendencies regarding these interactions have already been noted in the literature. Recall Marslen-Wilson's (1987) observation about "bottom–up priority" in lexical processing. Working in the domain of auditory word recognition, Marslen-Wilson observed that the computation of lexical information seems to dominate the effects of contextual constraints during lexical processing. The Kawamoto (1988, 1993) model instantiates this view, insofar as it was structured so that the associations between different types of lexical information (alternative meanings, orthography, phonology) were stronger than the associations between contextual information and specific parts of the lexical entry (e.g., one of the meanings). We can now see that bottom–up priority derives from two general characteristics of the processing system. First, there are facts about the nature of contextual constraints. The kinds of information provided by natural language contexts tend to be very useful in deciding between alternatives at a given level of ambiguity. However, they tend to be less effective at preselecting one of the alternatives (Seidenberg et al., 1982). For example, consider how contexts might affect the resolution of the morphological ambiguity associated with *raced*. Given the structure of English, it is often the case that a context will admit only the past-tense (or only the past-participle) form. Following a context of "The man who . . . ," for example, *raced* can only be a past-tense form. The question then is how the processing system makes use of this information. One possibility is that knowledge that only a past tense would be grammatical in this context obviates the morphological ambiguity entirely. Thus, when *raced* is recognized, only the past tense is activated. This is the way that context is assumed to work in selective-access models of lexical ambiguity resolution (Simpson & Krueger, 1991; Swinney & Hakes, 1976).

This description does not appear to characterize how contextual constraints function in general, however. The context "The man who . . ." does not dictate that the next word must be *raced,* or even that it must be a verb. Many other continuations are possible (e.g., "The man who people think . . ." "The man who slowly . . . ," etc.). Although the likelihood that the next word in "The man who . . ." will be a past participle is effectively zero, the likelihood that it is a past tense is not much higher, and it is unlikely that the processing system is set up to anticipate relatively low-frequency events.

One way to summarize these observations is to say that, although the architecture of the system affords the possibility of continuous interactions between contextual information and the lexicon, the effects of contexts tend to be more retroactive than proactive. The information provided by a context is often only weakly constraining, but it is typically quite sufficient to allow the comprehender to distinguish between a small number of alternatives (see Seidenberg et al., 1982, for discussion). Although the context "The man who . . ." does not specify that the next word must be a past-tense verb, once *raced* is identified as the next word, the only alternative morphological tense forms will be past tense or past participle, and the context will provide enough information to determine which is appropriate. In short, less information is needed to discriminate between two alternatives than to preselect one of them out of a whole range of possibilities. Thus, the nature of contextual constraints is such that they will typically provide useful information once lexical processing has yielded partial activation of multiple alternatives, but they typically do not provide sufficient information to restrict activation to the contextually appropriate alternative. Of course, these are general tendencies, rather than absolute restrictions. Clearly, there are some contexts that are so constraining as to make a particular word highly predictable ("I drink my coffee with cream and . . ."), and the processing system can apparently exploit this degree of contextual constraint when it is available (Fischler & Bloom, 1979; Juliano & Tanenhaus, 1993). However, words apparently achieve this high degree of predictability relatively infrequently, at least in English texts (Gough & Cosky, 1977).

A second crucial characteristic of the processing system is that properties of lexical processing limit the effects of contextual constraints even when they are strongly biasing. Consider again the Duffy et al. (1988) studies described earlier. They examined the processing of words with meaning ambiguities (e.g., *pitcher, port*) in contexts that provided clear disambiguating information. The effects of this contextual information were strongly limited by properties of lexical structure. When the context is consistent with the dominant (most frequent) meaning of an ambiguous word, the dominant meaning is assigned on line and the alternative, lower frequency meaning is not activated enough to be detected. Here, frequency is seen to have a significant impact on processing. For equibiased lexical ambiguities, a strongly constraining context promotes one reading to the point where the alternative is not activated enough to be detected using a measure such as fixation duration. Here, the context exerts a strong influence on the outcome, changing the pattern of activation within the lexicon. When the context favors the subordinate meaning of a nonequibiased ambiguity, both factors exert strong influences on processing. The context promotes the subordinate meaning to the point where it is activated enough to influence fixation durations. However, the influence of lexical structure is seen in the fact that the dominant meaning is still activated, now in parallel with the subordinate meaning. Thus, properties of processing within the lexicon—here, sensitivity to the frequency—limit the effects of even strong biasing contexts.

In summary, lexical items differ with respect to degree of ambiguity and the frequencies of the alternatives at each level of ambiguity, whereas contexts differ in terms of the degree to which they are informative about these ambiguities. The combination of these two general properties of language yields a processing system that is contextually constrained but lexically dominated. This account emerged largely from studies of meaning ambiguity. Given our view that syntactic ambiguities derive from the other types of lexical ambiguities, it follows that the processing of these ambiguities should exhibit similar characteristics vis-à-vis the interactions of lexical structure and contextual constraint. We discuss evidence bearing on this prediction next.

SYNTACTIC AMBIGUITY RESOLUTION

Given that much of syntactic ambiguity resolution involves lexical processing, we can now examine the extensive and often contradictory literature concerning ambiguity resolution for the MV/RR ambiguity. Discussions of this ambiguity within the garden-path model have focused on the fact that the two alternative interpretations result in two different phrase structures, but this ambiguity is also ambiguous at the lexical level in at least three ways (see Trueswell & Tanenhaus, this volume, for similar points). First, there is an ambiguity of tense morphology—the *-ed* ending on the ambiguous verb is interpreted as a past tense in the main-verb interpretation and as a past participle in the reduced-relative interpretation. Second, there is the argument structure ambiguity—the reduced-relative interpretation requires the transitive argument structure, whereas the main-verb interpretation may take a variety of structures (i.e., transitive, intransitive, etc). Finally, there is a voice ambiguity—the verb is interpreted in active voice in the main-verb structure, and passive in the reduced-relative structure.

Our hypothesis is that these three levels of ambiguity—tense, argument structure, and voice—are coded in the lexical representation of verbs. Like other lexical representations, these representations would include frequency information and would be affected by context in the way that other lexical ambiguities have been shown to be (Duffy et al., 1988). Given these assumptions concerning lexical representation and process, we predict that ambiguity resolution should be modulated by frequency effects over these three levels of lexical representation, and also by context effects, although with the same bottom–up priority that Marslen-Wilson (1987) noted for other aspects of lexical processing. We explore these predictions later for two of these representations, tense and argument structure, and examine the extent to which frequency and context information modulate ambiguity resolution for the MV/RR ambiguity. We omit the active–passive voice representation from this discussion because we know of no data available concerning the frequency of alternative voices of English verbs. We predict that the same principles should apply to voice information, however.

Frequency Effects in MV/RR-Ambiguity Resolution

The focus on phrase structure in the garden-path model has resulted in a lack of attention to frequency effects in the resolution of the MV/RR and other ambiguities, because it has been assumed that frequency information is not relevant to constructing syntactic representations. Frequency is very much a part of the lexically based view that we and Tanenhaus and colleagues advocate, however. Our claim is that there are several different lexical representations that are crucial to this ambiguity, and the relative frequencies of the alternatives at each level guide ambiguity resolution.

First, consider the past-tense versus past-participle tense morphology ambiguity that is present in all but a very few irregular verbs in English. Because the main-verb construction requires the past-tense and the reduced-relative construction requires the past-participle, we would expect that the frequency with which a verb appears in these two tenses in English could influence MV/RR ambiguity resolution, by way of influencing the activation levels of the alternative tenses in the lexical representation of the verb (Trueswell & Tanenhaus, this volume; Trueswell et al., in press). Although no experiments have explicitly manipulated the relative frequency of past-tense and past-participle uses for ambiguous verbs, suggestive evidence for the importance of frequency information comes from a reanalysis of one of our previous studies (Pearlmutter & MacDonald, 1992). This study was an extension of the plausibility manipulation conducted by Trueswell et al. in press) and examined the extent to which ambiguity effects in reading times could be predicted from off-line norming data that assessed the strength of the plausibility effects in the stimuli. Pearlmutter and MacDonald found a reliable relationship between plausibility and reading times, such that the more plausible the reduced-relative interpretation, the smaller the ambiguity effect in reading times. Our reanalysis concerned these normative data and their effects on the reading times. We investigated whether the plausibility ratings were themselves a function of the relative frequency of past- *vs* past-participle tenses in the ambiguous verbs, as measured by Francis and Kučera (1982) and supplemented by our own examination of the *Wall Street Journal* corpus for some verbs with very low Francis and Kučera frequencies. We found that within the items that had been designed to be plausible in the reduced-relative interpretation, a higher percentage of past-participle uses relative to past-tense uses of the ambiguous verb was associated with higher plausibility ratings in the normative data ($r = .54, p < .01$). Thus tense frequency was one of the factors that contributed to the plausibility differences that were a reliable predictor of reading times in Pearlmutter & MacDonald (1992). Tabossi et al. (in press) report a similar result for their own data. These results show that an important factor that contributed to the plausibility of the alternative interpretations in Pearlmutter and MacDonald's stimuli was a lexical one, the relative frequency of the alternative tense interpretations.

The lexical account suggests that a similar effect should obtain with the relative frequency of alternative argument structures. The main-verb interpretation can accommodate several argument structures, including both transitive and intransitive, but the reduced-relative interpretation requires the transitive argument structure. Therefore, argument structure frequency should have a substantial effect on MV/RR ambiguity resolution: The lower the frequency of the transitive argument structure relative to other alternatives for a verb, the less likely an MV/RR ambiguity will be resolved with a reduced-relative interpretation. MacDonald (in press, Experiment 3) tested this prediction by investigating comprehension difficulty in a self-paced reading experiment for ambiguous sentences resolved with the reduced-relative interpretation, in which the verbs varied in argument structure frequency. In one condition, the verbs (e.g., *pushed, carried*) had higher frequency transitive than intransitive argument structures (as measured in Connine, Ferreira, Jones, Clifton & Frazier, 1984). In another condition, the verbs were more frequent in their intransitive than transitive structures (e.g., *moved, raced*). MacDonald found that comprehenders had difficulty resolving the ambiguous reduced-relative sentences only in the second condition, where the required transitive argument structure was lower in frequency than the intransitive structure, evidenced by longer reading times at the disambiguation compared with the same region for unambiguous controls. When the ambiguous verbs were more frequent in the transitive than in the intransitive structure, however, the ambiguous sentences were no more difficult than unambiguous controls. This example conforms to the pattern of effects in lexical ambiguity resolution: Item-specific information (in this case the frequency of a verb's alternative argument structures) modulates the extent to which one interpretation is preferred over another. Again, such a result is not predicted by minimal attachment—accommodation within the garden-path model requires the stipulation that, after application of the minimal-attachment strategy has caused all ambiguities to be assigned the main-verb interpretation, some of them are later reanalyzed with the reduced-relative interpretation. No evidence of reanalysis is revealed in MacDonald's reading-time data. Indeed, analyses of some critical regions in this experiment suggest that the argument structure frequency information guided ambiguity resolution from the first introduction of the ambiguity, so that invoking minimal attachment as an explanation in this case leads to incorrect predictions about the ambiguity resolution process.

The literature provides no data for how these two frequency effects (tense morphology and argument structure) might be related to one another because no study has explicitly manipulated both of these factors. However, a simple statisti-

TABLE 6.2
Tense-Morphology and Argument-Structure
Conjoint Probabilities

Tense Morphology and Argument Structure	Verb	
	Raced	Carried
Past tense, intransitive	.82	.03
Past tense, transitive	.10	.45
Past participle, intransitive	.07	.03
Past participle, transitive	.01*	.49*

Note. The argument-structure and tense-morphology combination that is necessary for the RR construction is marked with an asterisk.

cal analysis reveals that the conjunction of the two should be quite powerful in guiding the ambiguity resolution process because the reduced-relative interpretation requires the conjunction of both the past-participle tense and the transitive argument structure. Consider again the example of "The horse raced past the barn fell," compared with the situation in which *carried* replaces *raced*. The two verbs differ on past-tense versus past-participle frequency (Francis & Kučera, 1982): *Raced* is used as a past participle only 8% of the time, whereas *carried* is a past participle 52% of the time. The verbs also differ on argument structure frequencies: *Raced* is transitive about 11% of the time, whereas *carried* is transitive about 94% of the time (Connine et al., 1984). Table 6.2 shows the probabilities of different combinations of these alternatives. The table shows that *raced* is overwhelmingly unlikely to be introducing a reduced relative because the probability of *raced* having both the transitive argument structure and past-participle interpretation of the *-ed* ending is less than 1%. By contrast, the conjoint probability of *carried* being both a past participle and transitive is 49%. This result does not mean that *carried* appears in reduced relatives 49% of the time—there are still other uses of transitive past participles that do not involve a reduced relative, including uses like *had carried, was carried,* and so on. The point is that some enabling conditions exist that make *carried* a possible candidate to be introducing a reduced relative clause, whereas these conditions do not exist for *raced*.[2] The conjunction of several different kinds of frequency information is therefore likely to be extremely important for resolving this ambiguity, and the table shows that there are substantial differences across verbs in the frequencies that are relevant for this ambiguity.

---

[2]We have made the simplifying assumption here that tense morphology and argument structure probabilities are independent, but this need not be true for some or all verbs.

The Effects of Context

In addition to lexical-frequency information, the MV/RR ambiguity is also affected by constraints from the surrounding context. Consider the animacy manipulation investigated by Trueswell et al. (in press) in sentences like "The witness/evidence examined by the lawyer was useless." Trueswell et al. hypothesized that these sentences provide a context that influences the plausibility of the order of thematic-role assignments: Although *witness* is a good agent for *examined, evidence,* being inanimate, is a highly implausible agent. Thus, the assignment of the thematic role of agent to the subject NP is favored in *witness examined,* whereas the theme role is favored for the subject in *evidence examined.* These plausibility effects should influence ambiguity resolution because the assignment of agent to the subject is possible only in the main-verb interpretation, whereas assignment of theme to the subject in this structure requires the reduced-relative interpretation. The Trueswell et al. results support this account. Ambiguous sentences resolved with the reduced-relative interpretation were more difficult than unambiguous controls when animacy information supported the incorrect main-verb interpretation (*defendant examined*), but not when the subject noun was inanimate (*evidence*), supporting the reduced-relative interpretation. These animacy effects have been replicated and extended to plausibility effects that do not depend on animacy (MacDonald, in press; Pearlmutter & MacDonald, 1992; Tabossi, Spivey-Knowlton, McRae, & Tanenhaus, 1993). In addition, following Crain and Steedman's (1985) suggestion, discourse-level context effects have also been demonstrated (Spivey-Knowlton et al., 1993; Trueswell & Tanenhaus, 1991, 1992).

At the same time, other studies have failed to find plausibility or discourse-context effects (Britt, Perfetti, Garrod, & Rayner, 1992; Ferreira & Clifton, 1986; Rayner, et al., 1983; Rayner, Garrod, & Perfetti, 1992). These conflicting findings have frequently been attributed to differences in methodologies (Ferreira & Clifton, 1986; Rayner et al., 1992) or to differences in context strength (McClelland, 1987; Trueswell et al., in press; Tyler, 1989). An additional hypothesis is that these differences are due to lexical frequency effects owing to the use of different stimuli across studies (Trueswell et al., in press). As discussed in the introduction, the Duffy et al. (1988) empirical investigation and the Kawamoto (1988, 1993) model of context and frequency effects in lexical ambiguity resolution suggested that context effects on lexical processing are constrained by frequency. Contextual support for a lower frequency meaning is generally not strong enough to eliminate the advantage of the higher frequency meaning. The same effects should hold for the other aspects of lexical representation considered here, in that contextual information should be able to affect the interpretation of the MV/RR ambiguity most clearly when the ambiguous verb is roughly equibiased in its alternative interpretations for tense morphology, argument structure, voice, and so on. When one alternative interpretation at a given level of representation is much more frequent than another, however, contextual factors supporting the subordinate interpretation are much less effective.

We explored the extent to which the conflicts in the literature concerning context effects were due to differing frequency biases in the ambiguous verbs in the different studies. The prediction is that the studies that yielded context effects used relatively equibiased verbs; hence, contextual information favoring the reduced-relative interpretation could be used to assign this structure on line. In contrast, the studies that failed to yield context effects are predicted to have used verbs that were strongly biased to the main-verb interpretation. Ideally, argument structure, voice, and tense-frequency biases should all be examined for verbs that have been used in previous experiments. However, data concerning voice frequency are not available as yet, and there is not enough information about the argument structure frequencies of English verbs to assess even 20% of those that have been used in previous studies. Therefore, an analysis using only morphological tense information (Francis & Kučera, 1982) was conducted. It revealed some very interesting relationships between morphological-tense frequency and context effects in the literature.

Table 6.3 reviews the 12 published studies of context effects in the MV/RR ambiguity that contained the relevant data in appendices. The second column of the table reports the percentage of past-participle uses in English for the verbs in each study (from Francis & Kučera, 1982). The studies are ordered from lowest to highest mean past-participle frequency. Additional columns indicate the type of context manipulation and the reading-time measure. The last column of the table indicates the results obtained in conditions when context favored the reduced-relative interpretation. Four studies found that subjects still had difficulty with the reduced-relative interpretation in the presence of helpful context information (the minimal-attachment result, in which helpful context is ignored), whereas six other studies found that comprehenders had little or no difficulty resolving the ambiguity in the presence of helpful context. As in the lexical semantic ambiguity research, the effectiveness of the context manipulation varied with the relative frequencies of the alternatives. The mean past-participle frequency for the four studies that found no context effects was 49.7%, whereas the eight studies that did find a context effect had a past-participle frequency of 62.1%—a reliable difference [$t(10) = 2.47$, $p < .05$]. As predicted, the studies that found that helpful context made it easy to interpret ambiguous sentences in favor of the reduced-relative interpretation are the studies that used verbs that more closely approximated equibiased items.[3] However, studies that used verbs

---

[3]Recall that it is the conjunction of several factors that is important for the reduced relative interpretation, including voice- and argument-structure frequencies, for which little data are available. Thus, although 49.7% past-participle frequency is quite close to equibiased for the tense-morphology level of representation, a 62.1% past-participle frequency is more likely to yield an equibiased conjunction of the several factors that are necessary for the reduced relative interpretation.

TABLE 6.3
Effects of Prior Context Modulated by Verb Tense Frequency Information

Study	%PPart	Manipulation of Prior Context	Measure	Early Effects in Helpful Context Condition
Rayner, Garrod, & Perfetti (1992)	44.4	Pragmatic	Eye tracking	Minimal attachment
Britt, Perfetti, Garrod, & Rayner (1992)	47	Pragmatic	SP-word	Minimal attachment
Ferreira & Clifton (1986)	47.4	Thematic-anim	Eye tracking, SP-phrase	Minimal attachment
Trueswell & Tanenhaus (1991, 1992)	47.6	Pragmatic	SP-phrase (1991), Eye tracking (1992)	Context helps
Ni & Crain (1990)	51.6	Pragmatic	SP-GJ	Context helps
Rayner, Carlson, & Frazier (1983)	60	Thematic-plaus	Eye tracking	Minimal attachment
Trueswell, Tanenhaus & Garnsey, 1993	61	Thematic-anim	Eye tracking, SP-word	Context helps
MacDonald (in press, Exp 2)	64.1	Thematic-anim	SP-word	Context helps
Burgess (1991)	65.5	Thematic-anim	SP-word, SP-phrase	Context helps (SP-phrase)
Tabossi, McRae, Spivey-Knowlton, & Tanenhaus (1993)	66.9	Thematic-plaus & anim	SP-phrase	Context helps
Spivey-Knowlton, Trueswell, & Tanenhaus (1993)	71.3	Pragmatic	SP-phrase, SP-word	Context helps
Pearlmutter & MacDonald (1992)	75.8	Thematic-plaus	SP-word	Context helps

Note. %PPart = Mean percentage of past-participle (vs. past-tense) usage of ambiguous verbs in stimulus materials, as measured by Francis and Kučera (1983); Thematic-anim = thematic-role manipulation using animacy; Thematic-plus = thematic-role manipulation using plausibility (with animacy controlled); Pragmatic = pragmatic manipulation of felicity of reduced relative interpretation; SP-word = self-paced reading, one word at a time; SP-phrase = self-paced reading, one phrase (usually 2–3 words) at a time; SP-GJ = self-paced reading with grammaticality judgment at each frame; Minimal attachment = presence of helpful context did not prevent garden pathing; Context helps = helpful context did prevent all or most garden pathing.

more strongly biased to the main-verb interpretation found that context could not promote the subordinate reduced-relative interpretation to the exclusion of the dominant (main-verb) one. The observed relationship holds, despite wide variations across the studies in type of context, strength of context, and reading-time measure. Indeed, it is worth noting, in light of the extensive criticism of self-paced reading (Ferreira & Clifton, 1986; Rayner et al., 1992), that Table 6.3 does not reveal a pattern in which eye-tracking data support the minimal-attachment model and self-paced data (by word or by phrase) support an interaction model. Instead, each of the three methods has produced data in support of minimal attachment, and the same three methods have also yielded early context effects.

In summary, the interpretation of the MV/RR ambiguity depends on at least two pieces of lexical information: the frequencies of the past-participle form and the transitive-argument structure. Given a verb with frequency biases that make the reduced-relative interpretation a viable option, contextual information can guide the comprehender to one or the other interpretation. This is the result that was obtained in six studies in Table 6.3, where helpful context eliminated any difficulty with the reduced-relative interpretation. However, the same contextual information will likely have little effect if the lexical biases of the ambiguous verb overwhelmingly favor the main-verb interpretation. This result replicates the pattern found by Duffy et al. (1988) for lexical semantic ambiguities. This parallel between the effects of context and frequency on meaning ambiguities (Duffy et al., 1988), and the effects of context and frequency in the MV/RR ambiguity noted here, is exactly what is expected if the MV/RR ambiguity is resolved through lexical processes.

GENERAL DISCUSSION

This chapter has sketched a generalized theory of ambiguity resolution that subsumes both syntactic and lexical types. A major component of this theory is a greatly enriched conception of the mental lexicon. This enrichment took two forms. We assumed that the lexicon is the repository for all types of knowledge associated with words, including their syntactic functions, and that rather than merely listing these different types of information, the lexicon encodes the grammatical and probabilistic relationships that hold among them. This approach permits a radical rethinking of the syntactic ambiguities that have been at the center of research on language comprehension. Rather than deriving from ambiguities with regard to the construction of phrase structure trees, they can be seen as deriving from ambiguities inherent in lexical items. Moreover, much grammatical knowledge (e.g., the fact that two types of information can or cannot co-occur; the fact that only some phrase structures are well formed) can be encoded by the structure of the lexicon (e.g., whether the connections between units representing different types of information are excitatory or inhibitory). Insofar as syntactic structures have a lexical basis, we predicted that syntactic processing should be governed by independently established principles concerning lexical processing, in particular lexical (i.e., meaning) ambiguity resolution. The factors implicated in the lexical ambiguity research include the structure of the ambiguous word (e.g., the relative frequencies of meanings) and the extent to which the context provides information relevant to distinguishing between the alternatives. This research also demonstrated that the effects of contextual constraints are modulated by lexical factors, and this was shown to carry over to the resolution of the MV/RR ambiguity.

This theory also sheds light on the question of the scope of contextual effects on processing. Previous research assessed whether information provided by the context could be used to "override" the minimal-attachment pattern, with the studies yielding a mixed pattern of results. From our perspective, framing the question in this way ignores two critical factors: (a) the nature of the information provided by the context, and (b) facts about the lexical items creating the ambiguity that constrain context effects. Contexts obviously differ in the extent to which they provide disambiguating information; contexts that are only weakly constraining would not be expected to have a large impact in anyone's theory. In the absence of an account of the factors that determine the strength of a contextual manipulation, the mere failure to override minimal attachment with a particular set of stimulus materials is not very informative. We have suggested that most contexts probably *are* weakly constraining, in the sense that they provide an effective basis for deciding between a small number of alternatives but are less effective in isolating a single alternative in advance. Moreover, the effects of contextual information are limited by lexical factors, specifically the frequencies of the alternatives at different levels. Putting these factors together yields a system that is "contextually constrained but lexically dominated." This theory admits a broad range of possible outcomes, including both minimal attachment and override of minimal attachment with appropriate stimulus materials. With the emergence of a theory of relevant aspects of lexical structure and contextual information, it is possible to replace the question of whether the parser does or does not follow the minimal-attachment principle with questions concerning the ways in which a variety of grammatical and probabilistic constraints interact to yield the range of outcomes that are observed.

This alternative conception of the ambiguity resolution process is in no way less "theoretical" or "principled" than previous accounts such as the garden-path model, which characterized parsing as the result of general structural principles such as minimal attachment. The lean principled look for the first-stage parser in the garden-path model is deceptive because it was purchased at the expense of underspecifying the second-stage thematic processor and the interaction between the two stages. This model also failed to yield a correct account of the factors that modulate syntactic ambiguity resolution, as shown in Table 6.3. Our account instead incorporates a broader set of principles under which both lexical and syntactic ambiguity can be subsumed, and which captures both frequency and context effects. The general principles we invoke include: (a) frequency-sensitive representations, (b) the nature of constraint-satisfaction mechanisms, and (c) the (typically weak) effect of context on lexical processes. An account of the probabilistic effects that predominate language processing is not less principled than a structural account that ignores these effects.

This change in theoretical emphasis necessitates important changes in the design of sentence-processing experiments and in the analysis of reading-time data. Studies of the garden-path model have typically employed factorial designs, in which the goal was to assess a main effect of ambiguity. Thus, longer latencies for sentences resolved with the reduced-relative reading in the MV/RR structure compared with unambiguous controls were taken as evidence for the minimal-attachment strategy. Parsing preferences depend on item-specific factors such as the frequencies of the argument structures associated with verbs, which differ in degree. These effects may not be apparent from an omnibus analysis of variance, but they do emerge when appropriate correlational analyses are performed (MacDonald, in press; Pearlmutter & MacDonald, 1992; Tabossi et al., 1993; Trueswell & Tanenhaus, this volume). Moreover, in assessing strategies such as minimal attachment, it will be important to take care in evaluating the status of the particular verbs that are employed in stimulus materials with regard to the factors now seen to control parsing preferences.

Our approach provides additional perspective on the debate between "modular" and "interactive" models. The phenomena that were taken as evidence for a modular lexicon (e.g., the multiple-access pattern; Swinney, 1979) or a modular parser (e.g., the garden-path effect) are seen as arising from more basic facts about the structure of the lexicon and the nature of contextual constraints. The basic processing mechanism is constraint satisfaction over all available sources of information. It may be convenient to think of lexical knowledge as a "module" if that means a distinct type of knowledge. However, the assumption that it is encapsulated (Fodor, 1983) cannot be maintained. Insofar as syntactic information can be represented and computed within the lexicon, it is an open question whether there is anything uniquely attributable to a separate parsing module.

The view outlined in this chapter promotes further investigation into how grammatical and probabilistic constraints interact in the course of ambiguity resolution. Areas of particular interest include: (a) whether other syntactic ambiguities can similarly be analyzed as stemming from lexical processes (see MacDonald, Pearlmutter & Seidenberg, 1993; Sedivy & Spivey-Knowlton, this volume; Trueswell, Tanenhaus & Kello, 1993); (b) the boundaries on the types of lexical frequency information that comprehenders possess (Juliano & Tanenhaus, 1993); (c) the essence of what makes a context constraining at a given level of linguistic processing; and (d) the extent to which all syntactic processes can be represented as part of lexical representations. We consider such a wide array of questions—many of which have received very little attention under more traditional theories of ambiguity resolution—both a challenge and an opportunity for research on the nature of human language comprehension.

ACKNOWLEDGMENT

This article is adapted from MacDonald et al. (1993). Our research was supported by National Science Foundation grant DBS-9120415, a grant from the Zumberge Research Innovation Fund at the University of Southern California (MCM), an NSF predoctoral fellowship at MIT (NJP), and National Institute of Mental Health grant MH-47566 (MSS).

REFERENCES

Altmann, G.T.M., & Steedman, M. (1988). Interaction with context during human sentence processing. *Cognition, 30,* 191–238.

Barsalou, L. W. (1987). The instability of graded structure: Implications for the nature of concepts. In U. Neisser (Ed.), *Concepts and conceptual development.* (pp. 101–140). Cambridge, England: Cambridge University Press.

Bever, T. G. (1970). The cognitive basis for linguistic structure. In J. R. Hayes (Ed.), *Cognitive development of language.* (pp. 279–363). New York: Wiley.

Boland, J. & Tanenhaus, M. (1991). The role of lexical representations in sentence processing. In G. B. Simpson (Ed.), *Understanding word and sentence.* (pp. 331–366). Amsterdam: North-Holland.

Bresnan, J. (1982). *The mental representation of grammatical relations.* Cambridge, MA: MIT Press.

Britt, M. A., Perfetti, C. A., Garrod, S., & Rayner, K. (1992). Parsing in discourse: Context effects and their limits. *Journal of Memory and Language, 31,* 293–314.

Burgess, C. (1991). *Interaction of semantic, syntactic and visual factors in syntactic ambiguity resolution.* Unpublished doctoral dissertation, University of Rochester.

Carlson, G. N., & Tanenhaus, M. K. (1988). Thematic roles and language comprehension. In W. Wilkins (Ed.) *Syntax and semantics, Vol. 21: Thematic relations.* (pp. 263–289). London: Academic Press.

Chomsky, N. (1965). *Aspects of the theory of syntax.* Cambridge, MA: MIT Press.

Chomsky, N. (1981). *Lectures on government and binding.* Dordrecht, The Netherlands: Foris.

Connine, C., Ferreira, F., Jones, C., Clifton, C., & Frazier, L. (1984). Verb Frame Preferences: Descriptive Norms. *Journal of Psycholinguistic Research, 13,* 307–319.

Conrad, C. (1974). Context effects in sentence comprehension: A study of the subjective lexicon. *Memory & Cognition, 2,* 130–138.

Crain, S., & Steedman, M. (1985). On not being led up the garden path: The use of context by the psychological syntax processor. In D. R. Dowty, L. Karttunen, & A. M. Zwicky (Eds.). *Natural language processing* (pp. 320–358). Cambridge, England: Cambridge University Press.

Duffy, S., Morris, R., & Rayner, K. (1988). Lexical ambiguity and fixation times in reading. *Journal of Memory and Language, 27,* 429–446.

Elman, J. L., & McClelland, J. L. (1984). Speech perception as a cognitive process: The interactive activation model. In N. Lass (Ed.), *Speech and language* (Vol. 10, pp. 337–374). New York: Academic Press.

Ferreira, F., & Clifton, C. (1986). The independence of syntactic processing. *Journal of Memory and Language, 25*, 348–368.

Fillmore, C. J. (1968). The case for case. In E. Bach & R. Harms (Eds.), *Universals in linguistic theory.* (pp. 1–90). New York: Holt, Rinehart & Winston.

Fischler, I., & Bloom, P. (1979). Automatic and attentional processes in the effects of sentence contexts on word recognition. *Journal of Verbal Learning and Verbal Behavior, 18*, 1–20.

Fodor, J. A. (1983). *Modularity of mind.* Cambridge, MA: MIT Press.

Fodor, J. D. (1978). Parsing strategies and constraints on transformations. *Linguistic Inquiry, 9*, 427–473.

Ford, M., Bresnan, J., & Kaplan, R. M. (1982). A competence-based theory of syntactic closure. In J. Bresnan (Ed.), *The Mental Representation of Grammatical Relations,* (pp. 727–796). Cambridge, MA: MIT Press.

Francis, W. N., & Kučera, H. (1982). *Frequency analysis of English usage: Lexicon and grammar.* Boston: Houghton Mifflin.

Frazier, L. (1979). *On comprehending sentences: Syntactic parsing strategies.* Bloomington, IN: Indiana University Linguistics Club.

Frazier, L. (1989). Against lexical generation of syntax. In W. Marslen-Wilson (Ed.), *Lexical representation and process* (pp. 505–528). Cambridge, MA: MIT Press.

Frazier, L., & Rayner, K. (1987). Resolution of syntactic category ambiguities: Eye movements in parsing lexically ambiguous sentences. *Journal of Memory and Language, 26*, 505–526.

Gough, P., & Cosky, M. J. (1977). One second of reading again. In N. J. Castellan, Jr., D. B. Pisoni, & G. R. Potts (Eds.), *Cognitive theory* (Vol. 2, pp. 271–288). Hillsdale, NJ: Lawrence Erlbaum Associates.

Grimshaw, J. (1990). *Argument structure.* Cambridge, MA: MIT Press.

Gruber, J. (1976). *Lexical structures in syntax and semantics.* Amsterdam: North-Holland.

Hinton, G. (1986). Learning distributed representations of concepts. *Proceedings of the Eighth Annual Meeting of the Cognitive Science Society* (pp. 161–188). Hillsdale, NJ: Lawrence Erlbaum Associates.

Hogaboam, T., & Perfetti, C. (1975). Lexical ambiguity and sentence comprehension. *Journal of Verbal Learning and Verbal Behavior, 14*, 265–274.

Jackendoff, R. (1972). *Semantic interpretation in generative grammar.* Cambridge, MA: MIT Press.

Juliano, C., & Tanenhaus, M. K. (1993). Contingent frequency effects in syntactic ambiguity resolution. In *Proceedings of the Fifteenth Annual Conference of the Cognitive Science Society.* (pp. 593–598). Hillsdale, NJ: Lawrence Erlbaum Associates.

Kawamoto, A. (1988). Interactive processes in the resolution of lexical ambiguity. In S. Small, G. Cottrell, & M. K. Tanenhaus (Eds.), *Lexical ambiguity resolution: Computational, linguistic, and psychological perspectives* (pp. 195–228). San Mateo, CA: Morgan Kaufman.

Kawamoto, A. (1993). Nonlinear dynamics in the resolution of lexical ambiguity: A parallel distributed processing account. *Journal of Memory and Language, 32*, 474–516.

Levin, B., & Rappaport, M. (1986). The formation of adjectival passives. *Linguistic Inquiry, 17*, 623–661.

MacDonald, M. C. (in press). Probabilistic constraints and syntactic ambiguity resolution. *Language and Cognitive Processes*.

MacDonald, M. C., Just, M. A., & Carpenter, P. A. (1992). Working memory constraints on the processing of syntactic ambiguity. *Cognitive Psychology, 24*, 56–98.

MacDonald, M. C., Pearlmutter, N. J., & Seidenberg, M. S. (1993). The lexical basis of syntactic ambiguity resolution. Manuscript submitted for publication.

Mackworth, A. K. (1977). Consistency in networks of relations. *Artificial Intelligence, 8*, 99–118.

MacWhinney, B., & Bates, E. (Eds.) (1989). *The crosslinguistic study of sentence processing.* Cambridge, England: Cambridge University Press.

Marslen-Wilson, W. D. (1987). Functional parallelism in spoken word-recognition. *Cognition, 25,* 71–102.

McClelland, J. L. (1987). The case for interactionism in language processing. In M. Coltheart (Ed.), *Attention and performance XII: The psychology of reading.* (pp. 3–36). London: Lawrence Erlbaum Associates.

McClelland, J. L., & Rumelhart, D. E. (1981). An interactive activation model of context effects in letter perception: Part 1. An account of basic findings. *Psychological Review, 88,* 375–407.

McClelland, J. L., Rumelhart, D. E., & Hinton, G. E. (1986). The appeal of parallel distributed processing. In D. E. Rumelhart & J. L. McClelland (Eds.), *Parallel distributed processing.* (pp. 3–44). Cambridge, MA: MIT Press.

Merrill, E. C., Sperber, R. D., & McCauley, C. (1981). Differences in semantic encoding as a function of reading comprehension skill. *Memory & Cognition, 9,* 618–624.

Morton, J. (1969). Interaction of information in word recognition. *Psychological Review, 76,* 165–178.

Ni, W., & Crain, S. (1990). How to resolve structural ambiguities. *Proceedings of the 20th annual meeting of the North Eastern Linguistic Society.*

Pearlmutter, N. J., & MacDonald, M. C. (1992). Plausibility and syntactic ambiguity resolution. In *Proceedings of the Fourteenth Annual Conference of the Cognitive Society.* (pp. 498–503). Hillsdale, NJ: Lawrence Erlbaum Associates.

Pearlmutter, N. J., Daugherty, K., MacDonald, M. C., & Seidenberg, M. S. (1993, March). Constraint satisfaction in main verb/reduced relative ambiguities. Poster presented at the Sixth Annual CUNY Conference on Human Sentence Processing, Amherst, MA.

Prince, A., & Smolensky, P. (in press). *Optimality theory.* Cambridge, MA: MIT Press.

Rayner, K., Carlson, M., & Frazier, L. (1983). The interaction of syntax and semantics during sentence processing. *Journal of Verbal Learning and Verbal Behavior, 22,* 358–374.

Rayner, K., & Duffy, S. A. (1986). Lexical complexity and fixation times in reading: Effects of word frequency, verb complexity, and lexical ambiguity. *Memory and Cognition, 14,* 191–201.

Rayner, K., Garrod, S., & Perfetti, C. A. (1992). Discourse influences during parsing are delayed. *Cognition, 45,* 109–139.

Rumelhart, D. (1977). Toward an interactive model of reading. In S. Dornic (Ed.), *Attention & performance VI* (pp. 573–603). Hillsdale, NJ: Lawrence Erlbaum Associates.

Seidenberg, M. S., Tanenhaus, M. K., Leiman, J. M., & Bienkowski, M. (1982). Automatic access of the meanings of ambiguous words in context: Some limitations of knowledge-based processing. *Cognitive Psychology, 14,* 489–537.

Simpson, G. (1981). Lexical ambiguity and its role in models of word recognition. *Psychological Bulletin, 96,* 316–340.

Simpson, G., & Krueger, M. (1991). Selective access of homograph meanings in sentence context. *Journal of Memory & Language, 30,* 627–643.

Spivey-Knowlton, M., Trueswell, J., & Tanenhaus, M. K. (1993). Context and syntactic ambiguity resolution. *Canadian Journal of Psychology, 47,* 276–309.

St. John, M., & McClelland, J. L. (1990). Learning and applying contextual constraints in sentence comprehension. *Artificial Intelligence, 46,* 217–257.

Stabler, E. (1993). *The logical approach to syntax: Foundations, specifications, and implementations of theories of government and binding.* Cambridge, MA: MIT Press.

Stowe, L. A. (1989). Thematic structures and sentence comprehension. In G. N. Carlson & M. K. Tanenhaus (Eds.) *Linguistic structure in language processing* (pp. 319–357). Dordrecht, The Netherlands: Kluwer.

Stowell, T. (1981). *Origins of phrase structure.* Unpublished doctoral dissertation, Massachusetts Institute of Technology, Cambridge, MA.

Swinney, D. A. (1979). Lexical access during sentence comprehension: (Re)consideration of context effects. *Journal of Verbal Learning and Verbal Behavior, 18,* 645–660.

Swinney, D. A., & Hakes, D. (1976). Effects of prior context upon lexical access during sentence comprehension. *Journal of Verbal Learning and Verbal Behavior, 15,* 681–689.

Tabossi, P. (1988). Accessing lexical ambiguity in different types of sentential context. *Journal of Memory and Language, 27,* 324–340.

Tabossi, P., Colombo, L., & Job, R. (1987). Accessing lexical ambiguity: Effects of context and dominance. *Psychological Research, 49,* 161–167.

Tabossi, P., Spivey-Knowlton, M., McRae, K., & Tanenhaus, M. K. (1993). Semantic effects on syntactic ambiguity resolution: Evidence for a constraint-based resolution process. In C. Umilta & M. Moscovitch (Eds.), *Attention & Performance XV.* Hillsdale, NJ: Lawrence Erlbaum Associates.

Tanenhaus, M. K., & Carlson, G. (1989). Lexical structure and language comprehension. In W. Marslen-Wilson (Ed.), *Lexical Representation and Process* (pp. 527–561). Cambridge, MA: MIT Press.

Tanenhaus, M. K., Leiman, J. M., & Seidenberg, M. S. (1979). Evidence for multiple stages in the processing of ambiguous words in syntactic contexts. *Journal of Verbal Learning and Verbal Behavior, 18,* 427–440.

Trueswell, J. C., & Tanenhaus, M. K. (1991). Tense temporal context and syntactic ambiguity resolution. *Language and Cognitive Processes, 6,* 339–350.

Trueswell, J. C., & Tanenhaus, M. K. (1992). Consulting temporal context during sentence comprehension: Evidence from the monitoring of eye movements in reading. *Proceedings of the Fourteenth Annual Conference of the Cognitive Society* (pp. 492–497). Hillsdale, NJ: Lawrence Erlbaum Associates.

Trueswell, J. C., Tanenhaus, M. K., & Garnsey, S. M. (in press). Semantic influences on parsing: Use of thematic role information in syntactic disambiguation. *Journal of Memory and Language.*

Tyler, L.K.T. (1989). The role of lexical representations in language comprehension. In W. Marslen-Wilson, (Ed.), *Lexical Representation and Process* (pp. 439–462. Cambridge, MA: MIT Press.

7
Toward a Lexicalist Framework for Constraint-Based Syntactic Ambiguity Resolution

John C. Trueswell
University of Pennsylvania

Michael K. Tanenhaus
University of Rochester

There is general agreement within the neuroscience and cognitive-science communities that complex multidimensional stimuli are represented and processed in at least partially independent subsystems or "modules." However, real-time processing typically results in local indeterminacy or ambiguity within a module because each subsystem is operating with a limited amount of information. Two general approaches for resolving these indeterminacies have been explored in depth within the cognition and perception literature. One approach is to incorporate domain-specific decision principles into each module. This preserves encapsulation (processing modularity) at the cost of inconsistent solutions across modules that later have to be reconciled. The other approach, which we argue for, is to make use of correlated information from within and across domains, without appealing to domain-specific principles. Although this approach violates the more traditional views of processing encapsulation, consistent solutions across domains can be rapidly coordinated. Within language comprehension, these approaches have been reflected in two-stage parsing models and in interactive or constraint-based models.

Most research on syntactic-ambiguity resolution has been guided by two-stage parsing models, in which an encapsulated syntactic processor within a modular architecture plays a privileged role in structuring the initial input to the language-comprehension system. During the first stage, the system makes an initial commitment to a single structure based on a restricted domain of purely syntactic information. Information that is not used in making initial commitments is then used to evaluate and, if necessary, revise the initial structure (e.g., Clifton, 1993; Clifton, Speer, & Abney, 1991; Ferreira & Clifton, 1986; Ford, 1988; Frazier,

1987, 1989; Frazier & Rayner, 1982; Mitchell, 1987, 1989; Mitchell, Corley, & Garnham, 1992; Pritchett, 1992).

Two-stage models can, of course, differ in what information is used in initial syntactic processing and in what decision principles they propose. The most influential two-stage model is the "garden-path" model originally proposed by Frazier and Rayner (1982) and further developed in more recent work by Frazier, Clifton, Rayner, and Ferreira (e.g., Clifton et al., 1991; Ferreira & Clifton, 1986; Ferreira & Henderson, 1990, 1991; Frazier, 1987, 1989, 1991; Rayner, Carlson, & Frazier, 1983; Rayner, Garrod, & Perfetti, 1992). In this model, the first-stage parser "attaches" each word into the structure it is building by using phrase-structure rules that apply to syntactic categories. At points of ambiguity, attachments follow a few structurally defined parsing principles such as minimal attachment (make the syntactically simplest attachment). These parsing principles are domain specific. They allow the syntactic module to initially structure the input without appealing to lexically specific syntactic information or to potentially relevant constraints from other domains (e.g., semantics and/or discourse context). Processing difficulty due to syntactic misanalysis (i.e., a garden path) is predicted to occur whenever a sentence with a local-syntactic ambiguity turns out to have a syntactic structure different from that predicted by the parsing principles.

In contrast, interactive or constraint-based models have assumed that multiple alternatives are at least partially available, and that ambiguity resolution is accomplished by the use of correlated constraints from other domains (e.g., Mac-Donald, in press; Marslen-Wilson, 1973; McClelland, St. John, & Taraban, 1989; Spivey-Knowlton, Trueswell, & Tanenhaus, 1993; Trueswell, Tanenhaus, & Garnsey, in press). Within a constraint-based architecture, ambiguity resolution is a continuous, constraint-satisfaction process. The effectiveness of a non-syntactic constraint at a point of ambiguity will depend on its strength and relevance (e.g., how strongly correlated it is with a syntactic alternative) and the availability of the alternative that it biases at the point of the ambiguity (Spivey-Knowlton et al., 1993). Processing difficulty occurs when there is inconsistent biasing information (e.g., a prior context that supports a less frequent alternative, a subsequent disambiguating phrase that favors an unsupported alternative).

Recent constraint-based models have emphasized the use of rich lexical representations that incorporate information about how a word combines syntactically and semantically with other words in a sentence (e.g., MacDonald, 1993, in press; Trueswell, Tanenhaus, & Kello, 1993; Trueswell et al., in press). Information that is accessed when a word is recognized is used to define a set of syntactic and semantic possibilities (within a circumscribed domain), as well as to provide many of the constraints relevant to evaluating the possibilities. Thus, information accessed during word recognition provides much of the temporary parallelism necessary to make available alternatives over which constraints can apply. The lexicalist approach allows most attachment ambiguities involving verbs to be treated as lexical/argument-structure ambiguities (see also MacDonald, Pearl-mutter, & Seidenberg, chapter 6, this volume). This approach predicts two important similarities between syntactic-ambiguity resolution and word-recognition phenomena. First, the availability of alternative argument structures will be determined, in part, by their frequency. Second, the effectiveness of a contextual constraint will interact with the frequency of the argument structure that it biases.

The syntactic and semantic aspects of verb-argument structure are clear examples of combinatory lexical information. Verb-*subcategorization* information describes the set of syntactic complements, or arguments, that can occur with a particular verb. Verb-*thematic-role* information describes the conceptually defined participants associated with a verb sense, as well as the relationship between these roles and the verb's syntactic complements.

From the perspective of an on-line processing system, thematic information could provide strong constraints on syntactic ambiguity. The semantic fit between a phrase and the thematic role with which it is assigned in different argument structures could serve as a useful constraint for deciding among these structures. The following example illustrates this interdependency:

(1) a. The fossil examined . . . .
     b. The archeologist examined . . . .

The ambiguity in these fragments arises because the form *examined* can be either a past tense or a passive participle. These forms have different argument structures associated with them. In the past-tense form, the fragment is a main clause, with the preceding noun phrase (NP) being the subject of the verb. The entity denoted by the NP plays the role of agent in the event denoted by the verb. In the passive-participle form, the verb is the start of a reduced-relative clause, and the NP is the (logical) object of the verb. In this case, the noun would play the role of theme. Thus, the verb *examined* in (1) is likely to be part of a reduced-relative clause when the preceding NP is a good theme and a poor agent of the verb (e.g., "The fossil examined by the archeologist was . . ."), whereas the same verb is likely to be part of a main clause when the preceding NP is a good agent and a poor theme (e.g., "The archeologist examined the fossil").

The semantic fit between a phrase and a possible thematic role is clearly an example of a correlated (nonsyntactic) constraint. Although constraint-based systems make use of this information during initial ambiguity resolution, two-stage models predict that thematic information should not influence initial syntactic commitments because it does not fall within the proper domain of syntax.

In this chapter, we present evidence that the semantic fit between an NP and a potential argument position has immediate effects on syntactic-ambiguity resolution for sentences with reduced-relative clauses. In addition, we show that data patterns that have been interpreted as evidence for the delayed use of thematic constraints actually provide strong empirical support for constraint-based models with rich lexicalist representations. We further show that these models provide a better framework for understanding results that have been interpreted as evidence for the delayed use of verb-specific syntactic (subcategorization) constraints.

THEMATIC-ROLE INFORMATION AND THE STRENGTH OF CONSTRAINT

Our discussion of thematic effects on parsing focuses on a set of results from two similar experiments. One experiment is reported in Ferreira and Clifton (1986, Experiment 1), and the other is reported in Trueswell et al. (in press). Both are eye-movement reading experiments that varied the animacy of a noun preceding a reduced-relative clause, as in Sentences 2a and 2b. Unambiguous unreduced relatives (Sentences 2c and 2d) were used as controls.

(2) a. The defendant examined by the lawyer turned out to be unreliable.

b. The evidence examined by the lawyer turned out to be unreliable.

c. The defendant that was examined by the lawyer turned out to be unreliable.

d. The evidence that was examined by the lawyer turned out to be unreliable.

We begin by outlining a constraint-based model of syntactic-ambiguity resolution, focusing on the relative-clause ambiguity (see Trueswell et al., in press). This provides a framework for understanding the various predictions. The model is similar in spirit to recent proposals developed by MacDonald and her colleagues (e.g., MacDonald, in press; MacDonald et al., chapter 6, this volume).

The principles that underlie the approach are simple. Structures are partially activated with the strength of activation dependent on their likelihood given the input. The effects of contextual constraint will depend on its strength and the availability of the alternative structures. To a first approximation, these are the same factors that are important for lexical-ambiguity resolution (MacDonald, in press; Tabossi, Spivey-Knowlton, McRae, & Tanenhaus, in press; Tanenhaus, Dell, & Carlson, 1987). Syntactic- and lexical-ambiguity resolution are viewed as similar and interrelated processes because many syntactic ambiguities depend on lexical ambiguities. Indeed, this becomes particularly clear when one takes into account the alternatives provided by aspects of combinatory lexical information such as argument structure.

Consider the evidence that a lexically based constraint-satisfaction system might use when encountering an ambiguous verb in the context of an NP. We assume that the verb will provide partial evidence/activation for both he past-tense and participial forms, with the strength of the evidence being determined by relative frequency (Burgess & Hollbach, 1988; Tabossi et al., in press). The question of how to calibrate frequency for lexical-structural ambiguity is just beginning to be explored (Gibson & Pearlmutter, chapter 8, this volume; Hindle & Rooth, 1990; Juliano & Tanenhaus, 1993; MacDonald, 1993; Mitchell & Cuetos, 1991; Trueswell et al., 1993). However, to a first approximation, it appears that frequency is determined by the specific lexical item (i.e., how frequent the past-tense and participial forms are for the particular verb) conditionalized on the frequency with which the forms occur in specific syntactic environments (Juliano & Tanenhaus, 1993). Corpus analyses indicate that, at the beginning of a sentence, a morphologically ambiguous verb that follows an NP is much more likely to be a past-tense verb in a main clause than a passive participial in a reduced-relative clause (Tabossi et al., in press). Thus, at the verb, there will be a clear frequency-based bias in favor of the past-tense/main-clause structure, although the participial/relative-clause structure will also be partially activated. In addition, we assume that verb forms activate the sets of thematic-conceptual roles associated with each form and its corresponding syntactic mappings (Carlson & Tanenhaus, 1988; Cottrell, 1985; McClelland & Kawamoto, 1986; Pearlmutter & MacDonald, 1992; Tanenhaus, Carlson, & Trueswell 1989). The thematic fit of a potential argument is immediately evaluated with respect to the active alternatives.

In thinking about what data patterns to expect and how to interpret them, it is helpful to consider the results of reading studies that have examined other types of lexical ambiguities. Eye-movement research has demonstrated that, for semantically ambiguous words having two equiprobable meanings, reading times are longer to the word when the prior context is neutral or only weakly biasing, compared with when the context strongly biases one meaning. Reading times to an ambiguous word are also longer when the context supports a subordinate, rather than a dominant, meaning (Duffy, Morris, & Rayner, 1988; Rayner, Pacht & Duffy, 1994; see also Rayner & Pollatsek, 1987).

Consider now how this data pattern would be reflected in the relative-clause ambiguity. A good semantic fit between the noun and the agent role ("The defendant examined . . .") is comparable to having a biasing context supporting the dominant meaning of a ambiguous word because a good agent biases the more frequent past-tense alternative. Thus, under these conditions, readers should not have any processing difficulty when reading the ambiguous verb, but should have difficulty with a by-phrase that is inconsistent with the main-clause structure. In contrast, a poor agent and a good patient/theme ("The evidence examined . . .") is comparable to having a biasing context supporting the less frequent alternative because the thematic fit of the noun supports the less active passive participle and runs against the more active past tense. In this case, readers should have increased processing difficulty at the ambiguous verb and less processing difficulty at the by-phrase. The magnitude of the difficulty at the verb should be correlated with the availability of the passive participle and the strength of the constraint provided by thematic fit. Whether there is any residual difficulty at the by-phrase should also depend on the strength of the semantic constraint and the relative availability of the past-tense and participial forms.

Ferreira and Clifton's (1986) study of reduced-relative clauses found elevated reading times at the verb and the by-phrase for inanimate nouns (nouns that tend to support a relative-clause structure), whereas they only found elevated times at the by-phrase for animate nouns (nouns that tend to support a main-clause structure). This data pattern was used to argue for the delayed use of semantic-thematic information in syntactic processing. Although readers were initially aware of the incongruity of the inanimate noun as the agent, they were still unable to use this information to avoid a main-clause parse, as evidenced by a large "garden-path," or misanalysis, effect at the by-phrase. On this explanation, the Ferreira and Clifton data pattern is the strongest type of evidence that can be marshaled in favor of a modular subsystem that is using domain-specific constraints. A correlated constraint from another domain is available, yet it is not affecting the decisions being made by another module.

However, the Ferreira and Clifton data pattern is also what one would expect when a contextual constraint supports a lower frequency alternative, and/or when the contextual constraints are only weakly biasing. What crucially distinguishes among the two-stage and constraint-based accounts of the data is what happens when the availability of the alternatives and the strength of the constraint is varied. As it turns out, our studies provide the relevant data.

Like Ferreira and Clifton, we (Trueswell et al., in press) monitored eye movements as subjects read reduced- and unreduced-relative clauses preceded by an animate or inanimate NP. Because we believed that many of the Ferreira and Clifton inanimate nouns were not highly biasing, we attempted to develop a new set of inanimate items that did not permit the main-clause alternative (see Trueswell et al., in press). We also included a second set of control conditions with unambiguous reduced-relative clauses, making use of verbs with unique participial forms such as *stolen.*

Shown in Fig. 7.1A are the first-pass (initial) reading times for four different regions of the target sentences: the NP "the defendant," the ambiguous verb *examined,* the disambiguating by-phrase "by the lawyer," and the first two words of the matrix verb phrase "turned out."

As can be seen in the figure, the basic data pattern is quite different from the Ferreira and Clifton results: There are rapid effects of thematic information. First consider the results for the animate nouns (i.e., nouns that were good agents). At the ambiguous verb *examined,* the reduced relative (the filled triangle) is no more difficult than the unreduced (the open triangle). However, at the disambiguating by-phrase, reading times to the reduced relatives are considerably longer than the unreduced relatives (a significant effect), suggesting that readers mistakenly took the preceding verb as part of a main clause. This pattern, no difficulty at the ambiguous verb and difficulty at the by-phrase, is consistent with a prior context

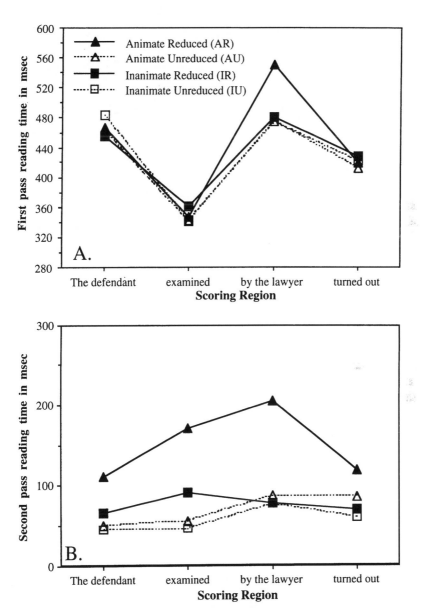

FIG. 7.1. Reading times from Trueswell, Tanenhaus, and Garnsey (in press) for reduced- and unreduced-relative clauses with ambiguous verbs preceded by animate and inanimate nouns. A. First-pass reading times. B. Second-pass reading times.

having supported either an equiprobable or dominant alternative. Now consider the results for the inanimate nouns (i.e., nouns that were poor agents). Even though reduced relatives (the filled squares) were slightly longer than the unreduced (the open squares) at the ambiguous verb, there were no significant differences between these two conditions at any position.[1] Thus, processing difficulty with the inanimate nouns seems to be diminished, if not eliminated. This pattern, slight difficulty at the ambiguous verb and no difficulty at the by-phrase, is consistent either with a biasing context that supports a somewhat subordinate alternative, or with a less biasing context that supports an equiprobable alternative.

Now consider the second-pass reading times (the re-reads), which are plotted in Fig. 7.1B. Reduced-relative clauses with animate NPs were re-read far more often than their unreduced counterparts (this difference was significant at the verb and the by-phrase). Reduced-relative sentences with inanimate nouns were re-read only slightly more often than their unreduced counterparts. Thus, as was the case with the first-pass reading times, there was only minimal processing difficulty with the inanimates.

The results for the reduced and unreduced relatives containing unambiguous verbs (e.g., *stolen*) should tell us whether there is any processing difficulty with reduced-relative clauses that is unrelated to syntactic misanalysis. As can be seen in Fig. 7.2, both first- and second-pass reading times resemble the results we just saw for the inanimate nouns followed by ambiguous verbs: There were only small differences at the verb in both the first- and second-pass readings, all of which were unreliable. Thus, difficulties with unambiguous items pattern onto the ambiguous conditions containing inanimate nouns.

In summary, the data showed rapid effects of thematic information. A breakdown of the items into categories, via a standard analysis of variance (ANOVA), revealed a statistical pattern in which thematic information completely eliminated any processing difficulty with ambiguous reduced relatives. Reduced-relative clauses with animate nouns showed clear signs of a misanalysis, whereas reduced relatives with inanimate nouns showed no reliable elevations in processing difficulty. However, as outlined in the predictions, constraint-based accounts crucially predict graded effects of semantic constraint. One should find some processing difficulty with inanimate nouns, depending on how much the semantic information supports the relative-clause alternative.

As mentioned earlier, the strongest semantic constraints in support of a reduced-relative clause come from nouns that are both poor agents *and* good patients or themes. When selecting inanimate nouns, we made sure the nouns were poor agents of their corresponding verbs. However, we did not worry about

---

[1]At the by-phrase, the interaction between animacy and the type of relative clause was significant because the animate condition showed an effect of relative-clause type, whereas the inanimate condition showed no such effect.

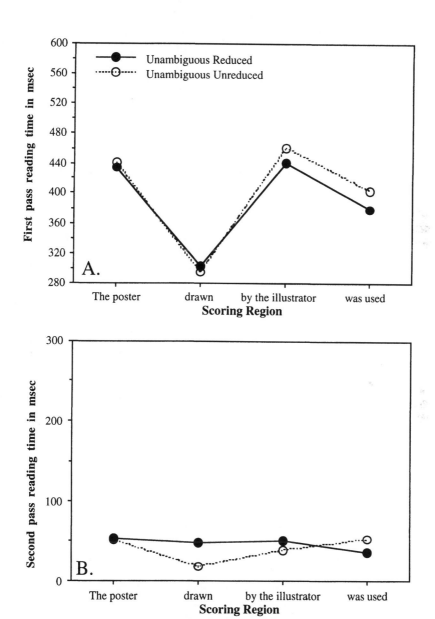

FIG. 7.2. Reading times from Trueswell et al. (in press) for reduced-
and unreduced-relative clauses with unambiguous verbs. A. First-pass
reading times. B. Second-pass reading times.

TABLE 7.1
Examples of Patient Typicality Ratings

Noun	Verb	Patient/Theme Rating*
The textbook	loved	1.9
The jewelry	identified	4.4
The evidence	examined	6.3

*1 = bad; 7 = good.

whether they were also good patients or themes. It turned out that the materials do indeed vary along this dimension. As part of a norming project conducted at the University of Southern California by MacDonald and Pearlmutter, in collaboration with Tanenhaus, McRae, and Spivey-Knowlton, a large group of subjects rated the typicality of the patient/theme relationship for each individual verb–noun pair by rating a question like "How typical is it for evidence to be examined by someone?" on a 7-point scale, with 1 as not typical at all and 7 as very typical. As can be seen from the examples in Table 7.1, patient-typicality ratings varied considerably from item to item, ranging from poor patients to good patients. Thus, students do not find textbooks to be very lovable, but evidence is a good thing to examine.

If ambiguity resolution for reduced-relative clauses is related to strength of thematic fit, increases in processing difficulty for individual reduced relatives should depend on the potential fit of the noun as a patient or theme of the verb. That is, the largest increases in processing difficulty with ambiguous reduced-relative clauses should occur for those inanimate items that are poor patients of their verbs. This is exactly what we found. Regression analyses that compared typicality ratings with increases in processing difficulty revealed reliable negative correlations for first-pass reading times at the by-phrase and for second-pass reading times at the first two regions. In addition, there were suggestive negative correlations at other positions (see Table 7.2). These negative correlations are consistent with immediate, but graded, use of semantic constraints. The goodness of fit of an NP as a potential argument predicts how much difficulty readers have with reduced relatives. When the noun is a relatively poor patient or theme, readers have some difficulty. When the noun is a good patient or theme, readers have little or no difficulty.

The conditions with morphologically unambiguous verbs provide an important control. If the correlations with typicality really reflect ambiguity resolution, typicality should not predict reading times for the reduced-relative clauses with morphologically unambiguous verbs. In fact, there were no significant correlations in either the first-pass or second-pass reading times for these conditions.

Before going on, we should mention that a complete replication of the ambiguous-verb conditions has been conducted in a second eye-tracking study

TABLE 7.2
Correlations Between Patient/Theme Typicality
and Processing Difficulty

Region	First Pass	Second Pass
The evidence	—	$R = -.52*$
examined	$R = -.42$	$R = -.56*$
by the lawyer	$R = -.51*$	$R = -.40$
turned out		$R = -.38$

Note. Negative correlations indicate that the better the patient/theme relation, the less the processing difficulty.
$*p < .05$.

using mostly new target sentences (also reported in Trueswell et al., in press). The means and statistical patterns are virtually identical between the two experiments. The ANOVA revealed little or no processing difficulty for reduced relatives with inanimate nouns. Moreover, correlations showed graded semantic effects similar to those reported here.

To illustrate more clearly the graded nature of the constraints, we can compare the inanimate items that had the strongest semantic constraints (i.e., those items with high patient/theme-typicality ratings) with those items that were less constraining. Figure 7.3 plots the reduction effect (reading times to the reduced relative minus the reading times to the unreduced relative) for first-pass reading times at the verb and the by-phrase for both the more constraining inanimate items (filled squares) and the less constraining inanimate items (filled triangles). Reduction effects are reading times to the reduced-relative clauses minus the unreduced. So, positive numbers represent increases in processing difficulty for the reduced. As can be seen in figure, the less constraining items show increases in processing difficulty at both the verb and the by-phrase (+44 ms and +46 ms, respectively), whereas the more constraining items show little or no increases at either position (+7 and −9 ms). In fact, the more constraining items show essentially the same pattern as the morphologically unambiguous verbs (plotted as open squares), which are +7 ms at the verb and −20 ms at the by-phrase. When semantic constraints are strongest, reduced relatives with ambiguous and unambiguous verbs behave similarly.

Finally, Fig. 7.4A replots the less constraining inanimates (filled triangles) and compares them with the animate noun condition (open triangles). At the verb, there is processing difficulty for the inanimates, but not the animates. Then, at the by-phrase, both show some processing difficulty. As you might recall, this is the data pattern reported in Ferreira and Clifton (1986; see Fig. 7.4B). With this result alone, it could be argued that readers are initially aware that the inanimates are poor agents of the verb, but that they still cannot use this

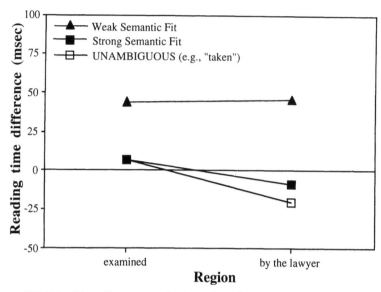

FIG. 7.3.   Mean first-pass reduction effects (reduced-relative relatives minus unreduced relatives) for the verb and the by-phrase. Positive numbers indicate increases in processing difficulty for the reduced relative. Inanimate nouns with weak semantic fit and strong semantic fit as compared with unambiguous controls.

information to avoid a syntactic misanalysis. However, in the context of our other results, the Ferreira and Clifton items indicate a data pattern associated with less constraining items.

The data we have presented map nicely onto a constraint-based account of sentence processing, in which syntactic-ambiguity resolution shares many of the properties known to hold for lexical-ambiguity resolution. At first glance, however, there appears to be a problem with this account. As we mentioned earlier, an NP–verb context has a large frequency asymmetry in favor of the past tense/main clause, making the past tense the dominant alternative and the participial the subordinate alternative. Thus, one might expect to see difficulty at the verb when a noun is a poor agent, even when it is also a good theme. (This would be an example of a context biasing a subordinate alternative.) Inconsistent with this prediction, we find that the inanimate items with the strongest semantic constraints behave almost exactly like the unambiguous items.

However, treating the participle as a subordinate alternative does not take into account the effects of parafoveal information on availability. It is well know that short function words (e.g., *by, the, was, that*) are typically skipped in reading because the word can be seen when fixating on the preceding word (Just & Carpenter, 1980; Rayner & McConkie, 1976). In fact, an analysis of fixation

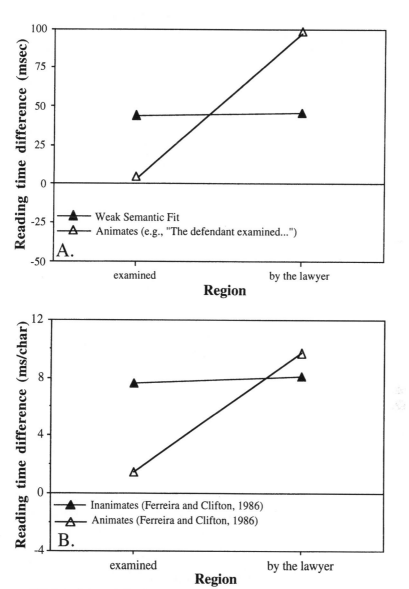

FIG. 7.4.   Mean first-pass reduction effects (reduced-relative relatives minus unreduced relatives) for the verb and by-phrase. Positive numbers indicate increases in processing difficulty for the reduced relative. A. Results for the inanimate nouns with weak semantic fit as compared with the animate nouns (Trueswell et al., in press). B. Results for inanimate and animate nouns, as determined from Ferreira and Clifton (1986).

patterns (see Trueswell et al., in press) revealed that readers rarely fixated on the *by*, indicating that it was read parafoveally during fixations on the ambiguous verb. It is likely that this would have increased the availability of the participial/relative-clause structure, making the situation more like that of an ambiguous word with two equally frequent senses. Note that the word *by* is ambiguous and not necessarily inconsistent with a past tense/main clause. Tabossi et al. (in press) showed that *by* following an NP–verb is frequently taken to be a manner or a locative preposition in a main clause when the noun is a good agent, but it is nearly always taken to be an agentive preposition in a relative clause when the noun is a poor agent. Thus, elevations at the verb for weakly biasing inanimates are simply an ambiguity effect related to the nature of the context.

Recent work by Burgess (1991) provides important empirical support for some of our conjectures about the significance of parafoveal support. Burgess conducted two self-paced reading studies using the materials that we modified slightly for Experiment 2. In one study, the sentences were presented one word at a time. In the other study, they were presented two words at a time, with the verb and *by* presented together (e.g.,/The evidence/ examined by/ . . .). Burgess found immediate effects of animacy with two-word presentation, but not with one-word presentation. Thus, strongly biasing nouns had immediate effects only when there was parafoveal support for the less frequent participial form.

SUBCATEGORY INFORMATION AND FREQUENCY

Thus far we have argued that thematic effects on syntactic processing depend on both the strength of the contextual constraint and the availability of the syntactic alternatives. We also suggested that the frequency with which argument structures occur plays an important role in determining availability, although we did not present any direct evidence. In the remainder of this chapter, we briefly review some recent results of the sentence-complement ambiguity that provide more direct support for our assumptions about frequency. In addition, these results address the superficial conflict between the interpretation of the thematic results just presented, which requires immediate access to alternative argument structures, and recent results that have been interpreted as evidence for delayed use of verb-specific argument-structure (subcategorization) information.

Sentence complements can occur immediately after verbs (as in Sentence 3a), or they can be introduced explicitly by the complementizer *that* (as in Sentence 3b).

(3) a. The chef remembered *the recipe was easy to make.*

b. The chef remembered *that the recipe was easy to make.*

An NP immediately after a verb like *remembered* is temporarily ambiguous because *remember* subcategorizes for either an NP complement or a sentence complement. The phrase "the recipe" could be the object of the verb (e.g., "The chef remembered the recipe") or the subject of a sentence complement (e.g., "The chef remembered the recipe was easy to make"). Considerable research has demonstrated that readers typically take the NP to be the object of the verb, resulting in longer reading times at the verb phrase in the sentence complement (e.g., "was easy . . .") for *that*-less complements, compared with *that*-complement controls (e.g., Ferreira & Henderson, 1990; Holmes, Stowe, & Cupples, 1989; Trueswell et al., 1993). This result is predicted by the minimal-attachment parsing principle because an NP-complement attachment requires at least one fewer node than the sentence-complement attachment.

Recently, Ferreira and Henderson (1990) found that readers experience difficulty at the verb phrase ("was easy . . ."), even when the verb strongly prefers to be followed by a sentence complement and typically does not permit an NP complement, e.g., *insist* as in Sentences 4a and 4b (but cf. Holmes et al., 1989). It was concluded that there is a misanalysis, or "garden-path," in sentences like these, even when the main verb does not license a direct object. On this interpretation, these results lend strong support to two-stage models that initially ignore lexically specific information, and are problematic for constraint-based approaches like the one outlined here.

(4) a. The chef insisted the recipe was easy to make.

   b. The chef insisted that the recipe was easy to make.

However, we have found results that shed a different light on these findings. As in the case of thematic constraints, the full data pattern actually provides strong evidence for the key assumptions underlying constraint-based approaches with rich lexical representations, especially those assumptions concerning frequency and argument structure.

The first set of data comes from Trueswell et al. (1993) and Garnsey and Lotocky (1992), who demonstrated that, with carefully normed materials, verb-subcategory information is used to eliminate a reanalysis effect at the verb phrase "was very . . ." in sentences like (4) as compared with sentences like (3). For verbs with a strong NP-complement bias (NP-bias verbs, e.g., *remember*), reading times are longer at the verb phrase for *that*-less complements, compared with *that* controls, whereas there is, at best, a small and unreliable difference for sentence-complement-bias verbs (sentence-bias verbs, e.g., *insist*). For a detailed explanation of why Ferreira and Henderson found a different pattern, see Trueswell et al. (1993).

However, Trueswell et al. (1993) and Garnsey and Lotocky (1992) did find that readers have difficulty with *that*-less sentence complements at the NP when the preceding verb was sentence-biased (e.g., "insisted *the recipe* . . ."). It is possible that this effect is due to rapid lexical filtering. On this account, the parser attached the NP as the object of the verb and then immediately revised the analysis. This interpretation can be ruled out for two reasons. First, the same effect occurs for completely unambiguous sentences, even when subcategorization information is available. Second, the effect is related to frequency: Difficulty with the NP goes away when the preceding sentence-bias verb is of high frequency. Both of these results, outlined next, reveal patterns consistent with a constraint-based approach to syntactic-ambiguity resolution.

The first result comes from a cross-modal naming study in Trueswell et al. (1993, Experiment 1). In the experiment, subjects heard an auditory-sentence fragment, after which they had to name a visually presented target word. On the trials of interest, the fragment ended with an NP-bias or sentence-bias verb (e.g., "The old man accepted/insisted," and the target word was a case-marked pronoun, either *he* or *him*). These were compared with fragments ending with the complementizer *that* (e.g., "The old man accepted/insisted that"). This kind of task is sensitive to grammaticality effects: Naming latencies are longer when the listener has to name an ungrammatical continuation of the sentence fragment (Cowart, 1987; Tyler & Marslen-Wilson, 1977).

Naming latencies to *him* (plotted in Fig. 7.5A) revealed that subcategorization information is available to the listener immediately after hearing the verb. The results show a grammaticality effect that depends on the use of subcategorization information. The pronoun *him* after a sentence-bias verb (e.g., "The old man insisted . . ."—*him*) is ungrammatical because the verb can only be used intransitively. Indeed, naming latencies to *him* in this condition were just as long as naming latencies to the ungrammatical *that* conditions (e.g., "The old man insisted/accepted that"—*him*). Only the grammatical NP-bias verb condition ("The old man accepted"—*him*) was reliably faster.

However, as Fig. 7.5B shows, naming times to *he* were longer when the fragment did not end in the complementizer *that*. Thus, there was a complementizer effect even when the noun was completely unambiguous: An unambiguous subject NP (*he*) is difficult to process following a verb (i.e., in a *that*-less sentence complement). Why should this be the case? The explanation hinges on the relationship between verb frequency and the availability of argument structure.

An NP after a verb can only be integrated if there is an argument structure available to determine the structural relationship. The complementizer *that* is sufficient to introduce the sentence-complement structure, whereas the pronoun *he* is not. This is because a complementizer's lexical structure, by definition, includes the sentence-complement relationship, whereas a pronoun's lexical structure does not. When no complementizer is present, the integration of the noun depends on information made available by the verb. Thus, difficulty in integrating the noun with the verb depends on the availability of verb information

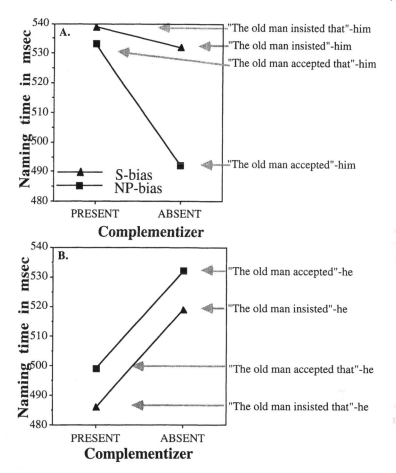

FIG. 7.5.   A. Mean latencies for naming *im* aloud after the four different types of sentence fragments. B. Mean latencies for naming *he* aloud after the four different types of sentence fragments (Trueswell, Tanenhaus, & Kello, 1993).

concerning the sentence-complement argument structure. The assumption that frequency of occurrence is related to availability predicts that processing difficulty with a subject pronoun after a verb will depend on the frequency with which the sentence-complement argument structure occurs with that particular verb. Thus, processing difficulty should correlate with the frequency of the verb and the frequency with which the verb occurs with a sentence-complement argument structure without a complementizer, which Trueswell et al. termed a *that preference*. These two frequencies are so highly correlated that it is difficulty to tease them apart, therefore we use them interchangeably.

The prediction that ease of integration of a case-marked pronoun will be

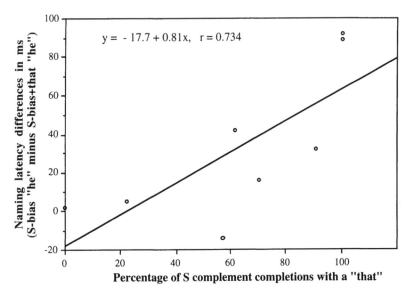

FIG. 7.6. Scattergram plotting the *he* complementizer effect in ms against the percentage of sentence-complement completions that began with a *that* for each Sentence-bias verb (Trueswell et al., 1993).

correlated with *that* preference and verb frequency has been confirmed in several of the experiments reported in Trueswell et al. (1993) and Juliano and Tanenhaus (1993). Figure 7.6, taken from Trueswell et al., illustrates the correlation between *that* preference and naming times to *he* following *that*-less fragments from the study just described.

Now we turn to the second result, which was that processing time for an NP after a sentence-complement verb is (also) correlated with the frequency of the verb. The integration explanation described earlier clearly would explain (and predict) this data pattern. However, there may be another factor at play as well. It is possible that some of the processing difficulty with unmarked nouns is due to the overlap in encoding lexically specific verb information. If access to argument structures is frequency based, some of the syntactic-regularity effects that are captured by parsing principles might emerge from item-specific frequencies, as it has been argued that they do in other lexical domains (e.g., spelling—sound correspondence; e.g., Seidenberg & McClelland, 1989). The preference to take an NP as the object of a verb, rather than as the subject of a sentence complement, is a likely candidate. Because an NP that follows a verb is typically an object, a system that is coding lexically specific co-occurrences will develop an NP bias, as long as we make the noncontroversial assumption that representations for verbs are at least partially distributed (i.e., all verbs will share some similarities). Moreover, verbs that violate this regular pattern (e.g., sentence-bias verbs) should have difficulty overcoming this regularity, provided that the verb is not highly frequent.

This suggests an interpretation of the complementizer effect that is similar to that given by constraint-based models for the "frequency by regularity" interactions reported in the word-recognition literature (e.g., Seidenberg & McClelland, 1989). For instance, consider the spelling–sound correspondences in English. Although there is a reasonably consistent mapping between letter strings and pronunciation, there are many exceptions. For instance, most syllables ending in *-aste* are pronounced with a long vowel (e.g., *waste, paste, taste*). Words that run against this regular pattern or rule (e.g., exception words like *caste*) typically take longer to read aloud than regular words. However, the difficulty with exception words is modulated by frequency. There is little or no penalty for naming a high-frequency exception word (e.g., *have*), whereas there is a large penalty for naming a low-frequency exception word (e.g., *caste*).

Figure 7.7, taken from Juliano and Tanenhaus (1993), illustrates this frequency-by-regularity interaction in parsing an NP after a verb. Reading times to *the* are longer following a sentence-bias verb than following an NP-bias verb. The magnitude of the difficulty for the sentence-bias verbs interacts with verb frequency (and with *that* preference). A determiner after a verb is typically the beginning of a NP complement. Verbs that do not allow NP complements

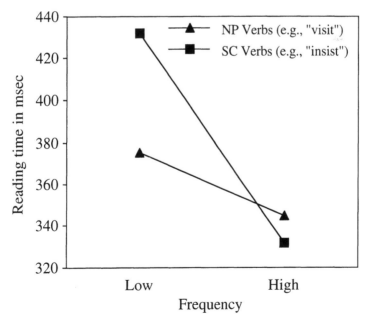

FIG. 7.7.   Reading time to the word *the* as a function of the frequency and type of the preceding verb (Juliano & Tanenhaus, 1993).

(sentence-bias verbs) are exceptions to this general pattern. As in word recognition, difficulty with the exceptional pattern should depend on frequency (i.e., how familiar the system is with the particular item). Thus, some of the processing difficulty for an NP after a *that*-less complement may be due to competition from the regular pattern.

Although we have no direct evidence for a competition effect above and beyond an integration effect, we do have clear evidence from a closely related domain. Note that the word *that* after a verb is actually ambiguous. It could be a demonstrative determiner, or it could be a complementizer. However, a *that* after a verb is more frequently a complementizer than a determiner, and readers parse it accordingly (Juliano & Tanenhaus, 1993). On the kind of distributed competition account outlined previously, readers should have difficulty processing the word *that* when it follows a transitive verb that does not permit a sentence complement (e.g., ". . . visited that . . . ," where the *that* is a determiner, not a complementizer). The reason is that the interpretation of *that* as a determiner runs counter to a highly regular pattern in the language. This is exactly what we find. Readers have difficulty with the word *that* in a sentence such as "Bill visited that museum" (Juliano & Tanenhaus, 1993). This is essentially the obverse of the effects we discussed earlier for Sentence-bias verbs. Now the preference for an NP structure runs counter to the general pattern in the language.

Note that the set of results we have just discussed, summarized next, is unified by the lexicalist framework outlined previously. As in the case of thematic effects, a subset of the effects is consistent with two-stage models, in which use of lexical information is delayed. However, when the full range of phenomena are considered, the data strongly support the constraint-based model with rich lexical representations.

Phenomena

1. That *preference for case-marked pronouns.* The difficulty of processing an unambiguous case-marked subject pronoun (e.g., *he, she,* or *they*) after a sentence-bias verb is correlated with its *that* preference and with the verb's frequency of occurrence. *That* preference is the percentage of times that a sentence complement after a verb begins with the overt complementizer *that* (Trueswell et al., 1993).

2. That *preference effects for determiners.* Reading times to a determiner that immediately follows a strong sentence-bias verb are correlated with the verb's *that* preference and with its frequency of occurrence (Juliano & Tanenhaus, 1993; Trueswell et al., 1993).

3. That *complementizer bias.* The word *that* is taken to be a complementizer after an NP-bias verb and after a sentence-bias verb (Juliano & Tanenhaus, 1993).

4. That *conflict effect*. *That* is difficult to process when it follows a verb that does not allow a sentence complement (e.g., "John visited that . . ."; Juliano & Tanenhaus, 1993).

In summary, these results converge on the importance of contingent-frequencies effects in syntactic processing, including effects that emerge from the frequencies with which argument structures occur with particular words and word patterns. The data provide strong support for the assumptions that we outlined about frequency and availability in our discussion o thematic effects on ambiguity resolution for reduced-relative clauses. They are clearly encouraging for approaches to ambiguity resolution that adopt a rich lexicalist framework, in which parsing preferences are not the result of domain-specific principles, but rather emerge from the constraints available from the language.

CONCLUSIONS

The results reviewed herein provide strong support for constraint-based approaches to ambiguity resolution and, in particular, approaches that exploit the richness of lexical representation. We have demonstrated that a syntactically correlated constraint—thematic fit—has immediate effects on syntactic-ambiguity resolution. Moreover, we have shown that the full pattern of results, which emerge when one takes strength of constraint into account, are explained by a lexicalist model, in which the availability of argument structures is determined in part by frequency. We then demonstrated that a set of effects with sentence-complement constructions can also be explained by this framework.

In future work, it will be important to provide a broader empirical base and to implement models that incorporate these principles. The work reported by Pearlmutter, Daugherty, MacDonald, and Seidenberg (1993) is an important step in this direction. In collaboration with Cornell Juliano, we are currently engaged in a modeling effort to determine whether the results outlined previously for the sentence complement will emerge from a system sensitive to co-occurrence patterns of words and argument structures.

It is unlikely that all parsing preferences can be reduced to argument-structure frequency effects. We argue that any successful constraint-based system will need to make use of the kinds of syntactically relevant discourse information emphasized in referential models of sentence processing (Altmann & Steedman, 1988; Crain & Steedman, 1985; Ni & Crain, 1990). However, to the extent that accessing the discourse model depends on contextually dependent "triggering" expressions within a sentence, discourse constraint will interact with—and often depend on—the kinds of local factors we have identified. Spivey-Knowlton and Tanenhaus (chapter 17, this volume) develop this argument in detail and argue that it unifies the literature on referential effects in syntactic processing (see also

Sedivy & Spivey-Knowlton, chapter 16, this volume, for some related discussion).

In developing this approach, we have focused on the combinatory constraints of verbs. Verb argument-structure ambiguities, particularly in a language like English, in which a verb precedes most of its arguments, are a natural domain for exploring hypotheses about rich lexical representation within a constraint-based framework. However, it is likely that the same processing principles will hold in other languages, although not necessarily with the same lexical categories. In fact, in English, we would predict argument-structure co-occurrence effects for lexical items other than verbs. Examples include the *that*-preference effects for sentence-complement structures following adjectives and nouns (e.g., "The man was afraid [that] his plane," "The hypothesis the lexicon is . . .") and co-occurrence effects with function words (e.g., co-occurrence effects between specifiers and prepositions, and the structures that they introduce).

Finally, it should be clear from our discussion that, in contrast to some interactive comprehension systems, we are outlining an approach that is both constrained by, and compatible with, the notions of a richly articulated linguistic system. The fact that thematic constraints can influence syntactic-ambiguity resolution does not mean that there is no distinction between semantic and syntactic information. Nor does it mean any kind of semantic information can affect syntactic processing. Only information that is correlated with syntactic alternatives will have effects. These correlations are most likely to occur at the interfaces between linguistic subsystems (e.g., the discourse function of a syntactic structure, or when a system such as lexical representation cuts across different aspects of representation). Thus, constraint-based systems rely heavily on both the richness of linguistic representation and the fact that different systems make use of the same forms (e.g., the word *the* participates in, and has consequences for, several different systems). It is this basic aspect of natural language that makes on-line processing possible and allows for constraints to be rapidly coordinated. Ultimately, constraint-based systems resolve ambiguity by making use of those constraints that are defined as relevant by linguistic structure and language use, along with an appeal to principles that are characteristic of processing systems in general.

ACKNOWLEDGMENTS

We would like to thank Michael Spivey-Knowlton for his helpful comments. Some of the research presented here was supported by NIH grants HD-22271 and HD-27206, NSF grant BNS-8617738, and the NIH/NEI grant EY-01319 to the Center for Visual Science at the University of Rochester.

REFERENCES

Altmann, G.T.M., & Steedman, M. J. (1988). Interaction with context during human sentence processing. *Cognition, 30,* 191–238.

Burgess, C. (1991). *Interaction of semantic, syntactic, and visual factors in syntactic ambiguity resolution.* Unpublished doctoral dissertation, University of Rochester, Rochester, NY.

Burgess, C., & Hollbach, S. C. (1988). A computational model of syntactic ambiguity as a lexical access process. In *Proceedings of the Tenth Annual Cognitive Science Society Meetings* (pp. 263–269). Hillsdale, NJ: Lawrence Erlbaum Associates.

Carlson, G. N., & Tanenhaus, M. K. (1988). Thematic roles and language comprehension. In W. Wilkens (Ed.), *Syntax and semantics* Vol. 21, pp. 263–287). New York, NY: Academic Press.

Clifton, C., Jr. (1993). The role of thematic roles in sentence processing. *Canadian Journal of Psychology, 47,* 222–246.

Clifton, C., Jr., Speer, S., & Abney, S. P. (1991). Parsing arguments: Phrase structure and argument structure as determinants of initial parsing decisions. *Journal of Memory and Language, 30,* 251–271.

Cottrell, G. (1985). *A connectionist approach to word sense disambiguation.* Unpublished doctoral dissertation, University of Rochester, Rochester, NY.

Cowart, W. (1987). Evidence for an anaphoric mechanism within syntactic processing: Some reference relations defy semantic and pragmatic considerations. *Memory & Cognition, 15,* 318–331.

Crain, S., & Steedman, M. J. (1985). On not being led up the garden path: The use of context by the psychological parser. In D. Dowty, L. Karttunen, & A. Zwicky (Eds.), *Natural language parsing: Psychological, computational, and theoretical perspectives* (pp. 320–357). Cambridge, England: Cambridge University Press.

Duffy, S. A., Morris, R. K., & Rayner, K. (1988). Lexical ambiguity and fixation times in reading. *Journal of Memory and Language, 27,* 429–446.

Ferreira, F., & Clifton, C., Jr. (1986). The independence of syntactic processing. *Journal of Memory and Language, 25,* 348–368.

Ferreira, F., & Henderson, J. M. (1990). The use of verb information in syntactic parsing: A comparison of evidence from eye movements and word-by-word self-paced reading. *Journal of Experimental Psychology: Learning, Memory and Cognition, 16,* 555–568.

Ferreira, F., & Henderson, J. M. (1991). How is verb information used during syntactic processing? In G. B. Simpson (Ed.), *Understanding word and sentence* (pp. 305–330). North Holland, The Netherlands: Elsevier Science.

Ford, M. (1988). Parsing complexity and a theory of parsing. In G. Carlson & M. Tanenhaus (Eds.), *Linguistic structure and language processing* (pp. 239–272). The Netherlands: Kluwer.

Frazier, L. (1987). Sentence processing: A tutorial review. In M. Coltheart (Ed.), *Attention and performance XII: The psychology of reading* (pp. 554–586). Hillsdale, NJ: Lawrence Erlbaum Associates.

Frazier, L. (1989). Against lexical generation of syntax. In W. D. Marslen-Wilson (Ed.), *Lexical representation and process* (pp. 505–528). Cambridge, MA: MIT Press.

Frazier, L. (1991). Exploring the architecture of the language-processing system. In G.T.M. Altmann (Ed.), *Cognitive models of speech processing* (pp. 409–433). Cambridge, MA: MIT Press.

Frazier, L., & Rayner, K. (1982). Making and correcting errors during sentence comprehension: Eye movements in the analysis of structurally ambiguous sentences. *Cognitive Psychology, 14,* 178–210.

Garnsey, S. M., & Lotocky, M. (1992). *Verb-usage knowledge in sentence comprehension.* Paper presented at the 33rd annual meeting of the Psychonomic Society, St. Louis, MO.

Hindle, M., & Rooth, M. (1990). Structural ambiguity and lexical relations. In *Proceedings of the 28th Annual Meeting of the Association of Computational Linguistics* (pp. 229–236).

Holmes, V. M., Stowe, L., & Cupples, L. (1989). Lexical expectations in parsing complement-verb sentences. *Journal of Memory and Language, 28*, 668–689.

Juliano, C., & Tanenhaus, M. K. (1993). Contingent frequency effects in syntactic ambiguity resolution. In *Proceedings of the 15th Annual Meeting of the Cognitive Science Society* (pp. 593–598). Hillsdale, NJ: Lawrence Erlbaum Associates.

Just, M. A., & Carpenter, P. A. (1980). A theory of reading: From eye fixations to comprehension. *Psychological Review, 87*, 329–354.

MacDonald, M. (in press). Probabilistic constraints and syntactic ambiguity resolution. *Language and Cognitive Processes.*

MacDonald, M. (1993). The interaction of lexical and syntactic ambiguity. *Journal of Memory and Language, 32*, 692–715.

Marslen-Wilson, W. D. (1973). Linguistic structure and speech shadowing at very short latencies. *Nature, 244*, 522–523.

McClelland, J. L., & Kawamoto, A. (1986). Mechanisms of sentence processing: Assigning roles to constituents of sentences. In J. McClelland & D. Rumelhart (Eds.), *Parallel distributed processing: Part 2. Psychological and biological Models* (pp. 272–325). Cambridge, MA: MIT Press.

McClelland, J. L., St. John, M., & Taraban, R. (1989). Sentence comprehension: A parallel distributed processing approach. *Language and Cognitive Processes, 4*, 287–336.

Mitchell, D. C. (1987). Lexical guidance in human parsing: Locus and processing characteristics. In M. Coltheart (Ed.), *Attention and performance XII: The psychology of reading.* Hillsdale, NJ: Lawrence Erlbaum Associates.

Mitchell, D. C. (1989). Verb-guidance and other lexical effects in parsing. *Language and Cognitive Processes, 4*, 123–154.

Mitchell, D. C., Corley, M.M.B., & Garnham, A. (1992). Effects of context in human sentence parsing: Evidence against a discourse-based proposal mechanism. *Journal of Experimental Psychology: Learning, Memory and Cognition, 18*, 69–88.

Mitchell, D. C., & Cuetos, F. (1991). *The origins of parsing strategies.* Unpublished manuscript.

Ni, W., & Crain, S. (1990). How to resolve structural ambiguities. *Proceedings to NELS, 20*(2), 414–427.

Pearlmutter, N. J., Daugherty, K., MacDonald, M. C., & Seidenberg, M. (1993, March). *Constraint satisfaction in main verb/reduced relative ambiguities.* Poster presented at the *sixth annual CUNY conference on Human Sentence Processing*, University of Massachusetts, Amherst, MA.

Pearlmutter, N. J., & MacDonald, M. C. (1992, March). *Garden-paths in "simple" sentences.* Poster presented at the *fifth annual CUNY conference on Human Sentence Processing*, City University of New York.

Pritchett, B. L. (1992). *Grammatical competence and parsing performance.* Chicago, IL: The University of Chicago Press.

Rayner, K., Carlson, M., & Frazier, L. (1983). The interaction of syntax and semantics during sentence processing. *Journal of Verbal Learning and Verbal Behavior, 22*, 358–374.

Rayner, K., Garrod, S., & Perfetti, C. A. (1992). Discourse influences during parsing are delayed. *Cognition, 45*, 109–139.

Rayner, K., & McConkie, G. W. (1976). What guides a reader's eye movements? *Vision Research, 16*, 829–837.

Rayner, K., Pacht, J. M., & Duffy, S. A. (1994). *Effects of prior encounter and discourse bias on the processing of lexically ambiguous words: Evidence from eye fixations.* Manuscript submitted for publication.

Rayner, K., & Pollatsek, A. (1987). Eye movements in reading: A tutorial review. In M. Coltheart (Ed.), *Attention and performance XII* (pp. 327–362). Hillsdale, NJ: Lawrence Erlbaum Associates.

Seidenberg, M. S., & McClelland, J. L. (1989). A distributed developmental model of word recognition and naming. *Psychological Review, 96,* 523–568.

Spivey-Knowlton, M. J., Trueswell, J. C., & Tanenhaus, M. K. (1993). Context effects in syntactic ambiguity resolution: Parsing reduced relative clauses. *Canadian Journal of Psychology, 47,* 276–309.

Tabossi, P., Spivey-Knowlton, M. J., McRae, K., & Tanenhaus, M. K. (1993). Semantic effects on syntactic ambiguity resolution: Evidence for a constraint-based resolution process. In C. Umilta & M. Moscovitch (Eds.), *Attention & Performance XV.* Hillsdale, NJ: Lawrence Erlbaum Associates.

Tanenhaus, M. K., Carlson, G. N., & Trueswell, J. C. (1989). The role of thematic structures in interpretation and parsing. *Language and Cognitive Processing, Special Edition, Parsing and Interpretation, 4,* 211–234.

Tanenhaus, M. K., Dell, G. S., & Carlson, G. (1987). Context effects in lexical processing: A connectionist perspective on modularity. In J. Garfield (Ed.), *Modularity in knowledge representation and natural language understanding* (pp. 83–108). Cambridge, MA: MIT Press.

Trueswell, J. C., Tanenhaus, M. K., & Garnsey, S. M. (in press). Semantic influences on parsing: Use of thematic role information in syntactic ambiguity resolution. *Journal of Memory and Language.*

Trueswell, J. C., Tanenhaus, M. K., & Kello, C. (1993). Verb-specific constraints in sentence processing: Separating effects of lexical preference from garden-paths. *Journal of Experimental Psychology: Learning, Memory and Cognition, 19*(3), 528–553.

Tyler, L. K., & Marslen-Wilson, W. D. (1977). The on-line effects of semantic context on syntactic processing. *Journal of Verbal Learning and Verbal Behavior, 16,* 683–692.

8

A Corpus-Based Analysis of Psycholinguistic Constraints on Prepositional-Phrase Attachment

Edward Gibson
Massachusetts Institute of Technology

Neal J. Pearlmutter
University of Illinois at Urbana-Champaign

Most empirical psycholinguistic data are currently obtained by performing experiments on subjects (e.g., measuring reading times or eye movements associated with the processing of sentences). The advent of large on-line corpora, along with computational tools for processing these corpora, provides us with a new psycholinguistic testing ground. In particular, it is now possible for researchers studying psycholinguistic complexity to measure the frequencies of target-linguistic constructs in corpora relative to the frequencies of control-linguistic constructs. Our claim is that, other factors being equal, structures that are harder to understand (as measured, e.g., by reading times) should be less frequent than structures that are easier to understand, so that the relative frequency measurements of two or more constructions are inversely related to the relative comprehension-complexity ranking of the constructions.

Before we discuss reasons for believing this claim, note that the claim we are making here is *not* the following, more general claim, which is too strong: That the frequency of a structure varies inversely with its complexity alone. This stronger hypothesis is false because many factors other than complexity are involved in determining the frequency of a structure. One structure may be frequent, yet still relatively complex, whereas another might be easy to comprehend, yet rare for reasons other than complexity. Therefore, when attempting to make conclusions about relative syntactic complexities on the basis of frequency information, it is necessary to ensure that there are no differences between the target and control structures other than the complexity difference that is being studied. For example, if two constructions function in different ways, and thus relay different kinds of meaning, then no conclusions can be drawn about their relative syntactic complexities based on frequency comparisons because the difference in frequencies may be primarily due to the difference in function of the two constructions. Thus, it would not be appropriate to compare the number of declarative structures of a certain form to the number of interrogative structures of a similar form because, although declaratives and interrogatives may be closely linked syntactically, their functions are very different.

However, if factors such as function can be controlled for, and a sufficient quantity of target and control items can be observed, then our claim applies: The frequency of the target construction relative to the control construction varies inversely with the relative complexity of the two constructions. One instance where such a comparison seems reasonable is in the area of ambiguous attachment of a constituent (e.g., a prepositional phrase [PP]). Suppose that we can obtain a large number of instances of a structure S containing n prospective attachment sites, where each S token is followed by the same kind of constituent C, so that C attaches to one of the n prospective attachment sites in S. If the tokens of S and C are the same in all relevant aspects, then attachments to sites within S that C attaches to more frequently are less complex than attachments that occur less frequently.

There are two main reasons to believe the hypothesis relating the relative comprehension complexities of two constructions to the inverse of their relative frequencies. First, because most on-line corpora are collections of sentences that were produced naturally, it is clear that the relative frequencies of two or more constructions are inversely related to the relative complexities of these constructions with respect to the human sentence-production mechanism. This complexity measurement may also directly reflect the human sentence-processing mechanism (HSPM), if the comprehension and production systems are closely linked to one another and rely on similar definitions of complexity. Although the specific nature of the relationship between the two systems is yet unclear, the existence of some connection between the comprehension and production systems is uncontroversial. At the very least, the two systems must access some of the same lexical representations, and, presumably, the same grammatical knowledge must be applied in each system, regardless of how it is encoded. Currently, there is no evidence distinguishing the complexity measures of the two systems. Until such evidence appears, the null hypothesis is that the two systems share the same complexity measures, so that measurements of production frequencies should reflect comprehension processing difficulty.

An additional reason to expect that corpus frequencies should reflect human sentence-processing complexity is that most of the text currently available in on-line corpora has been edited at some stage to make it more understandable (e.g., newspaper stories, etc.). Thus, naturally generated constructions that are too complex for the human sentence processor will often be edited to make them easier. For example, some types of ambiguity, which often give rise to processing difficulty, might not be noticed in the generation process, but might be filtered out by an editing process.[1]

Therefore, we expect to find the same patterns of complexity in corpus analyses as in comprehension data. If such patterns are observed, we can infer the existence of some combination of an effect of editing and a link between production and processing systems, at least in terms of shared complexity measures. In this case, corpus-based analyses can at least supplement data from comprehension experiments, and, given enough support across a range of comparisons, corpus data could be taken as independent evidence for or against processing hypotheses.

However, it is possible that the production and comprehension systems do not share the same complexity measures, and/or that the effects of editing are relatively weak, resulting in two other possible general patterns of data from corpus-based analyses:

1. Frequency data from corpus analyses might be unrelated to complexity data from comprehension experiments, indicating that the production and processing systems are relatively isolated from each other, and that editing processes do not have a strong effect.

2. Frequency data might reflect comprehension data only in certain aspects, making direct conclusions about the processing system on the basis of corpus data along somewhat suspect. In this case, a characterization of how the two sources of data differ—in the form of a range of comparisons between corpus and comprehension data (and possibly other independent production data)—could help to determine the relationship between the processing and production systems.

As an initial test of these claims, this chapter compares the results of a corpus analysis with the experimental results reported by Gibson, Pearlmutter, Canseco-Gonzalez, and Hickok (1993). Gibson et al. performed off- and on-line reading experiments on ambiguous noun phrases (NPs) of the following form, where the relative clause (RC) attached to one of NP_1, NP_2, or NP_3 (Prep = preposition, N = noun):

(1) $[_{NP_1} \ldots N_1 \, [_{PP_1} \, Prep_1 \, [_{NP_2} \ldots N_2 \, [_{PP_2} \, Prep_2 \, [_{NP_3} \ldots N_3 \,]]]]]$ RC

---

[1]Note that this observation means that edited corpora may not be as directly relevant to the human sentence-production mechanism as unedited corpora. Thus, a better source of measurements relevant to the sentence-production mechanism would be naturally occurring speech, or naturally occurring dialogues where editing is somehow minimized (e.g., electronic mail interactions), as in studies of naturally occurring speech errors, where editing has clearly not occurred (see, e.g., Dell, 1986; Garrett, 1975).

The constructions analyzed had the additional constraint that PP_2 attached to NP_2, so that the RC could syntactically attach to any one of NP_1, NP_2, or NP_3.[2] In addition, the head nouns and RC were constructed so that the RC agreed in number with only one of the three possible NP attachment sites, as in the following NPs:

(2) a. the computer near the models of the buildings that was destroyed in the fire

   b. the computers near the model of the buildings that was destroyed in the fire

   c. the computers near the models of the building that was destroyed in the fire

The intuitions are fairly clear: (2c), in which the RC attaches to NP_3, is easy to process and seems perfectly acceptable. (2a), in which the RC attaches to NP_1, is somewhat harder to process, but is still relatively easy to understand. However, (2b), in which the RC attaches to the intermediate site NP_2, is very difficult to process and seems ungrammatical, giving rise to a noticeable garden-path effect.

Accordingly, the results from the off-line grammaticality judgment experiment reported by Gibson et al. indicated that NPs like (2a) and (2c) are usually perceived as grammatical (66% and 69% of the time, respectively), whereas NPs like (2b) are perceived as grammatical much less often (only 29% of the time). An on-line reading-time experiment also found that attachment to NP_2 was the hardest to comprehend. Furthermore, in the on-line task, attachments to NP_3 were significantly easier to process than attachments to NP_1, resulting in a difficulty ordering of the three sites as follows (easiest to hardest): NP_3, NP_1, NP_2.

To explain these effects, Gibson et al. proposed that the human parser contains the following independent preference factors:

1. Recency preference (cf. right association; Kimball, 1973, and late closure; Frazier, 1978, 1987; Frazier & Fodor, 1978), which states that the human parser prefers attachments to more recent words in the input stream over attachments to less recent words; and

2. Predicate proximity (cf. Frazier, 1990; Gibson, 1991; Gilboy et al., 1993), which states that the human parser prefers attachments to be as close as possible to the head of a predicate.

---

[2]If PP_2 attached to NP_1, then attachment of the RC to NP_2 would be syntactically blocked by a prohibition against crossed branches.

Given a RC following three potential NP attachment sites, as in (1), recency preference results in a preference for attachment to the most recent, or lowest, NP—NP_3. On the other hand, predicate proximity results in a preference for attachment to NP_1, the highest site, because NP_1 is structurally closer to the head of a predicate to follow (as its potential subject) than either NP_2 or NP_3 .[3] Recency wins out in this case, partially because the attachment to NP_1 is so distant, with an intermediate attachment site NP_2 also available. The ranking of the intermediate (middle) site, NP_2, as least preferred derives from the fact that this site has neither recency preference nor predicate proximity in its favor. (See Gibson et al. (1993) for details.[4]) Other possible accounts of the observed complexity ordering include the tuning theory of Cuetos and Mitchell (1988), Mitchell (1993) and the references there, and the automaton theory of Langendoen and Langsam (1987), among other possibilities.[5]

The current chapter explores whether this on-line psycholinguistic result is replicated in corpus frequencies. The prediction is that, when a large number of instances of constructions of the form in (1) are considered, the frequency of low attachment (to NP_3) should be highest, followed by the frequency of high attachment (to NP_1), with middle attachments (to NP_2) least frequent of all. To evaluate this hypothesis, we examined most (as many as we could identify) of the NPs from the one million-word Brown corpus (Kučera & Francis, 1967) having a form similar to (1). In this analysis, any of the three attachments of the final modifying phrase (the RC in (1)) can be viewed as the target, relative to the two other attachment cases as controls. As predicted, we found that attachments to intermediate sites are indeed the most rare, and attachments to the most recent site (NP_3) are most common, with attachments to NP_1 falling in between. As a result, we conclude that corpus analysis can provide a useful additional method to test psycholinguistic hypotheses, either as a first test or as a validating measurement.

---

[3]Note that, at the point of attaching the RC, the predicate has not yet been processed. Thus, we are implicitly assuming a predictive-parsing algorithm—one that expects NP_1 to be subject of a matrix verb to follow. See Kimball (1973, 1975), Frazier and Fodor (1978), and Gibson (1991) for evidence that the human parser uses a predictive-parsing algorithm. See Gibson (1991) for an algorithm that is appropriate for use with predicate proximity.

[4]It should be noted that the presented theory also accounts for numerous other English parsing preferences. Furthermore, it is parameterized to account for the Spanish attachment results reported in Cuetos and Mitchell (1988), Mitchell, Cuetos, and Zagar (1990), and Mitchell and Cuetos (1991).

[5]An explanation for these findings on the basis of the serial-position effect from the memory and free-recall literature (e.g., Murdock, 1962; Tulving, 1968; and the references in each) might also seem possible, with recency effects and primacy effects corresponding to preference for low and high attachments, respectively. However, such an approach is empirically inadequate to explain a range of contrasts in attachment preferences beyond those described here, as discussed in Gibson et al. (1993).

ANALYSIS OF PP MODIFIERS OF NPS IN THE BROWN CORPUS

To test the psycholinguistic attachment-complexity hypotheses put forward by Gibson et al. (1993), we examined most of the NPs from the Brown corpus having the form in (3), which is the same as (1), but including a third PP modifier in the place of the RC:[6]

(3) $[_{NP_1} \ldots N_1 [_{PP_1} \text{Prep}_1 [_{NP_2} \ldots N_2 [_{PP_2} \text{Prep}_2 [_{NP_3} \ldots N_3]]]]]$
$[_{PP_3} \text{Prep}_3 NP_4]$

Using text-extraction tools (from the CLARIT project; Evans, Handerson, Lefferts, & Monarch, 1991) that are based on the work of de Marcken (1990) and Grefenstette (in press), every complex NP containing three or more prepositions was extracted from the Brown corpus, resulting in over 4,000 such phrases. However, many of these extracted phrases did not match the desired pattern, for a number of reasons:

1. Failure to conform to (3) because of poor category taggings.
2. One of the PPs attached to a site other than NP_1, NP_2, or NP_3. For example, in (4), "his supervision with a reduction in the number of forest fires in the state" was identified as a possible candidate NP. This particular sequence of words was ruled out because the PP "with a reduction" attaches to a preceding verb "credits," rather than to the NP "his supervision"[7]:

   (4) A citation from Conservation Commissioner Salvatore A. Bontempo credits his supervision with a reduction in the number of forest fires in the state.

3. An intermediate modifying phrase (other than a PP, as in a conjunction or a verb phrase) was attached to NP_1 or NP_2, making attachment to NP_2 and/or NP_3 impossible.

Thus, all of these kinds of examples were eliminated from consideration. Furthermore, we considered only the first three PPs that satisfied our requirements in a given example. Finally, we ruled out examples in which one of the prospective NP attachment sites was not a possible site for attachment. In particular, we eliminated examples in which one of the identified PPs was part of a

---

[6]Patterns of the form in Sentence (3) are much more common than are patterns of the form in Sentence (1), so that better statistics can be computed on the former.

[7]Although the pattern initiated by "his supervision" is not an appropriate item for our analysis, the NP that immediately follows the preposition "with" in Sentence (4)—"a reduction in the number of forest fires in the state"—satisfies the target pattern, and thus was included.

complex proper noun, such as "the United States of America," "Massachusetts Institute of Technology," or "Doctor of Philosophy." Such examples were eliminated because they contain only one possible attachment site for following modifiers, rather than two possible sites as in other NP–Prep–NP cases. Similarly, we ruled out examples that contained pronouns as one of the NP sites because pronouns in general do not allow modifier attachment.

Examples were also ruled out in which one of the identified NPs in the target template was a quantifier, such as "one of," "some of," "all of," or "many of." These examples were eliminated because attachment of a following modifier to the quantifier is extremely marked, and perhaps ungrammatical (except in appositive constructions, which are rare). Of the 69 examples we observed that contained such quantifiers, few contained a following modifier that could attach to the quantifier rather than the quantified NP.

The remaining 543 tokens were independently hand parsed by both authors, each resulting in a parse in which each of PP_1, PP_2, and PP_3 is attached to one of NP_1, NP_2, or NP_3. Because of the way the NPs were selected, PP_1 unambiguously attaches to NP_1 in all of the examples. The first ambiguity occurs at PP_2, which can attach to either NP_1 or NP_2. Of the 543 tokens, 202 are clear examples of NP_1 attachment, whereas 319 clearly attach to NP_2. Choosing a preferred attachment site in the remaining 22 cases is difficult because the meaning of the phrase is very similar with either attachment (cf. similar observations by Hindle & Rooth, 1993; Hobbs & Bear, 1990). Many of these ambiguous tokens involved the attachment of a locative PP; some of these are shown in (5), with the phrase to be attached in brackets:

(5) a. the topic for a round-table discussion [at the Bayerische Rundfunk in Munich]

  b. The inventories of unsold houses [in some areas of the country]

For these examples, a (slightly) preferred attachment of NP_1 was agreed on in 12 cases (as in (5a)), with the other 10 favoring NP_2 in our opinion (as in (5b)). Thus, there were 214 tokens of NP_1 attachment of PP_2, along with 329 tokens of NP_2 attachment (see Table 8.1). Therefore, we find a general preference to attach PP_2 to the most recent attachment site, although there are still many examples that violate this preference. This result replicates similar findings reported by

TABLE 8.1
Preferred Attachment Sites of PP_2

Attachment Site	Number of Tokens (%)
NP_1	214 (39)
NP_2	329 (61)

TABLE 8.2
Preferred Attachment Sites of PP_3

Attachment Site	Number of Tokens (%)
NP_1	62 (19)
NP_2	63 (19)
NP_3	204 (62)

Whittemore, Ferrara, and Brunner (1990), Hobbs and Bear (1990) and Hindle and Rooth (1993).

Examples in which PP_2 attached to NP_1 were then removed from consideration because such examples do not allow attachment of PP_3 to NP_2 (crossed branches would result). Of the 329 remaining examples, 62 prefer PP_3 attachment to NP_1, and 63 prefer PP_3 attachment to NP_2, with the remaining 204 preferring PP_3 to attach to NP_3. These results are presented in Table 8.2.

The results for attachment of PP_3 (Table 8.2) clearly indicate that the attachment pattern is not random [$\chi^2(2) = 121.72, P < .001$], with attachments to NP_3 occurring far more often than would be expected [vs. NP_1: $\chi^2(1) = 74.74, p < .001$; vs. NP_2: $\chi^2(1) = 73.41, p < .001$], and the frequency of attachments to NP_1 and NP_2 obviously not differing.[8,9]

The preference for attachments to NP_3 is as expected; this attachment is preferred in Gibson et al. (1993) as well. The lack of a difference between the number of attachments to NP_1 and NP_2 does not follow Gibson et al., but this is also not surprising because the set of 329 PP_3 attachment tokens includes: (a) tokens in which the three prospective attachment sites all have the same adjunct–argument status (i.e., either all adjunct sites or all argument sites), and (b) tokens in which one of the prospective sites has a different adjunct–argument status than the others (i.e., one or two of the sites are adjunct sites, and one or two sites are argument sites). It is well known that argument attachments are generally preferred over adjunct attachments, often even in cases in which recency favors the nonargument attachment. For example, Frazier's (1978, 1987) minimal-attachment principle favors argument attachments over adjunct attachments because argument attachments involve fewer phrase-structure nodes. Similarly, Pritchett's (1988, 1992) and Gibson's (1991) proposals involving the local satisfaction of the theta criterion (Chomsky, 1981) generally cause preferences for

---

[8]In order to use a chi-square test, we need to assume that each observation is independent, which, as pointed out by Don Mitchell (personal communication August 12, 1993), need not necessarily be the case because it is possible that some of the tokens come from the same passage in the corpus. However, independence seems to be a reasonable initial assumption.

[9]All chi-square tests with exactly one degree of freedom in this chapter have Yates' correction for continuity applied (Hays, 1988).

argument attachment over adjunct attachments (see also Hobbs & Bear, 1990; Whittemore et al., 1990, for corpus-based evaluations of parsing heuristics based partially on preferences for argument attachments). Thus, we would not expect the cases involving a heterogeneous set of adjunct–argument attachment sites to pattern in the same way as those involving homogeneous sites because, in the heterogeneous cases, attachment to the argument sites will tend to be preferred for independent reasons. Hence, the examples that we are interested in are those with homogenous attachment sites: either all prospective adjunct sites or all prospective argument sites.

As a result, we determined by hand for all 329 complex NPs whether the prospective attachment of PP_3 to each of NP_1, NP_2, and NP_3 was an argument attachment, satisfying a thematic role assigned by one of the NPs, or whether the attachment was an adjunct attachment (cf. Hindle & Rooth, 1993, who attempted to obtain related lexical information automatically). Standard syntactic tests for argumenthood (see, e.g., Pollard & Sag, 1987) were used to make this judgment. Most decisions were uncontroversial, although there were a few difficult cases decided by discussion between the authors. Representative examples of argument attachments to each of NP_1, NP_2, and NP_3 are given in (6a), (6b), and (6c), respectively. Representative examples of adjunct attachments to NP_1, NP_2, and NP_3 are given in (7a), (7b), and (7c), respectively. The attaching phrase is in brackets in each example.

(6) Argument attachment:
a. NP_1: the relation of the figure of the dancer [to light and color]
b. NP_2: the host of novel applications of electronics [to medical problems]
c. NP_3: the lack of scientific unanimity on the effects [of radiation]
(7) Adjunct attachment:
a. NP_1: periodic surveillance of the pricing practices of the concessionaires [for the purpose of keeping the prices down]
b. NP_2: headmaster of a private school for boys [in Louisiana]
c. NP_3: an area about the size of Rockefeller Center [in New York]

In (6a), the noun "relation" subcategorizes for a PP headed by "to". Similarly, "application" subcategorizes for a PP headed by "to" in (6b), and "effect" subcategorizes for a PP initiated by "of" in (6c). In contrast, there is no subcategorization relationship involved in the attachment of PP_3 in the adjuncts attachment examples: In (7a), "surveillance" does not subcategorize for a PP headed by "for"; in (7b), "school" does not subcategorize for a PP headed by "in"; and in (7c), "Rockefeller Center" does not subcategorize for a PP headed by "in". These are all adjunct attachments.

Of the 329 cases, 155 are examples in which all of the prospective attachments are adjunct attachments, whereas 174 involve at least one argument site.

TABLE 8.3
Adjunct Attachments of PP_3

Attachment Site	Number of Attachments (%)
NP_1	39 (25)
NP_2	23 (15)
NP_3	93 (60)
Totals	155 (100)

Of these 174 cases, almost all involve exactly one prospective argument-attachment site and two prospective adjunct-attachment sites. Because of the extremely low number of instances in which all three potential sites are argument sites, we restrict our analysis to the homogeneous adjunct-attachment cases.[10] The breakdown of adjunct-attachment location of PP_3 is presented in Table 8.3.

A chi-square analysis including all three attachment types reveals a significant effect [$\chi^2(2) = 52.08$, $p < .001$]. As in the analysis including arguments, the number of adjunct NP_3 attachments is far higher than would be expected on a random distribution of attachments [vs. NP_1: $\chi^2(1) = 21.28$, $p < .001$; vs. NP_2. $\chi^2(1) = 41.04$, $p < .001$]. Furthermore, the higher frequency of NP_1 versus NP_2 adjunct attachments is now apparent, although the effect is not quite significant [$\chi^2(1) = 3.63$, $p < .06$].[11]

As discussed earlier, however, it is difficult to unambiguously determine the attachment site for some modifiers because attachment to more than one site may result in identical or nearly identical interpretations. The counts in Tables 8.1, 8.2, and 8.3 reflect our intuitions about preferred attachments. In a number of cases, an alternative attachment still results in the same meaning. The existence of the possibility of alternate parses complicates the argument that the attachment site ordering presented in Table 8.3 reflects a complexity ordering. In particular, it could be that many sites that we have marked as high or low attachments also allow middle-site attachment to yield the same interpretation. Alternatively, it could be that many sites that we have tagged as middle attachments also allow high or low attachment. Thus, we examined all the adjunct PP_3 attachments and

---

[10]Another reason to restrict our analysis to the adjunct-attachment cases is that the experiments reported by Gibson et al. (1993) were also restricted to adjunct-attachment cases. Thus, although the Gibson et al. theory predicts that the pattern in homogeneous argument-attachment cases should be the same as in homogeneous adjunct cases, we do not yet have evidence that this is the case.

[11]In the 174 cases involving an argument attachment site, frequencies of attachment were 111 to NP_3, 40 to NP_2, and 23 to NP_1 (all three differ, $ps < .05$). This pattern can be partially explained by noting that PP_1 and PP_2 often attach as arguments, so that PP_3 is often a second argument for NP_1 or NP_2, but only a first argument for NP_3. Assuming that more NPs take one argument than take two or more, second arguments will be rarer than first arguments, and thus NP_3 attachments will be more common than higher attachments.

TABLE 8.4
Unambiguous PP_3 Attachments*

Attachment Site	Number of Tokens (%)
NP_1	27 (26)
NP_2	10 (10)
NP_3	68 (65)
Totals	105 (100)

Note. Adjuncts only.

determined which of these contained PP_3-attachment ambiguity. The unambiguous examples were then tabulated. The results are shown in Table 8.4.

These results provide further evidence for the complexity ordering (NP_3, NP_1, NP_2), from least to most complex. As with the preceding analysis, a chi-square test, including all three attachment categories, reveals a significant effect [$\chi^2(2) = 50.80$, $p < .001$], and all three categories differ significantly, with NP_3 attachments most frequent [vs. NP_1: $\chi^2(1) = 16.84$, $p < .001$; vs. NP_2. $\chi^2(1) = 41.65$, $p < .001$] and NP_1 attachments more frequent than NP_2 attachments [$\chi^2(1) = 6.92$, $p < .01$]. Therefore, the corpus analysis corroborates the complexity ordering given in Gibson et al. (1993).

Of the remaining 10 middle (NP_2) attachments, most are still relatively easy to understand, despite the comprehension result demonstrating the difficulty of interpreting middle attachments. In two of these cases, the lack of difficulty can be explained by the presence of what seems to be a path constituent, which consists of two separate PPs: [$_{PP}$ from . . .] followed by [$_{PP}$ to . . .], as in (8):[12]

(8) the tendency of some psychologists [from Heraclitus] [to Pirandello]

Because the PPs "from Heraclitus" and "to Pirandello" form a unit, they attach to the same location, which happens to be a middle (NP_2) attachment site in this example.

In some of the other leftover middle attachments, NP_3 is a proper NP, whereas NP_1 and NP_2 are headed by common nouns. Although proper nouns do allow some PP modifications (usually nonrestrictive attachments, as in "John Doe of Cambridge"), proper nouns do not readily allow the attachment of many PPs (those that are not easily interpreted nonrestrictively). Hence, if NP_3 is a proper NP to which PP_3 cannot attach, then there are effectively only two possible attachment sites for PP_3 (NP_1 and NP_2), as in (9), in which the PP "as the only effective method" is not permitted as a modifier of the proper NP "Cuba":

(9) the imposition of a naval blockade of Cuba [as the only effective method]

---

[12]Thanks to an anonymous reviewer for providing this analysis.

In other middle attachments, the attachment of PP_3 to one of NP_1 or NP_3 results in a meaning that is closely related to the meaning that results from attachment to NP_2, although this meaning is potentially distinct. It is possible that people do not notice this difference in most contexts, so that these NPs are interpreted based on a low or high attachment instead. For example, in (7b), the attachment of the PP "in Louisiana" to NP_2 or NP_3 might yield the same meaning, given an appropriate context (e.g., (7b): headmaster of a private school for boys [in Louisiana]).

Thus, the remaining middle-attachment examples that are present in the corpus are not overly difficult to understand. Of course, the lack of observed difficult middle-attachment examples in the corpus does not mean that all middle attachments are easy to understand. The middle-attachment stimuli in the experiments performed by Gibson et al. (1993) are examples of middle attachments that are difficult to understand. Furthermore, we can construct examples from the corpus of NP_1- and NP_3-attachment items in which attachment to NP_2 is forced semantically/pragmatically. These examples should be difficult to understand. For example, the NPs in (10b)–(10d) were constructed from NP_1-attachment examples by rewriting PP_3 so that the only plausible attachment was to NP_2. As expected, the constructed examples with forced middle attachment ((10b) and (10d)) are much more difficult to understand than the corresponding high-attachment versions:

(10) a. a program of prepayment of health costs [with absolute freedom of choice guaranteed]

b. # a program of prepayment of health costs [with a credit card]

c. a pile of wire cages for mice [from his time as a geneticist]

d. # a pile of wire cages for mice [with small doors]

GENERAL DISCUSSION

The corpus-analysis results described here corroborate the results of Gibson et al. (1993), replicating in corpus frequencies the pattern that Gibson et al. found in reading times and in grammaticality judgments: In ambiguous modifier attachments to NP sites, attachments to the lowest site are preferred over attachments to high and middle sites, and attachments to high sites are preferred over attachments to middle sites. However, as discussed previously, we might have found that the frequencies of different attachment types in our corpus were unrelated to the complexity ordering in Gibson et al. (1993), or that the frequency results replicated only part of the experimental pattern, so that, for example, low attachments were most frequent, but middle attachments were more frequent than high attachments. The fact that the current results agree with independent experimental findings casts doubt on the hypothesis that corpora and comprehension data are completely independent.

We do not yet have enough data to answer more detailed questions about the relationship between corpus frequencies and comprehension data, but we can speculate: Although editing processes probably play a role in determining corpus frequencies, we do not think that they can provide a full account of the apparently similar corpus and comprehension data patterns. Thus, we would expect to find the same similarity between the Gibson et al. results and frequency data derived from more spontaneously produced corpora. This prediction remains to be investigated.

Furthermore, if editing processes are not the sole cause of similarities between corpus-frequency data and comprehension data, we are faced with the question of what other factors are responsible. One possibility is that raised by the linguistic tuning theory (Cuetos & Mitchell, 1988; Mitchell, 1993), which, in its most general form, suggests that processing decisions in comprehension reflect construction frequencies in the environment, so that the more frequent interpretation of an ambiguity will be the preferred one when the ambiguity is encountered during the course of comprehension. Thus, linguistic tuning suggests that, at least in the case of ambiguity, comprehension difficulty and corpus frequency will be closely matched because the latter determines the former—no additional factor is present. The comprehension system simply keeps track of (at least certain types of) frequency information. Although many details of linguistic tuning remain to be specified (see Gibson et al., 1993, for some discussion), it is certainly compatible with the results presented here.

However, the theory involving recency preference and predicate proximity, described earlier and discussed in detail in Gibson et al. (1993), suggests an obvious alternative relationship between corpus and comprehension data, in which the two preference factors, already implicated in comprehension, apply in production as well. The details of how these preferences would operate in a sentence-production system remain to be worked out. One possibility would be to allow the production system to generate, in parallel, possible partial candidate syntactic structures for a given message to be expressed (perhaps along the lines of Garrett, 1975), with the two preference factors applying to select a single structure for use or to rank the alternatives. (See Gibson, 1991, for this conception of such preference factors in a comprehension system.) Alternatively, it is possible that the effects of the preference factors might follow from other properties of the production system: For example, recency might be a natural property of a production system that relies on the notion of spreading activation. Regardless of exactly how the preference factors end up being incorporated into the production system, on this approach the underlying explanation for the similarity between corpus-frequency and comprehension-difficulty data is that the systems responsible for generating the two patterns depend on the same underlying measure(s).

The data available so far are obviously much too limited to decide these issues. At the very least, the fact that the corpus-analysis results closely corroborate experimental results suggests that corpora can provide a useful supplement to experimental evidence in evaluating psycholinguistic processing theories. With further examinations of corpora and comparisons to related experimental data, it should be possible to develop a better understanding of how corpus statistics such as frequency are related to measurable properties of the comprehension process, and how such information can be used to evaluate psycholinguistic theories.

In addition to the psycholinguistic implications of these results, there are at least two relevant computational ramifications. First, the results reported here provide additional support for the conclusion that semantic-pragmatic information is necessary to achieve practically useful disambiguation (e.g., Crain & Steedman, 1985; Hirst, 1987; Hobbs & Bear, 1990; Schubert, 1984, 1986; Taraban & McClelland, 1988; Whittemore et al., 1990; Wilks, Huang, & Fass, 1985; among many others). In particular, although more than half of the PP_2 attachments in our corpus are to the most recent NP, 39% attach to the less recent NP. Even if the parser has access to argument- and/or lexical-preference information (cf. Ford, Bresnan, & Kaplan, 1982), it will get only 88 more of the 214 attachments to NP_1 correct (see Table 8.1), for a success rate of 79% on a single attachment decision.[13] Such a success rate is not practically useful, especially considering that a parse of a complete sentence may involve many such decisions. If only three decisions of this kind are necessary, the probability of a successful parse is only 49%. Thus, syntactic and lexical preferences are not sufficient for PP-attachment disambiguation in a practical natural-language processing (NLP) system.

---

[13]This success rate, using lexical preferences and recency, is somewhat low compared with several others in the recent computational literature: Whittemore et al. (1990) reported a success rate of 92% for a similar algorithm, and Hindle & Rooth (1993) achieved 85% success using automatically-acquired lexical preferences alone (no recency), when their algorithm's confidence in an attachment is 95% or higher. Furthermore, Hobbs & Bear (1990) reported a rate of 86% for a lexical preference/recency algorithm on cases not involving PPs headed by the preposition *of*. If we also exclude cases involving *of*, the success rate of the lexical preference/recency algorithm is only 61% in the current study.

A detailed consideration of the differences among these rates is beyond the scope of this chapter, but a major contributor to the lower success rate reported here is probably the difference in homogeneity of the attachment sites (in addition to differences in corpora). In particular, when potential attachment sites are homogeneous (of the same category), as in the current study (all NPs), the power of lexical preferences is likely to be degraded compared with attachment ambiguities involving heterogeneous sites. For example, certain prepositions strongly prefer to attach to nouns (e.g., *of*), whereas others (e.g., *during*) prefer to attach to events, which are canonically realized syntactically as verbs. When potential attachment sites are of heterogeneous categories, these preferences will often eliminate some sites from contention, whereas when all potential attachment sites are of the same category, strong category-based preferences will be irrelevant.

Second, when attempting to disambiguate an adjunct attachment in constructions of the form discussed here, an NLP system should adopt a search ordering of NP_3, NP_1, NP_2. More generally, when three or more NP sites are present, the most recent should be attempted first, followed by the least recent (followed by an as yet undetermined order of the other NP sites).

Previous NLP work in PP-attachment disambiguation has usually assumed a general recency preference, but no interacting high-attachment preference to lead the parser to rank NP_1 above NP_2. For example, Woods' (1973) selective modifier placement (SMP) heuristics ranked sites primarily by semantics, and then by recency if one site did not emerge as best. Schubert (1984, 1986) and Wilks et al. (1985) discussed similar semantics-based disambiguation methods.[14] These methods will fail on examples with three NP sites where (a) the most recent site is semantically blocked from attachment, and (b) there is no semantic difference between attaching to either of the two other sites. Examples of such constructions involving RC attachment are given in (11a) and (11b) (attaching clause in brackets):

(11) a. the sign above the memo to the committee [that was written in black ink]

b. the article on the movie about the murder [that was incorrect in many details]

Although people tend to prefer the attachment of the RC to the high-attachment site ("the sign" in (11a), "the article" in (11b)), the semantics/recency schemes will result in an attachment to the middle site. Naturally occurring examples of such high-attachment preferences are also present in the corpus discussed here. Two are given in (12a) and (12b):

(12) a. periodic surveillance of the pricing practices of the concessionaires [for the purpose of keeping the prices down]

b. a prohibition upon the withholding of patent rights [among A.L.A.M. members]

In Sentence (12a), the PP "for the purposes of keeping the prices down" cannot attach to NP_3 "the concessionaires" for semantic reasons. Attachment to either NP_1 "periodic surveillance" or NP_2 "pricing practices" is acceptable semantically, although the two readings have different meanings. Thus, the NLP systems of Woods (1973), Schubert (1984), and Wilks et al. (1985) would

---

[14]Some of these approaches rank attachments to a matrix verb phrase as better than a less recent NP attachment when semantics does not disambiguate, but none ranks a less recent NP attachment as better than a more recent one when semantics does not disambiguate.

probably choose NP_2. However, high attachment (NP_1) is preferred by people and turns out to be correct in context. Similarly, in Sentence (12b), attachment of the PP "among A.L.A.M. members" to NP_3 "patent rights" is semantically less preferred than attachment to either of the deverbal NPs (NP_1 or NP_2). Furthermore, there seems to be no semantic preference for either NP_1 or NP_2, so that NP_2 would be the choice of the semantics/recency heuristics. Here again, however, high attachment seems to be preferred and turns out to be correct in context. Thus, a system that relies on the ordering we have identified would have a better chance of rapidly finding the appropriate attachment site.

In further work, it should be possible to refine this ordering criterion by examining its performance on a wider range of constructions, both through corpus analysis and through comprehension experiments, considering differences across attachment-site type, attaching-site type, and, perhaps, languages. Results from a combination of corpus analyses and experimental methodologies should therefore be relevant for both computational and psycholinguistic perspectives.

ACKNOWLEDGMENTS

We would like to thank the following people for helpful discussions about the work reported here: Bob Berwick, Enriqueta Canseco-Gonzalez, David Evans, Greg Hickok, Judith Klavans, Don Mitchell, Teddy Seidenfeld, Gregg Solomon, audiences at MIT and Carnegie Mellon, and an anonymous reviewer. Of course, none of the views expressed here necessarily reflects the views of these people, and all remaining errors are our own. The second author was supported by an NSF graduate fellowship administered with funds provided to MIT under NSF grant RCD 9054772. Parts of this chapter were completed with equipment provided by the McDonnell-Pew Center for Cognitive Neuroscience at MIT.

REFERENCES

Chomsky, N. (1981). *Lectures on government and binding.* Dordrecht, The Netherlands: Foris.

Crain, S., & Steedman, M. (1985). On not being led up the garden path: The use of context by the psychological parser. In D. Dowty, L. Karttunen, & A. Zwicky (Eds.), *Natural language processing: Psychological, computational and theoretical perspectives* (pp. 320–358). Cambridge, England: Cambridge University Press.

Cuetos, F., & Mitchell, D. C. (1988). Cross-linguistic differences in parsing: Restrictions on the use of the Late Closure strategy in Spanish. *Cognition, 30,* 73–105.

Dell, G. S. (1986). A spreading-activation theory of retrieval in sentence production. *Psychological Review, 93,* 283–321.

de Marcken, C. G. (1990). Parsing the LOB corpus. *Proceedings of the 28th Annual Meeting of the Association for Computational Linguistics,* 243–251.

Evans, D. A., Handerson, S. K., Lefferts, R. G., & Monarch, I. A. (1991). *A summary of the CLARIT project* (Tech. Rep. No. CMU-LCL-91-2). Pittsburgh, PA: Carnegie Mellon University, Laboratory for Computational Linguistics.

Ford, M., Bresnan, J., & Kaplan, R. (1982). A competence-based theory of syntactic closure. In J. Bresnan (Ed.), *The mental representation of grammatical relations* (pp. 729–796). Cambridge, MA: MIT Press.

Frazier, L. (1978). *On comprehending sentences: Syntactic parsing strategies.* Unpublished doctoral dissertation, University of Connecticut, Storrs, CT.

Frazier, L. (1987). Sentence processing: A tutorial review. In M. Coltheart (Ed.), *Attention and performance XII* (pp. 559–586). Hillsdale, NJ: Lawrence Erlbaum Associates.

Frazier, L. (1990). Parsing modifiers: Special purpose routines in the human sentence processing mechanism? In D. A. Balota, G. B. Flores d'Arcais, & K. Rayner (Eds.), *Comprehension processes in reading* (pp. 303–330). Hillsdale, NJ: Lawrence Erlbaum Associates.

Frazier, L., & Fodor, J. D. (1978). The sausage machine: A new two-stage parsing model. *Cognition, 6,* 291–325.

Garrett, M. F. (1975). The analysis of sentence production. In G. Bower (Ed.), *Psychology of learning and motivation* (Vol. 9, pp. 133–177). New York, NY: Academic Press.

Gibson, E. (1991). *A computational theory of human linguistic processing: Memory limitations and processing breakdown.* Unpublished doctoral dissertation, Carnegie Mellon University, Pittsburgh, PA.

Gibson, E., Pearlmutter, N., Canseco-Gonzalez, E., & Hickok, G. (1993). *Cross-linguistic attachment preferences: Evidence from English and Spanish.* Unpublished manuscript, Massachusetts Institute of Technology, Cambridge, MA.

Gilboy, E., Sopena, J. M., Clifton, C., Jr., & Frazier, F. (1993). *Argument structure and association preferences in Spanish and English complex NPs.* Unpublished manuscript, University of Barcelona, Barcelona, Spain.

Grefenstette, G. (in press). SEXTANT: Extracting semantics from raw text. *Heuristics: Journal of Knowledge Engineering.*

Hays, W. (1988). *Statistics* (4th ed.). Orlando, FL: Holt, Rinehart & Winston.

Hindle, D., & Rooth, M. (1993). Structural ambiguity and lexical relations. *Computational Linguistics, 19,* 103–120.

Hirst, G. (1987). *Semantic interpretation and the resolution of ambiguity,* Cambridge, England: Cambridge University Press.

Hobbs, J. R., & Bear, J. (1990). Two principles of parse preference. *Proceedings of the Thirteenth International Conference on Computational Linguistics, 3,* 162–167.

Kimball, J. (1973). Seven principles of surface structure parsing in natural language. *Cognition, 2,* 15–47.

Kimball, J. (1975). Predictive analysis and over-the-top parsing. In J. Kimball (Ed.), *Syntax and semantics* (Vol. 4, pp. 155–179). New York, NY: Academic Press.

Kučera, H., & Francis, W. N. (1967). *Computational analysis of present day American English.* Providence, RI: Brown University Press.

Langendoen, T., & Langsam, Y. (1987). On the design of finite state transducers for parsing phrase-structure languages. In A. Manaster-Ramer (Ed.), *Mathematics of language* (pp. 191–235). Philadelphia, PA: John Benjamins.

Mitchell, D. C. (in press, 1994). Sentence parsing. In M. A. Gernsbacher (Ed.), *Handbook of psycholinguistics* (pp. 375–409). New York, NY: Academic Press.

Mitchell, D. C., & Cuetos, F. (1991). The origins of parsing strategies. In C. Smith (Ed.), *Conference proceedings: Current issues in natural language processing* (pp. 1–12). Austin, TX: University of Texas at Austin.

Mitchell, D. C., Cuetos, F., & Zagar, D. (1990). Reading in different languages: Is there a universal mechanism for parsing sentences? In D. A. Balota, G. B. Flores d'Arcais, & K. Rayner (Eds.), *Comprehension processes in reading* (pp. 285–302). Hillsdale, NJ: Lawrence Erlbaum Associates.

Murdock, B., Jr. (1962). The serial position effect of free recall. *Journal of Experimental Psychology, 64,* 482–488.

Pollard, C., & Sag, I. (1987). *An information-based syntax and semantics* (CSLI Lecture Notes, NO. 13). Menlo Park, CA.

Pritchett, B. (1988). Garden path phenomena and the grammatical basis of language processing. *Language, 64,* 539–576.

Pritchett, B. (1992). *Grammatical competence and parsing performance.* Chicago, IL: University of Chicago Press.

Schubert, L. K. (1984). On parsing preferences. *Proceedings of the Tenth International Conference on Computational Linguistics.* 247–250.

Schubert, L. K. (1986). Are there preference tradeoffs in attachment decisions? *Proceedings of the American Association of Artificial Intelligence,* 601–605.

Taraban, R., & McClelland, J. R. (1988). Constituent attachment and thematic role assignment in sentence processing: Influences of content-based expectations. *Journal of Memory and Language, 27,* 597–632.

Tulving, E. (1968). Theoretical issues in free recall. In T. R. Dixon & D. L. Horton (Eds.), *Verbal behavior and general behavior theory* (pp.2–36). Englewood Cliffs, NJ: Prentice-Hall.

Whittemore, G., Ferrara, K., & Brunner, H. (1990). Empirical study of predictive powers of simple attachment schemes for post-modifier prepositional phrases. *Proceedings of the 28th Annual Meeting of the Association for Computational Linguistics,* 23–30.

Wilks, Y., Huang, X., & Fass, D. (1985). Syntactic preference and right attachment. *Proceedings of the International Joint Conference on Artificial Intelligence 1985,* 779–784.

Woods, W. A. (1973). An experimental parsing system for transition network grammars. In R. Rustin (Ed.), *Natural language processing* (pp. 111–154). New York, NY: Algorithmics Press.

9 Unbounded Dependencies, Island Constraints, and Processing Complexity

Martin Pickering
University of Glasgow

Stephen Barton
University of Glasgow

Richard Shillcock
University of Edinburgh

This chapter discusses the processing of unbounded dependencies such as "whom does Fred think Mary loves?". It seeks to determine whether a first-resort strategy is employed in normal reading, and whether such a strategy is affected by the "island" constraints on possible unbounded dependencies. The first part of the chapter discusses theoretical and experimental evidence that suggests that a first-resort strategy is used in processing unbounded dependencies. Indeed, the processor appears to set up the dependency immediately when the subcategorizer is reached, before the purported trace location. However, this processing evidence does not resolve the issue of how island-constraint information is employed. We then describe some experimental evidence that supports the claim that the first-resort strategy is employed in normal reading, and suggests that much island-constraint information is in fact ignored during initial processing.

If island-constraint information is ignored during initial processing, then the processor tries to form dependencies even if they would be ungrammatical. This initially appears to be a bizarre strategy, but it is consistent with an extremely strong first-resort strategy under which the processor attempts to form dependencies at the first opportunity. On this account, island-constraint information would be used to check a structure that has already been built, rather than to constrain structures that could be built in the first place.

The main experiment reported here finds a localized processing load at the point where the unbounded dependency would be formed if a first-resort strategy is employed immediately after the subcategorizer is reached. This effect is found in both eye tracking and self-paced reading, and suggests that the first-resort strategy is used in normal reading. In addition, essentially the same pattern of results is found with the normal unbounded dependencies and those involving island constraints. This lends support to the view that island-constraint information is ignored during initial processing—an issue of potential linguistic interest.

The chapter also raises some additional issues. Processing complexity at the point of unbounded-dependency formation may not be due to this act of formation per se, but rather to the fact that, when this association is formed, the processor reaches a natural point to perform additional semantic processing. This may be because the processor has normally reached a point at which the sentence might conceivably end. If such a point has not been reached, no processing load may be found. This appears to explain some earlier experimental evidence, as well as some further experimental evidence reported here. The final issue raised is whether the coordinate structure constraint may be different in nature from other island constraints, in that it may be implicated in initial processing even if the other island constraints are ignored. We provide some tentative experimental evidence for this suggestion.

UNBOUNDED DEPENDENCIES WITH AND WITHOUT GAPS

In transformational grammar (e.g., Chomsky 1965), unbounded dependencies such as (1) are derived tranformationally.

(1) Whom does Fred think Mary loves?

There is an underlying level of deep structure at which *whom* is located after *loves,* but a transformation moves this element to its surface position. In recent transformational grammar (e.g., Government and Binding [GB] theory; Chomsky 1981), movement leaves a "trace" after *loves,* and this trace is coindexed with the moved element to provide the required interpretation. Sentence (1) is represented as in (2).

(2) [Whom]$_i$ does Fred think Mary loves t$_i$?

No such process occurs in most other kinds of sentences (e.g., "Fred thinks Mary loves John"), where there are only local dependencies and no movement occurs. This fundamental distinction differentiates unbounded-dependency constructions from most other sentence types.

In some recent alternatives to transformational grammar, in particular Generalized Phrase Structure Grammar (GPSG; Gazdar, Klein, Pullum, & Sag 1985), the appeal to traces in the canonical argument location remains, even though no movement is employed. An alternative analysis of unbounded dependencies does not make use of traces, but instead assumes that there is a direct relationship between the extracted element and the word that subcategorizes for it. On this account, (1) can be represented as in (3).

(3) [Whom]$_i$ does Fred think Mary [loves]$_i$?

This account is employed in various nontransformational theories, such as Categorial Grammar (Moortgat, 1988; Pickering & Barry, 1993; Steedman, 1987), Word Grammar (Hudson, 1984, 1990), and reformulations of Lexical-Functional Grammar (Kaplan & Zaenen, 1988) and Head-Driven Phrase-Structure Grammar (Pollard & Sag, 1993; chapter 9).

Assuming a reasonable transparent relationship between grammar and processor, the linguistic reality of empty categories could have some bearing on how unbounded dependencies are processed. The standard assumption, derived from transformational grammar, is that an association is set up between the moved element, or *filler,* and the trace, or *gap:* This process is known as *gap filling* (Fodor, 1978). First, the filler is identified and stored in memory. It is often assumed that this involves a specialized component of working memory (such as the store known as a HOLD cell in augmented transition networks [Wanner & Maratsos, 1978] or a "co-reference processor" [Nicol & Swinney, 1989], which may also deal with overt anaphora). Then the gap is located, and the filler is associated with the gap, setting up the coindexation relationship and causing gap filling to occur. Finally, the filled gap has to be related to the element subcategorizing for the gap (here, *loves*).

On the trace-free account, the filler is associated directly with its subcategorizer: We can call this *direct association* (Pickering, 1993). There clearly has to be a mechanism for dealing with this kind of association, but there is no reason to assume that it must be a separate mechanism from that which deals with local or bounded dependencies. The filler has to be remembered until its subcategorizer is reached, but this is a standard process for all associations. For example, the association between subject and verb can be interrupted by an arbitrary amount of intervening material (e.g., "John, who I know well, left"). This alternative view is clearly more compatible with linguistic theories that eschew traces.

Pickering and Barry (1991) argued that, in many instances, the two accounts cannot be easily distinguished because the trace is adjacent to its subcategorizer: This is the case in Sentences (1–3). But it is possible to distinguish the two models by separating the subcategorizer and the trace, as in (4).

(4) On which tray did you put the cup?

If there is a trace, it comes after *the cup,* as in (5a); but if there is no trace, the association is with *put,* before *the cup,* as in (5b):

(5a) [On which tray]$_i$ did you put the cup t$_i$?

(5b) [On which tray]$_i$ did you [put]$_i$ the cup?

Pickering and Barry provided evidence that the processor does not wait until the trace location before constructing the unbounded dependency, and hence provided support for the direct-association account. They argued that the short argument "the cup" can be replaced with arguments of arbitrary complexity without making the sentence impossible to process. The strongest evidence for direct association comes from nested constructions (for more details, see Pickering & Barry, 1991; Pickering, 1993).

Pickering and Barry's data are clearly compatible with having no traces. But as Gibson and Hickok (1993) pointed out, the data are also compatible with a "predictive" account employing traces, but where the trace is postulated in a top–down manner immediately when the verb is reached (see also Crocker, 1992; Gorrell, 1993). Pickering argued that the data are more parsimoniously explained in a totally gap-free theory, but it is clear that a trace-based account is compatible with the data. For present purposes, we assume that unbounded dependencies can be resolved at the subcategorizer, before the purported trace location is reached, and we do not talk in terms of gap filling. In the experiments discussed later, the subcategorizer and the trace are always adjacent, so the differences between the accounts are not fundamental to this chapter.

Strategies for Forming Unbounded Dependencies

The main question within the psycholinguistic literature on unbounded dependencies has been what the processor does in cases of local ambiguity. Consider Sentence (6).

(6) Which woman did you question Fred about?

There is a local ambiguity at the point of *question;* it is possible, but not certain, that *which woman* is the extracted object of *question.* In fact, it turns out that *Fred* is the object of *question,* and *which woman* is associated with the preposition *about.* Hence, if a dependency were formed between *which woman* and *question,* it would have to be undone, presumably causing a garden-path effect. In Fodor's (1978) terminology, there is a *doubtful gap* after *question.* In most cases, doubtful gaps will have to be resolved one way or the other by the end of the sentence, but sometimes this is not so, as in "who do you want to lose?", where there is a genuine (global) ambiguity. In all cases of doubtful gaps, the processor has to decide whether to form the dependency immediately.[1]

---

[1]Note that we are simply assuming (in line with other research in this area) that the relevant aspects of sentence processing take place in serial. However, the approach is equally compatible with a ranked parallel account.

There is no intuitive evidence that the unbounded dependency is wrongly formed in Sentence (6); the sentence does not appear to involve a garden path. Fodor proposed that the processor adopts a strategy that only assumes a gap if the next constituent could not serve as the argument of the verb instead of the gap (see also Wanner & Maratsos, 1978). In addition, Fodor proposed that a doubtful gap is only located if the verb preferentially takes an argument of the same category as the filler. In Sentence (6), *question* is preferentially transitive, so an object argument is expected, but no gap location occurs because *Fred* serves as the object. Hence, no garden path is predicted. On this account, the processor is likely to form relatively few erroneous dependencies, but processing will be slowed down if the dependency is correct, and dependencies will fail to be formed when an intransitive-preference verb is in fact used transitively. This account is purely intuitive and is not based on experimental research: There may be an unconscious garden path.

In contrast, more recent experimental evidence has tended to support a "gap as first resort" model, under which the processor does not wait until the next constituent has been analyzed before forming a dependency (e.g., Clifton & Frazier 1989). The best known line of evidence involves the so-called "filled-gap" effect (Crain & Fodor, 1985). In brief, the argument is that a first-resort strategy will sometimes be wrong and lead to reanalysis, causing a minor garden-path effect. For instance, in (6), *Fred* is the real object of *question,* rather than *which woman,* and it is clear that this is the case immediately after *Fred* is reached. Hence, if *which woman* is immediately treated as the object of *question,* as the first-resort strategy dictates, encountering *Fred* should cause reanalysis. The filled-gap effect is the fact that processing difficulty on *Fred* is often found in self-paced reading (e.g., Crain & Fodor, 1985; Frazier & Clifton, 1989; Stowe, 1986). We return to this point later.

Evidence for immediate forming of the unbounded dependency also comes from other experimental techniques. For example, Tanenhaus, Stowe, and Carlson (1985) used word-by-word self-paced reading and found plausibility effects compatible with the immediate formation of the unbounded dependency. They found a faster reading time on *asked* in (7a) than in (7b):

(7a) The district attorney found out which witness the reporter asked anxiously about.

(7b) The district attorney found out which church the reporter asked anxiously about.

The point is that both sentences are globally plausible, but there is a local plausibility difference at *asked* if a first-resort strategy is used: It is plausible to ask a witness, but not to ask a church. Hence the difference found on *asked* indicates that the first-resort strategy must be used. Similar effects have been demonstrated with event-related potentials (ERPs; Garnsey, Tanenhaus, & Chapman, 1989), which are sensitive to anomalies or predictability. Tanenhaus and his colleagues have conducted many similar experiments demonstrating immediate anomaly effects that are straightforwardly explained by a first-resort account (see, e.g., Tanenhaus, Boland, Mauner, & Carlson, 1993).

Another source of evidence is from cross-modal priming (e.g., Nicol & Swinney, 1989; Swinney, Ford, Frauenfelder, & Bresnan, 1988). The lexical decision or naming time for an associate of the filler is found to be speeded up (compared with a control) after the subcategorizer is encountered. This suggests that properties of the filler are reactivated at this point, and this implies that the unbounded dependency has been formed. This reactivation can be detected at the offset of the subcategorizer, suggesting that the unbounded dependency is formed right away. There is also some evidence that reactivation still occurs even if the next word indicates that the unbounded dependency is wrong. Swinney, Ford, Frauenfelder, and Nicol (reported in Swinney et al.) found a reactivation effect for an associate of doctor immediately after *advised* in "the boxer visited the doctor that the swimmer at the competition had advised him to see about the injury." This unbounded dependency is in fact ruled out by the next word *him*, and yet it still appears to be formed. This is strong evidence for a first-resort strategy. On the basis of all of this evidence, we assume that a first-resort strategy is employed during sentence processing.

Filled-Gap Effects

A first-resort strategy of course entails that sentences like (6) involve reanalysis. Therefore, it would seem likely that this reanalysis can be detected experimentally. However, there is good reason to suspect that any filled-gap effect is likely to be quite small. It is quite clear that the processor does not particularly mind reanalysis in these cases, as the ease of processing Sentence (8) would suggest.

(8) What did John say Fred believed Mary reckoned Sue did?

Here, backtracking should occur at *Fred, Mary,* and *Sue,* yet there is no marked garden path.

The lack of a clear garden-path effect is explicable if we assume an analysis like Pritchett's (1992a). Here, we simply sketch why we would expect this. It is well known that some garden-path effects are much stronger than others. For instance, Sentence (9) involves a clear garden path, yet (10) does not.

(9) While Mary was eating the pudding went cold.
(10) Bill knows the dinner is ready.

In Sentence (9), *the pudding* appears to be initially analyzed as the object of *eating,* but is then reanalyzed as the subject of the main clause. It loses any connection with *eating* because it has "moved out" of the subordinate clause.

More specifically, its final position is not governed or dominated by its initial position, which is Pritchett's criterion for reattachment being nonautomatic. In Sentence (10), *the dinner* starts off as the object of *knows,* but is then reanalyzed as the subject of the complement of *knows.* This is not hard to process because the location of *the dinner* is dominated by its old location. Intuitively, it ceases to be an argument of *knows,* but remains as part of an argument of this word. Pritchett predicted severe disruption around *went* in Sentence (9), but no conscious effect around *is* in Sentence (10). A minor, unconscious effect is possible in Sentence (10), but Pritchett was not concerned with any such effects.

Without needing to assume every detail of Pritchett's account, we can accept that there is a basic difference between reanalysis within a verbal domain and reanalysis outside a domain. Surprisingly, Pritchett did not systematically consider the analysis of unbounded dependencies within his framework, although some data are discussed in Pritchett (1992b). In unbounded dependencies, reanalysis is normally predicted to be unproblematic because the extracted element is reanalyzed from being one argument of the embedded verb to being part of an argument of the same verb, as in the following sentences.

(11) What did John say Fred did?

(12) What did Fred paint the picture with?

In Sentence (11), *what* starts as the object of *say* and ends up as the object of the complement of *say.* In Sentence (12), *what* starts as the object of paint and ends up as part of the prepositional object of *paint.* This appears to hold of most "complex" cases of unbounded dependencies, except those involving island constraints (as discussed later). For the other cases, any garden-path effect that can be demonstrated with unbounded dependencies is likely to be small.

In Stowe's (1986) Experiment 1, subjects performed word-by-word self-paced reading on the following sentences.

(13a) My brother wanted to know if Ruth will bring us home to Mom at Christmas.

(13b) My brother wanted to know who will bring us home to Mom at Christmas.

(13c) My brother wanted to know who Ruth will bring home to Mom at Christmas.

(13d) My brother wanted to know who Ruth will bring us home to at Christmas.

Stowe found that subjects took longer to process *us* in (13d) than in (13a) or (13b). The conclusion that she drew is that the unbounded dependency is formed between *who* and *bring* in (13d), and that it is undone when *us* is reached. Hence, the introspectively unobservable reanalysis appears to cause a measurable processing difficulty.

An important issue is whether processing difficulty is localized to the word that indicates the filled gap. Certainly, the experimental evidence suggests that the effect is greatest at this point. Crain and Fodor (1985) found an increase in processing difficulty relative to the immediately preceding and two following regions, and Stowe (1984) and Frazier and Clifton's (1989) results certainly show an increase in complexity at this point. But Stowe's experiments at least show some increase in complexity on the preceding region as well. The difference between *us* in (13d) compared with the mean of (13a) and (13b) is 192 ms, but there is an 81 ms difference on *bring*. In her second experiment, the comparable differences are 281 ms and 77 ms. In neither experiment is there any hint of an effect before this point. These differences might suggest that there is some difficulty with processing the embedded verb as well as the filled-gap effect. This could be due to the initial formation of the unbounded dependency. However, no such difference was found in Frazier and Clifton's first study (there is effectively no difference on the embedded verb). This discussion is of some importance when considering the experimental results presented later.

Another question is whether the increase in processing complexity found in these studies is due to the formation of the unbounded dependency and its later undoing per se. An alternative possibility is that processing complexity is tied to additional processing that takes place after the dependency has been formed. Such additional processing would be related to the extent to which the respective fragments are interpreted. There is an intuitive contrast between the fragments up to *bring* in Sentences (13c) and (13d); only (13c) appears to be "complete," in the sense that *bring* has an object argument in place. Of course, this assumes a first-resort strategy.

The obvious way to define this vague notion of completeness is that a complete fragment is one where a potential end of sentence has been reached. Clearly, this is the case at *bring* in (13c), but not in (13d). At this point, the processor might start additional processing, which could perhaps be associated with the notion of "wrap up." On this account, the filled-gap effect does not demonstrate simply the undoing of an unbounded dependency, but rather the undoing of semantic processing that is triggered by a potential end of sentence being reached. The formation of any "hanging" unbounded dependency is clearly a necessary, but not a sufficient, condition for this. At this point, we have provided no evidence for this suggestion, but it is taken up in the discussion of island-constraint phenomena.

This account is derivative from the *completeness hypothesis* of Goodluck, Finney, and Sedivy (1991; see also Bourdages, 1992). They claimed that gap filling is delayed until a potential end of sentence is reached, and they found evidence consistent with this position. Note that this is not our claim: We are not suggesting that the formation of an unbounded dependency is delayed until such a point is reached. Some evidence against this account is discussed by Pickering (1993). But the idea that processing complexity may be linked to a potential end of sentence may well be a good one, and it proves important in the later discussion of the experiments.

ISLAND CONSTRAINTS

Grammar

The notion of an "island" to extraction is due to Ross (1967). In our terms, it is impossible to form associations between fillers and subcategorizers within certain environments. In English, these environments include subject noun phrases (NPs) and relative clauses, as in the following sentences.

(14) *Who did a book about annoy John?

(15) *That's the man who the girl who loved knew the truth.

In fact, (15) is unacceptable on two separate counts because *who* is extracted from a relative clause forming part of the subject NP "the girl who loved." We pay particular attention to these two types of island-constraint violations in this chapter.

There appear to be two types of approach to island constraints within linguistic theory. The first is that they should be excluded as part of the basic syntax, so that sentences violating island constraints should be no different in kind from other ungrammatical sentences. The second position is the "overgeneration" account: Sentences violating island constraints are generated by the basic syntax, but are ruled out by a separate filter, which might be syntactic or semantic in nature. Perhaps the most obvious assumption is that they are straightforwardly ungrammatical like any other ungrammatical sentence. For example, if there is a single set of phrase-structure rules that generates all grammatical sentences and none of the ungrammatical ones, then sentences involving island-constraint violations should not be generated (whereas grammatical unbounded dependency constructions should be). In recent years, this has been a goal of work within GPSG (Gazdar, 1981; Gazdar et al., 1985), as well as other approaches such as Steedman's (1987) Combinatory Categorial Grammar. One obvious problem with this approach is that the acceptability of some types of extraction appear to vary in a manner that cannot be straightforwardly explained in syntactic terms:

(16a) ?*Which man did you read no books about?

(16b) ?Which man did you read two books about?

(16c) Which man did you read a book about?

In order to capture such distinctions syntactically, some very fine-grained distinctions regarding categorization have to be made.

The alternative is to assume that sentences containing island constraints are ruled out by means of some component of the grammar that is distinct from the basic grammatical rules. The basic rules then generate sentences such as (14–16), with constraints being subsequently applied by a different component of the grammar. One such approach is used by GB Theory, where the phrase-structure component of the theory is contained in an X′ module, and where extractions are dealt with by separate modules of the grammar. Obviously it is still necessary to find some way to distinguish examples (16a), (16b) and (16c); it is far from clear how this can be done by a purely syntactic component of the grammar.

However, it is important to note that the separation of basic grammatical rules from island constraints is not only compatible with GB. First, there is no straightforward account of island-constraint phenomena within GPSG or categorial grammar.[2] This suggests that such theories need additional components to deal with island constraints. A semantic account could be employed, which would not be dependent on the basic syntax. One relevant proposal is due to Szabolsci and Zwarts (1992), although they are only concerned with "weak" island effects such as those in Sentences (16a–16c). Szabolsci and Zwarts associated their semantic account with flexible categorial grammar. Hence, it is certainly possible to treat island-constraint phenomena separately from "core" syntax within monostratal theories of grammar.

An important possibility is that island constraints are not homogeneous, with some sentences being ruled out by the core syntax and others being eliminated by a filter. There are many possibilities here. One is that "weak" and "strong" islands differ, but we do not consider this here. Instead, we look at the coordinate structure constraint, as exemplified by Sentence (17) (e.g., Williams, 1978).

(17)   *I know who John loves Mary and Fred hates.

However, it is possible to say (18), where extraction occurs "across the board."

(18)   I know who John loves and Fred hates.

The generalization is that it is impossible to extract from a conjunct in a coordinate expression unless all conjuncts are (simultaneously) extracted from.

---

[2]In combinatory categorial grammar, Steedman's (1987) attempt to explain the complex NP constraint is problematic. For example, he ruled out "Beans, I met a man who likes" by preventing "a man who likes" from being a constituent. However, this also prevents legitimate coordinations such as the following (Pickering & Barry, 1993): (a) "I met a man who likes, and a woman who hates, sonatas by Mozart." Another problem (see Pickering, 1991) is that incremental comprehension of right-branching structures would be comprised if strings like "a man who likes" are not constituents.

A reasonable conjecture is that this constraint may be fundamentally syntactic, even if other island constraints should be regarded as semantic in nature. This is suggested because it is straightforward to deal with the coordinate structure constraint within a basic syntax. This was demonstrated by Gazdar (1981) in the context of early GPSG. Assume that conjuncts can coordinate if and only if they have the same category. In GPSG, the body of an RC such as "John loves" in Sentence (18) is given the category S/NP, meaning a sentence with an NP missing to its right. Now, "Fred hates" can also be given this category, and so coordination is possible: "John loves and Fred hates" also gets the category S/NP. But in Sentence (17), "John loves Mary" has category S because there is no missing NP, and this cannot be coordinated with "Fred hates." This simple account of coordination is only possible in an extended theory of categories such as employed by GPSG (for a number of complications that need to be addressed, see Pickering & Barry, 1993). For these purposes, a similar style of account is proposed within flexible categorial grammar (Moortgat, 1988; Pickering & Barry, 1993; Steedman, 1987). As mentioned previously, no such straightforward account has been formulated of other island constraints.

Another point is that the coordinate-structure constraint (CSC) is quite possibly a language universal, whereas most other island constraints are language specific. For example, the complex NP constraint is less restrictive in Italian (Rizzi, 1982) or Swedish (Engdahl, 1986) than in English; other constraints such as the *that*-trace filter disappear entirely in some languages (Maling & Zaenen, 1978). On the other hand, exceptions to the CSC are rare: In some languages, it is possible to coordinate a conjunct with an extracted NP with one with a resumptive pronoun (e.g., Georgeopolous, 1983), but resumptive pronouns are clearly unlike normal lexical NPs (see Sells, 1984). In English, cases like "what did you go and buy?" are presumably not really instances of coordination, but the example "how much can you drink and stay sober?" may be more problematic (Lakoff, 1986). However, the bulk of the evidence suggests CSC is more rigid than other island constraints, and it may be that they are fundamentally different in kind. Could it be that CSC violations are simply ungrammatical, but that this is not the case for other island constraints?

Processing

We have isolated two different approaches to the grammatical characterization of island constraints: one where island constraints are to be excluded as part of basic syntax, and the other where they are generated by the syntax, but are subsequently ruled out by a syntactic or semantic filter. We have also suggested that there is no reason to suspect that all islands should be explained in the same way. These two approaches to the linguistics of island constraints strongly suggest different accounts of the role of island-constraint information in language comprehension. Here we assume a reasonably "transparent" (Berwick & Weinberg,

1984) relationship between processor and grammar, with the processor applying rules of the grammar and reflecting any distinctions found in the grammar.

If sentences with island-constraint violations are regarded as simply ungrammatical in the same way that any other word-order violations are (e.g.,* "walks John"), there will never be a stage at which a transparent parser ignores these constraints. Alternatively, if the basic set of grammatical rules (e.g., the phrase-structure component of a grammar) does not rule out island-constraint violations, the processor will at least have the option of initially ignoring these constraints. Obviously, the constraints have to be applied eventually so that the appropriate acceptability judgments are obtained.

A useful way to consider these different positions is that the first model makes use of island-constraint information in a manner associated with structure building, whereas the second model uses this information in a structure-checking manner. This distinction is due to Mitchell (1989), who was concerned with the question of whether lexical information such as the subcategorization properties of verbs is employed immediately when major category information is accessed. He argued (along with Clifton & Frazier, 1989) that structure checking is correct. On this basis, he explained his (Mitchell, 1987) controversial evidence that a following NP is initially treated as the object of a strictly intransitive verb, but that this analysis is quite rapidly revised.

One of these approaches is presumably correct: Either islandhood information is applied immediately, or else it is applied rapidly after the initial phrase-structure analysis has been computed. Hence, this *structure-building/checking* terminology is preferable to that of *overgeneration,* as introduced by Freedman and Forster (1985). These authors found evidence on the basis of a sentence-matching task that there was a level of representation at which sentences with island-constraint violations behaved like grammatical sentences rather than un-grammatical ones. We do not consider this debate any further here because it is far from clear how their results should be interpreted (see Crain & Fodor, 1987; Forster & Stevenson, 1987; Stowe, 1992, for various accounts).

As Fodor (1989) noted, there has been very little on-line research on the processing of island-constraint information, and very little is known for certain. She discussed two studies, making use of extractions from subject NPs. Both experiments had rather weak results, and they went in opposite directions. Stowe (1986, Experiment 2) found no filled-gap effect in simple self-paced reading with sentences such as Sentences (19a and 19b).

(19a) The teacher asked if the silly story about Greg's older brother was supposed to mean anything.

(19b) The teacher asked what the silly story about Greg's older brother was supposed to mean.

(19c) The teacher asked if the team laughed about Greg's older brother fumbling the ball.

(19d) The teacher asked what the team laughed about Greg's older brother fumbling.

Stowe was concerned with the time spent reading *Greg's* in the four conditions. She found it took longer to read in (19d) than in (19c), indicating that the filled-gap effect is found in normal unbounded dependencies (although there is some question about the acceptability of (19d)). But no comparable effect is found between (19a) and (19b). On this basis, she suggested that island-constraint information is employed in structure building. First, we note that the theoretically crucial interaction is not significant by items. But a more interesting theoretical point is that *about* in (19b) does not constitute a potential end of sentence, even if island-constraint information is ignored. This is because it does not have a verb in the embedded clause. Hence, it is possible that the unbounded dependency is formed between *what* and *about,* but that the processor does not integrate the interpretation of this with other knowledge. If so, no filled-gap effect would be predicted even if the unbounded dependency had been formed.

Clifton and Frazier (cited in Frazier, 1985) found the opposite result using an end-of-sentence ungrammaticality task with visually presented materials. They found quicker responses to (20b) than to (20a), suggesting that subjects attempt to form the disallowed unbounded dependency in (20a).

(20a) What did John think the girl who always won received?
(20b) What did John think the girl who always excelled received?

Again, this result was rather weak, and there are alternative explanations of the results. For example, it may be that the processor is expecting an NP object for *won* in (20a), but not for *excelled* in (20b), because *won* is preferentially a transitive verb, whereas *excelled* is intransitive. Hence, the processor may be surprised by encountering the verb *received* in (20a), but not in (20b). It is also possible that *won* and *excelled* differ in some other way.

If both of these results are correct, there must be a fundamental difference between the materials or experimental method. One possibility is that there is an important linguistic difference between the constructions, causing the formation of the unbounded dependency in Clifton and Frazier's experiment, but not in Stowe's. The problem with this is that, if there is any difference, it is likely to go the other way. Clifton and Frazier's sentences are ruled out for two strong reasons: It is impossible to extract from subject NPs, and it is impossible to extract from a relative clause. Stowe's islands also occur in subject position, but extracting from a complex NP like "the silly story about Greg" is marginal, as Sentence (11) demonstrates. This suggests that the difference cannot be explained by a relevant linguistic difference. Possibly, the difference is due to the methodologies employed. Stowe used word-by-word self-paced reading, which is considerably slower than normal reading. If island constraints are applied very quickly as part of structure checking, it could be that their effect has already been felt while *about* is read and before *Greg* is even presented. This explanation is compatible with a hint of a greater reading time on *about* in (19b) compared with (19a), but the evidence is weak.

An alternative explanation is that the difference is purely a processing effect relating to the end-of-sentence issue. It may be that Clifton and Frazier's materials allow the processor to form a potential sentence at the embedded verb, so long as the island constraint is ignored. Hence, the processor must form sentences that can be compared with the declarative "John thinks the girl who always won the race." This is dependent on such examples being treated as sentences. In this example, this may not be the case because *think* cannot take an animate NP object, but has to take an S complement. However, it is likely that many of Clifton and Frazier's materials could be complete sentences at this point because there are not many verbs like *think* in this respect, and it would be these other materials that cause the effect. We return to this point when discussing experiments later.

Some evidence favoring the structure-checking account comes from the fact that "parasitic gap" constructions are possible where the parasitic gap occurs in an island in subject position (Engdahl, 1983).

(21) That's the person that everyone who meets likes a lot.

The fact that such sentences are possible suggests that an unbounded dependency is initially set up between the filler and the verb *meets,* although it is in an island position. If the verb in the main clause also has a missing argument, then a dependency is set up there as well, and the parasitic dependency is permitted. This does not explain why such a parasitic dependency is permitted (this is presumably to be explained by linguistic theory), but it is more plausible than the alternative processing model, under which the processor is initially prepared to accept that *meets* has no object, forms an unbounded dependency with *likes,* and then backtracks to form a parasitic dependency with *meets* (which would then have to be undone if it were subsequently to turn out that *likes* had an object and hence the sentence were ungrammatical). A final piece of evidence for structure checking is that there appear to be a few cases where nonparasitic extractions from subject position may be at least marginally acceptable.

(22) ?You're the only person I know who all my conversations with consist entirely of insults.

It is hard to see how these could ever be generated if the processor employed island-constraint information in assembling structure. Hence, there are some reasons to suspect that island-constraint information is not bound in with basic phrase-structure rules.

One other point is that Pritchett's account would suggest that some island-constraint violations would be hard to process if the islandhood information were not applied. For instance, "who does the man who loves Mary hate?" should be hard to process because *who* would be initially associated with *loves,* and would then be reanalyzed to a position that is not governed or dominated by its initial position as the object of *loves* (the argument does not change if we employ the language of empty categories). However, it may be a function of island constraints to make such processing more straightforward, by blocking this illegal unbounded dependency before it makes processing difficult (either in structure building or fast structure checking).

Let us briefly contrast the islands under discussion with the CSC. We have already suggested that it probably should be dealt with as part of basic syntax, and therefore (assuming transparency) should be employed in structure building rather than structure checking. Thus, there would be no attempt to form an unbounded dependency in an environment where that dependency is unambiguously ruled out by the CSC. Consider Sentence (23).

(23) I know what you hit the cupboard and broke the mirror with today.

In this sentence, the processor should form the unbounded dependency between *what* and *hit* as normal. Hence, reanalysis should be necessary on "the cupboard," leading to a filled-gap effect: *What* is not in fact the object of *hit*. When *broke* is encountered, it should not be possible for a dependency to be set up between *what* and *broke* if the CSC is obeyed. Hence, there should be no filled-gap effect on "the mirror." Therefore, an experiment should be looking for an interaction between these two object NPs, compared with a suitable control.

EXPERIMENTS

In this section of the chapter, we summarize a range of experiments on the processing of unbounded dependencies. The principal aim of these experiments was to investigate whether island-constraint information is applied immediately during sentence processing, or whether it acts in a structure-checking manner. The experiments all employ the logic of the filled-gap studies discussed earlier. However, the most important point to stress is that it is far from clear that solid support is provided for the assumptions of earlier filled-gap studies. We do find processing-load effects, as we describe. However, these effects cannot be straightforwardly equated with standard filled-gap effects, which is rather surprising.

These experiments were conducted using both eye tracking and self-paced reading. The three studies described were run together, with subject being exposed to the first study and one of the other two studies. In addition, there were two other experiments, which employed declarative sentences. Exactly the same conditions were employed in the eye-tracking and self-paced reading studies, with the same presentation order. Hence, direct comparison between the methods was possible. The eye-tracking study employed 24 subjects in the first study and 12 in each of the other two, whereas the self-paced reading study employed 32 subjects in the first study and 16 in the other two.

We employed a Stanford Research Institute Dual Purkinje Generation 5.5 eye tracker and monitored the position of the right eye every millisecond. The visual display unit was 70 cm from the position of the eye. For self-paced reading, we employed the moving window technique, with word-space information provided by underlines throughout the presented sentence. Unfortunately, there were problems with the data from the final words in each sentence because the reading times were not always recorded. Hence, we have omitted them from our analyses. All sentences were presented on a single line, and there were simple yes/no questions after about one third of our trials.

Experiment 1: Extraction from Nonislands and from Relative Clauses in Subject Position

Twenty-four items were constructed of the following form.

(25a) I realise what the artist painted the large mural with today.
(25b) I realise that the artist painted the large mural with skill.
(25c) I realise what the artist who painted the large mural ate today.
(25d) I realise that the artist who painted the large mural ate cakes.

Sentence (25a) involves an unbounded dependency between (roughly) *what* and *with*. However, when *painted* is reached, there might be a dependency between *what* and *painted*. Under a first-resort strategy, this dependency should be momentarily formed, but it should be undone immediately when *the* is reached.[3] The standard filled-gap account predicts an increased reading time on *the* (or possibly just downstream) as a result of reanalysis, compared with Sentence (25b), where there is no unbounded dependency. In light of the discussion of Pritchett's theory, we might expect this effect to be quite small.

In Sentence (25c), an unbounded dependency between *what* and *painted* is impossible, and the processor could be aware of this at *painted* (with the caveats discussed previously). Hence, we might predict that any difference between (25a) and (25b) in the critical region would not be found in (25c) and (25d). But if the processor overgenerates and ignores initial island violations, the difference would be expected.

---

[3]This point is true assuming that the processor does not interpret *the* as the beginning of a modifier such as "the other day." It would be very odd to adopt such an analysis over the direct-object analysis, but it does remain a remote possibility.

However, our experimental evidence does not fit very closely with the filled-gap predictions, although it does provide evidence for a localized processing complexity that can be associated with the formation of the unbounded dependency. Let us consider the eye-tracking data first. We divided the materials into the following regions.

(26a) I realise what the artist/ painted the/ large mural/ with today.

(26b) I realise that the artist/ painted the/large mural/ with skill.

(26c) I realise what the artist who/ painted the/ large mural/ ate today.

(26d) I realise that the artist who/ painted the/ large mural/ ate cakes.

Our second region included the word *the* because short function words such as *the* are regularly skipped, with the standard assumption being that the word is processed during the previous fixation.

We found the first-pass results shown in Table 9.1 measured in terms of milliseconds per character.[4] The critical finding is that "painted the" takes longer on extraction Sentences (26a) and (26c) than their declarative controls ($F1: p <$ .05; $F2: p = $ .05). The difference between the means for (26c) and (26d) reached statistical significance, but the difference between (26a) and (26b) did not. In the other regions, no differences between the extraction conditions and the controls were reliable.

The explanation most consistent with previous research is that this difference reflects a real, but very early, filled-gap effect. In addition, this effect appears to hold for the island cases, making us suspect that overgeneration does occur (*contra* Stowe, 1986). However, we also considered the first-pass times for the slightly different regions *painted* and "the large mural." Here, we found an effect on *painted* ($F1: p <$ .05, which was also significant when comparing the means of (26a) and (26b)), but not on "the large mural." This is still consistent with a filled-gap effect, but it is also possible that the effect reflects an increase in processing complexity on *painted*, related to the process of forming the unbounded dependency, rather than to a filled-gap effect. These possibilities cannot be distinguished because *the* might be processed whilst *painted* is fixated.

Let us briefly consider the total time spent in the various regions of the sentences, shown in Table 9.2. Very strong differences were found between the extraction conditions and their controls for the first two regions; in the third region, the difference merely approached significance. These results surely reflect the greater complexity of the extraction conditions. The most interesting point about these results is that the pattern of results is very similar for the island

---

[4]*First pass* is defined as the *total* time spent in a region before leaving the region to the right or to the left. Additionally, if the eye skips a region, the first-pass time is taken to be zero. Notice that we do not remove within-region regressions. The total time measure is simply the total time spent in a region while reading that sentence. Our critical regions are identical, and all regions are exactly matched for characters (and words). Hence, the transformation should not be problematic.

TABLE 9.1
Experiment 1: Eye Tracking First-Pass Reading Times

	Region			
Sentence	Region 1	Region 2	Region 3	Region 4
26a	33.5	31.9	36.8	35.3
26b	33.4	29.7	35.3	36.9
26c	31.9	31.7	35.2	46.4
26d	31.4	27.7	34.4	44.9

Note. Times are recorded in milliseconds per character.

and nonisland conditions, with no hint of an interaction. This gives some support to the claim that the islandhood information does not affect the way in which unbounded dependencies are processed.

In the self-paced reading study, we measured the reading time for all words of the sentence except the final word, and looked at differences between the extraction and the nonextraction conditions. There were no significant differences before *painted* (all $Fs < 1$). The means for "painted the large mural with/ate" are given in Table 9.3. For *painted,* the difference between extraction and nonextraction conditions was significant ($F1$: $p < .001$; $F2$: $p < .01$). Planned comparisons on the island condition means were significant ($F1$: $p < .01$; $F2$: $P < .05$), but on the nonisland conditions, the $F1$ was significant ($p < .05$), but not the $F2$ ($p = .10$). In contrast, the difference on *the* did not approach significance, and indeed no other differences were reliable.

These results suggest a very localized effect on *painted.* Hence, there appears to be no reason to assume a classical filled-gap effect. But an increased processing difficulty is found at the point where the unbounded dependency is initially formed (assuming a first-resort strategy), which is not found before this point. The fact that this effect is so localized strongly suggests that it is not due to an increased processing load associated with remembering a filler (as in Wanner and

TABLE 9.2
Experiment 1: Self-Paced Reading Times

	Word				
Sentence	Painted	The	Large	Mural	With/Ate
26a	584	540	540	536	538
26b	527	500	507	534	486
26c	557	489	492	564	541
26d	487	478	520	559	558

Note. Times are recorded in miliseconds.

TABLE 9.3
Experiment 1: Eye Tracking Total Reading Times

Sentence	Region			
	Region 1	Region 2	Region 3	Region 4
26a	61.8	55.5	57.6	58.6
26b	49.0	44.0	51.4	57.8
26c	64.5	58.6	61.1	73.4
26d	52.1	47.2	58.3	73.1

Note. Times are recorded in milliseconds per character.

Maratsos' (1978) HOLD cell hypothesis). In other words, the experiment provides good evidence that the initial formation of the unbounded dependency occurs at the point predicted by the first-resort strategy, and that this leads to a measurable processing cost.

In addition, we can be certain that this effect is significant for island-constraint conditions (26c) and (26d). Therefore, it is reasonable to conclude, on the basis of this experiment and the eye-tracking experiment, that island-constraint information does not block the initial formation of the unbounded dependency. This is in keeping with Clifton and Frazier's results (cited in Frazier, 1985), which made use of the same construction type. The structure-checking model appears to be supported. We can conclude that the processor makes use of a first-resort strategy that is so "active" that it ignores island-constraint information.

It is now necessary to discuss why there is no good evidence for a classical filled-gap effect. First, *all* sentences involved a "filled gap." There were no conditions in which the unbounded dependency was really between *what* and *painted* (this is necessary for the island conditions because an unbounded dependency is not possible). This was not the case in Stowe's (1986) Experiment 1. But it was the case for Stowe's (1986) Experiment 2 and Frazier and Clifton's (1989) Experiment 1, so the lack of a filled-gap effect cannot be explained in this way. In addition, our self-paced reading method involved underscoring, so that subjects might guess that the next word would be *the* before the button was pressed. This contrasts with Frazier and Clifton (1989) and Stowe (1986), who presented all words in the center of the screen without preview. It is difficult to rule out this explanation completely (although it would suggest that the self-paced reading task is greatly affected by minor changes in procedure). However, the great similarity between the eye-tracking and self-paced reading versions of the current experiment suggest that the pattern of results is reliable.

Now let us try to explain why our results are different from Stowe's Experiment 2 on island constraints. The increased processing time on *painted* may simply be due to the increased processing load due to forming an unbounded dependency, or possibly due to a filled-gap effect, but it may also be due to the fact that, in the nonisland case at least, the fragment "I realise what the artist painted" is a complete proposition; in the terms employed by Goodluck et al. (1991), it is a "potential end-of-sentence." We have already argued that this cannot explain when unbounded dependencies are formed, but it can explain why we find increased processing load under some conditions. "I realise what the artist painted" is of course only a complete proposition if the unbounded dependency has been formed. In the island-constraint sentence, the fragment "I realise what the artist who painted" could also be a complete proposition if the island constraint is ignored (in many materials, the matrix verb, such as *know* or *notice,* could more appropriately take an NP object).

On this account, it is not surprising that Stowe found no effect in her experiment because the potential unbounded dependency occurs before the verb. Hence, it may be that the processor does form a dependency between *what* and *about* in the fragment "the teacher asked what the silly story about," but no processing difficulty is incurred because the processor does not reason with this fragment. Therefore, our results are more compatible with Clifton and Frazier's study.

Experiment 2: Extraction from Complex NPs in Subject Position

In this light, we ran the following study comparing two conditions only, in both eye tracking and self-paced reading, using 12 sentence pairs (the slashes define the regions in the eye-tracking study).

(27a) I know what/ a book about/ the local election/ discussed the most.

(27b) I know that/ a book about/ the local election/ discussed the poll.

It is easy to summarize this experiment: No significant first-pass effects were found in eye tracking, nor were there any in self-paced reading. For example, under self-paced reading, all Fs on *about* and *the* were < 1.

On the basis of this experiment, it might seem that the processor does pay attention to island constraints during first-pass processing, in accord with Stowe (1986). This would then contrast with Experiment 1 discussed previously. We would like to conclude that the lack of an effect in this experiment is because the fragment "I know what a book about" is not a possible sentence, even when the island-constraint information is ignored. This would explain the difference between Experiments 1 and 2 in a manner that does not appeal to some putative linguistic distinction between the constructions.

Experiment 3: The Coordinate-Structure Constraint

Let us summarize one further experiment, again run both on self-paced reading and eye tracking. The purpose of this experiment was to investigate the

TABLE 9.4
Experiment 3: Eye Tracking First-Pass Reading Times

Sentence	Region					
	Region 1	Region 2	Region 3	Region 4	Region 5	Region 6
28a	39.2	39.6	32.3	37.8	25.6	41.0
28b	36.5	39.5	29.9	35.3	29.0	44.4

Note. Times are recorded in milliseconds per character.

coordinate-structure constraint (CSC) to see whether there was any evidence that it was ignored during first-pass processing. We contrasted the following sentences, again using 12 materials (again slashes are for eye-tracking regions only).

(28a) I know what/ you hit/ the cupboard/ and broke/ the mirror/ with today.

(28b) I know that/ you hit/ the cupboard/ and broke/ the mirror/ with force.

We would expect a processing difficulty in the first conjunct. Earlier studies suggest that this would be found on *the,* but Experiment 1 suggests that it might be found on *hit.* If the CSC is obeyed on-line, we predict no effect in the second conjunct. We have suggested that the CSC may be entirely syntactic, and in this respect unlike other island constraints, and therefore this result would not be surprising even in the light of Experiment 1.

The first-pass data for the eye-tracking study is given in Table 9.4 The only significant difference is on Region 5, "the mirror," where the reading time is longer in Sentence (28b) (control) than experimental Sentence (28a) ($F1: p < .05$).

We give the self-paced reading data for the words from *hit* to *with* in Table 9.5. There were no effects before *hit.* Significant differences were found at the first *the* (Word 6) ($F1, F2: p < .05$) and at Word 8 ($F1: p < .005; F2: p < 05$). The difference on *the* is explicable as a standard filled-gap effect. It is compatible with the nonsignificant tendency in the same direction on "the cupboard" in the eye-tracking study. In contrast, there was no effect on *hit* (Word 5), which

TABLE 9.5
Experiment 3: Self-Paced Reading Times

Sentence	Word Number							
	5	6	7	8	9	10	11	12
28a	524	570	548	588	558	520	536	531
28b	511	486	509	493	509	488	530	488

Note. Times are recorded in milliseconds.

contrasts with the first study. Let us begin by considering the data concerning this first conjunct.

Why should a standard filled gap be found in this experiment but not in Experiment 1? We do not have a clear answer to this. The first point to note is that the subjects would have no obvious way of telling that the sentences would continue in different ways. In addition, the embedded verbs used in the two experiments are rather similar: 4 of the 12 used in the first conjunct of Experiment 3, for instance, are used in Experiment 1. The only systematic difference is that the first experiment employed a two-word definite NP-embedded subject, whereas the CSC experiment used a one-word proper name or pronoun. We have to conclude that the differences are unlikely to be the result of syntactic distinctions. This suggests that the difference is probably found for very peripheral reasons: The effect may migrate one word "downstream" in Experiment 3 because the phrase is shorter and subjects are likely to press the button a few times before pausing to integrate what they have read. If there is a statistical artifact in one set of data, it must surely be in Experiment 3 because the results of Experiment 1 are robust across eye tracking and self-paced reading. Thus, we should conclude that Experiment 3 does not really provide a good replication of the filled-gap effect.

Now let us look at the second conjunct, which provides a test for the CSC. In the self-paced reading study, there was a filled-gap effect in the first conjunct, but not in the second. This would suggest that the CSC may be applied on line in a structure-building manner. This would be compatible with the linguistic proposals of Gazdar (1981), Steedman (1987), and Pickering and Barry (1993), where the CSC is integrated into the basic syntax. However, the interaction between the conditions and the first and second *the* (i.e., Words 6 and 10) was not significant. The eye-tracking study is more confusing because Region 5, "the mirror," is actually slower in the control condition. Although this clearly does not go against the claim that the CSC is applied on line, we do not have an explanation for the effect. Finally, we have no good explanation for the strong difference found on *and* in the self-paced reading study.

Although this study gives some weak evidence for the on-line application of the CSC, there are too many unexplained effects to draw strong conclusions on this issue. The differences found between the two experimental methods suggests that the materials may simply have been too complex to allow the processing of the CSC to be tested satisfactorily. However, it is far from clear how a relevant study could be done with less complex materials.

CONCLUSIONS

It would be premature to draw strong conclusions on the basis of these results. Our clearest findings come from Experiment 1, where we find a localized increase in processing load at the embedded verb, regardless of whether that verb is within an island to extraction. This appears to be indicative of the initial process of the formation of the unbounded dependency, and it does not appear to be sensitive to island-constraint information. On this basis, we suggest that island-constraint information is used in the process of structure checking rather than in structure building. This is consistent with Clifton and Frazier's results (cited in Frazier, 1985) discussed previously.

The fact that we do not find processing difficulty in Experiment 2 (in keeping with Stowe, 1986) may initially suggest that this island-constraint information is implicated in structure building. Linguistically, this seems very unlikely, given that the islands in Experiment 1 are certainly no weaker than those in Experiment 2. However, this difference can be explained if the processing difficulty in Experiment 1 does not reflect the simple process of unbounded dependency formation, but rather the process of forming the dependency and integrating the interpretation of the fragment with other knowledge. This may well be something that happens at positions that are potential ends of sentences. In more intuitive terms, "I realise what the artist painted" or "I realise what the artist who painted" may be points at which readers may stop and think because they momentarily appear to be complete units. This is because *painted* is momentarily considered to have an object argument. Readers are less likely to stop and think after reading the fragment "I realise that the artist (who) painted" because no possible object argument has been encountered. In addition, readers will not stop and think after reading "I know what a book about" because the end of the sentence could not have been reached even if the island constraint is ignored. Finally, Experiment 3 provided some very tentative evidence that the CSC may be applied as part of structure building.

We propose that the processor employs a first-resort strategy of the formation of unbounded dependencies in which most island-constraint information is initially ignored. Information about island-constraint information acts instead as part of a checking mechanism applied after initial structure building. This is in the spirit of the proposals of Mitchell (1989), although there is no need for us to be committed to other aspects of his proposal, such as the claim that subcategorization information is initially ignored. This proposal is not only consistent with GB theory, but is consistent with any theory in which island constraints are not encoded into the syntax.

The effects that we are attempting to tap into are extremely subtle, and settling the issues raised in this chapter may be very difficult. The problem seems to be that any effects that can be tied to the formation of unbounded dependencies are liable to be extremely small, as is evidenced by the fact that there is no evidence for any conscious garden paths with respect to these phenomena. In addition, there is the worry that it may be impossible to construct relevant experimental materials that do not stretch the boundaries of normal processing. It will be necessary to run many related studies if we are to make close investigation of the relationship between linguistic theory and sentence processing.

ACKNOWLEDGMENTS

We would like to thank Holly Branigan, Elisabet Engdahl, Simon Garrod, Alasdair Robertson, Andrew Stewart, and Matthew Traxler for their comments and assistance. This research was supported by an ESRC grant number R000243647 to Richard Shillcock and Martin Pickering, and by SERC Postdoctoral Fellowship B/90/ITF/293 and a British Academy Postdoctoral Fellowship to Martin Pickering.

REFERENCES

Berwick, R., & Weinberg, A. (1984). *The grammatical basis of linguistic performance: Language use and acquisition.* Cambridge, MA: MIT Press.

Bourdages, J. (1992). Parsing complex NPs in French. In H. Goodluck & M. Rochemont (Eds.), *Island constraints: Theory, acquisition and processing* (pp. 61–88). Dordrecht: Kluwer Academic Publishers.

Chomsky, N. (1965). *Aspects of the theory of syntax.* Cambridge, MA: MIT Press.

Chomsky, N. (1981). *Lectures on government and binding.* Dordrecht, The Netherlands: Foris.

Clifton, C., & Frazier, L. (1989). Comprehending sentences with long distance dependencies. In G. N. Carlson & M. K. Tanenhaus (Eds.), *Linguistic structure in language processing* (pp. 273–317). Dordrecht, The Netherlands: Kluwer Academic.

Crain, S., & Fodor, J. D. (1985). How can grammars help parsers? In D. R. Dowty, L. Karttunen, & A. M. Zwicky (Eds.), *Natural language parsing: Psychological, computational and theoretical perspectives* (pp. 94–128). Cambridge, England: Cambridge University Press.

Crain, S., & Fodor, J. D. (1987). Sentence matching and overgeneration. *Cognition, 26,* 123–169.

Crocker, M. (1992). *A logical model of competence and performance in the human sentence processor.* Unpublished doctoral thesis, University of Edinburgh, Scotland.

Engdahl, E. (1983). Parasitic gaps. *Linguistics and Philosophy, 6,* 5–34.

Engdahl, E. (1986). *Constituent questions: The syntax and semantics of questions, with special reference to Swedish.* Dordrecht, The Netherlands: Reidel.

Fodor, J. D. (1978). Parsing strategies and constraints on transformations. *Linguistic Inquiry, 9,* 427–473.

Fodor, J. D. (1989). Empty categories in sentence processing. *Language and Cognitive Processes, 3*(4), 155–209.

Forster, K., & Stevenson, B. (1987). Sentence matching and well-formedness. *Cognition, 26,* 171–186.

Frazier, L. (1985). Modularity and the representational hypothesis. *Proceedings of North Eastern Linguistics Society, 15,* 131–145.

Frazier, L., & Clifton, C. (1989). Successive cyclicity in the grammar and the parser. *Language and Cognitive Processes, 4,* 93–126.

Freedman, S., & Forster, K. (1985). The psychological status of overgenerated sentences. *Cognition, 19,* 101–131.

Garnsey, S., Tanenhaus, M., & Chapman, R. M. (1989). Evoked potentials and the study of sentence comprehension. *Journal of Psycholinguistic Research, 18,* 51–60.

Gazdar, G. (1981). Unbounded dependencies and coordinate structure. *Linguistic Inquiry, 12,* 155–182.

Gazdar, G., Klein, E., Pullum, G., & Sag, I. (1985). *Generalized Phrase Structure Grammar.* Cambridge, MA: Harvard University Press.

Georgeopolous, C. (1983). Trace and resumptive pronouns in Palauan. *Papers from the 19th Regional Meeting of the Chicago Linguistics Society, 19,* 134–145.

Gibson, E., & Hickok, G. (1993). Sentence processing with empty categories. *Language and Cognitive Processes, 8,* 147–161.

Goodluck, H., Finney, M., & Sedivy, J. (1991). Sentence completeness and filler-gap dependency parsing. In P. Coopmans, B. Schouten, & W. Zonneveld (Eds.), *OTS Yearbook 1991* (pp. 19–31). Utrecht, the Netherlands: University of Utrecht Press.

Gorrell, P. (1993). Evaluating the direct association hypothesis: A reply to Pickering and Barry. *Language and Cognitive Processes.* 8, 129–146.

Hudson, R. A. (1984). *Word grammar.* Oxford: Basil Blackwell.

Hudson, R. A. (1990). *English word grammar.* Oxford: Basil Blackwell.

Kaplan, R. M., & Zaenen, A. (1988). Long-distance dependencies as a case of functional uncertainty. In M. Baltin & A. Kroch (Eds.), *Alternative conceptions of phrase structure* (pp. 17–42). Chicago, IL: University of Chicago Press.

Lakoff, G. (1986). Frame semantic control of the coordinate structure constraint. *Proceedings of the Chicago Linguistics Society 22.2, 22,* 152–167.

Maling, J., & Zaenen, A. (1978). The non-universality of a surface filter. *Linguistic Inquiry, 9,* 475–497.

Mitchell, D. (1987). Lexical guidance in human parsing: Locus and processing characteristics. In M. Coltheart (Ed.), *Attention and performance XII: The psychology of reading* (pp. 601–618). Hillsdale, NJ: Lawrence Erlbaum Associates.

Mitchell, D. (1989). Verb guidance and other lexical effects in parsing. *Language and Cognitive Processes, 3*(4), 123–154.

Moortgat, M. (1988). *Categorial investigations: Logical and linguistic aspects of the lambek calculus.* Dordrecht, The Netherlands: Foris.

Nicol, J., & Swinney, D. (1989). The role of structure in coreference assignment during sentence comprehension. *Journal of Psycholinguistic Research, 18,* 5–19.

Pickering, M. J. (1991). *Processing dependencies.* Unpublished doctoral thesis, University of Edinburgh, Scotland.

Pickering, M. J. (1993). Direct association and sentence processing: A reply to Gorrell and to Gibson and Hickok. *Language and Cognitive Processes, 8,* 163–196.

Pickering, M. J., & Barry, G. (1991). Sentence processing without empty categories. *Language and Cognitive Processes, 6,* 229–259.

Pickering, M. J., & Barry, G. (1993). Dependency categorial grammar and coordination. *Linguistics, 31,* 855–902.

Pollard, C., & Sag, I. A. (1993). *Head-Driven Phrase Structure Grammar.* Chicago, IL: University of Chicago Press.

Pritchett, B. (1992a). *Grammatical competence and parsing performance.* Chicago, IL: University of Chicago Press.

Pritchett, B. (1992b). Parsing with grammar: Islands, heads and garden paths. In H. Goodluck & M. Rochemont (Eds.), *Island Constraints: Theory, Acquisition and processing* (pp. 321–349). Dordrecht, The Netherlands: Kluwer Academic.

Rizzi, L. (1982). Violations of the Wh-island constraint and the subjacency condition. In L. Rizzi (Ed.), *Issues in Italian syntax* (pp. 49–76). Dordrecht, The Netherlands: Foris.

Ross, J. R. (1967). *Constraints on variables in syntax.* Unpublished doctoral dissertation, Massachusetts Institute of Technology, Cambridge, MA.

Sells, P. (1984). *The syntax and semantics of resumptive pronouns.* Unpublished doctoral dissertation, University of Massachusetts, Amherst, MA.

Steedman, M. (1987). Combinatory grammars and parasitic gaps. *Natural Language and Linguistic Theory, 5,* 403–439.

Stowe, L. A. (1984). *Models of gap location in the human language processor.* Bloomington, IN: Indiana University Linguistics Club.

Stowe, L. A. (1986). Parsing WH-constructions: Evidence for on-line gap location. *Language and Cognitive Processes, 1,* 227–245.

Stowe, L. A. (1992). The processing implications of syntactic constraints: The sentence matching debate. In H. Goodluck & M. Rochemont (Eds.), *Island constraints: Theory, acquisition and processing* (pp. 419–443). Dordrecht, The Netherlands: Kluwer Academic.

Swinney, D., Ford, M., Frauenfelder, U., & Bresnan, J. (1988). On the temporal course of gap-filling and antecedent assignment during sentence comprehension. Unpublished manuscript.

Szalbolsci, A., & Zwarts, F. (1992). Weak islands and algebraic semantics for scope taking. *Natural Language Semantics, 1,* 235–284.

Tanenhaus, M., Boland, J., Mauner, G., & Carlson, G. (1993). More on combinatory lexical information: Thematic structure in parsing and interpretation. In G. Altmann & R. Shillcock (Eds.), *Cognitive models of speech processing: Psycholinguistic and computational perspectives II* (pp. 297–319). Cambridge, MA: MIT Press.

Tanenhaus, M., Stowe, L. A., & Carlson, G. (1985). The interaction of lexical expectation and pragmatics in parsing filler-gap constructions. *Proceedings of The Seventh Annual Cognitive Science Meeting.*

Wanner, E., & Maratsos, M. (1978). an ATN approach to comprehension. In M. Halle, J. Bresnan, & G. A. Miller (Eds.), *Linguistic theory and psychological reality* (pp. 119–161). Cambridge, MA: MIT Press.

Williams, E. (1978). Across-the-board rule application. *Linguistic Inquiry, 9,* 31–43.

10

German Verb-Final Clauses and Sentence Processing: Evidence for Immediate Attachment

Markus Bader*
Universität Stuttgart/Institut für Linguistik

Ingeborg Lasser
Max-Planck-Institut für Psycholinguistik

One central question in sentence processing concerns the relationship between knowledge of language and the way this knowledge is put to use. This relationship between *competence* and *performance,* to use traditional terms, has received a great deal of attention in the discussion of models of the human parsing mechanism. The human parsing mechanism is that part of our language-comprehension system that is responsible for computing syntactic structures. Despite this attention, the issue of how linguistic knowledge is used during sentence comprehension is far from being settled. The goal of this chapter is to narrow down the number of possible parsing models by introducing some on-line data from German.

From the earliest days when language-processing models first drew on the theory of generative grammar, until the present time, attempts have been made to make the relationship between the grammar and the parser as transparent as possible. In discussing this relationship, we must distinguish the output of the parser (*what* it computes) from the operational process of the parser (*how* it computes). Accordingly, two different notions of grammar–parser transparency must be distinguished. The first notion concerns the relationship between the representations computed by the human parser and the structures defined by the competence grammar. It is generally assumed that this relationship is transparent in the sense that the parser computes structures that are defined by the competence grammar. We share this assumption without further discussion. The second, and more controversial, notion of transparency is concerned with the relationship between the parsing process and the grammatical knowledge. It is in this sense that we use the term *transparency* in the following. For instance, assuming a rule-based grammar model, transparency can be implemented by a

---

*Markus Bader is now at the Universitaet Jena.

parsing algorithm that accesses and uses the rules stored in the competence grammar (see, e.g., Berwick & Weinberg, 1984; Miller & Chomsky, 1963).

In the principles and parameters theory (see Chomsky, 1986; Chomsky & Lasnik, 1993), which is the grammatical theory we adopt, the grammar consists of a set of principles. In this chapter, we discuss a particular class of parsers that assumes both principles and parameters theory and a transparent grammar–parser relationship. We call these parsers *head-driven licensing parsers*. On the basis of experimental evidence from German verb-final structures, we reject the particular interpretation of grammar–parser transparency found in these parsers. We present and discuss the empirical evidence later. Before discussing the experiment, we introduce certain properties of current syntactic theory and then show how these properties have found their way into head-driven licensing parsers. We also show the predictions that these parsers make for verb-final clauses. In the concluding section, we discuss the role of grammar–parser transparency in models of the human parser.

HEAD-DRIVEN APPROACHES TO PARSING

In this section, we discuss the role that lexical heads play in a principles and parameters grammar, and we introduce the concept of a head-driven licensing parser. The two most prominent properties of this concept are that syntactic structure is built exclusively from heads in the input string, and that every attachment must be licensed by an element in the already existing structure.

Heads and Licensing

In some models of generative grammar (such as earlier transformational models and some current nontransformational models), syntactic representations are derived by the application of rules. In the framework assumed here, rules have been excluded from the theory of grammar as a result of work initiated by Chomsky (1970) and continued by Stowell (1981) and Speas (1990). As an overall result of this elimination, projection of syntactic structure occurs directly from the lexicon in accordance with certain general principles, and without application of phrase-structure rules.[1]

The grammar consists of rich lexical entries that interact with a set of general well-formedness principles (e.g., binding principles, projection principle, theta-criterion). For a syntactic structure to be well formed, no such principle may be violated. In addition, each element that appears in it "must be licensed in one of a small number of available ways" (Chomsky, 1986, p. 93), or in short:

---

[1]For a detailed illustration of how projection from the lexicon works, see Speas (1990).

(1) The licensing condition: Every element in a structure must be licensed. (Speas, 1990, p. 26)

A number of different licensing relationships have been proposed in the literature, where a basic distinction is drawn between the licensing of maximal projections and the licensing of nonmaximal projections. Nonmaximal projections are licensed by the X-bar schema, which constrains the structure of all phrases. The X-bar schema determines the form in which phrases are projected. The actual categorical features of each phrase are determined by its head. For example, if the head is a verb, the maximal phrase directly dominating it is a verb phrase (VP). Thus, a particular phrase is determined both by a general principle (X-bar theory) and specific lexical information (the syntactic category of its head).

Maximal projections are licensed by specific relationships to other elements in the structure. The core case of licensing a maximal projection is the licensing of a phrase as an argument of a verb. This kind of licensing is accomplished by the mechanism of theta marking. Each verb is associated with a theta grid, and in a well-formed structure there is a one-to-one mapping between arguments and positions in the theta grid.[2] This mapping is regulated by the theta criterion, which is given here in a simplified version:

(2) Theta criterion: Every argument must be associated with a theta role, and every theta role has to be associated with an argument.

Because theta grids are associated with heads, one can say that maximal projections are licensed by their relationship to a head. Thus, heads carry two types of grammatically relevant information: First, they determine the categorical features of phrases; second, they are associated with certain "licensing information" like a theta grid and thus function as licensors for other maximal phrases. In the next section, we see how these two aspects of heads have been used in parsing theory.

Head-Driven Licensing Parsers

Head-driven licensing parsers are parsers that contain the following two parsing principles.

(3) Head projection (HP): Build a maximal phrase if its head has been encountered in the input.

(4) Attachment by licensing (AbL): Attach a phrase into the current tree

---

[2]These are only the simplest assumptions. For more sophisticated analyses, see Grimshaw (1990) and Rappaport and Levin (1988).

when it is licensed by an element in the current tree. (Attach a phrase in accordance with the syntactic-licensing conditions.)

HP and AbL determine what the parser does with the two types of information contained in lexical entries: HP determines how and when categorical information is used in projecting phrases, whereas AbL determines how and when selectional information is used in attachment decisions. Thus, the organization of the parser corresponds to the organization of lexical entries into two types of grammatically relevant information.

An important assumption that head-driven licensing parsers make is that both structure building and attachment actions are input driven. Thus, HP determines that only heads in the input string can initiate the building of new structure, and, according to AbL, attachment of a phrase occurs only when it is licensed by an element in the already existing structure.[3]

Two points are crucial for our discussion. One is that a parser obeying HP cannot hypothesize a new phrase prior to the occurrence of the head of that phrase in the input. This kind of hypothesizing is inherently illicit for a parser that abides by HP. This is true irrespective of whether a specific hypothesis is doubtful. For example, after the occurrence of a complementizer in the input string, it would be without risk to insert an IP projection as a sister to C^0, although no Infl element has as yet occurred in the input. This is so because IP is the obligatory complement of C^0. Because of the strict nature of HP, a head-driven parser cannot exploit this fact. The second important point is that a phrase must be attached when and only when it is licensed.

Two parsing models that integrate both HP and AbL are found in Abney (1989) and Pritchett (1991, 1992), respectively. In Abney's model, the structure-building mechanism is the SHIFT action, which projects a word of Category X in the input string to XP. Thus, the categorical information of a head X is used to build a phrase of type XP. Attachment of that XP into the current tree occurs in accordance with specific licensing principles. Another model that aims at implementing grammatical licensing is Pritchett's. In his (1991) article, he introduced the notion of "head-driven" parsing: "A node cannot be projected before the occurrence of its head, since the relevant features which determine its categorical identity and license both its own and its arguments' attachments are theretofore undetermined" (p. 252). Attachment in Pritchett's model occurs in such a way that licensing principles are maximally satisfied at each point in time during on-line processing (see his 1992 generalized theta-attachment principle). Although Pritchett's model differs from Abney's in certain ways, it is similar to it in that all structure building originates from heads in the input,[4] and phrases are attached

---

[3]We do not address here the problem of how adjuncts get integrated into syntactic representations. Specific problems arise there that are beyond the scope of this chapter.

[4]Pritchett's (1992) model makes no explicit reference to a head-driven mechanism. However, it is clearly an implementation of a head-driven approach. This can be seen from his discussion of Japanese (pp. 151–153).

exclusively into the structure that has been projected by that head-driven procedure.

The significance of head projection and attachment by licensing can best be seen by considering how they affect the projection of the VP of a clause. According to HP, to build a VP, the lexical head that projects to V must already have occurred in the input string. Prior to this, no satellites of VP, such as arguments or adverbial phrases, can be attached to that VP. Such a parser model has strong implications for verb-final structures. Any noun phrase (NP) or prepositional phrase (PP) of a clause must remain unattached until the verb occurs for two reasons. First, their attachment is not licensed by any other element in the previous input; second, the phrase (VP) into which they would have to be attached is not projected yet because its lexical head has not yet occurred in the input. In the next section, we introduce the structure of German verb-final clauses and derive the predictions for their processing by a head-driven licensing parser.

VERB-FINAL CLAUSES AND PROCESSING

We now consider how a head-driven licensing parser would process German verb-final sentences. In declarative root clauses, German exhibits the verb-second phenomenon (i.e., the verb must always appear as the second constituent, presumably in C^0). Although interesting questions with respect to parsing arise from verb-second structures, we focus here exclusively on embedded verb-final structures. With respect to these structures, we report findings that are not predicted by a head-driven licensing parser.

German Verb-Final Clauses

With respect to headedness, German is a mixed language (i.e., NP, PP, and CP are head initial, whereas AP and VP are head final). In this chapter, we act as if German syntax did not contain an IP level. We do this solely for expository reasons. The question of whether there are functional projections between CP and VP in a German clause (an IP in the simplest case) is one of the most debated questions about German syntax. Because this question has no bearing on the interpretation of the experimental results, we omit IP to simplify the exposition. The fact that verbs are base generated in clause-final position is seen in embedded clauses introduced by a complementizer. In these clauses, all verbal elements occur to the right of their objects.

(5) *Maria dachte . . .*
    Mary thought . . .
    . . . [CP *daß* [VP *Hans* [VP *das Buch gelesen hat*]]]
    . . .   that   John   the book read   has
    "that John has read the book"

In Sentence (5), the complementizer *daß* introduces the complement clause selected by the higher verb *dachte. Daß* is obligatory and cannot be dropped.[5] The elements following the complementizer are the complements of the embedded verb, namely *Hans* and *das Buch.* The main verb of the embedded clause in (5) is a participial form (*gelesen*), and the finite auxiliary (*hat*) concludes the clause.

Predictions of the Head-Driven Licensing Model for Verb-Final Clauses

Next, let us consider how a verb-final structure like (5) would be processed by a head-driven licensing parser. The question to ask is: Which decisions about the syntactic structure of a verb-final clause can the parser make before encountering the main (theta-assigning) verb? A head-driven licensing parser can make two kinds of decisions before encountering the verb in a sentence like (5): At the complementizer, the parser can construct the topmost phrase CP. The parser can also assemble those phrases that will later be attached to VP—for instance, NPs and PPs. Both of these processes are in accordance with head projection. A snapshot of the parsed structure just prior to the occurrence of the verb can be schematized as in (6):

(6) . . . *daß Hans das Buch* . . .

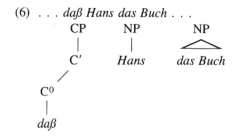

What a head-driven licensing parser cannot do is attach the NPs to any existing structure. To do this, the parser would need the VP projection, which mediates between the highest projection (CP) and the argument phrases. To a head-driven licensing parser, the VP does not become available until the end of the clause, when the verb arrives in the input string. Thus, in verb-final clauses, such a parser delays attachment of arguments until the end of the clause.

Although head-driven licensing parsers make this clear prediction with regard to the time course of parsing actions, it is not a trivial matter to find linguistic structures that can serve as a convincing test case for this prediction. Take for

---

[5]Embedded clauses exist without a complementizer. However, these clauses show the verb-second structure of root clauses. Thus, in German declaratives, C⁰ is either filled by a complementizer or the finite verb. As with root verb-second clauses, we do not consider embedded verb-second clauses here.

example PP-attachment ambiguities in German or Dutch. In this case, we have a configuration like in (8), where the PP can be attached either to NP or to VP, depending on the verb at the end of the clause.

(7) Comp [$_{VP}$ . . . NP PP . . . V]

In the case where the PP can plausibly be an argument of the NP, examples have been reported where there is a preference for attachment of PP to NP, until the verb disambiguates the sentence. Thus, a garden-path experience occurs when the PP is required as an argument of the verb (see Crocker, 1992). This speaks in favor of parsing models incorporating AbL because, when PP attachment is licensed by the head of NP, this attachment is in fact carried out. On the other hand, consider the situation where the PP could be either an adjunct of the NP or an argument of the VP. Frazier (1987b) found that processing is faster when the disambiguating verb is compatible with the argument interpretation of the PP (PP attached to VP), and has explained this by the minimal-attachment strategy. This result can be predicted by a licensing parser only under special assumptions. If it is stipulated that a phrase is left unattached if it cannot be licensed as an argument, the PP will not be attached to the NP.[6] Afterward, when the verb is encountered, it may be assumed that it is easier for the parser to compute the structure with PP attached to VP as an argument than to compute the structure with PP attached to NP. All in all, PP-attachment ambiguities have not led to a decision between licensing parsers and parsers assuming immediate attachments also for verb-final structures.

AN EXPERIMENT WITH GERMAN VERB-FINAL CLAUSES

Data from verb-final languages are crucial for head-driven licensing parsers because these parsers predict a different time course of attachment decisions for verb-final languages than for verb-initial languages. In this section, we report an experiment that aims to test the prediction of head-driven licensing parsers for verb-final clauses; namely, that, in these clauses, all attachments have to be delayed until the end of the clause. For reasons of space, we concentrate on the main points of the experiment. More details as well as results from follow-up experiments can be found in Bader (in preparation).

---

[6]That this is a stipulation follows from the fact that leaving a phrase unattached means that this phrase will not be licensed. On the other hand, attachment as an adjunct would make the phrase a licensed phrase because adjuncts are also licensed in some way, although the licensing of adjuncts may not be as obvious as the licensing of arguments. That is, in the case of PP attachment, it has to be stipulated that the parser prefers unlicensed phrases to phrases licensed as adjuncts.

Method and Predictions

Because the structure of the experimental sentences might seem somewhat complex to the untrained eye, we first introduce their syntactic structure in some detail. Overall, the experimental sentences consisted of a verb-second main clause that embedded a finite verb-final clause that embedded a verb-final infinitival clause. Because we are interested in the processing of verb-final clauses, the relevant part of this construction is the finite verb-final clause with its infinitival complement. This part of the structure is shown in sentence (8).

(8) [$_{CP2}$ *daß* . . . [$_{CP1}$ . . . V1] V2]

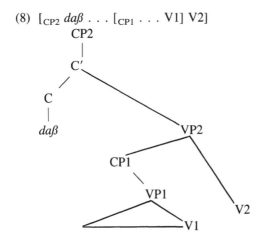

Although we have two levels of embedding, sentences of this kind are fully acceptable sentences of German. They may be part of a somewhat formal register, but their grammatical status is in no way marginal. The crucial point to note about (8) is that the infinitival clause (CP1) is embedded to the left of the verb by which it is selected (V2). The experimental sentences involved a serialization of constituents as in Sentence (9).

(9) . . . *daß* NP PP V1 V2

V1 and V2 are both heads of head-final VPs. V2 is the finite verb of the clause introduced by the complementizer *daß*. V1 is the head of the infinitival complement of V2. V1 is optionally transitive with a bias toward transitivity.

The ambiguous sentences in our study involved a phrase-structure ambiguity for the NP. By using appropriate verbs for V2, the NP had to be attached to one of two possible attachment sites. One choice of V2 had the effect that the NP had to be attached as a direct object under the VP headed by V1; the other choice had the effect that it had to be attached as the subject of the *daß* clause, whose verb is the sentence-final V2. The two cases are illustrated by Sentences (10a) and (10b), respectively.

(10) a. . . . . [$_{CP2}$ *daß*   [$_{CP1}$ NP PP V1] V2]
     b. . . . . [$_{CP2}$ *daß* NP [$_{CP1}$ PP V1] V2]

In what follows, we refer to CP2 as the matrix clause (disregarding that it is a dependent clause) and to CP1 as the embedded clause (equally disregarding that it is not the only embedded clause). The disambiguating element is V2 at the end of the sentence. In those cases where the structure is disambiguated, as in (10b), NP serves as the subject of the *daß* clause (CP2). When the structure is disambiguated, as in (10a), NP is the object of the embedded clause (CP1).

Consider the predictions for a head-driven licensing parser here. Prior to disambiguation, AbL will favor attachment of NP to VP1, as in (10a), because, according to AbL, NP has to be attached as soon as a licensor becomes available. Because V1 is (optionally) transitive, it is a potential licensor for NP; consequently, a licensing parser must attach NP as a daughter to VP1. This is so because licensed structure (i.e., attached structure) is always preferred over nonlicensed structure. Thus, when V2 occurs, NP is already attached and is not available as an argument of V2 anymore. Hence, only a V2 that is compatible with the structure in (10a) will be processed smoothly. If V2 requires a structure like (10b), processing breakdown will occur because the initially built structure needs to be reanalyzed.

Because of this prediction with respect to processing of V2 at the very end of the entire sentence, this ambiguity can be used to test the hypothesis that the human parser works in accordance with HP and AbL. If it should turn out that perceivers do not take NP as a complement to V1 (i.e., that Sentence (10b) is the preferred structure until the sentence gets disambiguated by V2), we would have found strong evidence against head-driven licensing parsers.

The sentences tested in the experiment we report here were of just the kind abstractly shown in (8) and (10). (11) is a typical experimental sentence, where (as in all test sentences) V2 consists of a participle (here, *erlaubt*) and an auxiliary (AUX), and the ambiguity is resolved by the auxiliary part of V2.

(11) [*daß* sie$_{NOM/AKK}$ [*nach dem Ergebnis*] *zu fragen tatsächlich erlaubt*   AUX]
      that she/her   for the result   to ask   indeed   permitted AUX

Four factors conspire to give the ambiguity of (11):

- The NP *sie* following *daß* is ambiguous between nominative and accusative case.
- V1 (*zu fragen*) is optionally transitive.
- The nonfinite part of V2 (*erlaubt*—past participle of *erlauben,* "to permit") can be used either with a perfect auxiliary to form an active perfect tense and with a passive auxiliary to form a passive verb.

- Disambiguation occurs through the auxiliary following all arguments and verbs of the structure.

If a sentence like (11) ends with an active auxiliary, then *erlaubt* must be a perfect participle. Consequently, the pronominal *sie* is nominative and thus the subject of the matrix clause. The resulting structure is (12).

(12)a. [*daß* *sie*~NOM~ [~CP1~ *nach* *dem* *Ergebnis* *zu fragen*] *tatsächlich* *erlaubt*   HAT]
       [that   she   for   the   result   to ask   indeed   permitted   has
       "that she indeed has given permission to ask for the result"

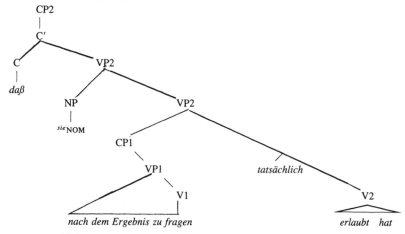

By contrast, if the sentence terminates in a passive auxiliary, *erlaubt* is the passive participle. In this case, *sie* is accusative and thus object of the embedded clause. The corresponding structure is shown in (13):

(13)a. [*daß* [~CP1~ *sie*~akk~ *nach* *dem* *Ergebnis* *zu fragen*] *tatsächlich* *erlaubt* WORDEN IST]
       [that   her   for   the   result   to ask   indeed   permitted been   is
       "that permission indeed has been given to ask her for the result"

b.

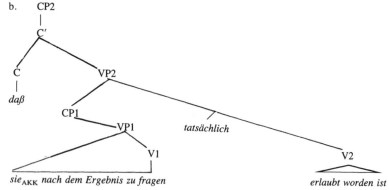

In terms of surface strings, the only difference between Sentences (12) and (13) is the auxiliary at the very end of the sentence (i.e., the auxiliary is the point of disambiguation). Such a structure involving a temporary local ambiguity with subsequent disambiguation is of course typical of garden-path sentences. The first thing to see about a predicted garden-path sentence is whether one of the two disambiguations is associated with a surprise reaction, or even processing breakdown. It turns out that the cases where the matrix verb V2 is passive, as in Sentence (13), are very hard to process. Native German speakers consistently report confusion upon hearing a sentence like (13). This off-line result suggests that listeners prefer Sentence (12) until the sentence-final auxiliary disambiguates the sentence. Such a preference indicates that, prior to disambiguation, listeners take the ambiguous NP *sie* to be part of the matrix clause CP2, which is not predicted by head-driven licensing parsers. If listeners took it to be part of the embedded clause CP1, we would expect a sense of surprise for Sentence (12), but not for Sentence (13). If listeners did not decide on the phrase-structure position of the ambiguous NP, we should observe equal ease of processing for both sentences.

At this point, it might be objected that processing complexity associated with passive sentences like Sentence (13) could be the reason for the reported intuitions. Fortunately, this possibility can be controlled by taking into account sentences with masculine pronouns. For masculine pronouns, there is no nominative/accusative ambiguity; the nominative form is *er,* whereas the accusative form is *ihn.* Unambiguous sentences with masculine pronouns were thus included in the tested materials as controls.

In (14), we show the four tested structures. (14a) and (14b) correspond to (12) and (13) respectively; (14a′) is the structurally equivalent control to (14a), containing a nominative-marked masculine NP, and (14b′) is parallel to (14b), except that it contains an accusative-marked masculine pronoun.

(14) a. [*daß sie*$_{NOM}$ [$_{CP1}$ *nach dem Ergebnis zu fragen*] *tatsächlich erlaubt* HAT]
      that she   for the result   to ask   indeed   permitted has
      "that she indeed has given permission to ask for the result"

  a′. [*daß er*$_{NOM}$ [$_{CP1}$ *nach dem Ergebnis zu fragen*] *tatsächlich erlaubt* HAT]
      that he   for the result   to ask   indeed   permitted has
      "that he indeed has given permission to ask for the result"

  b. [*daß* [$_{CP1}$ *sie/*$_{ACC}$ *nach dem Ergebnis zu fragen*] *tatsächlich erlaubt* WORDEN IST]
      that   her   for the result   to ask   indeed   permitted been is
      "that permission indeed has been given to ask her for the result"

  b′. [*daß* [$_{CP1}$ *ihn*$_{ACC}$ *nach dem Ergebnis zu fragen*] *tatsächlich erlaubt* WORDEN IST]
      that   him   for the result   to ask   indeed   permitted been is
      "that permission indeed has been given to ask him for the result"

The main point of interest is how subjects treat the NP following the complementizer on line. Twenty-four sentences were tested in a self-paced reading experiment with noncumulative word-by-word presentation, along with 75 filler sentences. For the experimental sentences and some of the filler sentences, a comprehension question followed the sentences. Twenty-four native German speakers (students at the University of Stuttgart) were tested.

Results

Table 10.1 shows the reading times in ms. for the finite auxiliaries in sentences like (14), which are the last word of their sentences. For the active Sentences (14a) and (14a′), this is the word *hat*. For the passive Sentences (14b) and (14b′), this is the word *ist*. As can be seen in Table 10.1, in the ambiguous, feminine case, reading times were significantly longer for the passive auxiliary than for the active auxiliary, while in the unambiguous, masculine case, reading times for the two auxiliaries were nearly identical. (factor attachment: $F_{it} = 5.05$, $p < .035$; $F_{vp} = 7.27$, $p < .013$; factor gender: $F_{it} = 19.63$, $p < .001$; $F_{vp} = 8.49$, $p < .008$; interaction between gender and attachment: $F_{it} = 10.71$, $p < .003$; $F_{vp} = 5.12$, $p < .033$). The results show that subjects took longer to process those ambiguous sentences where the auxiliary reveals that the ambiguous NP must be the object of the embedded verb V1. Crucially, for the unambiguous control case, no such difference exists. The off-line garden-path experience of native German speakers in the ambiguous case with a passive auxiliary is thus confirmed by the experimental results.

Discussion

Our findings argue against attachment by licensing. In the ambiguous sentences, *sie* is licensed by V1, but nevertheless it does not get interpreted as its object. If the parser had obeyed AbL, the ambiguous pronoun should have been interpreted as the object of V1 as soon as this verb was encountered. Under such a structural

TABLE 10.1
Reading Times in ms. for the finite *hat* and *ist*
of the Experimental Sentences Described in the Text

| | Gender | | |
| | Ambiguous | Unambiguous | |
Attachment	Feminine	Masculine	Mean
Low in CP1 ist	1496	972	1234
(passive)			
High in CP2 hat	1073	996	1035
(active)			
Mean	1285	984	1134

representation, a garden path should have occurred when the active auxiliary was processed, and we should have obtained the opposite results. Thus, the data suggest that the human parser does not, at every point during processing, attempt to build a structure that makes every possible licensed attachment.

The immediate question arising from this conclusion is: What should cause the parser to leave an NP without a theta role in the presence of a theta-role assigner? What is needed to explain the results is a kind of mechanism that protects the ambiguous pronoun from becoming a complement of V1. As an answer, we suggest that the NP is incorporated into the current structure as soon as it is encountered, and thus before V1 arrives in the input string. Hence, it is unavailable as a complement of V1.

In order for *sie* to be incorporated immediately into the current phrase marker, the attachment site of *sie* must have been made available prior to this attachment. Because the attachment site of *sie* is below VP2, VP2 must be hypothesized long before its head has been encountered. Of course, this cannot be achieved by head projection. Thus, a different parsing strategy is called for here. One possibility is left-corner parsing, which integrates both top–down and bottom–up processing. In this case, hypothesizing of the VP node is independent of the occurrence of the head of VP in the input string.

Let us derive the experimental results under such an alternative parsing strategy. First, the parser encounters a complementizer and projects CP2. Next, it finds an ambiguous NP and attaches it as a constituent of this CP. To do this, the parser must hypothesize a maximal VP projection from which to hang the NP. When V1 is encountered, because it is an infinitive, it cannot be the finite matrix verb of CP2. Therefore, an embedded clause, CP1, must be projected. Because the NP is already attached inside CP2, it is impossible to attach it as a sister to V1. The participle is inserted without problem as the head of VP2, which has already been projected and which has *sie* in subject position. When the final auxiliary turns the matrix into an active sentence, these attachments are confirmed and processing occurs smoothly, accounting for the faster reaction times in the active case than in the passive case. However, when the final auxiliary turns CP2 into a passive, reanalysis is necessary, giving rise to parsing difficulty and resulting in the slower reaction times that have been found.

The crucial step is that the NP *sie* becomes attached into the matrix clause as soon as it is encountered. At that point, the verbal head that would license this attachment in a head-driven licensing parser has not yet occurred in the input string. In fact, no verbal head has occurred. Crucially, we believe it is the immediate attachment of the NP that protects it from becoming an argument of V1. At this point, we do not defend any specific reason why this attachment is made, and defer speculations about this to a later section. However, besides immediate attachment of the NP—for whatever reason—there seems to be no other reason why the NP does not get interpreted as an object of V1 prior to disambiguation.

We conclude that the human parser hypothesizes a VP and also attaches phrases to it before the head of that VP has occurred in the input. Thus, the specific predictions of head-driven licensing model of human parsing are not borne out. Our results are clearly incompatible with such strictly bottom–up models. Our results go against AbL, and the explanation we have just given explicitly rejects projection from the head as the only operative principle for postulating maximal projections.

REQUIREMENTS OF A UNIVERSAL
SENTENCE PROCESSOR

In this last section, we first consider in more detail what kind of parsing model could provide an explanation for our data. Then, we express some theoretical considerations about the notion of licensing and its relevance for human parsing.

Head Direction and Human Sentence Processing

We have concluded that our experimental results speak strongly against parsing models that assume versions of either HP or AbL. Because Abney's (1989) and Pritchett's (1991, 1992) models were developed with English in mind, the question naturally arises whether we now have to assume distinct parsing mechanisms for English and German. Fortunately, this is not the case. For English too, with its consistently head-initial phrases, on-line evidence has been gathered that contradicts pure head-driven licensing parsers. For instance, Clifton, Speer, and Abney (1991) investigated PP-attachment ambiguities. They found that, in first-pass parsing, PPs are immediately attached to the VP irrespective of the specific lexical information associated with the verb and noun that preceded the PP. This is consistent with an item-independent strategy like minimal attachment, but not with strategies that are based solely on lexical information. Furthermore, Ferreira and Henderson (1990) presented evidence that verb information is not used immediately in assigning syntactic structures, but only later in the reanalysis stage of the parser (but see also Trueswell, Tanenhaus, & Kello, 1993).

All in all, the German examples discussed previously give the picture of a parser making at least some, or perhaps all, initial attachment decisions independent of specific lexical information. The question now is whether something more can be said than just that. If the parser's initial decisions are not made on the basis of lexical information, other parsing strategies are called for that do not depend on this kind of information. Frazier's minimal-attachment principle (cf. Frazier, 1987a) is a plausible candidate here (see also Inoue & Fodor in press, for a discussion of Japanese with regard to this question). However, it is premature to draw any strong conclusions about the decision principles of the human parser because too many questions have yet to be answered.

To illustrate two of these questions, consider again the experimental sentences as discussed earlier. First, there seems to be a problem with regard to the control clauses with unambiguous masculine pronouns. Why is the accusative pronoun *ihn* not attached into the matrix clause as an object to the hypothesized matrix verb? In this case, it would be unavailable for interpretation with the embedded infinitive, and clauses with *ihn* should also lead to parsing problems, which, however, they do not. If the parser were to attach *ihn* into the matrix clause, it would have to assume a structure like in Sentence (15).

(15) [*daß* Object [Infinitival clause] Subject Verb]

Sentences with a structure as in (15) are not totally impossible in German, as shown by Sentence (16). However, they are highly marked with respect to discourse properties and grammatical only under very special intonational and discourse factors.

(16) [*daß ihn* [PRO *abzureisen*] *sogar der Vater aufgefordert hatte.*]
     that him   to leave   even the father asked   had
     "that even the father had asked him leave"

It seems that the human parser is aware of such facts as marked versus unmarked word orders, and that it prefers unmarked ones over marked ones, at least without a marked context.

One could also wonder whether the use of pronouns in all experimental sentences has any bearing on the results. It has been argued (Schwartz, 1990; Schwartz & Tomaselli, 1990) that subject pronouns stand in a somewhat privileged relationship with the COMP position, in that the two must be immediately adjacent (nothing can intervene between COMP and a subject pronominal). Thus, subject pronouns have been said to cliticize to the COMP position at S structure. Therefore, it is possible to argue for the previous test sentences that the complementizer somehow attracts the pronoun in a special way, and that this leads to a preferred interpretation of the ambiguous pronoun as subject.

What would happen in the experiment if the pronouns were replaced by full lexical NPs? In follow-up experiments (discussed more fully in Bader, (in preparation)), this question was addressed by taking proper names into account. Like the feminine pronoun, proper names are ambiguous between nominative and accusative. Preliminary results show that, with proper names, the same kind of garden-path effect occurs as with pronouns. Therefore, we conclude that the effect is not in any way due to a preferred interpretation of pronouns as subjects.

Interestingly, however, the garden-path effect is smaller with proper names than with pronouns. We interpret this to mean that pronouns are more difficult to reanalyze as the object of the embedded clause than proper names. Our reasoning is as follows: Initially, the parser attaches both pronouns and proper names into the matrix clause (that is why we get an effect for both cases). In the case of pronouns, when the passive auxiliary at the end of the sentence requires reanalysis, it is necessary to dissolve the special clitic relationship between the position of the complementizer and the pronoun in order to reanalyze the latter as object of the embedded clause. In the case of proper names, because there is no special relationship between complementizer and proper name, no such relationship has to be dissolved, and accordingly reanalysis is easier. Thus, we interpret the stronger effect with pronouns to stem from extra load during the reanalysis process, and not from any first-pass process. If the results reported earlier were only due to a privileged status of subject pronouns, we would not expect to obtain a similar effect for full NPs.

Transparency in Parsing Theory

In summary, we come back to the notion of transparency in the relationship between the grammar and the parser, as discussed in the introduction. The motivation for the head-driven licensing model has been to implement transparency between the grammar and the parser. Thus, head-driven licensing approaches have a certain theoretical motivation, but there are strong indications that they cannot be confirmed empirically. We have argued against head-driven licensing parsers, but we agree with one of the assumptions found in them— namely, the attempt to construct a model of the parser whose decision principles do not involve any language-specific properties and therefore can be taken as potentially innate.

It is not necessary to implement transparency between the grammar and the parser in the way in which this has been done in head-driven licensing parsers. Pritchett's and Abney's assumptions, as summarized in HP and AbL, are only one way of obtaining a transparent parsing model. Note again that HP and AbL operate solely on the basis of elements that have already occurred in the input. Although it is certainly not a good idea to assume that the parser engages in wild speculation, we suggest that a certain amount of constrained predictive hypothesizing is performed during on-line parsing.

With other researchers (cf. Crocker, 1992), we believe that the human parser uses the X-bar component of universal grammar to build syntactic structure in a top–down fashion. For instance, consider that a complementizer necessarily introduces a proposition in the form of an IP (or VP in our IP-less grammar for German). It is reasonable for the parser to assume that an NP following the complementizer is part of that proposition. Expressed in syntactic terms, C^0 licenses its complement IP (or VP). This maximal projection can then be used as an attachment site for further incoming phrases like NPs or PPs. This amounts to the on-line use of functional selection information by the parser (see also Crocker, 1992) because C^0 f-selects its complement IP (VP). Perhaps this kind of selection can be derived directly from universal grammar. Grimshaw (1991) suggested that head-complement relationships are universal in the sense that lexical projections (NP, VP, AP, PP) have unique functional projections associated with them. Conversely, each functional projection has a unique lexical complement.

We have shown that strictly head-driven models make wrong predictions for the on-line processing of certain verb-final clauses. We have proposed that our experimental results can only be explained if the parser projects structure using X-bar theoretic information on line. In this way, the parser can hypothesize obligatory maximal phrases whose heads have not yet occurred in the input. We leave open for future research the exact principles that guide attachment decisions, and the revision routines that must be employed in case of reanalysis. We find it a particularly fruitful approach to test hypotheses about the time course of sentence processing in both head-initial and head-final structures.

ACKNOWLEDGMENTS

We thank Josef Bayer, Janet Fodor, Lyn Frazier, Christine Haag-Merz, and Janet Randall for discussion of the issues raised in this chapter.

REFERENCES

Abney, S. P. (1989). A computational model of human parsing. *Journal of Psycholinguistic Research, 18*, 51–60.

Bader, M. (in preparation). *Syntaktische Verarbeitung im Deutschen* [*Syntactic processing in German*]. Unpublished doctoral dissertation, University of Stuttgart, Germany.

Berwick, R. C., & Weinberg, A. S. (1984). *The grammatical basis of linguistic performance.* Cambridge, MA: MIT Press.

Chomsky, N. (1970). Remarks on nominalizations. In R. Jacobs & P. Rosenbaum (Eds.), *Readings in English transformational grammar* (pp. 184–221). Waltham, MA: Ginn.

Chomsky, N. (1986). *Knowledge of language: Its nature, origin, and use.* New York: Praeger.

Chomsky, N., & Lasnik, H. (1993). Principles and parameters theory. In J. Jacobs, A. von Stechow, W. Sternefeld, & T. Vennemann (Eds.), *Syntax: An international handbook of contemporary research* (pp. 506–569). Berlin: Walter de Gruyter.

Clifton, C., Jr., Speer, S., & Abney, S. P. (1991). Parsing arguments: Phrase structure and argument structure as determinants of initial parsing decisions. *Journal of Memory and Language, 30*, 251–271.

Crocker, M. W. (1992). *A logical model of competence and performance in the human sentence processor.* Unpublished doctoral dissertation, University of Edinburgh, Scotland.

Ferreira, F., & Henderson, J. M. (1990). Use of verb information in syntactic parsing: Evidence from eye movements and word-by-word self-paced reading. *Journal of Experimental Psychology: Learning, Memory, and Cognition, 16*, 555–568.

Frazier, L. (1987a). Sentence processing: A tutorial review. In M. Coltheart (Ed.), *Attention and performance XII. The psychology of reading* (pp. 559–586). Hillsdale, NJ: Lawrence Erlbaum Associates.

Frazier, L. (1987b). Syntactic processing: Evidence from Dutch. *Natural Language and Linguistic Theory, 5,* 519–559.

Grimshaw, J. (1990). *Argument structure.* Cambridge, MA: MIT Press.

Grimshaw, J. (1991). *Extended projections.* Unpublished manuscript.

Inoue, A., & Fodor, J. D. (in press). Information-paced parsing of Japanese. In R. Mazuka & N. Nagai (Eds.), *Japanese syntactic processing.* Hillsdale, NJ: Lawrence Erlbaum Associates.

Miller, G. A., & Chomsky, N. (1963). Finitary models of language users. In R. D. Luce, R. R. Bush, & E. Galanter (Eds.), *Handbook of mathematical psychology* (Vol. 2, pp. 419–490). New York: Wiley.

Pritchett, B. L. (1991). Head position and parsing ambiguity. *Journal of Psycholinguistic Research, 20,* 251–270.

Pritchett, B. L. (1992). *Grammatical competence and parsing performance.* Chicago: The University of Chicago Press.

Rappaport, M., & Levin, B. (1988). What to do with theta-roles. In W. Wilkins (Ed.), *Thematic roles. Syntax and semantics* (Vol. 21, pp. 7–36). New York: Academic Press.

Schwartz, B. D., & Tomaselli, A. (1990). Some implications from an analysis of German word order. In W. Abraham, W. Kosmeijer, & E. Reuland (Eds.), *Issues in Germanic syntax.* Berlin: Mouton de Gruyter.

Speas, M. J. (1990). *Phrase structure in natural language.* Boston: Kluwer.

Stowell, T. (1981). *Origins of phrase structure.* Unpublished doctoral dissertation, Massachusetts Institute of Technology.

Tomaselli, A. (1990). COMPO as a licensing head: An argument based on cliticization. In J. Mascarò & M. Nespor (Eds.), *Grammar in progress. GLOW essays for Henk van Riemsdijk* (pp. 433–445). Dordrecht: Foris.

Trueswell, J. C., Tanenhaus, M. K., & Kello, C. (1993). Verb-specific constraints in sentence processing: Separating effects of lexical preference from garden-paths. *Journal of Experimental Psychology: Learning, Memory, and Cognition, 19,* 528–553.

IV SYNTACTIC PROCESSING AND COMPUTATIONAL MODELS

11

On the Nature of the Principle-Based Sentence Processor

Matthew W. Crocker
The University of Edinburgh

Theories of linguistic performance have long sought direct psycholinguistic evidence for the representations and mechanisms posited by theories of syntactic competence. The line of reasoning that underlies this program of research can be summarized as follows: Theories of syntax claim to provide an account of a person's knowledge of language. The human sentence-processing mechanism (HSPM) must presumably make use of knowledge of language. Thus, the most parsimonious models are those where the processing mechanism makes direct use of the rules and representations of syntax. The view has been expressed as the strong competence hypothesis (SCH), which holds that the process model must make direct use of the principles of grammar—what Berwick and Weinberg (1984) called *type transparency.*

However, the emergence of transformational grammar (TG) lead to a divergence in the paths taken by linguists and psycholinguists. This occurred for a number of reasons: The derivational theory of complexity (DTC), which advanced the view that sentence-processing complexity should be proportional to the number of transformations involved in the analysis, was quite convincingly falsified. Because the DTC was tacitly believed to be the only natural model for the perceptual realization of TG (i.e., the so-called "standard theory"), a close grammar–parser relationship seemed out of reach. This, combined with the clear distinction between theories of competence and performance that was argued for by Chomsky, was enough to deflate the interests of psycholinguists in pursuing TG-based theories of sentence processing (see Berwick & Weinberg, 1984, for thorough review and discussion). Perhaps the final blow was that parsing theory, which was particularly well understood for phrase-structure grammars, was rather less understood for transformational grammars. This gap in technology widened further with the shift from rule-based TG to so-called "principle-based" grammatical theories in the late 1970s.

However, recent years have witnessed a renewed initiative in this area of cognitive science: one in which modern linguistic theory, high-resolution psycholinguistic evidence, and sophisticated computational techniques are being brought to bear in developing rich and explanatory accounts of human linguistic performance. There are several reasons for the rebirth of this multidisciplinary research program. Perhaps most notably, early attempts at reconciling transformational grammar with models of human parsing, such as the DTC, were based on a misconception: They tacitly assumed that the SCH (i.e., a direct grammar–parser relationship) was uniquely realizable. That is, they assumed that, for a given competence theory, there was precisely one parsing model that satisfied the SCH—namely, a parsing model where the number of transformational operations involved in recovering a syntactic analysis should be directly proportional to the human parsing complexity. However, theories of computation tell us that this is naive.[1] In the case of current principle-based grammars, the range of possible parsing architectures is expanded even further.[2]

The "one-to-many" nature of the direct grammar–parser relationship is further confounded by the fact that we know rather little about the nature of the computational architecture in which the sentence-processing mechanism is embedded. For example, although many assume the HSPM pursues only one analysis at a time, Gibson (1991) advocated pursuing several possible (ranked) analyses in parallel. In a different vein, Crocker (1991) argued that a range of empirical evidence may best be explained by assuming a modular, distributed syntactic-processing architecture where various aspects of a (single) syntactic analysis are recovered in parallel. The space of possibilities and permutations for the grammar, processor, and architecture lead to numerous possible models, which often differ only subtly in their empirical coverage and predictions.

Indeed, in constructing a relatively complete principle-based model of sentence processing, the number of degrees of freedom are vast: How are structures generated? How are principles applied? What order are they applied in? What particular instantiation of the competence theory is assumed? (See Berwick, 1991; Berwick, Abney, & Tenny, 1991, for a clear and thorough overview of these issues.) Therefore, it seems rather unlikely that any of the extant models is correct in every respect; not surprisingly, few claim to be. Although this fact in itself is not a damning one, it does make it difficult to ascertain which aspects of

---

[1]In particular, we know that for a given declarative grammar, there are numerous parsing algorithms, all of which must be considered equally direct in their relationship to the grammar. Considering a context-free grammar, for example, possible parsing algorithms include recursive–descent (top–down), shift–reduce (bottom–up), left-corner (a combined strategy) techniques, and so on (Aho & Ullman, 1972).

[2]See Johnson (1989), Crocker (1991), Fong (1991), Gibson (1991), and Merlo (1992) for examples and discussion.

the existing models are most strongly supported, and should be addressed by future work.

In this chapter, my aim is a more modest one. The overriding aim is to contribute further to the view that a principle-based theory of linguistic performance is possible, natural, and desirable. Furthermore, based on a few simple assumptions, I argue for some relatively strong conclusions about the nature of the principle-based HSPM. First, it must operate incrementally, in at least a partially top–down manner. Second, it must employ an active gap-filling strategy, which identifies traces top–down, before the string position has been encountered. I do not attempt to embed these mechanisms within a highly complex (and possibly arbitrary) processing system, but simply leave them unadorned (see, however, Crocker, 1991, for the detailed exposition of a system that incorporates these mechanisms). In this way, I hope to clarify what the substantive certainties are, thereby defining a class of plausible principle-based performance models. I then consider the implications of our results for current processing accounts, and, in particular, I argue that the range of principle-based performance models that are head driven, as proposed by Pritchett (1992) and Abney (1989), are untenable. Finally, I propose an underlying principle, the principle of incremental comprehension, as the explanatory force behind our claims concerning the properties of the HSPM.

CURRENT THEORIES OF SENTENCE PROCESSING

The status of a distinct syntactic subsystem within the human language processor is one of the most fundamental concerns in psycholinguistics. Particularly active is the debate as to whether the syntactic processor is autonomous. Although it is widely agreed that semantic interpretation begins before the end of an utterance, some propose that it does not occur soon enough to actually influence the actions of the parser (i.e., it has been argued that the sentence processor structures incoming utterances purely on the basis of syntactic knowledge and parsing strategies; see Frazier, 1978; Kimball, 1973). An alternative position is that the parser interacts with postsyntactic systems when choosing which analysis to favor (i.e., permitting semantics to direct the actions of the syntactic analyser; see Altmann & Steedman, 1988; Crain & Steedman, 1985; Tanenhaus, Carlson, & Trueswell, 1989, as examples).

I avoid here a reconstruction of the data and conclusions in the literature: There are substantial and compelling presentations from both camps. Rather, I begin with the assumption that the syntactic processor is strictly autonomous, at least with respect to the so-called "first pass,"[3] and directly consider only those

---

[3]There are various definitions of *first pass* in the literature; here we simply mean that the initial construction of a syntactic representation is done strictly by the parser, without recourse to nonsyntactic knowledge sources. We leave aside the issue of how or whether semantics is used for reanalysis.

other models that fall into this category. However, at the end of the chapter, I briefly return to this issue.

Complexity-Based Models

Traditional hypotheses concerning the parsing strategies and algorithms of the HSPM are founded on some notion of syntactic *complexity*. This view argues that increases in processing complexity incurred during parsing are the result of some increased load on the syntactic processor, where *increased load* is determined by either the time or space complexity of syntactic processing. Perhaps the best known account that attempts to minimize space, or memory load, is Frazier's garden-path theory, which incorporates the minimal-attachment strategy (Frazier, 1978): "Minimal Attachment: Attach incoming material into the phrase marker being constructed using the fewest nodes consistent with the well-formedness rules of the language" (p. 76). As is clear from the minimal-attachment strategy, the parser will attempt to construct the simplest analysis consistent with current initial substring, and in so doing will minimize the amount of memory required to store the representation of the analysis.

In contrast to Frazier's model based on "representational parsimony," Marcus (1980) advocated the construction of a deterministic parsing model—a parser that operates in linear time (with respect to the length of the input). His motivation was the observation that, for most utterances, people are able to construct an interpretation in real time, and without any conscious effort. The model further predicted that those sentences that could not be parsed deterministically were precisely the ones that cause a conscious garden-path effect for people.

The parser developed by Marcus has since been refined by Berwick and Weinberg (1984). Significantly, they proposed *informational monotonicity,* rather than determinism, as the relevant underlying computational constraint on the parser. That is, once a representation is constructed, no subsequent action of the parser can destroy it. They proposed an LR parser that uses a state table based on single-item lookahead, bounded left context, and relevant lexical information (such as subcategorization frames) to determine the next action the parser should take. The parser acts serially, constructing only one analysis of the utterance, but cannot be considered incremental. The machinery of the parser allows lexical items or phrases to remain unstructured—in the input buffer—until necessary disambiguating information is found. Perhaps the most interesting result of their effort is that the use of bounded left context provides a functional, processing account of *c-command* and *subjacency*—two central notions in grammatical theory. This supports the possibility of the parser determining, at least in part, the principles of grammar.

Grammar-Based Models

In addition to the complexity-based approaches outlined previously, an alternative basis for the development of a performance theory has been identified: what

I term the *grammar-based approach*. This view takes syntactic relationships to be fundamental in determining the actions taken by the parser during processing, and shifts the emphasis away from the abstract notions of computational or representational complexity, which are fundamental to the models outlined in the last section. Rather, grammar-based accounts assume that the sentence processor is driven by the desire to construct a well-formed analysis of an utterance, and in this regard employs strategies that take into consideration syntactic relationships such as licensing conditions (e.g., theta and case assignment). This approach is theoretically attractive, in that it supports the notion of a close grammar–parser relationship, suggesting the HSPM is strongly principle based.

As psycholinguists turn their attention to the recent *principles and parameters* model of linguistic competence, two particular properties demand the attention of SCH proponents:

1. The theory makes use of a set of interacting, heterogeneous principles, rendering traditional parsing technologies insufficient because there is only a minimal phrase-structure component.
2. The principles and parameters model makes use of multiple levels of syntactic representation, and posits the existence of empty categories in subcategorized, adjoined, and intermediate positions.

These issues have sparked research into a range of computational and psychological models of how principles of grammar may be used directly in parsing (see, e.g., Crocker, 1991; Fong, 1991; Gibson, 1991; Pritchett, 1988). This conception takes the sentence-processing problem (particularly in the context of principle-based grammars) to be one of constraint satisfaction. In other words, the on-line process of recovering a syntactic analysis is essentially one of satisfying the necessary grammatical principles (i.e., constraints) as the input string is received. This view is perhaps best represented in the work of Pritchett (1992), and also the computational work of Johnson (1989). It is interesting to note that, if one imagines unresolved or unsatisfied grammatical constraints to cause an increase in complexity, a natural strategy appealing to the computational arguments of the previous section is to adopt the analysis that maximally satisfies any constraints (e.g., case theory, theta theory, etc.). This is in fact precisely the strategy adopted by Pritchett in his model:

(1) Theta Attachment: The θ-criterion attempts to apply at every point during parsing given the maximal θ-grid. (p. 12)

Roughly this says attach constituents so as to saturate the θ-roles of given lexical items. The central assumption of this is that lexical entries are fully specified for thematic roles, and that such information is immediately accessed and used to drive parsing. Pritchett then argued that such a strategy can be generalized to include all the principles of grammar, what he called *generalized* Θ *attachment*.

Although Pritchett has not emphasized implementation of his theory, Abney (1989) proposed a licensing parser that operates in a manner largely consistent with Pritchett's principles. In particular, he constructed an LR parser that uses thematic information to drive parsing in a head-driven manner as advocated in Pritchett (1991). One important property of such a head-driven model, however, is that it entails nonincremental parsing, particularly in head-final languages, because attachment decisions must be delayed until the necessary thematic information is available.

Discussion

As mentioned earlier, I have only considered those models based on an autonomous syntactic processor. It is perhaps not surprising, then, that these approaches are based fundamentally on the isolation of the parsing task. That is, they are isolated in the sense that the syntactic-processing strategies are insensitive to the more general comprehension task. The parsing models proposed are motivated purely by a desire to minimize syntactic complexity, be it representational, computational, or grammatical. Although it is reasonable to assume that all will be relevant contributors to overall sentence-processing complexity, it is possible that their importance may be overshadowed by the complexity of the more general comprehension task. In other words, simple time and space complexity considerations within the syntactic processor might not be of paramount importance, and thus processing strategies therein may rather be oriented toward the concerns of global comprehension. To put it another way, the hypothesis of an autonomous syntactic processor does not entail the use of strategies that are syntactically oriented (although they must only have access to syntactic knowledge).

AN ALTERNATIVE

On the grounds just outlined, the model I propose does not take the minimization of computational, representational, or grammatical complexity to be fundamental. Rather, I assume that the sentence processor strives to optimize local, incremental comprehension of the input utterance as it is perceived. I propose that decisions about the current syntactic analysis are made incrementally (for each input item) on the basis of principles that are intended to maximize the overall interpretation. The philosophy that underlies the position is that the syntactic processor's primary objective is to provide a maximal, partial interpretation of an utterance as input is received, such that it may be quickly integrated into the current context, thereby meeting the real-time demands of comprehension. As such, syntactic analysis proceeds first and foremost in a manner that satisfies this objective. In summary, I propose that the operations of the autonomous syntactic processor are not determined by internal syntactic factors, but rather by the external demand for a maximal incremental analysis. I dub this the *principle of incremental comprehension* (PIC), defined as follows: "The sentence processor operates in such a way as to maximize the interpretation and comprehension of the sentence at each stage of processing (i.e., as each lexical item is encountered)." At first consideration, this would seem satisfiable by any of the standard assumptions of incremental syntactic processing, such as Frazier's left-to-right constraint (Frazier & Rayner, 1988). As is seen, however, there is an important difference. Although the traditional incremental parsing requirement is subsumed by PIC (i.e., each lexical item must be incorporated into the current "connected" partial syntactic analysis as it is encountered), there is the additional implication that any structure that can be built (according to the principles of grammar) must be built. As is seen, this is especially relevant for the characterization of both attachment and gap-filling preferences. The latter phenomenon, in particular, is not considered by traditional definitions of *incremental interpretation.*

RECOVERING PHRASE STRUCTURE

The task of parsing with principle-based grammars is particularly challenging because the syntax incorporates only a minimal phrase-structure component— namely, $\bar{X}$-theory. Furthermore, $\bar{X}$-theory is typically postulated as a D-structure component, licensing the underlying structure of the sentence, rather than its surface structure. One solution is to "compile out" the principles of $\bar{X}$-theory with the other modules of grammar to obtain a set of phrase-structure rules as advocated in Frazier (1987).[4] However, such an approach is at odds with my desire for a model that directly exploits the principles of syntax. Furthermore, recent developments in principle-based parsing have demonstrated technologies that make incremental, principle-based parsing possible (see Crocker, 1991; Johnson, 1989; Stabler, 1991). In the present, discussion, I am less concerned with the particular technology used for the recovery of phrase structure. Rather, I focus on how such a parsing mechanism should behave, thereby identifying the *class* of psychologically possible, principle-based parsers.

The PIC, as introduced in the previous section, essentially demands that the syntactic processor make maximal use of all available information during parsing, such that it constructs a maximal, partial, syntactic analysis. Following my assumption of an autonomous syntactic processor, there are essentially two sources of information that can be brought to bear by the parsing mechanism: the fixed principles of grammar to which all utterances of the language must conform, and the syntactic properties of lexical items as they are encountered by the

---

[4]Frazier's basis for this argument was influenced by principle-based parsers at that time, which took such an approach (e.g., Dorr, 1987).

sentence processor. Given these two types of information, how can the parsing mechanism best satisfy the PIC? As noted in my earlier discussion, the obvious importance of lexical items appears to countenance a bottom–up, and possibly even a head-driven, algorithm, whereas some aspects of grammatical knowledge seem best exploited by a predictive, top–down system. To this end, I argue for an architecture that employs a combined strategy of prediction (top–down) and projection (bottom–up), and I demonstrate that such an architecture is indeed the only one that can successfully account for the full range of data.

Although it is reasonably apparent how the input items of an utterance may be recruited by a "projection" component, the "predictive" element of the parser requires greater consideration. Recalling that my model is constrained to make direct use of grammatical principles (not a compiled out set of phrase-structure rules, e.g.), consider that component of the grammar that is most directly involved in the licensing of phrase structure (i.e., $\bar{X}$-theory) and the properties of the categories that may instantiate the $\bar{X}$-schema. In its simplest form, $\bar{X}$-theory may be stated as follows.

(2) $X^i \rightarrow X^j \, Y^{max}$,
     where $0 \leq j \leq i \leq max$, and max $= 2$.

I assume that the order of satellites (Y^{max}) is not specified, but parameterized for particular languages and categories. For example, in English, this yields the following general structure for all phrases, where X is the category of the phrase (e.g., one of N, V, A, P, DET, INFL, COMP).

(3)

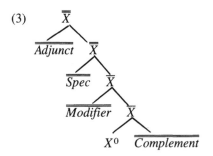

Furthermore, current syntactic theory partitions the set of categories on the basis of different clusters of properties. These have been succinctly enumerated in Cowper (1992, p. 173) as follows:

(4) a. LEXICAL CATEGORIES (N, V, A)
         —have substantive meaning
         —assign θ-roles to their arguments
         —are open classes (new words can be created)
         —permit indefinite recursion on $\bar{X}$

b. FUNCTIONAL CATEGORIES (COMP, INFL, DET)
   —lack substantive meaning
   —do not assign θ-roles
   —are closed classes (no new words can be created)
   —do not permit recursion on $\overline{X}$

An additional property of functional categories is that their c-selection[5] properties are fixed. That is, DET always c-selects for an $\overline{N}$ complement, COMP for $\overline{I}$, and INFL for $\overline{V}$. Given that functional categories are so fixed with regard to their configurations, they are an obvious source of predictive information. Thus, one is presented with a natural way in which to carve up the top–down and bottom–up components of the parser, based on the distinction between functional and lexical categories, respectively.

The general idea is this: Given a functional node (e.g., CP [formerly, $\bar{S}$] or IP [formerly, S], I can immediately engage syntactic knowledge to predict the structure of the clause. However, given a lexical category (e.g., VP or NP), predictions about its internal structure would be guesswork, and bottom–up attachment into the VP seems more sensible. Evidence for the top–down strategy has been particularly forthcoming in verb-final languages such as Dutch, where arguments are encountered before the verb is reached (Frazier, 1987). Frazier demonstrated this for sentences of the following sort.

(5) a. [CP *dat* [IP *het meisje* [VP [PP *van Holland*] *houdt*]]]
       that the girl Holland likes

    b. [CP *dat* [IP [NP *het meisje* [PP *van Holland*]] *glimlachte*]]
       that the girl from Holland smiled

If I consider how the utterance might be processed prior to encountering the final verb, there are basically three possibilities:

(6) a. the prepositional phrase (PP) is incrementally attached as a modifier of the noun phrase (NP),

    b. the PP is incrementally attached into the verb phrase (VP), as an object, or

    c. the PP (and possibly NP) are left unattached because they are not lexically licensed.

Options (6a) and (6b) predict faster reading times when the final verb is consistent with relevant attachment, whereas the head-driven model, option (6c),

---

[5]*C-selection* refers to the phrasal category selected as the complement of a head (see Chomsky, 1986).

predicts no difference because the verb will direct the parser toward the appropriate attachment, whatever it may be.[6] Although the first two options are consistent with my assumption of incremental processing, the latter option entails the buffering of constituents until their licensing head appears. That is, (6c) corresponds with the head-driven models of Abney (1989) and Pritchett (1991), which Frazier characterized as the *head-projection hypothesis* (Frazier, 1987).

In a reading-time experiment, Frazier demonstrated a clear preference for sentences consistent with the VP–object analysis as in (5a), suggesting that option (6b) is, in fact, the analysis adopted. To be more concrete, this suggests that, before the verb is reached, the following is the preferred structure:

(7)

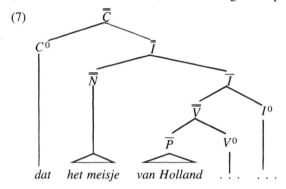

Regardless of the particular strategy used to account for this preference,[7] this result has two important consequences: First, the simple existence of a significant preference (had it been for option (6a) or (6b) supports our assumption of incremental interpretation over the "buffering" mechanism implicit in the head-driven option (6c). Second, the fact that option (6b) is obtained entails that the VP node exists as a potential site for attachment, despite that the verb has yet to be parsed. This is both a refutation of the head-projection hypothesis and corroborating evidence in my case for a partially top–down, predictive mechanism. Indeed, if I assume the prediction of functional structure suggested earlier, the VP node would be posited top–down as a necessary, c-selected complement of the functional head I (and IP would, in turn, have been predicted as the complement of C).

In addition to Frazier's findings for Dutch, similar results have been obtained for the corresponding constructions in German (Bader, 1990). However, there is some controversy regarding these findings. In particular, Konieczny, Hemforth, Scheepers, and Strube (1993) criticized the presentation method used by both

---

[6]Although see Pritchett (1991) for an argument that some preference for argument attachment can be explained.

[7]It is consistent with both the minimal-attachment strategy (Frazier, 1979) and Crocker's argument-attachment principle (Crocker, 1991).

Frazier and Bader, which involves presenting the materials in segments, roughly as follows.

(8) a. *[Ik weet dat* [$_{NP}$ *de man]/*[$_{PP}$ *in Holland] investeert]*
        that the man in Holland invests

     b. *[Ik weet dat* [$_{NP}$ *de man]/*[$_{PP}$ *in Spanje]/*[$_{PP}$ *in Holland] investeert]*
        that the man from Spain in Holland invests

Konieczny et al. argued that methods used in these studies bias against the complex NP preference (option (6a) above), due to the a priori chunking of phrases in the presentation. Citing evidence from (Hemforth, Hoelter, Konieczny, Scheepers, and Strube, 1991), they noted that these finding were replicated using the same method and materials. However, when the method was changed to word-by-word presentation with almost identical materials, they obtained opposite results. That is, the word-by-word presentation, which is arguably less biasing, indicated a preference for the complex subject NP (option (6i)). If this is the correct result, how does it impact on the claims I have made up to this point? The preference for attaching the PP into the complex subject NP, rather than the VP, means that top–down prediction of the VP is no longer entailed, although it is not explicitly refuted either.[8] Nonetheless, the preference is still compatible with the assumption of incremental interpretation, and contradicts the head-projection hypothesis: the PP is clearly not left unattached until the licensing verbal head is reached, as claimed by Pritchett (1991), i.e. option (6c).

Indeed, if the findings are correct, the thematically driven licensing models of Pritchett (1991) and Abney (1989) seem to completely break down. However, the data of Hemforth et al. (1991) also question whether the (complex) subject NP is attached as the subject, in the top–down manner proposed here, before the verb is reached. That is, preferred integration of the PP with the preceding NP is consistent with both a top–down and (nonhead-driven) bottom–up procedure. However, there is independent evidence bearing on this issue: In a recent study, Bader and Lasser (chapter 10, this volume) considered sentences of the following sort.

(9) *[daß sie [nach dem Ergebnis zu fragen] erlaubt hat]*
     that she for the result to ask permitted has
     that she has given permission to ask for the result

(10) *[daß [sie nach dem Ergebnis zu fragen] erlaubt werden ist]*
     that her for the result to ask permitted has
     that permission was given to ask her for the result

---

[8]That is, the VP may still be predicted top-down, but it is simply not the preferred attachment site given the two options available.

The pronoun *sie* is ambiguous for the nominative or accusative case, which means that it can potentially be attached as either the subject of the matrix clause (i.e., of *erlaubt*), as in (9), or as the object of the embedded clause (i.e., *zu fragen*), as in (10). The top–down, incremental model advocated here predicts a preference for the continuation, which is consistent with the matrix subject attachment. However, the bottom–up models (including Pritchett's & Abney's head-driven model), predict that *sie* should be attached into the embedded clause, which is encountered before the matrix verb, and is hence the first licensing θ-role assigner available. In a self-paced, word-by-word reading study, Bader and Lasser obtained faster reading times for sentences of the sort in (9), confirming the predictions made here and contradicting the predictions of bottom–up (including head-driven) architectures in general.

PARSING EMPTY CATEGORIES

A distinguishing feature of modern transformational grammar is its use of empty categories, or *traces,* to explicitly represent positions vacated by movement. Although this is a perfectly reasonable mechanism in the construction of syntactic theory, it poses an interesting question to psycholinguists: Are traces "psychologically real"? Are traces explicitly recovered and represented during comprehension of an utterance, or are they merely some formal mechanism of the competence theory (thereby weakening the SCH)? In the strict principle-based model I am assuming here, its is assumed that traces are real because they are necessary participants in the formation of chains. At the end of this chapter, I return to this issue and consider whether the evidence presented actually favors the reality of empty categories or is merely consistent with it.

Of all the gap-filling strategies that have been proposed, perhaps the most descriptively successful is the active filler strategy (AFS), which has been defended by Frazier and her colleagues. AFS can be most simply defined as follows: "When a filler has been identified, rank the possibility of assigning it to a gap above all other options" (Frazier & Clifton, 1989, p. 292). To illustrate the strategy, Clifton and Frazier (1989) presented the globally ambiguous examples given next, for which they obtained a strong preference for Sentence (11b):

(11) a. Who$_i$ did Fred tell Mary ε_i left the country.

      b. Who$_i$ did Fred tell ε_i Mary left the country.

The preference for (11b) suggests that, at the point immediately following the verb *tell,* the parser prefers to posit a trace in the direct-object position over attaching *Mary* into it. These data are highly suggestive of a process that incrementally processes the utterance, identifying the antecedent *who* and attempting to recover its originating trace position as soon as possible. Further, they pointed to the experiments conducted by Crain and Fodor (1985) and Stowe (1986), on sentences of the type in (12), which yield significantly longer reading times for *us* in (12b) than in (12a) or (12c). This suggests that the AFS is operative, assigning the filler to the gap after *bring,* and that some expense results from revising this analysis.

(12) a. My brother wanted to know who$_i$ ε_i will bring us home at Christmas.

    b. My brother wanted to know who$_i$ Ruth will bring (* ε_i) us home to ε_i at Christmas.

    c. My brother wanted to know if Ruth will bring us home to Mom at Christmas.

For further evidence and discussion, the reader is referred to Clifton and Frazier (1989). In the remainder of this chapter, I consider some recent evidence that challenges traditional assumptions about the manner in which long-distance dependencies are processed. Specifically, I argue that, if a trace-based account is to be maintained, the postulation of traces must obey a radical version of Frazier's AFS, but that the revised strategy is, in fact, derivable from the PIC.

Evidence Against Traces

In a recent article, Pickering and Barry (1991) argued against the reality of empty categories, particularly traces, in the sentence-processing mechanism. They contrasted the trace-based mechanism of current transformational theories with a "dependency-grammar," account, wherein a filler is associated directly with its subcategorizer and not mediated via a gap. This contrast is illustrated by the following pair of sentences.

(13) a. [Which man]$_i$ do you think Mary loves ε_i?

    b. [Which man]$_i$ do you think Mary loves$_i$?

The transformational model of grammar, including the principles and parameters theory that I have assumed throughout, posits a gap in the object position of *loves,* as in (13a), whereas a dependency-grammar account assumes that the filler is directly associated with *loves,* as in (13b). Pickering and Barry pointed out that, although there is significant evidence supporting the psychological reality of processing unbounded dependencies (see McElree & Bever, 1989), and references cited therein), the evidence is equally consistent with the alternative grammatical account discussed earlier because the filler and subcategorizer are typically adjacent.

This stalemate demands that we investigate sentences where the subcategorizing element and the position of the proposed trace are separated by intervening material. Consider the following PP extraction.

(14) a. [In which tin]$_i$ did you put the cake ε_i?

      b. [In which tin]$_i$ did you put$_i$ the cake?

Pickering and Barry argued that a trace-based parsing model prohibits the resolution of the filler-gap relationship until the end of the sentence, whereas the dependency account permits this to be resolved immediately upon encountering *put*. They then pointed out that the gap-free model appears to permit a greater degree of incremental interpretation, which seems intuitively borne out if the direct object is lengthened.

(15) [In which tin]$_i$ did you put$_i$ the cake that your little sister's friend baked for you?

It seems that readers are quite capable of recovering the fact that *in which tin* is the indirect object of *put* long before they finish processing the direct-object NP. Indeed, if we do not pied pipe the preposition, forcing the interpretation of the indirect object to be delayed until the preposition is reached (because it is the subcategorizer of the NP), the sentence becomes rather unwieldly.

(16) [Which tin]$_i$ did you put the cake that your little sister's friend baked for you in$_i$?

Pickering and Barry went on to consider examples with multiple long-distance dependencies, which provide further evidence that filler-gap constructions are resolved at the subcategorizer. However, I argue that all their evidence can be accounted for within a trace-based theory of performance that employs a uniform processing strategy. My model makes identical predictions to the system of Pickering and Barry for the type of evidence they considered. At the end of this section, however, I also cite evidence that, although predicted by the trace-based model, cannot be naturally accounted for within their dependency-grammar approach.

Parsing with Traces: The Second Dimension

The arguments of Pickering and Barry clearly must be addressed by any model that claims to be principle based. However, traditional models of gap filling have tacitly assumed that empty categories may only be posited once the relevant position in the string has been reached. In this way, traces are treated much as lexical items, despite that they lack inherent phonological content. An alternative is to assume that empty categories do not constitute part of the Phonetic Form (PF) level of representation (i.e., the phonetic, S-structure yield of a syntactic analysis). Indeed, current transformational syntax does not posit the existence of empty categories at any level except the syntactic levels of representation,

S-Structure (SS) and Logical Form (LF). Rather, empty categories are simply another representational device in the syntactic structure of an utterance, with a psychological status similar to say, the branches of the phrase-structure tree. If I adopt this view, then there is no a priori reason to delay positing a trace once an attachment site exists in the constituent structure (i.e., there is no reason to hold off until the corresponding string yield position is reached). Having relaxed this (arguably unmotivated) constraint on gap postulation, reconsider the following sentence, assuming the use of traces.

(17) [In what tin]$_i$ did you put the cake ε_i?

If one follows this suggestion, then—once the verb *put* and its VP projection are incorporated into the structure—there is no reason to delay the postulation of the PP trace as a complement.

(18)

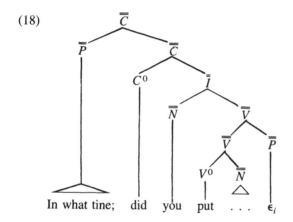

Once this structure is built, one can proceed to parse the remaining lexical material (i.e., the *cake*): Whether the remaining input precedes the trace (i.e., intervenes in the structure) or follows it is of no concern as long as the independent principles of grammar are upheld.

If at first this proposal seems controversial, it is because our existing perception of gap filling has been shaped by the use of one-dimensional characterizations of syntactic analyses, i.e., the string in (17) represents only the linear, terminal yield of the S-structure tree in (18), which is fundamentally a two-dimensional structure (i.e., a hierarchical representation of constituents and attachment). One can see that the one-dimension characterization has the potential to misguide one's intuitions about processing, which is inherently concerned with the recovery of the two-dimensional structure. Furthermore, empty categories should not be considered a priori part of the PF yield, and may therefore be processed as soon as the current partial syntactic representation permits.

This revised view entails that the AFS, as proposed by Frazier, be ammended to operate such that it posits a trace in any potentially vacated position made available by the current partial analysis, regardless of where that position is in the string yield. This might be descriptively characterized as a hyperactive filler strategy—what I dub the *active trace strategy* (ATS). Thus, a trace may be postulated even sooner than was dictated by the AFS, as motivated earlier. In fact, the ATS is equivalent to the AFS, but is less "inhibited" given my revised interpretation of the status of empty categories. Indeed, just as I argued that the active prediction of a (functionally selected) constituent structure was derived from the PIC, I similarly claim that PIC forces the postulation of traces in an equally "active" manner, so as to ensure that antecedent–trace relationships are resolved incrementally and at the earliest possible moment.

Consider some additional support for my approach that demonstrates that the ATS applies for traces resulting from both X^{max} (phrasal) and X^{min} (head) movement. To illustrate this, consider the following example.

(19) *Das Mädchen sah das Buch*
     The girl saw the book.

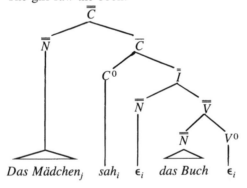

I follow the standard transformational analysis in assuming that the canonical clause structure of German and Dutch is verb final.[9] However, in both languages, the highest verb (either auxiliary or main) raises to the beginning of the sentence (to C^0), followed by movement of some phrase to the [Spec,CP] position—the so-called verb-second, or V-2, phenomenon. Both the English and German sentences have similar word order, but the structure illustrates that, in German, the D-structure position of the verb occurs at the end of the sentence. If I assumed the traditional gap-filling strategies, then German and Dutch hearers would be forced to delay the use of the verb's selectional information until the

---

[9]That is, the head of VP, and indeed IP, are assumed to occur at the rightmost positions of their respective structures. I omit the head I^0 in the tree because it is not essential to the analysis and nothing hinges on it.

end of the sentence, after all the complements have been parsed, the verb's trace identified, and thematic assignment performed.[10] This contrasts with Stowe's evidence for English, which seems to demonstrate the incremental use of thematic information during processing (Stowe, 1989). Thus, the traditional assumptions about gap filling imply that, for sentences with virtually identical word order, English hearers have the advantage of using thematic information incrementally, whereas German hearers do not. However, given the account motivated earlier, I predict an equivalent degree of incrementality for both language types. Consider the structure for the following partial input.

(20) *Das Mädchen sah . . .*

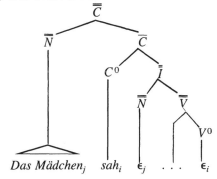

Given the prediction of functional constituent structure argued for earlier, the parser can posit both the subject trace (in [Spec,IP]) and the trace for the head of the VP immediately because the necessary structure exists for the postulation of these traces (recall the functional prediction of IP by C, and of VP by I). This in turn permits the relevant thematic structure to be recovered, allowing the selectional properties of the verb to be consulted immediately. Thus, if the sentence fragment was "Das Buch sah . . ," the parser could quickly determine that the topicalized NP was not a plausible agentive subject, and reanalyze.

A similar proposal for early trace postulation was advanced by Gibson and Hickok (1993) and briefly considered in Gorell (1993). The parsing model suggested by Gibson and Hickok postulates a *wh*-trace immediately once the subcategorizer is found. Indeed, the model they proposed should behave identically to that of Pickering and Barry. In contrast, the present model does not stipulate that the parser should wait for a subcategorizer, but rather that the trace should be postulated as soon as an attachment site is available. Thus, although all models successfully account for the indirect *wh*-PP object examples previously, both Pickering and Barry and Gibson and Hickok failed to explain the broader evi-

---

[10]Although in the example there is only one complement, there could be more and of arbitrary length.

dence for early trace postulation. In particular, their subcategorization-driven parsers will be at a disadvantage in the case of verb-final languages such as Dutch. Consider the following examples from Frazier (1987).

(21) a. *Jan houdt niet van de Amerikaanse die de Nederlander wil uit-nodigen.* (Amb.)
John liked not the American who the Dutchperson wants to invite.
John liked not the American who wants to invite the Dutchperson.

b. *Karl hielp de mijnwerkers die de boswachter vonden.*(Unamb.)
Karl helped the mineworkers who found-PL the forester.

c. *Karl hielp de mijnwerkers die de boswachter vond.*(Unamb)
Karl helped the mineworkers who the forester found-SG.

In each of these sentences, there exists a relative clause (RC) introduced by the relative pronoun (RP) *die*. This pronoun will ultimately be bound as either the subject or object of the RC. According to the parsing mechanism proposed here, once *die* is encountered, causing the RC (CP) to be identified, I predict (top–down) the IP that is c-selected by C. This IP now provides an attachment site in the subject position, and the ATS will cause a trace to be postulated there and bound to the RP, leading to a preference for the subject-gap reading, illustrated by the following structure.

(22)

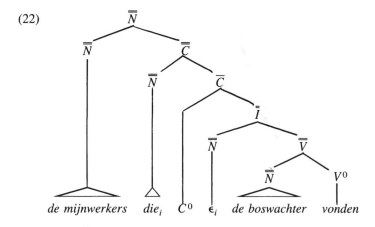

de mijnwerkers   die$_i$ C^0 ϵ_i de boswachter   vonden

For the data in (21), Frazier obtained the preference for the subject-gap reading (21b) even where the final verb forces an object-gap reading. These data are consistent with both the AFS and ATS, assuming the functional prediction of the subject NP I argued for here. Clearly, waiting for the subcategorizer, as Gibson and Hickok implied, will not explain this phenomenon. Such a model would simply leave the intervening lexical NP ("*de boswachter*") unattached, or possibly attach it as the subject because this is the first available site. Only when the verb is reached will the parser try to posit the trace. If the NP is unattached, no preference is predicted either way (the agreement on the verb will unambiguously solve the problem). If the NP is preferentially attached as a subject, they predicted a preference for object relative, contra Frazier's evidence. It is also clear that this preference is not captured by a direct-association mechanism of Pickering and Barry. Indeed, it is difficult to see how a nontrace-based theory could account for these data given that a presubcategorizer preference is obtained, thus providing at least some positive evidence for the psychological reality of empty categories.

CONCLUSIONS

In this chapter, I demonstrated that, to account for incremental processing data, particularly from verb-final languages, the sentence processor must operate at least partially top–down, as concluded in Frazier (1987). However, this does not entail a "compiled out" phrase-structure component as Frazier suggested. Indeed, the degree of top–down processing required to capture the existing data has a natural and principled explanation in terms of the properties of functional categories, whose selectional properties are highly fixed. In particular, I argued that the prediction of functional structure is entailed by the PIC in an effort to make maximal use of predetermined, syntactic knowledge.

I have further outlined the process of resolving antecedent–trace relationships. On the basis of the recent and rather convincing observations of Pickering and Barry, I argued that traces are not part of the PF yield for a syntactic structure, as has been tacitly assumed,[11] but are manifest in the syntax alone. Given this, the notion of "encountering" a gap during sentence comprehension is simply not well formed, and the postulation of such traces must therefore be driven by the parser. Insofar as this is the case, there is no reason to delay the postulation of traces until its string position is reached. This relaxation on trace postulation, combined with the requirement for maximal, incremental interpretation as dictated by the PIC, predicts that a trace will be postulated (and bound to its antecedent) as soon as an appropriate position in the syntactic structure exists. Crucially, such early trace postulation hinges on the top–down operation of the parser, as illustrated in the case of Dutch RCs. This ATS not only accounts for the relevant data presented by Pickering and Barry, but also for the standard range of data from English and Dutch hitherto accounted for by the ATS's predecessor—Frazier's AFS. Furthermore, I showed how prediction of functional structure and the ATS conspire to permit incremental processing in German V-2 constructions.

---

[11]This is not to deny that the existence of a trace may influence PF, as in the ubiquitous *wanna*-contraction.

The processes of functional, top–down prediction and the ATS are proposed as necessary mechanisms of the syntactic processor, particularly in the context of principle-based performance accounts. I argued that attachment decisions are not dependent on subcategorization information, as suggested by the delayed-attachment, head-driven parsing model of Abney (1989) and Pritchett (1991). Similarly, I showed that a trace-based account of long-distance dependencies does exist, despite the arguments of Pickering and Barry (1991). The recovery of these dependencies can occur independently of subcategorizer, in contrast with the proposals of both Pickering and Barry, and the mechanism implied therein (Gibson & Hickok, 1993). In summary, I conclude that any principle-based model of sentence processing must operate incrementally, partially top–down, and employ an ATS. Furthermore, all of these mechanisms can be seen as instantiations of the broader PIC.

REFERENCES

Abney, S. (1989). A computational model of human parsing. *Journal of Psycholinguistic Research,* *18*(1), 129–144.

Aho, A., & Ullman, J. (1972). *The theory of parsing, translation, and compiling* (Vol. 1). Englewood Cliffs, NJ: Prentice-Hall.

Altmann, G., & Steedman, M. (1988). Interaction with context during human sentence processing. *Cognition, 30,* 191–238.

Bader, M. (1990). *Syntaktische Prozesse beim Sprachverstehen: Theoretische Überlegungen und experimentelle Untersuchungen* [Syntactic processes in understanding language: Theoretical considerations and experimental investigations. Magisterarbeit [Masters Thesis], Albert-Ludwigs-Universtaet Freiburg.

Berwick, R. C. (1991). Principle-based parsing. In P. Sells, S. Sheiber, & T. Wasow (Eds.), *Foundational issues in natural language processing* (pp. 115–226). Cambridge, MA: MIT Press.

Berwick, R. C., Abney, S. P., & Tenny, C. (Eds.). (1991). *Principle-based parsing: Computational and psycholinguistics.* Dordrecht, The Netherlands: Kluwer.

Berwick, R. C., & Weinberg, A. S. (1984). *The grammatical basis of linguistic performance.* Cambridge, MA: MIT Press.

Chomsky, N. (1986). *Knowledge of language: Its nature, origin and use.* New York: Praeger.

Clifton, C., & Frazier, L. (1989). Comprehending sentences with long-distance dependencies. In G. Carlson & M. Tanenhaus (Eds.), *Linguistic structure in language processing* (pp. 273–317). Dordrecht, The Netherlands: Kluwer.

Cowper, E. A. (1992). *A concise introduction to syntactic theory.* Chicago, IL: University of Chicago Press.

Crain, S., & Fodor, J. D. (1985). How can grammars help parsers? In D. R. Dowty, L. Karttunen, & A. M. Zwicky (Eds.), *Natural language parsing* (pp. 94–128). Cambridge, England: Cambridge University Press.

Crain, S., & Steedman, M. (1985). On not being led up the garden path: The use of context by the psychological syntax processor. In D. R. Dowty, L. Karttunen, & A. M. Zwicky (Eds.), *Natural language parsing* (pp. 320–358). Cambridge, England: Cambridge University Press.

Crocker, M. W. (1991). *A logical model of competence and performance in the human sentence processor.* Unpublished doctoral dissertation, University of Edinburgh, Scotland.

Dorr, B. (1987). UNITRAN: *A Principle-based approach to machine translation*. Unpublished master's thesis, MIT, Cambridge, MA.

Fong, S. (1991). *Computational properties of principle-based grammatical theories*. Unpublished doctoral dissertation, MIT, Cambridge, MA.

Frazier, L. (1978). *On comprehending sentences: Syntactic parsing strategies*. Unpublished doctoral dissertation, University of Connecticut, Storrs, CT.

Frazier, L. (1987). Syntactic processing: Evidence from Dutch. *Natural Language and Linguistic Theory, 5,* 519–559.

Frazier, L., & Clifton, C. (1989). Successive cyclicity in the grammar and parser. *Language and Cognitive Processes, 4*(2), 93–126.

Frazier, L., & Rayner, K. (1988). Parameterizing the language processing system: Left- vs. right-branching within and across languages. In J. Hawkins (Ed.), *Explaining linguistic universals* (pp. 247–279). Oxford: Basil Blackwell.

Gibson, E. (1991). *A computational theory of human linguistic processing: Memory limitations and processing breakdown*. Unpublished doctoral dissertation, Carnegie Mellon University, Pittsburgh, PA.

Gibson, E., & Hickok, G. (1993). Sentence processing with empty categories. *Language and Cognitive Processes, 8,* 147–161.

Gorrell, P. (1993). A note on the direct association hypothesis: A reply to Pickering and Barry (1991). *Language and Cognitive Processes, 8,* 129–146.

Hemforth, B., Hoelter, M., Konieczny, L., Scheepers, C., & Strube, G. (1991). Kognitive Modellierung und empirische Analyse von Prozessen der Satzverarbeitung. In *Zwischenbericht im DFG-Schwerpunktprogramm Kognitive Linguistik,* No. 4 [Cognitive modelling and empirical analysis of sentence processing. In: Intermediate report of the DFG-main subject program in cognitive linguistics]. Ruhr-Universitaet Bochum.

Johnson, M. (1989). Use of knowledge of language. *Journal of Psycholinguistic Research, 18*(1), 105–128.

Kimball, J. (1973). Seven principles of surface structure parsing in natural language. *Cognition, 2*(1), 15–47.

Konieczny, L., Hemforth, B., Scheepers, C., & Strube, G. (1993). Semantikorientierte Syntaxverabeitung. In C. Habel & G. Rickheit (Eds.), *Kognitive Linguistik: Repraesentationen und Prozesse* [Semantically orientated processing of syntax. In: Cognitive linguistics: Representations and processes]. Opladen: Westdeutscher Verlag.

Marcus, M. P. (1980). *A theory of syntactic recognition for natural language*. Cambridge, MA: MIT Press.

McElree, B., & Bever, T. G. (1989). The psychological reality of linguistically defined gaps. *Journal of Psycholinguistic Research, 18*(1), 21–36.

Merlo, P. (1992). *On modularity and compilation in a government-binding parser*. Unpublished doctoral dissertation, University of Maryland, College Park, MD.

Pickering, M., & Barry, G. (1991). Sentence processing without empty categories. *Language and Cognitive Processes, 6*(3), 229–259.

Pritchett, B. (1988). Garden path phenomena and the grammatical basis of language processing. *Language, 64,* 539–576.

Pritchett, B. L. (1991). Head position and parsing ambiguity. *Journal of Psycholinguistic Research, 20*(3), 251–279.

Pritchett, B. L. (1992). *Grammatical competence and parsing performance*. Chicago, IL: University of Chicago Press.

Stabler, E. P. (1991). Avoid the pedestrians paradox. In R. C. Berwick, S. P. Abney, & C. Tenny (Eds.), *Principle-based parsing: Computational and psycholinguistics* (pp. 199–238). Dordrecht, The Netherlands: Kluwer.

Stowe, L. (1986). Parsing wh-constructions: Evidence for on-line gap location. *Language and Cognitive Processes, 1,* 227–246.

Stowe, L. A. (1989). Thematic structures and sentence comprehension. In G. Carlson & M. Tanenhaus (Eds.), *Linguistic structure in language processing* (pp. 319–357). Dordrecht, The Netherlands: Kluwer.

Tanenhaus, M., Carlson, G., & Trueswell, J. (1989). The role of thematic structures in interpretation and parsing. *Language and Cognitive Processes: Special Issue on Parsing and Interpretation, 4,* 211–234.

12 A Processing Model for Free Word-Order Languages

Owen Rambow and Aravind K. Joshi
University of Pennsylvania

German is a verb-final language. Like many verb-final languages, such as Hindi, Japanese, and Korean, German displays considerable word-order freedom: There is no syntactic constraint on the ordering of the nominal arguments of a verb, as long as the verb remains in final position. This effect is referred to as *scrambling,* and is interpreted in transformational frameworks as leftward movement of the arguments. Furthermore, arguments from an embedded clause may move out of their clause; this effect is referred to as *long-distance scrambling*. Although scrambling has recently received considerable attention in the syntactic literature, the status of long-distance scrambling has only rarely been addressed. The reason for this is the problematic status of the data: Not only is long-distance scrambling highly dependent on pragmatic context, but it also is strongly subject to degradation due to processing constraints. As in the case of center embedding, it is not immediately clear whether to assume that observed unacceptability of highly complex sentences is due to grammatical restrictions, or whether we should assume that the competence grammar does not place any restrictions on scrambling (and that, therefore, all such sentences are in fact grammatical), and the unacceptability of some (or most) of the grammatically possible word orders is due to processing limitations. In this chapter, we argue for the second view by presenting a processing model for German.

German is an interesting language to study from the perspectives of competence syntax and performance because it allows scrambling as well as topicalization of arguments. *Topicalization* refers to the movement of a single element into the sentence-initial position in the root clause. Because German is a verb-second language, in every sentence some element must topicalize. Like scrambling (and like topicalization in English), topicalization in German can create unbounded dependencies. However, the two types of movement differ in terms of their linguistic properties. For example, scrambling can create new anaphoric bindings, whereas topicalization cannot (Webelhuth, 1989). In addition to the linguistic differences, there is also a processing difference: Long-distance topicalization into sentence-initial position appears to be easier to process than long-distance scrambling of the same element over a similar distance. A simple processing account that somehow measures the number of intervening lexical items must fail.

Thus, not only do the German data call for a processing model, but the model must be sensitive to subtle differences in the constructions involved. Our processing model for free word-order languages has two important properties:

- The processing model provides a metric that makes predictions about processing difficulty on an open-ended scale. This property allows us to verify our model with respect to the results from psycholinguistic experiments as well as from native-speaker intuition.
- The processing model is tightly coupled with the competence grammar, in the sense that the grammar directly determines the behavior of the parser. This tight coupling means that if two superficially similar constructions have rather different linguistic analyses, their processing behavior may well be predicted to be different.

The chapter is structured as follows. In the next section, we discuss the relevant issues in German syntax and isolate two phenomena for which we derive a processing model. We then present a grammar formalism—tree-adjoining grammar (TAG)—and an associated automaton, bottom-up embedded pushdown automaton (BEPDA). After that, we give linguistic examples and show that the model makes correct predictions with respect to certain cross-linguistic psycholinguistic data. We thereupon discuss the extensions to the basic model that are required to handle long-distance scrambling. We show how the extended model makes plausible predictions for the two phenomena that we identify in the data section.

GERMAN DATA

German is a verb-final language. In addition, it is verb second, which means that, in a root clause, the finite verb (main verb or auxiliary) moves into the second position in the clause (standardly assumed to be the COMP position).[1] This divides the root clause into two parts: the position in front of the finite verb,

---

[1]Note that in the case of clauses with simple tensed verbs, the final position in the clause for the nonfinite verb remains empty.

the *Vorfeld* or ("forefield," VF), and the positions between the finite and non-finite verbs, the *Mittelfeld* ("Middlefield," MF). The VF must contain exactly one constituent, which can be any element (an argument or an adjunct, or the nonfinite verb). Three types of word-order variation ("movement" in transformational frameworks) are possible: In *extraposition*, embedded clauses appear behind the nonfinite verb; *topicalization* fills the VF with an element from the MF; and *scrambling* permutes the elements of the MF. We discuss them in turn.

Extraposition

Although nominal arguments must appear in the MF, clausal arguments may appear behind the verb in the clause-final position. (In fact, finite subclauses *must* appear in this position.)

(1) a. ... *daß Peter dem Kunden   den Kühlschrank   zu reparieren zu helfen versucht*
      ... that Peter the client (DAT) the refrigerator (ACC) to repair   to help   tries
      ... that Peter tries to help the client repair the refrigerator

    b. ... *daß Peter versucht, dem Kunden zu helfen, den Kühlschrank zu reparieren*

    c. ... *daß Peter versucht, dem Kunden den Kühlschrank zu reparieren zu helfen*

Sentence (1a) shows the unextraposed, center-embedded order. Sentence (1b) is the fully extraposed order, whereas (1c) shows that an extraposition of a center-embedded two-clause structure is possible. The fully extraposed version is by far the preferred one in both spoken and written German, especially in situations with more than two clauses.

Topicalization

We give some examples of topicalization.

(2) a. *Der Lehrer   hat den Kindern   dieses Buch   gegeben*
      the teacher (NOM) has the children (DAT) this book (ACC) given
      The teacher has given this book to the children

    b. *Dieses Buch hat der Lehrer den Kindern gegeben*

In (2a), the default word order, the subject is topicalized into the VF. In (2b), the direct object has topicalized into the VF, so that the subject remains in the MF. An adjunct could also occupy the VF, so that all three arguments of *geben* ("to give") would be in the MF. In the case of embedded clauses, the V-2 phenomenon does not occur if there is an overt complementizer, and hence there is no topicalization. The finite verb is in clause-final position.

(3) *Ich glaube, daß der Lehrer   den Kindern   dieses Buch   gegeben hat*
   I   think   that the teacher (NOM) the children (DAT) this book (ACC) given   has
   I think that the teacher has given this book to the children

If we are only interested in scrambling or extraposition, we give examples of subordinate clauses so that we do not have to deal with the orthogonal issue of topicalization.

Can elements topicalize out of embedded clauses? In the presence of a complementizer, topicalization out of embedded finite clauses is degraded in Standard German. However, extraction out of nonfinite embedded clauses is fine, regardless of whether the embedded clause has extraposed. There is no intonation break (or comma) between fronted element and matrix-finite verb.

(4) a. [*Dieses Buch*]$_i$ *habe ich* [*PRO den Kindern t$_i$ zu geben*] *versucht*
this book (ACC) have I   the children (DAT) to give   tried
This book I have tried to give the children

  b. [*Dieses Buch*]$_i$ *habe ich versucht,* [*PRO den Kindern t$_i$ zu geben*]

Scrambling

Scrambling in German is the movement of arguments (nominal or clausal) within the MF (rather than into the VF). The following example is from Haider (1991).

(5) . . . *daß* [*eine hiesige Firma*]   [*meinem Onkel*] [*die Möbel*]   [*vor drei Tagen*]
. . . that a local company (NOM) my uncle (DAT) the furniture (ACC) three days ago
[*ohne Voranmeldung*]   *zugestellt hat*
without advance warning delivered has
. . . that a local company delivered the furniture to my uncle three days ago without advance warning

As Haider pointed out, "any permutation of these five elements (5! = 120) is grammatically well-ordered" (p. 12). We conclude that scrambling of more than one element is possible.

If there are embedded clauses, scrambling can move elements out of the embedded clauses (long-distance scrambling). However, in German, scrambling can never proceed out of tensed clauses. It has been suggested that embedded infinitival clauses form a "clause union" (Evers, 1975). If this is the case, then there is no long-distance scrambling in German because no clause boundary is crossed. However, the clause-union analysis has not gone uncontested (Kroch & Santorini, 1991). For the sake of the development in this chapter, it is irrelevant whether clause union takes place and whether a clause boundary is actually crossed. The important fact is that an argument or adjunct can scramble into the domain of an (originally) different predicate. We continue to refer to this effect as long-distance scrambling.

(6) a. . . . *daß niemand*   [*PRO den Kühlschrank zu reparieren*] *versprochen hat*
. . . that no one (NOM) the refrigerator (ACC) to repair   promised   has
. . . that no one has promised to repair the refrigerator

  b. . . . *daß* [*den Kühlschrank*]$_i$ *niemand* [*t$_i$ zu reparieren*] *versprochen hat*

There is no bound on the number of clause boundaries over which an element can scramble.

(7) a. . . . *daß* [*den Kühlschrank*]*ᵢ*   *niemand*   [[t*ᵢ* *zu reparieren*]
       . . . that the refrigerator (ACC) no one (NOM)   to repair
       zu versuchen] *versprochen*   hat
       to try   promised   has
       . . . that no one has promised to try to repair the refrigerator

     b. . . . *daß* [*den Kühlschrank*]*ᵢ*   *niemand*   [[t*ᵢ* *zu reparieren*]
       . . . that the refrigerator (ACC) no one (NOM)   to repair
       zu versuchen]   *zu versprechen bereit   ist*
       to try   to promise   ready   is
       . . . that no one is ready to promise to try to repair the refrigerator

Furthermore, an element scrambled (long distance or not) from one clause does not preclude an element from another clause from being scrambled, and scrambling does not obey a "path-containment" condition (Pesetsky, 1982), which would require that dependencies between moved element and trace are nested, but not crossed.

(8) . . . *daß* [*dem Kunden*]*ᵢ*   [*den Kühlschrank*]*ⱼ*   *bisher noch*
     . . . that the client (DAT) the refrigerator (ACC) so far as yet
     niemand   t*ᵢ* [[t*ⱼ* *zu reparieren*]   *zu versuchen*] *versprochen hat*
     no one (NOM)   to repair   to try   promised   has
     . . . that so far, no one yet has promised to repair the refrigerator

We conclude that scrambling in German is "doubly unbounded": There is neither a bound in the competence syntax on the distance over which each element can scramble, nor is there a bound in the competence syntax on the number of unbounded dependencies that can occur in one sentence. This generalization does not mean that all sentences in which "doubly unbounded" scrambling has occurred will be judged equally acceptable. Clearly, scrambling is constrained by pragmatic and processing factors, and perhaps also by semantic factors.[2] In this chapter, we propose a competence model that allows doubly unbounded scrambling, and an associated processing model that predicts the degree of acceptability of scrambled sentences.

---

[2]Analyses of the pragmatic and semantic issues involved in scrambling (see, e.g., Höhle, 1982; Lenerz, 1977; Moltmann, 1990) are still somewhat sketchy. However, although they provide constraints on word order, they do not provide evidence that the generalization of "double unboundedness" must be abandoned. The contextual and semantic restrictions on word order do not translate into general rules that would categorically rule out certain formally definable orders (such as, say, word orders derived by multiple long-distance scrambling), irrespective of the particular choice of lexemes and context.

Whereas processing load appears to increase with an increasing number of scrambled elements, the increase in processing load is gradual, providing us with a range of acceptability judgments. This picture is further complicated by the fact that long-distance scrambling, which degrades acceptability, can interact with extraposition, which improves acceptability.

(9) a. (ok) . . . *daß niemand   den Kühlschrank   zu reparieren*
       . . . that no one (NOM) the refrigerator (ACC) to repair
       zu versuchen   versprochen hat
       to try   promised has
       . . . that no-one has promised to repair the refrigerator

   b. ok . . . *daß niemand versprochen hat, zu versuchen, den Kühlschrank zu reparieren*

   c. ok . . . *daß niemand versprochen hat, den Kühlschrank zu reparieren zu versuchen*

   d. ? . . . *daß niemand den Kühlschrank zu versuchen zu reparieren versprochen hat*

   e. ?? . . . *daß den Kühlschrank niemand zu reparieren zu versuchen versprochen hat*

Sentence (9a) is prescriptively grammatical, and native-speaker judgment can therefore not serve as an indication of processing difficulty (this is indicated by the parentheses around the judgment). However, it is well known that center embedding presents processing difficulties. Sentence (9b) is the much preferred and perfectly acceptable fully extraposed word order. The other example sentences represent variations in decreasing order of acceptability. Sentence (9d) and (9e) include long-distance scrambling, which degrades them further.

In the case of three levels of embedding, with two of the clauses having one overt argument each and the third clause having none (as in (9)), we end up with 30 possible word orders. Six of these are ruled out straightforwardly by a linguistic account (with only minimal assumptions about phrase structure, these word orders would necessarily result in unbound traces). The remaining 24 sentences display acceptabilities ranging from "perfectly acceptable" to "flat out." This "grey zone" of acceptability has not, to our knowledge, been investigated in either the linguistic or the psycholinguistic literature. This is the first phenomenon for which we would like our processing model to account.

Topicalization and Scrambling: Two Distinct Types of Movement

We have seen that German has two distinct types of (leftward) movement: topicalization, which is movement of a single constituent (argument/adjunct) into the VF; and scrambling, which is movement of any number of constituents

within the MF. There are formal differences between these two types of movement. Topicalization can be handled by a simple TAG, whereas scrambling is
beyond the formal power of TAGs (we discuss this later on in more detail). The
question arises whether this formal difference is accompanied by any linguistic
differences between the two types of movement. There is evidence that the two
types of movement do in fact have different linguistic properties, in particular
with respect to the binding possibilities from the surface position (see Webelhuth,
1989, for anaphoric binding; Frank, Lee, & Rambow, 1994, for bound-variable
and principle C binding facts). Interestingly, the two types of word-order variation also appear to have different effects on the processor. Consider the following
minimal pair.

(10) a. Sentence with long-distance scrambling:
      ? Der Meister hat den Kühlschrank   niemandem   zu reparieren versprochen
      the master   has the refrigerator (ACC) no one (DAT) to repair   promised
      The master has promised no one to repair the refrigerator

    b. Sentence with long-distance topicalization:
      Den Kühlschrank   hat der Meister   niemandem   zu reparieren versprochen
      the refrigerator (ACC) has the master (NOM) no one (DAT) to repair   promised
      The master has promised no one to repair the refrigerator

In both sentences, the argument "*den Kühlschrank*" ("the refrigerator") of the
embedded clause has moved out of the clause and to the left. In the scrambled
sentence, the surface position is just after the finite verb; in the topicalized
sentence, the landing site is just before the finite verb. Nonetheless, (10b) is
significantly more acceptable than (10a). We propose that this difference in
acceptability is due to processing constraints, and it is the second phenomenon
that we want our processing model to be able to predict.

TAGS AND BEPDAS

The processing model that we present in this chapter is based on Joshi (1990).
Joshi proposed to model human sentence processing with a formal automaton
called the *embedded pushdown automaton* (EPDA). The EPDA is equivalent to
TAG: For every TAG there is an EPDA that accepts exactly the set of strings that
the TAG generates, and for every EPDA there is a TAG that generates exactly the
set of strings that the EPDA accepts. In this chapter, we use the bottom–up
variant of the EPDA, called BEPDA,[3] which is also formally equivalent to TAG.
This formal equivalence is crucial to our point: TAG has been used for the
representation of competence syntax. We propose that, through the formal equivalence, we can relate in a motivated manner formal models of competence

---

[3]We would like to thank Yves Schabes for suggesting the use of the BEPDA (rather than the
EPDA) in modeling human sentence processing.

directly to formal models of performance. Therefore, we carefully introduce the formal notions that we need for the remainder of our exposition. We do so using abstract formal language examples because linguistic examples might obscure the underlying formal mechanisms. We return to linguistic facts in the next section.

We start out by describing TAG, which underlies our model. We then describe the automaton and proceed to show how an automaton can be derived from a grammar.

Context-Free Grammar and Tree-Adjoining Grammar

We first briefly review context-free grammars (CFG). Although they have been all but abandoned as a basis for linguistic description in the linguistic and computational literature, they are quite familiar as a formalism and therefore useful as a starting point for the exposition of TAGs. Recall that in a CFG, we have string rewriting rules that specify how a single symbol, called a *nonterminal,* can be rewritten as a sequence of other symbols. We start out with a special nonterminal symbol, say *S* for *sentence,* and successively apply string rewriting rules until we have no more nonterminal symbols left in the string, but only terminal symbols (such as "John likes Mary"). (In the process, we create a derivation tree that records how we rewrite each nonterminal symbol: The symbols we replaced it with appear as its daughters.)

Just as CFG is a string rewriting system, TAG is a tree rewriting system: We start with elementary trees, and then can replace nonterminal nodes in the tree with entire trees. A TAG consists of a set of such elementary trees. Two tree-combining operations are used to derive larger trees: *substitution* and *adjunction.* Substitution is shown in Fig. 12.1: Tree α_1 if the root node of α_2 has the same label as a nonterminal node on the frontier of α_1 that has been specially marked for substitution (a "substitution node"; substitution nodes are marked with down

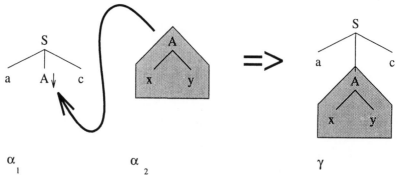

FIG. 12.1.   The substitution operation.

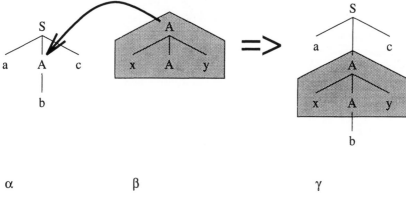

FIG. 12.2.   The adjunction operation.

arrows). Adjunction is shown in Fig. 12.2. Tree α (called an *initial tree*) contains a nonterminal node labeled *A;* the root node of Tree β (an *auxiliary tree*) is also labeled *A,* as is exactly one nonterminal node on its frontier (the foot node). All other frontier nodes are terminal nodes or substitution nodes. We take Tree α and remove the subtree rooted at its node *A*, insert in its stead tree β, and then add at the footnode of β the subtree of α that we removed earlier. The result is Tree γ. As we can see, substitution rewrites a node on the frontier, whereas adjunction can rewrite an interior node, thus having the effect of inserting one tree into the center of another. For a more extensive introduction to TAGs, see Joshi (1987) and Joshi, Vijay-Shanker, and Weir (1991).

TAG is an appealing formalism for the representation of linguistic competence because it allows local dependencies (in particular, the subcategorization frame and *wh*-dependencies) to be stated on the elementary structures of the grammar and to be factored apart from the expression of recursion and unbounded dependencies. This in turn allows us to develop a lexicon-oriented theory of syntax: Because the entire subcategorization frame of a lexical item can be represented in a single tree, we can "lexicalize" the grammar so that every tree is associated with exactly one lexical item (be it a word or a multiword idiom). It is this lexicalized version that has been used in the development of TAG grammars for English, French, German, and Japanese, and that we use in the remainder of this chapter.

The Pushdown Automaton and the Bottom–Up Embedded Pushdown Automaton

The EPDA was introduced by Vijay-Shanker (1987) and proved to be formally equivalent to TAG. Schabes (1990) proposed a bottom–up version called *BEPDA*. We only describe the BEPDA here.

First, we briefly recall the definition of the pushdown automaton (PDA), which is known to recognize exactly context-free languages. A PDA[4] consists of (a) a stack of stack symbols, (b) an input tape with a read head, and (c) a finite state control. The read head scans the input once from left to right. A transition relationship determines the moves of the automaton, based on the current state, the input symbol being scanned, and the symbol currently on the top of the stack. Two types of moves are possible:

- The automaton can shift the input symbol onto the stack (a SHIFT move).
- The automaton can remove a number of stack symbols and replace them by a single symbol (a REDUCE move).

In either case, the automaton can transition to a new state. The automaton accepts the input if, upon reading it completely, its stack is empty. It should be noted that a PDA (in general) is nondeterministic: For a given state, input symbol, and top of stack, several different moves are possible. Given a context-free grammar, it is easy to construct a corresponding PDA (although it will not be the only one that corresponds to that CFG): We simply need to SHIFT any nonterminal from the input tape onto the stack and to interpret the context-free rules as REDUCE moves (if the right-hand side of a rule is on the top of the stack, it REDUCEs to the left-hand side). Now let us turn to the BEPDA. Like the PDA, the BEPDA consists of a pushdown store, an input tape with a one-way read-only scanner, and a finite state automaton that controls the actions of the automaton. The pushdown store of the BEPDA has a more complex structure than that of a PDA: It is a stack of stacks of stack symbols, rather than a simple stack of stack symbols. A transition relation is defined for the automaton between triples consisting of the current state, the input symbol, and the stack symbol on the top of the top stack on the one hand and pairs consisting of a new state and new material to be put on the pushdown store on the other hand. The actions are as follows:

- The SHIFT move first creates a new (empty) stack on the top of the stack of stacks and then pushes a single symbol onto it.
- The UNWRAP operation is an extension of the PDA REDUCE move. This operation is illustrated in Fig. 12.3. In an UNWRAP move, finite (and possibly empty) sequences of stacks are removed immediately below (stacks $\beta_1, \ldots, \beta_{k_b}$ in the figure) and above (stacks $\alpha_1, \ldots, \alpha_{k_a}$) a designated stack (which becomes the new top stack). (We say that these stacks are "UNWRAPped around" the new top stack.) Then, a sequence of (possibly empty) stack symbols on the new top stack is popped (γ in the figure) and replaced by a single new stack symbol (a in the figure).

---

[4]We give a particular definition of PDA; other equivalent ones are possible.

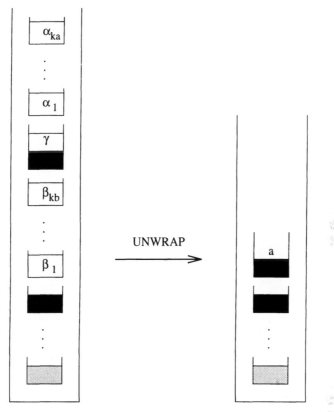

FIG. 12.3. UNWRAP move of the BEPDA.

There are several "degenerate" UNWRAP moves that are used often and therefore have special names. They are degenerate because some of the stack symbols involved in the definition of the UNWRAP move are specified to be the empty string. For example, if the stacks below and above the new top stack are empty (i.e., the new top stack is the old top stack), and if the new stack symbol is also empty, we have simply removed stack symbols from the top stack. We call this move a POP. However, if in addition to the stacks below and above, the new top stack γ is also empty (i.e., we do not remove any stack symbols at all, but just push a new stack symbol on to the top stack), we call the move a PUSH move.

It is the UNWRAP move that extends the power of the BEPDA beyond that of the PDA and its REDUCE move: The stacks removed above and below the new top stack correspond to adjoined material. We illustrate this by giving an automaton for the sample of Fig. 12.2.

The automaton has a single state, q. We then have the following transition rules:

1. Any scanned input symbol (a, b, c, x, or y) is SHIFTed onto the stack of stacks.

2. A top top-stack symbol of b is replaced by A_α (a degenerate form of UNWRAP).

3. If the top top-stack symbol is A_α, A_β may be PUSHed on top of it.

4. If the top stack consists of the element y (and nothing else), the third stack of the element x (and nothing else), and if the top of the second stack is A_β, then x, A_β, and y can be UNWRAPped around the second stack and another copy of A_β pushed onto it.

5. A_β on the top of the top stack can be POPped.

6. If the top stack consists of the element c (and nothing else), the third stack of the element a (and nothing else), and if the top of the second stack is A_α, then x, A_α, and y can be UNWRAPped around the second stack and S pushed onto it.

7. S on the top of the top stack can be POPped.

For every TAG, there are many different equivalent BEPDAs. We have constructed this BEPDA in a specific manner, which is particularly straightforward in that it establishes a close relationship between the grammar and the automaton. We call this construction the *simple method*. First, we have distinguished nodes in different trees that bear the same label by subscripts. The stack symbols are the terminal symbols and the nonterminal nodes (identified by their label and the tree index) from the trees of the grammars, so we speak (somewhat sloppily) of a tree node being in the pushdown store. We have then constructed the rules as follows. Apart from the SHIFT moves (Rule 1), we have "exploded" the trees in the TAG into a set of context-free rules, each describing a node and its daughters. We have then associated one UNWRAP move with each of these context-free rules (Rule 4 for Tree α and Rule 6 for Tree β). Furthermore, at each node at which an adjunction is possible, we have added a rule that PUSHes the foot node of each adjoinable tree onto that node. In our example, the only possible adjunction is of Tree β into Tree α at the node labeled *A (Rule3). Finally, any root node of a tree can be POPped off the automaton (Rule 5 for Tree α and Rule 7 for tree β). We now present a run of this automaton as it accepts the input string axbyc.* The pushdown store is shown "sideways," with the top to the right. The symbol '[' denotes the bottom of a stack.

(11) Step	In State	Store	Input Consumed	Rule Used
0	q			
1	q	[a	a	(1)
2	q	[a [x	x	(1)

Step	In State	Store	Input Consumed	Rule Used
3	q	$[a\ [x\quad [b$	b	(1)
4	q	$[a\ [x\quad [A_\alpha$	—	(2)
5	q	$[a\ [x\quad [A_\alpha\ A_\beta$	—	(3)
6	q	$[a\ [x\quad [A_\alpha\ A_\beta\ [y$	y	(1)
7	q	$[a\ [A_\alpha\ A_\beta$	—	(4)
8	q	$[a\ [A_\alpha$	—	(5)
9	q	$[a\ [A_\alpha\ [c$	c	(1)
10	q	$[S$	—	(6)
11	q		—	(7)

We observe two crucial points about how the automaton recognizes the adjoined tree. First, the automaton "decides" to start stimulating an adjunction in Step 5 by PUSHing the foot node of the auxiliary tree onto the top stack. The automaton proceeds in Steps 6 and 7 by recognizing the auxiliary Tree β completely independently from the initial Tree α into which it is adjoined. The only sign that Tree α has been partially recognized is the A_α node in the stack (at the top of the stack of stacks after Steps 5 and 7, the second from the top after Step 6). But because A_α is not at the top of any stack, it does not affect the processing of the automaton during the recognition of Tree β. Here it becomes apparent why we need a stack of *stacks* (because we need to store information about partially recognized trees) and why we need an UNWRAP move (the automaton needs to manipulate the top of stacks without affecting the information stored in them below). Second, once Tree β has been fully recognized, its root node is at the top of the top stack. In Step 8 (after recognizing the y), the node is POPped from the pushdown store. Thereafter, there is no trace at all of Tree β ever having been recognized. The automaton continues as if it were simply recognizing the string *abc*, whose derivation requires no adjunction.

A FORMAL MODEL OF SYNTACTIC PROCESSING

In this section, we use the machinery introduced in the previous section to model human syntactic processing. We first give examples of how processing models are derived from competence grammars, and then we show how the automaton can be equipped with a metric to predict processing load.

Linguistic TAGs and Associated BEPDAs

As we have previously pointed out, the formal equivalence between TAG and BEPDA means that, for every tree adjoining language L, there is at least one BEPDA M that recognizes exactly L, and typically there is an infinite number of such automata. However, the existence of *some* automaton that makes psycholinguistically relevant predictions is not of interest unless we know how to choose the right automaton from among those that are formally equivalent (but not all of which make the right predictions). We propose that the simple method introduced in the previous section will derive the right automaton. From a linguistically motivated grammar it will derive an automaton that models syntactic processing in a plausible way. This approach shifts the problem of providing a principled account of how to construct models of the syntactic processor (i.e., automata) to the problem of how to construct (competence) grammars, which of course is the object of syntax. This point is important because it affects the question of the universality of the parser. The processor behaves differently for different languages. If we want to explain this variation in a principle and parameter-type methodology, we have two options: Either we can assume that the processor is parametrized on its own (although the parameter setting may be linked to the setting of the linguistic parameters), or we can deduce the cross-linguistic variation among processors from cross-linguistic variation among competence grammars and the way in which the (universal) processor interacts with the competence grammar. The latter view is adopted by Inoue and Fodor (1993), who termed it *as-if-parametrized*. Our approach falls into this paradigm as well.

We now turn to linguistic grammars and show how the simple method derives automata. Let us consider the grammar for a fragment of German given in Fig. 12.4. In this grammar, matrix clauses are adjoined into their subordinate clauses at the root S node. This analysis is motivated by facts about *wh*-extraction out of subordinate clauses as discussed by Kroch (1987, 1989). If we assume that the *wh*-word is included in the same tree as its governing verb (at an S′ node) and

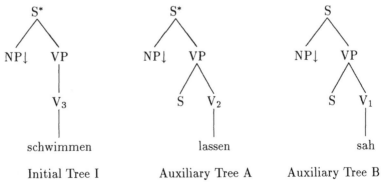

Initial Tree I   Auxiliary Tree A   Auxiliary Tree B

FIG. 12.4.   The German grammar.

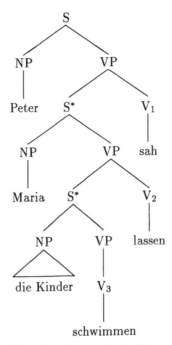

FIG. 12.5.   German derived tree.

adjoin the matrix clause at the S node, then we get subjacency effects "for free."
Further cross-linguistic evidence for this analysis of clausal embedding comes
from Dutch. Kroch and Santorini (1991) gave extensive syntactic evidence for
the grammar given in Fig. 12.6. Again, the correct derivation of the cross-serial
dependencies relies on the adjunction of the matrix clause into its subordinate.
Therefore, we adopt this approach. Note that it is motivated by purely linguistic
considerations—no processing issues intervened in the formulation of this grammar. The grammar in Fig. 12.4 can generate center-embedded sentences such as
the following:

(12) *daß Peter Maria die Kinder   schwimmen lassen   sah*
     that Peter Maria the children (ACC) swim (inf) let (inf) saw
     N_1 N_2 N_3 V_3 V_2 V_1
     that Peter saw Maria let the children swim

German Sentence (12) is derived by first substituting the nominal arguments into
the noun phrase (NP) substitution nodes of Trees I, A, and B. Then, auxiliary
Tree A is adjoined into initial Tree I at the root node of I, and auxiliary Tree B is
adjoined into the root node of the derived tree (which is, in fact, the root node of
auxiliary Tree A). The resulting structure, the derived tree, is shown in Fig. 12.5.

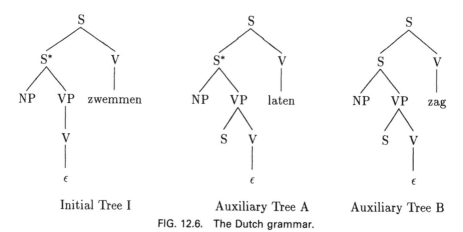

Initial Tree I   Auxiliary Tree A   Auxiliary Tree B

FIG. 12.6.   The Dutch grammar.

We now construct an automaton using the simple method. We start out by "exploding" the trees into context-free rules. For Tree I, we obtain the following context-free rules.

(13) Derived context-free rules for Tree I in Fig. 12.4:

$S_I \rightarrow NP_I \; VP_I$
$VP_I \rightarrow V_I$
$V_I \rightarrow schwimmen$

As we have stressed during the discussion of the TAG formalism, the elementary structures of a TAG are trees, therefore we can associate every elementary structure with a single lexical item (*lexicalization*). Because the automaton mimics the derivation in a TAG, we can interpret the moves of the BEPDA as establishing connections between lexical items. This view of the processor—as manipulating lexical items and not phrase-structure nodes—is somewhat different from the view of processing that arises when one starts from context-free grammars. To emphasize the lexical orientation of the BEPDA model, we follow Joshi (1990) in giving the stack symbols quasicategorical labels, rather than the standard labels. Suppose we have a clausal tree (anchored on a verb) that has substitution nodes $\alpha_1, \ldots, \alpha_n$. Recall that substitution nodes are nodes at which substitution must occur in order to make the tree a complete initial or auxiliary tree. Linguistically, they correspond to nominal arguments. We associate with the verb and each of the nodes in its projection (labeled V (verb), VP (verb phrase), and S (sentence) in this case) a label of the form $V \{\alpha_1, \ldots, \alpha_k\}$, where the α_i are labels of substitution nodes that have not yet been filled. Thus, linguistically, the list represents unfulfilled nominal subcategorization requirements. It is important to note that this notation is entirely equivalent to the notation used in writing the trees themselves: In our sample trees, the VP corresponds to V{NP}, and the top S node to V{ }. The rules of the BEPDA that we obtain are as follows.

(14) BEPDA rules derived from Tree I in Fig. 12.4:
- SHIFT *die Kinder* and *schwimmen* onto the pushdown store.
- UNWRAP [*schwimmen* and replace by [V_i{NP}
- UNWRAP [NP around [V_i{NP} and replace by [V_i{ }
- POP [V_i{ }

The first rule in (14) implements the principle of the simple method to push any scanned input symbols onto the pushdown store. The second rule represents the projection of *schwimmen* to the VP and corresponds to the second and third context-free rules from (13). In the third rule, the subject and the VP are combined to form the sentence, corresponding to the first context-free rule of (13). Finally, the fourth rule implements the principle that root nodes of fully recognized trees are removed from the automaton. Note that we assume that all NP symbols (both stack symbols and those in the subcategorization set) are marked with case information. Furthermore, we assume that we have a syntax of NPs that will allow us to recognize full NPs; we omit the details.

The BEPDA is defined as a nondeterministic automaton. This is not appealing as a model of human sentence processing. We observe that the notion of incremental processing means that the syntactic processor performs as much computation as it can on a given input token, rather than wait for the complete sentence before processing initial parts of it. Therefore, we assume the following ordering principle on the application of BEPDA rules.

(15) Ordering Principle for BEPDA rules:
- Perform all possible UNWRAP and POP moves first.
- SHIFT a new input item only when no further UNWRAP moves are possible.

This, of course, does not address the problem that arises when two UNWRAP moves are possible, which represents cases of true syntactic ambiguity such as prepositional phrase (PP) attachment. Such syntactic ambiguity does not arise in the cases we are interested in in this chapter, and the automaton does not immediately make predictions about preferences. We return briefly to the issue of syntactic ambiguity in the conclusion.

As an example, suppose we want to use the BEPDA to recognize the sentence fragment "*die Kinder schwimmen.*" The run of the automaton would be as follows.

(16)

Step	Rule Applied	Pushdown Store Configuraton
1	SHIFT *die Kinder* (Rule 1)	[*die Kinder*
2	Use NP BEPDA rules to derive	[NP
3	SHIFT *schwimmen* (Rule 1)	[NP [*schwimmen*
4	UNWRAP *schwimmen* (Rule 2)	[NP [V_I{NP}
5	UNWRAP NP (Rule 3)	[V_I
6	POP (Rule 4)	

The empty pushdown store at the end indicates a successful recognition of a clausal unit. Because, the rules derived from the three trees in the grammar in Fig. 12.4 are structurally similar, we can group them together as in the following.

(17)   Automaton for German:

Rule	Read Head Scans	Top of Stack is	Action
1	N	*anything*	SHIFT N
2	V	*anything*	SHIFT V
3	*anything*	[N [. . . V{N}	UNWRAP N around [. . . V{N}
4	*anything*	[. . .V [V'	UNWRAP V' around [. . . V

In the third rule, V must have an unfulfilled subcategorization requirement for a noun (indicated by the {N}; in the fourth rule, V' must have an unfilled subcategorization requirement for a clause. Now let us turn to recognition of German center-embedded Sentence (12). In (18), the "Input Scanned" column shows the symbol being scanned by the read head.

(18)

Step	Rule	Store	Input Read	Input Scanned
0	0			
1	1	[N_1	N_1	N_1
2	1	[N_1 [N_2	N_2	N_2
3	1	[N_1 [N_2 [N_3	N_3	N_3
4a	2	[N_1 [N_2 [N_3 [V_3{N_3}	V_3	V_3
4b	3	[N_1 [N_2 [V_3{}	—	V_2

Step	Rule	Store	Input Read	Input Scanned
5a	2	$[N_1$ $[N_2$ $[V_3\{\}$ $[V_2\{N_2\}$	V_2	V_2
5b	4	$[N_1$ $[N_2$ $[V_3\{\}$ $V_2\{N_2\}$	—	V_1
5c	3	$[N_1$ $[V_3\{\}$ $V_2\{\}$	—	V_1
6a	2	$[N_1$ $[V_3\{\}$ $V_2\{\}$ $[V_1\{N_1\}$	V_1	V_1
6b	4	$[N_1$ $[V_3\{\}$ $V_2\{\}$ $V_1\{N_1\}$	—	—
6c	3	$[V_3\}\}$ $V_2\{\}$ $V_1\{\}$	—	—
6d	POP	$[V_3\{\}$ $V_2\{\}$	—	—
6e	POP	$[V_3\{\}$	—	—
6f	POP			

In Steps 1–3, the NPs are recognized and stored in separate stacks in the push-down store. In Step 4a, a verb is read in. The UNWRAP rule derived from Tree I applies and the nominal subcategorization requirement of V_3 is fulfilled. Note that we have now recognized Tree I to the root node. However, it cannot be removed from the automaton because a further adjunction at the root node (in terms of the automaton, a further UNWRAP) may occur, and in fact does occur in our example. Therefore, we read in the next input V_2 (Step 5a), which can be UNWRAPped around the top stack (Step 5b). After Step 5c, the top stack contains $V_2\{$ } on top of $V_3\{$ }, representing the fact that we have recognized V_2's Tree A (with its nominal argument substituted) adjoined into V_3's Tree I (with its nominal argument substituted). Finally, in Steps 6a and 6b, we read in V_1, and UNWRAP it and N_1 around the top stack. We have now recognized V_1's Tree B, adjoined into V_2's Tree B, which in turn is adjoined into V_3's Tree 1. We can now pop $V_1\{$ }, followed by $V_2\{$ }, and finally $V_3\{$ }.

We now briefly discuss Dutch. We use the grammar for Dutch given in Kroch and Santorini (1991), repeated in Fig. 12.6. Kroch and Santorini gave extensive syntactic evidence for their grammar, but did not consider processing issues at all. The Dutch cross-serial dependencies are derived by adjoining Tree B into Tree A at the node marked S^*, and then adjoining the combination into Tree I, again at the node marked S^*. Note that the cross-serial dependencies are a result only of head movement (verb raising) that has occurred locally in each clause, not of multiclausal ordering rules or verb-complex formation.

We derive an automaton in an analogous manner to the German case. However, there is one complication: the empty category that results from head movement of the verb. Because the bottom–up recognition of a tree can only proceed once the empty head has been posited, the automaton must have a rule for hypothesizing empty heads. Clearly, we do not want it to do so nondeterministically, and we must extend our algorithm for deriving automata from competence grammars. We do so by defining the following two conditions on processing empty heads, or, more precisely, subtrees whose yield is the null string and that contain a head trace ("headed null-subtrees"). Both conditions must be met.

- Bottom–up condition: The automaton assumes the recognition of a headed null-subtree only if it has recognized its sister subtree and it can perform an UNWRAP operation involving the headed null-subtree.
- Top–down condition: A headed null-subtree can only be posited if it is licensed top–down by a previously processed licensor (in which case the licensing relationship must be indicated on the top of the pushdown store by features), or if the input symbol the read head is currently scanning licenses an empty head of the appropriate type.

We denote the projection from a (verbal) head trace by V^{h-}, whereas we will use V^{h+} to indicate an overt full lexical head. With this approach, our Dutch automaton looks as follows (we omit the details of the construction):

(19) Automaton for Dutch:

Rule	Read Head	Top of Stack	Action
1	N	*anything*	SHIFT N
2	V^{h+}	*anything*	Assume V^{h-} (an empty V head projection) and UNWRAP
3	V^{h+}	V^{h-}	SHIFT V^{h+} and UNWRAP

Recall that all possible UNWRAP moves are performed before any possible SHIFT moves. Consider the following sentence.

(20) *omdat   Piet Marie de kinderen zag   laten   zwemmen*
    because Piet Marie the children   saw   let   swim
           N_1 N_2 N_3 V^{h+}_1 V^{h+}_2 V^{h+}_3
    because Piet saw Marie let the children swim

Given the input N_1 N_2 N_3 V^{h+}_1 V^{h+}_2 V^{h+}_3, the automaton executes the following steps.

(21)

Step	Rule	Store			Input Read	Input Scanned
0	0					
1	1	$[N_1$			N_1	N_1
2	1	$[N_1$	$[N_2$		N_2	N_2
3	1	$[N_1$	$[N_2$	$[N_3$	N_3	N_3

Step	Rule	Store	Input Read	Input Scanned
4a	2	$[N_1 \quad [N_2 \quad [V_3^{\natural-}\{\}$	—	$V_1^{\natural+}$
4b	2	$[N_1 \quad [N_2 \quad [V_3^{\natural-}\{\}\ V_2^{\natural-}\{N_2\}$	—	$V_1^{\natural+}$
4c	2	$[N_1 \quad [V_3^{\natural-}\{\}\ V_2^{\natural-}\{\}$	—	$V_1^{\natural+}$
4d	2	$[N_1 \quad [V_3^{\natural-}\{\}\ V_2^{\natural-}\{\}\ V_1^{\natural-}\{N_1\}$	—	$V_1^{\natural+}$
4e	2	$[V_3^{\natural-}\{\}\ V_2^{\natural-}\{\}\ V_1^{\natural-}\{\}$	—	$V_1^{\natural+}$
5a	3	$[V_3^{\natural-}\{\}\ V_2^{\natural-}\{\}\ V_1^{\natural-}\{\} \quad [V_1^{\natural+}$	$V_1^{\natural+}$	$V_1^{\natural+}$
5b	3	$[V_3^{\natural-}\{\}\ V_2^{\natural-}\{\}\ V_1^{\natural+}\{\}$	—	$V_2^{\natural+}$
5c	POP	$[V_3^{\natural-}\{\}\ V_2^{\natural-}\{\}$	—	$V_2^{\natural+}$
6a	3	$[V_3^{\natural-}\{\}\ V_2^{\natural-}\{\}\ [V_2^{\natural+}$	$V_2^{\natural+}$	$V_2^{\natural+}$
6b	3	$[V_3^{\natural-}\{\}\ V_2^{\natural+}\{\}$	—	$V_3^{\natural+}$
6c	POP	$[V_3^{\natural-}\{\}$	—	$V_3^{\natural+}$
7a	3	$[V_3^{\natural-}\{\}\ [V_3^{\natural+}$	$V_3^{\natural+}$	$V_3^{\natural+}$
7b	3	$[V_3^{\natural+}\{\}$	—	—
7c	POP		—	—

First, the three nouns are read into the pushdown store on separate stacks. Before Step 1, the bottom–up condition for positing a headed null-subtree is not met. Before Steps 2 and 3, the bottom–up condition is met, but not the top–down condition: No licensing verbal head has been read, nor is the input head scanning a potential licensor. The latter condition is met after Step 3, so that in Steps 4a–4e headed null-subtrees are posited and the appropriate UNWRAP moves are performed. At the end of Step 4, the empty heads with saturated subcategorization requirements are stacked on one stack, representing that Tree A is adjoined into Tree I, and Tree B into Tree A, with the adjunctions taking place below the lexical verb but above its trace. Then, in Steps 5, 6, and 7, the lexical heads are read in, UNWRAPped with the top of the stack, and the completed structures are popped off the pushdown store.

Measuring Processing Load

Bach, Brown, and Marslen-Wilson (1986) showed experimentally that native German speakers take longer to process sentences with nested dependencies than native Dutch speakers take to process equivalent sentences with cross-serial dependencies. Joshi (1990) showed how a processing model based on an (top–down) EPDA predicts these facts. In this section, we show that the BEPDA model proposed in this chapter makes the same predictions.

We associate a metric with the run of the automaton. Joshi proposed two metrics: a simple one that simply registers the maximum number of items stored during processing of a given input sentence, and a more complex one that also takes into account how long each item spends in the pushdown store. We adopt the second approach, although we modify it slightly. The basic idea is to record for each step how many items are stored in the pushdown store (each lexical item is given a score of 1), and then sum up the scores for all steps. A *step* is defined as a move of the automaton, regardless of whether input is read.[5] For center-embedded sentences, the automaton for German gives us the following score.

(22)

Step	Store	Input Read	New Score	Cumulative Score
0				0
1	$[N_1$	N_1	1	1
2	$[N_1 \; [N_2$	N_2	2	3
3	$[N_1 \; [N_2 \; [N_3$	N_3	3	6
4a	$[N_1 \; [N_2 \; [N_3 \; [V_3\{N_3\}$	V_3	4	10
4b	$[N_1 \; [N_2 \; [V_3\{\}$		4	14
5a	$[N_1 \; [N_2 \; [V_3\{\} \; [V_2\{N_2\}$	V_2	5	19
5b	$[N_1 \; [N_2 \; [V_3\{\}V_2\{N_2\}$		5	24
5c	$[N_1 \; [V_3\{\} \; V_2\{\}$		5	29
6a	$[N_1 \; [V_3\{\} \; V_2\{\} \; [V_1\{N_1\}$	V_1	6	35
6b	$[N_1 \; [V_3\{\} \; V_2\{\}V_1\{N_1\}$		6	41
6c	$[V_3\{\} \; V_2\{\} \; V_1\{\}$		6	47
6d	$[V_3\{\} \; V_2\{\}$		4	51
6e	$[V_3\{\}$		2	53
6f				

New Score refers to the score contributed by that step, when a Cumulative Score is the total up to and including that step. Note that a verb with its subcategorization requirements fulfilled contributes a score corresponding to the verb and its nominal arguments. Now consider the Dutch automaton:

---

[5]Joshi (1990) defined a *step* to be a move in which input is read, which explains the different values given in that article and here. The difference between the EPDA and the BEPDA models is not relevant. If we use the original convention for scoring for the BEPDA model, we obtain exactly the same scores as Joshi.

(23)

Step	Store	Input Read	New Score	Cumulative Score
0				0
1	[N_1	N_1	1	1
2	[N_1 [N_2	N_2	2	3
3a	[N_1 [N_2 [N_3	N_3	3	6
	[N_1 [N_2 [$V_3^{\flat-}\{\}$		3	9
3b	[N_1 [N_2 [$V_3^{\flat-}\{\}$ $V_2^{\flat-}\{N_2\}$		3	12
3c	[N_1 [$V_3^{\flat-}\{\}$ $V_2^{\flat-}\{\}$		3	15
3d	[N_1 [$V_3^{\flat-}\{\}$ $V_2^{\flat-}\{\}$ $V_1^{\flat-}\{N^1\}$		3	18
3e	[$V_3^{\flat-}\{\}$ $V_2^{\flat-}\{\}$ $V_3^{\flat-}\{\}$		3	21
4a	[$V_3^{\flat-}\{\}$ $V_2^{\flat-}\{\}$ $V_1^{\flat-}\{\}$ [$V_1^{\flat+}$	$V_1^{\flat+}$	4	25
4b	[$V_3^{\flat-}\{\}$ $V_2^{\flat-}\{\}$ $V_1^{\flat+}$		4	29
4c	[$V_3^{\flat-}\{\}$ $V_2^{\flat-}\{\}$		2	31
5a	[$V_3^{\flat-}\{\}$ $V_2^{\flat-}\{\}$ [$V_2^{\flat+}$	$V_2^{\flat+}$	3	34
5b	[$V_3^{\flat-}\{\}$ $V_2^{\flat+}\{\}$		3	37
5c	[$V_3^{\flat-}\{\}$		1	38
6a	[$V_3^{\flat-}\{\}$ [$V_3^{\flat+}$	$V_3^{\flat+}$	2	40
6b	[$V_3^{\flat+}\{\}$	—	2	42
6c		—	0	42

Our model is based on the assumption that the automaton manipulates representations of lexical items. This assumption dictates a conventions about scoring that we have made above: empty heads do not contribute to the score because they are not associated with any lexical item. The scores by number of clauses are as follows:

(24)

Level of Embedding	Dutch	German
1	5	5
2	18	23
3	39	53
4	72	95

Finally, without going into much detail, we give a run of an automaton for a German sentence with extraposition, N_1 V_1 N_2 V_2 N_3 V_3. The grammar is as given in Fig. 12.4, except that in Trees A and B, the S node follows, rather than precedes, the V node.[6]

(25)

Step	Store	Input	New	Cum
0			0	0
1	$[N_1$	N_1	1	1
2a	$[N_1 [V_1\{N_1\}$	$V_1\{N_1\}$	2	3
2b	$[V_1\{\}$		2	5
2c			0	5
3	$[N_2$	N_2	1	6
4a	$[N_2 V_2\{N_2\}$	$V_2\{N_2\}$	2	8
4b	$[V_2\{\}$		2	10
4c			0	10
5	$[N_3$	N_3	1	11
6a	$[N_3 [V_3\{N_3\}$	$V_3\{N_3\}$	2	13
6b	$[V_3\{\}$		2	15
6c			0	15

We see that we can remove each clause as it is recognized because we start with the matrix clause. In extraposed constructions, the scores grow linearly with the number of embedded clauses, whereas in center-embedded constructions, the scores grow with the square of the number of embeddings. The following refers to German data.

(26)

Level of Embedding	Center Embedded	Extraposed
1	3	5
2	23	10
3	53	15
4	95	20

The automaton model predicts strongly that extraposition is preferred over center embedding, particularly at levels of embedding beyond two. This prediction is

---

[6]*Lassen* ("to let") does not allow extraposition. Any verb that takes a *zu*-infinitive does and can be used instead.

confirmed by native-speaker intuition, and we conjecture that psycholinguistic experiments or corpus-based studies would come to the same conclusions.

The Principle of Partial Interpretation

Why does the BEPDA automaton model make different predictions for Dutch and German sentences of comparable levels of embedding? The main reason is that, in the Dutch sentences, clauses are removed from the pushdown store as soon as the first verb is read in, whereas in German, clauses are only removed once the last verb of the sentence has been processed. Bach et al. (1986) interpreted their experimental data as suggesting such a behavior by the processor, and suggested that this behavior arises because structures can only be removed from the processor once there is a place for them "to attach to" (i.e., an embedded clause cannot be removed while its matrix clause is still in the processor). Joshi (1990) proposed to formalize this intuition by defining a restriction on the way that automaton works, called the *principle of partial interpretation* (PPI). The PPI makes the following two stipulations:

1. Structures are only discharged from the automaton when they are a properly integrated predicate-argument structure. More precisely, a clausal structure must contain all of the nominal arguments for which it subcategorizes.

2. A structure is discharged only when it is either the root clause or it is the immediately embedded clause of the previously discharged structure.

In our discussion so far, we have not appealed to the PPI. For the types of structures under consideration, we have not needed to do so: The PPI is simply a consequence of the simple method used to derive the automaton from the competence grammar and independently motivated ways in which the competence grammar is defined. The reason for this is that adjunction in the grammar is simulated in the automaton by recognizing the adjoined tree bottom–up and then removing any trace of it once its root node has been reached (UNWRAPping). Thus, the first material to be removed from the automaton corresponds to the last tree adjoined. On the other hand, substitution is handled differently: The material corresponding to the substituted tree is not removed from the automaton; in fact, it is treated as if it were part of the tree into which it was substituted. Thus, we see that the first part of the PPI follows from the fact that, in the competence grammar, we substitute nominal arguments into the trees of their governing verbs. The second part of the PPI follows from the fact that, in the competence grammar, we adjoin matrix clauses into their subordinate clauses. We intend to investigate further whether the PPI is required as an independently stated principle of processing by considering other constructions from other languages.

HANDLING LONG-DISTANCE DEPENDENCIES

How do we handle long-distance scrambling? It has been formally shown that TAGs are not powerful enough to derive the full range of scrambled sentences (Becker, Joshi, & Rambow, 1991; Rambow, Becker, & Niv, 1992).[7] Therefore, we introduce a multicomponent extension of TAG called *V-TAG* (vector TAG; see Rambow (1994) for a formal definition). In multicomponent TAG systems, several trees are grouped together into a set. In V-TAG, there is no "locality" restriction on where we may adjoin trees from one set as there are in the so-called "linear context-free rewriting systems" (LCFRS; Weir, 1988). There is also no requirement that trees from one set be adjoined simultaneously, nor that the trees from one set be adjoined one immediately following the other. We can first adjoin one tree from a set, then go on and adjoin some trees from a second set, and then return to the first set to adjoin the remaining trees. The only requirement is that, at the end of the derivation, either no or all trees from a given instance of a tree set must have been adjoined. Furthermore, the trees in a set are connected by *dominance links* (indicated by dotted lines in the figures). A dominance link indicates that when the derivation has terminated, the nodes linked by the dominance link must be in a relation of (not necessarily immediate) dominance. Linguistically, we use dominance links to enforce a c-command relationship between related elements. Let us consider as an example the tree set for *versprechen* "to promise"), shown in Fig. 12.7. We can think of this tree set as representing a head (the verb) and its projection (as is done in the use of simple TAG; see Frank, 1992, for a full discussion). However, the position in the projection of the overt direct object is not specified, and it can move away from the verb while still receiving θ-role and case marking. Note that we have chosen to label all nodes in the projection of the verb with *VP;* the functional information expressed by separate node labels in recent syntactic theories (IP, CP, AgrSP, etc.) we express as features (not shown here for simplicity). We do not discuss the linguistic issues involved in using such sets as the formalism for representing linguistic competence (for details see Rambow & Lee, 1993).

How can we derive sentences with long-distance scrambling? Consider Sentence (27) (Sentence (9c) repeated here for convenience).

(27) *daß* *[den Kühlschrank]ᵢ* *niemand* *[[tᵢ zu reparieren] zu versuchen] verspricht*
that the refrigerator (ACC) no-one (NOM) to repair to try promises
Comp₁ N₃   N₁   V₃   V₂ V₁
because no one promises to repair the refrigerator

---

[7]In fact, linear context-free rewriting systems (LCFRS) are also not powerful enough. LCFRSs were introduced in Weir (1988) as a generalization of TAGs.

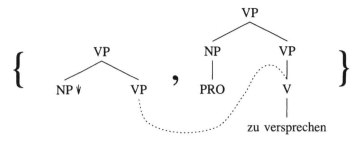

FIG. 12.7. Multicomponent tree set for *versprechen* ("to promise").

The accusative NP "*den Kühlschrank*" ("the refrigerator") has been scrambled out of the most deeply embedded clause into the matrix clause.[8] A complete grammar is given in Fig. 12.8. There are two auxiliary trees for the matrix Verb V_1 *versprechen* ("to promise"; β_1) and for the intermediate Verb V_2 *versuchen* ("to try"; β_2). Finally, there is the tree set introduced earlier for the most deeply embedded Verb V_3 *reparieren* ("to repair") containing auxiliary Tree β_{31} and initial Tree α_{32}. In the interest of readability, we use abbreviations for the terminal symbols, and we omit empty categories (PRO). These issues do not affect our discussion.

The derivation is shown by the arrows in Fig. 12.8. We start out by adjoining the intermediate clause into the verbal tree (α_{32}) of the most deeply embedded clause at its root node, and then we adjoin the matrix clause into the intermediate clause at the root of the intermediate clause. Because we have not yet used the nominal argument tree from the most deeply embedded clause (Tree β_{31}), the derivation is not yet complete. We choose to adjoin the most deeply embedded argument into the matrix clause at the VP node between the complementizer and its nominal argument. This choice corresponds to long-distance scrambling. The resulting derived tree is shown in Fig. 12.9.

Now let us turn to our processing model. Because the BEPDA is formally equivalent to TAG, and because TAG is formally inadequate for the long-distance phenomenon we are interested in, we must extend our automaton model as well. We do this by using an indexed version of the BEPDA, called the *I-BEPDA* (Rambow, 1994). In the I-BEPDA, every stack symbol in the push-down store is associated with a set of indices. Intuitively, these indices represent trees that still need to be adjoined for the derivation to be successful. Because we are using auxiliary trees in sets to represent nominal arguments, we can think of

---

[8]Of course, Sentence (27) is embedded in some other clause that we consistently omit in order to avoid the complications of the verb-second effect. Our use of the term *matrix clause* to denote the topmost of the recursively embedded clauses is thus sloppy, but the intended meaning is clear.

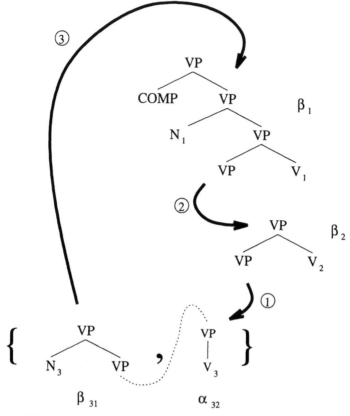

FIG. 12.8.   Grammar for German long-distance scrambling.

these sets as unfulfilled (nominal) subcategorization requirements. We see that
the notation is consistent with the quasicategorical notation we adopted previously. If we do not allow stack symbols to pass subcategorization requirements to
other stack symbols, we simply have a BEPDA that just recognizes tree-
adjoining languages. However, if we allow symbols in the same stack of the
pushdown store to pass a subcategorization requirement to a stack symbol immediately above or below it, we increase the power because we can now simulate
the "detaching" of nominal arguments from their verbs. We illustrate the func-
tioning of the I-BEPDA by showing how it performs on Sentence (27).

(28)

Step	Store	Input	New	Cum
0			0	0
1	[Comp$_1$	Comp$_1$	1	1

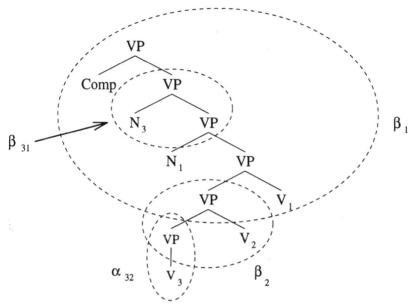

FIG. 12.9. Derived tree for Sentence 27.

Step	Store	Input	New	Cum
2	[Comp₁ [N₃	N₃	2	3
3	[Comp₁ [N₃ [N₁	N₁	3	6
4	[Comp₁ [N₃ [N₁ [V₃{N₃}	V₃	4	10
5a	[Comp₁ [N₃ [N₁ [V₃{N₃} [V₂{}	V₂	5	15
5b	[Comp₁ [N₃ [N₁ [V₃{N₃} V₂{}		5	20
6a	[Comp₁ [N₃ [N₁ [V₃{N₃} V₂{} [V₁{N₁}	V₁	6	26
6b	[Comp₁ [N₃ [N₁ [V₃{N₃} V₂{} V₁{N₁}		6	32
6c	[Comp₁ [N₃ [N₁ [V₃{N₃} V₂{} V₁{}		6	38
6d	[Comp₁ [N₃ [V₃{} V₂{N₃} V₁{}		6	44
6e	[Comp₁ [N₃ [V₃{} V₂{} V₁{N₃}		6	50
6f	[Comp₁ [V₃{} V₂{} V₁{}		6	56
6g	[V₃{} V₂{} V₁{}		5	61
6h	[V₃{} V₂{}		3	64
6i	[V₃{}		2	66
6j				66

In Steps 1–3, the complementizer and the two nouns are read in. In Step 4, Verb V_3 is read in, but no UNWRAP is possible because V_3 is not next to its nominal argument. In Steps 5a and 5b, Verb V_2 is read in and UNWRAPped. In Steps 6a, 6b, and 6c, the last Verb V_1 is read in and UNWRAPped around the stack of verbs and its nominal argument. At this point, no further reduction is possible without passing index symbols within a stack. This happens in Steps 6d and 6e. When V_1 has "inherited" the subcategorization requirement of V_3, N_3 can be discharged. The fact that N_3 is UNWRAPped around V_1 corresponds to the fact that it has scrambled into the clause of V_1.

If we apply this method to the other sentences in (9), we get the following results.

(29)

No.	Sentence	Score	Judgment
(9b)	$Comp_1$ N_1 V_1 V_2 N_3 V_3	17	ok
(9c)	$Comp_1$ N_1 V_1 N_3 V_3 V_2	24	ok
(9a)	$Comp_1$ N_1 N_3 V_3 V_2 V_1	52	(ok)
(9d)	$Comp_1$ N_1 N_3 V_2 V_3 V_1	58	?
(9e)	$Comp_1$ N_3 N_1 V_3 V_2 V_1	66	??

Sentence (9b) is fully extraposed: The score is low because material can be removed from the processor as soon as a clause is complete. In Sentence (9c), the two most embedded clauses have been extraposed behind the matrix clause, but they have been left in a center-embedded construction. Thus, the matrix clause can be removed from the automaton before any embedded clause is reached, but the items must remain in the automaton until the whole sentence has been read in. Sentence (9a), which is prescriptively acceptable, is simply the fully center-embedded version; all lexical items must remain in the automaton until the entire sentence has been read in. This is also true for Sentence (9d), but the score gets even worse because N_3 has been long-distance scrambled out of the most deeply embedded clause (which has been extraposed) into the second clause. Finally, Sentence (9e) is worst of all because there is long-distance scrambling over two clause boundaries. We see that the ordering of scores corresponds to the ordering by acceptability that we proposed earlier, and that, generally speaking, extraposition improves sentences, whereas long-distance scrambling degrades them.

Now let us address the second area that requires explanation—the apparent difference in processing load between long-distance topicalization and long-distance scrambling (over comparable distances). We repeat the contrasting sentences, first given as (10):

(30) a. Sentence with long-distance scrambling:
      ? *Der Meister hat   den Kühlschrank   niemandem*
      the master   has   the refrigerator (ACC) no one (DAT)
      N_{11} Aux_1 N_2 N_{12}

zu reparieren   versprochen
to repair   promised
V_2 V_1
The master has promised no one to repair the refrigerator

b. Sentence with long-distance topicalization:

Den Kühlschrank   hat   der Meister   niemandem
the refrigerator (ACC) has   the master (NOM)   no one (DAT)
N_2 Aux_1 N_{11} N_{12}
zu reparieren versprochen
to repair   promised
V_2 V_1
The master has promised no one to repair the refrigerator

Let us first consider the processing of the sentence with long-distance scrambling. The run of the automaton is similar to the one for Sentence (27), except that we now have a full sentence with a matrix auxiliary in second position. We assume it has been adjoined to the matrix verb and contributes features in a manner similar to the complementizer in our previous example.

(31)

Step	Store	New	Cum
1	$[N_{11}$	1	1
2	$[N_{11}\ [Aux_1$	2	3
3	$[N_{11}\ [Aux_1\ [N_2$	3	6
4	$[N_{11}\ [Aux_1\ [N_2\ [N_{12}$	4	10
5	$[N_{11}\ [Aux_1\ [N_2\ [N_{12}\ [V_2\{N_2\}$	5	15
6a	$[N_{11}\ [Aux_1\ [N_2\ [N_{12}\ [V_2\{N_2\}\ [V_1\{N_{11}, N_{12}\}$	6	21
6b	$[N_{11}\ [Aux_1\ [N_2\ [N_{12}\ [V_2\{N_2\}\ V_1]N_{11}, N_{12}\}$	6	27
6c	$[N_{11}\ [Aux_1\ [N_2\ [V_2\{N_2\}\ V_1\{N_{11}\}$	6	33
6d	$[N_{11}\ [Aux_1\ [N_2\ [V_2\{\}\ V_1\{N_{11}, N_2\}$	6	39
6e	$[N_{11}\ [Aux_1\ [V_2\{\}\ V_1\{N_{11}\}$	6	45
6f	$[N_{11}\ [V_2\{\}\ V_1\{N_{11}\}$	5	50
6g	$[V_2\{\}\ V_1\ \{\}$	5	55
6h	$[V_2\{\}$	2	57
6i		0	57

Again, the long-distance scrambling is achieved by passing the subcategorization requirement from a verb to its governing verb (in Step 6d), which represents that N_2 has scrambled into the matrix clause. Now let us consider the run of the automaton in the topicalized case.

(32)

Step	Store	New	Cum
1	$[N_2$	1	1
2	$[N_2$ $[Aux_1$	2	3
3	$[N_2$ $[Aux_1$ $[N_{11}$	3	6
4	$[N_2$ $[Aux_1$ $[N_{11}$ $[N_{12}$	4	10
5	$[N_2$ $[Aux_1$ $[N_{11}$ $[N_{12}$ $[V_2\{N_2\}$	5	15
6a	$[N_2$ $[Aux_1$ $[N_{11}$ $[N_{12}$ $[V_2\{N_2\}$ $[V_1\{N_{11}, N_{12}\}$	6	21
6b	$[N_2$ $[Aux_1$ $[N_{11}$ $[N_{12}$ $[V_2\{N_2\}$ $V_1\{N_{11}, N_{12}\}$	6	27
6c	$[N_2$ $[Aux_1$ $[N_{11}$ $[V_2\{N_2\}$ $V_1\{N_{11}\}$	6	33
6d	$[N_2$ $[Aux_1$ $[V_2\{N_2\}$ $V_1\{\}$	6	39
6e	$[N_2$ $[V_2\{N_2\}$ $V_1\{\}$	5	44
6f	$[N_2$ $[V_2\{N_2\}$	2	46
6g	$V_2\{\}$	2	48
6h		0	48

In the case of topicalization into sentence-initial position, we see that it is not necessary to pass subcategorization requirements among verbs. Instead, once the matrix clause has been removed (Step 6e), the embedded verb is adjacent to its argument, which can UNWRAP in the usual manner. This results in a lower score (48 as opposed to 57).

This difference in the behavior of the automata reflects the difference in the linguistic analysis in the competence grammar: whereas scrambling is achieved by adjoining NP arguments separately and in arbitrary order, topicalization is achieved by choosing a different elementary tree prior to the derivation. In topicalization, the long-distance effect is achieved by adjoining the matrix clause below the topicalized element, thus stretching it away from its verb. The difference in representation of scrambling and topicalization in the competence grammar is justified by the linguistic differences between the two word-order variation types that we mentioned previously. (For example, anaphoric binding behavior could be related to the fact that topicalization occurs within a single tree, whereas scrambling involves tree sets. We do not propose to work out the details of a TAG-based binding theory here.) Once again, we see that the independently motivated competence theory leads to automata models that make highly plausible predictions.

CONCLUSION

We have presented a model of human syntactic processing that makes plausible predictions for a range of word-order variation phenomena in German (and Dutch). Our model of the human syntactic processor is directly linked to a TAG-based model of human syntactic competence. This direct link gives our model two major characteristics that differentiate it from other models:

- The processor is not concerned directly with phrase-structure trees, but with relations between lexical items.
- The processor is defined in terms of a set of formally defined operations, which may at first appear arbitrary.

We briefly discuss these two points in turn, and finish with a brief note on syntactic ambiguity.

The parser simulates a derivation in the formalism of the competence theory, TAG. TAG is a tree rewriting system, and therefore derivations in a TAG are not recorded by a phrase-structure tree (as in the case for CFG), but by the so-called "derivation tree," which is a tree that represents adjunctions and substitutions performed during the derivation. Each node in the derivation tree corresponds to one elementary tree, and a dominance relation represents adjunction (or substitution) of the tree represented by the daughter node into the mother. Because the representation of competence exploits the lexicalizability of TAG, each tree in our competence grammar is associated with one lexical item. This means that the parser is, in fact, establishing direct dependencies between lexical items (heads). However, our approach does not build a phrase-structure tree (although one can be derived from its actions, just as one can be derived form the derivation tree). Although explanatory approaches such as minimal attachment are less appealing in our model (because no phrase-structure tree is explicitly represented during the parse), licensing properties of lexical items can be represented in straightforward manner. In this respect, our approach is close to licensing-based or head-driven approaches (Abney, 1986; Pritchett, 1991). Lexical licensing relations, in particular θ-role assignment, also play a crucial role in approaches that are not head driven (Gibson, 1991; Inoue & Fodor, 1993). We suspect that such conditions will find a straightforward representation in our processing model. Furthermore, the lexicon-oriented processing model allows for an elegant integration of lexical co-occurrence effects, which, it is generally believed, play a crucial role in parsing.

The second characteristic of our model that we would like to discuss is its very precise definition, which may seem somewhat arbitrary at first: Why does the pushdown store contain stacks of stack symbols, and why may each stack symbol be associated with an index set? The justification for this machinery comes from a careful study of the requirements of competence syntax. It is known that (case-marked) cross-serial dependencies are not context free (Shieber, 1985). Therefore, the representation of competence syntax cannot be based on a transformation-free CFG, nor can the parser be, say, a simple PDA. Therefore, the representation of competence must either include transformations, in which case we give up formal constraints and any hope that a formal analysis can guide us in modeling the parser, or we can look for other (more powerful, yet still constrained) formalisms for the expression of competence. We do not argue for our choice (TAG and its extension, V-TAG) here (the reader is referred to Becker et al., 1991; Joshi, 1985; Rambow, 1994), but we claim that the complexity of the machinery of the processing model is justified by the details of the competence model. If the processing model makes empirically interesting predictions, the complexity of its operations and data structures should not be held against it (on the basis of scientific parsimony) because they are independently motivated.

Finally, we need to address the issue of ambiguity. The model, as presented in Joshi (1990) and extended and modified here, does not address the issue of the resolution of syntactic ambiguity. (The reader will have observed that, in all of our examples, the syntactic structure is in fact unambiguous, partly due to the case marking. Furthermore, in all cases, the processing difficulties are not of the garden-path variety because they persist even when the reader is primed for the syntactic structure.) A priori, it seems that our model can be integrated into a variety of ambiguity-resolution models, including parallelism, limited parallelism, deterministic with lookahead, and serial with (limited) backtracking. In further work, we intend to investigate whether the particular features of our model favor one or the other of these approaches.

ACKNOWLEDGMENTS

This work was partially supported by the following grants: ARO DAAL 03-89-C-0031; DARPA N00014-90-J-1863; NSF IRI 90-16592; and Ben Franklin 915-3078C-1. We would like to thank an anonymous reviewer for insightful and helpful comments, and Michael Niv for helpful discussions.

REFERENCES

Abney, S. (1986). Licensing and parsing. In *Proceedings of the 16th Annual Meeting of the North Eastern Linguistics Society*. Graduate Linguistics Students Association, University of Massachusetts.

Bach, E., Brown, C., & Marslen-Wilson, W. (1986). Crossed and nested dependencies in German and Dutch: A psycholinguistic study. *Language and Cognitive Processes, 1*(4), 249–262.

Becker, T., Joshi, A., & Rambow, O. (1991). Long distance scrambling and tree adjoining grammars. In *Proceedings of the 5th Conference of the European Chapter* (pp. 21–26). ACL, Berlin.

Evers, A. (1975). *The transformational cycle in Dutch and German*. Unpublished doctoral dissertation, University of Utrecht, The Netherlands.

Frank, R. (1992). *Syntactic locality and tree adjoining grammar: Grammatical, acquisition and processing perspectives*. Unpublished doctoral dissertation, University of Pennsylvania, Philadelphia.

Frank, R., Lee, Y.-S., & Rambow, O. (1992). Scrambling as non-operator movement and the special status of subjects. In *Proceedings of the Third Leiden Conference for Junior Linguists* (pp. 135–154). Leiden: LCJL.

Gibson, E. (1991). *A computational theory of human linguistic processing: Memory limitations and processing breakdown*. Unpublished doctoral dissertation, Carnegie Mellon University, Pittsburgh, PA.

Haider, H. (1991). [Argument structure: Semantic basis and syntactic effects.] Class notes from the 3rd European summer school in language, logic and information, Saarbrücken, Germany.

Höhle, T. (1982). Explikation für "normale Betonung" and "normale Wortstellung." [Explication for "normal intonation" and "normal word order."]. In W. Abraham (Ed.), *Satzglieder im Deutschen* (pp. 75–153). Tübingen: Gunter Narr Verlag.

Inoue, A., & Fodor, J.D. (1993). Information-paced parsing of Japanese. In R. Mazuka & N. Nagai (Eds.), *Japanese syntactic processing*. Hillsdale, NJ: Lawrence Erlbaum Associates.

Joshi, A. K. (1985). How much context-sensitivity is necessary for characterizing structural descriptions—Tree adjoining grammars. In D. Dowty, L. Karttunen, & A. Zwicky (Eds.), *Natural language processing—theoretical, computational and psychological perspective* (pp. 206–250). New York: Cambridge University Press.

Joshi, A. K. (1987). An introduction to tree adjoining grammars. In A. Manaster-Ramer (Ed.), *Mathematics of language* (pp. 87–115). Amsterdam: John Benjamins.

Joshi, A. K. (1990). Processing crossed and nested dependencies: An automaton perspective on the psycholinguistic results. *Language and Cognitive Processes, 5*(1), 1–27.

Joshi, A. K., Vijay-Shanker, K., & Weir, D. (1991). The convergence of mildly context-sensitive grammatical formalisms. In P. Sells, S. Shieber, & T. Wasow (Eds.), *Foundational issues in natural language processing* (pp. 31–81). Cambridge, MA: MIT Press.

Kroch, A. (1987). Subjacency in a tree adjoining grammar. In A. Manaster-Ramer (Ed.), *Mathematics of language* (pp. 143–172). Amsterdam: John Benjamins.

Kroch, A. (1989). Asymmetries in long distance extraction in a tree adjoining grammar. In M. Baltin & A. Kroch (Eds.), *Alternative conceptions of phrase structure* (pp. 66–98). Chicago, IL: University of Chicago Press.

Kroch, A., & Santorini, B. (1991). The derived constituent structure of the West Germanic verb raising construction. In R. Freidin (Ed.), *Principles and parameters in comparative grammar* (pp. 269–338). Cambridge, MA: MIT Press.

Lenerz, J. (1977). *Zur Abfolge Nominaler Satzglieder im Deutschen* [On the sequence of nominal sentence constituents in German]. Tübingen: Narr.

Moltmann, F. (1990). *Scrambling in German and the specificity effect*. Unpublished manuscript.

Pesetsky, D. (1982). *Paths and categories*. Unpublished doctoral dissertation, Massachusetts Institute of Technology, Cambridge, MA.

Pritchett, B. (1991). Head positions and parsing ambiguity. *Journal of Psycholinguistic Research, 20*(3), 251–270.

Rambow, O. (1994). *Natural language syntax and formal systems*. Unpublished doctoral dissertation, University of Pennsylvania, Philadelphia.

Rambow, O., Becker, T., & Niv, M. (1992). *Scrambling is beyond LCFRS*. Paper presented at MOL3.

Rambow, O., & Lee, Y.-S. (1993). *Word order variation and tree adjoining grammar*. Manuscript submitted for publication.

Schabes, Y. (1990). *Mathematical and computational aspects of lexicalized grammars*. Unpublished doctoral dissertation, University of Pennsylvania, Philadelphia.

Shieber, S. B. (1985). Evidence against the context-freeness of natural language. *Linguistics and Philosophy, 8*, 333–343.

Vijay-Shanker, K. (1987). *A study of tree adjoining grammars*. Unpublished doctoral dissertation, University of Pennsylvania, Philadelphia.

Webelhuth, G. (1989). *Syntactic saturation phenomena and the modern Germanic languages*. Unpublished doctoral dissertation, University of Massachusetts, Amherst.

Weir, D. J. (1988). *Characterizing mildly context-sensitive grammar formalisms*. Unpublished doctoral dissertation, University of Pennsylvania, Philadelphia.

13 The Finite Connectivity of Linguistic Structure

Edward P. Stabler
University of California, Los Angeles

While there is no interesting limitation on the degree of right-embedding in acceptable sentences, center-embedding is severely restricted. Similarly, while there is no interesting bound on the number of nouns that can occur in acceptable noun compounds, there is a very low bound on the number of causative morphemes that can occur in the verb compounds of agglutinative languages. Turning to the clause-final verb clusters of West Germanic languages, we find another similar bound. A cluster including verbs from one embedded clause may be acceptable, but clusters formed from the verbs of two or three or even more deeply embedded clauses are much more awkward (regardless of whether the subject–verb dependencies are crossing or nested). And in languages that allow multiple *wh*-extractions from a single clause, extractions of more than one element with a given case quickly become unacceptable. More careful experimental study of the nature of these limitations is needed, in a range of languages, but here a preliminary attempt is made to subsume them all under a single generalization— a version of the familiar idea that the human parsing mechanism is limited in its ability to keep track of many grammatical relations of the same kind. To make this idea more precise, I assume in the first place,

(1) Weak competence hypothesis: Human syntactic analysis typically involves the explicit recognition of all grammatical relations.

Then I define the *connectivity* of each constituent α in a linguistic structure as the number of linguistic relations which relate α (or any part of α) to any constituent external to α. I conjecture that there is a universal finite bound on the connectivity of acceptable structures in every language. In fact, I argue that the bound is not only finite, but extremely low. Relativizing the measure to a typology of relations, I propose the following hypothesis about the connectivity of both completed constituents and those partial constituents constructed during parsing. (For the moment, a partial constituent can be regarded as a set of nodes completed at any point during a human parse.)

(2) Bounded connectivity hypothesis: There is a natural typology of linguistic relations such that the psychological complexity of a structure increases quickly when more than one relation of any given type connects a (partial) constituent α (or any element of α) to any constituent external to α.

I can make this claim more specific as follows. In advance of more careful experimental study, and subject to qualifications that are discussed later, I predict significant increases in complexity when more than one relation of any kind crosses a (partial) constituent boundary; structures with connectivity two are slightly awkward or marginal; and three and four connecting relations are always unacceptable.[1] I defend this claim by beginning the articulation of an appropriate typology of relations—one that yields the desired results about acceptable structures and one that is fairly natural given recent syntactic theory. Surprisingly, if (2) is on the right track, it appears that neither θ-assignment relations in general, nor the particular types of θ-assignment relations (agent, theme, experiencer, etc.), should be included in the typology relevant to characterizing acceptability bounds, contrary to the proposals of Pritchett (1988, 1992), Gibson (1991), Stabler (1992), and many others.

The bounded connectivity hypothesis interacts with another familiar sort of hypothesis that I formulate as follows.

(3) Left-to-right incremental parsing hypothesis: Human syntactic analysis is typically incremental, in the sense that people typically incorporate each (overt) word into a single, totally connected syntactic structure before any following words. Incremental interpretation is achieved by interpretation of this single connected syntactic structure. The psychological complexity of a structure increases quickly when processing proceeds with more than one independent completed substructure.

Hypotheses (1)–(3), which have been accepted in one form or another by many linguists and psychologists, have some surprising consequences. In particular, it follows that human syntactic analysis is not achieved by any standard top–down, bottom–up, left corner, or head-driven phrase-structure analysis strategy. When

---

[1]It is important to notice that high connectivity is being proposed as a *sufficient* condition for unacceptability. Of course, a structure can be unacceptable for other reasons too.

one considers what kind of parser is needed, it appears that our linguistic resources have a definite finite structure that imposes particular limitations on processing, not like a machine with a potentially infinite, homogenous tape or stack, but like a machine with a finite number of registers whose roles are tightly constrained. The restrictions that hypothesis (2) aims to account for are specifically linguistic structural constraints, and are *not* due to a general restriction on a (potentially infinite) available memory store. Some informal considerations in favor of this view are mentioned here, but a more careful development of a computational model along these lines is beyond the scope of this preliminary study (see Stabler, 1993).

A LIMITATION ON CAUSATIVIZATION

In Swahili, there are a couple of causative suffixes, one of which is *-lish,* translated as *-make,* in (5):[2]

(4) *Msichana a-li-u-fungu-a*   *mlango.*
    girl   SUBJ-PAST-OBJ-open-IND door
    The girl opened the door.

(5) *Mwalimu a-li-m-fungu-lish-a*   *msichana mlango.*
    teacher   SUBJ-PAST-OBJ-open-make-IND girl   door
    The teacher made the girl open the door.

It is impossible to causativize the verb twice.

(6) * *Mwalimu a-li-m-fungu-lish-ish-a*   *msichana mlango.*
    teacher   SUBJ-PAST-OBJ-open-make-make-IND girl   door
    The teacher made someone make the girl open the door.

Considering that it makes perfect sense to have someone make the girl open the door, this inability to iterate the causative morpheme may be surprising, but morphological restrictions of this sort are common. However, there are other languages that allow iteration of causatives.[3] These are of particular interest

---

[2]In this chapter, SUBJ stands for subject marker, OBJ stands for object marker, TOP stands for top marker, IND for indicative, PROG for progressive, FUT for future, NEG for negative, CMP for complementizer, S for singular, PL for plural, DAT for dative, ACC for accusative, ERG for ergative, INS for instrumental, BEN for benefactive, GEN for genitive, LOC for locative, DEL for delimitative, DUR for durative, POSS for possessive, REFL for reflexive, and EMP for emphatic elements. Sentences (4) and (5) are essentially those of Comrie (1976), with minor changes for the dialect of my consultant, Deogratias Ngonyani. The inability to iterate the Swahili causative that I observe in (6) is also noted in other Bantu dialects by Givón (1976) and Abasheikh (1978).

[3]This is found in Hungarian (Hetzron, 1976), Turkish (Zimmer, 1976), Kashmiri (Syeed, 1985),

because they may indicate what limits there are on iteration when there is no
reason to think that general morphological, syntactic, and semantic principles
disallow iteration in general.

Consider the following constructions from Bolivian Quechua, an SOV language with the causative suffix *-chi*, which we see in Sentences (8) and (10).[4]

    (7) *Tata-y-pis*   *Mama-y-pis*   *wañu-sa-nku*
         father-POSS1S-EMP mother-POSS1S-EMP die-PROG-3PL
         My father and mother are dying.

    (8) *Tata-y-ta-pis*   *mama-y-ta-pis*   *yarqay-manta.*
         father-POSS1S-ACC-EMP mother-POSS1S-ACC-EMP hunger-from
         wañu-chi-sa-nku
         die-make-PROG-3PL
         They are starving my father and mother.

    (9) *Řiku-ni.*
         see-1S
         I see it.

   (10) *Řiku-chi-ni.*
         see-make-1S
         I show it or I make him see it.

Double causatives are found in Bolivian Quechua, and they are typically semantically regular, although they are often slightly awkward.

   (11) *Řiku-chi-chi-ni.*
         see-make-make-1S
         I have it shown.

   (12) *Tata-s-niy-ta*   *wañu-chi-chi-sa-nku.*
         father-PL-POSS1S-ACC die-make-make-PROG-3PL
         They are having my parents killed.

Interestingly, there seems to be some sort of complexity boundary here. There is
some variability among speakers, but in general verbs with more than two
occurrences of *-chi* are extremely awkward or impossible.[5]

Kannada (Schiffman, 1976), Kuki (Mahajan, 1982), Amharic (Hetzron, 1976), Awngi (Hetzron,
1969), West Greenlandic (Fortescue, 1984), Chicheẁa (Alsina, personal communication), Malagasy
(Keenan, personal communication), and other languages.

    [4]The Quechua judgments in this chapter are those of Jaime Daza, from Cochabamba. Sentence
(7) is from a popular folk song.

    [5]A construction with three occurrences of *-chi* is listed in Herrero and Sánchez de Lozada's
(1978) descriptive grammar of Cochabamba Quechua:

   (a) Susanitapaj t'impuchichichiy lecheta
      'Have someone make boiling milk for Susanita' (p. 216).

(13) *Řiku-chi-chi-chi-ni

(14) *Tatasniyta wañuchi-chi-chi-chi-sa-nku

The possibility of two causatives as in Sentences (11) and (12) shows that the problem here is not simply due to an inability to repeat an affix, and is certainly not due to some absolute upper limit on the number of affixes that can appear on a verb stem. Many more complex forms are perfectly acceptable.

(15) Suldadu-s wañu-chi-chi-lla-sa-nku-ña-puni.
soldier-PL die-make-make-DEL-PROG-3PL-DUR-EMP
Soldiers are still just having people killed as always.

Nor does the lack of productivity have any apparent semantic explanation. Notice that the causal morpheme makes a regular semantic contribution in all of the acceptable examples shown here, and so it is puzzling that we do not accept and interpret Sentence (13) in the regular way.[6] This lack of productivity in morphological causatives has been noted before in various dialects of Quechua and in every other language in which morphological causatives have been studied.[7] The collection of languages known to respect the bound includes both verb-final languages like Quechua, and also verb-initial languages like Amharic (Hetzron, 1976) and Arabic (Comrie, 1976).

Two basic types of theoretical approaches to morphological causatives and other valency-changing affixes can be distinguished in the literature. One approach with a long history maintains that these constructions are derived from biclausal syntactic structures by some kind of incorporation of the verb from the lower clause into the higher causative. Recent prominent views of this sort are provided by Baker (1988), Marantz (1984), and Perlmutter and Postal (1983), for example. Baker argues that causatives are formed by verb raising in the syntax—

However, the translation given by Herrero and Sánchez de Lozada for this triple causative is the one shown here—the one expected for the simpler double causative t'impuchichiy. It is interesting that Mohanan (1982) also lists a triple causative in Malayalam, but gave it the same translation as the corresponding double causative. In Turkish as well, verbs like göster- (show) can take two causatives (yielding a verb that means "make someone have something shown"), and when further causative affixes are added they do not introduce additional intermediate causees, but add only an emphatic or humorous effect (M. Kural, personal communication). In short, iteration beyond two causatives ceases to be valency increasing. In Quechua, such forms are certainly very awkward and quite rare. Jaime Daza, my consultant from Cochabamba, Bolivia, finds (a) just as bad as (13) and (14). I have been unable to find any triple causatives at all in any other Quechua literature. Hetzron (1969, 1976) describes two Awngi constructions as triple causatives, but does not provide detailed information about their interpretation. It would be interesting to study these exceptional constructions more carefully with speakers who find them acceptable.

[6]Like other languages with morphological causatives, some Quechua causatives have irregular, idiomatic meanings. No surprise here—all languages have idiomatic phrases.

[7]On the limitations in various dialects of Quechua, see Muysken (1977), Weber (1989), and Cole (1985). For the general claim, see Comrie (1981).

an instance of head movement. I can schematize the basic idea of such approaches with a picture like the following.

(16) Syntactic causativization
$$[_{VP} \ldots [_V \text{make-}V_i] \ldots [_{VP} \ldots t_i \ldots]]$$

Baker treats other reflexive and reciprocal markers similarly—as independent syntactic units that are incorporated into the verb.

(17) Syntactic reflexivization
$$[_{VP} \ldots [_V \text{V-self}_i] \ldots [_{DP} t_i]]$$

The order of constituents in these schemata is irrelevant, and for present purposes it does not matter whether one supposes that the parts of a causative complex come together by movement. The important point is that causatives are treated like verbs with their own syntactic phrasal projections and argument positions, somehow incorporating or merging with verbs from an embedded phrase that also have their own argument positions. At some level of representation, there is a connection between the valency-changing elements of the complex verb and other syntactic positions.

An alternative approach treats the combination of the causative morpheme with a verb as a lexical operation. Causatives induce a certain lexical mapping between argument structure and syntactic expression, a certain "morpholexical operation on argument structure." I use the following sort of picture to indicate that causativization adds an argument position.[8]

(18) Morpholexical causativization
$$\varnothing$$
$$\Downarrow$$
$$\langle \theta \ldots \theta_{causer} \ldots \rangle$$

Reciprocalization and reflexivization are similarly treated as morpholexical operations that "suppress" one role of the verb, as indicated in the following schema.

---

[8]This schema for causativization is modeled on Bresnan and Moshi's (1990) schema for applicative, and the following schema for reflexivization is exactly the one they suggested for reciprocalization. Clearly, these representations suppress details about what the operations involve. In his study of causatives in Chicheŵa, Alsina (1992) proposed that the Chicheŵa causative denotes a three-place relationship among a causer, a patient, and the caused event, and that when this morpheme combines with another "embedded" predicate, the patient argument of the causative is fused with some argument of the embedded predicate. For present purposes, this account fits the scheme in Sentence 18 because the net increase in arguments is one. Mohanan (1982) also proposed a morpholexical analysis of causatives in Malayalam.

(19) Morpholexical reflexivization

$$\langle \theta_i \; \ldots \; \theta_i \; \ldots \rangle$$
$$|$$
$$\emptyset$$

Thus, this approach fits with the general program of resisting the "syntacticiza-tion of grammatical phenomena" by providing a purely lexical account of causa-tivization.

In the present context, it is clear that nothing in either of these basic ap-proaches to causatives explains the limitations on causative morpheme iteration. On the syntactic approach, morphological causatives are derived from complex syntactic structures, and yet periphrastic causatives do not seem to be subject to the same sort of restriction.

(20) The private killed the reporter.

(21) The sergeant always made the private kill the reporter.

(22) The general made the sergeant make the private kill the reporter.

(23) The president made the general make the sergeant make the private kill the reporter.

(24) The corporate executives made the president make the general make the sergeant make the private kill the reporter.

(25) ? No one makes the corporate executives make the president make the general make the sergeant make the private kill the reporter.

Since complex periphrastic causatives like these are acceptable, what explains the restriction on morphological causatives?[9] Similarly, the puzzle remains un-solved in the morpholexical approach. Since it is plausible that at least some morpholexical operations can iterate, as one sees in double and triple causatives, what explains the restriction on iteration?

This chapter argues that the restriction on causatives follows from a simple and intuitive complexity bound on syntactic structures. Because this bound can be independently motivated, it actually supports a syntactic analysis like Baker's rather than threatening it, whereas the morpholexical approach would have to propose a separate morphological restriction, despite the striking similarity be-tween this restriction and other syntactic restrictions.

---

[9]Baker (1988) points out that one can always assume that there are special morphological filters that simply rule out unacceptable forms that would have been predicted, on syntactic grounds, to be well formed. Two points about this idea should be discussed. First, this is clearly a move of last resort. There are certainly regularities here that are not understood yet, and it is not clear exactly what *morphological* filtering will be needed. Second, notice that, even in the extreme case where every morphological causative is assumed to be learned separately, one would still face a version of our basic puzzle in trying to explain why languages tend not to call on the child to learn double or triple causatives, and never quadruple causatives. Compare Pinker (1984) on the peculiarities of causatives and how lexically based variations on their productivity might be learned.

EXPLAINING THE LIMITS ON CAUSATIVIZATION

The complexity of a constituent is sometimes gauged by the number of morphemes it contains, but I do not assume that there is any interesting bound on the number of morphemes in X^0 constituents in general. For example, English noun compounds can have many nouns and still be perfectly acceptable.

(26) The customer asked about [$_N$ ticket validation].

(27) The customer asked about [$_N$ parking ticket validation].

(28) The customer asked about [$_N$ parking lot ticket validation].

(29) The customer asked about [$_N$ grocery parking lot ticket validation].

(30) The customer asked about [$_N$ grocery store parking lot ticket validation].

So what explains the difference between compounds like these and the complex verbs formed with causative morphemes?

One idea is based on the observation that, unlike noun compounding and unlike affixation of tense, aspect, and emphasis markers, causativization increases the number of arguments taken by the verb. So the limits of causativization might be due to an absolute upper bound on the number of arguments any verb can take—a bound on "semantic valency." This idea does not explain, though, why transitive and intransitive verbs seem to have the same limits on iteration of the causative affix. Surely transitives take one more argument than intransitives, but intransitives do not regularly allow one more causative than transitives, as was seen in the Quechua examples (Sentences 7–14) with the intransitive *wañu-* and the transitive *řiku-*.[10] And in the second place, three causatives are not allowed even in the presence of an apparently valency-decreasing affix like a reflexive. In Quechua, reflexives seem to make both double and triple causatives more complex, not less complex.

(31) *Řiku-chi-ni*   *wawa-y-ta*   *dujtur-man.*
see-make-REFL-PROG-1S child-POSS1S-ACC doctor-GOAL
I had the doctor see my child.

(32) *Řiku-chi-ku-ni.*
see-make-REFL-PROG-1S
I have myself seen (e.g., by a doctor) or I give myself away.

---

[10]Comrie (1976) suggests that, when all the causatives allowed by all languages are considered, causative forms of transitive verbs are less common than causative forms of intransitives. It is not clear how to assess this idea. In languages with quite productive causativization like Quechua or Turkish, how can one count the numbers of forms allowed? In languages where all causative verbs are just lexical items, would one expect an interesting theoretical basis for a trend toward causative intransitives? In any case, because the facts about causatives vary so significantly across languages, it is hard to know what would follow from the conjectured trend.

(33) *Ři̇ku-chi-chi-ku-ni.

(34) *Ři̇ku-chi-ku-chi-ni.

(35) *Ři̇ku-ku-chi-chi-ni.

Hence, although one can agree that there may be a limit on the number of valency-changing affixes that any stem can host, the reason is not simply that there is an upper bound on the number of arguments that any verb (complex or not) can take.

A second idea about the limits on causativization is that there is a bound on the number of positions in any clause where the arguments of the causatives could go, perhaps for case reasons.[11] This idea does not seem quite right either. It shares the main defect of the previous proposal: It does not explain why transitives and intransitives have the same limits on causativization. Further-more, the noted restrictions on causativization hold equally in languages with rich case marking and pre- or post-positional systems like Quechua, and in languages where all the intermediate agents need not, and even cannot, be mentioned with overt determiner phrases (DPs).

As suggested in the introduction, a more satisfactory idea is that the operation of forming a causative compound increases syntactic "connectivity" because it forms a constituent that enters into more relations of a particular kind. Various proposals along these lines are possible. If the verb raises from an embedded clause to amalgamate with the higher verb, there is a verb-movement relation to keep track of. If double causatives involve two verb-movement relations, per-haps keeping track of movements of this kind is difficult enough to account for the rather marginal status of double causatives, and the unacceptability of triple causatives. Assuming that verb movements are one of the relevant types of relations, the observed limitation on causatives is subsumed by the bounded connectivity hypothesis, repeated here:

(2) There is a natural typology of linguistic relations such that the acceptabil-ity of a structure degrades quickly when more than one relation of any given type connects a (partial) constituent α (or any element of α) to any constituent external to α.

This proposal has the advantage that it predicts the same complexity bound for transitives and intransitives because the transitivity of the embedded verb does not affect the number of verb movements involved in forming the causative compounds.

---

[11]Something like this is suggested by Givòn's (1976) speculation that the reason iteration of causatives is blocked in Bantu languages is due to "the lack of sufficient case markings to differentiate the semantic function of the various object nominals following the verb, since every application of lexical causativization increases the transitivity of the verb by one nominal object" (p. 337).

A different (but compatible) hypothesis about the connectivity bound in causatives is that the arguments of the embedded clause must also be moved up into
the higher clause to get case, but the theoretical accounts of the case-marking
relations in these constructions are less settled, so I do not pursue this idea.[12] Yet
another idea (proposed in Stabler, 1992) is that the causative compound must
enter into multiple θ-marking relations of the same kind, taking more than one
agent, but this idea is disconfirmed by some of the multiple-extraction constructions discussed later, and it is also rather difficult to assess because, unlike case
marking, θ-marking is not overtly indicated by the morphology.

Notice that these connectivity hypotheses do not predict a restriction on noun
compounds analogous to the one seen in morphological causatives because additional nouns in a noun compound do not generally increase the connectivity of
the complex.[13]

A challenge to the idea that one has trouble keeping track of multiple verb
movements comes from the clause-final verb clusters of Dutch and German.
Here, it is quite possible to have more than two verbs in a cluster, as in the
following Swiss-German example from Shieber (1985).

(36) *mer d'chind   em Hans   es   huus   haend wele   laa.*
      we   the children-ACC Hans-DAT the house-ACC have   wanted let
      hälfe aastriiche
      help paint
      We have wanted to let the children help Hans paint the house.

---

[12]In Bolivian Quechua, the intermediate objects always receive a distinct case marking from any
of the overt arguments to the highest verb, suggesting that the objects may all raise to the matrix
clause. On the other hand, Jake (1985) reports that in Ecuadorian Imbabura Quechua it is possible for
both the direct object of the highest verb and an intermediate causee to get ACC case marking,
suggesting that the intermediate causee may get case in the embedded clause from the lower verb.
(See, e.g., Baker, 1988; Johnson, 1991, for other perspectives on object raising and case assignment.)

[13]Ward, Sproat, and McKoon (1991) point out that internal elements of noun compounds and
other X^0 elements may sometimes increase connectivity because they may be involved in anaphoric
relationships as in:

(1) Although [cocaine$_i$ use] is down, the number of people using it routinely has increased.

(2) [[McCarthy]$_i$ites] are now puzzled by him$_i$.

However, the anaphoric relations here are pronoun–antecedent relations, which are not local in the
way most grammatical relations are. Berwick and Weinberg (1984) argued that, because pronoun–
antecedent relationships apparently extend well beyond the local domain needed to make structural
decisions and because a speaker's determination of these relations is apparently based on inferences
from general background knowledge, it is plausible that these relations are not computed by the same
mechanism that builds syntactic structure. This argument continues to be persuasive, and so I do not
assume that pronoun–antecedent relations are subject to the same sorts of low finite bounds that apply
to other types of linguistic relations. That is, I assume that there is a finite bound on the number of
pronoun–antecedent relations that any acceptable expression can involve, but it does not seem to be
an interestingly low bound of the sort seen with other dependencies.

According to some analyses, these clusters are formed by verb raising, in which a verb in an embedded clause moves to get its inflection and then up into the higher clause, with the resulting complex moving to combine with the verb of the higher clause, and so on up to the matrix clause.[14] In this framework, one natural idea is that, in the course of this derivation, auxiliary verbs form units with their associated main verbs, and so the relevant factor is how many main verbs occur in the cluster.

I do not have data about the on-line processing difficulty for (36), but Bach, Brown, and Marslen-Wilson (1986) studied similar constructions in both Dutch and German.

(37) *dat* [*Jan* [*Piet* [*Marie* t$_3$] t$_2$] t$_1$] [*zag* [*laten zwimmen$_3$*]$_2$]$_1$ (Dutch)
that Jan Piet Marie   saw make swim
that Jan saw Piet make Marie swim

(38) *dass Jan* [*Piet* [*Marie* t$_3$] t$_2$] t$_2$ [[*schwimmen$_3$ lassen*]$_2$ *sah*]$_1$ (German)
that Jan Piet Marie   swim   make saw
that Jan saw Piet make Marie swim

Because the dependencies in the German examples are nested and the dependencies in the Dutch examples are crossing, it is remarkable that they were found to have similar psychological complexity. In both constructions, there was a significant jump in psychological complexity when a third main verb was added to the clause-final clusters. Many German speakers find Sentence (38) to be completely unacceptable. Bach et al. found the center-embedded German structures were actually slightly less intelligible than the Dutch. It would be interesting to account for this slight difference, but the more striking result is the similar jump in complexity in both constructions when a third verb is added. This is what the connectivity bound (2) would predict, if we assume that the verbs raise to the clause-final cluster in both German and Dutch.[15]

---

[14]For example, Den Besten and Edmondson (1983), Besten and Rutten (1989), Hoeksema (1988), Haegeman and van Riemsdijk (1986), and Koopman (1993).

[15]A different account of these constructions has been proposed by Kroch and Santorini (1991), according to which the clause-final sequences of verbs in Dutch and German do not form a constituent. Rather, in Dutch, the embedded verbs are extraposed, adjoining to the main clause, forming structures like the following:

(1) *dat* [[[*Jan* [*Piet* [*Marie* t$_3$] t$_2$] zag] *laten$_2$*] *zwimmen$_3$*],   (Dutch)

whereas in German the embedded verbs can stay in place:

(2) *dass* [*Jan* [*Piet* [*Marie schwimmen*] *lassen*] *sah*]   (German)

Even on this alternative analysis, my proposals predict the observed limitations. Notice that in Sentence (1), if the minimal indicated boundary containing *Jan . . . zag* is regarded as a real constituent boundary, one can see that two verb movements cross that boundary. On the other hand, the

CONNECTIVITY BOUNDS IN MULTIPLE EXTRACTION

Although English allows multiple questions when one or more *wh*-phrases are left in situ, it only marginally allows A-bar extractions of more than one *wh*-phrase (here I use italics to indicate stress on the in situ *wh*-constituent).

(39) Who$_1$ did you ask [t$_1$ to fix the car *how*]?

(40) ? Who$_1$ did you ask how$_2$ [t$_1$ to fix the car t$_2$]?

Other languages are much more liberal. For example, Mahajan (1990) points out that in Hindi there are cases where *wh*-phrases cannot be left in situ, but must be extracted.

(41) * [rām-ne   kahā ki   kɔn kis-ko   māregā]
     Ram-ERG said that who whom-DAT hit-FUT
     Who did Ram say will hit who?

(42) kɔn$_1$ kis-ko$_2$ [rām-ne   kahā ki   t$_1$ t$_2$ māregā]
     who whom-DAT Ram-ERG said that   hit-FUT
     Who did Ram say will hit who?

Extraction of two or three *wh*-elements is not uncommon, although sometimes slightly awkward.[16]

(43) ? kis-ne$_1$ kɛse$_2$ [rām-ne   kahā ki   t$_1$ t$_2$ gaRīThīk kī]
     who-ERG how Ram-ERG said that   car   fixed?
     Who did Ram say fixed the car how?

(44) ? kis-ne$_1$ kis-ko$_2$ kyā [rām-ne   sītā-ko   batāyā
     who-ERG whom-DAT what Ram-ERG Sita-DAT told
     kī t$_1$ t$_2$ t$_3$ diyā hogā]
     that   gave-FUT
     Did Ram tell Sita who gave what to whom?[17]

(45) ? kɔn$_1$ kis-ne$_2$ t$_1$ socā   ki   mohan-ko   t$_2$ maregā
     who who-ERG   thought that Mohan-DAT hit-FUT
     Who thought that who hit Mohan?

German construction becomes a center-embedding construction. As indicated earlier, this is ruled out by the application of the connectivity bound to partial structures created during parsing, as I discuss in detail in the next section.

  [16]Like the previous Hindi examples, Sentence (43) is from Mahajan (1990). Thanks to Anoop Mahajan for providing the additional examples and judgments herein.

  [17]The Hindi sentence here can be interpreted either as a multiple question or as a multiple indirect question where the *wh*-elements have been topicalized.

However, when we have more than one A-bar chain with any particular case crossing any boundary, the construction really becomes unacceptable.

(46) ??? *kis-ko₁   rām-ne   kis-ko₂   t₁ t₂ kahā ki   sar   dard hɛ*
who-DAT Ram-ERG who-DAT   tell   that head pain is
Who did Ram tell that who has a headache?

These limitations in Hindi suggest a possible way to elaborate the connectivity hypothesis (2). If one counts outstanding A-bar movement relations, or outstanding θ-marking relations, one sees that three or more can occur with only slight awkwardness. In (45), we even have two A-bar extractions of elements with the same type of θ-roles (agent). However, if A-bar DP movement relations are classified by their case, the extremely low bounds can be maintained, allowing structures like Sentences (42)–(46) while predicting the difficulty of Sentence (46) because it has two A-bar extractions with dative case.[18]

CONNECTIVITY BOUNDS ON CENTER EMBEDDING

Connectivity bounds for linguistic constituents do not predict the well-known unacceptability of deeply center-embedded sentences. This can be seen by observing that, in a simple constituent structure tree, as in any context-free grammar derivation tree, regardless of the depth of center embedding, every constituent is connected to the rest of the structure by only one constituency relation—the relation represented by the arc drawn from the constituent to its parent.[19] English center-embedded clauses presumably have somewhat greater connectivity than context-free languages because different kinds of relations are involved, but connectivity need not increase with depth of embedding. For example, in the following examples, there is some modification relation between each embedded clause and the N′ phrase it modifies, but there are not increasing numbers of connections to elements in the matrix clause when a second or third center-embedded clause is added.

(47) The house [(that) the malt lay in] was built by Jack.

(48) * The house [(that) the malt [(that) the rat ate] lay in] was built by Jack.

So why should center embedding be subject to such similar bounds as the other constructions surveyed earlier? As in the other cases, when there are two clauses,

---

[18]It remains unclear how to classify A-bar adjunct extractions of elements other than DP because they may not bear case. This question is currently under study.

[19]If precedence is counted as a relevant linguistic relation, there is perhaps also an immediate precedence relation to a sister node.

as in Sentence (47), the construction is perhaps significantly more complex, but still within bounds of normal acceptability. But with three center-embedded clauses, as in Sentence (48), the construction is extremely awkward or impossible.

To capture the difficulty of these center-embedded constructions, it suffices to assume that not only completed constituents, but also the partial constituents constructed by the parser, are subject to the connectivity bound. For the moment, there is no need to be precise about what the partial structures are like. They can be regarded as sets of nodes, as descriptions of some sort, or as sequences or stacks of subtrees. The relevant parameter is the number of relations connecting nodes in any partial structure to nodes that are not in that partial structure. If parsing proceeds from the beginning of a sentence to the end (and if it never involves the prediction of overt, lexical elements), then, after seeing the first two DPs in Sentence (48), the parser presumably has a structure with something like the following form.

(49) [The house [(that) the malt . . .] . . .]

This structure already has two DPs, each of which must be assigned nominative case by constituents that have not yet been found. It is natural to assume that each type of case-assignment relation (nominative, accusative, etc.) is relevant for the bounded connectivity hypothesis. Then, at the step indicated by Sentence (49), the parse is already complex because it is connected by two relations of the same kind to the rest of the structure. As the parse continues, the following structure is built:

(50) [The house [(that) the malt [(that) the rat . . .] . . .]. . .]

But now the elaboration of this structure to get Sentence (48) would involve relating three DPs by nominative case marking to elements outside of this partial structure, and so the connectivity hypothesis correctly predicts that the structure should be extremely awkward or impossible. Notice that this is predicted no matter how much of the syntactic structure is built for these elements, since whatever the structure is, it will somehow involve relations to three case-marking elements that have not been found yet. According to recent theories in the transformational framework, this element could be any tensed inflection node, which might be filled by a modal like *will,* for example.

It is widely observed that although it is unacceptable to have two center-embedded relative clauses in subject position, two relative clauses in object position is not quite so bad. Compare the subject relative in Sentence (48) with the following sentence.

(51) ?? She loves the house [(that) the malt [(that) the rat ate] lay in].

The contrast with Sentence (48) is predicted, because after parsing the following structure (52),

(52) She loves the house [(that) the malt [(that) the rat . . .] . . .]

there are just two DPs with outstanding case-assignment relations. This is because *loves* has already case marked its object. There are not three relations as in the partial structure (50) of (48). So (51) is correctly predicted to be better than (48), whereas (53) should be just as bad as (48) (assuming other contributors to complexity are approximately alike).

(53) * She loves the house [(that) the malt [(that) the rat [(that) the cat chased] ate] lay in].

The previous discussion and the heading of this section might have given the impression that degree of center embedding per se is the contributor to complexity. That idea is corrected by these examples. Connectivity of constituents does not increase with center embedding. On the other hand, connectivity of the partial structures built by a left-to-right parser does tend to increase with depth of center embedding, but even here the two measures cannot be equated.[20]

I turn now to sentential subjects. It has often been observed that a relative cause inside a sentential subject is not as bad as a relative clause inside a relative clause in a subject DP, nor is it as bad as a sentential subject inside a sentential subject. Consider relative clauses in sentential subjects first, as in Sentence (54).

(54) ? [That the rat [who the cat chased] lives in the house] surprised Jack.

Here, the parser presumably builds a partial structure like the following.

(55) [$_{CP}$ That the rat [who the cat . . .] . . .]

In this structure, there seems to be two DPs that need case, and also a complementizer phrase (CP) in subject case position, so why isn't the structure as awkward as the structure (48) beginning with (50)? This question is easily answered when the structure of sentential subjects is considered more carefully. For example, Stowell (1981) observes the contrast between structures like Sentences (56)–(57) on the one hand, and topicalization and dislocation structures like Sentences (58–59) on the other.[21]

---

[20]Similarly, in an implementation, there is no requirement that stack depth should correlate perfectly with depth of center embedding. Contrast Church (1980), for example.

[21]Sentences (57–59) are said to involve *topicalization* when they do not include the parenthesized pronouns, and they are called *left dislocation* structures when they do include the parenthetical material. I discuss some of the differences between these constructions later.

(56) * Is that the rat lives in the house likely?

(57) * John doubts (that) that the rat lives in the house is likely.

(58) That the rat is in the house, Mary could not doubt (it) for a minute.

(59) That the rat is in the house, who could possibly doubt (that)?

Examples like these suggest that a *that* clause, a finite CP, can occur in the position of a topic or left dislocation, but cannot occur in a subject or object position. Stowell proposes that there is a "case resistance principle" at work here: A tensed CP (and certain other categories) cannot appear in case-marked positions. But then one must conclude that the "sentential subject" in Sentence (54) is misnamed in the sense that the CP is not really in subject position at all, but is rather in a non-case-marked A-bar position—a position that may somehow license an empty subject. Many other linguists have come to similar conclusions. I tentatively assume something along the lines of Koster's (1978) and Safir's (1985) proposal that sentences with sentential subjects, like (54) or the simpler (60), have the structure (61).

(60) [$_{TopicP}$ [$_{CP}$ That the rat lives in the house] [$_{CP}$ e$_1$ e$_1$ surprised Jack]].

(61) [$_{TopicP}$ CP [$_{CP}$ e$_1$ [$_{IP}$ e$_1$ I']]].

The fronted CP in these structures is not part of a case-marked chain, but is in the position of a left-dislocated phrase that stands in a special "control" relation to the indicated empty positions. Such an analysis provides exactly what is needed to explain the relative acceptability of (54). The partial structure (55) has only two DPs with case relations to elements outside of that structure because the fronted CP is not in a case position. Of course, the unacceptability of more complex structures like Sentence (62) is still predicted.

(62) * [That the rat [who the cat [who the dog bit] chased] lives in the house] surprised Jack.

Now consider sentential subjects within sentential subjects. It is widely noted that these are completely unacceptable, as seen in Sentence (64).

(63) [That the rat ate the malt] surprised Jack.

(64) * [That [that the rat ate the malt] surprised Jack] bothered Mary.

I suggested earlier that sentential subjects are in the position of a topic or dislocation. The earlier examples did not show this, but Baltin (1982), Lasnik and Saito (1992), and others have observed that left dislocation is more awkward than topicalization in embedded clauses, as is seen in the following examples.

(65) a. The basic theorem, Mary has proven (it).

    b. I know that the basic theorem, Mary has proven.

    c. * I know that the basic theorem, Mary has proven it.

(66) a. I know that Mary could not doubt that the rat is in the house.

    b. ? I know that the rat is in the house, Mary could not doubt.

    c. * I know that the rat is in the house, Mary could not doubt it.

On the basis of examples like these, these linguists propose that left dislocation involves base generation of the topic in a topic phrase position, (TopicP), whereas topicalization involves movement inside of CP. (Perhaps, as Lasnik and Saito suggested, topicalization is an adjunction to the inflection phrase, IP.) This idea fits perfectly with the earlier idea that sentential subjects have the structure (61), where the two indicated empty categories are related by an A-bar movement. This also leads one to expect to find similar subtle differences between left-dislocated and topicalized clauses in sentential subject constructions. This prediction is borne out in the following sentences.

(67) ? [[That the rat ate the malt] surprised Jack], it bothered Mary.

(68) * [That [that the rat ate the malt] it surprised Jack] bothered Mary.

(69) * [[That the rat ate the malt] it surprised Jack], it bothered Mary.

These data clearly suggest that the sentential subjects in Sentences (64), (68), and (69) are not bad simply because of the way the clauses are nested. Rather, something specific about topicalization structures causes the problem. Furthermore, in contrast to the DPs with relative clauses in sentence (51), these bad sentential subjects are not significantly improved by being embedded as complements to a verb.

(70) * I know [(that) [that the rat ate the malt] surprised Jack] bothered Mary.

So a grammatical account of these observations seems more appropriate than a performance or connectivity-based account. In fact, assumptions already introduced provide the account that is needed. Notice that, given the structural assumptions, both Sentences (64) and (68) try to form a phrase from the complementizer *that* and a TopicP, but complementizers combine with IPs. TopicP is a different category from IP, and it is no surprise that complementizers do not combine with them. On the other hand, the unacceptability of Sentence (69) and the subtle contrast with Sentence (67) are explained by the mentioned generalization that standard left dislocation can only occur in a matrix clause.[22]

---

[22]This generalization is discussed by Lasnik and Saito (1992). It would be nice to derive this special property of left-dislocation constructions from deeper principles, and the prospects for doing so look good, but this would take us too far afield.

INCREMENTAL PROCESSING

If the hypothesized connectivity bounds hold up to further empirical study and elaboration, they will support the intuitive idea that the human parsing mechanism is limited in its ability to keep track of many grammatical relations of the same kind. Furthermore, the bounds are distinctively linguistic and sensitive to the detailed articulation of linguistic relations. They are also very low, with difficulties arising when the *unary* bounds are exceeded, much like grammatical constraints (cf. subjacency). These ideas do not fit well with performance models, according to which the human processing mechanism has available a homogenous memory store of some kind with some fixed, linguistically arbitrary bound. If that picture were right, it would follow, for example, that instead of keeping track of two verb movements, two constituency relations, and two nominative case-assignment relations, the parser could keep track of just six constituency relations, or five verb movements and one case relation. But this is exactly the kind of thing that is not found. The *wh*-movements in languages that allow extractions, or the arguments of various cases that appear before the verb in SOV languages, do not each impose a unit of additive complexity. Rather, as long as the relations are different and few in number (essentially one), parsing may proceed easily. These observations suggest quite a different picture, according to which the human parser has a very rigid and limited memory store, with fixed registers for various roles—registers that cannot be redeployed for other purposes.

This picture of a parsing mechanism with strict connectivity bounds imposed by its architecture interacts in an interesting way with the hypothesis that interpretation is "incremental," typically proceeding morpheme by morpheme.[23] Let us assume that incremental interpretation results from processing a connected syntactic structure—an idea that has been proposed in a number of places.[24] This kind of view is expressed by the left-to-right incremental processing hypothesis, repeated here:

(3) Human syntactic analysis is typically incremental, in the sense that people typically incorporate each (overt) word into a single, totally connected syntactic structure before any following words. Incremental interpretation is achieved by interpretation of this single connected syntactic structure. The psychological complexity of a structure increases quickly when processing proceeds with more than one independent completed substructure.

Stabler (1991) points out that one could make the alternative assumption, according to which unconnected pieces of syntactic structure are interpreted incremen-

---

[23]For example, see Marslen-Wilson (1989).

[24]For example, see Frazier and Rayner (1988) and Steedman (1989).

tally. Johnson and Shieber (1993) point out that an interpretive component could even make assumptions about relationships among unconnected pieces before the parser has connected them. But (3) yields a simpler, more natural, and more restrictive theory. Here, I observe some consequences that this simpler idea has when taken together with the bounded connectivity hypothesis (2).

Standard top–down (LL) parsers for context-free grammars have the property that the partial structures they build in the course of a parse always form a single, connected structure. In standard stack implementations, interpretation of this completed structure can begin while the stack keeps track of constituents that have been predicted but not found yet. Unfortunately, as is well known, these parsers cannot handle left recursion. Standard bottom–up (LR) parsers can handle left recursion because they build subconstituents before attaching their parents, using the stack to keep constituents that have been built but not attached to parents yet. However, there is no bound on the amount of memory required to process simple right-branching structures with this strategy.[25] If one wants to find a parsing strategy whose resource demands predict appropriate acceptability bounds, corresponding to those characterized with the notion of connectivity, one must consider strategies that mix top–down prediction with bottom–up analysis.

Perhaps the most familiar mixed strategy is "left-corner" (LC) parsing. The left corner of any constituent is its leftmost immediate subconstituent. The intuition behind LC parsing is this: Begin working bottom–up, but after completing each constituent, each left corner, build its parent and predict any potential siblings of the left corner. An LC parse of a sentence can be diagrammed by circling the nodes that have been completed at each step. This is done for the first 10 steps of a LC parse in Fig. 13.1.[26] The steps indicated there are the following, beginning with the smallest circle.

  i. The word *the* is heard.

 ii. The parent D is built because *the,* its left corner, has been completed.

iii. The parent D' is built because its left corner D is complete, and the sibling NP is predicted. Notice that completed categories are indicated by upward arcs across each circle, and predicted categories are indicated by downward arcs. The arcs that connect the completed structure to the rest of the structure are what must be kept on the stack in standard stack-based implementation strategies. These are the points in the structure that the parser still needs to be working on, so they must be held in memory.[27]

---

[25]This is a familiar point, at least since Miller and Chomsky (1963). For recent discussions, see Gibson (1991) and Abney and Johnson (1991).

[26]The structure here is obviously considerably simplified. In particular, there is evidence that I and D projections both have more structure than shown here, syntactic features have not been indicated, and only constituency relations are drawn.

[27]See Johnson and Stabler (1993) for more detailed discussion.

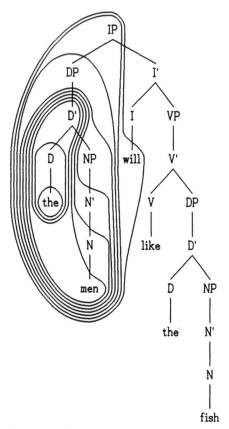

FIG. 13.1. A structure (showing only constituency relations) and the first 10 steps of an LC parse.

  iv. The word *men* is heard.

   v. The parent N is built because its left corner is complete.

  vi. The parent N' is built because its left corner is complete.

 vii. The parent NP is built because its left corner is complete, and this constituent is attached as the predicted NP.

viii. The parent DP is built because its left corner D' is complete.

  ix. The parent IP is built because its left corner DP is complete.

   x. The word *will* is heard.

The LC parser continues in this way until the whole structure is built. Notice that at Step iv, the parser has defined two disconnected subtrees: the D' and the N. This can be seen in Fig. 13.1: The third largest circle encloses two separate subtrees, and the nodes inside this circle are connected to the rest of the structure by three constituency arcs. The two subtrees are not joined until Step vii. Then again at Step x, two separate subtrees are being processed. At every step, the nodes in the partial structures all have completed left corners; the node to be processed next is also one whose left corner is complete; the other nodes are all those whose left corners have not been completed.

Two pertinent aspects of this parsing strategy are easily seen. First, at the points where disconnected subtrees are waiting, the connectivity of the partial structure increases. This increased connectivity translates into an increased burden on the memory resources of the parsing mechanism. Second, this strategy does not conform to our incremental processing hypothesis, since disconnected subtrees can end up waiting to be completed and assembled. This problem is seen more clearly in the primarily right-branching structure of Fig. 13.2, in which I have indicated with a solid line the stage in the LC parse at which the connectivity of constituency relations is highest. There are six outstanding connections: three arcs leaving the loop downward to indicate predicted categories, and three arcs leaving the loop upward to indicate categories that need to be attached when they are completed.

Notice that a parsing strategy that tried a little harder to maintain a single connected structure could have done so with the structure in Fig. 13.2 just by attaching N' to a predicted NP, and by attaching D' to DP as specifier of the predicted IP, before they were complete. This would reduce memory demands significantly, leaving only a single outstanding prediction, indicated by the dotted loop. Let us call this alternative strategy a *left-attaching* (LA) parse. For the moment, let it be like LC parsing, with additions that can be roughly described as follows.

a. If XP has been predicted, and if the next word is a head X, this item can be projected to XP and attached (predicting siblings at each level, left-corner style).

b. If XP has been predicted and allows a specifier YP, and if the next word is a head Y, this item can be projected to YP and attached as specifier of XP (predicting siblings at each level).

Some further aspects of these additions are discussed in the next section, but it may be helpful to quickly sketch how the LA parsing strategy is intended to apply to some of the constructions considered earlier.

Fig. 13.3 shows a center-embedded construction, with relativization on the subject position. The stage of the LC parse with maximum memory demands is again indicated by a solid line, and here we see that the partial structure has four disconnected subtrees, connected by 11 constituency relations to other parts of the structure (six arcs leaving the loop upward, indicating constituents to be attached, and five arcs leaving the loop downward, indicated predicted constitu-

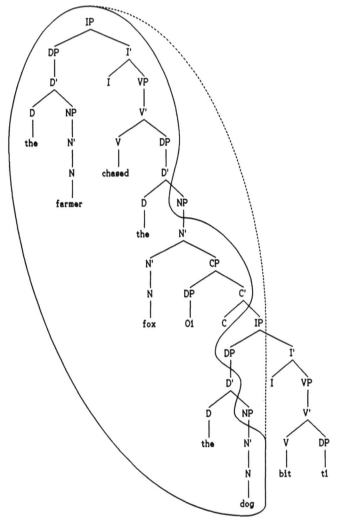

FIG. 13.2. A structure (showing only constituency relations), with a stage in an LC parse shown by the solid line, and a stage in an LA parse shown by the dotted line.

ents). On the other hand, the corresponding stage of the LA parse, indicated by the dotted loop, defines one totally connected structure, with two outstand pre-dictions of exactly the same category.[28] It is accordingly predicted that this

---

[28]The sentences in Figs. 2 and 3 are Gibson's (1991) examples (110) and (113), respectively. Gibson reports that in his LC parser, the unacceptable sentence (110) requires only six stack ele-ments, whereas the acceptable sentence (113) requires seven elements. He concludes that "the

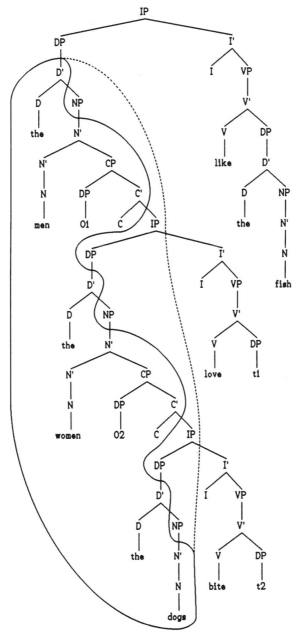

FIG. 13.3. A center-embedded structure (showing only constituency relations), with a stage in an LC parse shown by the solid line, and a stage in an LA parse shown by the dotted line.

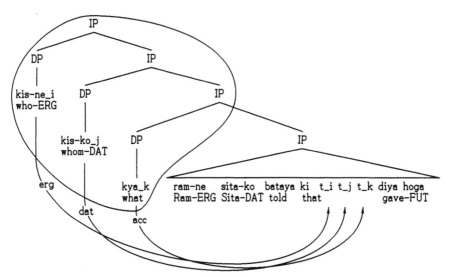

FIG. 13.4. A structure (showing only constituency and *wh*-movement relations), with a loop indicating a stage in an LA parse.

structure should be difficult, as it is, now assuming that constituency relationships are bounded by the bounded connectivity hypothesis. In fact, the prediction follows even if constituency relations are classified according to category or "role" since in this case, there are two predictions of exactly the same type of constituent.

Considering the treatment of multiple A-bar extractions, I tentatively adopt the idea that extracted *wh*-elements are adjoined to IP (Mahajan, 1990). Then for a sentence like Sentence (44), the structure might have roughly the form indicated in Fig. 13.4. That figure again indicates a stage in the LA parse of this acceptable sentence. At the indicated stage, three A-bar movement relations connect the partial structure to unbuilt elements, but these three A-bar chains each have a distinctive case. Notice that in a left-to-right parse of this structure, five DPs are encountered before any case or θ-assigners. This poses a problem for any theory of psychological complexity that assumes that each of these DPs simply adds a unit of load to the parse, but it can be accommodated once the various case roles are distinguished, as suggested previously.

---

number of categories locally stored by a left corner parsing algorithm does not give a satisfactory metric for sentential complexity" (p. 52). I chose these examples to show that we get quite different results here, emphasizing the important point that Gibson's conclusion depends on the details of both is parsing algorithm and his grammar. There is a wide range of parsing strategies, such as the "arc-eager" LC or LA strategies described here, which with plausible structural assumptions, have significantly different memory requirements. See Johnson and Stabler (1993) and Stabler (1993) for further discussion.

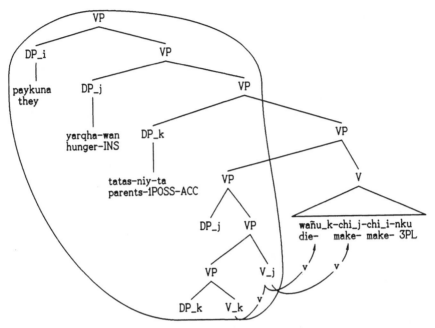

FIG. 13.5. A structure (showing only constituency and V-movement relations), with a loop indicating a stage in an LA parse.

The structure of Quechua clauses is still a matter of controversy. But adapting the proposals of Lefebvre and Muysken (1988), I tentatively suppose that a Quechua verb phrase (VP) has a structure like the one shown in Fig. 13.5, with VP-internal subjects. A stage of an LA parse is shown just before the complex verb has been parsed. At this point, two V-movement relations and one predicted constituent are outstanding. Clearly, if the verb had three causatives, the partial structure would have too many V-movement relations, as suggested previously.

INCREMENTAL PROCESSING AND THE SURFACE-RECURSION RESTRICTION

A fundamental problem arises for any parsing strategy that tries to bound memory requirements while maintaining a connected structure. The puzzle begins with the observation that there is no interestingly low bound on the length of left branches, even when they are not on the left frontier of the sentence structure. Consider the example of English possessive structures first.

(71) He saw [Dave's] car.

(72) He saw [[Dave's] mother's] car.

(73) He saw [[[Dave's] mother's] brother's car.

(74) He saw [[[[Dave's] mother's] brother's] friend's] car.

In any left-to-right parse of these sentences that respects the incremental parsing hypothesis, the length of the branch that connects the DP "Dave's" to the V′ must be increasing, and presumably the connectivity of the first partial structure incorporating this VP is increasing, too. Yet acceptability is not decreasing in the way that the bounded connectivity hypothesis would predict. For example, consider the partial structure indicated by the loop in Fig. 13.6.[29] Something has to give way here. The bounded connectivity hypothesis and left-to-right parsing, do not allow a single connected structure. To handle left-recursive structures like the one in Fig. 13.6, the human parser must, at least briefly, define sets of nodes from two independent subtrees. Linguists have observed that there are, cross linguistically, significant restrictions on recursion in these left-branching structures, suggesting that they impose a special, additional processing load. But the observed restrictions can be explained without any new assumptions, as discussed below. This makes the present account entirely consistent with Frazier and Rayner's (1988) failure to find any significant increases in on-line complexity associated with left branching per se.

To handle left-recursive determiner phrases with bounded connectivity, the LA parsing strategy can be elaborated in something like the following way. On hearing the first three words of (74) including the possessive marker, the parser builds the following connected structure, with one predicted NP (in the position of the ellipsis).

(75) $[_{IP}$ He $[_{VP}$ saw $[_{DP}$ Dave's . . .]]]

After attaching *mother* to get,

(76) $[_{IP}$ He $[_{VP}$ saw $[_{DP}$Dave's mother]]]

the parser hears the possessive marker and realizes that a mistake has been made. At this point, the current analysis is revised. The attachment of the DP "Dave's mother" as the complement of V is revised by making this DP the specifier of a new DP parent, attaching this new DP as the V complement, and predicting the new D′. While this revision is occurring, the completed nodes of the parser form two independent subtrees. The next possessive marker is attached as D and projected to attach to the predicted D′, with a predicted NP sibling. Continuing

---

[29]See Footnote 26 for my caveat about the structures depicted in this chapter. In particular, it is important that my proposals do not hang on the assumption that the English possessive marker is the head D of DP. Szabolcsi (1993) points out that, cross linguistically, possessives and determiners are not complementary, as can be seen in sentences like "Dave's every move was watched by the police."

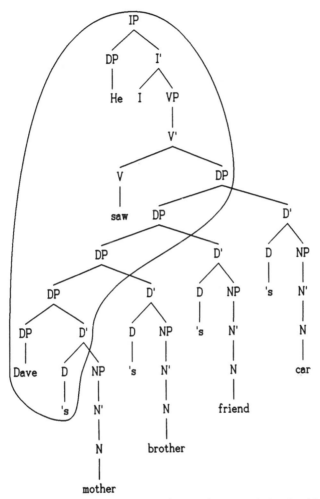

FIG. 13.6. A structure (showing only constituency relations), with a hoop indicating a partial structure with high connectivity.

in this way, one can see that there is never more than one outstanding predicted category, no matter how deep the left recursion in the possessive. There are various ways to execute this sort of strategy in a computational model, as discussed in Stabler (1993). Note that it is not essential to assume that revision is involved (although, in advance of experimental studies, it is a natural assumption). To get the right structure on the first parse, the strategy would simply build up the first DP, attach it to a higher one, and so on until attachment to the predicted complement of V′ is the correct thing to do. Again, it is clear that during this process of building up the possessive DP, there are two independent subtrees.

There is evidence from a number of languages that this process imposes a burden on the human parser. Notice first that not just any DP can occur in English possessive constructions.

(77) a. I saw the [[famous Peruvian] author]'s car.
  b. ? I saw the [author [of my favorite book about laughter]]'s car.
  c. ?? I saw the [man [who just left]]'s car.

It seems that prenominal modifiers on the left side of the CP are fine, but a relative clause to the right of N is very awkward. Horvath (1985) reports similar contrasts in Hungarian, where the VP is right branching. A preverbal NP, presumably left adjoined to a projection of V, cannot have a relative clause on its right.

(78) a. *Az asztal, ami   az erkélyen   állt   bepiszkolódott.*
      the table   which the balcony-on stood dirty-got
      The table that stood on the balcony got dirty.
  b. **Mari [az asztalra, ami   az erkélyen   állt] tette*
      Mary the table-onto which the balcony-on stood put
      az edényeket.
      the dishes
      Mary put the dishes on the table that stood on the balcony.

What explains this restriction on recursion in these NPs?

A plausible account is ready at hand, given the parsing strategy just described. The problem is that, in these constructions, there are configurations of center embedding. The English construction (77c) is as awkward as the center-embedded, relativized object in (51), but not as bad as the center-embedded, doubly relativized object in (53), and the account here can be similar. Consider the partial structures formed in analyzing (77c). Using the parsing strategy described earlier, the correct parse will be one that posits two separate structures. The partial structure might be depicted as follows.

(79) [I saw . . .] [$_{DP}$ the man who$_i$ t$_i$ . . .]

where a DP complement has been predicted in the position of the first ellipsis, and the DP currently being built is *not* the predicted one. In this circumstance, the DP currently being constructed has an outstanding case-marking relation (to the possessive marker that I have not yet heard), and the (empty) subject of the relative clause has an outstanding case relation to the verb that has not been heard. So there are two outstanding case-marking relations, exactly as in the partial structure (52) of the marginal (51).

Emonds (1976) suggests that the restriction seen in Sentences (77c) and (78) is an instance of a very general "surface-recursion restriction"—a restriction that also explains the very slight awkwardness of (77b) and the following much more severe contrasts.

(80) a. He saw the [weary] student.

   b. * He saw the [weary [of his girlfriend]] student.

(81) a. He was [magnificently] attired.

   b. * He was [magnificently [to his admirers]] attired.

(82) a. He [quickly] reads the paper.

   b. * He [quickly [to the end]] reads the paper.

Giorgi and Longobardi (1991) describe similar contrasts in Italian.

(83) a. *una triste avventura*
     a   sad   adventure

   b. * *una triste per Mario avventura*
        a   sad   for Mario adventure

(84) a. *Quell' uomo d' affari,   ora sorpredentemente ricco, era partito*
     That   businessman, now surprisingly   rich, had left
     dall' Italia in condizioni miserevoli
     Italy   in conditions miserable

   b. * *Quell' uomo d' affari,   ora sorpredentemente per noi ricco,*
        That   businessman, now surprisingly   for us rich,
        era partito dall' Italia in condizioni miserevoli
        had left   Italy   in conditions miserable

The proposed restriction (Emonds, 1976; Giorgi & Longobardi, 1991) can be stated roughly as follows.

(85) Surface-recursion restriction: If a lexical category X takes complements on the right (left), and if YP attaches to a projection of X on the left (right), the lexical part of YP cannot branch to the right (left).

This proposal is very different from most grammatical principles, but it is un-surprising from a processing perspective because alternating direction of branch-ing is exactly what causes center embedding. However, I suspect that it is a mistake to assume that all of the restrictions mentioned should be subsumed under this single idea. To begin with, notice that Sentence (77b) is much better than any of the latter examples (i.e., Sentences 80b–84b).

The latter examples are sometimes assumed to be ruled out by a special head-final filter (HFF; Williams, 1982), but I think that the facts actually follow in a natural way from fundamental properties of adjectives and other modifiers. Abney (1987) proposes that prenominal As are not adjuncts, but heads selecting DP. Then Sentences (83b), (84b), and (85b) could be ruled out on the grounds that the modifiers only can take one complement—the DP. It is natural to extend this idea to adverbs, and this would fit well with Rochette's (1990) arguments for the view that adverbs select their VPs. If these proposals are on the right track, or if the HFF is right, then Sentences (80b–84b) are out because they violate basic grammatical principles.[30]

Many related problems deserve much more attention than they can be given here. Notice that posthead-adjunct modifiers in English are fully recursive, although on traditional conceptions of phrase structure they also can form long left branches. To handle these, the extensively studied "closure conditions" for these constructions, conditions that restrict the range of attachment options in the human parser, are obviously of critical importance.[31] But an examination of how these ideas should be accommodated in the present framework must be left to another occasion. Obviously, these rough sketches need to be worked out in much more computational detail before they can be properly assessed.

CONCLUSIONS

Most of the data discussed in this chapter are drawn from conventional linguistic study. The acceptability judgments that underpin this work need more careful experimental verification, but they seem fairly clear and robust, and they suggest a picture of the language processor that is at odds with the traditional one. The limitations observed here do not appear to be linguistically arbitrary. On the contrary, they are clearly sensitive to structural detail. And they do not appear to be uninterestingly high limitations, like a limitation to 6 or 12 cells in a stack automaton. Rather, they appear to be essentially unary, like most other interesting linguistic constraints. If these ideas hold up under further exploration, it will be interesting to explore the possibility that they reflect fundamental properties of the architecture of the human sentence processing mechanism.

Some first steps in this direction are taken here. This chapter suggests that, in

---

[30]Giorgi and Longobardi (1991) defend a generalization of Emonds' idea on the basis of facts about the positions of prepositional particles (PPs) in German and Dutch. A careful study of this argument is beyond the scope of this chapter, but it appears that these facts can be handled by independently motivated "incorporation" analyses of Dutch and German PPs (Koopman, 1991, 1993).

[31]For example, Frazier and Fodor (1978), Church (1980), Frazier and Rayner (1988), Frazier (1990), Gibson, Perlmutter, Canseco-Gonzalez, and Hickok (1993), and Langendoen and Langsam (1984).

addition to "locality constraints," human languages respect the following very general connectivity constraint:

(2) There is a natural typology of linguistic relations such that the psychological complexity of a structure increases quickly when more than one relation of any given type connects a (partial) constituent α (or any element of α) to any constituent external to α.

Evidence was presented that the relevant typology includes V-movement relations, case-assignment relations for each case, A-bar chain relations for each case, and constituency relations (although perhaps these will need to be subcategorized further according to the role of the constituent). I speculate that it will include specifier-head agreement relations, control relations, local binding relations and others as well. Furthermore, it appears that, at least for the range of constructions considered here, the bounded connectivity hypothesis can be maintained in conjunction with a simple incremental processing hypothesis. It is tentatively suggested that, together, these hypotheses fit with a picture of the parsing mechanism that may explain Emonds' surface-recursion restriction, which has been attested in a range of languages.

In a more speculative vein, it is suggested that the human processing mechanism may have tightly constrained, finite resources, with something like registers alloted for particular tasks. This idea about the human sentence processing mechanism fits well with attempts to design parsers that could be realized in finite asynchronous networks lacking a (potentially infinite) recursively accessible memory store. Then, rather than assuming that acceptable or intelligible structures whose connectivity exceeds one relation of each kind are processed recursively, it is natural to consider the idea that, in these cases, the human parser must resort to limited and special purpose mechanisms to assemble whatever results it can deliver. This idea would motivate an important qualification to the tentative construal of the bounded connectivity hypothesis presented in the introduction. I suggested there that, for all types of constructions, structures with a connectivity of two are awkward, whereas structures with three or more connections of the same kind should always be unacceptable. But the examples presented show that, beyond one relation of a given kind, different kinds of structures break down differently. It appears that the attempt to define *acceptability bounds* more precisely, on any approach, will have to carefully distinguish the various properties of different kinds of structures.

ACKNOWLEDGMENTS

Early (and quite different!) versions of some of this material were presented at the CUNY93 Sentence Processing Conference and in a technical report (Stabler,

1992). Discussions of this work and stimulating comments on previous drafts from Robert Berwick, Jaime Daza, Janet Fodor, Lyn Frazier, Ted Gibson, Mark Johnson, Ed Keenan, Terry Langendoen, Anoop Mahajan, Stuart Shieber, Dominique Sportiche, Mark Steedman, Tim Stowell, and Amy Weinberg were especially helpful.

REFERENCES

Abasheikh, M. I. (1978). *The grammar of Chimwïni causatives*. Unpublished doctoral dissertation, University of Illinois, Urbana-Champaign.

Abney, S. P. (1987). *The English noun phrase in its sentential aspect*. Unpublished doctoral dissertation, Massachusetts Institute of Technology, Cambridge.

Abney, S. P., & Johnson, M. (1991). Memory requirements and local ambiguities of parsing strategies. *Journal of Psycholinguistic Research, 20*, 233–249.

Alsina, A. (1992). On the argument structure of causatives. *Linguistic Inquiry, 23*, 517–556.

Bach, E., Brown, C., & Marslen-Wilson, W. (1986). Crossed and nested dependencies in German and Dutch: A psycholinguistic study. *Language and Cognitive Processes, 1*, 249–262.

Baker, M. (1988). *Incorporation: A theory of grammatical function changing*. Chicago: University of Chicago Press.

Baltin, M. (1982). A landing site theory of movement rules. *Linguistic Inquiry, 13*, 1–38.

Berwick, R., & Weinberg, A. (1984). *The grammatical basis of linguistic performance*. Cambridge, MA: MIT Press.

Bresnan, J., & Moshi, L. (1990). Object asymmetries in comparative Bantu syntax. *Linguistic Inquiry, 21*, 147–186.

Chomsky, N. (1986). *Barriers*. Cambridge, MA: MIT Press.

Church, K. W. (1980). *On memory limitations in natural language processing* (Tech. Rep. TR-245). Cambridge, MA: Massachusetts Institute of Technology, Laboratory for Computer Science.

Cole, P. (1985). *Imbabura Quechua*. London: Croom Helm.

Comrie, B. (1976). The syntax of causative constructions: Cross-language similarities and divergences. In M. Shibatani (Ed.), *Syntax and semantics: Vol. 6. The grammar of causative constructions* (pp. 261–312). Academic Press.

Comrie, B. (1981). *Language universals and linguistic typology*. Oxford: Basil Blackwell.

den Besten, H., & Edmondson, J. (1983). The verbal complex in continental West Germanic. In W. Abraham (Ed.), *On the formal syntax of West Germania* (pp. 155–216). Amsterdam: Benjamins.

den Besten, H., & Rutten, J. (1989). On verb raising, extraposition, and free word order in Dutch. In D. Jaspers, W. Klooster, Y. Putseys, & P. Seuren (Eds.), *Sentential complementation and the lexicon* (pp. 41–56). Dordrecht, The Netherlands: Foris.

Emonds, J. (1976). *A transformational approach to English syntax*. New York: Academic Press.

Fortescue (1984). *West Greenlandic*. London: Croom Helm.

Frazier, L. (1990). Parsing modifiers: Special purpose routines in the human sentence processing mechanism? In D. A. Balota, G. B. Flores d'Arcais, & K. Rayner (Eds.), *Comprehension processes in reading* (pp. 303–330). Hillsdale, NJ: Lawrence Erlbaum Associates.

Frazier, L., & Fodor, J. D. (1978). The sausage machine: A new two-stage parsing model. *Cognition, 6*, 291–325.

Frazier, L., & Rayner, K. (1988). Parameterizing the language processing system: Left- vs. right-branching within and across languages. In J. Hawkins (Ed.), *Explaining linguistic universals* (pp. 247–279). New York: Basil Blackwell.

Gibson, E. (1991). *A computational theory of human linguistic processing*. Unpublished doctoral dissertation, Carnegie-Mellon University, Pittsburgh, PA.

Gibson, E., Perlmutter, D., Canseco-Gonzalez, E., & Hickok, G. (1993). *Cross-linguistic attachment preferences: Evidence from English and Spanish.* Manuscript submitted for publication.

Giorgi, A., & Longobardi, G. (1991). *The Syntax of noun phrases.* New York: Cambridge University Press.

Givón, T. (1976). Some constraints on Bantu causativization. In M. Shibatani (Ed.), *Syntax and semantics: Vol. 6. The grammar of causative constructions* (pp. 325–352). New York: Academic Press.

Haegeman, L., & van Riemsdijk, H. (1986). Verb projection raising, scope, and the typology of movement rules. *Linguistic Inquiry, 17,* 417–466.

Herrero, S. J., & Sánchez de Lozada, F. (1978). *Grammatica Quechua: Estructura del Quechua Boliviano Contemporaneo.* Cochabamba: Editorial Universo.

Hetzron, R. (1969). *The verbal system of Southern Agaw.* Berkeley: University of California Press.

Hetzron, R. (1976). On the Hungarian causative verb and its syntax. In M. Shibatani (Ed.), *Syntax and semantics: Vol. 6. The grammar of causative constructions* (pp. 371–398). New York: Academic Press.

Hoeksema, J. (1988). A constraint on governors in the West Germanic verb cluster. In M. Everaert, A. Evers, R. Huybregts, & M. Trommelen (Eds.), *Morphology and modularity: In honour of Henk Schultink.* Dordrecht, The Netherlands: Foris.

Horvath, J. (1985). *Focus in Hungarian and the theory of grammar.* Dordrecht, The Netherlands: Foris.

Jake, J. L. (1985). *Grammatical relations in Imbabura Quechua.* New York: Garland.

Johnson, K. (1991). Object positions. *Natural Language and Linguistic Theory, 9,* 577–636.

Johnson, M., & Shieber, S. (1993). *Variations on incremental interpretation.* Manuscript submitted for publication.

Johnson, M., & Stabler, E. (1993). *Topics in principle-based parsing.* Unpublished manuscript, LSA 1993 Summer Linguistic Institute. Revised version forthcoming.

Koopman, H. (1991). *The verb particle construction and the syntax of PPs.* Unpublished manuscript.

Koopman, H. (1993). Licensing heads. In N. Hornstein & D. Lightfoot (Eds.), *Verb movement.* New York: Cambridge University Press.

Koster, J. (1978). Why subject sentences don't exist. In S. J. Keyser (Ed.), *Recent transformational studies in European languages* (pp. 53–64). Cambridge, MA: MIT Press.

Kroch, A. S., & Santorini, B. (1991). The derived constituent structure of the West Germanic verb raising construction. In R. Friedin (Ed.), *Principles and parameters in comparative grammar* (pp. 269–338). Cambridge, MA: MIT Press.

Langendoen, D. T., & Langsam, Y. (1984). The representation of constituent structures for finite-state parsing. *COLING '84 Proceedings of the 10th International Conference on Computational Linguistics* (pp. 24–27).

Lasnik, H., & Saito, M. (1992). *Move-α: Conditions on its application and output.* Cambridge, MA: MIT Press.

Lefebvre, C., & Muysken, P. (1988). *Mixed categories: Nominalizations in Quechua.* Boston: Kluwer.

Mahajan, A. K. (1982). *Causative constructions in the Indian subcontinent.* Unpublished doctoral dissertation, University of Delhi, India.

Mahajan, A. K. (1990). *The A/A-bar distinction and movement theory.* Unpublished doctoral dissertation, Massachusetts Institute of Technology, Cambridge.

Marantz, A. P. (1984). *On the nature of grammatical relations.* Cambridge, MA: MIT Press.

Marslen-Wilson, W. (Ed.). (1989). *Lexical representation and process.* Cambridge, MA: MIT Press.

Miller, G. A., & Chomsky, N. (1963). Finitary models of language users. In R. D. Luce, R. Bush, & E. Galanter (Eds.), *Handbook of mathematical psychology* (Vol. 2, pp. 419–492). New York: Wiley.

Mohanan, K. P. (1982). Grammatical relations and clause structure in Malayalam. In J. Bresnan (Ed.), *The mental representation of grammatical relations* (pp. 504–589). Cambridge, MA: MIT Press.

Muysken, P. (1977). *Syntactic developments in the verb phrase of Ecuadorian Quechua*. Dordrecht, The Netherlands: Foris.

Perlmutter, D. M., & Postal, P. (1983). Some proposed laws of basic clause structure. In D. M. Perlmutter (Ed.), *Studies in relational grammar 1* (pp. 81–128). Chicago: University of Chicago Press.

Pinker, S. (1984). *Language learnability and language development*. Cambridge, MA: Harvard University Press.

Pritchett, B. L. (1988). Garden path phenomena and the grammatical basis of language processing. *Language, 64*, 539–576.

Pritchett, B. L. (1992). *Grammatical competence and parsing performance*. Chicago: University of Chicago Press.

Rochette, A. (1990). The selectional properties of adverbs. In *papers from the 26th Regional Meeting of the Chicago Linguistic Society, CLS 26* (pp. 379–392).

Safir, K. J. (1985). *Syntactic chains*. New York: Cambridge University Press.

Schiffman, H. (1976). *A reference grammar of spoken Kannada*. Seattle, WA: University of Washington.

Shieber, S. (1985). Evidence against the context-freeness of natural language. *Linguistics and Philosophy, 8*, 333–343.

Stabler, E. P. (1991). Avoid the pedestrian's paradox. In R. C. Berwick, S. P. Abney, & C. Tenny (Eds.), *Principle-based parsing: Computation and psycholinguistics*. Boston: Kluwer.

Stabler, E. P. (1992). The finite connectivity of linguistic structure. *UCLA Working Papers in Syntax and Semantics*, No. 11 (pp. 87–133).

Stabler, E. P. (1993). *Syntactic analysis with connectivity bounds*. Unpublished manuscript, UCLA. Revised version forthcoming.

Steedman, M. J. (1989). Grammar, interpretation, and processing from the lexicon. In W. Marslen-Wilson (Ed.), *Lexical representation and process* (pp. 463–504). Cambridge, MA: MIT Press.

Stowell, T. (1981). *Origins of phrase structure*. Unpublished doctoral dissertation, Massachusetts Institute of Technology, Cambridge.

Syeed, S. M. (1985). *Morphological causatives and the problems of the transformational approach*. Bloomington, IN: Indiana University Linguistics Club.

Szabolcsi, A. (1993). The noun phrase. In F. Kiefer & E. Kiss (Eds.), *The syntax of Hungarian: Vol. 27. Syntax and semantics*. New York: Academic Press.

Ward, G., Sproat, R., & McKoon, G. (1991). A pragmatic analysis of so-called anaphoric islands. *Language, 67*, 439–473.

Weber, D. (1989). *A grammar of Huallaga (Huánuco) Quechua*. Berkeley: University of California Press.

Williams, E. (1982). Another argument that passive is transformational. *Linguistic Inquiry, 13*, 160–163.

Zimmer, K. E. (1976). Some constraints on Turkish causativization. In M. Shibatani (Ed.), *Syntax and semantics: Vol. 6. The grammar of causative constructions* (pp. 399–412). New York: Academic Press.

V REFERENTIAL PROCESSING

14 Resolving Pronouns and Other Anaphoric Devices: The Case for Diversity in Discourse Processing

Simon Garrod
University of Glasgow

Over the last 15 years, there has been considerable psycholinguistic interest in the time course of anaphoric resolution: the process by which a reader or listener determines the antecedent for an anaphoric expression (Clark & Sengul, 1979; Dell, McKoon, & Ratcliffe, 1983; Garrod & Sanford, 1977; Gernsbacher, 1989). This research indicates that resolving anaphora is an integral part of sentence comprehension that can often occur at the earliest possible point in reading or spoken-language comprehension (Dell et al., 1983; Gernsbacher, 1989; Marslen-Wilson, Tyler, & Koster, 1993). However, most of the discussion in psycholinguistics treats anaphoric interpretation as an isolated process only loosely associated with overall resolution of the sentence against its discourse context (Sanford & Garrod, 1989). This is very much in contrast with the treatment in the linguistic literature, where different anaphoric devices have been associated with a range of discourse functions signaling different ways in which a sentence should be resolved (Ariel, 1990; Givon, 1983; see also Marslen-Wilson, Levy, & Tyler, 1982, for a more process-oriented discussion). The present chapter sets out to reconsider some of the processing assumptions about anaphoric resolution in the light of these linguistic analyses.

By way of background, I begin with a brief account of what is entailed in resolving a sentence, as opposed to just resolving the anaphora it may contain. This then leads into a discussion of the various discourse functions associated with different anaphoric devices (i.e., pronouns, definite descriptions, proper names, etc.), and how they might be expected to direct the sentence-resolution process. The main body of the chapter then looks at the evidence for differences in the on-line processing of sentences containing the different anaphora and how this can be related to their discourse functions.

SENTENCE RESOLUTION AS AN ANCHORING PROCESS

To understand an extended discourse, one has to create a coherent representation of the whole thing; as each sentence is read, it will have to be resolved against this representation and integrated into it. Therefore, sentence resolution can be conceived as a process of anchoring the sentence to the existing discourse representation. The anchoring comes about through links that establish what linguists call *cohesion* and *coherence* (Brown & Yule, 1983; Halliday & Hasan, 1976). Cohesive links are explicitly signaled in the sentence itself (e.g., by the use of pronouns). They typically involve establishing referential relationships between elements in the sentence and elements in the discourse representation. On the other hand, coherence comes from establishing the logical or causal relationships needed to make sense of the events and situations being portrayed in the context of the discourse representation as a whole.

A simple case of cohesive referential anchoring is illustrated in the following sentences.

(1) Bill wanted to lend $Susan_1$ some $money_2$.
(2) She_1 was hard up and really need it_2.

These two sentences form a connected discourse because the pronoun *she* in (2) refers to *Susan* in (1) and the pronoun *it* in (2) refers to the *money* in (1). As a result, Sentence (2) becomes anchored to the discourse representation set up by Sentence (1), through links of common reference. However, sentence resolution also depends on anchoring as a result of coherence relations. For instance, Sentences (3) and (4) form a perfectly satisfactory discourse, but there are no explicit referential links between the two.

(3) Bill wanted to lend Susan some money.
(4) It is not nice to have friends who are hard up.

What is important in this case is a coherence link. The reader will take it that the unpleasantness of having friends who are hard up is the reason that Bill wants to lend Susan some money and, by implication, that Susan is Bill's friend. Thus, a text's coherence comes from establishing the logical and psychological links (i.e., the causes and reasons why) between the events and states portrayed (Trabasso & van den Broek, 1985).

From a processing point of view, cohesion and coherence often have to be considered together. Establishing referential cohesion may depend on establishing coherence, and vice versa (Hobbs, 1979). For instance, consider the following further variant of Sentences (1) and (2).

(5) $Bill_1$ wanted to lend his $friend_2$ some money.

(6) He$_2$ was hard up and really needed it.

(7) However, he$_1$ was hard up and couldn't afford to.

The same pronoun in almost identical clauses takes on different referential interpretations depending on the different coherence relationships between the two sentences. At the same time, the form of coherence relationship differs depending on the assignment of the pronoun. For instance, whereas his being hard up in (6) is taken as a reason for Bill's wanting to lend money, his being hard up in (7) is taken as an obstacle to Bill's lending the money.

Not only are cohesion and coherence often interrelated, but there are also circumstances when sentences may be anchored to the discourse representation directly through a special form of referential link, established on the basis of coherence. For instance, consider Sentences (8) and (9).

(8) Keith drove Δ_1 to London yesterday.

(9) The car$_1$ kept overheating.

Sentence (9) relates to the discourse representation set up by Sentence (8) because "the car" is taken to refer to the vehicle that Keith must have used to drive to London. Thus, although there is no explicit antecedent reference for the car, the referential relationship is forced on the reader through establishing a coherence link between the sentences; namely, that Sentence (9) is an elaboration of Sentence (8). Garrod and Sanford (1990) argued that these referential coherence links anchor referents in terms of their situational roles in the discourse representation. Hence, "the car" in sentence (9) is anchored to the representation by filling the role "vehicle used to drive to London." As is seen later, only certain kinds of referential expression seem able to signal such role-anchoring links.

It should be clear from even this limited range of examples that sentence resolution is basically a process of anchoring interpretations of the sentence as a whole and its fragments (e.g., referential expressions, temporal expressions, etc.) to the discourse representation. The anchors reflect referential links or more general coherence relationships between the sentence and the representation. The main issue to be addressed here is how different anaphoric devices affect this anchoring process and, as a consequence, the on-line interpretation of the sentence. The next section considers a scheme for classifying anaphora in terms of their discourse functions and enables me to set up some hypotheses about on-line interpretation of the sentences containing them.

CLASSIFYING ANAPHORIC DEVICES IN TERMS OF THEIR DISCOURSE FUNCTION

It turns out that every known language possesses a range of anaphoric expressions that vary in terms of their lexical specificity (Ariel, 1990). In English, the range goes from various forms of zero anaphora ($\emptyset$ and gaps), through un-

TABLE 14.1
Part of the Referential Hierarchy for English Anaphoric Expressions
Illustrating Functional Differences

Position	Form	Contextual Presupposition	Referential Role	Antecedent Identifiability
High	Pronoun (*he, it*) Demonstrative NP ("this man")	High	Ref. maint.	Low
Medium	Definite NP ("the man") Def. NP + modifier ("the man in the hat")	Moderate	Referential maintenance + establishment	Moderate
Low	Proper name (*John*)	Low	Ref. establ.	High

stressed and stressed pronouns, demonstratives, definite descriptions with or without modification, to proper names with or without modification. Each of these may be used anaphorically to pick up its interpretation from some other reference in the text. Some examples are shown.

(10) Jim bumped into Bill and ∅ fell over.

(11) Jim bumped into Bill and he fell over.

(12) Jim bumped into Bill and the fool fell over.

(13) Jim bumped into Bill and Bill fell over.

A number of linguists have argued that the different forms constitute a kind of referential hierarchy, with the lexically attenuated ones at the top and the fuller forms at the bottom (Ariel, 1990; Silverstein, 1976). Table 14.1 illustrates part of the hierarchy for English and shows some of the characteristics of the different expressions that are relevant to their usage.

In general, items at the top act as prototypical anaphora (e.g., pronouns), whereas those at the bottom may serve other functions as well (e.g., proper names, which often introduce new individuals into the model). Not surprisingly, this difference in anaphoricity correlates with a number of other differences in discourse function that should have consequences for how the expressions are processed. Three dimensions of variation are indicated in the table: *contextual presupposition, referential function,* and *antecedent identifiability.*

Contextual Presupposition

The first dimension on which anaphoric expressions may vary is contextual presupposition: the degree to which their interpretation is governed by the surrounding text. Items at the top of the hierarchy tend to be high in contextual presupposition. For instance, the interpretation of zero anaphora is completely constrained by the immediate syntactic context. Whereas the $\emptyset$ in Sentence (10) can only refer to *Jim* as subject of the previous clause, the pronoun in Sentence (11) is ambiguous between *Jim* and *Bill*. A similar contrast can be made between pronouns and definite descriptions, with the pronoun generally being more contextually constrained than the fuller form. For instance, consider the following short text.

> (14) Mary likes to go to Vanentino's for lunch. She fancies a waiter$_1$ there. For dinner she prefers Le Grand Bouffe, where the food is better but the waiter$_2$/*he$_1$ is not nearly so handsome.

Whereas the pronoun in Sentence (14) has to take its meaning from the antecedent *waiter* supplied by the context, the matching definite description does not. Instead, it takes its meaning from the situation of dining at the Grand Bouffe, where the referent is treated as filling the situational role "waiter at the restaurant." To this extent, the full noun phrase (NP) interpretation is less constrained by the prior discourse context than is the pronoun interpretation.

This contrast between pronouns and fuller forms is reflected in their distribution in written text. Whereas referential pronouns are hardly ever used in the absence of an explicit text antecedent, Fraurud (1990) found that 60% of definite descriptions in a large corpus of text occurred as first mentions without any explicit discourse antecedents.

The difference in contextual presupposition is associated, in part, with the degree to which the expression signals a *cohesion* relationship as opposed to a *coherence* relationship. Items high in the hierarchy tend only to serve as cohesion devices with a purely discourse anaphoric interpretation. Thus, zero anaphora, pronouns, and demonstrative NPs usually cannot be used to signal referential coherence of the kind discussed in the previous section. This can be illustrated by substituting the definite reference to "the car" in Sentence (9) with a pronoun or a demonstrative NP. Notice that neither Sentence (16) nor Sentence (17) make an acceptable discourse following Sentence (15), even though they are fine following Sentence (18).

> (15) Keith drove Δ_1 to London yesterday.
>
> (16) It$_1$ kept overheating.
>
> (17) This car$_1$ kept overheating.
>
> (18) Keith took a car$_1$ to London yesterday.

(19) It$_1$ kept overheating.

(20) This car$_1$ kept overheating.

Thus, one way in which different kinds of anaphora vary is in terms of their contextual presupposition. In general, the more attenuated the expression, the more its interpretation relies directly on the immediate linguistic context. This difference in contextual presupposition relates to the second feature associated with the hierarchy—namely, *referential function*.

Referential Function

Referential expressions can serve to establish new referents in a discourse, to reestablish old referents no longer in focus,[1] or to maintain reference to something still in focus. In general, expressions that are high in the hierarchy tend to serve purely as reference maintenance devices, whereas expressions lower in the hierarchy serves as reference (re)introduction devices.

The correlation between referential function and hierarchical position is clearly seen in narrative text where the same character may be referred to on different occasions by name, definite description, or pronoun. In one of the earliest studies of the distribution of the different forms of reference, Marslen-Wilson et al. (1982) analyzed a long monologue where a subject retold a comic book story. First they blocked the narrative into successive story episodes and event sequences within each episode. They then classified each character reference in terms of its specificity, along similar lines to the hierarchy in Table 14.1. It turned out that the choice of referential device was almost completely determined by how the context in which the reference occurred related to the context of antecedent mention. Therefore, proper names with further modifications (e.g., The Hulk, the one with the green chest . . .) were only used when the character was first introduced into the story; subsequent use of the name alone depended on whether the antecedent had been mentioned in the current story episode. Hence, reintroduction at the beginning of a new episode always led to renaming of the antecedent. A similar pattern emerged with the use of pronouns and zero anaphora, where the distribution depended on whether the clause maintained reference to the same event as in the clause containing the antecedent mention. It was particularly striking that these relationships between anaphoric and antecedent contexts were just as important in determining use of the pronouns as the degree of potential ambiguity in the reference.

A similar observation was made by Fox (1987) when analyzing a written corpus taken from four modern novels. She examined the patterns of use of

---

[1]For the present purposes, *in focus* can be taken as meaning "currently under discussion," although there is much more that can be said about what might determine a referent's degree of focus at any point (for further discussion, see Garrod & Sanford, 1990; Grosz, 1977).

pronouns versus proper names or definite descriptions as references to key characters in these stories. Looking first at gender-unambiguous pronouns, she found that they only occurred when no other active referent intervened between the sentence and the last mention of the referent in question; otherwise, the writer reverted to a proper name or fuller description. This is important because it again shows that the reference maintenance function of the pronoun is more significant than the potential ambiguity of the interpretation because these were all gender-disambiguated uses. The second situation in which the fuller descriptions were used, even without intervening mention of alternative characters, was when they occurred in sentences that introduced a new *narrative unit* or *episode,* in the Marslen-Wilson et al. terminology. Again, the pattern was very much one where proper names (or definite descriptions) were used to reestablish referents already given, either because they had gone out of focus due to intervening reference to an active character or because the story was entering a new narrative episode. The same pattern of results was found for the ambiguous pronouns. Basically, fuller descriptions were only used when the competing antecedents had just been mentioned in the previous sentence, or if the writer needed to refer to the character not involved in the last mentioned main event.

Thus, position in the hierarchy relates to the referential function of the anaphoric device. Not surprisingly, items toward the top of the hierarchy that have a high degree of contextual presupposition tend to be used to maintain reference to highly focused and so currently available antecedents. Lower items tend to be used to introduce fresh referents into the discourse or reintroduce old referents no longer in focus. Interestingly, this differentiation in terms of function depends only partially on the degree to which the anaphora unambiguously identifies its antecedent.

Antecedent Identifiability

One of the main differences between the various devices in Table 14.1 relates to antecedent identifiability, and this has received considerable attention in the psychological literature. As Gernsbacher (1989) pointed out, pronouns are in a sense lexically transparent; their interpretation is only very weakly constrained by their lexical content. This means that, in most contexts, a pronoun by itself could map onto many different textual antecedents. Demonstrative and other definite NPs have more semantic content, but they are also commonly used to identify antecedents that do not uniquely match this content (Garnham, 1984; Garrod & Sanford, 1977). However, when used anaphorically, names usually serve as unique identifiers. Thus, the different devices range along an explicitness continuum in terms of the degree to which they uniquely identify their discourse antecedents. As is seen later, this difference has been used to account for apparent differences in the time course of resolution of the different types of anaphora, where it has been suggested that the more explicit the expression the more rapidly it is resolved (Gernsbacher, 1989). However, this is a somewhat contentious point to which I return later.

Associated with differences in antecedent identifiability is another referential characteristic of the different forms—what Sanford, Moar, and Garrod (1988) called *referential rigidity*. Referential rigidity reflects the degree to which the referential interpretation of different tokens of the same expression is fixed within any stretch of text. In general, items low in the hierarchy, such as proper names and to a lesser extent definite descriptions, receive the same interpretation whenever they are used within the same stretch of text. On the other hand, higher items, such as pronouns, tend to take on quite different interpretations within the same text episode or even within the same sentence (see Marslen-Wilson et al., 1982, for some interesting examples of this in natural discourse).

Again, position in the hierarchy relates to the degree to which an expression uniquely identifies its discourse antecedent and the degree to which its interpretation is fixed within any stretch of text. Next, I argue that each of the dimensions represented in the table affect the on-line interpretation of sentences containing the anaphora. But comparing the different dimensions in this way highlights a processing paradox.

RESOLUTION PROCESSES IN RELATION TO THE DISCOURSE FUNCTION OF DIFFERENT TYPES OF ANAPHORA

The prior discussion identified three dimensions along which anaphoric devices vary, and one would expect them to be reflected in some way in on-line processing. Consider first the functional consequences of contextual presupposition. If an expression is high in terms of contextual presupposition, its contribution to understanding the sentence crucially depends on recovery of the relevant contextual information. Therefore, recovering this information should be a high priority in on-line processing. In terms of immediacy, one would therefore expect items high in the hierarchy to instigate early recovery of relevant contextual information. This is for two reasons: First, holding off interpretation requires holding an uninterpreted place marker[2] in memory, thereby increasing memory load; second, any delay in recovering the information would inevitably hinder the overall resolution of the sentence. On this count, pronouns should, where possible, instigate more immediate recovery of relevant contextual information than fuller forms such as names or definite descriptions.

This hypothesis is also consistent with the referential function of the different

---

[2]Note that unresolved pronouns have almost no semantic content in contrast with either proper names or definite descriptions, whose semantic content is immediately available once the expression has been identified.

kinds of expression. I noted previously that items high in the hierarchy tend to be used in contexts that continue discussion of the same story episode or event. In other words, they occur in sentences that can be immediately anchored into the currently active discourse representation—sentences that maintain reference both to the currently focused individual and the currently focused event or episode. This contrasts with the general use of the fuller anaphora, which tend to occur in sentences that either instigate a new episode in the story, establish a new referent (albeit a contextually identifiable one), or reestablish an old one. In such cases, it may be beneficial for the processor to delay full resolution of the sentence until more information has been sampled because such sentences are likely to trigger the construction of a new component of the discourse representation only partially integrated with what is currently active (see Vonk, Hustinx, & Simons, 1992).

Hence, according to their discourse characteristics, one would predict that items high in the hierarchy most strongly motivate early resolution. But there is a problem with this hypothesis because it is just those expressions that tend to be low in terms of antecedent identifiability. Whereas a pronoun's strength of contextual presupposition and its referential function motivate early recovery of contextual information, the low antecedent identifiability associated with a pronoun would seem to make it that much more difficult to do this. It seems that both sides of this processing paradox are reflected in the experimental findings. As is seen later, evidence on the speed of antecedent reactivation favors items low in the referential hierarchy. Thus, proper names or definite descriptions that readily identify their antecedents seem to trigger rapid reactivation of antecedent information. However, evidence on when this information is incorporated into the resolution of the sentence indicates earlier integration of information associated with items high in the hierarchy such as pronouns. To make sense of this paradox, the data need to be examined more closely.

The most influential methodology for studying the time course of reactivation is antecedent probe recognition. A context containing some antecedent is presented, typically one word at a time, and then either immediately before presentation of the anaphor or at some predetermined time after presentation, a memory-recognition probe appears. Comparison between pre- and postprobe recognition time yields a measure of antecedent reactivation that can then be used to infer the time course of the resolution process. Results from the original studies using this technique tended to suggest that the more explicit the anaphor, the more rapid the reactivation of its antecedent. For instance, Gernsbacher (1989) demonstrated both immediate reactivation of the antecedent and suppression of nonantecedents using a repeated name probe-recognition task. A similar result was found by Dell et al. (1983) for definite description anaphors. They measured probe-recognition latency for an antecedent such as *burglar* following the anaphor *the criminal* and found immediate activation (i.e., within 250 ms) as compared with a nonanaphoric control condition. Taken together, the two studies suggest that antecedent reactivation occurs soon after encountering an explicit anaphor like a name or definite description. However, the results from similar studies with pronouns produce a much more confusing picture.

There is some evidence for early nonantecedent suppression effects associated with unambiguous pronouns presented in speech. Shillcock (1982) used a cross-modal priming procedure to test for differential activation of associates of the antecedent as compared with associates of the nonantecedent with materials like the following.

(21) The teacher$_1$ did not board the train$_2$ for the simple reason that it$_2$/he$_1$ was not going to the south of England.

He found evidence of immediate suppression of the nonantecedent probes compared with a prepronoun baseline, but there was no evidence for activation of the antecedent probes at this point. Studies using Gernsbacher's probe-recognition procedure have been even less successful in demonstrating early effects of pronoun resolution with visual presentation. Thus, although Gernsbacher detected some suppression of the nonantecedent probe for an unambiguous pronoun, this was only after a long delay. Similarly, MacDonald and MacWhinney (1990) were only able to detect delayed suppression relative to a nonanaphoric baseline. Others have not been able to detect any activation at all even well downstream of the pronoun (Greene, McKoon, & Ratcliffe, 1992). On the basis of these findings, Gernsbacher suggested that it is necessary to have an explicit anaphor to detect strong effects of activation of the antecedent and suppression of nonantecedents. This, of course, goes against my discourse-motivated hypothesis that predicts quite the opposite pattern.

However, the comparison between probe-recognition studies with explicit anaphora versus pronouns is more complicated than it seems. First, there is good reason to suspect that antecedent focusing may play an important part in resolving pronouns as compared with the more explicit anaphora (Garrod & Sanford, 1988; Gordon, Grosz, & Gilliom, in press[3]; Sanford et al., 1988), and focus was not systematically manipulated in the studies cited earlier. In fact, a more recent probe-recognition experiment with unambiguous pronouns demonstrated some early reactivation of the antecedent probes, but only when they were topicalized in the prior sentence (Speelman & Kirsner, 1990). Also, Vonk et al. (1992) found earlier reactivation of the antecedent for unambiguous pronouns as compared with proper name anaphors when the sentence was embedded in text that clearly identified the antecedent as the topic character in the story. Hence, even in relation to the probe-recognition technique, there is some evidence to support the

---

[3]Gordon et al. used the term *centering* to cover what I have been calling *focusing,* but it reflects the same basic concept.

hypothesis that pronouns may, on occasion, instigate earlier antecedent reactivation when they are used in appropriate contexts.

The second problem with comparing the two kinds of materials relates to the nature of the probe-recognition task itself. Cloitre and Bever (1988) pointed out that facilitation effects for the referent in the repeated name conditions may simply reflect repetition priming for the probe word that the subject has just seen twice before, and so may not signal antecedent identification as such. They reported a number of experiments that suggest that noun anaphora only immediately reactivate surface information about their antecedents, whereas pronouns activate deeper conceptual information. The experiments compared the same materials using a number of different probe tasks. In general, they found that tasks that tapped recovery of conceptual information about the antecedent, such as category decision, produced earlier effects following the pronoun than the noun anaphora, whereas the opposite was true for lexical decision tasks with the same materials. At the same time, they found that secondary effects associated with conceptual properties of the antecedent, such as its concreteness, emerged in the immediate responses following the pronoun, but not the noun anaphora. Thus, it is possible that the different referential devices are initially recovering different types of information from the prior discourse. Pronouns may have a privileged status in terms of access to conceptual information about their antecedents, whereas fuller forms may only produce immediate reactivation of the surface information.

Although the results from the various probe-recognition studies tend to indicate that the speed of an antecedent's reactivation relates to its identifiability, there is some uncertainty about what this tells us about the time course of the resolution process. Sanford (1985; see also Garrod & Sanford, in press; Sanford & Garrod, 1989) drew a distinction between two aspects of anaphoric processing: antecedent *bonding* and reference *resolution*. Bonding is envisaged as a low-level automatic matching process that highlights the anaphora–antecedent link, but without necessarily committing the processor to any particular semantic interpretation at that point. This contrasts with reference resolution, which is seen as the process of incorporating a particular semantic interpretation of the anaphora—maybe in terms of identity of sense or of reference—into the semantic representation being constructed for the sentence. The distinction was originally drawn to explain why readers become garden pathed with examples such as Sentence (23), but have no trouble with Sentence (24) as compared with Sentence (25), even though these are very similar.

(22) Keith drove to London$_1$ last week.

(23) It$_1$ kept breaking down.

(24) It was a beautiful day.

(25) It$_1$ is a beautiful city.

It was suggested that, in all cases, the pronoun initially bonds onto *London* as potential antecedent, but whether the bond is actually cashed in depends on what happens later in the sentence. From the present point of view, what is important is that the conditions for immediacy of resolution may be somewhat different from the conditions on immediacy of bonding, and the probe-recognition studies can only tap into the bonding process. Other techniques are required to establish the time course of resolution; there have been a few recent studies that do this.

The first of these are speech experiments reported by Tyler and Marslen-Wilson (1982) and Marslen-Wilson et al. (1993). In both cases, they used a technique where subjects were required to name a visually presented probe (either the pronoun *him* or *her*) following one of the auditorily presented text fragments (Sentence 27a, 27b, or 27c) illustrated next.

(26) As Phillips was walking back from the shop, he saw an old woman trip and fall flat on her face. She seemed to be unable to get up again.

(27) a. Philip ran toward . . . <u>him</u>/<u>her</u>.
   b. He ran toward . . .<u>him</u>/<u>her</u>.
   c. Running toward . . . <u>him</u>/<u>her</u>.

The probes were chosen in such a way that one (e.g., *her*) was always pragmatically consistent with the contextual interpretation of the fragment at that point, whereas the other (e.g., *him*) was not. Tyler et al. reasoned that any advantage in terms of naming latency for the appropriate probe could only arise if the listener had already resolved the anaphora at that point, and so combined this information with the interpretation of the verb. In other words, it would reflect an immediate and continuous process of sentence resolution.

The results from their first study indicated that, in all conditions, such an advantage occurred. Therefore, they concluded that zero anaphora (as in Sentence 27c) as well as pronouns (as in Sentence 27b), and names (as in Sentence 27a) are all resolved by the time the reader has finished interpreting the main verb of the sentence. In a more recent extension, Marslen-Wilson et al. replicated this finding for pronouns and zero anaphora, as well as demonstrated the immediate effects of gender agreement and antecedent focusing on the resolution of sentences containing these expressions.

Although these results are consistent with the early resolution of pronoun and zero anaphora, the technique does suffer from the disadvantage that it only enables a test somewhat downstream of the anaphora. There is also the objection that the task may force listeners to resolve the anaphora earlier than under uninterrupted listening conditions. The second set of studies by Garrod, Freudenthal, and Boyle (1994) got around this objection by measuring eye movements during normal reading without imposing any secondary task requirements. They also made it possible to establish whether the anaphor has been resolved at the time of encountering the next word in the text.

TABLE 14.2
Materials Using the Full Anaphora from Garrod et al. 1994

Flying to America

Joan$_1$ wasn't enjoying the flight at all. The dry air in the plane made her really thirsty.
Just as she was about to call him, she noticed the steward$_2$ coming down the aisle
with the drinks trolley
(1) Right away Joan ordered$_1$ a large glass of Coke.
(2) Right away Joan poured$_2$ a large glass of Coke.*
(3) Right away the steward poured$_2$ a large glass of Coke.
(4) Right away the steward ordered$_2$ a large glass of Coke.*

Name

Right away *Joan* /ordered/ a large glass of Coke/. no conflict
/poured / a large glass of Coke/. conflict

Definite Description

Right away *the steward* /poured / a large glass of Coke./ no conflict
/ordered/ a large glass of Coke./ conflict
[]   []
/VERB /   POSTVERB   /

Note. Consistency effect = Conflict–no conflict (in first-pass fixation time for the
region).
*Anaphoric verb conflict.

We contrasted proper name and definite description anaphora with both ambiguous and unambiguous pronouns. The rationale behind the experiments is
most clearly explained by considering the contrasts between the texts presented.
For the full anaphoric conditions, subjects were given texts of the kind shown in
Table 14.2. Hence, each passage introduced two antecedent characters: one
always named (i.e., *Joan*) and established as the focused character through
pretests on the materials, and the other introduced by definite description (i.e.,
the steward) and established as unfocused in the pretests. The critical sentences
(1–4 in the table) then contained repeated name or definite description anaphora.
It is possible to test for the time course of resolution using the contrast between
the two kinds of verb in the sentences. For the name anaphora, Sentence (1)
contains a verb contextually consistent with Joan as agent (i.e., ordering a drink),
whereas Sentence (2) contains an inconsistent verb (i.e., pouring a drink). The
converse is true for Sentences (3) and (4) with the definite description anaphora,
so it is appropriate for the steward to pour a drink (Sentence 3), but not to order
one (Sentence 4). We argued that any reading-time differences between the
consistent and inconsistent conditions can only arise when the reader has resolved the reference in favor of that character. In terms of overall reading time for
the sentences, a marked consistency effect was detected with both name and

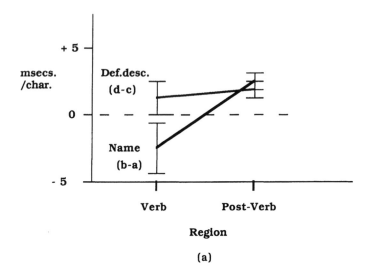

(a)

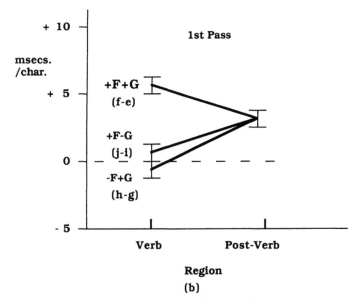

(b)

FIG. 14.1. The magnitudes of the consistency effects (inconsistent–consistent fixation time) for the first-pass fixations in the verb and postverb regions of the critical sentences (from Garrod, Freudenthal, & Boyle, 1994). (A) The times for the full anaphoric conditions (d–c) and conditions (b–a). (B) The matched times for the pronoun conditions (f–e), (h–g), and (j–i).

TABLE 14.3
Materials Using the Pronoun Anaphora from Garrod et al. (1994)

Flying to America

Joan$_1$ wasn't enjoying the flight at all. The dry air in the plane made her really thirsty. Just as she was about to call him, she noticed the steward$_2$/stewardess$_3$ coming down the aisle with the drinks trolley.

(5) +F+G: **Right away she$_1$ ordered$_1$ a large glass of Coke.
(6) +F+G: Right away she$_1$ poured$_2$ a large glass of Coke.*
(7) −F+G: Right away he$_2$ poured$_2$ a large glass of Coke.
(8) −F+G: Right away he$_2$ ordered$_1$ a large glass of Coke.*
(9) +F−G: Right away she$_{1/3}$ ordered$_1$ a large glass of Coke.
(10) +F−G: Right away she$_{1/3}$ poured$_3$ a large glass of Coke.*

*Anaphoric verb conflict.
**+F indicates that pronoun is consistent with focused antecedent (i.e. Joan). −F indicates that it is consistent with non-focused antecedent (i.e. steward). +G indicates that pronoun is gender disambiguating. −G indicates that pronoun is not gender disambiguating.

definite description anaphora. However, when we looked at the initial first-pass fixations on the verb and postverb regions, no reliable consistency effect was present in these conditions (see Fig. 14.1).

A comparable experiment was then carried out with the pronoun anaphoric materials shown in Table 14.3. The first contrast was between unambiguous pronouns that either referred to the focused antecedent (Sentences 5 and 6) or the nonfocused antecedent (Sentences 7 and 8). The second was between the gender-unambiguous pronouns (Sentences [5]–[8]) and matched ambiguous pronouns (Sentences 9 and 10), with the same consistent versus inconsistent verb contrasts in each case. Here the pattern of first-pass reading times was very different as is shown in Fig. 14.1. When the pronoun was used appropriately (i.e., was gender unambiguous and maintained reference to the currently focused antecedent), there was a highly reliable consistency effect emerging at the first-pass reading of the verb and continuing into the postverb region. Even for the other four conditions (i.e., Sentences [7]–[10]) a reliable first-pass effect of consistency emerged in the postverb region of the sentence. Hence, we were able to conclude that when a pronoun is used in a way consistent with its discourse function, it is resolved immediately and the antecedent information is incorporated directly into the interpretation of the rest of the sentence.

These results, together with those from the speech studies cited earlier, indicate that when an expression high in the referential hierarchy is used in an appropriate manner, it instigates immediate resolution. Interestingly, the results from the eye-tracking study also suggests that when an expression low in the hierarchy, such as a name, is substituted for the pronoun it leads to delayed resolution of the reference. This result is similar to the Gordon et al. repeated name penalty in overall reading time, which they observed under similar conditions.

I am now in a position to relate the range of experimental findings more clearly to the discourse characteristics of the different anaphoric devices. The three basic dimensions of antecedent identifiability, contextual presupposition, and referential function are all seen to impact in various ways on the resolution of the sentence and its anaphora. If I follow Sanford's distinction between bonding and resolution processes, comparison of the various probe-recognition results suggest that bonding is very much affected by differences in antecedent identifiability. Other things being equal, expressions low in the referential hierarchy, such as the fuller anaphora, rapidly bond with their discourse antecedents (cf. Gernsbacher, 1989). For pronouns, on the other hand, antecedent identifiability depends on both the degree to which the pronoun's number and gender select a unique antecedent in the discourse and the degree to which this antecedent is currently in focus. Evidence for immediate bonding is limited to cases where a pronoun is used to refer to a currently focused and uniquely matching antecedent (cf. Vonk et al., 1992). If this conclusion is correct, antecedent identifiability would only act as a lower bound on the speed of resolution.

By contrast, the results from the Garrod et al. experiment suggest that it is the contextual presupposition of the anaphora that actively drives the resolution process. As pointed out at the beginning of this section, there are good reasons for expecting this to be the case. First, there is the memory cost associated with holding an uninterpreted expression having little semantic content. If a referential interpretation is not recovered for a pronoun, there is little information available to help the processor interpret the rest of the sentence. This contrasts with the situation for names and definite descriptions that contribute semantic content to the interpretation of the rest of the sentence. Furthermore, it may turn out that the referential interpretation of the fuller expression is not that of a matching antecedent because it could be establishing a new referent in a contextually determined role. This means that there are special costs that may come from early commitment to a particular referential interpretation of the fuller forms that do not apply to expressions such as pronouns or zero anaphora. The second reason relates to referential function. As noted earlier, items high in the hierarchy tend to be used when referring to a currently focused antecedent in a context that effectively continues the same story topic. Therefore, an efficient sentence-resolution system should attempt to incorporate the interpretation of the sentence and its elements directly into the currently active discourse representation where this is possible. This contrasts with the standard use of fuller anaphora, which seems to signal either the beginning of a new discourse segment or the return to a previous segment that is no longer active in the discourse representation.

SUMMARY AND CONCLUSIONS

This chapter set out to reappraise the psycholinguistic work on anaphoric resolution processes in the light of the discourse linguistic treatment. Whereas the psycholinguistic work centers around questions of immediacy of processing, the linguistic discussion is more concerned with how different anaphoric devices signal such things as topic continuity in the discourse as a whole (e.g., Givon, 1983).

The referential hierarchy served as a framework for the reappraisal by identifying three dimensions along which different types of anaphora vary. The first was contextual presupposition: the degree to which the interpretation of the expression is determined solely by its linguistic context. The second was referential function: the degree to which that type of expression is used to main reference to focused antecedents. The third was antecedent identifiability: the degree to which the expression uniquely specifies its antecedent reference. It has been possible to show that all these factors are reflected in some way in the overall process of resolving a sentence against its discourse context.

Antecedent identifiability predicts the speed of antecedent reactivation as measured using probe-recognition techniques. On the other hand, contextual presupposition seems to be important in motivating early integration of the antecedent information into the overall interpretation of the sentence. It can be argued that this is also consistent with the different referential functions of different kinds of anaphor. To reconcile these two findings, one has to maintain a processing distinction between antecedent bonding and referential resolution. Bonding is best thought of as an automatic process only loosely associated with the incremental interpretation of the sentence. By analogy with syntactic parsing, it might correspond to identifying an expression's syntactic category without making a commitment to its position in the tree. On the other hand, resolution requires making a referential commitment that can then be incorporated into the interpretation of what follows.

Evidence for immediate resolution is therefore evidence of incremental discourse processing, with each element of the sentence being directly integrated into the overall representation. Evidence for immediate bonding, as in the probe-recognition studies, does not lead to such a strong conclusion. In fact, it is not clear the extent to which referential integration even requires any explicit identification of the form of antecedent mention. Thus, a reader may recognize that it is the same character responsible for the various events portrayed in a complex Russian novel without reactivating the name *Bogoyavlenskaya,* for instance, every time they encounter a pronominal reference to that character. At the very least, systematic comparison of the results from studies using a variety of methodologies is required before one can come to any firm conclusion about the relationship between antecedent reactivation and referential resolution.

REFERENCES

Ariel, M. (1990). *Accessing noun-phrase antecedents*. London: Routledge.

Brown, G., & Yule, G. (1983). *Discourse analysis*. Cambridge, England: Cambridge University Press.

Clark, H. H., & Sengul, C. J. (1979). In search of referents for nouns and pronouns. *Memory and Cognition, 7*, 35–41.

Cloitre, M., & Bever, T. G. (1988). Linguistic anaphors, levels of representation and discourse. *Language and Cognitive Processes, 3*, 293–322.

Dell, G. S., McKoon, G., & Ratcliffe, R. (1983). The activation of antecedent information during the processing of anaphoric reference in reading. *Journal of Verbal Learning and Verbal Behavior, 22*, 121–132.

Fox, B. A. (1987). Anaphora in popular written English narratives. In R. S. Tomlin (Ed.), *Coherence and grounding in discourse* (pp. 157–195). Amsterdam: John Benjamins.

Fraurud, K. (1990). Definiteness and the processing of NPs in natural discourse. *Journal of Semantics, 7*, 395–434.

Garnham, A. (1984). Effects of specificity on the interpretation of anaphoric noun-phrases. *Quarterly Journal of Experimental Psychology, 36A*, 1–12.

Garrod, S., Freudenthal, D., & Boyle, E. (1994). The role of different types of anaphor in the on-line resolution of sentences in a discourse. *Journal of Memory and Language, 33*, 39–68.

Garrod, S., & Sanford, A. J. (1977). Interpreting anaphoric relations: The integration of semantic information while reading. *Journal of Verbal Learning and Verbal Behavior, 16*, 77–90.

Garrod, S., & Sanford, A. J. (1988). Thematic subjecthood and cognitive constraints on discourse structure. *Journal of Pragmatics, 12*, 519–534.

Garrod, S., & Sanford, A. J. (1990). Referential processing in reading: Focusing on roles and individuals. In D. A. Balota, G. B. Flores d'Arcais, and K. Rayner (Eds.), *Comprehension Processes in Reading*. Hillsdale, N.J.: Lawrence Erlbaum Associates. 465–486.

Garrod, S., & Sanford, A. J. (in press). Resolving sentences in a discourse context: How discourse representation affects language understanding. In M. Gernsbacher (Ed.), *Handbook of psycholinguistics*. New York: Academic Press.

Gernsbacher, M. A. (1989). Mechanisms that improve referential access. *Cognition, 32*, 99–156.

Givon, T. (Ed.). (1983). *Topic continuity in discourse: A quantitative cross-language study*. Amsterdam: John Benjamin.

Gordon, P. C., Grosz, B. J., & Gilliom, L. A. (in press). Pronouns, names and the centering of attention in discourse. *Cognitive Science*.

Greene, S. B., McKoon, G., & Ratcliffe, R. (1992). Pronoun resolution and discourse models. *Journal of Experimental Psychology: Learning, Memory, and Cognition, 18*, 266–283.

Grosz, B. (1977). *The representation and use of focus in dialogue understanding* (Tech. Note 15). SRI International Artificial Intelligence Center, Menlo Park, Cal.

Halliday, M.A.K., & Hasan, R. (1976). *Cohesion in English*. London: Longman.

Hobbs, J. R. (1979). Coherence and coreference. *Cognitive Science, 3*, 67–90.

MacDonald, M. C., & MacWhinney, B. (1990). Measuring inhibition and facilitation for pronouns. *Journal of Memory and Language, 29*, 469–492.

Marslen-Wilson, W., Levy, E., & Tyler, L. K. (1982). Producing interpretable discourse: The establishment and maintenance of reference. In R. J. Jarvella & W. Klein (Eds.), *Speech, place and action* (pp. 339–378). Chichester, England: Wiley.

Marslen-Wilson, W., Tyler, L. K., & Koster, C. (1993). Integrative processes in utterance resolution. *Journal of Memory and Language, 32*, 647–666.

Sanford, A. J. (1985). Aspects of pronoun interpretation: Evaluation of search formulations of inference. In G. Rickheit & H. Strohner (Eds.), *Inferences in text processing* (pp. 183–204). North-Holland: Elsevier Science Publishers.

Sanford, A. J., & Garrod, S. (1989). What, when and how? Questions of immediacy in anaphoric reference resolution. *Language and Cognitive Processes, 4,* 235–262.

Sanford, A. J., Moar, K., & Garrod, S. (1988). Proper names as controllers of discourse focus. *Language and Speech, 31,* 43–56.

Shillcock, R. (1982). The on-line resolution of pronominal anaphora. *Language and Speech, 25*(4), 385–404.

Silverstein, M. (1976). Hierarchy of features and ergativity. In R.M.W. Dixon (Ed.), *Grammatical categories in Australian languages.* NJ: Humanities Press.

Speelman, C. P., & Kirsner, K. (1990). The representation of text-based and situation-based information in discourse comprehension. *Journal of Memory and Language, 29,* 119–132.

Trabasso, T., & van den Broek, P. (1985). Causal thinking and the representation of narrative events. *Journal of Memory and Language, 24,* 612–630.

Tyler, L. K., & Marslen-Wilson, W. D. (1982). Processing utterances in discourse contexts: On-line resolution of anaphors. *Journal of Semantics, 1,* 297–315.

Vonk, W., Hustinx, L., & Simons, W. (1992). The use of referential expressions in structuring discourse. *Language and Cognitive Processes, 7,* 301–335.

15 Referential Context Effects on Syntactic Processing

Wayne S. Murray
Simon P. Liversedge
University of Dundee

Probably the longest-running debate in psycholinguistics concerns the question of whether there are contextual influences on the process of syntactic parsing. The precise nature of this question has changed somewhat over the years, but its underlying basis has remained substantially the same. It boils down to the question of whether there is a stage of sentence processing that can appropriately be described as an *autonomous syntactic parser*.

The question is central for two reasons: First, it is part of the debate concerning the overall architecture of language processing, both in terms of the modularity of language processes (Fodor, 1983) and the modularity of the various subcomponents within the language-processing system (Forster, 1979). However, perhaps more fundamentally than this, it bears on the question of whether there is, in some sense, a psychological level of representation of a sentence that can be considered to be purely syntactic. There now appears to be general acceptance of the psychological reality of grammatical structure and its role in the process of decoding the meaning of a sentence, but to say that we consider (at least some) aspects of syntactic structure in the decoding process is not the same as saying that a complete, detailed, structural representation of a sentence is *ever* derived.

SYNTACTIC PARSING

There is surprisingly little direct evidence for the psychological reality of grammatical processing per se. The results from the majority of early studies investigating the question are, at best, equivocal (see Fodor, Bever, & Garrett, 1974), and there is, in fact, very little evidence bearing on even the most fundamental aspects of the question. For example, although it is generally assumed that two clause sentences are more difficult to process than those containing a single clause (see, e.g., Holmes, Kennedy, & Murray, 1987), there appears to be only one study that ever directly tackled the question (Forster & Ryder, 1971). However, perhaps the idea that it is possible to *directly* investigate the effects of syntactic structure is ill-conceived, since there will always be a correspondence between structure and meaning, and it may well prove impossible to disentangle the effects of one from the other.[1]

The indirect evidence for the psychological reality of syntactic structure (in processing terms) derives, almost entirely, from studies that have employed so called "garden-path" sentences, where the reader's initial parsing of the sentence turns out to be incorrect and reanalysis or reassignment is required. The assumption here is that the reader has been pursuing a particular structural analysis that he or she later finds to be incorrect. Thus, the argument goes: "If the structural analysis was incorrect, it must be the case that the reader was analyzing the sentence on a structural basis" (i.e., deriving a syntactic representation of the input). However, if we find that the initial analysis that the reader applied to the input was driven by a number of factors, of which apparent syntactic form is only one, this suggests that *some* syntactic analysis is pursued, but there then seems to be no pressing reason to suggest that this extends to computing a complete, detailed, structural representation of the sentence.

The issue is whether a processor exists that computes structural relationships *and nothing else*. If there is, there will be, at some level of description, a representation of the input that is purely syntactic in form (see, e.g., the discussion by Forster, 1987, of the relation between representation and process). If we are unable to find evidence for the existence of a purely syntactic representation, then we have little reason to posit the existence of a syntactic parser. This is not the same as saying that processing is unaffected by structure. Syntactic rules may take part in a more general process that could be referred to simply as "sentence parsing" or "interpretation" (see, e.g., the proposals by Crain & Steedman, 1985; Marslen-Wilson & Tyler, 1987), but this is not syntactic parsing. If context conspires with structural factors in determining the initial analysis that will be applied to an input string, then, as these authors suggest, it may be quite inappropriate to talk about syntactic parsing itself as a process. Perhaps we will find that this is correct and that a process of interpretation derived from multiple

---

[1]A possible exception to this is in experiments by Murray (1982) using a same–different sentence-matching task. Although this task is normally sensitive to sentence meaning, with some combinations of response and stimulus configuration it is possible to find effects of structure without any effect of meaning (sentence plausibility), arguably because the fastest level of comparison of the sentences, under these circumstances, is on the basis of syntactic representations. (See also experiments by Freedman & Forster, 1985, using this task.)

sources of evidence is a good representation of what is actually happening, but the question is clearly a fundamental one. As a theoretically entity, a syntactic parser exists only in as much as we can show limitation in the influence of other factors upon its operation, since, if two processes interact with one another in a completely unconstrained manner, it can be argued that there is no theoretical basis for distinguishing between them.

TYPES OF CONTEXT

So far, we have been using the term *context* in a very general sense, but it is worth distinguishing between three broad classes of context effects. The first can be described as *lexically based*. Here we refer to the possibility that parsing decisions may be influenced by information associated with the individual lexical items in a string. For example, initial structural decisions may be influenced not only by information about the major form class of words (noun, verb, etc.), but also by subcategorization features (e.g., transitivity or ability to take a sentential complement) or even, as suggested by Ford, Bresnan, and Kaplan (1982), by the extent to which a verb "prefers" to take a particular structural role (as assessed by its frequency of occurrence in various structures). Also, structural decisions could be influenced by lexical-semantic information. For example, there may be circumstances under which a different parsing decision would be made following the occurrence of an animate noun than following an inanimate one.

The second class involves possible effects of sentence-internal semantic or pragmatic constraints on parsing decisions. By this we mean factors such as phrasal, clausal, or sentential plausibility. For example, the meaning of a previously processed part of a sentence might influence later parsing decisions by promoting a particular structural analysis which will lead to an interpretation of a portion of the sentence that is more plausible than some alternative.

Finally, in the third class, we include a variety of extrasentential context types. These cover a range from situational real-world contexts through to textual discourse context. They are based on the possibility that factors such as locally defined plausibility or expectation, or referential cohesion, may exert an effect on parsing decisions, again by promoting an analysis that is in some way semantically preferred.

Although the possibility of context effects of the first type remains controversial, their existence or otherwise is perhaps not critical for the issue of syntactic autonomy. Evidence for such effects bears on the question of the sources of evidence that may be employed by the parser in making structural decisions. But if this information is indeed stored with the individual lexical items, there is no reason to suggest that such effects need necessarily violate any principle of syntactic autonomy. Clearly, however, if parsing decisions are affected by contextual manipulations of the latter two types, this would seriously compromise the idea of an autonomous syntactic processor.

TYPES OF INTERACTION

In addition to distinguishing between types of context, it is also necessary to distinguish two types of interaction. On the one hand, a context could predispose a particular structural analysis or guide the parser along a particular path (perhaps even to the extent of that analysis not being one that is fully licensed by the available structural information). Such "strong" interaction with *contextual guidance* would certainly call into question any idea of there being a separate stage of processing devoted purely to syntactic parsing.

It was this type of context effect that was investigated in studies of the effect of "reversibility" on the processing of passives by Slobin (1966) and Herriot (1969). In Sentences (1) and (2), there is only one structural analysis licensed by the syntax. Thus, if the structural analysis of Sentence (1) is aided by semantic information, this suggests that context caused a particular analysis to be initially proposed that turned out to be correct. However, in Sentence (3), a similar initial proposal would be structurally incorrect. Thus, with a strong, contextual guidance system, both syntactic and nonsyntactic sources of information would be used to guide parsing decisions (even if, finally, analyses not licensed by the syntax were discarded).

(1) The chicken was eaten by the girl.
(2) The horse was chased by the girl.
(3) The girl was eaten by the chicken.

However, if this were the case, it would become somewhat implausible to suggest that the output of the analysis must necessarily be a fully-detailed, pure structural description of the input string. If a combination of types of information is used to compute the nature of the relationships among words in the string, then there is no compelling reason to suggest that the relationships are purely syntactic in form. However, the evidence in favor of such a contextual guidance system seems fairly unconvincing (see, e.g., Forster & Olbrei, 1973, for evidence against this interpretation of the results of Slobin and Herriot; and Forster, 1979; Garnham, 1985, for discussions of the experiment reported by Steedman & Johnson-Laird, 1978). Even the classic experiment by the prime proponents of such a "strong" interactive model (Tyler & Marslen-Wilson, 1977) can more readily be interpreted in terms of the second type of interaction.

This is often referred to as "weak" interaction and can be characterized as a *contextual adjudication* or *disposal* system. Here the interaction results from the use of contextual information to decide between two (or more) alternative structural analyses of an input string. As a result of either local or global structural ambiguity, both potential analyses are licensed by the syntax, and context is used to adjudicate between them. For example, in Tyler and Marslen-Wilson's famous example (4), "landing planes" is structurally ambiguous, but, it is argued, the preceding context causes the selection of the verbal form (the act of landing planes) rather than the nominal (planes that are landing).

(4) If you have been trained as a pilot, landing planes . . .

Although there are alternative interpretations of the results of Tyler and Marslen-Wilson (see, e.g., Cowart, 1981; Forster, 1979), it appears to be the question of the existence of this type of interaction, involving contextual adjudication, that remains at issue today.[2] In a nutshell, the question is: Can context ever influence the initial structural analysis of an input string?

It is, however, a deceptively simple question. Even if we agree to limit use of the word *context* to influences of the latter two types, there is an additional problem that arises with the word *ever*. The question is not whether all contexts influence syntactic processing (since it seems obvious that it will always be possible to find ineffective contexts even with a system that would normally make use of such information), but whether it is possible for at least some contexts, perhaps even only under certain highly constrained conditions, to influence the syntactic analysis.

But perhaps the thorniest problem of all comes with the suggestion that the effect must be on the *initial* structural analysis. That is, evidence against this suggestion would need to show that there is a point during the initial structural analysis at which the context had the potential to influence the analysis, but that, nevertheless, a structural choice was made that was uninfluenced by context, regardless of whether the context eventually influenced the finally chosen analysis of the sentence. For example, as has been frequently pointed out, it is not sufficient to show that the eventual analyses of Sentences (5) and (6) differ, with a preference for the attachment of the final prepositional phrase (PP) in Sentence (5) to the verb (as the instrument) and in Sentence (6) to the noun phrase ([NP] as a modifier).

(5) The cop shot the man with the pistol.

(6) The cop shot the man with the banana.

---

[2]Proponents of interactive constraint-satisfaction models of processing (e.g., MacDonald, in press; McClelland, St. John, & Taraban, 1989; Spivey-Knowlton, Trueswell, & Tanenhaus, 1993) might wish to argue that the distinction between *guidance* and *adjudication* models is a spurious one when input from all sources may be simultaneously affecting the level of activation of alternative analyses. However, even under these circumstances, the distinction can still be made on the basis of whether alternatives that are not licensed by the syntax ever receive a higher level of activation than those that are.

What needs to be shown is that the initial proposed attachment of the PP differs. Also, of course, if a syntactic parser proposed alternative analyses in parallel, and some higher level process eventually decided between them, this would not violate principles of autonomy.

SOURCES OF EVIDENCE

As mentioned, the primary source of evidence for the application of a particular structural analysis has been to show instances where the reader is "garden pathed." That is, cases where an incorrect analysis was initially pursued and, when later found to be incorrect, reanalysis was performed, with an associated processing cost. But, of course, increases in apparent processing load at points in a sentence need not necessarily be associated with initial misanalysis. They could arise from differences in structural complexity (see, e.g., the debate between Frazier & Rayner and Kennedy & Murray on apparent "garden pathing" in reduced-complement structures: Frazier & Rayner, 1982; Holmes et al., 1987; Kennedy, Murray, Jennings, & Reid, 1989; Rayner & Frazier, 1987), differences in processing strategies (e.g., the reader pursuing parallel, rather than a single-preferred, analysis of an ambiguous segment), or effects of meaning. For example, if (6) were found to be more difficult to process than (5) this may be due to garden pathing in (6), with the initial verb phrase (VP) attachment of the PP requiring revision. Alternatively, perhaps revision never occurred, and the effect was a consequence of the semantic implausibility of the use of a banana as a weapon.

Although this last interpretation is still consistent with readers having pursued a structurally preferred analysis, it does point up a potential complication arising with the use of semantic disambiguation (i.e., that it is never clear whether the effects arise from semantic or syntactic processes, or at exactly what points effects of both types might be found). In addition, there are two other considerations that suggest that the use of PP attachment ambiguities may not be optimal in the study of context effects. First, it is not entirely clear that there is, in fact, a clear bias (in the absence of context) for one attachment over the other (e.g., Taraban & McClelland, 1988). Second, the Minimal-Attachment (Frazier, 1978; Frazier & Fodor, 1978) proposal for a bias in favor of the VP attachment rests critically on a detail of the structural description (which, in some formalisms, would show no complexity difference between the two attachments).

To provide a clear test of possible contextual influences on syntactic analysis, it is preferable to use a structure: (a) that, on anybody's analysis, will be expected (without context) to provide clear garden pathing at a well-defined point in the sentence; (b) where the disambiguation is syntactic and unequivocal; (c) where no meaning artifacts could potentially influence the results (i.e., it must be clear that differences between the garden-path items and comparison controls cannot be attributed to semantic effects such as differences in plausibility); and (d) where we can be sure that the context employed is one that would, on independent grounds, be of the right type and strong enough to potentially influence the syntactic analysis.

One structure that appears to fulfill the first three requirements is the now infamous reduced relative. Considering examples such as Sentences (7) and (8), it is clear that readers have considerable difficulty with them, and that this would be predicted by any parsing theory that suggests that readers pursue a single preferred analysis. Regardless of whether this comes about as a result of the application of Minimal Attachment, the Canonical Sentoid Strategy (Fodor, Bever, & Garrett, 1974), or any other processing heuristic, it seems clear that minor modifications to the grammar will not affect the predictions made.

(7) The boat sailed on the pond sank.

(8) The man dressed as a woman looked ridiculous.

Further, the point of disambiguation is clearly and unequivocally signalled structurally by the occurrence of the second verb. Finally, it is possible to compare the processing of these items to controls with identical meaning and structure—the unambiguous, unreduced forms, such as (9) and (10).

(9) The boat that was sailed on the pond sank.

(10) The man who was dressed as a woman looked ridiculous.

(11) The woman shown the photograph recognized her uncle.

It is also possible to make a comparison with unambiguous forms, such as Sentence (11), where the correct structure is signaled by the form of the first verb. But clear conclusions may not be so easy to draw in this case because there is some change of meaning with a lexical substitution and the possibility of other confounds. For example, it assumes that verb subcategorization information is immediately available and serves to clearly disambiguate the structure. As mentioned, this is a controversial issue, and there is at least some evidence that argues against the suggestion (e.g., Mitchell, 1989).

If we now consider studies that have looked for effects of sentence-internal semantic or pragmatic cues on the resolution of this form of ambiguity, the conclusions seem fairly clear, although perhaps not totally unequivocal. Rayner, Carlson, and Frazier (1983) showed that sentences containing a pragmatic cue to the correct structure, such as Sentence (12), showed just as much evidence of garden pathing as those containing a misleading cue, such as Sentence (13).

(12) The actress sent the flowers was very pleased.

(13) The florist sent the flowers was very pleased.

Murray and Liversedge (1991) verified this conclusion in an eye-movement study that, arguably, employed stronger semantic and pragmatic cues, and that compared the processing of both of these reduced forms to their unambiguous, unreduced counterparts. One complication, however, is the suggestion that such constraints may not be strong enough to affect parsing in these items, because the relevant information frequently comes only toward the end of the ambiguous VP. Although in our study we did attempt to avoid this by employing as many pragmatically or semantically constrained initial NP–Verb combinations as possible, use of this information could possibly still have been delayed until after an initial incorrect assignment had been made (although we found no evidence of such effects during the processing of the ambiguous VP). Thus, these results may fall foul of the fourth requirement listed—the ability to show, on independent grounds, that the context has the potential to influence the syntactic analysis before decisions are made. In addition, there are conflicting results from experiments by Ferreira and Clifton (1986), Trueswell, Tanenhaus, and Garnsey (in press), Tabossi, Spivey-Knowlton, McRae, and Tanenhaus (in press), and MacDonald (in press) examining the effects of semantic factors on the processing of reduced-relative ambiguities,[3] But, as we argue later, these may critically depend on the particular form of the ambiguity that was used in those experiments.

REFERENTIAL CONTEXT

Consider now sentence-external contexts; there has been much discussion in recent years of the possibility of discourse context influencing parsing. Although the question has broadened a little recently, it has its roots in the suggestion that referential context may bias parsing decisions involving structures that could be analyzed as containing a complex (restrictively modified) NP. As argued by Crain (1980), Crain and Steedman (1985), and Altmann and Steedman (1988), a complex NP containing a modifier carries with it the presupposition that there is a set of entities to which the noun could refer, and that the modifier in some way restricts this set. Thus, for example, in Sentence (12), the authors would argue that the presupposition is that there are a number of actresses to whom the sentence may be referring, but that the reference is restricted to only the one who was sent the flowers.

On the basis of a principle of parsimony (that the reader will prefer an analysis containing the smallest number of unsatisfied presuppositions), Altmann and Steedman argued that parsing decisions will be affected by what they refer to as a Principle of Referential Support: An NP analysis that is referentially supported (one that has all its referential presuppositions supported by the context) will be favored over one that is not. For example, if a preceding context contained

---

[3]Although it is sometimes arguable in these studies whether the semantic manipulation is of the first type (lexically based) or one of sentence-internal pragmatics.

reference to two entities to which an NP could refer, the theory predicts that, given a choice between a simple NP analysis and one involving an NP modifying expression, the parser will be biased toward the latter. Conversely, if there was only one (or perhaps no) entity in the preceding context to which the NP could refer, the bias would be toward a simple NP analysis. For example, if the preceding context contained reference to more than one actress, the simple NP analysis of the initial portion of Sentence (12) would be rejected in favor of the (correct) complex reduced-relative interpretation; whereas, if there was no prior reference to more than one actress, the reader would be expected to initially mis-parse the item as a simple direct object.

Although there has been considerable debate over the conclusions to be drawn from studies that have manipulated this type of context (see, e.g., Altmann, Garnham, & Dennis, 1992; Clifton & Ferreira, 1989; Mitchell & Corley, in press; Mitchell, Corley, & Garnham, 1992; Spivey-Knowlton, Trueswell, & Tanenhaus, 1993, it nevertheless appears to be one of the best contenders for a potential effect of context on syntactic parsing. Most strongly in its favor is the fact that, unlike sentence-internal pragmatics, with referential context, there can be little argument concerning whether the potential bias existed before process-ing decisions were made. Also, it is clear that the strength of such biases should be relatively easy to assess.

If the "Incremental Interactive" theory proposed by Altmann and Steedman is correct, it should be the case that when a reader encounters a definite NP that could refer to more than one specific entity in a preceding context, they will anticipate that it should be followed by an appropriate NP modifier, such as a relative clause. Therefore, if subjects are given a context of this type to read, followed by a sentence fragment beginning with such an NP, and asked to complete the sentence, it would be expected that they should, with high proba-bility, begin the completion with an NP-modifying expression. This prediction was tested in the first experiment.

EXPERIMENT 1

Method

Twenty-four subjects were asked to read a number of short passages and to complete the final sentence in each. Each passage consisted of two sentences, which formed the context, and the beginning of a third sentence. They were told that their task was to read each passage and then write out a completed version of the last sentence, adding at least six words.

Following two practice items, they were given 72 passages to complete. Of these, 36 were experimental items, and the remainder were fillers of varying construction. In all cases, the third sentence of the passage began with a definite NP bearing some anaphoric relationship to the two preceding context sentences.

TABLE 15.1
Examples of Contexts Used for the Sentence-Completion Task in Experiment 1

Context	Example
Double	
	The restaurant was deserted apart from the two people who were about to order their meals. One was a woman who ordered beer with her meal and the other was a woman who ordered wine. The woman. . . .
Single	
	The restaurant was deserted apart from the two people who were about to order their meals. One was a man who ordered beer with his meal and the other was a woman who ordered wine. The woman. . . .

Each of the experimental items was constructed in two forms. In one, the preceding context contained two potential referents for the following NP; in the other, the structure of the context was maintained, but it contained only one potential referent, as can be seen in Table 15.1. On half of the occasions where a context contained only one potential referent, this was the first mentioned of the two individuals. In the other half, the relevant individual was mentioned second. For each subject, half of the experimental items contained a single referent, while the other half contained two referents. A counterbalanced design was used such that half of the 24 subjects saw each item in one condition, while the other half saw it in the other condition.

Results and Discussion

When subjects' completions were classified in terms of whether or not they contained an NP-modifying expression, the results were clearly in the direction predicted by referential theory. Following "single" contexts, only 9.0% of the completions contained NP modifiers; following "double" contexts, this figure rose to 85.6%. Not only is the difference highly significant [$F1$ (1,22) = 270.90, $p < .001$; $F2$ (1,34) = 770.44, $p < .001$], but it follows the predictions of the theory very closely indeed. Modifiers were seldom produced when not required, and nearly always produced when there was a referential ambiguity. Also, not surprisingly, 92.1% of the modifiers produced were relative clauses (with 15.8% of these being reduced relatives).

Thus, these results clearly indicate that subjects will expect sentences beginning with a definite NP to continue with an NP-modifying expression, most probably a relative clause, if that NP could refer to either of two entities in a preceding context. However, they will not anticipate a modifying expression if there is only one potential referent for the NP in the preceding context.

It therefore appears that contexts of this sort are capable of setting up precisely the type of structural expectation that Altmann and Steedman predicted. This result not only supports their arguments concerning referential support, but clearly demonstrates that this is a context type strong enough to have the potential to affect parsing decisions. In addition, it appears that the type of modifying expression most likely to be expected is a relative clause.

EXPERIMENT 2

To test whether this type of context does have an on-line effect on syntactic parsing strategies, we conducted a study that employed exactly the contexts used in Experiment 1, but in which we monitored subjects' eye movements while they read a following experimental item. These items were, as shown in Table 15.2, of three different forms:

1. A reduced-relative clause construction where the first VP was locally ambiguous between a relative clause and a direct object.

TABLE 15.2
Examples of Contexts and Experimental Items Used in Experiment 2

Context	Example
Double Context	
	After the auditions two people had been chosen to perform in a local village pantomime.
	One was a man who was playing the prince and the other was a man who was playing an old witch.
Single Context	
	After the auditions two people had been chosen to perform in a local village pantomime.
	One was a woman who was playing the prince and the other was a man who was playing an old witch.

Experimental Item	Example
1. Reduced Relative	1 3 4
	The man | dressed as a woman | looked quite ridiculous.
2. Unreduced Relative	1 2 3 4
	The man | who was | dressed as a woman | looked quite ridiculous.
3. Direct Object	1 3 4
	The man | dressed as a woman | and | looked quite ridiculous.

Note. Sentence analysis zones are numbered and marked by vertical lines.

2. An unambiguous, unreduced, relative clause form of this item, to provide a baseline control.

3. A locally ambiguous version, identical with Item 1, up until the end of the initial VP, but where the final resolution of the structure is as a direct object.

The prediction, of course, is that if referential context is effective in influencing parsing decisions, the classic garden-path effect found with these reduced-relative clause constructions should be eliminated following an appropriate context containing two potential referents, since referential theory predicts that a complex NP analysis will be preferred under these circumstances. At the very least, the context should increase the probability of the reader pursuing the correct analysis, and reduce the average size of the garden-path effect. Thus, compared with baseline processing time in the unambiguous, unreduced relatives, where no garden pathing would be anticipated, there should at least be evidence for a smaller garden-path effect in the reduced relatives that follow a "double" context than those that follow a "single" context.

Further, the theory predicts what might be called a "reverse garden-path effect" where, following a context containing two potential referents, subjects should be garden pathed in the items that end up being resolved as the simpler direct-object structure. However, this would not be expected when such an item follows a context containing a single referent. The inclusion of this condition not only provides a situation in which an opposing garden-path effect would be predicted, and therefore provides the basis for a stronger test of contextual influences on garden pathing in reduced relatives, but also a condition in which both the theory and the results of our completion study predict that garden pathing should occur with the simpler of the two possible structures.

Method

Thirty-six experimental item triples, of the type shown in Table 15.2, were constructed. Each of the triples could complete a discourse that began with the two sentences in one of the base contexts. In each triple, one version of the item was a reduced relative clause construction containing a locally ambiguous VP of between three and five words in length, one was the unreduced relative clause form of this item, and the third was a direct-object construction, identical to the unreduced relative except that it was disambiguated as a direct object by the inclusion of a conjunction immediately preceding the second verb.

Following six practice items, each of the 24 subjects tested saw 36 experimental items mixed in with 36 fillers of varying structure. Preceding each filler and each experimental item, there were two context sentences. These were identical with the contexts used in the first experiment. In half of the items, the individual referred to in the experimental sentence was mentioned first in the context and in the other half was the second-mentioned. On a proportion of the trials, a question requiring a yes/no answer followed the third sentence of the set. This question referred to either the context or the target sentence, and was included to ensure that subjects were paying attention to the meaning of both the contexts and the targets. Similarly to the first experiment, a counterbalanced design was used, with the 36 experimental items assigned evenly to each of the six experimental conditions (three item types in each of two contexts), with no subject seeing more than one version of the same base item and with each item occurring in all conditions over the set of six item files.

Four subjects were tested on each of the six experimental files. Their head movement was constrained by the use of a dental composition bite bar and chin rest, and their eye movements were monitored using a conventional infrared limbus-tracking device mounted on spectacle frames. The subject's horizontal line of regard was sampled every 10 ms, and the data were stored for off-line analysis. Calibration of the equipment was carried out immediately preceding each second discourse (every six sentences). The calibration and clustering algorithm used to detect fixations employed statistical procedures to maximize resolution for each subject, and average resolution was to better than one character position. Each of the context and experimental sentences was presented singly on one line of a high-resolution display. Eye movements were recorded throughout, but analysis was performed only on the eye movements made while subjects read the target sentences.

Results and Discussion

Subjects were clearly paying close attention to the meaning of both context and target sentences. The average correct response rate to the comprehension questions was 90.3%, and no subject answered fewer than 75% correctly. There were no significant differences in comprehension question accuracy among the three target sentence types.

For the eye-movement analysis, experimental items were divided into four zones, as indicated in Table 15.2. The first zone was the initial NP; the second zone, which occurred only in the unreduced relatives, was comprised of the relative pronouns; the third zone was the following VP (locally ambiguous in the reduced-relative and direct-object items); and the fourth zone was the disambiguating region at the end of the sentence, beginning with the second verb. In the case of the direct-object items, fixations falling on the conjunction were analyzed separately, but this was not considered to be the beginning of the fourth zone in these items as it is only the combination of this word with the following verb that provides complete disambiguation.

In the discussion of the results, we focus primarily on what have been referred to as first-pass eye movements. It is generally supposed that these provide the most sensitive index available of the consequences of initial parsing decisions.

TABLE 15.3
Experiment 2: First-Pass Reading Time per Word (ms) in Zone 1

Context	Unreduced	Reduced	Direct Object	Mean
Single	194	187	182	188
Double	176	172	182	177
Mean	185	180	182	

Eye-movement measures have the potential to provide, under relatively normal reading conditions, very detailed information about exactly when a process occurs. Where a parse has gone wrong, it is expected that this will be reflected in the first-pass inspection of parts of the sentence that contain information indicating the error. More generally, it is suggested that longer first-pass reading times in particular regions of a sentence can be taken to indicate a heavier processing load in that region.

We then consider second-pass reading times and patterns of reinspection. These measures appear to be sensitive to whether a mis-parsing has occurred and, if it has, the time and difficulty involved in reconstructing the parse.

As can be seen in Table 15.3, somewhat surprisingly, there was evidence of an effect on first-pass reading time found in Zone 1—the initial NP. Subjects tended to spend more time reading this zone when it was preceded by a single context than when preceded by a double [$F1$ $(1,18) = 3.45, p = 1.07, F2$ $(1,30) = 5.15, p < .05$]. Our only interpretation of this result is in terms of a priming or recency effect as a consequence of the more frequent repetition of the NP in the double context. No other main effects or interactions approached significance in Zone 1. The 11 ms per word size of this main effect of context carried over into Zone 2— the relative pronouns—but was far from significant in this region (single: 164 ms/word; double: 153 ms/word[4]). Although the precise interpretation of this effect may be uncertain, it at least provides a clear indication of subjects' sensitivity to the context during processing in the early part of the sentence.

By Zone 3—the locally ambiguous VP—differences in processing time between items following single and double contexts have disappeared ($F1$ & $F2 < 1$). However, as can be seen from the results in Table 15.4, sentence-structure effects are clearly present, with longer reading times in the unreduced relatives

---

[4]These mean times include calculation of the small number of case's where the relative pronouns were never directly fixated (and were presumably processed parafoveally) as 0 ms. Treating these cases instead as missing data results in a 13-ms mean difference, which is again not significant in either the subject or item analysis. In all other zones, lack of first-pass fixation was rare (only one case occurred in the critical Zones 3 and 4), and treatment as missing data results in a change of no more than 2 ms in the size of any main effect or interaction, and no change at all in the significance or otherwise of any of the results.

TABLE 15.4
Experiment 2: First-Pass Reading Time per Word (ms) in Zone 3

Context	Unreduced	Reduced	Direct Object	Mean
Single	238	210	197	215
Double	223	213	210	215
Mean	231	212	203	

$[F1 \ (2,36) = 6.81, p < .005; F2 \ (2,60) = 4.89, p = .01]$. This could, as MacDonald (in press) suggested with a similar type of effect, be due to greater syntactic processing complexity in the unreduced relatives. Alternatively, it could reflect referential work being performed in these items at this point; or, indeed, it could be a combination of the two. The only indication of the most plausible interpretation of the effect is that, although there was no significant interaction between sentence type and context $[F1 \ (2,36) = 1.34, p > .2; F2 \ (2,60) = 0.69$, ns] and no significant main effect of context in the unreduced relatives alone, the direction of the reading-time difference in these items is at least consistent with the suggestion that some part of the effect may be due to referential work, with a tendency toward longer times in the single condition where a modifying expression was unnecessary. The apparent small difference between reduced-relative and direct-object items in this zone is far from significant $[F1 \ (1,18) = 1.43, p > .2; F2 \ (1,30) = 0.61$, ns].

However it is Zone 4—the disambiguating region—in which we would expect to find clear indications of garden-path effects and any influence of referential context upon them. We have shown previously (Murray & Liversedge, 1991) that garden-path effects can be found on first fixation durations in this region; and, as the results in Table 15.5 show, this is indeed the case here. First fixation durations in this zone were longer in reduced-relative items than in either of the other two structures $[F1 \ (2,36) = 3.74, p < .05; F2 \ (2,60) = 3.09, p = .05]$—a clear early indication of garden pathing in this structure. However, no effects of context type were found. There was no main effect of context $[F1 \ (1,18) = 0.56$, ns; $F2 \ (1,30) = 1.04, p > .3]$, and no indication of any interaction between context and sentence structure $(F1 \ \& \ F2 < 1)$. A comparison between first

TABLE 15.5
Experiment 2: First-Fixation Duration (ms) in Zone 4

Context	Unreduced	Reduced	Direct Object	Mean
Single	256	280	271	269
Double	259	279	256	265
Mean	258	279	264	

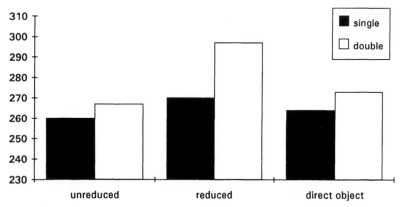

FIG. 15.1. Experiment 2: First-pass reading time per word (ms) in Zone 4 (the disambiguating region).

fixation durations in just the reduced and unreduced relatives shows this even more clearly. There were significantly longer first fixation durations in reduced than in unreduced relatives [$F1$ (1,18) = 7.53, $p < .02$; $F2$ (1,30) = 6.63, $p < .02$], but no main effect of context and no hint of an interaction (all Fs < 1). In the relative clause items, the words surrounding the location of the first fixation are identical, whereas in the direct objects it is preceded by a different short high-frequency word (the conjunction) and, although there was no context effect on gaze duration on the conjunction (single: 124 ms; double: 126 ms; $F1$ & $F2$ < 1), it seems likely that the initial processing in Zone 4, of direct objects, could be influenced by parafoveal preview during the inspection of this word.

Figure 15.1 shows first-pass reading times over the zone as a whole. It is apparent that the garden pathing in reduced relatives continues throughout the region, with, if anything, a context effect that goes in the opposite direction to that predicted by the Incremental Interactive theory. Reading times tended to be longer in reduced relatives following double contexts. However, the main effect of context over the region was not statistically reliable [$F1$ (1,18) = 3.77, $p = .07$; $F2$ (1,30) = 1.84, $p = .18$], and there was no significant difference in the size of the context effect for any of the three structures [$F1$ & $F2$ < 1].

If we just consider the contrast between reduced and unreduced relatives, the same story emerges. Reduced relatives show longer first-pass times than unreduced [$F1$ (1,18) = 4.96, $p < .05$; $F2$ (1,30) = 3.62, $p = .06$]. There is a marginal main effect of context [$F1$ (1,18) = 4.56, $p < .05$; $F2$ (1,30) = 2.46, $p = .12$], but no significant interaction between structure and context [$F1$ (1,18) = 1.20, $p > 0.2$; $F2$ (1,30) = 0.86, ns]. A comparison between the two locally ambiguous structures that were predicted to be oppositely affected by the context manipulation (reduced relatives and direct objects) completes the picture. As is apparent from Fig. 15.1, direct objects behave similarly to unreduced relatives, with no indication of any garden pathing having occurred. There is a significant main effect of sentence type with longer first-pass reading times in reduced relatives than in direct objects [$F1$ (1,18) = 5.72, $p < .05$; $F2$ (1,30) = 6.46, $p < .05$], but no main effect of context [$F1$ (1,18) = 0.50, ns; $F2$ (1,30) = 1.22, $p > .2$] and no interaction between sentence type and context [$F1$ & $F2 < 1$], which in any case goes marginally in the opposite direction to that predicted by the theory.

The conclusions to be drawn from the first-pass measures are clear. Main effects of context type are found early in the sentences. There are also indications of context effects later on, but in no case is there any indication of a significant interaction between context type and sentence structure, as predicted by the theory and shown in our results from Experiment 1. In fact, the trends that do exist show a tendency toward going in the opposite direction.

What then of second-pass measures? There may be considerable controversy about whether context influences initial parsing decisions, but it is fairly widely agreed that it will exert some influence on reanalysis procedures when the initial processing has gone wrong. However, this certainly has not been a consistent feature of all results. In at least one experiment examining the effects of pragmatic cues on parsing, we found influences of context on processing *strategies,* but failed to find any overall advantage of a "supporting" context (Murray & Liversedge, 1991). The same appears to be true here. As can be seen from the second-pass reading times shown in Fig. 15.2, there is again a clear indication of the

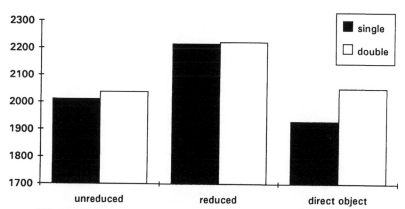

FIG. 15.2. Experiment 2: Total second-pass reading time (ms) for the three sentence types following single and double contexts.

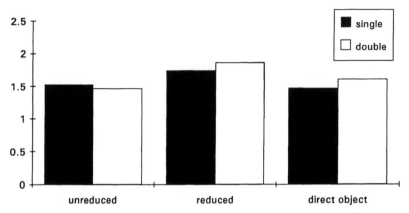

FIG. 15.3. Experiment 2: Number of regressive saccades made from Zone 4 (the disambiguating region) to earlier regions of the sentence.

difficulty of processing reduced relatives, with a main effect of sentence type significant by subjects [$F1$ (2,36) = 4.45, $p < .02$; $F2$ (2,60) = 2.20, $p = .12$], but no interaction between sentence type and context [$F1$ & $F2 < 1$] and with the only hint of a context effect for direct-object items. This difference is not significant [$F1$ (1,18) = 1.07, $p > .3$; $F2$ (1,30) = 2.67, $p > .1$], but would appear, if anything, to be related to the problems readers may face in integrating the meaning of this structure with the preceding context *after having processed it.* That is, a difficulty sometimes found when attempting to integrate the meaning of a simple direct-object sentence containing reference to one, unspecified, NP, when there are two potential referents for it in the preceding context.

Analysis of the total number of regressive saccades made from the disambiguating region in each item, as shown in Fig. 15.3, shows a similar pattern of effects. There were more saccades out of the region in reduced-relative items [$F1$ (2,36) = 10.26, $p < .001$; $F2$ (2,60) = 11.70, $p < .001$], but no significant main effect of context [$F1$ (1,18) = 1.73, $p > .2$; $F2$ (1,30) = 2.57, $p > .1$] and no interaction between sentence type and context [$F1$ (2,36) = 1.47, $p > .2$; $F2$ (2,60) = 0.89, ns]. Again, the largest apparent context effect is in direct-object items, but this fails to achieve statistical significance [$F1$ (1,18) = 2.00, $p > .1$; $F2$ (1,30) = 2.68, $p > .1$].

Focusing just on the class of regressions most likely to be associated with mending an incorrect parse—those from the final region into the locally ambiguous VP—the results are clear. As can be seen from Fig. 15.4, there is garden pathing in the reduced relatives only [$F1$ (2,36) = 26.53, $p < .001$; $F2$ (2,60) = 33.34, $p < .001$], no significant main effect of context [$F1$ (1,18) = 1.94, $p > .1$; $F2$ (1,30) = 3.84, $p > .05$], and no hint of an interaction between sentence structure and context [$F1$ & $F2 < 1$].

Regressions from Zone 4 to Zone 3

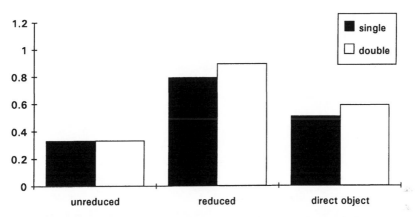

FIG. 15.4. Experiment 2: Number of regressive saccades made from Zone 4 (the disambiguating region) to Zone 3 (the ambiguous VP).

Should we therefore conclude that referential context is ineffective in influencing all syntactic processing? Clearly not. The effects shown in the production task were huge and exactly as predicted by referential theory. Of course, this also shows that the contexts we used were effective in influencing subjects' expectations concerning the way that the following item should continue. Hence, the lack of effects in the reading study clearly cannot be attributed to the use of poor contexts. However, effects of context were not entirely lacking in this study either. Main effects of context were found, showing that they had been effectively processed by the subjects. What is lacking is any indication that they influenced parsing decisions.

On the face of it, this seems fairly compelling evidence against the suggestion that referential context plays a part in initial on-line parsing decisions. But before resting with this conclusion, we need to examine two alternative explanations of the results. The first is based on the suggestion that the completion study results may not truly reflect the type of processing bias that we have assumed. If subjects expect the initial NP to be followed by a *subject relative*, then this cannot be reduced and it would therefore not be surprising if the bias were not shown when subjects processed the reduced forms in this experiment. However, the evidence is against this suggestion. Although a large number of irreducible relatives were produced in Experiment 1 (we believe largely due to subjects' repetition of the form of the modifiers used in the preceding context), if just reducible relatives are considered, a clear bias still exists, with continuations of this type occurring 2.4% of the time after single contexts and 24.7% of the time after double contexts.

The second alternative is, as suggested by Altmann (1987), that effects of referential context may be blocked by the need for the subject to perform inferencing in order to make the connection between the NP modifier and an entity in the preceding context. For example, the subject would need to work out, in the item in Table 15.2, that "the man dressed as a woman" is the one who was "playing an old witch," or that "the manager who owned a fax machine" was the one "who was faxed a message." In no case in this experiment did we use the same verb in the context and in the target sentence, so some inferencing would always be required. However, our reason for this was because of a fear of possible repetition effects contaminating the results. In a subsequent experiment (Liversedge & Murray, 1993), we used items with explicit repetition of the form of the relative clause and of the verb used, and with minimal inferencing required. However, the results from this experiment also provide no evidence for the predicted effect of referential context. What they do show is an apparent effect of a type of priming. This includes aspects of syntactic priming (e.g., Bock, 1986; Frazier, Taft, Roeper, Clifton, & Ehrlich, 1984) together with effects tied to the precise form of and entities referred to in the relative clause. There is other evidence for effects of syntactic repetition priming on processing (M. Pickering, personal communication, September, 1993), and it is interesting to speculate to what extent those studies that have apparently shown effects of referential context on processing may have been influenced by such a process. For example, in the study reported in Altmann (1987), the "inferencing" condition, which showed no effect, did not involve repetition, whereas in the "minimal-inferencing" condition, where effects were found, there was explicit repetition of phrases of up to five words in length.

Thus, it appears that neither of these explanations can account for the results. In this experiment we have shown that the contexts are capable of producing suitable effects; that they do influence some aspects of first-pass reading time; but, at the same time, that they do not in any way influence the magnitude of garden-path effects in these items. However, before resting with this conclusion, we should consider at least one possible alternative interpretation.

A Constraint-Satisfaction Interpretation

Proponents of "constraint-satisfaction" approaches to parsing (e.g., MacDonald, in press; McClelland, St. John and Taraban, 1989; Spivey-Knowlton et al., 1993; Tabossi, Spivey-Knowlton, McRae, & Tanenhaus, in press; Trueswell, Tanenhaus, & Garnsay, in press) have placed great emphasis on the effects on parsing of information potentially carried by the verb. They suggest that the level of activation of alternative structural interpretations of the input string will depend on, among other things, how likely, a priori, it is that the particular verb form will enter into structures of the various possible types. They also reported results that correlate the apparent size of garden-path effects with this a priori probability, as assessed by completion studies, rating studies, or analyses of corpora. (See also MacDonald, Pearlmutter, & Seidenberg, chapter 6, this volume; Sedivy & Spivey-Knowlton, chapter 16, this volume; Trueswell & Tanenhaus, chapter 7, this volume; Spivey-Knowlton & Tanenhaus, chapter 17, this volume). Further, they suggest that there will be an interaction between the effects of context and the "availability" of alternative structural analyses. Context effects will be apparent when the level of activation of the appropriate structural alternative is high enough, but will be reduced in size as its level of activation drops—until a point where even a strong contextual manipulation will exert no effect if the availability of the appropriate structural analysis is sufficiently low. For example, Trueswell et al. (1993) suggested that the contextual manipulation used by Ferreira and Clifton (1986) was ineffective because there were aspects of the particular items used in that study that made the reduced-relative analysis so unavailable that it could not be affected by context, but that this context manipulation is effective under conditions where the availability of the relative clause analysis is maintained.

Following this line of argument, it could be suggested that whatever biases were present when the initial NP of our experimental items was read, these were effectively "killed off" when the verb was processed because of an extremely low a priori probability of it occurring in a relative clause in that form. That is, the initial biases (of better than 80%), that existed when the NP was processed, were ineffective in the light of evidence obtained when the verb was identified and information accessed about its "structural preferences."

Although it must be admitted that such an interpretation is at least possible, we are unconvinced by it for a number of reasons. First, it would suggest that activation levels of alternative structural descriptions went from being very strongly biased in a particular direction on one word to being irretrievably low only one word later—so low, in fact, that this alternative interpretation must have been completely unavailable at the point when its level of activation should once again have been boosted by the occurrence of the second verb. It seems unclear why a structural alternative should become irretrievable, based on a summation of conflicting probabilistic information, unless, of course, it is suggested that constraints imposed by probabilistic information carried by the verb are many orders of magnitude stronger than any other. It may prove possible to construct an interactive-activation type model of this type, in which the activation levels of the alternatives flip–flop word by word in such a manner, but our suspicion is that it will prove considerably more difficult than the proponents of this approach may wish to imply. Activation levels would need to be driven so low that large differences that existed at the initial NP became effectively zero. If there was any continuing difference, it would be expected to influence the magnitude of the garden-path effect when the subject encountered the disambiguating information in Zone 4.

Further, implicit in this suggestion is the implication that such structures are so unlikely or so unnatural that a parser would obviously wish to "kill this off" as a structural alternative (despite, it seems, no obvious cost associated with a continuing lower level of activation of alternative structural descriptions). However, this is by no means a necessary conclusion with this structure. Consider the example shown in Table 15.2 or the following.

(14) The woman sent the letter was amazed at what she read.

(15) The man poured the beer drank it quickly.

It also appears that there must be no processing load associated with either the killing off or maintenance of alternative structural options. If there were, we would expect to have seen evidence of this in Zone 3, with differences in load when the alternative analysis was initially highly favored compared with the case where it was already at a very low level of activation (following a single context). However, if there is no cost associated with changing the level of activation of alternative structural descriptions, it is difficult to see why such a system would be unable to maintain one initially highly favored structural alternative at a level somewhat above "oblivion."

However, the detailed parameters of such constraint-satisfaction parsers are rather underspecified at present and, with the use of an appropriate number of parameters, it may be possible to model such a pattern of results within an interactive-activation framework. Therefore arguments based on apparent plausibility can be no more than that. However, using the methodologies already employed, a more direct test of the proposal can be undertaken. If information carried by the verb reduces the availability of the reduced-relative structural interpretation to a level so low that it cannot possibly influence later processing, we would expect a completion study that included the verb to show absolutely no effects.

EXPERIMENT 3

Method

The items and procedure used were identical with those employed in Experiment 1, except that the third sentence fragment in each item began with the initial NP and verb used in Experiment 2. Twenty-four subjects, who had not taken part in either Experiment 1 or Experiment 2, were tested.

Results and Discussion

Subjects' completions were again classified in terms of whether or not they contained a NP-modifying expression. Not surprisingly, in this case, all NP modifiers produced were reduced-relative clause constructions. Also not surprisingly, the proportion of modifier completions dropped dramatically between

Experiment 1 and this experiment, but the addition of the verb did not give rise to a complete obliteration of the effect. Following double contexts, subjects produced relative clauses on 10.0% of occasions. Following single contexts, this occurred only 4.2% of the time. The difference is highly reliable [$F1$ (1,22) = 6.13, $p < .02$; $F2$ (1,34) = 9.09, $p < .005$].

The availability of the reduced-relative structural interpretation, as assessed by subjects' sentence-fragment completions, certainly appears to decrease following the processing of the verb, but by no means is it completely unavailable. If it were, we would expect completion rates very much closer to zero and, more importantly, no evidence of modulation of its availability by context. It obviously follows that something which is unavailable cannot be modulated in terms of its availability.

Is it still possible then to save the constraint-satisfaction interpretation of the results of Experiment 2? Well, perhaps, if it is suggested that subjects' completions are not necessarily a good indicator of processing availability. This is a view with which we have some sympathy. For example, had the results of Experiment 3 shown absolutely no reduced-relative completions at all, we would have been tempted to argue that this does not necessarily represent complete unavailability—it simply shows no preference for producing this, as a first alternative, in a production task. In fact, the extent to which production data, especially when it involves off-line "considered" completions, can be used to assess processing availabilities is more than a little open to question. It may provide some useful indications, but great caution should be exercised both in terms of the methodologies employed and the implied equivalence between processes of production and perception.

Nevertheless, short of suggesting that this type of completion data is completely useless for assessing structural availabilities, it appears to be very difficult to argue that the alternative of a reduced relative was completely unavailable after the verb had been processed. This leaves only the possibility that it was still available at this point, was modulated by preceding referential context, but was nevertheless at such a low level that it could never play an active role again, or that, throughout the remainder of the locally ambiguous VP, it continued to fall to such a level. That could, potentially, be tested by yet another completion study, with fragments terminating later in the VP, but we feel that, whatever the result, it would be unlikely to convince proponents on either side of the debate.

We concede that our results cannot necessarily rule out a very highly constrained version of a constraint-satisfaction parser, but then again it is difficult to imagine what results could. However, the evidence does suggest that the parser cannot operate "strong" contextual guidance, or even what would generally be referred to as *contextual adjudication*. Instead, it can be no more than contextual "tipping of the scales" in cases where the alternatives were finely balanced. It certainly could not be a parser that, in any logical sense, did not operate very much on a principle of primacy of syntax. However, it seems to us far more parsimonious to suggest that parsing, in these cases, proceeds on the basis of an initial, single preferred analysis, and that the choice of this analysis is not influenced by referential context.

This interpretation fits well with these results and others in the literature that have failed to find evidence of context effects on the initial analysis of a reduced-relative/direct-object ambiguity (e.g., Britt, Perfetti, Garrod, & Rayner, 1992; Ferreira & Clifton, 1986; Rayner et al., 1983; Rayner, Garrod, & Perfetti, in press). However, it must be said that there are a number of recent articles that contain results apparently calling this conclusion into question (e.g., Mac-Donald, in press; Spivey-Knowlton et al., 1993; Tabossi et al., in press; True-swell et al., 1993). In the final section, we briefly explain why we find the interpretation offered in these articles to be relatively unconvincing.

THE SHORT REDUCED RELATIVE

A large number of recent studies have employed the reduced-relative/direct-object ambiguity as a means of assessing possible context effects on syntactic parsing, but with a slightly different form to the structure than that used in Experiment 2. These studies typically used items similar to Sentence (16).

(16) The witness examined by the judge turned out to be unreliable.

(17) The witness examined by the window the evidence he had found.

The critical distinction is that, in these items, the ambiguous verb is immediately followed by a PP. This does not necessarily immediately disambiguate the structure because it could be the beginning of a "parenthetic," specifying mode or location as in Sentence (17), but it does indicate that there is not an immediately following direct object, and it can be suggested that it acts as a probabilistic disambiguation. Since such by-phrases are far more commonly used in relative clause constructions and are usually felt to be rather clumsy, inelegant, or awkward when interposed in a transitive structure, it would not be surprising if they were taken as strong (but not necessarily critical) evidence for a relative clause. Unfortunately, therefore, in these items we are left with two potential points of disambiguation at which we might look for garden-path effects. Critically, also, the length of the ambiguous region in these items could be argued to be very small (one word) before there is a structural cue to the correct analysis (albeit not an unequivocal one).

We know from other evidence (Frazier & Rayner, 1982; Holmes, Stowe, & Cupples, 1989; Kennedy & Murray, 1984) that the length of a locally ambiguous region may influence the extent of garden pathing, with little or no effect found following short ambiguous regions. This suggests that final commitment to a particular structural analysis may be delayed for at least a word or two (not surprisingly, when disambiguation frequently relies not on the presence of a single word, but on a combination of two or more). Therefore, in this type of item, we are left with a situation where a parser that operates on a principle of pursuing a single preferred analysis would not necessarily commit itself to the (incorrect) direct-object interpretation immediately upon encountering the verb, and may be expected to take into account information about the likely structural role played by the following by-phrase (i.e., a situation in which such a parser would not necessarily be expected to be garden pathed at all).

However, the results suggest that the situation cannot be quite as simple as this because at least some studies do find garden-path effects with this type of structure. But, as Trueswell et al. (1993) pointed out, this may critically depend on aspects of the items and their presentation mode. They reported the results of studies by Burgess (1991), which show that, with self-paced reading using a moving-window display mode where only one word is visible at a time, garden-path effects are found and that they are unmodulated by context, but that this is not true for a two-word display mode where the verb and the following "by" are presented simultaneously. Some caution must be exercised in the interpretation of these results because, as suggested by Kennedy and Murray (1984) and Kennedy et al. (1989), such moving-window self-paced displays are not the best simulation of normal reading. They preclude a normal, and perhaps necessary, aspect of it—the ability to reinspect prior text—and they may show very different patterns of results from those obtained with good "cumulative" displays, which most closely model the results found with eye-movement studies. Nonetheless, what seems clear is that garden-path effects in these items are most likely to occur in situations in which an unnatural segmentation of processing is forced when the verb is read, but that they may be avoided when there is no restriction on the speed with which the following by-phrase can be processed (regardless of whether, as argued by Trueswell et al., any of it is processed parafoveally during the inspection of the verb—as this will depend on not just the length of the verb and whether the "by" itself is ever fixated, but also on the location of the first [or subsequent] fixation falling on the verb; see discussions of the Optimal Viewing Position and its influence on lexical access procedures in Kennedy & Murray, 1991; McConkie, Kerr, Reddix, & Zola, 1988; O'Regan, 1990; Pynte, Kennedy, & Murray, 1991).

We are therefore left with a situation in which a "syntax first," "single preferred analysis" parsing procedure would not necessarily be expected to show garden-path effects with these items (depending on the nature of the items and the parameters of the display mode employed), and where the predictions derived from a constraint-satisfaction parser may be very similar. The advantage that a constraint-satisfaction parser appears to have in explaining the results is in the way it suggests that the size of the garden-path effect will *sometimes* be modulated by contextual influences. If there is clear evidence of this, then it must be said that the constraint-satisfaction approach has the edge. However, we argue that the evidence is not yet clear for the following reasons. First, as suggested, there are situations under which it seems rather implausible that the constraint-satisfaction approach would not predict at least some effect, and yet none is found. Second, the statistical evidence in many of the studies apparently showing modulation of garden-path effects by context is not particularly strong: In many cases, the results show a significant garden-path effect in one context condition, but not in the other. However, the critical interaction, showing a statistical *difference* in the size of the effects, is either not reported or fails to achieve statistical significance over subjects, items, or both (e.g., MacDonald in press; Spivey-Knowlton et al., in press, Experiments 2 & 3; Tabossi et al., in press; Trueswell et al., 1993, Experiments 1 & 2, but significant when combined). This is frequently then followed by the argument that the strength of the constraint imposed is a continuous variable, and that a correlational analysis is a more appropriate procedure. However, where statistically significant correlations over items are found, although they are certainly suggestive of the type of results that would be expected following the constraint-satisfaction approach, they cannot in any way be taken as robust statistical evidence for the effect. These are item analyses only; they consequently do not show evidence of the generality of the effect over subjects (the most basic criterion usually employed). In addition, being correlations, they do not, of course, show evidence of generality over items. In fact, it is possible to find significant correlations of this type with only a small minority of cells in a subject–item matrix showing any indication of an effect.[5]

This second criticism is not necessarily damming since it must be admitted that the results in many of the studies show exactly the trends that would be predicted from a constraint-satisfaction approach. The correlations provide some additional suggestive evidence, and a lack of robust statistical effects does not in itself provide evidence against a proposal, but we feel that these uncertainties, together with the other criticisms, certainly leave the debate in a situation where "the jury is out."

---

[5]In a typical experimental design involving 24 items (or item pairs) tested on 32 subjects, with a continuous constraint variable, it is, in principle, only necessary for 2 cells of the 768 in the entire subjects–item matrix to show an indication of an effect before a significant correlation ($r = .479$, $p < .05$) between item effect and the constraint can be found (i.e., less than 0.3% of the total number of data points in the experiment). For a correlation of $r = .709$, $p < .001$, only 5 cells (0.65%) need to show the effect. (These calculations are based on the assumption of a rectangular distribution of the constraint variable and all cells containing zero effects except for the number specified, which contain effect sizes directly related to the two or five strongest constraints. Other distribution types will result in slightly different sized effects. But the general principle holds that significant correlations result when only a small proportion of subjects—as few as one—show's effects on only a very small number of items. It is plausible, of course, that the items on which any subject is most likely to show an effect will be those with the strongest constraint.)

CONCLUSIONS

Because of the uncertainties in the evidence provided for constraint-satisfaction approaches and because of the relative parsimony in the interpretation of the results in terms of a "syntax first," "single preferred analysis" parsing procedure, we are inclined to argue for the latter on the basis of current evidence. Perhaps more highly specified versions of the constraint-satisfaction approach will prove capable of providing an equally effective explanation of these types of results, but our suspicion is that once the parameters in such a model are specified and set, it will prove extremely difficult to distinguish the predictions made by both types of model.

It seems clear, however, that the type of syntactic ambiguity best suited to testing such models is one in which there is a single, unequivocal point of syntactic disambiguation, and that this should occur at a potentially variable distance from the point at which the ambiguity is established. The similarity noted by MacDonald, Perlmutter, and Seidenberg (chapter 6, this volume) between the effects of lexical ambiguity and the apparent effects of syntactic ambiguity in short relative clause items may not be so much an indication that a constraint-satisfaction approach is correct, as an indication that the effects in this case are ones of lexical ambiguity, rather than parsing processes. If it is to be argued that the type of reduced-relative ambiguity used in Experiment 2 is, in a sense, "too difficult" to be influenced by contextual factors, then an alternative that satisfies the same criteria is clearly required.

Finally, these results and our interpretation of them provide no support for the suggestion that referential context affects on-line parsing decisions, although they certainly do provide evidence that such contexts may influence subjects' conscious expectations.

ACKNOWLEDGMENTS

The work reported here was supported by an SERC (UK) postgraduate studentship to the second author. We would like to thank Gerry Altmann, Maryellen MacDonald, Ken McRae, Don Mitchell, Mike Tanenhaus, John Trueswell, and Michael Spivey-Knowlton for helpful discussion and suggestions, and for making available as yet unpublished accounts of their work. We would also like to thank Chuck Clifton for his helpful comments on an earlier draft of this chapter.

REFERENCES

Altmann, G. T. M. (1987). Modularity and interaction in sentence processing. In J. L. Garfield (Ed.), *Modularity in knowledge representation and natural language understanding* (pp. 249–258). Cambridge, MA: MIT Press.

Altmann, G. T. M., Garnham, A., & Dennis, Y. I. L. (1992). Avoiding the garden path: Eye movements in context. *Journal of Memory and Language, 31,* 685–712.

Altmann, G. T. M., & Steedman, M. (1988). Interaction with context during human sentence processing. *Cognition, 30,* 191–238.

Bock, J. K. (1986). Syntactic persistence in language production. *Cognitive Psychology, 18,* 355–387.

Britt, M. A., Perfetti, C. A., Garrod, S., & Rayner, K. (1992). Parsing in discourse: Context effects and their limits. *Journal of Memory and Language, 31,* 293–314.

Clifton, C., & Ferreira, F. (1989). Ambiguity in context. *Language and Cognitive Processes, 4,* 77–103.

Cowart, W. (1981). *Cataphoric co-reference and the resolution of structural ambiguity.* Unpublished manuscript, Queens College, City University of New York.

Crain, S. (1980). *Pragmatic constraints on sentence comprehension.* Unpublished doctoral dissertation, University of California at Irvine.

Crain, S., & Steedman, M. (1985). On not being led up the garden-path: The use of context by the psychological syntax processor. In D. R. Dowty, L. Karttunen, & A. M. Zwicky (Eds.), *Natural language parsing: Psychological, computational and theoretical perspectives.* (pp. 320–358). Cambridge, England: Cambridge University Press.

Ferreira, F., & Clifton, C. (1986). The independence of syntactic processing. *Journal of Memory and Language, 25,* 348–368.

Fodor, J. A. (1983). *The modularity of mind.* New York: McGraw-Hill.

Fodor, J. A., Bever, T. G., & Garrett, M. F. (1974). *The psychology of language.* New York: McGraw-Hill.

Ford, M., Bresnan, J. W., & Kaplan, R. M. (1982). A competence based theory of syntactic closure. In J. W. Bresnan (Ed.), *The mental representation of grammatical relations* (pp. 727–796). Cambridge, MA: MIT Press.

Forster, K. I. (1979). Levels of processing and the structure of the language processor. In W. E. Cooper & E. C. T. Walker (Eds.), *Sentence processing: Psycholinguistic studies presented to Merrill Garrett* (pp. 27–81). Hillsdale, NJ: Lawrence Erlbaum Associates.

Forster, K. I. (1987). Binding, plausibility and modularity. In J. L. Garfield (Ed.), *Modularity in knowledge representation and natural language understanding* (pp. 63–82). Cambridge, MA: MIT Press.

Forster, K. I., & Olbrei, I. (1973). Semantic heuristics and syntactic analysis. *Cognition, 2,* 319–347.

Forster, K. I., & Ryder, L. A. (1971). Perceiving the structure and meaning of sentences. *Journal of Verbal Learning and Verbal Behavior, 10,* 285–296.

Frazier, L. (1978). *On comprehending sentences: Syntactic parsing strategies.* Unpublished doctoral dissertation, University of Connecticut, Storrs, CT.

Frazier, L., & Fodor, J. D. (1978). The sausage machine: A new two-stage model of the parser. *Cognition, 6,* 291–325.

Frazier, L., & Rayner, K. (1982). Making and correcting errors during sentence comprehension: Eye movements in the analysis of structurally ambiguous sentences. *Cognitive Psychology, 14,* 178–210.

Frazier, L., Taft, L., Roeper, T., Clifton, C., & Ehrlich, K. (1984). Parallel structure: A source of facilitation in sentence comprehension. *Memory & Cognition, 12,* 421–430.

Freedman, S., & Forster, K. I. (1985). The psychological status of overgenerated sentences. *Cognition, 19,* 101–131.

Garnham, A. (1985). *Psycholinguistics: Central topics.* London: Methuen.

Herriot, P. (1969). The comprehension of active and passive sentences as a function of pragmatic expectation. *Journal of Verbal Learning and Verbal Behavior, 8,* 166–169.

Holmes, V. H., Kennedy, A., & Murray, W. S. (1987). Syntactic structure and the garden path. *Quarterly Journal of Experimental Psychology, 39A,* 277–293.

Holmes, V. H., Stowe, L., & Cupples, L. (1989). Lexical expectations in parsing complement-verb sentences. *Journal of Memory and Language, 28*, 668–689.

Kennedy, A., & Murray, W. S. (1984). Inspection times for words in syntactically ambiguous sentences under three presentation conditions. *Journal of Experimental Psychology: Human Perception and Performance, 10*, 833–849.

Kennedy, A., & Murray, W. S. (1991). The effects of flicker on eye movement control. *Quarterly Journal of Experimental Psychology, 43A*, 79–99.

Kennedy, A., Murray, W. S., Jennings, F., & Reid, C. (1989). Parsing complements: Comments on the generality of the principle of minimal attachment. *Language and Cognitive Processes, 4*, 51–76.

Liversedge, S. P., & Murray, W. S. (1993 September). *Referential context effects on garden paths in relative clause constructions.* Paper presented at international conference on the Psychology of Language and Communication, Glasgow, Scotland.

MacDonald, M. C. (in press). Probabilistic constraints and syntactic ambiguity resolution. *Language and Cognitive Processes.*

Marslen-Wilson, W., & Tyler, L. K. (1987). Against modularity. In J. L. Garfield (Ed.), *Modularity in knowledge representation and natural language understanding* (pp. 37–62). Cambridge, MA: MIT Press.

McClelland, J. L., St. John, M., & Taraban, R. (1989). Sentence comprehension: A parallel distributed approach. *Language and Cognitive Processes, 4*, 287–335.

McConkie, G. W., Kerr, P. W., Reddix, M. D., & Zola, D. (1988). Eye movement control during reading: I. The location of initial eye fixations on words. *Vision Research, 28*, 1107–1118.

Mitchell, D. C. (1989). Verb guidance and other lexical effects in parsing. *Language and Cognitive Processes, 4*, 123–154.

Mitchell, D. C., & Corley, M. M. B. (in press). Immediate biases in parsing: Discourse effects or experimental artifacts? *Journal of Experimental Psychology: Learning, Memory and Cognition.*

Mitchell, D. C., Corley, M. M. B., & Garnham, A. (1992). Effects of context in human sentence parsing: Evidence against a discourse-based proposal mechanism. *Journal of Experimental Psychology: Learning, Memory and Cognition, 18*, 69–88.

Murray, W. S. (1982). *Sentence matching: The influence of meaning and structure.* Unpublished doctoral dissertation, Monash University.

Murray, W. S., & Liversedge, S. (1991). *Effects of context on syntactic parsing and reanalysis.* Paper presented to Experimental Psychology Society, Sussex, England.

O'Regan, J. K. (1990). Eye movements and reading. In E. Kowler (Ed.), *Eye movements and their role on visual and cognitive processes* (Vol. 4, pp. 395–453). *Reviews of Oculomotor Research*). Amsterdam: Elsevier.

Pynte, J., Kennedy, A., & Murray, W. S. (1991). Within-word inspection strategies in continuous reading: Time course of perceptual, lexical and contextual processes. *Journal of Expeirmental Psychology: Human Perception and Performance, 17*, 458–470.

Rayner, K., Carlson, M., & Frazier, L. (1983). The interaction of syntax and semantics during sentence processing: Eye movements in the analysis of semantically biased sentences. *Journal of Verbal Learning and Verbal Behavior, 22*, 358–374.

Rayner, K., & Frazier, L. (1987). Parsing temporarily ambiguous complements. *Quarterly Journal of Experimental Psychology, 39A*, 657–673.

Rayner, K., Garrod, S., & Perfetti, C. A. (in press). Discourse influences during parsing are delayed. *Cognition.*

Slobin, D. I. (1966). Grammatical transformations and sentence comprehension in childhood and adulthood. *Journal of Verbal Learning and Verbal Behavior, 5*, 219–227.

Spivey-Knowlton, M. J., Trueswell, J. C., & Tanenhaus, M. K. (1993). Context effects in syntactic ambiguity resolution: Discourse and semantic influences in parsing reduced relative clauses. *Canadian Journal of Psychology, 47*, 276–309.

Steedman, M. J., & Johnson-Laird, P. N. (1976). A programmatic theory of linguistic performance.

In R. N. Campbell & P. T. Smith (Eds.), *Recent advances in the psychology of language: Formal and experimental approaches.* (pp. 171–192). New York: Plenum.

Tabossi, P., Spivey-Knowlton, M. J., McRae, K., & Tanenhaus, M. K. (in press). Semantic effects on syntactic ambiguity resolution. In *Attention and Performance XV.*

Taraban, R., & McClelland, J. L. (1988). Constituent attachment and thematic role assignment in sentence processing: Influences of content-based expectations. *Journal of Memory and Language, 27,* 597–632.

Trueswell, J. C., Tanenhaus, M. K., & Garnsey, S. M. (in press). *Semantic influences on parsing: Use of thematic role information in syntactic disambiguation.* Manuscript submitted for publication. *Journal of Memory and Language.*

Tyler, L. K., & Marslen-Wilson, W. D. (1977). The on-line effects of semantic context on syntactic processing. *Journal of Verbal Learning and Verbal Behavior, 16,* 683–692.

16

The Use of Structural, Lexical, and Pragmatic Information in Parsing Attachment Ambiguities

Julie Sedivy
Michael Spivey-Knowlton
University of Rochester

It is by now a commonplace observation that many sentences occurring in natural language are at least temporarily ambiguous between more than one interpretation. Given that language comprehension takes place in a rapid and incremental fashion, such that the sentence processor attempts to integrate each word into a partially constructed interpretation, an important focus of research is to specify the mechanisms by which the processing system decides on an analysis at a point in time when the input is compatible with multiple interpretations. Recent work in sentence processing has identified a variety of sources of information, both linguistic and nonlinguistic, which could in principle be used in the resolution of ambiguity. Existing proposals differ with respect to when various sources of information become available to the parser, and the manner in which they interact. In this chapter, we focus on one particular ambiguous construction as a case study for evaluating the nature of the contribution of various information sources in the process of comprehending structurally ambiguous sentences. Although the discussion and the experiments we report are centered on the ambiguous attachment of prepositional phrases (PPs), we assume that the mechanisms under discussion are of a general nature and are involved in a variety of different structural ambiguities.

We begin by discussing various attempts to account for experimental data dealing with the resolution of PP-attachment ambiguities. The existing proposals fall into roughly three classes: models that emphasize the role of structural information, those that emphasize the importance of lexically based information, and those that focus on the use of discourse-related constraints. We review data relevant to each class of model. The body of the chapter is concerned with our own attempts to test the predictions made by each class of model, and to identify more clearly the information that is used in parsing PP-attachment ambiguities. The first experiment we report examines the predictions made by a discourse-based model that accords an important role to referentially based pragmatic presuppositions. In this experiment, we find that referential factors are important in influencing early parsing decisions, although they cannot be entirely responsible for the pattern of data we obtain. Examination of corpus data and sentence-completion data suggests that lexical information pertaining to individual verbs might be relevant for early parsing commitments. Our second experiment tests this hypothesis by introducing a class of verbs (consisting of verbs of perception and psychological predicates) that differs semantically from the kinds of verbs that have typically been used in reading-time experiments with PP-attachment ambiguities (predominantly prototypical action verbs). We find that the verbs used in the second experiment show strikingly different parsing effects from the verbs in the previous experiment. We conclude that, minimally, early parsing commitments are made on the basis of discourse-related information *and* lexically specific information. We discuss the type of model we believe is most appropriate for accounting for the currently existing body of data on ambiguity resolution, and conclude by posing a few questions about the role of frequency-based information in parsing.

The ambiguity involved in attaching PPs is one of the most widely studied structural ambiguities. The construction is illustrated in the following sentence:

(1) The gang leader hit the lawyer with a whip before getting off the subway.

There are two possible interpretations of this sentence, corresponding to two possible structural assignments. If the PP "with a whip" is attached to the verb phrase (VP), we interpret the sentence as meaning that the gang leader used a whip in hitting the lawyer. On the other hand, if the PP is attached to the noun phrase (NP) "the lawyer," the sentence means that the gang leader, in some unspecified manner, hit the lawyer who had a whip. There is general agreement that it is *not* the case that both interpretations are given equal consideration until a point at which disambiguating evidence of either a structural or semantic nature becomes available. Preference for one analysis often manifests itself early on and is strong enough to be intuitively accessible. For Sentence (1), the reading that emerges as dominant is the VP-attached structure (i.e., the interpretation in which the gang leader uses a whip to inflict violence on the lawyer). The preference for VP attachment in this case becomes particularly salient when we consider a related sentence in which attachment of the PP to the VP results in an absurd interpretation.

(2) The gang leader hit the lawyer with a wart before getting off the subway.

Research suggests that the preference for VP attachment over NP attachment is quite robust. A number of reading-time studies have shown that, when presented with sentences containing V–NP–PP sequences, people take longer to read the PP when its semantic content demands an NP attachment than when it is compatible with a VP attachment (e.g., Altmann, 1986; Ferreira & Clifton, 1986; Frazier, 1978; Rayner, Carlson, & Frazier, 1983; Rayner, Garrod, & Perfetti, 1992; but see Taraban & McClelland, 1988). This is generally taken as evidence that people initially assign such ambiguous strings a structure in which the PP is initially attached to the VP, and are forced to revise this analysis when it turns out to be meaningless or pragmatically deviant.

However, there is considerable disagreement about the specific mechanisms responsible for the observed preference, as well as the representational vocabulary to which they are assumed to have access. We briefly review a number of different proposals that have been generated in an attempt to account for the on-line resolution of ambiguous constructions. We then discuss the diverging predictions made by the various proposals with respect to the conditions under which misanalysis effects are expected to occur.

SOURCES OF CONSTRAINT

Constraints on the Construction of Phrase Markers

One of the most influential proposals, developed by Lyn Frazier and colleagues (e.g., Frazier, 1978, 1987; Frazier & Fodor, 1978; Rayner et al., 1983), assumes an architecture of the language processing system consisting of informationally encapsulated subprocessors that interact with one another in limited ways. For instance, the module that builds syntactic structure is claimed to have access only to information about possible phrase markers, and to be blind to all lexical information except categorial information that is associated with incoming lexical items. Clearly, this subdomain of linguistic information is not sufficient to resolve structural ambiguities in favor of one analysis over another. Proponents of this model have argued that what induces the parser to commit to one structural analysis at the point of ambiguity is the existence of parsing-specific principles that are independent of the grammar, but are stated in terms of the representational vocabulary that is assumed to be available to the processor at the structure-building stage. The specific principle that is claimed to be relevant for parsing PP-attachment ambiguities is the Minimal Attachment principle, which states that the parser initially builds only the simplest phrase marker when more than one phrase structure is compatible with the input at that point in time. Structural simplicity is stated in terms of the fewest number of nonterminal nodes required to build a phrase marker. With respect to the PP-attachment ambiguity, this principle predicts that the parser will always initially construct an analysis in which the PP is attached to the VP because attachment to the NP results in the creation of an additional node, following certain assumptions regarding the building of phrase structure made explicit in Frazier (1990).[1] The output of this structure-building component is then sent to an evaluative component (termed the *thematic processor;* Frazier, 1990, 1991; Rayner et al., 1983) that determines the semantic well formedness or plausibility of the initial parse. If the structure submitted by the syntactic parser is deemed to be semantically deviant, the thematic processor rejects the initial structure and guides a subsequent reanalysis of the ambiguous string.

The predictions made by this model are straightforward: A PP nonminimally attached to the NP rather than the VP should always yield a misanalysis effect. Although factors pertaining to semantic plausibility or pragmatic appropriateness may have a discernible effect on the speed of recovery from the misanalysis, they are not expected to eliminate the initial misanalysis. Several experiments report persistent effects of Minimal Attachment despite semantic or contextual factors biased in favor of an NP attachment (Ferreira & Clifton, 1986; Rayner et al., 1983, 1992).

Constraints from the Lexicon

In contrast to the garden-path model, which places very strong limitations on the nature of the lexical information that is available to the structure-building component, there is a class of approaches that accords an important role to more articulated lexical information in the resolution of ambiguities. Within this class of approaches, there are differences as to the nature of the lexical information that is considered to be relevant.

Information from Argument Structure.   A number of different researchers have proposed that syntactic argument frames associated with specific lexical items play a crucial role in the structural commitments that are made by the parser (e.g., Fodor, Bever, & Garrett, 1974; Ford, Bresnan, & Kaplan, 1982). Information pertaining to the argument structure of a verb has been shown to be important for parsing constructions with long-distance dependencies (Boland & Tanenhaus, 1991; Kurtzman, 1989; Tanenhaus, Boland, Garnsey, & Carlson, 1989), and ambiguities concerning nominal versus sentential complements (Trueswell, Tanenhaus, & Kello, 1993). With respect to PP-attachment ambiguities, it has been argued (Abney, 1989; Britt, Perfetti, Garrod, & Rayner, 1992) that the parsing preference exhibited for such structures is due not to constraint on the building of phrase structures, but rather to a general preference to relate material encoded in a PP as an argument of some head rather than as an

---

[1]Frazier (1990) argued that the constraints on phrase structure building that are relevant to the parser are not necessarily isomorphic with grammatical constraints on phrase structure. Most relevantly, she assumed that the structure-building component permits ternary branching, and that it does not introduce intermediate nodes at the X-bar level unless they branch.

adjunct. Examination of the experimental materials used in some studies looking at ambiguously attached PPs shows that, for many of the sentences in the VP-attachment conditions, the PP occurred as the argument of the verb, whereas the NP-attached PPs were all instances of adjunction (cf. Ferreira & Clifton, 1986; Rayner et al., 1983, 1992), suggesting that the parsing preference may reduce to an argument/adjunct distinction. The argument structure information associated with individual lexical entries specifies whether a PP complement is possible for that entry, thus determining the possibility of attaching the PP as an argument to that head. Under the view that PPs are preferentially attached as arguments, it is easy to imagine that attachment might be mediated by the availability of a PP argument in the verb's subcategorization frame. Furthermore, it has been suggested that it is not only the mere presence or absence of a PP complement in the argument structure for a lexical entry that is relevant for the attachment of PPs; rather, the parser also takes into account the strength of the preference for a PP complement in the argument structure (Britt et al., 1992; Ford et al., 1982). Lexical items with strong preferences for PP complements should show greater penalties when the PP is not realized as an argument of that item. Systematic studies mapping measures of argument frame preferences on an item-by-item basis onto detectable on-line misanalysis effects are lacking at the moment for this construction type, but the patterns of data across some experiments are consistent with this prediction. For instance, Britt (1991) found that contextual manipulations were more effective in eliminating the garden-path effect typical of NP-attached PPs when the verb preceding the PP was a locative verb that permitted, but did not require, the surface realization of the Goal argument (e.g., *throw*) than when the verb required the realization of the Goal argument (e.g., *put*). Similarly, in a study that demonstrated the successful elimination of the VP-attachment preference due to contextually biasing factors, the postverbal PP was almost always an adjunct rather than an argument (Britt et al., 1992), whereas the study by Ferreira and Clifton (1986), which failed to show contextual override of the VP-attachment preference, used verbs that selected for a PP complement.[2]

Conceptual-Semantic Information. A number of researchers have proposed that the lexical information relevant for parsing is even more fine-grained than this, and not limited to structural aspects of lexical entries such as argument selection frames. Rather, it has been argued that the semantic content of each constituent is taken into consideration and evaluated with respect to the role it plays in the event being described (Taraban & McClelland, 1988, 1990). These authors have pointed out that differences in the attachment of PPs also imply differences with respect to the thematic role that is assigned to the object of the

---

[2]However, the reported imperviousness of parsing preferences to context may be due, at least in part, to characteristics of the contextual manipulations. See Britt et al. (1992) and Spivey-Knowlton and Tanenhaus (chapter 17, this volume) for a discussion of effective bias in context manipulations.

preposition, and suggest that attachment preferences are guided by the conceptual representations being constructed in tandem with syntactic structure. Under this view, garden-path effects reflect violations of expectations for particular thematic roles within an event, rather than resulting from the construction of phrase markers that turn out to be ultimately incorrect. The idea is that, upon encountering the preposition *with* in the sentence "The gang leader hit the lawyer with . . . ," the semantic content of the preposition in combination with the preceding lexical material evokes the expectation of an Instrument role, rather than some other role such as Accompaniment (e.g., "hit the lawyer with his fellow gang members") or the expectation of a nominal modifier (e.g., "hit the lawyer with a wart"). If this expectation is not met, processing difficulty results and reanalysis takes place. Empirical support for this view comes from experiments that determined a priori thematic expectations by means of sentence completion and rating measures. The experiments found that when thematic expectations were consistent with attachment of the PP to the NP, reading times following the disambiguating word were actually slower for sentences containing VP-attached PPs than for sentences containing NP-attached PPs.

Clifton, Speer, and Abney (1991) argued that the expectations proposed by Taraban and McClelland to be of primary importance in processing actually reflect a number of different parsing influences—among them, the preference for argument over adjunct attachment. They suggested that the degree to which a verb produces an expectation for a specific thematic role coincides with the status of a postverbal phrase as argument or adjunct. Although experimental subjects appear to be sensitive to the conceptual relatedness between a verb and specific thematic roles, they may in fact be using information limited to the argument structure of the verb. The two accounts make a number of distinguishable and clearly testable predictions, however. For one, the view that parsing decisions are driven by available argument frames makes no predictions about preferred attachment sites for phrases that are not subcategorized elements. For example, it would not predict that attachment of a PP as an adjunct to a VP would be preferable to attachment as an adjunct to the NP, yet this reflects the pattern of experimental results for a number of studies testing sentences in isolation or with purportedly neutral contexts (Britt et al., 1992; Clifton et al., 1991).[3] However, this preference could, in principle, be accounted for by the thematic expectations account—if it could be shown that a bias exists for these materials such that the thematic roles encoded by the objects of the preposition in the VP-attached conditions are more consonant with expectations than the roles for the NP-attached conditions.[4]

---

[3]There is considerable disagreement as to what constitutes an appropriate diagnostic for determining argumenthood or adjuncthood. The studies just cited are ones that test phrases that appear to behave more like adjuncts than arguments.

[4]Abney (1989) hypothesized the existence of a parsing principle in addition to, and subordinate to, the prefer-adjunct principle, which would account for the preference to attach adjuncts to the VP

In addition, Taraban and McClelland (1990) reported that manipulating the content of the direct-object noun preceding the PP also modulates attachment preferences, such that the presence of certain nouns yields stronger expectations for modification and results in reading-time penalties for the conditions in which the phrase is attached to the VP. For instance, the sentence beginning as "The dictator viewed the masses from . . . " yielded longer reading times for NP-attached PPs, whereas a sentence such as "The dictator viewed the petitions from . . ." had longer reading times for VP-attached PPs. Because this manipulation did not alter the argument structure of any lexical items, these results would also be outside of the predictive domain of the argument-frame account.

Finally, the semantic expectations account leads to stronger predictions about the effects of finer grained lexical differences that fall within the broader categories of *argument* or *adjunct*. Taraban and McClelland (1990) showed that, even when the PP encodes the preferred thematic role, manipulating the typicality of the object of the PP as a participant in this role results in differences in reading times (e.g., "The janitor cleaned the storage area *with the broom*" [typical] vs. *with the solvent* [not typical]). Ideally, for the semantic expectations story to be truly compelling, we would expect to see off-line expectations correlating with reading times on an item-by-item basis. This kind of analysis is not reported in the studies by Taraban and McClelland, but correlations of this sort have been found to hold for studies looking at the resolution of the ambiguity associated with reduced relative clauses (cf. Pearlmutter & MacDonald, 1992; Spivey-Knowlton & Tanenhaus, chapter 17, this volume; Tabossi, Spivey-Knowlton, McRae, & Tanenhaus, in press, Trueswell & Tanenhaus, chapter 7, this volume; Trueswell, Tanenhaus, & Garnsey, in press). Thus, there is an emerging body of evidence that indicates that parsing decisions are sensitive to lexical information that is more intricate and semantically specific than categorial or subcategorial information alone. Whether it will be possible to reduce all the effects apparently related to argument structure to semantic expectations is another question altogether. On the one hand, whether a PP has the status of an argument of some head appears to be intricately bound with the degree to which the information expressed by the PP is an inherent part of the event described by the head.[5] On

---

rather than the NP. This second principle states that attachment to a theta-assigner is preferred to attachment to a non theta-assigner. Clifton et al. (1991) simultaneously manipulated the possibilities of attaching phrases either as arguments or adjuncts and the possibility of VP or NP attachment. They found that the preference to attach to the VP takes precedence over the preference to attach a phrase to an argument, and they interpreted these results as supportive of the immediacy of the Minimal-Attachment principle.

[5]Dowty (1982) introduced a semantic argument/adjunct distinction where the relationship between the adjunct phrase and the event is determined by applying that phrase's meaning to the meaning of any verb, such that any specific type of adjunct phrase will have a constant meaning across all VPs it occurs in. In contrast, the relationship between the argument phrase and the event is determined by the meaning of the verb itself. Dowty stated that there is a strong, but not exact, correspondence between semantic and syntactic notions of argumenthood and adjuncthood.

the other hand, given that there appears to be some degree of lexical idio-syncrasy, such that words that stand for conceptually similar events have different argument frames (e.g., *put* vs. *place*), it is likely that reference to argument structure, as well as reference to semantic content and conceptual representa-tions, will be necessary.

Lexical Frequency Information.   Another type of lexically related informa-tion that needs to be taken into account is information about the frequency of co-occurrence for various kinds of constructions or lexical items. Hindle and Rooth (1993) suggested that sensitivity to the frequency of co-occurrence of specific noun-verb-preposition sequences, in the absence of access to semantic or con-ceptual representations, would yield the observed attachment preference for each such sequence. It will be difficult to establish the precise role of frequency information in parsing. To date, the work on frequency of co-occurrence has consisted largely of demonstrating that predictions based on frequency informa-tion correlate with human parsing preferences (Hindle & Rooth, 1993; Juliano & Tanenhaus, 1993; Mitchell, Cuetos, & Corley, 1992). It is not at all clear how this information is actually used by humans in making parsing decisions. Specifi-cally, to make claims about the relationship between frequency counts and pars-ing effects, one must know more about what sort of information or categories frequency effects are conditionalized over. The answer to this question is not necessarily obvious from looking at patterns of distribution. To give an illustra-tion with respect to our lead-in example sentence, a number of hypothetical frequency statements could, in principle, account for the garden-path effect (VP-attachment preference) observable in the sentence "The gang leader hit the law-yer with a wart." Among them might be: (a) a simple pattern in which VP attachments are more common than NP attachments in the English language; (b) a pattern in which VP attachments are more common than NP attachments for the preposition *with,* but not necessarily for other propositions; (c) a pattern in which the preposition *with* by itself occurs most frequently as selecting an Instrument role; (d) a pattern in which transitive action verbs occur more frequently with an instrumental phrase than with a direct object modifier; and (e) a pattern in which the preposition *with* introduces an instrumental phrase more frequently than other kinds of phrases when it occurs with the verb *hit.* These examples by no means exhaust all the logical possibilities—a number of which may actually hold for the English language. We discuss in more detail the nature of frequency effects later on in the chapter. For the moment, we acknowledge that this information source remains a possible candidate in accounting for a number of the parsing effects under discussion, and note the difficulty in empirically establishing its role.

Constraints from Discourse

In contrast with the local nature of the parsing strategies discussed previously, a referential account of the processing of attachment ambiguities attributes parsing preferences to the way in which the parser attempts to establish referential links with a mental discourse model. It has been argued that, although experiments typically present sentences in isolation, it is incorrect to assume that null contexts are equivalent to neutral contexts because the interpretation of these sentences must still take place with relation to the building of a discourse model (Altmann, Garnham, & Dennis, 1992; Altmann & Steedman, 1988; Crain & Steedman, 1985). These researchers pointed out that the experiments that have shown a preference for VP attachment of PPs have typically contained definite NPs immediately prior to the ambiguously attached PP. They suggested that the VP-attachment preference has its roots in the discourse properties of definite NPs. The theory hinges on the notion that a "simple" (i.e., unmodified) definite NP presupposes the existence of a unique referent denoted by the noun. On the other hand, a "complex" (i.e., modified) definite NP presupposes the existence of multiple referents denoted by the head noun, one of which must be distinguished by virtue of the property picked out by the modifier.[6] In the absence of preceding context, a complex NP interpretation requires accommodating more unsatisfied presuppositions of the discourse model than a simple NP interpretation. When faced with an ambiguously attached PP, the parser will be able to avoid the more presuppositionally complex analysis by initially attaching the PP to the VP, rather than attaching it as a modifier to the NP. If the PP turns out to actually be attached to the NP, a misanalysis effect will result.

The most compelling evidence for the referential theory comes from the effect of introducing contexts containing two NP referents corresponding to the direct object noun in the target sentence. This results in a preference for a complex NP analysis (i.e., a modified NP that hosts the ambiguous PP; Altmann & Steedman, 1988). In Altmann and Steedman's study, contexts with two NP referents not only eliminated the reading-time misanalysis effect for NP-attached PPs, but they also produced a misanalysis effect in VP-attached PPs. Similar effects of this kind of context, using self-paced reading and measures of eye movements during reading, have since been found for PP-attachment ambiguities (Britt et al., 1992; Spivey-Knowlton, 1992; but see Clifton & Ferreira, 1989), for sentence complement/relative clause ambiguities (Altmann et al., 1992; Altmann, Garnham, & Henstra, in press; but see Mitchell, Corley, & Garnham, 1992; Mitchell & Corley, in press), and for reduced-relative clause ambiguities (Spivey-Knowlton

---

[6]The precise status of the presupposition associated with modified definite NPs is not clear. Steedman and Altmann (1989) explicitly stated that they are considering a pragmatic, rather than a semantic, notion of presupposition, but did not discuss in detail the specific nature of such presuppositions. Portner (1989) and Clifton and Ferreira (1989) argued that this type of presupposition has its origins in Gricean-style conversational implicature. They claimed that, as such, it is highly unlikely to be accessible quickly enough to influence initial parsing decisions. We are making no theoretical claims about the status of such presuppositions, but we tend to agree with Rayner et al. (1992) that modifiers serve the general attentional function of supplying additional information that is needed either to establish a unique referent among a number of possible referents, or to orient attention to a referent that is not in discourse focus.

& Tanenhaus, chapter 17, this volume; Spivey-Knowlton, Trueswell, & Tanenhaus, in press; but see Murray & Liversedge, chapter 15, this volume).

However, showing that context can modulate a parsing preference does not
necessarily indicate that the preference can be reduced to these contextual factors. It is, of course, possible that referential factors form one of a number of
constraints that are at work in parsing ambiguities. The rest of this chapter
focuses on some of our attempts to identify the types of constraints (structural,
lexical, and/or pragmatic) that are relevant to resolving syntactic ambiguities on
line.

EFFECTS OF NP DEFINITENESS ON ATTACHMENT
PREFERENCES

We designed an experiment to determine whether a clear parsing preference
exists for materials that do not involve the kind of referential presuppositions just
described, as compared with materials that do. We acknowledge that null contexts cannot be said to be neutral because, even in the absence of context,
interpretations must take place with respect to a discourse model. Nonetheless, it
is possible to create sentences that are presuppositionally neutral in the relevant
sense (i.e., sentences in which the NP preceding the ambiguous PP is indefinite).
Because the function of an indefinite is to introduce a new discourse entity, and
an indefinite carries with it no presuppositions of existence or uniqueness (Heim,
1982), a modified indefinite NP is presuppositionally equivalent to an unmodified one. Therefore, if referential factors are responsible for all of the
misanalysis effect, we would expect to find the standard VP-attachment preference in sentences containing definite NPs, but no such effect for sentences
containing indefinite NPs.

There was an additional motivation to examine the effects of referential factors sentence internally: We had some concerns about the explanation for the
context effects found in studies that modeled their contexts on the Crain and
Steedman (1985) materials. One possibility is that the presence of two NP
referents satisfies the presuppositions required by definite complex NPs. However, there is a possible alternative account for the effect of the context manipulations that were used. To illustrate, consider the following NP-attachment supporting context, taken from Altmann and Steedman (1988).

(3) A fireman was running to the scene of a fire carrying a heavy axe. He had
     to smash down a door. When he got to the scene of the fire, he found a
     door which had a rusty lock and a door which was nailed shut.

Like this story, the contexts in Altmann and Steedman's study typically introduced a minimal pair of entities into a discourse in which it was established that

one would play a special role. For instance, in passage (3), we have been told in advance that the fireman will smash down a door; when we encounter the two NPs denoting doors, we are unsure as to which is the relevant one in this event. This indeterminacy may create a powerful expectation that subsequent discourse will provide information to choose between these two doors. If this is indeed the nature of the context effect, it would be a very interesting result, but one that is subtly different from the claim being made by Referential Theory. That is, the context effect may not have so much to do with accommodating presuppositions associated with definite constructions as with developing expectations as to the informational content that is likely to be relevant (cf. Spivey-Knowlton, 1992). This latter account similarly predicts that contexts containing two NP referents will induce a preference for complex over simple NPs. However, the trigger for the preference is not the definiteness of the NP, but the content of the narrative. If modification of the NP is deemed informationally important in selecting one element (from a set) to play a special role, the parser may avoid closing off the NP until a modifier is encountered that allows for the selection to be made. We reasoned that comparing constructions that require the satisfaction of referential presuppositions with ones that do not, in the absence of context, should allow us to test the predictions made by Referential Theory in a manner that avoids the possibility of this alternative explanation.

For the purpose of conducting a reading time experiment, we collected sentences with ambiguously attached PPs and manipulated the definiteness of the direct object NP, as in (4) and (5) below:[7]

(4) a. The fireman smashed down the door with the rusty lock but smoke overcame him.

    b. The fireman smashed down the door with the heavy axe but smoke overcame him.

(5) a. The fireman smashed down a door with a rusty lock but smoke overcame him.

    b. The fireman smashed down a door with a heavy axe but smoke overcame him.

The sentences in (4) contain definite direct objects, where as the Sentences in (5) contain indefinite direct objects. Sentences (4a) and (5a) represent NP-attached PPs for both definiteness conditions, and Sentences (4b) and (5b) represent the VP-attached versions.

The referential theory would predict a preference for VP over NP attachment only for those sentences containing definite NPs prior to the ambiguous PP. To

---

[7]To draw as direct a comparison as possible between extrasentential context effects and intrasentential referential effects, we used sentences adapted from Altmann and Steedman (1988), for which effects of referential context were obtained.

motivate this prediction, we sought to determine whether definiteness is, in fact, an effective predictor of attachment in naturally occurring language. To do this, we conducted a corpus analysis on one half of the Brown corpus (Kucera & Francis, 1967). Because all of the experimental items chosen for inclusion in our reading time study contained the preposition *with* as the head of the ambiguously attached PP, we limited the analysis to instances of this preposition. We initially analyzed a restricted set of sentences that closely mirrored the structure of the sentences used in the reading time experiment (i.e., a potentially ambiguous PP following a verb with an NP complement). A classification of these sentences by attachment site revealed that, although there was an overall preference for VP attachment over NP attachment, sentences with definite NPs differed markedly from sentences with indefinite NPs. For the sentences containing definite NPs immediately preceding the ambiguously attached PP, there was a clear preference for VP attachment, which is what one would expect if modification of definite NPs is limited to those (probably uncommon) contexts in which the modifier serves to pick out one member out of a presupposed set. In contrast, sentences containing indefinite NPs actually displayed a higher proportion of NP attachments over VP attachments. Analysis of a less restricted set of sentences containing PPs headed by *with* showed a similar pattern. This set of sentences contained not only the sentences in the subset described earlier, but also sentences where *with* followed an earlier postverbal PP adjunct, or where the potentially ambiguous PP followed a passive verb and an agent by-phrase. Frequency counts are given in Table 16.1. The results of the corpus analysis suggest that modification of an NP complement by means of a PP is constrained by the definiteness of the complement, and consequently provide some motivation for the referential account of on-line parsing preferences for ambiguous PP attachment.

To observe the on-line effects of NP definiteness, we presented sentences of

Table 16.1
Frequency Counts of Sentences from the Brown Corpus

Set	Restricted		
	NP Attached	*VP Attached*	*Totals*
Definite NP	12	82	94
Indefinite NP	53	29	82
Totals	65	111	176
	Unrestricted		
Definite NP	16	96	112
Indefinite NP	63	32	95
Totals	79	128	207

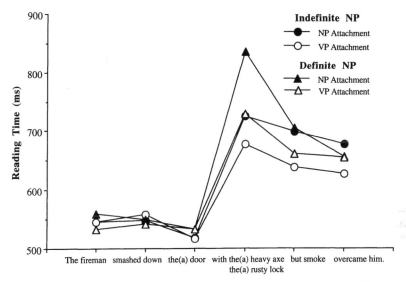

FIG. 16.1. Sentences adapted from Altmann and Steedman (1988). Reading time across sentence region as a function of NP definiteness and PP attachment. Notice at the PP the small but positive increase from open circles to closed circles (indefinite NPs). In contrast, the difference between open and closed triangles (definite NPs) at the PP is large.

the sort exemplified in Sentences (4) and (5) (taken from Altmann & Steedman, 1988) to subjects performing a phrase-by-phrase, noncumulative, self-paced reading task. The results of this study are depicted graphically in Fig. 16.1. We found a substantial VP-attachment preference at the PP for sentences with definite NPs. Sentences with indefinite NPs showed a smaller but statistically significant VP-attachment preference. The interaction between definiteness and attachment was marginally significant by subjects and items.

These results indicate that referentially based aspects of discourse cannot be entirely responsible for the misanalysis effect that we obtained for these sentences. If the attachment preference for these kinds of sentences reduced to choosing the analysis with the fewest unsatisfied presuppositions, we would not expect to have found that modified indefinite NPs should be less preferred than unmodified ones because neither case involves setting up referential presuppositions. Nonetheless, the marginal interaction between definiteness and attachment suggests that referential factors do contribute somewhat to the on-line parsing preference.[8]

---

[8]In this experiment, we intended to look at the effect of varying the definiteness of the NP preceding the PP. Because it is infelicitous to modify an indefinite NP with a PP containing a definite

At this point, it might be worth asking why the interaction between the definiteness of the direct objects and attachment was not as strong as might be expected on the basis of the patterns in the corpus analysis. Recall that the corpus study showed that sentences containing indefinite NPs were actually about twice as likely to attach the PP to the NP as to the VP. On the other hand, the on-line study showed a clear VP-attachment preference for both definite and indefinite conditions. Although referential factors seem to have some effect on on-line parsing decisions, there is a robust residual misanalysis effect that is in need of an explanation.

NONREFERENTIAL PARSING EFFECTS

Earlier we discussed possible candidates for explaining parsing preferences for PP-attachment ambiguities—among them, a structurally based parsing principle such as Minimal Attachment, the argument-frame account, and the semantic expectations account. Let us explore how each of these candidates fares in accounting for the pattern of data described in the previous section.

A structurally based principle such as Minimal Attachment is able to predict the overall preference for VP attachment in the reading time data. Under this account, the discrepancy between the corpus and on-line data never arises as a problematic issue. The Minimal Attachment principle is assumed to be specific to the parsing of linguistic input. As such, it does not necessarily make any predictions with respect to patterns of language production found in corpus data. However, given that the on-line VP-attachment preference is modulated to some degree by definiteness, we would have to allow for an on-line interaction between structurally based and discourse-based parsing mechanisms, which is prohibited by the two-stage model, from which Minimal Attachment stems (Frazier, 1990, 1991).

Along a different vein, the view that attachment decisions are driven by preferred argument frames (Britt, 1991; Britt et al., 1992) does not, in our opinion, have anything to say about the VP-attachment preference for these materials. All of the sentences in the experiments reported earlier used PPs

---

NP, the experiment simultaneously varied the definiteness of the noun within the PP as well. To ensure that the effect of definiteness on attachment that was obtained in this experiment was not due to the effect of changing the definiteness of the PP-internal NP, which we considered theoretically irrelevant, we conducted a control experiment that varied only the definiteness of the NP inside the PP, while the direct object NP remained definite across all conditions. We again found evidence for a VP-attachment preference. However, rather than seeing a reduction in the magnitude of this preference for sentences with indefinite NPs within the PP, these sentences showed a VP-attachment preference that was at least as large as the one obtained for their definite counterparts. The results of this control experiment reassured us that any interaction between definiteness and attachment in the previous experiment could safely be attributed to the definiteness of the NP preceding the PP rather than within it.

headed by *with,* and expressed either an instrumental phrase or an attribute of the preceding NP. Although the appropriateness of specific diagnostic tests for argumenthood is controversial, instrumental phrases certainly behave more as adjuncts than as arguments with respect to a number of standard constituency tests that appear to be sensitive in determining when a phrase is a subcategorized element of a verb. For instance, the pro-form "do so" is normally required to have as its antecedent a verb plus all of the arguments of that verb, yielding the ungrammaticality in Sentence (6) compared with Sentence (7).

(6) *John will place the book on the shelf and Bill will do so on the chair.

(7) John will visit Mary on Sunday and Bill will do so on Wednesday.

Thus, the PP "on . . ." is an argument of the verb *place* (in Sentence 6) and an adjunct of the verb *visit* (in Sentence 7). Note that when a VP contains an instrumental phrase, the subsequent use of the pro-form "do so" may refer back to the verb without the instrumental phrase:

(8) John will eat the cake with a fork and Bill will do so with a spoon.

Unlike argument PPs, instrumental phrases may be ordered after other adjuncts:

(9) *John will place the book in a hurry on the shelf.

(10) John will break the door down on Tuesday with a crowbar.

An emphatic reflexive may be inserted between the verb and an instrumental phrase, but not between a verb and one of its arguments:

(11) *John will place the book himself on the shelf.

(12) John will eat the cake himself with a fork.

In addition, *with* phrases are not restricted in their occurrence. They may appear relatively freely with almost any kind of verb, whereas subcategorized PPs are frequently very limited in terms of the specific verbs with which they co-occur. Furthermore, *with* phrases do not meet the semantic criteria for argumenthood either. The relationship of the instrumental phrase to the event is constant regardless of the particular verb to which it is attached (Dowty, 1982), and failure to syntactically realize in instrumental phrase does not necessarily express an open discourse role (cf. Carlson & Tanenhaus, 1988). For these reasons, we conclude that instrumental phrases are adjuncts, rather than arguments. Consequently, the argument-frame account cannot predict the VP-attachment preference that is evident in the reading times.

Alternatively, a semantic expectations view (Taraban & McClelland, 1988,

1990) could, in principle, account for the residual (i.e., nonreferentially based) VP-attachment preference, with respect to these materials, if it could be shown that the verbs typically expressed events that involved a semantic bias toward VP attachment of the preposition *with*. Because this account predicts a close correspondence between off-line biases and on-line parsing preferences, the discrepancy between the on-line and corpus data might be explained by verb class differences. That is, although the verbs were identical across both attachment conditions in the experimental task, there is no reason to expect that this should be the case for the types of verbs that naturally occur in environments containing VP-attached phrases as opposed to NP-attached phrases. In fact, a closer look at the verbs in the corpus suggested a systematic difference in the semantic class of those verbs preceding NP-attached phrases versus verbs with VP-attached phrases. The verbs that were usually followed by VP-attached PPs were almost exclusively action verbs taking an Agent as subject and an affected Theme as direct object. On the other hand, the corpus sentences with NP-attached PPs, contained a high proportion of verbs of perception of psychological predicates, as well as frequent instances of the verbs *have* and *be*.

The verbs we used in the on-line reading task were all action verbs typical of the verbs found in the VP-attached category of the corpus study. To determine attachment expectations for our experimental items, we decided to collect data from subjects on a sentence completion task based on the materials used in the on-line task. Subjects were asked to complete sentence fragments that included the portion of the sentence up to and including the ambiguous preposition (e.g., "The fireman smashed down the door with _____"). The results showed that our experimental items did, in fact, have a considerable VP-attachment bias, and were not representative of the general attachment patterns for verbs preceding ambiguously attached PPs in natural language. Although there was a statistically reliable effect of definiteness on attachment in the completion study, the vast majority of the completions, even for the sentences containing indefinite direct object NPs, indicated a VP attachment of the PP. Fragments with definite NPs were completed with a VP-attached PP 96% of the time, whereas fragments with indefinite NPs were completed as VP attachments 90% of the time. This bias toward VP attachment superseded the strength of the overall preference for VP attachment in the corpus study. Most significantly, where the corpus data showed an NP-attachment preference for sentences containing indefinite objects, the verbs in the completion study still elicited predominantly VP attachments of the PP even for the indefinite condition. This strong VP-attachment bias across both definiteness conditions in the completion study suggests that the experimental items in this case were restricted to a highly specific set of verbs that are not fully representative of those in the corpus. Given that the experimental materials exhibit such a heavy bias, it is perhaps surprising that the effect of NP definiteness was observable at all.

To explore the possibility that the residual VP-attachment preference is the result of semantic biases inherent to specific classes of verbs, we attempted to develop a new set of materials that did not exhibit a similar verb-based expectation for VP attachment. These materials consisted primarily of psychological predicates and verbs of perception. Norming of these materials by means of a sentence completion task suggested that these materials induced different expectations from the materials in the previous experiments reported in this chapter. Rather than displaying a very strong VP-attachment bias, these sentences fragments showed an overall preference for NP attachment over VP attachment. The definiteness of the NP preceding the ambiguous preposition had a clear effect as well: For sentences with indefinite NPs, the PP was attached to the NP 76% of the time, whereas for sentences with definite NPs, NP attachments made up only 46% of the completions, again suggesting an important role for referentially based factors in making attachment decisions.

Materials for a self-paced reading task were developed based on the sentences used in the norming study and manipulated both attachment site and definiteness of the direct object NP. Sample sentences are given here.

(13) a. The salesman glanced at the customer with ripped jeans and then walked away.

   b. The salesman glanced at the customer with suspicion and then walked away.

(14) a. The salesman glanced at a customer with ripped jeans and then walked away.

   b. The salesman glanced at a customer with suspicion and then walked away.

The results of this second experiment (shown in Fig. 16.2), taken in comparison with the previous on-line experiment, support a view in which both referential factors and semantic expectations play an important role in determining initial attachment expectations. We found that, for sentences containing indefinite direct objects, the commonly attested preference for VP attachment was eliminated entirely. In fact, NP-attached PPs were read 68 ms faster than VP-attached PPs in the indefinite condition. For definite conditions, however, the pattern was reversed: NP-attached PPs were read 63 ms slower than VP-attached PPs.

To summarize our empirical data so far, we have found that, for action verbs, there is a strong off-line expectation for VP attachment of a PP, which is reflected in an on-line task as a reading-time penalty for NP-attached PPs. This penalty is modulated somewhat by the definiteness of the object NP, but persists even with indefinite NP objects. A second verb class consisting of psychological predicates and verbs of perception indicates different attachment expectations. This class of verbs exhibits an overall NP-attachment bias in sentence completions as well as a substantial modulation of that preference by definiteness of the object NP. These attachment expectations are also reflected in an on-line reading task, where the

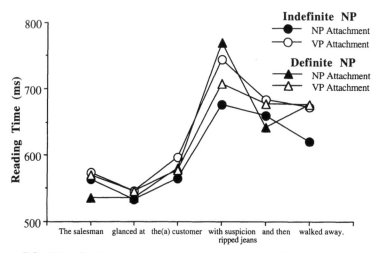

FIG. 16.2. Sentences using psych and perception verbs. Reading time across sentence region as a function of NP definiteness and PP attachment. Notice at the PP the small increase from closed circles to open circles (NP-attachment preference for indefinite NPs). In contrast, the closed triangles at the PP are greater than the open triangles (VP-attachment preference for definite NPs).

presuppositionally neutral indefinite condition yields slowed processing for VP-attached PPs. In contrast, the definite condition shows slowed processing for NP-attached PPs. This suggests that referential factors alone can induce an on-line preference for VP attachment with verbs that do not themselves show a VP-attachment preference. The results of our experiments are contrary to the predictions made by the Minimal Attachment account, and they identify referential factors and content-based semantic expectations as playing an important role in on-line parsing. These data suggest an architecture in which semantic and discourse-related information is accessible to the parser for the purpose of making immediate structural commitments. In the next section, we discuss the nature of the model that best accounts for these data.

A CONSTRAINT-BASED MODEL OF PARSING

Throughout the literature, studies report apparently conflicting results with respect to the nature of the interaction among various sources of information. However, once viewed within the perspective of a constraint-based model that allows for the combined influences of several well-motivated sources of information, the results of these studies are no longer inconsistent with one another. A number of chapters in this volume argue for precisely this kind of model. They show that effects on parsing decisions are predictable on the basis of the strength of cues such as referential context (Spivey-Knowlton & Tanenhaus, chapter 17, this volume) and semantic expectations (Trueswell & Tanenhaus, chapter 7, this volume), both of which are conditionalized upon the "availability" of the syntactic alternatives (Spivey-Knowlton & Tanenhaus) as determined by the contingent frequency of lexical items (MacDonald, Pearlmutter, & Seidenberg, chapter 6, this volume; Trueswell & Tanenhaus). Within the domain of studies on PP-attachment ambiguities, similar patterns seem to emerge. For example, discourse effects are more visible when the context is strongly constraining and when cues that conflict with discourse-based preferences are relatively weak (Britt et al., 1992). We have already pointed out that studies that showed clear effects of context in on-line attachment decisions (e.g., Britt et al., 1992) used target sentences that were less constrained by verb argument structure information than studies that failed to show similar effects (e.g., Ferreira & Clifton, 1986; Rayner et al., 1983, 1992). In a similar vein, the experiments we have reported in this chapter indicate that the effect of NP definiteness emerges most clearly when the strength of verb-based semantic bias is weakened.

In our opinion, a constraint-based system is particularly well suited to handling the graded effects observed across the literature. In such a model, all syntactically permissible structures are computed upon reaching a syntactic ambiguity, while frequency information determines the availability of those alternative structures, and semantic and discourse constraints provide continuous support for one or another of the available alternatives. Thus, if the semantic information for a given item provides strong support for a particular alternative, and discourse provides moderate support for the competing alternative (as with the definiteness effect in the action verbs), the influence of discourse may appear to be relatively weak. In contrast, if the semantic information for a given item provides only mild support for an alternative (as with the psych and perception verbs), that same discourse constraint will exhibit stronger and more immediate effects. This kind of model can account for a substantial portion of the graded variation in on-line parsing preferences across individual items (Spivey-Knowlton, 1994, Spivey-Knowlton & Tanenhaus, chapter 17, this volume; Trueswell & Tanenhaus, chapter 7, this volume), and has no need for structure-based parsing preferences.

On the other hand, it has been argued (e.g., Frazier, 1990) that the source of gradations in experimental effects is due not to initial parsing decisions, but to the speed with which revisions can be made, depending on the degree of accord between structural and nonstructural factors. Presumably, semantic information that is incompatible with the initial structural assignment made by the parser will serve as an early warning signaling the unviability of the original parse, whereas semantic information that confirms the initial structure will strengthen the processor's commitment to that analysis, resulting in exceptional difficulty should that analysis turn out to be incorrect. It is, of course, impossible for us to categorically rule out this interpretation if one wants to claim that revisions are made so quickly as to render the misanalysis effect undetectable. However, no matter how fast the revision effects are in a two-stage model, they can only account for a reduction (or elimination) or a Minimal Attachment preference; they cannot account for an initial preference for nonminimal attachment, as seen in the psych and perception verbs with indefinite object NPs. Moreover, several studies have used what is believed to be the most on-line measure of reading times (monitoring eye movements during reading) and have shown that lexically specific and discourse information immediately influence the resolution of syntactic ambiguity (Altmann et al., 1992, in press; Britt et al., 1992; Spivey-Knowlton & Tanenhaus, chapter 17, this volume; Trueswell & Tanenhaus, chapter 7, this volume).

Perfetti (1990) formulated a proposal that attempts to reconcile immediate effects of nonstructural information with an autonomous syntactic component that takes temporal precedence over a semantic component. This is accomplished by having the syntactic component build local constituents composed of syntactically categorized words plus their immediately dominating constituent heads without consulting nonstructural information, and by delaying more remote attachment decisions that may later be guided by the semantic processing component. Although we agree that the building of local constituents is accomplished largely without the help of nonstructural information, we propose that this is due to the relative irrelevance of such sources of information in constructing local constituents, rather than to an architecture that explicitly disallows nonstructural information from operating at the earliest stage in processing. The fact that nonstructural information has little to say about certain aspects of parsing gives rise to the appearance of processing autonomy. Thus, although syntactic information may be representationally autonomous, we see no reason to believe that it has any autonomy in a processing sense.

What Is the Role of Frequency-Based Information?

In the experiments reported in this chapter, once we take verb class information into account, we observe a relatively clean convergence in the data patterns from a variety of sources: frequency counts from the corpus analysis, off-line attachment preferences, and on-line parsing effects. It is easy to imagine that the situation could have been otherwise because the corpus reflects production data, whereas at the other end of the spectrum, the reading time study looks at on-line comprehension processes. The convergence of data from these disparate sources suggests either of two possibilities. On the one hand, it is consistent with the speculation that comprehension and production mechanisms have similar underlying constraints. The possibility that certain constraints permeate the language system is indeed an intriguing one, and is quite far removed from hypotheses postulating the existence of mechanisms that deal specifically with the requirements of the parser. On the other hand, the same convergence of data would be consistent with a situation in which production is constrained in a principled manner, but parsing is sensitive predominantly to information about statistical frequency. In other words, although linguistic and discourse ·principles may *underlie* the frequency patterns observable in natural language, parsing may take place to a lesser or greater degree independently of these principles. As noted earlier, the nature of frequency-based influences on parsing is extremely difficult to determine empirically because frequency information co-occurs with other sources of information that may, in fact, be ultimately responsible for the distribution patterns. However, evidence for parsing effects that are related to subtle contextual manipulations is not plausibly accounted for by a mechanism that is driven by lexical co-occurrences without making reference to conceptual or discourse representations. Such effects have been obtained by manipulating, to cite just a few examples, the referential context (Altmann et al., 1992; Altmann & Steedman, 1988; Spivey-Knowlton, 1992; Spivey-Knowlton et al., in press; Spivey-Knowlton & Tanenhaus, chapter 17, this volume) and the temporal properties of discourse (Trueswell & Tanenhaus, 1991, 1992). Therefore, there is considerable evidence that the parsing mechanism does have access to higher level semantic and discourse representations, and that it must rely on information other than lexical co-occurrence.

At the same time, we acknowledge that frequency-based information does play a constraining role in the parsing of ambiguities. MacDonald et al. (chapter 6, this volume) and Trueswell and Tanenhaus (chapter 7, this volume) discuss in detail a plausible model for frequency effects. Their model exploits the fact that many structural ambiguities actually hinge on lexical ambiguities of one sort or another. The relative frequencies of the possible instantiations of lexically ambiguous forms determine the initial availability of the syntactic structure that is associated with each instantiation. This view can account for some types of structural ambiguities appearing to be more impervious to contextual and semantic effects than others. For instance, difficulty with reduced relative clauses may persist in supportive contexts, whereas the VP-attachment preference is eliminated by supportive contexts (Britt et al., 1992). Britt et al. proposed that this difference is because, at the point of ambiguity for reduced relative clauses, the attachment of lexical items into local constituents takes place within the autonomous syntactic component. In contrast, the mechanism that attaches PPs is argued to be able to access semantic and discourse information. However, the difference in the behavior of the two ambiguity types is easily accounted for by a single mechanism within the frequency-based account because corpus analyses show that NP-verb"ed" sequences are far more likely to begin main clauses than reduced relatives (Tabossi et al., in press). By comparison, the PP-attachment ambiguity is much more evenly balanced among the possible alternatives (Hindle

& Rooth, 1993; also see the corpus analysis reported in this chapter). It is our opinion that the approach we briefly sketched earlier is a promising way in which to think about frequency effects. We maintain that frequency-based constraints operate in conjunction with other constraints that appeal to semantic and discourse information.

CONCLUSION

In this chapter, we have argued that the on-line parsing effects found with PP-attachment ambiguities cannot be accounted for by a single mechanism, whether it be structurally based, lexically based, or conditioned by referential presuppositions. Rather, a combination of constraints originating from different informational sources appears to guide the syntactic commitments that are made by the human parser. As a result of our experimental manipulations, we have identified two separate constraints that influence attachment decisions. Referential presuppositions associated with definite NPs can intensify an existing misanalysis effect for NP-attached phrases, and can even induce a misanalysis effect for NP-attached phrases in materials that otherwise show a preference for NP attachment. In addition, the semantic class of the verb is a strongly constraining factor, such that for prototypical action verbs, NP-attached PPs result in reading-time penalties even when NP attachment does not give rise to a more presuppositionally complex interpretation, as in the case of modified indefinite NPs. Moreover, when such referential presuppositions are not involved, psych verbs and verbs of perception actually show a preference for NP attachment.

These results suggest a multiplicity of factors that have immediate or extremely rapid effects in on-line processing. With increasing evidence for the early use of nonstructural information in making structural commitments, part of the research program for a constraint-based approach such as ours becomes specifying how information that is nonsyntactic, yet syntactically relevant, might be constrained and organized. The findings reported in this chapter can be seen as having methodological and theoretical import in demonstrating the difficulty of abstracting away from all of these factors in the construction of unbiased experimental materials designed to test specific hypotheses. Evidently, it is not safe to assume that all things other than the crucial manipulation are equal. It is our view that the careful examination of patterns found in corpus data will turn out to be increasingly useful, not only in establishing more clearly any existing link between frequency-based information and parsing effects, but also in identifying the full range of linguistic constructions that occur in natural language. Examining the semantic and discourse properties of specific items by means of off-line measures such as ratings or sentence-completion tasks will continue to be useful in understanding the nature of the experimental materials used for studying on-line comprehension processes.

ACKNOWLEDGMENTS

This work was partially supported by NIH grant HD-27206. In addition, the first author is a recipient of a Social Sciences and Humanities Research Council doctoral fellowship, and the second author holds a Graduate Research Fellowship from the National Science Foundation. We would like to extend warm thanks to Mike Tanenhaus, John Trueswell, and Gail Mauner for many helpful comments, and to Cornell Juliano for providing the computerized version of the corpus we used for the purpose of this study.

REFERENCES

Abney, S. (1989). A computational model of human parsing. *Journal of Psycholinguistic Research, 18*, 129–144.

Altmann, G. (1986). *Effects of context in human sentence parsing.* Unpublished doctoral dissertation, University of Edinburgh, Scotland.

Altmann, G., Garnham, A., & Dennis, Y. (1992). Avoiding the garden-path: Eye movements in context. *Journal of Memory and Language, 31*, 685–712.

Altmann, G., Garnham, A., & Henstra, J. (in press). Effects of syntax in human sentence parsing: Evidence against a structure-based proposal mechanism. *Journal of Experimental Psychology: Learning, Memory & Cognition.*

Altmann, G., & Steedman, M. (1988). Interaction with context during human sentence processing. *Cognition, 30*, 191–238.

Boland, J. & Tanenhaus, M. (1991). The role of lexical representation in sentence processing. In G. Simpson (Ed.), *Understanding word and sentence.* (pp. 331–366). Amsterdam: North Holland.

Britt, M. (1991). *The role of referential uniqueness and argument structure in parsing prepositional phrases.* Unpublished doctoral dissertation, University of Pittsburgh, PA.

Britt, M., Perfetti, C., Garrod, S., & Rayner, K. (1992). Parsing and discourse: Context effects and their limits. *Journal of Memory and Language, 31*, 293–314.

Carslon, G., & Tanenhaus, M. (1988). Thematic roles and language comprehension. In W. Wilkins (Ed.), *Syntax and semantics, Vol. 21: Thematic relations.* London: Academic Press.

Clifton, C., & Ferreira, F. (1989). Ambiguity in context. *Language & Cognitive Processes, 4*, 77–103.

Clifton, C., Speer, S., & Abney, S. (1991). Parsing arguments: Phrase structure and argument structure determinants of initial parsing decisions. *Journal of Memory and Language, 30*, 251–271.

Crain, S., & Steedman, M. (1985). On not being led up the garden path: The use of context by the psychological parser. In D. Dowty, L. Karttunen, & A. Zwicky (Eds.), *Natural language parsing* (pp. 320–357). Cambridge, England: Cambridge University Press.

Dowty, D. (1982). Grammatical relations and montague grammar. In P. Jacobson & G. Pullum (Eds.), *The nature of syntactic representation* (pp. 79–130). Dordrecht, The Netherlands: Reidel.

Ferreira, F., & Clifton, C. (1986). The independence of syntactic processing. *Journal of Memory and Language, 25*, 348–368.

Fodor, J. A., Bever, T., & Garrett M. (1974). *The psychology of language: An introduction to psycholinguistics and generative grammar.* New York: McGraw-Hill.

Ford, M., Bresnan, J., & Kaplan, R. (1982). A competence-based theory of syntactic closure. In J. Bresnan (Ed.), *The mental representation of grammatical relations* (pp. 727–796). Cambridge, MA: MIT Press.

Frazier, L. (1978). *On comprehending sentences: Syntactic parsing strategies.* Unpublished doctoral dissertation, University of Connecticut, Storrs, CT.

Frazier, L. (1987). Sentence processing: a tutorial review. In M. Coltheart (Ed.), *Attention & performance XII: The psychology of reading* (pp. 554–586). Hillsdale, NJ: Lawrence Erlbaum Associates.

Frazier, L. (1990). Parsing modifiers: Special purpose routines in the human sentence processing mechanism? In D. Balota, G. Flores d'Arcais, & K. Rayner (Eds.), *Comprehension processes in reading* (pp. 303–330). Hillsdale, NJ: Lawrence Erlbaum Associates.

Frazier, L. (1991). Exploring the architecture of the language-processing system. In G. Altmann (Ed.), *Cognitive models of speech processing* (pp. 409–433). Cambridge, MA: MIT Press.

Frazier, L., & Fodor, J. D. (1978). The sausage machine: A new two-stage parsing model. *Cognition, 6,* 291–325.

Heim, I. (1982). *The semantics of definite and indefinite nounphrases.* Unpublished doctoral dissertation, University of Massachusetts, Amherst.

Hindle, D., & Rooth, M. (1993). Structural ambiguity and lexical relations. *Computational Linguistics, 19,* 103–120.

Juliano, C., & Tanenhaus, M. (1993). Contingent frequency effects in syntactic ambiguity resolution. In *Proceedings of the 15th Annual Conference of the Cognitive Science Society* (pp. 593–598). Hillsdale, NJ: Lawrence Erlbaum Associates.

Kucera, H., & Francis, W. (1967). *Frequency analysis of English usage.* Boston: Houghton-Mifflin.

Kurtzmann, H. (1989). Locating Wh-traces. In C. Tenny (Ed.), *The MIT parsing volume, 1988–1989.*

Mitchell, D., Corley, M., & Garnham, A. (1992). Effects of context in human sentence parsing: Evidence against a discourse-based proposal mechanism. *Journal of Experimental Psychology: Learning, Memory & Cognition, 18,* 69–88.

Mitchell, D., & Corley, M. (in press). Immediate biases in parsing: Discourse effects or experimental artifacts? *Journal of Experimental Psychology: Learning, Memory & Cognition.*

Mitchell, D., Cuetos, F., & Corley, M. (1992, March). *Statistical vs. linguistic determinants of parsing bias: Crosslinguistic evidence.* Talk presented at the CUNY Sentence Processing Conference, New York.

Pearlmutter, N., & MacDonald, M. (1992). Plausibility effects in syntactic ambiguity resolution. In *Proceedings of the 14th Annual Conference of the Cognitive Science Society* (pp. 498–503). Hillsdale, NJ: Lawrence Erlbaum Associates.

Perfetti, C. (1990). The cooperative language processors: Semantic influences in an autonomous syntax. In D. Balota, G. Flores d'Arcais, & K. Rayner (Eds.), *Comprehension processes in reading* (pp. 205–230). Hillsdale, NJ: Lawrence Erlbaum Associates.

Portner, P. (1989). *Processing indefinite noun phrases in quantified sentences.* Unpublished manuscript, University of Massachusetts, Amherst.

Rayner, K., Carlson, M., & Frazier, L. (1983). The interaction of syntax and semantics during sentence processing: Eye movements in the analysis of semantically biased sentences. *Journal of Verbal Learning and Verbal Behavior, 22,* 358–374.

Rayner, K., Garrod, S., & Perfetti, C. (1992). Discourse influences during parsing are delayed. *Cognition, 45,* 109–139.

Spivey-Knowlton, M. (1992). Another context effect in sentence processing: Implications for the principle of referential support. In *Proceedings of the 14th Annual Conference of the Cognitive Science Society.* (pp. 486–491). Hillsdale, NJ: Lawrence Erlbaum Associates.

Spivey-Knowlton, M. (1994). Quantitative predictions from a constraint-based theory of syntactic ambiguity resolution. In M. Mozer, P. Smolensky, D. Touretzky, J. Elman, & A. Weigand (Eds.), *Connectionist models proceedings of the 1993 summer school.* (pp. 130–137). Hillsdale, NJ: Lawrence Erlbaum Associates.

Spivey-Knowlton, M., Trueswell, J., & Tanenhaus, M. (in press). Context and syntactic ambiguity resolution: Discourse and semantic influences in parsing reduced relative clauses [Special Issue]. *Canadian Journal of Experimental Psychology, 47,* 276–309.

Steedman, M., & Altmann, G. (1989). Ambiguity in context: A reply. *Language & Cognitive Processes, 4,* 105–122.

Tabossi, P., Spivey-Knowlton, M., McRae, K., & Tanenhaus, M. (in press). Semantic effects on syntactic ambiguity resolution: Evidence for a constraint-based resolution process. *Attention & Performance XV.* Hillsdale, NJ: Lawrence Erlbaum Associates.

Tanenhaus, M., Boland, J., Garnsey, S., & Carlson, G. (1989). Lexical structure in parsing long-distance dependencies. *Journal of Psycholinguistic Research, 18,* 37–50.

Taraban, R., & McClelland, J. (1988). Constituent attachment and thematic role expectations. *Journal of Memory and Language, 27,* 597–632.

Taraban, R., & McClelland, J. (1990). Parsing and comprehension: A multiple constraint view. In D. Balota, G. Flores d'Arcais, & K. Rayner (Eds.), *Comprehension processes in reading* (pp. 231–263). Hillsdale, NJ: Lawrence Erlbaum Associates.

Trueswell, J., & Tanenhaus, M. (1991). Tense, temporal context and syntactic ambiguity resolution. *Language and Cognitive Processes, 6,* 303–338.

Trueswell, J., & Tanenhaus, M. (1992). Consulting temporal context in sentence comprehension: Evidence from the monitoring of eye movements in reading. In *Proceedings of the 14th Annual Meeting of the Cognitive Science Society.* (pp. 492–497). Hillsdale, NJ: Lawrence Erlbaum Associates.

Trueswell, J., Tanenhaus, M., & Garnsey, S. (in press). Semantic influences in parsing: Use of thematic role information in syntactic disambiguation. *Journal of Memory & Language.*

Trueswell, J., Tanenhaus, M., & Kello, C. (1993). Verb-specific constraints in sentence processing: Separating effects of lexical preference from garden paths. *Journal of Experimental Psychology: Learning, Memory & Cognition, 19,* 528–553.

Trueswell, J. & Tanenhaus, M. (this volume). Toward a lexicalist account of syntactic ambiguity resolution.

17 Referential Context and Syntactic Ambiguity Resolution

Michael Spivey-Knowlton
Michael Tanenhaus
University of Rochester

A great deal of experimental evidence supports the intuition that language comprehension takes place immediately and incrementally. For example, listeners can shadow speech (repeat auditory language input) with a latency of as little as 250 ms (Marslen-Wilson, 1973). Unambiguous words are often recognized before the spoken input is even complete (Marslen-Wilson & Welsh, 1978). Given this immediacy of comprehension, combined with the many local indeterminacies in natural language, it is clear that at least partial commitments are being made to certain interpretations before completely disambiguating information is available. What sources of information do readers and listeners use when making these early commitments?

(1) a. The actress selected a blue dress.
     b. The actress selected by the director quit.

For example, Sentences 1a and 1b are temporarily ambiguous at the verb *selected.* "The actress selected" could continue as a main clause (1a) or as a reduced relative clause (1b). If the reader is understanding the sentence incrementally and on-line, he or she must make some form of commitment to an interpretation before completely disambiguating information is available. Since the early 1970s, a substantial portion of sentence processing research has addressed the question: What sources of information contribute to initial parsing commitments? A few broad categories of approaches have been taken. One approach assumes that syntactic processing is autonomous (i.e., syntactic decisions are informed only by syntactic information). Because the syntactic information is indeterminate, domain-specific decision principles must be postulated that cause the reader to initially prefer a particular type of syntactic structure over another. Nonsyntactic information can then assist in a reinterpretation of the input should the decision principles lead the reader "down the garden path." An influential example of this approach is the garden-path model (e.g., Frazier, 1987; Frazier & Fodor, 1978; Frazier & Rayner, 1982), in which the syntactically less complex alternative is initially pursued, regardless of the evidence from nonsyntactic information sources. Another approach has viewed initial parsing preferences as the result of informational biases set up by the discourse context. The best formulated account in this category is referential theory (e.g., Altmann & Steedman, 1988; Crain & Steedman, 1985; Steedman & Altmann, 1989), in which the syntactic alternative with the fewest unsatisfied referential presuppositions is initially pursued, regardless of structural complexity. Recently, a broadly interactive multiple constraints-driven account has been emerging (e.g., Mac-Donald, Pearlmutter, & Seidenberg, chapter 6, this volume; Spivey-Knowlton, Trueswell, & Tanenhaus, 1993; Taraban & McClelland, 1990; Trueswell, Tanenhaus, & Garnsey, in press), in which the available syntactic information defines the possible alternatives, but the likelihood (or availability) of these alternatives is modulated by their frequency of occurrence as well as other local factors. Simultaneously, a host of nonsyntactic constraints (e.g., lexical semantics and referential pragmatics) provide support for one or another of the available alternatives, thus determining which interpretation is initially pursued.

There are two critical issues that distinguish these approaches from one another. The first issue is whether initial activation of the syntactic alternatives is continuous and based largely on relative frequency of occurrence of the alternatives, or whether the alternatives of an ambiguity have discrete (binary) activations, in that an interpretation is either pursued or not pursued. Because Trueswell and Tanenhaus (chapter 7, this volume) and MacDonald et al. (chapter 6, this volume) discuss this issue in detail, we do not spend too much time on it. The second issue of importance is how and when contextual information modulates resolution of the syntactic ambiguity. Effects of intrasentential context are discussed in detail in this volume by Trueswell and Tanenhaus (chapter 7) and Sedivy and Spivey-Knowlton (chapter 16). In this chapter, we focus on the effects of extrasentential context—in particular, "referential contexts."

We review and integrate a range of seemingly conflicting results from several laboratories that have studied the effects of referential context in on-line resolution of syntactic ambiguity. We also present new results from our own laboratory, which support the claim that the constraint-based approach best accounts for the available data on this issue. We pay special attention to two general themes: availability of syntactic alternatives and strength of contextual constraint. We argue that much of the conflict in results throughout the literature can be accounted for by the availability of syntactic alternatives. If a given syntactic ambiguity has one alternative much less available than the other, due to frequency of occurrence as well as other "low-level" factors, then any contextual influence will take some time to activate that less available alternative and override the dominant alternative. Thus, we argue that results that have been used to argue against early effects of referential context may be due to highly skewed availability in the syntactic alternatives, rather than initial syntactic parsing being uninformed by context. In addition, the strength of contextual constraint also serves to resolve some of the conflict in the literature. Studies that have failed to find early effects of referential context have typically not demonstrated that the contextual constraint in question was present in their stimuli and available at the point of ambiguity. If the contextual constraint is not present in an off-line measure, such as sentence completion, then whether or not it influences on-line ambiguity resolution is a moot point. An important consequence of the dynamics between "availability" and "strength of constraint" is that slowed reading times (which have usually been interpreted as evidence of a garden path, and thus supporting a lack of contextual influence) may be the result of context immediately providing moderate activation to a less available alternative, thus causing competition between the two (now equally active) alternatives (Trueswell & Tanenhaus, chapter 7, this volume; Trueswell, et al., in press).

REFERENTIAL THEORY

Referential Theory, as it has come to be known, was initially proposed by Crain and Steedman (1985) as a discourse-based model of sentence processing that contrasted greatly with Frazier and Rayner's (1982) structure-based garden-path model of sentence processing. Whereas Crain and Steedman focused almost entirely on the role of definite noun phrase (NP) reference in syntactic ambiguity resolution, they also suggested a role for lexical semantics (such as noun animacy, or "typicality of agenthood"). Driven by an incremental "on-line" linking from referential expressions to context and their accompanying presuppositions, referential theory accounted for many of the parsing preferences observed by Frazier and colleagues (Frazier & Fodor, 1978; Frazier & Rayner, 1982; Rayner, Carlson, & Frazier, 1983), plus the effects of context observed by Crain (1980).

Crain and Steedman pointed out that many of the syntactic ambiguities studied by Frazier and colleagues hinged upon a definite NP (e.g., "the actress") being analyzed as a simple (unmodified) NP (as in "[The actress]$_{NP}$ selected a blue dress") or a complex (modified) NP (as in "[The actress selected by the director]$_{NP}$ quit"). The garden-path model's predictions (driven by a preference for the syntactic structure with the fewest nonterminal nodes) results in the simple NP analysis always being initially pursued, regardless of semantic or discourse context. In contrast, Crain and Steedman argued that the often-observed preference for the simple NP analysis was due to the complex NP analysis having a more costly presupposition than the simple NP analysis. The complex NP analysis presupposes a set of referents (two or more actresses in discourse), one of whom is distinguishable by virtue of having been selected by the director. This presupposition is computationally more expensive to accommodate than that of the simple NP analysis, which presupposes a unique referent (one actress) in the mental model of discourse. The crucial difference between this explanation and that of the garden-path model is that referential theory predicts an initial parsing preference toward the complex NP analysis when previous context satisfies its presupposition (by containing a set of referents)—that is, when context "referentially supports" the complex NP analysis. Altmann and Steedman (1988) generalized this hypothesis into the principle of referential support: An NP analysis that is referentially supported will be favored over one that is not.

Although this is indeed an interactive approach to sentence processing, Steedman and colleagues were quick to point out that referential pragmatics can only choose between alternatives proposed in parallel by syntax; they cannot instruct the parser to initially consider its favored alternative only. For this reason, they preferred the label *weak interaction,* as opposed to a strong interaction, in which the parser can be instructed by pragmatics or semantics to initially pursue a particular analysis. Referential theory posits a parallel consideration of syntactic alternatives from which a selection is immediately made by discourse-based principles. This proposal has two important differences from the constraint-based approach described in the introduction. First, although referential theory does not exclude effects of semantics, such as noun animacy (cf. Trueswell & Tanenhaus, chapter 7, this volume) or verb class (cf. Sedivy & Spivey-Knowlton, chapter 16, this volume), it has never proposed an explicit role for such sources of information. In contrast, by definition, a constraint-satisfaction theory of sentence processing maintains that any information source that is relevant to syntactic analysis can have immediate (although varying widely in strength) effects on parsing. Second, in referential theory, the syntactic alternatives are assumed to be equally available. In contrast, the constraint-based approach is driven by the relative availability of the syntactic alternatives.

The following sections discuss research that has tested referential theory's predictions with regard to discourse context effects in parsing three different types of syntactic ambiguity. Conflicting results exist for all three ambiguities. However, in each case, recent findings support a very early influence of referential context on the resolution of syntactic ambiguity. In the final section, we discuss the disparate findings as a whole, and argue that a constraint-satisfaction approach naturally accommodates all of the results.

SENTENCE-COMPLEMENT/RELATIVE-CLAUSE AMBIGUITY

Crain and Steedman (1985, Experiment 2) describe an experiment in which grammaticality judgments were recorded for complement sentences (2c) and for relative-clause sentences (2d) after contexts containing one NP referent (Sentence 2a) or two NP referents (Sentence 2b).

(2) a. One NP-referent context:
         A psychologist was counseling a married couple.
         One member of the pair was fighting with him but the other one was nice to him.

     b. Two NP-relevant context:
         A psychologist was counseling two married couples.
         One of the couples was fighting with him but the other one was nice to him.

     c. Complement target sentence (simple NP):
         The psychologist told the wife that he was having trouble with her husband.

     d. Relative target sentence (complex NP):
         The psychologist told the wife that he was having trouble with to leave her husband.

In target sentences (2c) and (2d), "the wife" can be a simple NP, in which case the subsequent clause must be a sentence complement of the verb *told;* or it can be a complex NP, in which case "that he was having trouble with" is a relative clause modifying "the wife." The garden-path model (Frazier & Rayner, 1982) argues that the sentence-complement analysis will always be initially pursued (regardless of context) because it has fewer nonterminal nodes in its syntactic structure. Thus, judgments of ungrammaticality should be more common for Sentence 2d than for Sentence 2c, regardless of which context preceded them. This is not what Crain and Steedman observed. In accordance with referential theory, the complex NP analysis of "the wife" (relative target sentence), which presupposes a set of NP referents (a set of wives), elicited 50% ungrammaticality judgments when preceded by the context containing one NP referent and only 22% ungrammaticality judgments when preceded by the context containing two NP referents. The simple NP analysis of "the wife" (complement target sentence), which presupposes a unique NP referent, elicited only 12% ungrammaticality judgments when preceded by the context containing one NP referent and 54% ungrammaticality judgments when preceded by the context containing two NP referents.

   Although this interaction between context and target sentence demonstrates the importance of referential pragmatics in parsing, the grammaticality judgment technique does not allow us to discriminate between immediate parsing preferences and subsequent reinterpretation processes. Therefore, the garden-path model, which posits an informationally encapsulated initial parsing mechanism based purely on structural principles (e.g., the syntactic simplicity preference of minimal attachment), followed by a thematic processor that evaluates the initial interpretation and, if necessary, quickly proposes a reinterpretation, can accommodate Crain and Steedman's results. More "on-line" measures of parsing preference are needed to distinguish between competing theories.

Mitchell, Corley, and Garnham (1992) used a self-paced reading task to study processing of critical regions of the target sentence. Subjects pressed a button to present portions of the sentence, and reading times were recorded. With an additional control sentence, Mitchell et al. examined reading times to an early disambiguating region for complement sentences and relative clause sentences. Sentence (3a) is the typical relative clause version, and Sentence (3b) is the typical complement version. (Presentation regions are delineated by slashes.) These sentences are disambiguated in Region 4. However, Sentence (3c), is disambiguated as a subject relative clause at Region 2. Thus, these three sentences allow an examination of early parsing preferences [by comparing reading times of Region 2 in Sentence (3c) with the mean reading times of the same region in Sentences (3a) and (3b)], and an examination of late ambiguity-resolution processes [by comparing reading times of Region 4 in Sentence (3a) with reading times of the same region in Sentence (3b)].

(3) a. The politician told the woman that he / had been / meeting / that he was going out to see the minister.
     b. The politician told the woman that he / had been / meeting / the minister responsible once weekly.
     c. The politician told the woman that / had been / meeting him / that he was going out to see the minister.

These three sentence types cross-indexed by two context conditions (one NP referent vs. two NP referents) produced a 2×3 experimental design. Unfortunately, the interaction between context and sentence type at Region 4 was only marginally significant. This failure to reliably observe their contexts influencing sentence processing at even such a late region makes it difficult to interpret their main finding: effects at Region 2. At Region 2, where immediate parsing preferences can be examined, Sentence (3c) was read more slowly than the mean of Sentences (3a) and (3b), and context did not appear to affect this slowed reading. Was the contextual constraint really ignored at the early disambiguation point? Or was the contextual constraint in these stimuli, as the effects at Region 4 may suggest, too weak to show up at all? Finally, it is arguable under the constraint-based approach that the slowed reading times at the early disambiguation point are not due to a misanalysis, but instead to competition between the syntactic alternatives. Given that the availability of alternatives in this syntactic ambiguity is strongly biased toward the sentence complement, an early influence of relative-supporting context may serve to activate the relative clause alternative up to about the same level as the sentence complement, resulting in close competition between the two—hence, slowed processing.

Around the same time, Altmann, Garnham, and Dennis (1992) reported eye-tracking results supporting effects of referential context on parsing complement/relative ambiguities. Subjects' eye movements were monitored while they read complement, relative clause, and unambiguous relative clauses sentences (Sentences 4a–4c, respectively) in or out of their corresponding supportive referential contexts. (Slashes represent regions for the purposes of analysis.)

(4) a. He / told / the woman / that he'd risked his life for / many people / in similar fines.
   b. He / told / the woman / that he'd risked his life for /to install / a smoke detector.
   c. He / asked / the woman / that he'd risked his life for / to install / a smoke detector.

Results showed no difference between the target sentences when preceded by respectively supportive contexts, and a reliable difference (slower first-pass reading times at the disambiguating region, "to install," of the ambiguous relative clause) in the absence of context. Although first-pass reading times for the disambiguating region alone were not statistically analyzed, the means and standard errors suggest a robust interaction between relative clause ambiguity (Sentence 4b vs. Sentence 4c) and context (supportive vs. null). Having two NP referents in context eliminated the difficulty in processing an ambiguous relative clause, as compared with an unambiguous relative clause. This was replicated in a second experiment (Altmann et al., 1992, Experiment 2).

In summary, although immediate effects of referential context on complement/relative ambiguities may be somewhat elusive, it does not appear that they are nonexistent. When referential context supports a simple NP analysis of the NP preceding the *that* clause, that analysis is usually pursued. When referential context supports a complex NP analysis of the NP preceding the *that* clause, that analysis is usually pursued. Nonetheless, we have not yet fully explained why Mitchell et al. (1992) did not find such context effects. Altmann, Garnham, and Henstra (in press) modified the Mitchell et al. materials and found what appear to be early effects of referential context, but Mitchell and Corley (in press) pointed out several criticisms of this work. In fact, we would argue that the difficulty in finding context effects with this ambiguity may be due, in part, to the availability of alternatives being highly skewed. The experimental stimuli for all of these experiments use the verb *told* almost exclusively (one of the target sentences in Altmann et al., 1992, used the verb *assured* instead of *told*). Interestingly, a computer search of the Brown corpus (Kucera & Francis, 1967) and the *Wall Street Journal* corpus (Marcus, Marcinkiewicz, & Santorini, 1992) for sequences of NP–"told"–NP–"that," which were temporarily ambiguous between beginning a sentence complement or a relative clause, revealed 79 entries, all of which are disambiguated as sentence complements. Thus, the ambiguity in the experiments just described has an unusually high degree of asymmetry in initial availability of the two syntactic alternatives. As it stands, the contexts in these studies appear to have supported the less available alternative (the relative clause) just enough to reveal close competition (indicated by processing difficulty) at the earliest measurement point, followed by contextual override at a slightly later measurement point.

PREPOSITIONAL PHRASE ATTACHMENT AMBIGUITY

In prepositional phrase (PP)-attachment ambiguities (Sentence 5a, verb phrase (VP) attached and Sentence 5b, NP attached), the availability of alternatives may be less skewed than in the complement/relative ambiguity (cf. Hindle & Rooth, 1993; Sedivy & Spivey-Knowlton, 1993). Consequently, early effects of referential context on this ambiguity are easier to find.

(5) a. The burglar / blew open / the safe / with the dynamite / and made off / with the loot.

(simple NP)

b. The burglar / blew open / the safe / with the new lock / and made off / with the loot.

(complex NP)

According to referential theory, the reader's preference for a simple NP analysis of "the safe" (Sentence 5a) or a complex NP analysis (Sentence 5b) of "the safe" depends on whether the discourse context contains a set of safes or only one safe.

Altmann and Steedman (1988) preceded sentences, such as Sentences (5a) and (5b), with contexts doing exactly that: providing either one or two referents for the NP preceding the ambiguously attached preposition. Subjects read the context by pressing a button to present each line and then the target sentence by pressing the button to present each phrase (slashes represent self-paced presentation regions). The reading times of interest are at the PP ("with the dynamite/new lock"). When the context contained one NP referent, the VP-attached PP (Sentence 5a) was read faster than the NP-attached PP (Sentence 5b). However, when the context contained two NP referents, the NP-attached PP was read faster than the VP-attached PP. Most importantly, the NP-attached PP was read faster in a two NP-referent context than in a one NP-referent context. Although the crucial interaction between context and attachment did not approach significance, the comparisons just described were statistically significant. Thus, once again, referential theory's predictions hold true.

However, self-paced reading may not be the best measure of immediate parsing preferences. The remainder of this section discusses studies that monitored eye movements during reading of the PP-attachment ambiguity. For example, Ferreira and Clifton (1986) compared VP-attached sentences with NP-attached sentences (Sentences 6a and 6b, respectively; slashes delineate regions for analysis only) in an eye-tracking study in which the sentences were preceded by contexts that were either neutral or referentially supportive of the target sentence's attachment.

(6) a. Sam loaded / the boxes on the cart / before his coffee break.
    b. Sam loaded / the boxes on the cart / onto the van.

Context (neutral vs. supportive) did not appear to affect first-pass or second-pass reading times in any way. The disambiguating region of the VP-attached sentence was initially read faster than that of the NP-attached sentence in both contexts. However, the majority of Ferreira and Clifton's (1986, Experiment 2) items used verbs such as *loaded* and *placed,* whose preferred argument structures include a PP after the NP. The crucial PP "on the cart" naturally fills the last argument of the verb, and thus forces a simple NP analysis of "the boxes." This argument-structure information biases the reader against an NP attachment, making effects of discourse context especially difficult to observe (cf. Sedivy & Spivey-Knowlton, chapter 16, this volume).

In a subsequent eye-tracking study, Britt, Perfetti, Garrod, and Rayner (1992, Experiment 2) compared "semantically resolved" VP-attached sentences (Sentence 7a) to "semantically resolved" NP-attached sentences (Sentence 7b, similar to Ferreira & Clifton's) and "pragmatically resolved" NP-attached sentences (Sentence 7c, similar to Altmann & Steedman's) in their respectively supportive contexts and in isolation (slashes delineate regions for analysis only).

(7) a. Peter read the books / on the chair / instead of lying in bed.
    b. Peter read the books / on the chair / instead of the other books.
    c. Peter read the books / on the war / instead of the other books.

Sentences (7a) and (7c) are disambiguated from one another at the PP ("on the chair/war"). Therefore, of interest here is the difference in first-pass reading times between Sentences (7a) and (7c) at the PP in isolation and in supportive context. In isolation, the VP-attached PP was read faster than the NP-attached PP. However, in their supportive contexts, the VP-attached PP was read at the same speed as the NP-attached PP. On the other hand, Sentences (7a) and (7b), are disambiguated from one another at the region following the PP ("instead of . . ."). Differences in first-pass reading times for this comparison at this region were exactly the same as in the previous comparison. Although the crucial interaction between context and attachment was not tested within the relevant regions, a reliable three-way interaction of context × attachment × region supported the conclusion that supportive context eliminated the NP-attachment penalty at the disambiguating region. These results were replicated in a self-paced reading task (Britt et al., 1992, Experiment 3).

Rayner, Garrod, and Perfetti (1992) also monitored eye movements during reading of VP-attached sentences and NP-attached sentences (Sentences 8a and 8b, respectively) in certain contexts (slashes delineate regions for analysis only). Although their contextual manipulation (discourse focus) does not bear on referential theory, an informal comparison of isolated target sentences (in one experiment) and target sentences preceded by their referentially supportive contexts (in another experiment) bears directly on referential theory. This is analogous to the comparison of Sentences (7a) and (7b) in isolation and in supportive context from the Britt et al. study.

(8) a. She decided to take / the cheese / from the farmer / rather than from / the grocery store.

b. She decided to take / the cheese / from the farmer / out of her bag / to eat for their lunch.

Looking at first-pass reading times of the disambiguating region ("rather than from" vs. "out of her bag"), they reported an NP-attachment penalty for sentences in isolation equal to that found in supportive contexts. Thus, context did not immediately eliminate the difficulty in processing an NP-attached preposition (complex NP analysis). However, the immediately subsequent nonregressive fixations (first-pass reading times of "the grocery store" vs. "to eat for their lunch") showed an NP-attachment penalty in isolation, but no difference in supportive contexts. Thus, referential context eliminated the NP-attachment penalty relatively early (within about 500 ms of encountering the disambiguating information), but not immediately. As discussed earlier, however, the fact that context did not eliminate processing difficulty immediately does not mean that it was not exerting an influence immediately. If context does not provide enough support for an alternative to cause its activation to greatly surpass that of its competitor, competition between these alternatives will result in some slowed processing.

In summary, attempts to find early effects of referential context in parsing PP-attachment ambiguities have been relatively successful. As was also the case with the complement/relative clause ambiguity, when the simple NP's presupposition of a unique discourse referent is satisfied by context, it is the analysis pursued, but when the complex NP's presupposition of a set of discourse referents is satisfied by context, it is the analysis pursued. As predicted by a process of constraint satisfaction, information provided by other constraints such as lexical semantics should be able to modulate the effects of referential context. Work on referential effects in the PP-attachment ambiguity by Sedivy and Spivey-Knowlton (chapter 16, this volume) has shown that different verb classes have different strengths of bias toward NP- or VP-attachment. For example, action-like verbs followed by an object NP and an ambiguously attached *with* phrase are strongly biased toward a particular attachment, and therefore reveal only weak effects of referential presupposition. In contrast, psych verbs and verbs of perception followed by an object NP and an ambiguously attached *with* phrase are only mildly biased toward a particular attachment, and therefore show quite clear modulation by referential presupposition.

REDUCED-RELATIVE/MAIN-CLAUSE AMBIGUITY

Attempts to find early effects of referential context in parsing reduced-relative clauses have, until very recently, met with considerably less success. This should not be surprising because the relative availability of the two syntactic alternatives is highly biased toward the main clause. A corpus analysis revealed that a sentence-initial NP-verb"ed" combination is 12 times more likely to begin a simple main clause than a reduced-relative clause (cf. Tabossi, Spivey-Knowlton, McRae, & Tanenhaus, in press).

In experiments comparing main-clause and reduced-relative sentences (Sentences 9a and 9b, respectively) in neutral and referentially supportive contexts, Ferreira and Clifton (1986) monitored eye movements and collected self-paced reading times. (Slashes delineate regions for analysis in eye-tracking and presentation in self-paced reading. The vertical line separates regions for self-paced reading only.)

(9) a. The editor | played the tape / and agreed / the story was big.
          (simple NP)

     b. The editor | played the tape / agreed / the story was big.
          (complex NP)

In the eye-tracking study, Ferreira and Clifton (Experiment 2) found that the slower first-pass reading times for reduced relatives, as compared with main clauses, did not change in the two contexts. However, in the self-paced reading task, readers actually had greater difficulty processing the reduced relative (as compared with the main clause) when it was preceded by a referentially supportive context. A reliable interaction between context and target sentence confirmed this observation. Thus, their contexts were having a reliable effect on initial parsing preference, but in the opposite direction. They suggested that this may have been due to readers simply failing to get the reduced-relative interpretation in the neutral contexts. In contrast, it may have been that the relative supporting contexts actually biased readers toward a main clause because the contextual constraint of these stimuli was not independently established (e.g., in a sentence completion task). However, because the availability of alternatives in this ambiguity is so highly biased toward the main clause, it is likely that the relative supporting contexts activated the relative clause interpretation just enough to cause close competition between the main-clause and reduced-relative alternatives. This increased competition between alternatives, due to an immediate influence from referential context, may have been responsible for the increased reading times.

Britt et al. (1992) compared reading times for main clauses and reduced relatives (Sentences 10a and 10b, respectively) in their referentially supportive contexts and in isolation (slashes delineate self-paced presentation regions).

(10) a. The woman / rushed to the hospital / without taking her laundry.

b. The woman / rushed to the hospital / had given birth safely.

For sentences in isolation, they observed that self-paced reading times of the disambiguating (last) region of the reduced-relative sentence were longer than for the main-clause sentence. As evidence against referential theory, this difference was still present (although slightly smaller) when the sentences were preceded by their own referentially supportive contexts. Unfortunately, their relative clause biased contexts may not have been as biasing as they hoped. Their own bias ratings, collected from subjects who read the entire context and target sentence, suggest a substantial bias toward the reduced-relative clause in those contexts. However, we tested their items in a sentence completion task to see what the off-line parsing preferences were at the point of ambiguity, and we found different results. Twenty subjects read the context and the target sentence up to and including the ambiguous verb, and were then asked to complete it as a grammatical, sensible sentence. In the main-clause-biasing contexts, the sentences were completed as main clauses 99% of the time. In the relative clause biasing contexts, the sentences were still completed as main clauses 83% of the time. Thus, the Britt et al. evidence against referential context effects in parsing reduced relatives may be due to a weak contextual manipulation.

Rayner et al. (1992) monitored eye movements in a similar experiment on reduced relatives in which almost half of their stimulus items were taken from Britt et al. (They split the Britt et al. disambiguating region into two regions.) As with their study on PP-attachment ambiguities, the Rayner et al. contextual manipulation (discourse focus) does not bear on referential theory. However, one can make an informal comparison of their separate data from isolated sentences with data from sentences in referentially supportive contexts to test referential theory's predictions regarding reduced relatives. For sentences in isolation, first-pass reading times of the disambiguating region were faster for main clauses than for reduced relatives. For sentences in their referentially supportive contexts, they were still faster for main clauses than for reduced relatives. Hence, referential context did not immediately resolve the ambiguity for the reduced-relative target sentences. As was the case with the Rayner et al. PP-attachment items, however, first-pass reading times of the region immediately following the disambiguating region did show an effect of context. In isolation, first-pass reading times of this region were faster in the main-clause sentences than in the reduced-relative sentences. In their respectively supportive contexts, there was no difference. This suggests a relatively early, although not immediate, elimination of processing difficulty due to referential context. As stated earlier, this lack of immediacy in the elimination of processing difficulty does not entail a lack of immediacy in the influence of referential context.

With an impressive number of stimulus items (36), Murray and Liversedge (Chapter 15, this volume) contrasted contexts containing one NP referent (Sentence 11a) with contexts containing two NP referents (Sentence 11b), and monitored eye movements during reading of main-clause sentences (Sentences 11c), reduced-relative sentences (Sentence 11d), and unreduced-relative sentences (Sentence 11e).

(11) a. Two people were discussing the food that had been prepared at the barbecue.
One was a guest who enjoyed meat while the other was a caterer who was a vegetarian.

b. Two people were discussing the food that had been prepared at the barbecue.
One was a guest who enjoyed meat while the other was a guest who was a vegetarian.

c. The guest grilled the steak and said it tasted nice.

d. The guest grilled the steak said it tasted nice.

e. The guest who was grilled the steak said it tasted nice.

They found that reading times for the disambiguating region of the reduced relative were reliably slower than those for the corresponding regions of the main clause and the unreduced relative, regardless of the preceding context. (For more details, see Murray & Liversedge, chapter 15, this volume). After careful examination of the items used in this study, this result points to an important, previously unstated component of effective referential contexts. The majority of Murray and Liversedge's relative-biasing contexts, although containing two referents for the crucial NP, do not include the event by which the relative clause discriminates the referring NP. In Sentence (11b), the context contains two guests, but does not mention someone grilling a steak for one and not the other. Thus, for the reader to interpret "The guest grilled the steak" as a reduced relative, he or she must infer this previously unmentioned event as already in the discourse. In contrast, interpreting it as a main clause simply means introducing a new event to the discourse. If revising the mental model of discourse by accommodating an inferred event is more costly than simply introducing a new event (cf. Altmann, 1987; Trueswell & Tanenhaus, 1991), then this constitutes a bias toward the main-clause alternative. Such inferencing can be avoided by having the two NP-referent contexts provide the event (or feature, in the case of PP-attachment ambiguities) that discriminates the crucial NP's reference (see Sentence 12b). Murray and Liversedge's results suggest that, in order to bias this type of ambiguity toward the complex NP analysis, a referential context must do more than satisfy the complex NP's presupposition of a set of referents. An effective referential context must also explicitly provide the event or feature that, in the modifying expression of the complex NP, discriminates one of the referents from the set.

In our own work concerning effects of referential context in parsing reduced relatives, the relative-biasing contexts do exactly that (cf. Spivey-Knowlton et al., 1993). However, in the case of the reduced-relative/main-clause ambiguity, the relative availability of the two alternatives is highly skewed toward the main clause. Therefore, even norming the stimulus items with sentence completions and using only those items that show the strongest off-line contextual constraint may not be enough to override the on-line parsing preference for the more common main-clause interpretation. One way to increase the initial availability of the relative clause alternative is to provide easily processed parafoveal information that probabilistically supports the relative clause (Burgess, 1991; Burgess & Tanenhaus, in preparation; Spivey-Knowlton et al., 1993). For example, a short, potentially agentive preposition such as *by* immediately following the ambiguous verb is still consistent with a main-clause continuation (i.e., "The animal hunted by night"), but is likely to continue as a relative clause (i.e., "The animal hunted by Elmer Fudd was casually eating a carrot"). Allowing *by* to be parafoveally processed during reading of the ambiguous verb should boost the availability of the relative clause interpretation (making the two syntactic alternatives closer to equal in availability), and thus allow contextual information to play a stronger role in determining the initial parsing preference.[1]

Using contexts selected from norming studies [one NP referent, Sentence (12a) and two NP referents, Sentence (12b)] and target sentences in which *by* began the relative clause [reduced relative, Sentence (12c), and unreduced relative, Sentence (12d)], Spivey-Knowlton et al. (1993) collected self-paced reading times (slashes delineate presentation regions).

(12) a. An actress and the producer's niece were auditioning for a play. The director selected the actress but not the niece.

   b. Two actresses were auditioning for a play. The director selected one of the actresses but not the other.

---

[1]It is important to note that we are saying the two-word presentation format allows parafoveal processing of *by* during reading of the verb, whereas the single-word presentation prohibits it. Because this experiment used self-paced reading, not eye tracking, we cannot know exactly what readers' eyes are actually doing when the verb + *by* is displayed. Nonetheless, eye-tracking of similar materials has shown that readers rarely (less than 25% of the time) fixate the *by*, indicating that it was processed parafoveally (Trueswell et al., in press).

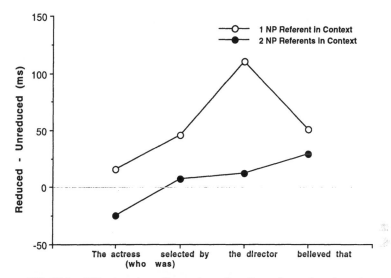

FIG. 17.1.   Difference in self-paced reading times for reduced- and unreduced-relative clauses as a function of sentence region. Open circles are for sentences preceded by contexts containing a unique referent. Filled circles are for sentences preceded by contexts containing a set of referents.

   c. The actress / selected by / the director / believed that / her performance / was perfect.

   d. The actress / who was / selected by / the director / believed that / her performance / was perfect.

The two-word presentation format allows *by* to be processed during reading of the ambiguous verb, yet maintains good resolution for locating where in the sentence any slowed processing occurs. Comparing only reduced and unreduced relatives allows us to equate string length and frequency of critical regions because the same words are used. At the verb + *by* region, reading times for the unreduced relatives were faster than for reduced relatives when context contained a unique referent (one NP referent). In contrast, when context contained a set of referents (two NP referents), the verb + *by* was read at the same speed in the unreduced relative as in the reduced relative (see Fig. 17.1). However, because the crucial interaction between context and target sentence was not significant at this region, a claim for immediate effects of referential context cannot be made. More importantly, this difference between reduction effects for the two context conditions is similarly present at the initial NP (although not at all approaching significance), making a clear interpretation of differences scores at the verb + *by* impossible.

At the following region (e.g., "the director"), the context-by-target sentence interaction was statistically reliable and clearly interpretable. In the one NP-referent context, the subject NP in the unreduced relative was read much faster than in the reduced relative. In the two NP-referent context, the subject NP in the unreduced relative was read only slightly faster than in the reduced relative. Similar to our examination of the Rayner et al. (1992) data, this supports an early, although perhaps not immediate, elimination of processing difficulty due to referential context.

In a second experiment, Spivey-Knowlton et al. compared ambiguous reduced relatives (Sentence 12c) with unambiguous reduced relatives (Sentence 13, in which the verb is morphologically unambiguous as a past participle) in corresponding contexts.

(13) The actress / chosen by / the director / believed that / her performance / was perfect.

Self-paced reading times at the verb + by revealed that the crucial interaction between context and target sentence was significant. In the one NP-referent context, this region was read faster in the unambiguous reduced relative than in the ambiguous reduced relative. In the two NP-referent context, this region was read slightly slower in the unambiguous reduced relative than in the ambiguous reduced relative (see Fig. 17.2). Reading-time differences for the subject NP were similar, and the context by target sentence interaction at that region was also significant. This result clearly supports an immediate effect of referential context in parsing reduced-relative clauses.

To test the importance of allowing by to be parafoveally processed during reading of the ambiguous verb, Spivey-Knowlton et al. conducted a third experiment in which the same items from Experiment 2 were presented in a single-word, self-paced format. With each button press revealing only one word at a time, by cannot increase the availability of the relative clause alternative during reading of the ambiguous verb. Therefore, effects of referential context should be weak and/or delayed.

This is exactly what was observed. At the determiner, noun, and matrix-verb positions (e.g., *the, director,* and *believed*), reading times were moderately slower for ambiguous versus unambiguous reduced relatives when preceded by a one NP-referent context, and only slightly slower for ambiguous versus unambiguous reduced relatives preceded by a two NP-referent context (see Fig. 17.3). However, the interaction between context and target sentence did not approach significance in any of these regions.

Thus, availability of the syntactic alternatives (as manipulated by the presence of by during presentation of the verb) has an important role in determining the strength and immediacy of context effects in syntactic-ambiguity resolution. When the relative availability is highly biased toward one alternative, referential

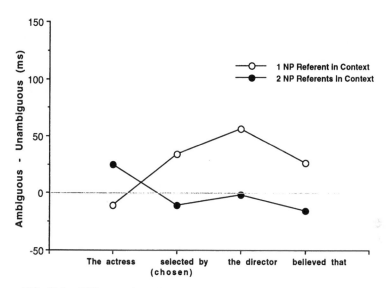

FIG. 17.2. Difference in self-paced reading times for ambiguous and unambiguous reduced-relative clauses as a function of sentence region. Open circles are for sentences preceded by contexts containing a unique referent. Filled circles are for sentences preceded by contexts containing a set of referents.

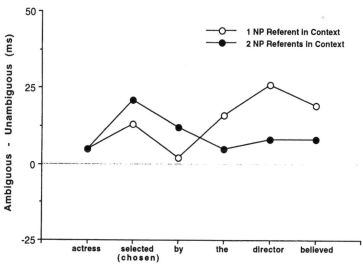

FIG. 17.3. Difference in self-paced reading times for ambiguous and unambiguous reduced-relative clauses as a function of word position. Open circles are for sentences preceded by contexts containing a unique referent. Filled circles are for sentences preceded by contexts containing a set of referents.

context will require some time to steer the interpretation toward the less available alternative. In contrast, when the two alternatives of a syntactic ambiguity are roughly equal in availability, referential context has a strong influence on which alternative is initially pursued. The same relationship has been observed for contextual influences from thematic constraint (cf. Trueswell & Tanenhaus, chapter 7, this volume). This one factor, "availability of alternatives," is likely to account for a substantial portion of the data patterns observed in studies of referential context effects on syntactic processing.

Still, it is arguable that the two-word, self-paced presentation format may introduce some strategy in the reader that does not apply to normal reading situations. Under such an explanation, this evidence for immediate effects of referential context and for the importance of the availability issue is questioned. To study reading of these stimuli under full-sentence presentation conditions, and thus test this alternative interpretation, Spivey-Knowlton and Tanenhaus (in preparation) conducted an eye-tracking experiment using the same items from Spivey-Knowlton et al. (1993, Experiments 2 and 3). First-pass reading times for the disambiguating *by*-phrase (e.g., "by the director") were much slower for ambiguous versus unambiguous reduced relatives when context contained only one NP referent. However, when context contained two NP referents, the *by*-phrase was read slightly faster in ambiguous versus unambiguous reduced relatives (see Fig. 17.4). A reliable interaction between context and target sentence

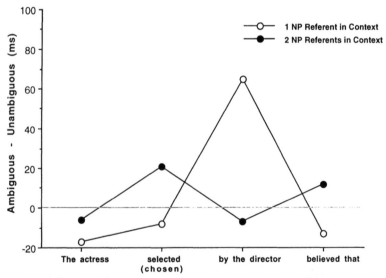

FIG. 17.4. Difference in first-pass reading times for ambiguous and unambiguous reduced-relative clauses as a function of sentence region. Open circles are for sentences preceded by contexts containing a unique referent. Filled circles are for sentences preceded by contexts containing a set of referents.

at this region confirmed the conclusion that referential context has an immediate influence in parsing reduced-relative clauses. This result discredits the alternative explanation of strategy effects causing the results of the two-word, self-paced reading experiments. Thus, the comparison between one-word and two-word presentation regions strongly supports the "availability of alternatives" explanation. Availability of alternatives determines the strength and latency of contextual influence.

In accordance with the constraint-based approach outlined in the beginning of this chapter, referential context should not be the only contextual factor relevant to initial parsing preferences. Semantic information, such as typicality of a given noun being the agent of a given verb, also appears to have early effects in parsing (MacDonald, in press; Pearlmutter & MacDonald, 1992; Tabossi et al., in press; Trueswell et al., in press; Trueswell & Tanenhaus, chapter 7, this volume; but see also Rayner et al., 1983). For example, a rating task (from 1 to 7) can provide an index of the typicality with which an entity plays the role of agent in an event (Sentences 14a–14c).

(14) a. How typical is it for an actress to select someone/something?
           mean rating: 2.1
       b. How typical it is for an actor to cover someone/something?
           mean rating: 3.1
       c. How typical is it for a senator to criticize someone/something?
           mean rating: 4.6

Such ratings were collected for the items used in Spivey-Knowlton et al. and matched (item by item) with the degree of slowed processing of the ambiguous reduced relative in the two NP-referent context only (Spivey-Knowlton & Tanenhaus, in preparation). At the verb + *by*, self-paced reading-time differences between reduced and unreduced relatives (Fig. 17.1) directly correlated, across stimulus items, with the agenthood ratings ($r^2 = .33, p < .02$). Thus, when the noun was a typical agent of the ambiguous verb, local semantic information supported the main-clause alternative and the reader had difficulty processing the ambiguous reduced relative. When the noun was an atypical agent of the ambiguous verb, the reader had little or no difficulty with the reduced relative. The same direct correlation was found between agenthood ratings and first-pass reading-time differences (between ambiguous and unambiguous past participles) at the verb itself ($r^2 = .47, p < .005$). Thus, in concert with referential context, local semantic context also influences immediate parsing preferences in the reduced-relative/main-clause ambiguity when the availability of alternatives is near equal. Moreover, these graded effects across different stimulus items are explicitly predicted by a constraint-based approach to syntactic-ambiguity resolution. When context provides strong support for the reduced relative (two NP referents) and local semantic context provides similarly strong support for the main clause (e.g., 6.1 agenthood), close competition between these alternatives results in high processing difficulty and greatly slowed reading times. With slightly weaker support from local semantic context (e.g., 5.1 agenthood), less competition will arise, and the degree processing difficulty will be slightly milder.

CONCLUSION

The majority of the data support immediate, or very early, effects of referential context in syntactic-ambiguity resolution. Referential expressions are linked with discourse immediately, and this linking to context allows discourse to partially determine which alternative of a syntactic ambiguity is initially pursued. However, it is not enough to point out successful referential context effects in all three types of syntactic ambiguities. To fully understand the phenomena, we must also be able to explain why certain studies have failed to find such context effects. The first point we discuss is methodological in nature: off-line norming. The second point is concerned with a theoretical aspect, availability of alternatives, which naturally leads us into the evidential, or constraint-based, approach to syntactic ambiguity resolution.

Off-Line Norming

An important consequence of the constraint-based approach to sentence processing, in which several factors simultaneously contribute to immediate parsing preferences, is that any two stimulus items are bound to vary along some relevant dimension(s). Thus, whereas one contextual constraint may be carefully controlled across all items in the experiment, variability in the uncontrolled constraints will produce great variability in the effectiveness of the contexts. The result is that an on-line influence of contextual constraint on parsing is tested with contexts that may not even show a consistent off-line influence on parsing preference. To avoid some of this variability in items, norming studies (such as sentence completion at the point of ambiguity) can be used to ensure that on-line measures are performed only on items in which the contextual constraint is clearly present off-line. Studies in which such norming was not done may have had stimulus items in which the contextual constraint was too weak to noticeably affect processing.

For example, this predicts that if sentence-completion norms were performed on Ferreira and Clifton's (1986) referential context stimuli, context would have little effect on the percentage of main-clause completions. Similarly, sentence-completion norms of the stimuli of Mitchell et al. (1992) and Rayner et al. (1992) should show weak effects of referential context. Unfortunately, norms on those stimuli have not been reported in the literature. Sentence completions have been conducted on the Britt et al. reduced-relative items (reported in this chapter) and on the Murray and Liversedge items (chapter 15, this volume), revealing a rather weak effect of referential context, which corresponds with their very small (or nonexistent) influence from referential context in on-line reading times.

Availability of Alternatives

Weak contextual constraint cannot account for all the failures to observe immediate effects of referential context. For example, in the Spivey-Knowlton et al. (1993) one-word presentation, self-paced reading experiment with reduced relatives, the contexts were carefully normed in advance. The reason immediate effects of referential context were not observed in that experiment is that the participial form of the verb (and hence the reduced relative) was not sufficiently available without *by* visible following it (as is the case with two-word presentation and in full-sentence eye-tracking). Work by Burgess and Tanenhaus (in preparation) showed similar effects of the presence of *by* in reduced relatives. Local semantic context (animacy of the initial NP) affected parsing preference when *by* was visible during reading of the verb (two-word presentation), but not when the verb was presented alone (one-word presentation).

MacDonald et al. (chapter 6, this volume) also discussed a form of "availability of alternatives," based on frequency of the critical verb being used as a simple past tense versus a past participle (cf. Kucera & Francis, 1967). Although the past participle is used in several constructions other than the reduced-relative clause, it is still an informative index of the availability of this uncommon structure for any given verb. In fact, MacDonald et al. found that, across many reduced-relative studies in the literature, the stimulus sets whose verbs had the highest past-participle frequency tended to find the earliest and strongest effects of semantic or discourse context. Clearly, availability of alternatives plays an important role in ambiguity resolution. Additionally, it is a fundamental component of the constraint-based approach to sentence processing.

Constraint-Based Syntactic Ambiguity Resolution

Although studies examining whether referential context influences initial syntactic commitments have reported superficially contradictory results, the literature can be unified when the availability of syntactic alternatives at the point of ambiguity and the strength of contextual constraint are taken into consideration. This observation has important theoretical implications for how we understand the syntactic ambiguity resolution process.

The fact that contextual constraints can have immediate effects is clearly problematic for models that claim that initial parsing commitments can use only syntactic information. As proposed by referential theory, discourse context provides important constraints that are exploited early on in processing to resolve many syntactic ambiguities. However, other types of nonsyntactic constraints, such as lexical semantics, operate in conjunction with referential constraints. In addition, there are strong local influences on parsing preferences (e.g., relative frequency) that are independent of discourse or semantic context. This pattern of results can be naturally accounted for within an evidential, or constraint-based, framework.

In the class of model that we have been developing, information associated with local input, such as the relative frequency of the verb occurring in one construction versus another as well as the parafoveal presence of the relative clause-supporting preposition *by*, determines the availability of the syntactic alternatives. Similar to referential theory (Altmann & Steedman, 1988; Crain & Steedman, 1985), semantic and discourse context can only support or refute one or more of those available parses. They cannot propose an interpretation disallowed by the structure and/or frequency characteristics of the current input. Unlike referential theory, the constraint-based approach posits that context will have only weak or delayed effects if only one alternative is sufficiently activated.

Although a model such as this can account for results that have been interpreted as support for opposing theories, it is important to note that constraint-based models cannot predict any possible pattern of results. When the factors that determine the availability of the syntactic alternatives and the strength of a contextual constraint are operationalized and independently quantified, and the resolution mechanism is specified, constraint-based models make precise and easily falsifiable predictions. Constraint-based models of syntactic ambiguity resolution are capable for accounting for a wide range of sentence processing data not because they contain multiple parameters, but because the constraints have graded effects. A constraint-based model does not predict discrete categorical parsing preferences for particular interpretations. It predicts continuously varying degrees of competition between available interpretations, which then map onto processing difficulty (slowed reading times) at regions of syntactic ambiguity. For example, a preliminary computational implementation, using data presented in Fig. 17.1, has demonstrated that immediate integration of lexical semantics, referential pragmatics, and conditionalized frequency information, followed by an explicit process of competition between the main-clause and reduced-relative alternatives, explains a substantial portion of the variance in slowed reading times at the point of syntactic ambiguity (Spivey-Knowlton, 1994).

The constraint-based approach to syntactic ambiguity resolution, with its continuous levels of activation of the alternatives and its immediate integration of various sources of relevant contextual information, may be best modeled within a connectionist-style framework. A connectionist learning rule allows the model to take advantage of, and internalize, statistical regularities that are present in the input. Although such statistical regularities may not account for discourse context effects, they do lead to emergent properties in the system that can account for many local influences in syntactic parsing (cf. Trueswell & Tanenhaus, chapter

7, this volume). Preliminary work on such an endeavor, with a feedforward network modeling the role of animacy in parsing reduced-relative clauses, has produced encouraging results (Pearlmutter, Daugherty, MacDonald, & Seidenberg, 1993). The constraint-based theory's strong claim that domain-specific decision principles are unnecessary to account for parsing preferences makes it a testable and falsifiable theory. Attempts (connectionist or otherwise) to provide quantitative predictions from a computational model and map them onto psycholinguistic data will be the crucial test of the constraint-based theory of syntactic ambiguity resolution.

ACKNOWLEDGMENTS

This work was supported by an NSF Graduate Student Research Fellowship to the first author and NIH grant #HD27206 to the second author. We are grateful to the volume editors and to Jen Saffran for helpful comments on an earlier draft.

REFERENCES

Altmann, G. (1987). Modularity and interaction in sentence processing. In J. Garfield (Ed.), *Modularity in knowledge representation and natural language understanding* (pp. 249–257). Cambridge, MA: MIT Press.

Altmann, G., Garnham, A., & Dennis, Y. (1992). Avoiding the garden-path: Eye movements in context. *Journal of Memory and Language, 31,* 685–712.

Altmann, G., Garnham, A., & Henstra, J. (in press). Effects of syntax in human sentence parsing: Evidence against a structure-based proposal mechanism. *Journal of Experimental Psychology: Learning, Memory and Cognition.*

Altmann, G., & Steedman, M. (1988). Interaction with context during human sentence processing. *Cognition, 30,* 191–238.

Britt, M. A., Perfetti, C. A., Garrod, S., & Rayner, K. (1992). Parsing and discourse: Context effects and their limits. *Journal of Memory and Language, 31,* 293–314.

Burgess, C. (1991). *The interaction of syntactic, semantic and visual factors in syntactic ambiguity resolution.* Unpublished doctoral dissertation, University of Rochester, Rochester, NY.

Burgess, C., & Tanenhaus, M. (in preparation). *The interaction of semantic and parafoveal information in syntactic ambiguity resolution.*

Crain, S. (1980). *Contextual constraints on sentence comprehension.* Unpublished doctoral dissertation, University of California, Irvine.

Crain, S., & Steedman, M. (1985). On not being led up the garden path: The use of context by the psychological parser. In D. Dowty, R. Kartunnen, & A. Zwicky (Eds.), *Natural language parsing,* (pp. 320–358). Cambridge, England: Cambridge University Press.

Ferreira, F., & Clifton, C. (1986). The independence of syntactic processing. *Journal of Memory and Language, 25,* 348–368.

Frazier, L. (1987). Sentence processing: A tutorial review. In M. Coltheart (Ed.), *Attention & performance XII: The psychology of reading* (pp. 554–586). Hillsdale, NJ: Lawrence Erlbaum Associates.

Frazier, L., & Fodor, J. D. (1978). The sausage machine: A new two-stage parsing model. *Cognition, 6,* 291–325.

Frazier, L., & Rayner, K. (1982). Making and correcting errors during sentence comprehension: Eye movements in the analysis of structurally ambiguous sentences. *Cognitive Psychology, 14*, 178–210.

Hindle, D., & Rooth, M. (1993). Structural ambiguity and lexical relations. *Computational Linguistics, 19,* 103–120.

Kucera, H., & Francis, W. (1967). *Computational analysis of present-day American English.* Providence, RI: Brown University Press.

MacDonald, M. (in press). Probabilistic constraints and syntactic ambiguity resolution. *Language & Cognitive Processes.*

Marcus, M., Marcinkiewicz, M., & Santorini, B. (1992). *The Penn Treebank Project* (Preliminary release, version 0.5). University of Pennsylvania: Linguistic Data Consortium.

Marslen-Wilson, W. (1973). Linguistic structure and speech shadowing at very short latencies. *Nature, 244,* 522–523.

Marslen-Wilson, W., & Welsh, A. (1978). Processing interactions and lexical access during word recognition in continuous speech. *Cognitive Psychology, 10,* 29–63.

Mitchell, D., & Corley, M. (in press). Immediate biases in parsing: Discourse effects or experimental artefacts? *Journal of Experimental Psychology: Learning, Memory and Cognition.*

Mitchell, D., Corley, M., & Garnham, A. (1992). Effects of context in human sentence parsing: Evidence against a discourse-based proposal mechanism. *Journal of Experimental Psychology: Learning, Memory and Cognition, 18,* 69–88.

Pearlmutter, N., Daugherty, K., MacDonald, M., & Seidenberg, M. (1993, March). *Constraint satisfaction in main verb/reduced relative ambiguities.* Poster presented at the 6th annual CUNY Sentence Processing Conference, Amherst, MA.

Pearlmutter, N., & MacDonald, M. (1992). Plausibility effects in syntactic ambiguity resolution. In *Proceedings of the 14th Annual Meeting of the Cognitive Science Society* (pp. 498–503). Hillsdale, NJ: Lawrence Erlbaum Associates.

Rayner, K., Carlson, M., & Frazier, L. (1983). The interaction of syntax and semantics during sentence processing: Eye movements in the analysis of semantically biased sentences. *Journal of Verbal Learning and Verbal Behavior, 22,* 358–374.

Rayner, K., Garrod, S., & Perfetti, C. (1992). Discourse influences during parsing are delayed. *Cognition, 45,* 109–139.

Sedivy, J., & Spivey-Knowlton, M. (1993). The effect of definiteness in parsing PP-attachment ambiguities. In A. Schafer (Ed.), *Proceedings of the North Eastern Linguistic Society* (pp. 447–461). Amherst, MA: Graduate Linguistic Student Association.

Spivey-Knowlton, M. (1994). Quantitative predictions from a constraint-based theory of syntactic ambiguity resolution. In M. Mozer, P. Smolensky, D. Touretzky, J. Elman, & A. Weigand (Eds.), *Proceedings of the 1993 Connectionist models summer school.* (pp. 130–137). Hillsdale, NJ: Lawrence Erlbaum Associates.

Spivey-Knowlton, M., & Tanenhaus, M. (in preparation). *Immediate effects of referential context in parsing: Evidence from eye movements during reading.*

Spivey-Knowlton, M., Trueswell, J., & Tanenhaus, M. (1993). Context effects and syntactic ambiguity resolution: Discourse and semantic influences in parsing reduced relative clauses. *Canadian Journal of Experimental Psychology, 47,* 276–309.

Steedman, M., & Altmann, G. (1989). Ambiguity in context: A reply. *Language and Cognitive Processes, 4,* 211–234.

Tabossi, P., Spivey-Knowlton, M., McRae, K., & Tanenhaus, M. (in press). Semantic effects on syntactic ambiguity resolution: Evidence for a constraint-based resolution process. In C. Umilta & M. Moscovitch (Eds.), *Attention and performance XV* Hillsdale, NJ: Lawrence Erlbaum Associates.

Taraban, R., & McClelland, J. (1990). Sentence comprehension: A multiple constraints view. In D. Balota, K. Rayner, & G. Flores d'Arcais (Eds.), *Comprehension processes in reading* (pp. 231–263). Hillsdale, NJ: Lawrence Erlbaum Associates.

Trueswell, J., & Tanenhaus, M. (1991). Tense, temporal context and syntactic ambiguity resolution. *Language and Cognitive Processes, 6,* 303–338.

Trueswell, J., Tanenhaus, M., & Garnsey, S. (in press). Semantic influences on parsing: Use of thematic role information in syntactic disambiguation. *Journal of Memory and Language.*

VI

SENTENCE PROCESSING AND LANGUAGE ACQUISITION

18 Learning, Parsing, and Modularity

Stephen Crain,*
Weijia Ni,*
Laura Conway
University of Connecticut
*and Haskins Laboratories

According to the *modularity hypothesis,* different components of the language apparatus obey different operating principles (cf. Crain & Shankweiler, 1991; Crain & Steedman, 1985; Fodor, 1983; Shankweiler & Crain, 1986). In this chapter, we argue that two subcomponents of the language apparatus are autonomous because of their different operating characteristics. One is the component responsible for language acquisition (i.e., the language acquisition device [LAD]). The other is the component used in resolving ambiguities (i.e., the sentence-parsing mechanism). We identify instances in which operating characteristics of these two components conflict due to the different demands placed on them. The principles of the LAD must be responsive to demands of learnability. To achieve learnability, the LAD must constrain learners' hypotheses to guarantee that linguistic representations that are not derived in the target language will not be formulated or, if formulated, can be disconfirmed by readily available evidence. By contrast, the sentence-parsing mechanism selects among the competing linguistic representations that are derived in a language. Selection is based on considerations of simplicity. It turns out that certain initial representations that are favored on learnability grounds are ones that are dispreferred by the sentence-parsing mechanism. Putting it the other way around, certain linguistic representations that are preferred by the sentence-parsing mechanism are ones that would create problems of learnability if they were initially adopted by learners. The upshot of these deliberations is that the principles of parsing must not guide learners in their formulation of grammatical hypotheses. Therefore, the principles of parsing and the principles of learning must be kept in distinct modules of the language faculty.

We assume the following model of the parser. In resolving ambiguities, the parser prefers representations that succeed in referring to entities that have already been introduced in the discourse, rather than ones that postulate the existence of entities not previously mentioned. In the absence of context, as in most studies of adult sentence processing, the parser begins to construct multiple representations (mental models) of an ambiguous sentence in parallel, but quickly curtails its operations once a viable representation is constructed. Lacking evidence from the discourse context, parsing decisions are guided by a principle that favors the representation that requires the fewest extensions (or accommodations of presuppositional failure) to the mental model. This is called the *principle of parsimony* (Crain & Steedman 1985).

Our assumptions about the operating principles of the LAD are quite different. These principles must enable learners to successfully converge on the target grammar on the basis of the available evidence. Presumably, the evidence available to learners consists primarily of sentences presented in circumstances that make them true. Sometimes more than one alternative interpretation of a sentence is made available by Universal Grummar (UG).[1] To complicate matters further, the alternative interpretations may sometimes form a subset–superset relationship (i.e., the circumstances that make the sentence true on one interpretation may be a proper subset of the circumstances that make it true on another interpretation). A semantic subset problem arises if the target language includes the subset interpretive option, but not the superset option. To avoid semantic subset problems, the interpretive options for sentences must be ordered in the LAD by a principle instructing learners to initially choose the representation that is true in the smallest set of circumstances.[2] This is called the *semantic subset principle* (Crain, 1992, 1993; Crain & Lillo-Martin, in press; Crain & Philip, 1993).

This chapter is concerned with conflicts between the basic operating principles of acquisition and parsing. The cases we discuss involve the focus operator—*only*. The next section sets the stage with a brief description of the syntactic and semantic properties of *only*. Following that, we discuss the principle of parsimony, which guides adults in parsing sentences with *only*. Finally, we discuss the semantic subset principle, which guides children in the acquisition of sentences with *only*.

---

[1]However, this does not entail that both options are derived in the target language. Some UG options may be available in the theory, but may not appear in some particular language. Such is the case with parameter settings, for example. Therefore, it is important not to confuse the state of affairs we are describing—where the child selects among competing grammatical options—with the state of affairs that confronts adults in processing structurally ambiguous sentences.

[2]This argument presupposes that negative semantic evidence is not available to learners. That is, we assume that learners are not informed with sufficient regularity about interpretations that cannot be assigned to sentences in the target language.

SYNTAX AND SEMANTICS OF *ONLY*

Syntactically, the focus operator *only* associates exclusively with elements that it c-commands.[3] This means that when *only* appears in preverbal position, it can focus on the entire verb phrase (VP), or on a constituent within the VP (e.g., the direct-object noun phrase [NP]). Because *only* can associate with more than one element on different occasions of use, sentences that contain *only* are often ambiguous. One ambiguity is illustrated in (1), where the boldface **F** indicates the element in focus. The alternative readings of (1) are paraphrased in (2).

(1) a. The big elephant only eats peanuts.
   b. The big elephant only <u>eats peanuts</u>.
      F
   c. The big elephant only eats <u>peanuts</u>.
      F

(2) a. The only thing the big elephant does is eat peanuts.
   b. The only food the big elephant eats is peanuts.

When it appears in preverbal position, as in (1), *only* cannot associate with the subject NP. For this to happen, *only* must appear in presubject position. In that position, it can associate with the entire NP, or with a nominal constituent within the NP. An example is given in (3), with the corresponding interpretations given in (3a–b).

(3) Only the big elephants eat peanuts.
   a. The only thing who eats peanuts is the big elephant.
   b. The only elephant who eats peanuts is the big elephant.

In presubject position, the c-command domain of *only* does not extent beyond the NP in which it appears, so it cannot associate from this position with the VP or with any element inside the VP.

The basic semantic function of focus operators generally, and *only* in particular, is to signal when the extension of some linguistic constituent is being contrasted with a set of alternatives. An example will clarify the point. Consider Sentence (4) (Willoughby's is a shop in New Haven, Connecticut, that sells really good coffee).

(4) In New Haven, only Willoughby's coffee is really good.

Sentence (4) is felicitous only if coffee from Willoughby's is being compared to coffee from other shops in New Haven. If the speaker had tried only Will-

---

[3]A constituent A c-commands another constituent B if, and only if, there is a path from A up to the first branching node above A and then down to B (cf. Reinhart, 1983).

oughby's coffee, we would be reluctant to say that the statement was appropriate. However, note that the sentence does not assert that a comparison is being made; rather, this is presupposed. The presupposition that coffee from other shops has been tried is triggered by the occurrence of *only*. We call the entities that are presupposed to exist a *contrast set*.

The meaning representation of a sentence with a focus operator has three parts. Two of these parts are concerned with the content of the sentence. Some of its content is background information, B, and some of its content is in focus, F. The third part of the meaning representation is pragmatic: There must be a contrast set of alternatives to the focus element within the domain of discourse. The contrast set, CON, is not mentioned in the sentence; rather, it is presupposed.

The meaning of an individual focus operator includes truth conditions that are specific to it. For sentences with *only* to be true, two conditions must be met. First, the information in background must apply to the focus element (i.e., the background must be true of the focus). Second, the background must not apply to any of the alternatives to the focus element. That is, the background must apply uniquely to the element in focus. The requirement of uniqueness can be paraphrased as follows: If the background applies to any alternative to the focus element, that alternative is the focus element. Formally, the semantic value of the focus operator *only* can be stated using the following rule (adapted from Krifka, 1991; also see Jackendoff, 1972; Rooth, 1985).

(5) Meaning rule for *only:* $B(F) \& \forall X[\{X \in CON(F) \& B(X)\} \rightarrow X = F]$, where X is variable of type F, and CON(F) is a set of contextually determined alternatives to F.

To unpack the contents of the meaning rule for *only,* let us examine it one piece at a time. The first conjunct, $B(F)$, states the requirement that the background must apply to the focus element. The second conjunct is the statement of uniqueness: $\forall X[\{ X \in CON(F) \& B(X)\} \rightarrow X = F]$. The universal quantifier ranges over a metavariable, X. The metavariable X may be replaced by real variables of different types, depending on the kind of entity that is being contrasted with the focus element. This gives the meaning rule the flexibility to handle alternative interpretations that may be assigned to sentences with *only*. Different interpretations are rendered by replacing the metavariable, X, with a variable of one kind or another. If the focus element is an individual, the contrast set will be individuals; therefore the metavariable in the meaning rule will be replaced by an individual variable: x, y, and so on. If the focus element is a property, as with a VP, the contrast set will consist of properties rather than individuals, therefore, the metavariable will be replaced by a variable of this type: P, Q, and so on. The meaning rule ends by guaranteeing the uniqueness of the focus element—for each member of the contrast set, if the background applies to it, that member is the focus element.

To illustrate how the meaning rule in (5) works, let us apply it to some examples, beginning with (6).

(6) The big elephant only eats peanuts.
a. The only food the big elephant eats is peanuts.
b. The only thing the big elephant does is eat peanuts.

We saw that when *only* is in preverbal position it can associate with at least two different elements, as indicated by the paraphrases in (6a–b). Therefore, we should be able to derive different logical representations from the meaning rule in (5), corresponding to these interpretations. We take them in turn. Interpretation (6a) can be stated informally as follows: There is something under consideration that the big elephant eats, namely, peanuts; if there is anything else that the big elephant eats, that thing is peanuts. This is a close paraphrase of the logical representation that follows from the meaning rule:

Logical Representation for Reading (6a)

The-Big-Elephant-Eats' (Peanuts') &
$\forall y[\{y \in$ CON(Peanuts') & The Big-Elephant-Eats' (y)$\} \rightarrow y =$ Peanuts']

(In the formula, the focus, F, is the direct object, whose semantic value is Peanuts'. The background, B, is represented as The-Big-Elephant-Eats'. Because the element in focus is an individual, the metavariable X from the meaning rule in (5) is replaced by an individual variable, viz. y.)

Next we derive interpretation (6b). Stating it informally, there is some activity the big elephant is engaged in, namely, eating peanuts; if there is any other activity that the big elephant is engaged in, then that activity is one of eating peanuts:

Logical Representation for Reading (6b)

The-Big-Elephant' (Eats-Peanuts') &
$\forall y[\{P \in$ CON(Eats-Peanuts') & The-Big-Elephant' (P)$\} \rightarrow P =$ Eats-Peanuts']

(Here, the element in focus is the VP, Eats-Peanuts'. Because this is a property, a variable that ranges over properties, viz. P, is substituted for the metavariable, X, in the meaning rule in (5).)

To end this section, we acknowledge another construction containing *only* that gives rise to ambiguity. This construction is illustrated in (7).

(7) The big elephant is the only one eating peanuts.

   a. The only thing eating peanuts is the big elephant.

   b. The only elephant eating peanuts is the big elephant.

As the paraphrases (a, b) show, the contrast set for (7) can either be the set of elephants or the entire domain of discourse. Although both interpretations of (7) are quite accessible for most people, there are reasons for thinking that the interpretation in (7b) is preferred. In the next section, we explain why this should be the case.

PARSING AMBIGUOUS SENTENCES WITH *ONLY*

This section outlines a model of how adults resolve semantic ambiguities. The model is called the *referential theory*. First, we show how the referential theory explains the differences that are found in parsing so-called "garden path" sentences with the definite article, such as Sentence (8), and ones with the focus operator *only*, such as Sentence (9).

(8) The horses raced past the barn fell.

(9) Only horses raced past the barn fell.

According to the referential theory, sentences like (9) should not evoke garden path effects. We explain why and provide some empirical support for this prediction. Then we turn to other constructions containing *only*, which we have recently investigated in a series of experiments, that compare the interpretations assigned by adults and those assigned by children.

The Referential Theory

The referential theory maintains that the preferred reading of an ambiguous sentence is determined by comparing the discourse representations associated with the alternative interpretations (Altmann & Steedman, 1988; Crain & Steedman, 1985; Ni & Crain, 1990). On this account, multiple syntactic analyses are computed as an ambiguous sentence is parsed. These analyses are input to the semantic-pragmatic processor, which selects the interpretation that best conforms to the surrounding context. The referential theory contends that the primary responsibility for resolving structural ambiguities does not rest with structural mechanisms, but with immediate, word-by-word evaluation of the alternative analyses by the semantic-pragmatic processor. The context in which the sentence is presented is checked, and the reading of the sentence that best fits the context is selected, as stated in the following principle (Crain & Steedman, 1985):

The Principle of Referential Success: If there is a reading that succeeds in refering to an entity already established in the perceiver's mental model of the domain of discourse, then it is favored over one that does not. (p. 331)

In most experimental work reported in the literature, ambiguous sentences are presented in the so-called null context. Therefore, the principle of referential success is not applicable. A related principle is operative, however. According to the referential theory, outside of any linguistic or nonlinguistic context, the perceiver actively attempts to construct a mental representation of a situation that is consistent with each of the alternative interpretations of the sentence. In addition to the characters and events depicted in the sentence, the construction of a mental model sometimes requires the perceiver to represent information that the sentence presupposes, not just what it asserts. The process of augmenting one's mental model to represent the presuppositional content of sentences has been called "accommodation for presupposition" by Lewis (1979, p. 340).

According to the referential theory, the accommodation of presuppositional failure plays a critical role in explaining which interpretation of an ambiguous sentence is preferred outside of a discourse context. The parser begins constructing all permissible representations of a sentence, but, due to limited computational resources, quickly settles on just one interpretation—the one that requires the fewest modifications in establishing a coherent discourse representation. Crain and Steedman advanced the following principle to explain such parsing preferences.

The Principle of Parsimony: If there is a reading that carries fewer unsatisfied but consistent presuppositions than any other, then that reading will be adopted and the presuppositions in question will be incorporated in the perceiver's mental model. (p. 333)

To wrap up our review of the referential theory, we note one further property of the principle of parsimony: It pertains only to ambiguous sentences. In processing unambiguous sentences, the parser has no choice but to construct a mental representation that accommodates all unmet presuppositions. This is why sentences like "The horse ridden past the barn fell" do not pose difficulties for the parser, even outside of context.

Experiment 1: Garden-Path Sentences with *Only*

This section presents the results of a recent experimental investigation of the principle of parsimony: it applies to garden-path sentences with the focus operator *only* presented without contextual support. The experiment manipulated the referential content of NPs by substituting the word *only* for the define determiner *the*. Test materials included sentences like (10)–(12).

(10) The students furnished answers before the exam received high marks.

(11) Only students furnished answers before the exam received high marks.

(12) Only dishonest students furnished answers before the exam received high marks.

These sentences are structurally identical at the point during processing at which the ambiguity arises; namely, at the word *furnished*. Sentence (10) is a variant of the classic garden-path sentence "The horse raced past the barn fell," therefore it should be expected to induce garden-path effects, on any theory. Accordingly, the referential theory predicts that Sentence (10) will produce garden-path effects. This expectation does not hold for Sentence (11), however. Because the modifier *only* has replaced the definite determiner, it follows from the referential theory that the parser will opt for the reduced-relative clause analysis of the ambiguous phrase beginning with "furnished answers. . . ."

As we discussed earlier, the focus operator *only* requires the perceiver to form a discourse representation that contrasts the element in focus with another set of entities. In (11), this requirement is most readily satisfied if the reduced-relative clause analysis of the ambiguous phrase is selected. Having already encountered the NP, "only students," the discourse representation makes reference to a set of students. At the point of the ambiguity, the parser has two options. One option is to analyze the ambiguous verb *furnished* as part of the main clause (i.e., to assign it the grammatical feature, past tense). This puts in focus the head of the NP containing *only,* as indicated in the following.

Only <u>students</u> . . .
        F

If this option is pursued, however, the parser still has to establish the set of alternatives to the focus set—*students*. The problem is that there is no information about the nature of the contrast set either from the context (because we are assuming that there is no discourse context) or from within the sentence. It follows from the principle of parsimony that creating a contrast set from scratch should be avoided if possible (see Heim, 1982, for a similar suggestion).

However, the option remains to interpret *furnished* as a past participle, beginning a reduced-relative clause.

Only <u>students furnished answers . . .</u>
             F

If this option is chosen, the problem of constructing a contrast set is solved. The reduced-relative clause provides the information needed to form the contrast set; the set in focus is subdivided. In the present example, the set of students is partitioned into those who were furnished answers before the exam and those who were not. In short, the requirements of *only* are satisfied more easily on the reduced-relative clause analysis of the local ambiguity. Consequently, garden-path effects should not occur.

In (12), by contrast, the appearance of the adjective *dishonest* in the subject NP helps the perceiver to establish the focus set (dishonest students) and its corresponding contrast set (honest students) before the ambiguity is encountered.

Only <u>dishonest students</u> . . .
$\qquad$ F

Hence, at the point of ambiguity, there is no longer any reason to favor the reduced-relative clause analysis. The same conditions obtain at this point in (12) as obtain at this point in (10). Therefore, the same analysis should be pursued and we should expect the reemergence of garden-path effects in sentences like (12). In summary, the referential theory makes the following predictions about garden-path effects for these sentences.

(a) The students—garden-path effects
(b) Only students—no garden-path effects
(c) Only dishonest students—garden-path effects

These predictions were tested in an experiment using a self-paced reading paradigm. Subjects read sentences one word at a time on a computer screen. They called up each new word by pressing one of two keys marked "yes" or "no." Subjects were instructed to press the "yes" key as long as each word could be grammatically incorporated into the material they had previously read. Either key press continued to bring up new words, which accumulated on the screen. The computer recorded the duration in milliseconds between the onset of each new word and the following key press.

There were 32 tests sentences and 16 control sentences with unambiguous verbs. They were interspersed among 92 filler sentences. Four lists of stimuli were composed so that each version of each test and control sentence appeared only once in any list. Eight subjects were tested on each list, thus 32 subjects participated in the experiment.

To analyze the data, mean reaction times for the test sentences and the controls were divided into four regions. The first region spanned the initial NP; the second region consisted of the first VP, which contained the ambiguous verb in the test sentences; the third region was the main verb; and the final region was the remainder of the sentence. Figure 18.1 presents the data for sentence of type (a), (b), and (c) in each region. The points in each region represent the average time subjects took to read each word in that region. Only those responses that correctly recognized the sentences as grammatical were used in the analysis.

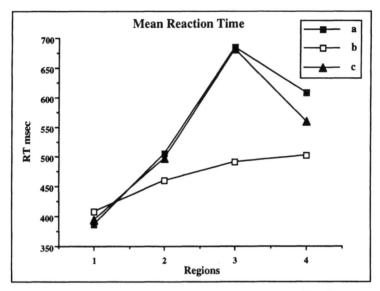

FIG. 18.1   Mean reaction time by region for three types of locally ambiguous sentences: (a) The N . . ., (b) only N . . ., (c) only adj N. . . .

a. The students	furnished . . .	received	high . . .
b. Only students	furnished . . .	received	high . . .
c. Only dishonest students	furnished . . .	received	high . . .
1	2	3	4

These were the findings: There were no significant differences in reaction
times among any of the sentence types in region 1. In region 2, type (a) and (c)
sentences grouped together and yielded slightly longer reaction times than type
(b) sentences. Region 3 presented significant differences among the sentence
types. Type (a) and (c) sentences took significantly longer to read than type (b)
sentences, which patterned like the unambiguous controls without any elevation
in response times. Thus, the parser was not disturbed in the on-line processing of
type (b) sentences in region 3. By contrast, responses times were elevated in
region 3 for sentence types (a) and (c). We interpret these data as showing that
type (a) and (c) sentences induced garden path effects at the point of disambiguation, but sentences of type (b) did not. To circumvent the criticism that word-by-
word monitoring tasks do not tap rapid on-line processing, we replicated the
present study using the technique of eye-movement recording (Ni & Crain,
1993). The findings were equally robust.

To summarize the findings of Experiment 1, garden-path effects appeared in
sentences with *the* and ones with *only* plus an adjectival modifier, but not when
only was directly followed by a noun. This is exactly as predicted by the referen-

tial theory. These findings underscore the conclusion reached by Crain and Steedman (1985) that there really is no such thing as a "null context." In the absence of an external context, the parser actively engages in internal, mental model building.

Minimal Commitments

The results of Experiment 1 support the claim that the principle of parsimony guides the on-line operation of the parser, outside of context. Crain and Hamburger (1992) suggest that the principle of parsimony is ultimately motivated by the need to minimize cognitive effort in response to limitations in working memory capacity. To conserve effort, unnecessary extensions to the mental model are avoided if possible. The advantage of such a "least effort" strategy for ambiguity resolution is to reduce the risk of making commitments that will need to be changed later. To coin a phrase, the parser is a "minimal commitment" component of the language apparatus.

To avoid unnecessary commitments, the parser selects the interpretation of an ambiguous sentence that makes it true in the largest set of circumstances.[4] To illustrate this operating characteristic of the parser, consider the ambiguity involving *only* in Sentences like (13).

(13) The big elephant is the only one playing the guitar.
  a. The only thing playing the guitar is the big elephant.
  b. The only elephant playing the guitar is the big elephant.

As the paraphrases in (a) and (b) indicate, there are two possible contrast sets. One is the set of elephants; the other is the entire set of individuals in the domain of discourse. On the (a) interpretation, everything in the domain of discourse is in the contrast set. This makes Sentence (13) true only in a limited set of circumstances, as compared with interpretation (b). In fact, the (a) interpretation of (13) is true in a subset of the circumstances that make it true on the (b) interpretation. That is, the (a) reading entails the (b) reading, but not vice versa: If the big elephant is the only elephant playing the guitar, it need not be the only thing playing it; on the other hand, if the big elephant is the only thing playing

---

[4]Any model of discourse that contains individuals or events whose existence is disconfirmed by new information will have to be modified appropriately to bring the model of the parser in line with that of the interlocutor. Mismatches between the mental models of a speaker and a hearer, or a writer and a reader, are apt to interfere with the flow of information between them. To facilitate the transfer of information, a perceiver must continuously attempt to align their mental model with that of the other participants in the discourse. Following the guidelines of the principle of parsimony, the strategy adopted by the parser is to avoid interpretations of ambiguous sentences that entail additional commitments about individuals and events within the domain of discourse.

the guitar, it must be the only elephant playing the guitar. If our inference is correct—that the parser favors the interpretation that makes a sentence true in the broadest range of circumstances—then adults should prefer the (b) interpretation of sentences like (13).

Another ambiguity occurs when *only* appears in preverbal position, as in example (14). The alternative readings are paraphrased in (a) and (b).

(14) The dinosaur is only painting a house.
    a.   The only thing the dinosaur is doing is painting a house.
    b.   The only thing the dinosaur is painting is a house.

Again, the (a) interpretation is true in a subset of the circumstances that correspond to the (b) interpretation. To minimize commitments, then, the parser should favor the (b) interpretation because this interpretation is consistent with a larger range of possible outcomes.

In contrast to our expectation that adults will prefer the (b) interpretation of sentences like (13) and (14), we argue in the next section that children adopt the (a) interpretation as their initial grammatical representation of such sentences. In other words, children sometimes initially hypothesize semantic representations that are dispreferred by adults. We examine this proposal by looking at children's understanding of sentences with the focus operator *only*.

ACQUISITION OF SENTENCES WITH *ONLY*

The LAD permits children to attain their target grammar(s) solely on the basis of positive evidence. Just as children lack negative syntactic evidence—evidence about the ungrammaticality of sentence forms—it also seems likely that they lack the kind of evidence needed to reject incorrect hypotheses about what sentences may and may not mean. Therefore, if a child were to commit semantic overgeneration (i.e., if he or she assigned sentence meanings beyond those assigned by the adult grammar), he or she would be hard pressed to recover from the error. As with negative syntactic evidence, if every semantic miscue must be corrected on the basis of experience, this would require an enormous supply of negative semantic feedback. To our knowledge, there is little empirical data on the matter. However, we think it highly unlikely that children expunge semantic errors on the basis of experience. Therefore, we explore the possibility that children avoid making semantic errors in the first place. We propose a principle of learnability to account for the absence of errors. The principle orders children's semantic hypotheses in advance, as follows: Default hypotheses are ones that will not subsequently need to be revised (i.e., they are realized universally), and additional (language-particular) hypotheses are added on the basis of positive evidence from the input.[5] The principle is called the Semantic Subset Principle (cf. Crain & Philip, 1993).

> Semantic Subset Principle: If the interpretative component of UG makes two inter-pretations, A and B, available for a sentence, S, and if interpretation A makes S true in a narrower range of circumstances than interpretation B does, then inter-pretation A is hypothesized before B in the course of language development.

Language acquisition is replete with potential learnability problems. A prob-lems arises in principle whenever a sentence can be mapped onto two different interpretations, such that one interpretation is true in a set of circumstances that constitutes a subset of the circumstances corresponding to the other interpreta-tion. To avoid such semantic subset problems, the semantic subset principle arranges grammatical options to ensure that learners initially hypothesize an interpretation that makes a sentence true in the smallest set of circumstances. In this way, learners are assured of formulating falsifiable hypotheses. To make sentences true in the narrowest possible set of circumstances amounts to making the maximal commitments about the entities and events in the domain of dis-course. In short, the LAD is a "maximal commitment" component of the lan-guage apparatus.

Let us consider some examples of the semantic subset principle in operation. We saw earlier that when *only* appears in preverbal position it can focus on the entire VP or it can focus within the VP, selecting the direct-object NP. This means that (17) is ambiguous, with the interpretations indicated in (17a-b).

(17) The dinosaur is only painting a house.

a.   The only thing the dinosaur is doing is painting a house.

b.   The only thing the dinosaur is painting in a house.

The circumstances in which these two readings are true vary depending on the contrast set for the focus operator *only*. The contrast set of both (a) and (b) include properties of individuals, rather than individuals themselves. The con-trast set for the (a) reading includes all of the properties of the dinosaur under consideration. For the sentence to be true on this reading, the dinosaur can only

---

[5]Even if UG makes alternative interpretive options available for a sentence, it is not necessarily ambiguous for the child. As in parameter setting, children may have a range of options available to them in the theory, but they may nevertheless hypothesize only certain of these values at any given time. There is an important difference between parameter setting and the case we are considering, however. In parameter setting, new parameters supplant old ones. In formulating semantic hypothe-ses, by contrast, children are seen to begin with a limited set of (universal) interpretive options, which is then extended to include additional (language-particular) options on the basis of positive evidence.

have one property—that of painting the house. The (b) reading is less restrictive. The sentence is true on this reading if the only thing the dinosaur is painting is a house, but this allows the dinosaur to have other properties as well, such as flying a kite, for instance.

Children and adults are both expected to find (17) inappropriate as a description of the situation in (18), but they should have different reasons for rejecting it. Assuming that adults have both readings available, they should adopt the (b) reading of (17) because this reading is consistent with a broader range of circumstances than the (a) reading. Putting it differently, the (b) reading makes fewer commitments than does the (a) reading, so the (b) reading is favored by the principle of parsimony. However, the context in (18) makes Sentence (17) false on this interpretation.

(18)

Children should also reject (17), but for a different reason. The circumstances corresponding to the alternative readings of (17) are in a subset–superset relationship. Therefore, the semantic subset principle compels children to initially hypothesize the (a) reading. This reading too is falsified by the context in (18). At a later point in development, the (b) reading will also become available, in response to evidence from the input. For example, one source of evidence would be Sentence (17) "The dinosaur is only painting a house," presented in a situation in which the only thing the dinosaur is painting is a house, but in which he is doing something else as well, say flying a kite. Once children have both readings available to them, they should behave like adults in resolving ambiguities such as (17) both in and out of context. That is, they will appeal to the principle of referential success and the principle of parsimony, respectively.

Another potential semantic subset problem arises with ambiguous sentences like (19). The ambiguity involves the reference of the proform *one*, which varies depending on what is taken to be the contrast set for the focus operator *only*.

(19) The big elephant is the only one playing a guitar.

a.   The big elephant is the only thing playing a guitar.

b.   The big elephant is the only elephant playing a guitar.

The circumstances in which the two readings of (19) are true are depicted in (20). The illustration makes it clear that the set of circumstances allowed by the two readings fall into a subset–superset relationship.

(20)

Maximal Commitment   **Minimal Commitment**

The (a) reading of (19) is depicted on the left. This is the maximal commitment interpretation. On this interpretation, the sentence is false if anything other than the big elephant is playing a guitar. The (b) interpretation is the minimal commitment interpretation. On this interpretation, the contrast set consists of elephants. The illustrations show that the maximal commitment interpretation (a) makes Sentence (19) true in a narrower set of circumstances than it is true on the minimal commitment interpretation (b). In fact, it is true in only one circumstance on the maximal commitment interpretation.[6] For the sentence to be true on the (b) reading, however, all that is required is that no other elephant besides the big elephant is playing a guitar. The activities of the octopus and the crane are not pertinent on this reading. The crucial observation here is that the (a) interpretation of (19) is true in a subset of the circumstances corresponding to the (b) interpretation. For learners, sentences like (19) represent a potential semantic subset problem. The semantic subset principle resolves the dilemma by compelling children to initially hypothesize the falsifiable interpretation (a) (cf. Hornstein & Lightfoot, 1981).

For the sake of argument, suppose that children initially guess the minimal commitment interpretation. Suppose further that the preferred adult interpretation is the maximal commitment interpretation. On this scenario, the preferred adult interpretation would be unlearnable for the children. This is because the interpretation that children assign will be confirmed in the contexts in which adults generally use sentences like (19). In these contexts, the big elephant will be the only individual that is playing a guitar. According to the children's interpretation, the big elephant just needs to be the only elephant playing a guitar. This requirement is clearly satisfied in the contexts in which adults generally use (19), because if nothing other than the big elephant is playing a guitar, then no other elephant is. This would raise a problem for learnability, however, because the analysis children assign would not require them to examine individuals who are not elephants. Therefore, children will not notice that no other individual besides the big elephant is ever playing a guitar in the contexts that adults use the sentence. But this is precisely what children must notice if they are to achieve the preferred adult interpretation. Hence, that interpretation will remain beyond their grasp. This outcome is clearly contrary to fact.

Suppose, then, that children start out with the maximal commitment hypothesis, (a). In this case, there will be positive evidence that can prompt them to add the minimal commitment reading (b) as a possible interpretation of the sentence. According to the maximal commitment hypothesis, nothing in the domain of discourse besides the big elephant can be playing a guitar. On some occasions, however, children will witness adults using a sentence like (19) in a situation that renders it false according to this interpretation. For example, they might encounter Sentence (19) in a situation where a crane is playing a guitar as well. Children will observe that such a situation is inappropriate on their hypothesis, which precludes the crane from playing a guitar. Given the reasonable assumption that children take adult sentence-meaning pairs as positive evidence for grammatical change, contexts of this kind will cause children to add semantic interpretation

---

[6]There is a positive correlation between the size of contrast set and the number of commitments being made. The interpretation with the smallest contrast set makes the fewest commitments, whereas the larger the contrast set the more commitments that are being made. The consequence of a large number of commitments is maximal falsifiability.

(b) to their grammars. Sentences like (19) will be ambiguous for children from that point on. Presumably, when more than one interpretive option becomes operative for a given sentence type (i.e., when that type of sentence becomes ambiguous for children), the same parsing preferences that characterize the adult processing system will also be invoked by children to resolve ambiguities.

EXPERIMENTS COMPARING LEARNING AND PARSING

We have reached quite different conclusions about the operating characteristics of the adult parser and those of the LAD. According to the referential theory, the parser favors representations that are true in the broadest range of circumstances (i.e., ones that make minimal commitments). By contrast, the semantic subset principle encourages learners to initially hypothesize representations that are true in the narrowest range of circumstances (i.e., ones that make maximal commitments).

Earlier we reported the results of an experiment examining on-line responses by adults to local structural ambiguities. We saw that the parser is sometimes able to circumvent garden path effects that would otherwise occur by pursuing the minimal commitment analysis of garden path sentences. There is an even more direct way to compare the decisions of the parser and those of the learner, however. In this section, we report the findings of two experiments that take advantage of this more direct approach—by considering how children and adults respond to globally ambiguous sentences with the focus operator *only*. The findings from two experiments are reported, demonstrating striking dissimilarities between children and adults.

Experiment 2: The focus of Preverbal *Only*

Experiment 2 was designed to assess the interpretations that children and adults assign to sentences like (21) in which the focus operator *only* can associate with either the entire VP or can focus more narrowly within the VP, associating with the direct object NP.

(21) The dinosaur is only painting a house.
   a. The only thing the dinosaur is doing is painting a house.
   b. The only thing the dinosaur is painting is a house.

A result from previous research on children's understanding of sentences with *only* played a vital role in the experiment. The result was obtained in a study by Crain, Philip, Drozd, Roeper, and Matsuoka (1992). The study asked children to respond to sentences in which the focus operator *only* preceded the subject NP and ones in which it preceded the VP, as in (22) and (23). The test sentences were used to describe pictures such as (24). If children interpreted the test sentence in the same way as adults do, they should have accepted (23) as a correct description, (24), but they should have rejected (22).

(22) Only the cat is holding a flag.
(23) The cat is only holding a flag.
(24)

The main finding was that 35 of the 38 three- to six-year-old children tested in this study assigned a nonadult interpretation to the test sentences. The majority of children ($n = 21$) consistently interpreted *only* as if it were construed with the VP, regardless of its surface position in the test sentence. These children correctly interpreted sentences like (23) with *only* in pre-VP position, but they interpreted sentences like (22) in the same way (i.e., they interpreted "Only the cat is holding a flag" as if it meant "The cat is only holding a flag").[7] Children who gave this pattern of responses are called VP-oriented children.

VP-oriented children are of special interest to us because six such children served as subjects in Experiment 2. Use of these children made it possible to avoid a potential problem in presenting sentences like (23), namely, the possi-

[7]Although adults adopt different semantic representations depending on the surface position of *only*, the findings show that children initially hypothesize just one of the interpretative option's from UG. As a consequence, they are forced to ignore surface position. The interpretations that are lacking in early child grammars are simply added on the basis of positive evidence, however. For example, VP-oriented children will encounter sentence-meaning pairs that are false on the interpretation they assign, but true on an alternative interpretation that is consistent with the circumstances they encounter.

bility that the prosodic contour of sentences could favor one reading or another. This problem was avoided because VP-oriented children would assign focus on the VP even when *only* preceded the subject NP. This allowed us to present sentences like (25) auditorily, with *only* in presubject position, to test children's assignment of focus within VPs.

(25) Only the dinosaur is painting a house.

Prosodic information from sentences like (25) could not provide cues about the speaker's intended focus of *only* because any stress by the experimenter would fall on the subject NP, and not on or within the VP.[8] Crucially, however, Sentence (25) has the same meaning for VP-oriented children as "The dinosaur is only painting a house." In the experiment, six VP-oriented children (mean age: 4 years, 9 months) were given four test trials in a picture-verification task.[9] The picture in (18) is representative of the test materials.

The main finding was that three of the six children always associated *only* with the entire VP of the test sentences, such as (25) not with the direct object NP. The response of these children clearly conform to the semantic subset principle. The circumstances corresponding to the alternative readings of (25) are in a subset–superset relationship. Therefore, the semantic subset principle compels children to initially hypothesize the reading that makes the maximal commitments. In the present example, this is the reading in which the only activity being performed by the dinosaur is that of painting a house. Three children's responses were exactly of this form. For example, they rejected (25) on the grounds that the dinosaur was flying a kite and painting a chair, as well as painting a house.

The responses of the remaining three children were difficult to interpret. The majority of their responses were rejections of the test sentences, but, in explaining their reasons for rejection, these children mentioned every event depicted in the picture, regardless of which character was involved. Although such responses are not inconsistent with our claims about the stepwise acquisition of VP focus, neither do they offer support for these claims. We speculate that these children were adopting a nonlinguistic strategy to derive their responses.

A different experimental design was used to test for adult preferences in assigning focus in sentences with *only*. Because we assume that all interpretations of an ambiguous sentence are available to adults, we thought it ill advised to present pictures that falsified more than one interpretation at the same time, as was true of the pictures we presented to children. Therefore, for adults, test

---

[8]Subjects were classified as VP-oriented on the basis of their response to intransitive sentences. For example, the intransitive sentences "Only Oscar is dancing," was presented in a context in which someone was dancing in addition to Oscar, and Oscar was drinking a Coke, as well as dancing. A child was classified as VP oriented if he or she rejected such sentences on all three of the test trials.

[9]There were also four intransitive verb controls and two unrelated filler sentence–picture pairs.

sentences were presented in written form, outside of context, and with *only* in preverbal position, as in (26).

(26) The dinosaur is only painting a chair.

We interviewed 10 adults. They were instructed to imagine a situation corresponding to each test sentence, but one in which the sentence was false. Then, they were asked to write down a description of that aspect of their imagined situation that made the sentence false. For example, in response to Sentence (26), we wanted to find out whether subjects would write things like "He also painted a table" or "He also flew a kite." Based on the principle of parsimony, we expected adults to prefer descriptions like "He also painted a table," indicating that they associated *only* with the direct object NP (the minimal commitment interpretation), rather than associating it with the entire VP (the maximal commitment interpretation). This expectation was clearly met. Twenty-eight of the 34 responses that we could interpret repeated the verb of the test sentence with a different direct object. For example, in response to example (26), subjects wrote, "The dinosaur is also painting a table" and "He's going to paint all the furniture." However, five subjects gave at least one maximal commitment response. This indicates that this interpretation is available to adults, although it is not easily accessed in the absence of context.

In summary, Experiment 2 was designed to assess the interpretations that children and adults assign to sentences in which the focus operator *only* can associate with either the entire VP or it can associate within the VP. We predicted that children and adults would associate the focus operator differently for such sentences. Children were expected to associate it with the entire VP, whereas adults were expected to associate it within the VP. The results were largely as predicted. Three of the children gave the maximal commitment interpretation to the test sentences in Experiment 2. The responses of the other children could not be counted for or against the experimental hypothesis. We interpret the positive finding from the three children whose responses were germane to the experimental hypothesis as evidence that they were guided by the semantic subset principle, which encourages learners to initially hypothesize representations that are true in the narrowest range of circumstances (i.e., ones that make the maximal commitments). By contrast, adults strongly favored the minimal commitment interpretation of the test sentences. We interpret this as evidence that adults were guided by the principle of parsimony, which instructs perceivers to favor representations that are true in the broadest range of circumstances (i.e., ones that make minimal commitments).

Experiment 3: The Interaction of *Only* and *One* Substitution

This experiment concerns the interaction between the focus operator *only* and the linguistic phenomenon known as *one substitution*. This term describes the use of the proform *one* to refer back to the contents of a nominal element mentioned earlier in a sentence. Sometimes more than one referent for the proform *one* is possible, as (27) illustrates. The ambiguity turns on which norminal element the proform *one* is interpreted as replacing.

(27) The big elephant is the only one playing a guitar.

a. The big elephant is the only thing playing a guitar.

b. The big elephant is the only elephant playing a guitar.

On the (a) interpretation, where *one* substitutes for the entire NP, Sentence (27) is true in a subset of the circumstances corresponding to the (b) interpretation, where *one* substitutes for the nominal *elephant*. For learners, these interpretations present a potential semantic subset problem. Consequently, the semantic subset principle compels children to initially hypothesize the maximally falsifiable interpretation—namely, (a). By contrast, adults are expected to favor the (b) interpretation of (27), because this interpretation makes fewer commitments as to who is playing a guitar.

Again, different tasks were administered to children and adults. To test for the influence of the semantic subset principle on children's initial grammatical representations, children were interviewed using the truth-value judgment task developed by Crain and McKee (1985). On a typical trial, a child and a puppet, Kermit the Frog (played by one experimenter), watched stories that were acted out (by a second experimenter) using toy figures and other props. In the course of a story, the experimenter identified each character, as he or she participated in the action. Following each story, Kermit the Frog reported what he thought happened in the story (using a test sentence). The child's task was to indicate if Kermit was correct by rewarding him with a bite of his favorite food. But if Kermit was wrong, the child was to encourage him to pay closer attention by pretending to feed him a bite of an old shoe. Whenever a child indicated that Kermit had said the wrong thing, we asked him or her, "What really happened?" Test sentences were presented with neutral intonation, especially within the subject NP. The stories were constructed so that a "yes" response indicated that the child assigned the minimal commitment interpretation; a "no" response indicated that the child rejected the minimal commitment interpretation. By asking the subject to explain what really happened, we ascertained whether some children at least assigned the alternative maximal commitment interpretation as predicted by the semantic subset principle.

The results were largely as expected. Eight of the twelve 3- to 5-year-old children we interviewed (mean age: 4 years, 8 months) consistently rejected sentences like "The big elephant is the only one playing a guitar" if any character other than the big elephant was playing a guitar. In theoretical terms, these children hypothesized the entire domain of discourse as the contrast set. These children rejected the alternative interpretation, according to which the contrast set consisted of just elephants. If this interpretation had been available to children, they would have presumably said "yes." The four remaining children occasionally did accept this interpretation, although three of the four children rejected it more often than they accepted it.

Adults' responses to test sentences like (27) were assessed using the procedure described in Experiment 2. Test sentences were presented in written form outside of context. Subjects were asked to imagine a situation corresponding to each sentence, but one in which the sentence was false. Subjects were asked to write down a description of that aspect of the situation that falsified the sentence. The referential theory predicts that adults should favor those interpretations of ambiguous sentences that are true in the broadest circumstances. In particular, adults should prefer the minimal commitment interpretation of ambiguous sentences such as (27), in contrast to the response's children gave to such sentences. Based on the principle of parsimony, we expected adults to respond to (27) with descriptions that mentioned another elephant, which was being contrasted with the big elephant.

The results confirmed this expectation. Sixteen of the 18 responses that were relevant to the experimental hypothesis indicated that the referent of the head noun of the subject NP was taken as the contrast set (e.g., the set of cats was the contrast set for the sentence, "The gray cat is the only one with a toy"). In response to this sentence, for example, subjects wrote, "The black cat also has a toy," "Black and white cats have toys too," and so on. Besides the predicted pattern of responses, many subjects mentioned some other reason why the sentence was false (e.g., "The cat was not gray," "The gray cat lost its toy"). Only two of the subjects' responses conformed to a maximal commitment interpretation, however. This indicates that the maximal commitment interpretation is highly dispreferred for adults, whereas the minimal commitment interpretation is readily accessible.

To summarize the findings of the two experiments reported in this section, the responses of children and adults to the same global ambiguities reveal a striking dissimilarity in their understanding of sentences with the focus operator *only*. We conclude by discussing the implications of these findings for the architecture of the mind.

RESOLVING THE CONFLICT: MODULARITY

Is it time to draw our final conclusions. These are based on theoretical considerations of learning and parsing, as well as the results of our empirical investigations of how children and adults interpret sentences with the focus operator *only*. One set of conclusions concerns language learnability. Languages differ in the availability of particular semantic interpretations, and certain interpretative options that distinguish languages are in a subset–superset relationship. To meet the demands of learnability in the absence of negative evidence from the environment, the learner must start with the most restricted interpretation and add additional interpretations to his or her grammar based on positive evidence from the linguistic community. To converge on the target grammar, children must initially hypothesize semantic representations that make a sentence true in the narrowest possible set of circumstances. To accomplish this, the interpretations children initially hypothesize are ones that make the greatest number of commitments. This is dictated by the semantic subset principle, used by the LAD to arrange grammatical hypotheses in the order in which they are to be evaluated by the learner.

Another set of conclusions concerns language processing. Every language contains massive ambiguity. To confront this problem, with only limited computational resources, the parser rapidly checks the context surrounding an ambiguous sentence to see which of the alternative interpretations is most appropriate. In the absence of an explicit context, the parser is guided by the principle of parsimony. According to this principle, the language perceiver selects the interpretation that makes the fewest commitments, so as to limit the number of revisions that may be required in the light of impending information. The interpretation that makes the minimal commitments is the one that is true in the broadest range of circumstances.

Given this opposition between the principles of learning and parsing, the final conclusion we draw is that an impasse can be avoided only if the architecture of the mind is modular. An "interaction" between components, according to which the parser influences grammar formation, would have disastrous consequences in cases like those described in this chapter. If learners hypothesized the interpretation preferred by the parser, this would render the target grammar unlearnable. To prevent the parsing device from interacting with the LAD in this fashion, the principle of parsimony and the semantic subset principle must be kept in distinct modules of the mind. Within a modular linguistic system, the principles that dictate adult parsing preferences need not influence decisions that are made within the LAD. Learnability problems will thereby be avoided. As a final comment, we would underscore a point we made earlier. Once the learner has expanded his or her interpretive options beyond the default interpretive options prescribed by the LAD, he or she is at liberty to invoke the same parsing principles as adults do in deciding among competing interpretations. This minimizes the difference between the language apparatus of the learner and the adult language user. The difference is that the learner has an additional component, the LAD. In our view, this is all that distinguishes learners and parsers.

ACKNOWLEDGMENTS

We wish to thank Chuck Clifton, Lyn Frazier, Jane Grimshaw, Nina Hyams, Donald Shankweiler, and Mark Steedman for their comments on an earlier draft of this chapter. Special thanks goes to Rosalind Thornton for helping with the design and execution of the experiments with children. We also thank the children, teachers, and administrators of the Child Development Laboratories at the University of Connecticut. Portions of this research were presented at Rutgers University, the University of California at Los Angeles, and at the 16th GLOW Colloquium, Lund, Sweden. The research was supported, in part, by a program project grant to Haskins Laboratories by the National Institute of Child Health and Human Development (HD-01994) and by a graduate fellowship from the National Science Foundation (to Laura Conway).

REFERENCES

Altmann, G. T. M., & Steedman, M. (1988). Interaction with context during human sentence processing. *Cognition, 30,* 191–238.

Crain, S. (1992, July). *The semantic subset principle in the acquisition of quantification.* Paper presented at the Workshop on the Acquisition of WH-Extraction and Related Work on Quantification, University of Massachusetts, Amherst, MA.

Crain, S. (1993). Continuity and modularity. In E. Clark (Ed.), *Proceedings of the 25th Annual Stanford Child Language Research Forum* Chicago, IL: University of Chicago Press.

Crain, S., & Hamburger, H. (1992). Semantics, knowledge and NP modification. In R. Levine (Ed.), *Formal grammar: Theory and implementation* (vol. 2, pp. 372–401). British Columbia: The University of British Columbia Press.

Crain, S., & Lillo-Martin, D. (in press). *Language and mind: An introduction to linguistic theory and natural language acquisition.* Oxford, England: Blackwell.

Crain, S., & McKee, C. (1985). Acquisition of structural restrictions on anaphora. In S. Berman, J.-W. Choe, & J. McDonough (Eds.), *Proceedings of the North Eastern Linguistic Society* (Vol. 16, pp. 94–110). Amherst, MA: GLSA, The University of Massachusetts.

Crain, S., & Philip, W. (1993). *Global semantic dependencies in child language.* Paper presented at the 16th GLOW Colloquium, Lund, Sweden.

Crain, S., Philip, W., Drozd, K., Roeper, T., & Matsuoka, K. (1992). *Only in child language.* Unpublished manuscript, University of Connecticut, Storrs, CT.

Crain, S., & Shankweiler, D. (1991). Modularity and learning to read. In I. G. Mattingly & M. Stuttert-Kennedy (Eds.), *Modularity and the motor theory of speech perception* (pp. 375–392). Hillsdale, NJ: Lawrence Erlbaum Associates.

Crain, S., & Steedman, M. J. (1985). On not being led up the garden path: The use of context by the psychological parser. In D. Dowty, L. Karttunen, & A. Zwicky (Eds.), *Natural language parsing: Psychological, computational, and theoretical perspectives* (pp. 320–358). Cambridge, England: Cambridge University Press.

Fodor, J. A. (1983). *Modularity of mind.* Cambridge, MA: MIT Press.

Heim, I. (1982). *The Semantics of definite and indefinite noun phrases.* Unpublished doctoral dissertation, University of Massachusetts, Amherst, MA.

Hornstein, N., & Lightfoot, D. (1981). Introduction. In N. Hornstein & D. Lightfoot (Eds.), *Explanation in linguistics: The logical problem of language acquisition* (pp. 9–31). New York: Longman.

Jackendoff, R. (1972). *Semantic interpretation in generative grammar.* Cambridge, MA: MIT Press.

Krifka, M. (1991). A compositional semantics for multiple focus constructions. Linguistische Berichte, Sonderheft, 4. (Also in Proceedings of Semantics and Linguistic Theory (SALT) I, Cornell Working Papers 11).

Lewis, D. (1979). Scorekeeping in a language game. *Journal of Philosophical Logic, 8,* 339–359.

Ni, W., & Crain, S. (1990). How to resolve structural ambiguities. In *Proceedings of the North Eastern Linguistic Society* (Vol. 20, pp. 414–427). Amherst, MA: GLSA, The University of Massachusetts.

Ni, W., & Crain, S. (1993). Up and down the garden path. Unpublished manuscript, The University of Connecticut, Storrs, CT.

Reinhart, T. (1983). Coreference and bound anaphora: A restatement of the anaphora questions. *Linguistics and Philosophy, 6,* 47–88.

Rooth, M. (1985). *Association with focus.* Unpublished doctoral dissertation, University of Massachusetts, Amhert, MA.

Shankweiler, D., & Crain, S. (1986). Language mechanisms and reading disorder: A modular approach. *Cognition, 24,* 139–168.

Author Index

Subject Index